A FOOTNOTE TO PLATO

An Introduction to Western Philosophy

JOHN DOUGLAS MILLER
OKLAHOMA STATE UNIVERSITY
OKLAHOMA CITY

—A Footnote to Plato. I don't get it.

—It's from Alfred North Whitehead. All of western philosophy is but a footnote to Plato.

—I still don't get it.

—Read the book, and we'll talk about it.

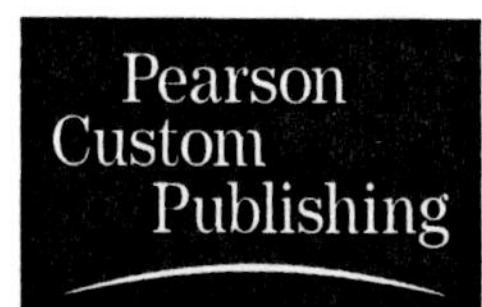

Printed in the United States of America

10 9 8 7 6 5 4

This manuscript was supplied camera-ready by the author(s).

Please visit our website at www.sscp.com

ISBN 0–536–01887–1

BA 98628

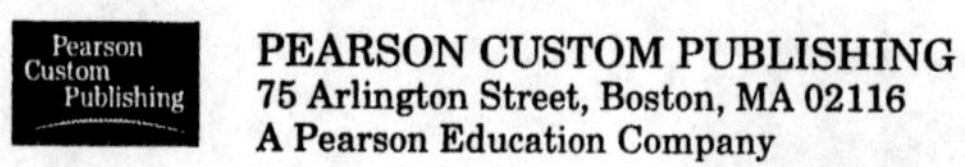

PEARSON CUSTOM PUBLISHING
75 Arlington Street, Boston, MA 02116
A Pearson Education Company

CONTENTS

Introduction

With a few exceptions, the verses that head up chapters in this book are my own. This proves that I can put words together and make them rhyme. But because philosophers and poets are notoriously unable to make a living rhyming and philosophizing I have spent the past sixteen years teaching philosophy in colleges. I am not sure how much I have been able to teach my students during that time, but they have certainly taught me a great deal. I have learned, for example, that bits of verse can serve didactic purposes, which is why I have placed my own poetry throughout this book, chiefly at the beginnings of chapters. I am, after all, trying to draw the attention of both student and teacher to my subject, for nowadays philosophy appears to need all the attention it can get. This is puzzling and bears examination.

Philosophy is the mother academic discipline, the vehicle of Plato, Kant, Descartes, at one time the most honored and revered of all scholarly undertakings. Today, we don't seem to know exactly where to fit it in. Frequently it is attached to humanities departments, taught by someone whose degree is in a field other than philosophy, and offered only because liberal arts degree plans usually call for a certain number of humanities hours. The students often seem uncertain about what to expect, and even about the value of what they are doing. Frequently they ask me what the point of philosophy is.

This is a fair question, and an important one.

I tell them that the most critical questions they will ever ask, and try to answer, will be philosophical ones, questions about truth and beauty, good and evil, morality, God, the ultimate meaning of life. I cannot imagine an even marginally educated person who hasn't at some time looked out at the cosmos, or in to heart and soul, and been seized with a sense of wonder.

Nor can I imagine anyone who has lived to be an adult who has never faced an ethical dilemma and wondered what to do. Pick up any newspaper or news magazine on most any day and you will be overwhelmed with philosophical questions begging for answers that go deeper than mere opinion. Abortion, divorce, euthanasia, capitol punishment, war, welfare, affirmative action, cloning. . . The list goes on and on. Opinions abound; clear thinking, unfortunately, does not.

Were I called on to set up a program in any university, there are certain philosophy courses which I would insist all students take before I granted them a bachelor's degree. No business major, for example, would graduate without having taken ethics; no one who had not taken epistemology would be granted a teaching degree; and every science major would have to take both logic and a course in the philosophy of science. Pre-law students would be required to minor in philosophy. History majors would be encouraged to take courses in philosophy, and political science majors would spend as much time in the philosophy department as they do in American Government. Symbolic logic would be a must for any student majoring in mathematics or computer science. I might even find a philosophical niche for home economics and agriculture majors.

I doubt I will ever see my dream fulfilled; but the dream is of some value. In the meantime, I can at least do something with those students who *do* come my way, and this brings me to the reason for this book. There are a number of excellent texts already on the market for use in teaching lower level philosophy courses, but I obviously find the need for another. Philosophy is difficult, and students who are coming to it for the first time need all the help they can get. To this end I have produced a text which avoids, to the degree possible, confusing language, long sentences, long paragraphs and convoluted lines of reasoning. Most of the texts with which I am familiar run from six-hundred to a thousand pages. Mine is considerably shorter. Every chapter in the book (there are a total of sixteen) may be read in a single sitting, assuming the reader is willing to apply himself or herself, and there will be few terms with which he or she is not already familiar. Of course, some new terms must be learned, and for these I have followed a course already used by others. Rather than defining them in a glossary at the end of the book, I have placed the definitions in the margins when they are introduced, and have highlighted them in the text. Thus, when the student reads of Socrates's ***epistemological*** concerns, he or she will have a definition immediately at hand.

The normal class is taught over a sixteen week period, so I have set the book up in four sections of four chapters each. The teacher may give a week to each chapter, with a test coming at the end of each section, and working through the entire book during a semester should be quite easy.

Every book must have some underlying idea that gives it coherence and unity. Mine is suggested by the title. The quote by Alfred North Whitehead is a familiar one to all philosophy students: "All philosophy is nothing more than a footnote to Plato." By this he meant that Plato, incredible genius that he was, laid the philosophical foundation for everything that would follow, identifying the main concerns of philosophy and its major sub-fields of metaphysics, epistemology, and ethics. Plato did not solve all the problems. Indeed, some of his suggested solutions seem quaint and curious to us today; but he did clearly *see* the problems, and his proffered solutions gave rise to the rich, complex, fruitful discipline we know as western philosophy.

For the student, this ought to be an intellectual adventure. At the end of the semester he or she should never again look at the universe in the same way, but rather should find that a quest for truth and beauty need never be justified by considering its ends. The justification, the reward, is in the quest itself.

Section I
A Brief History of Philosophy

We sat in the darkness for an age-long year,
Huddled together, shivering with fear,
Picking the cosmic dump to find a meal —
Until the Greeks struck flint against the steel.

Chapter 1
About Those Greeks

Said Plato to young Aristotle,
His student, "Please pass me the bottle.
"This thing with the forms
"Has created such storms
"That I think I'll get drunk and forgottle."

here is no convincing explanation, that I have ever heard, for Greece being the birthplace of western philosophy. The Greeks weren't more intelligent than other people, had no greater capacity for metaphysical wonder, didn't possess superior poetic ability or heightened mathematical skills. Every indication is that they were just as superstitious, just as given to explaining unknown things by appealing to the gods as were any other humans that inhabited the earth in the fifth century B.C. In fact, judging from what we know of India and China during this same period, the Greeks seem a bit backward, parochial and rustic by comparison. None would deny that they had been strongly influenced by the Egyptians, but the Egyptians remained tied to mythological explanations for many centuries while the Greeks left mythology for rationalism and in the process virtually created the western mind.

It might be well at this point to define **philosophy**. At its simplest it means nothing more than a love of wisdom, from the Greek words *philein* (love) and *sophia* (wisdom). But this is hardly enlightening. There is scarcely a culture we know of, present or past, in which wisdom is not desired and revered. This is why I specified at the outset of this chapter that the Greeks originated *western* philosophy. What the Greeks meant by philosophy (and what their western descendants subsequently came to mean) is indeed quite different from the meaning that most other peoples have given the word, and the difference is critical. Think of logic, of precise rational inquiry, of looking at the cosmos and saying, "This can all be understood without making reference to myth and fairy tale," and you are beginning to show

Philosophy: The word is derived from two Greek words, and means love of wisdom.

your kinship with the Greeks.

The Greek philosophers may be classified in a number of ways, **monists** versus **dualists**, for example, or **rationalists** versus **empiricists**, or **idealists** versus **materialists**. Though these are the sorts of terms that typically cause students a great deal of grief, none is particularly difficult to understand, and we will get to all of them in the course of this book. Just now, however, I wish to keep things a bit simpler by designating the Greek philosophers as pre- and post-Socratic. Socrates is, as we shall see, a philosophical watershed; after him western philosophy was changed, changed utterly. This is why Socrates is known as the father of western philosophy. But being the father does not, odd as it may seem, make him the first. There were others before him, and it is to these that we now turn.

Thales (c. 624-545 B.C.)

By universal consent the first western philosopher was named Thales, and he lived in the city of Miletus, in Ionia, a Greek-speaking area on the west coast of what is now Turkey. We know precious little about him, and we owe that little largely to Aristotle, who makes reference to him in the opening of the *Metaphysics*

> There is some one entity (or more than one) which always persists and from which all other things are generated...Thales...says the permanent entity is water (which is why he also propounded that the earth floats on water). Presumably he derived this assumption from seeing that the nutriment of everything is moist, and that heat itself is generated from moisture and depends upon it for its existence (and that from which a thing is generated is always its first principle). He derived his assumption, then, from this; and also from the fact that the seeds of everything have a moist nature, whereas water is the first principle of. . .moist things.[1]

There is not a great deal here, looking simply at the number of words Aristotle set down, but what we have is extraordinary, particularly when we consider that Thales lived over five hundred years before the birth of Christ. Notice that he is a **monist**, assuming that all of reality is reducible to one particular substance. **Metaphysically**, he is a **materialist**, because he clearly

---

[1] Aristotle, *The Metaphysics,* Books 1-1X, ed. Hugh Tredennick, Cambridge, Mass.: Harvard University Press, 1980, p. 19.

believes that the one substance of which all is made is a certain physical matter. But it is *why* he believes that water is the one substance from which all is generated that makes him a philosopher and not just another myth-maker. Notice what Aristotle says of him. He saw that the nutriment of everything was moist, that heat was generated from water, etc., and from this he derived his assumption. Aristotle criticized Thales for not being able to isolate and explain the mechanism (Aristotle refers to it as the "cause") by which all is generated out of and ultimately returns again to water. But the important thing is not that Thales produced viable theory or complete explanation, but rather that he attempted an explanation that was rational, physical, non-mythological. He probably didn't know it, but he had taken the first, faltering step toward one of the great intellectual achievements of ancient humanity; for beginning with Thales, the Greeks began moving toward an atomic theory, a theory not so very different from our own and to which we have added merely the fancy trimmings.

Heraclitus (dates of life unknown, c. 500 B.C.)

It was predictable that someone would say Thales got it wrong, that water was not the basic substance of creation, but that it was sawdust or apple butter. In fact, the next major pre-socratic philosopher, Heraclitus, said it was not water, but fire. I will not go into his reasons for thinking this but will invite the student to go to the library and look it up. It's a rather fascinating story in its own right. Just now I want to tell the story of the Greeks's slow progression toward an atomic theory. Heraclitus helped this along by his well-known observation that the only unchanging fact of the cosmos is change itself. To quote him, "One cannot step into the same river twice."

A moment of reflection will convince one of the truthfulness of this assertion, but Heraclitus means a much broader application than rivers and bathers; and it seems again that a brief moment of reflection is sufficient to convince one that he has spoken the truth. Everything is changing, though we do not always see the change. Our bodies are breaking down, all physical things are breaking down, seeds are changing into flowers, flowers back into seeds, and each seed or flower is different than all the others. Let us grant him his point, but let us also think about the full implications of what we have granted. What does this ongoing, irresistible, inevitable change do to our concept of truth and to our hope of ever finding it? If the very cosmos is changing beneath us, slip-sliding away and becoming something else, then we are left with only one truth, and that is the truth of change, and any statement we make about the truth of anything has become obsolete almost as soon as we have spoken it. It is not certain that Heraclitus understood the dead-end into which his conjecturing had driven philosophy, but it would be odd if a person of his intelligence did not see something so obvious. Perhaps nothing remained to be said, and the best thing for philosophers would have been to fold their tents and creep back to mythology. If they had, there is no doubt that the history of the west would have developed in a far different manner than it did. As it turned out, not everyone agreed with Heraclitus.

Enter:

Parmenides (lived during the fifth century B.C.)

Imagine, if you will, a man so brazenly self-confident, so willing to court ridicule, as to float a metaphysical theory that is absurd on its face. Parmenides announced that Heraclitus had it backwards! It was not that everything was changing, but that nothing was. He cannot have been serious. Oh, but he was. Not only was he serious in making the statement, but he was very serious about the philosophical argument he constructed to prove it.

Ontology: the study of being qua being. I frankly have always had some difficulty telling where metaphysics leaves off and ontology begins.

Nothing is changing! This must be ridiculous, for we can see change all about us every moment, from the houses in which we live, to the cars we drive, to the bodies we inhabit. If nothing is changing, then motion is not possible because all motion involves change; no one is growing older, for aging involves change; and no one is being born, because birth involves change. Horses are not running at Santa Anita, stars are not wheeling through the heavens, and ice cream is not melting in the cone. Was Parmenides a serious philosopher, a serious comedian, or a serious head case? The answer is, he was a serious philosopher, and in supporting his position he created a new area of philosophical inquiry, **ontology**, the study of being.

The so-called laws of inference, first identified by Aristotle, are the law of identification, the law of contradiction, and the law of the excluded middle. These are basic to logic and thinking.

"What **is, is,**" said Parmenides, "and what **is not, is not.**" Very well, we can probably grant him this point and say that the two propositions contained in this one compound sentence are both warranted by Aristotle's **law of identification** (a thing is equal to itself), which won't be formulated for another two hundred years or so, but must nevertheless be valid for the earlier philosophers as well. And since we are leaping ahead to borrow from Aristotle, there is no reason why we can't bring the **law of the excluded middle** to bear on the argument: what **is** either **is** or it **is not**. Now, adding the **law of contradiction** we get: what **is** cannot be both **is** and **is not** at the same time.

"Wonderful," I hear the student muttering, "but didn't you promise, sir, not to confuse us unduly with a lot of philosophical jargon?"

This is not confusing, it merely looks that way. All Parmenides is saying is that being exists and non-being does not; then he pushes on to identify non-being as no-thing-ness. There is no such thing as *nothing*, and to talk as if nothing exists is to reveal that one hasn't thought about the matter. Now, follow carefully as Parmenides shows us why change cannot actually occur, and that what appears to be change is just that, mere appearance. In order for something to change it must become what it was not, and at the same time that which it changes from must somehow metamorphose into nothing, and this gives us the strange (Parmenides says impossible) occurrence of *something* coming out of *nothing*.

Reductio ad absurdam: **a type of argument which attacks an opponent by taking the opponent's position, pushing it to its ultimate conclusion, and showing that the conclusion is absurd.**

Where did the old thing go, and from whence came the new? This sort of argument will be refined by later philosophers into the ***reductio ad absurdum***, in which the opponent's argument is destroyed by being pushed to its ultimate conclusion, which is then shown to be an absurdity.

Common sense tells us that somehow Parmenides has bungled things. It looks as if he has actually turned his *reductio* back upon himself and, as we say, shot himself in the foot. However, what he has actually done is discovered a very important principle, one which will bear a good deal of fruit for future generations: things are not always what they seem to be. And he may also have saved philosophy from an early death at the hands of skeptics.

A Brief Interlude

Now, where have we come from and where are we going? We have the pre-Socratic philosophers, convinced that there is some basic matter of which everything is made, faced with a problem of how the many things we see are generated out of the one, arguing over whether constant change or constant stability is the rule, and with no immediate solution in sight. Suppose we bring common sense to bear on the problem and see if that will help. We eat hot dogs, chew them up and swallow them, but we don't turn into hot dogs, or anything resembling them. Instead, somehow, the matter in the hot dogs becomes teeth, hair, eyeballs, bones, skin, an obvious fact which leaves us as puzzled as ever and drives us back to Heraclitus. Change is certainly taking place, but how? Hotdog becomes tooth...The truth, when stated in this way, indeed seems stranger than fiction.

Anaxagoras (c. 500-428 B.C.)

Pluralism: the belief that reality is composed of two or more elements, as opposed to monism, which holds that there is only one.

By the time Anaxagoras came on the scene things had gotten considerably more complicated. Monism was no longer the only game in town. There were now philosophers we have come to call **pluralists**, who did not believe that there was only one element, but that there were as many as four (earth, air, fire and water). Typical of these was one Empedocles, about whom I will have little to say except that he agreed with Parmenides, at least to a degree. If change did occur, he thought, then it must occur within the system itself, otherwise we are left in the insupportable position of saying that something can come from nothing. But we are still left to ask, how does change take place, how does the hotdog become the tooth?

From our vantage point, Anaxagoras's answer seems brilliant and insightful, but I can't help but think that to his contemporaries he must have appeared dangerously confused. What if everything were made up of tiny little seeds, Anaxagoras suggested, and what if everything had within it some of the tiny little seeds that belong to everything else? Then there would be little hot dog seeds in the tooth, and little tooth seeds in the hot dog, and little eyeball seeds in the tree, and so on, and these seeds would sort of be shuffled around through natural processes, and a thing would be given its outward appearance by the dominant seeds it possessed. "In everything," said Anaxagoras, "there is a portion of everything."

Once again we find ourselves looking backward over 2,000 years and benefiting from the excellence of our temporal vantage point. Nevertheless, we must be impressed as we see the rudiments of an atomic theory being drawn together, particularly when we consider that these early Greeks were propounding theories that in some cases ran contrary to common sense, and in any case were the result of armchair speculation without the benefit of any experimental data.

Democritus of Abdera (c. 460-370 B.C.)

The man actually credited with originating atomism, and with coining the term "atom" was Leucippus of Miletus, but Democritus developed Leucippus's ideas, smoothed them up, made them marketable, and history has given more attention to Democritus than to any other of the early atomists. To quote Kurt Vonnegut in *Slaughter House Five*, "So it goes."

The word **atom** comes from the Greek, *tome*, which means to divide, and the little Greek letter alpha (a), which when placed at the beginning of a word makes it a negative. We have, for example, *theos* (god) becoming *atheos* (no god, or atheist); *gnosko* (to know) becomes *agnosko* (not knowing, or agnostic); *bussos* (bottom) is changed into *abussos* (bottomless, or abyss); and *tome* (to divide) becomes *atome* (atom, not divisible). The Greek atomic theory is simple, elegant, aesthetically beautiful. Go back to Anaxagoras's tiny seeds. Now what could these seeds possibly be, supposing they actually exist? We might begin by dividing matter, any matter, and then re-dividing it, going down and down toward infinite smallness. The Greeks, however, had what must have amounted to a basic fear of infinity, for they seem uniformly to have assumed that an infinite regress was not possible -- in either direction. Sooner or later, dividing downward, one must reach a stopping point, a piece of matter that was no longer divisible, and this Democritus and his colleagues called the atom.

What was the early Greek atom like?

It certainly was not constructed like the atom in Niels Bohr's famous theory, a tiny solar system with protons and neutrons whirling about a nucleus. It was more like Anaxagoras's tiny seed. It was matter, and these early atomists (and all subsequent atomists, for that matter) were *materialists*,[2] that is, they assumed that the entire cosmos was reducible to matter. Further, these tiny atoms were indestructible. Why wouldn't they be, since they couldn't be divided? There were only so many of them, and thus the cosmos was limited in space by the fact that its building matter was limited. And finally, everything that we see is made up of these atoms, and the difference in the appearances of things is due to the differing number of their constituent atoms and the manner in which they are combined.

Does all of this have a familiar sound? It should, for as I said earlier, this atomic theory, formulated some four hundred years before the birth of Christ, is essentially the same theory our chemists and physicists are working with today. There is, moreover, in this theory, an ingenious solution to the problem posed by Heraclitus (all is changing) and Parmenides (change is an illusion), for the theory can neatly accommodate both positions. Indeed there is change all about us, but it is superficial, whereas underneath is a stable and unchanging structure which is merely shifted about over time.

---

2 This is true until we get to the twentieth century and the quantum physicists. Bohr, Schrödinger, Pauli, *et al.*, are in a mixed state, holding that whether the atom is matter or energy depends a great deal on what we choose to measure.

A Second Brief Interlude

This has been a woefully short and simplistic account of the pre-socratic philosophers. I have said nothing about the Pythagoreans, about the ***nous*** and the ***logos***, nothing about Zeno of Elia and his marvelous race between Achilles and the tortoise, and have not mentioned Anaximander and the ***apeiron***. Even the subject I have dealt with might have been expanded to book length, instead of being confined to the few pages I have given it. My purpose has been to whet the student's appetite for philosophy by showing him or her how some of the earliest of the remarkable Greeks began a search for the truth and wound up with an atomic theory. Clearly, they left many questions unanswered, and many of the answers they gave were the wrong ones, but in making the effort they set us on the road toward intellectual enlightenment, and they gave us three incredible geniuses, Socrates, Plato, and Aristotle.

Protagoras of Abdera (481-411 B.C.)

Sophistry, as it was defined by the Greeks, was the practice of arguing effectively for either side of a position. The important thing was winning — not being right or wrong.

Why Protagoras? Because without him it is impossible to understand Socrates and Plato. Protagoras was one of the class of philosophers we have come to call sophists, and his style of teaching is called (what else?) **sophistry**. Now to accuse someone of sophistry is not to pay that person a compliment, for a sophist deliberately plays fast and loose with the truth in order to prove a point. The main thing in arguing, for the sophist, is to win, no matter what one is arguing. Nowadays lawyers, whether rightly or wrongly, are seen as prime examples of sophistry, and this was probably true in Protagoras's day as well.

Look back now to an earlier sentence in the paragraph above, the one which says that sophists deliberately play fast and loose with the truth. A more direct way of saying this is that they lie, and yet neither Protagoras nor his followers would have taken kindly to being call liars, and would have denied that they were lying when they argued that white was black and black was white. Rather, what Protagoras said was that truth was **relative** to the one who holds it. Perhaps, for one person, white is black and black is white; and if this is the case, then what is the truth in the matter? If Protagoras is correct, then there is no such thing as objective truth, and calling someone a liar is to engage in nothing more than pointless slander. If there is no truth, then there can be no falsehood — only winners and losers in the great, ongoing argument.

Protagoras's most famous statement, quoted often by professors of both philosophy and humanities, is, "Man is the measure of all things." By this he meant just what we have been considering, that there are no objective truths, and that the final arbiters in any question are individuals.

Now this may sound tolerant and big-hearted, and indeed Protagoras was a cosmopolitan person whose vision encompassed a great deal more than the confines of the city of Athens, but one needn't think too deeply to realize that this position is something of a throwback to Heraclitus. With Heraclitus, truth was impossible to find because everything was changing at all times. With Protagoras, truth was irrelevant because what any individual believed to be truth was truth for him, and any view could be made to prevail over another, not by its correspondence with fact, but by the skill of its proponent in arguing his case.

Protagoras's view is still with us today, particularly in the areas of morals and aesthetics. It is called **relativism**. Very few philosophers subscribe to it, however, because it goes precisely nowhere, proves precisely nothing, leaves one precisely where one started, and renders the word "truth" devoid of substance. But it has great value in the rough and tumble of the market place where debaters sell their skills to the highest bidder.

Relativism: the view (particularly in ethics) that there are no hard and fast truths, but that everything is relative to the circumstances in which it occurs.

Socrates, a contemporary of Protagoras, would have none of it, and spent a good part of his life attempting to show that truth is not relative, but is objective, stable, eternal.

Socrates (c. 470-399 B.C.)
Plato (c. 427-348 B.C.)

I have placed Socrates and Plato together, not because they are the same person, but because I, for one, cannot tell where one leaves off and the other begins. This by itself does not demonstrate that I am abnormally obtuse. What has sometimes been called the "Socratic problem" has troubled philosophers and teachers across the centuries. The problem is that Socrates taught widely, talked constantly, became the acknowledged father of western philosophy, but wrote nothing. What we know of him is what was said about him by others, principally Xenophon and Plato.

What follows will pertain exclusively to Socrates when I discuss the particulars of his life, and exclusively to Plato when I discuss the particulars of his life. The student should be aware, however, that when the philosophies of these men are under discussion, it is never clear whether the views are those of Socrates, or Plato, or both.[3] It is ironic that Socrates, the apostle of irony, is one of the most influential men in the history of the west,

[3] Many scholars have argued that in the earlier dialogues Plato is faithfully giving Socrates's arguments, whereas in the later one he is merely making Socrates a mouthpiece for his own ideas. I, for what it is worth, have never felt comfortable with this theory.

and yet remains something of a mystery.

What, then, do we know of him?

He was born in about 470 B.C.in the great city-state of Athens. The fact that he was free-born and an Athenian citizen assumes considerable importance because slaves and foreigners had few rights, if any, and it is doubtful that he would have been a very effective philosopher chained to a laborer's bench. His father was probably a stonecutter, a trade which he also pursued off and on with little apparent enthusiasm. He seems never to have had much money, although his wife, Xanthippe, initially brought him a comfortable dowry. Xanthippe does not come off well in the accounts of Socrates's contemporaries, being described as a shrew, a nag, and so on, but moderns are apt to see her in a much more favorable light. She has always seemed to me to be a long-suffering woman, married to a man who, rather than earning a living, spent his time conversing in the ***agora*** with anyone who would listen. How was she to know that her ragged, ne'er-do-well husband would one day be considered an intellectual giant with few peers in the world.

Agora is the Greek word for market place. It was the center of most Greek cities of that day.

He was, to make matters worse, the ugliest man in Athens, a comic figure who made some people laugh and infuriated others to the point that they wanted nothing more than to get rid of him. They got their wish. In 399 B.C. he was tried before an Athenian court of 501 citizens, on charges of blasphemy and of corrupting the youth of Athens. The trial and Socrates's defense of himself is the subject of one of Plato's most famous dialogues, *The Apology.* At one point Socrates tells the Athenians that were they to acquit him and let him go on the condition that he cease philosophizing, he must respectfully refuse. The condition would be too drastic, tantamount to being less than a man, for "the unexamined life is not worth living." Unimpressed by Socrates's defense, the court found him guilty and sentenced him to death. He was executed in 399 B.C.

End of story. Well, not quite, for in his steps came his famous student, Plato, to write it all down in a series of philosophical dialogues which remain some of the finest pieces of literature ever produced in the west.

Plato was an aristocrat, also Athenian, whose real name was Aristides.[4] He lived through a period in the history of Athens that can only be described as chaotic. The Greek golden age of Pericles was fading away,

---

[4] Plato was a nickname, given to him by his peers, that stuck and became the name by which we know him. It means "the Broad." He was obviously large.

hastened to its close by the disastrous Peloponnesian War, which Athens lost to Sparta. The thirty tyrants were in charge of government and had inaugurated a sort of democracy that encouraged mob rule. And most distressing of all, from Plato's point of view, his friend and teacher Socrates had been executed on trumped-up charges. Philosophically, Protagoras was preaching **relativism**, Thrasymachus, another of the sophists, was pushing the view that might makes right, and Glaucon, who appears prominently in the *Republic*, taught a sort of psychological egoism which, if adopted, would have made ethics turn upon the simple principle of doing what is right for oneself, which is what everybody ultimately will do because they can't help themselves.

Into this strange and challenging mental world comes now our dual philosopher-hero, Socrates/Plato, to set western philosophy on a course which will cause later philosophers, in agreement with Whitehead, to say that since the fourth century B.C. we have all been supplying annotations to the work of Plato.

Later in his life Plato founded a school in Athens which he called the Academy, and which became the major center of higher learning in the west for another eight hundred years, until the Byzantine emperor Justinian closed it in the sixth century A.D.

The student ought to have noted by now that philosophy, like any other discipline, builds upon what has gone before. Thus it is not surprising to see Socrates and Plato producing work in reaction either to earlier philosophers or to those who are alive and operating during their lives. This reaction gives us, as we shall see, the modern beginnings of **epistemology**, **ethics** and **metaphysics**. We will look at each of these philosophical sub-fields in greater detail later. Just now I shall confine myself to general comments which serve the purpose of giving the student an overview of the history of western philosophy.

Epistemology: The study of knowledge, how one learns.

Ethics: The study of morals, right & wrong.

Metaphysics: The study of reality, or what is actually there.

The Platonic writing format is dialectical, which means that it is like a play, with characters who speak to one another and in so doing argue for whatever position they champion. The main character in the Platonic dialogues is always Socrates, and it will come as no surprise to the student that in whatever is being argued Socrates always prevails. The dialect, often called the "Socratic dialectic" or the "Socratic method," is an important device which will be used by philosophers, educators, and lawyers from then until now. In opposition to the empirical style of Aristotle and his more

Apodeictic: the basic idea is to postulate something as necessary rather than merely probable. In logic, it assumes reasoning from sound premises with a resultant conclusion that is certain.

logical progeny (for purposes of identification I will call Aristotle's the **apodeictic** style) the dialectical style aims to get at the truth by force of argument rather than pure deduction. The *reductio ad absurdam*, to which I referred earlier in discussing Parmenides, plays an important role in the socratic dialectic; for if an opponent's argument may be shown to be absurd, then he is down for the count.

This method also gives one a remarkable insight into the learning theory of Socrates and Plato. What counts as knowledge, and whence comes this knowledge, and how can it be gained and held by the student as a certainty? Socrates characterized himself as a philosophical midwife, another revealing sobriquet. A midwife does not conceive, nor give birth, to a child; she or he is simply there to aid the mother in its birthing. So with Socrates. He consistently called himself ignorant, said he knew nothing at all, and that this ignorance was the only true sign of his wisdom, for other men, who were just as ignorant and himself, compounded their ignorance by thinking themselves wise. He at least avoided this pitfall. The beginning of true wisdom is the admission therefore of one's ignorance and the willingness to learn.

> I asked myself: "Whatever does the god mean? What is his riddle? I am very conscious that I am not wise at all; what then does he mean by saying that I am the wisest?". . .For a long time I was at a loss as to his meaning; then I very reluctantly turned to some such investigation. . . I went to one of those reputed wise, thinking that there, if anywhere, I might refute the oracle. . .I thought that he appeared wise to many people and especially to himself, but he was not. I then tried to show him that he thought himself wise but he was not. As a result he came to dislike me. . .So I withdrew and thought to myself: "I am wiser than this man; it is likely that neither of us knows anything worthwhile, but he thinks he knows something when he does not, whereas when I do not know, neither do I think I know; so I am likely to be wiser than he to this small extent, that I do not think I know what I do not know." After this I approached another man, one of those thought to be wiser than he, and I thought the same thing, and so I came to be disliked both by him and by many others.[5]

This is another example of one of Socrates's famous teaching devices,

---

[5] Plato, *The Apology*, in *Five Dialogues*, trans. G.M.A. Grube, Indianapolis, Indiana: Hackett Publishing Co., 1981, p. 27.

irony. Can it really be that this man thought himself ignorant, or was he merely using feigned ignorance as a device for showing up the ignorance of his opponents? Probably a little of both; for one cannot help but see the chuckling ironist behind the mask of a humble and ignorant seeker of truth.

Let us see the master, the old ironist, at work as he takes on a self-assured young man named Euthyphro and leads him step by step down the primrose path to confusion and self-contradiction.

> Soc: What all the gods hate is impious, and what they all love is pious, and that what some gods love and others hate is neither or both? Is that how you now wish us to define piety and impiety?
>
> Eut: I would certainly say that the pious is what all the gods love, and the opposite, what all the gods hate is impious.
>
> Soc: Then let us again examine whether that is a sound statement, or do we let it pass, and if one of us, or someone else, merely says that something is so, do we accept that it is so? Or should we examine what the speaker means?
>
> Eut: We must examine it, but I certainly think that this is now a fine statement.
>
> Soc: Consider this: Is the pious loved by the gods because it is pious, or is it pious because it is loved by the gods?

After further exchange, Socrates leads Euthyphro to admit that something is loved because it is pious; it is not pious because it is loved. He does this through the reflection that if anything comes to be, it does not come to be because it is coming to be, but it is coming to be because it comes to be; it is not affected because it is being affected but because something affects it.

> Soc: What then do we say about the pious, Euthyphro? Surely that it is loved by all the gods. . .because it is pious, but it is not pious because it is loved.
>
> Eut: Apparently.
>
> Soc: The god-beloved is then not the same as the pious, Euthyphro, nor the pious the same as the god-beloved, as you say it is, but one differs from the other.

> Eut: How so, Socrates?
>
> Soc: Because we agree that the pious is beloved for the reason that it is pious, but it is not pious because it is loved. Is that not so?
>
> Eut: Yes.
>
> Soc: And that the god-beloved, on the other hand, is so because it is loved by the gods, by the very fact of being loved, but it is not loved because it is god-beloved.
>
> Eut: But Socrates, I have no way of telling you what I have in mind, for whatever proposition we put forward goes around and refuses to stay put where we established it.[6]

The problem in establishing the ethical condition of piety is not with Socrates, as Euthyphro seems to think (and would obviously have the onlooker believe), but with Euthyphro himself, with the fuzziness of his thinking and the looseness of his definitions. And here we have another of the timeless contributions of Socrates and Plato to the philosophical enterprise: exactness of definition. Socrates was one of the first to recognize that unless the parties to a debate can agree on what the things under discussion mean, they will typically wind up arguing past one another. He: All humans are created equal. She: You are wrong, some are stronger than others, some are more intelligent. The problem in this exchange is one that philosophers call equivocation, using the same term, "equal", but giving it two different meanings. Socrates sought to solve this problem by insisting on clarity of definition.

Now, I have stated that Socrates and Plato anticipated all of western philosophy by identifying in their dialect the major areas of philosophical inquiry: **ethics, metaphysics,** and **epistemology.**[7] Consider, for example, the brief excerpt from *Euthyphro* in which Socrates attempts to get Euthyphro to define piety, and asks whether something is pious because it is loved by the gods or is loved by the gods because it is pious. Clearly, this dialogue deals with a question of ethics, of right and wrong, morality and immorality. In brief, Euthyphro has had his father charged with murder because his

---

[6] *Euthyphro*, ibid., pp 15-16.

[7] These major fields of philosophy break down into subfield of course. Within ethics, for example, we have axiology, the study of values. Some say that logic is really a subfield of epistemology.

negligence resulted in the death of one their slaves, and Socrates asks Euthyphro whether he is so sure that he knows right from wrong (Socrates uses the term "piety") that he is willing to do something so serious as bring his father up on charges. As the discussion unfolds, Socrates asks Euthyphro to define piety, and Euthyphro replies that "the pious is to do what I am doing now, to prosecute the wrongdoer. . .whether the wrongdoer is your father or your mother or anyone else." But Socrates is not convinced. Hear his fascinating response:

> I did not bid you tell me one or two of the many pious actions but that form itself that makes all pious actions pious. . .Tell me what this form itself is, so that I may look upon it, and using it as a model, say that any action of yours or another's that is of that kind is pious.[8]

The student not familiar with philosophy cannot be expected to immediately grasp the full significance of this rejoinder, for simple as it may seem the implications are really profound and full of unseen problems. Recall the bit of verse with which I began this chapter, in which I have Plato complaining to Aristotle about the problems created by the "forms". Here we have the **forms** cropping up, in one of the early dialogues, and Socrates saying to Euthyphro that what he (Socrates) is after is the form of the pious, and not merely examples of piety. If he has the form, he states, then he can use it to determine of any action whether or not it is pious.

Think of the form, in this case, as a measuring staff or a benchmark of some sort. We can draw a line on the chalk board and then stand for hours debating its length, or we can simply take a ruler and measure it. Obviously the calibrated ruler is the thing we want in this case, and Socrates says that a similar thing exists for the determination of morality. There are metaphysical implications here, and epistemological implications, and ethical implications, and all within a seemingly simple request by a man who liked to pass himself off as ignorant, a philosophical gadfly, a mere intellectual midwife. What he is suggesting is that there is, somewhere in this universe, an abstract entity he calls a form, that this thing can be known, and that it can be used to determine ethical truth in a way that Protagoras would never have allowed. He is saying that there are existent absolutes.

Socrates and Plato did not stop with the form of piety. They were convinced that behind all particulars stand unseen, nonspatial, eternal forms.

---

[8] *Euthrphro*, ibid., p. 10.

I would be very surprised if the student who has never been exposed to this notion has been able to follow what I have said, so I shall try to illustrate. Suppose I am standing in front of a classroom and I ask my students to define the word **noun.** One of them would surely say it is a part of speech which denotes a person, place, or thing. I would pat him or her on the head with my compliments for paying attention in grade school. Then I might write a series of nouns in a column on the board, one after another: book, chair, dog, house, boy, tree, and so on. Now, in another column alongside the first I might write justice, beauty, courage, piety, wisdom. Suppose, then, that I asked my students which column of words were nouns. Both, they would say. But, when asked if they did not immediately perceive a difference in the sorts of nouns in the first column and the sorts of nouns in the second column, I would be told that the first column was composed of concrete things that we could all see and touch, and the second was composed of things that we could not see and touch, abstractions for which we might, at best, provide examples. We understand that the first group of nouns, the concrete particulars, all stand for things that are objective, real, recognizable. If I say, "Book," and someone points to a chair I immediately understand that he or she has not learned the language well, or that he or she is putting me on, or that he or she is mad.

Now for the critical question.

What of the second list? If I say, "Justice," to what would one be likely to point? The problem becomes instantly apparent. We all use these abstract nouns everyday, and we communicate with one another as if we all know what we intend when we use them. But do we? One must be impressed, when considering these abstractions, by their implicit importance. Justice. Truth. Beauty. These are words that humans over the centuries have lived and died for, and yet where are they?

Here we see Socrates and Plato diverging sharply from Protagoras, who had no particular problem with any of this. For him, these abstractions were culturally, even individually, defined, and what was beauty (for example) for one man was not necessarily beauty for another. Protagoras saw no difficulty in this, and neither have many people across the centuries. Socrates and Plato were terribly troubled, however, by the idea that things so important could not be known with certainty, for this left philosophy with a large blank slate that could never be filled in, and it left people to use words as if they knew what they meant when in fact they did not. This called for serious thought.

The necessity to explain how we can have true knowledge in these matters gave rise to a theory of reality and learning that has seemed very strange to many philosophers of subsequent generations, but in postulating the existence of the forms Socrates and Plato set philosophy on the course that would determine its future. All of western philosophy would indeed become but a footnote to Plato because all western philosophers would have to deal with the problems he raised.

I have had a good deal to say about the forms. I suppose I should have a go at describing them in greater detail. The forms are sometimes called **ideals** (though **form** is the preferred designation), and were called universals by Aristotle. Linguistically they are words that stand for classes of things. Max, Jim, and Albert have something in common, their masculinity; thus masculinity is one of these universals, an abstract noun which stands for the class in which Max, Jim, and Albert participate. But whereas Max, Jim, and Albert are individuals who exist in space and time, masculinity does not. So what is it? One possible answer is that it is merely a word which we learn to use as a communication device when we wish to refer to several men in general. Another possible answer is that the forms do in fact exist, more truly, more actually than do the particulars they represent. Socrates and Plato took the latter posture.

Even the Athenians, who lived for nothing more than to tell or to hear some new thing,[9] must have found this difficult to swallow. If the forms exist, and if they have greater reality than do the particulars of the waking world, then where are they and how can we know them?

When a question is raised about what is really there, we are dealing with metaphysics; and when a question is raised about how we can know that something is there we are dealing with epistemology. We will look more carefully at each of these areas, and ethics as well, a few chapters hence; but some overlap is unavoidable. I will mention *The Republic* later with regard to further developments in philosophy, but there is no better place to introduce it to the student than right now, when the subject is western philosophy and how it grew. Plato wrote widely and well, and as a result we probably know more about him than any other Greek philosopher. But he wrote nothing so influential as *The Republic*. This is, in fact, probably the most widely-read book on philosophy in the history of the west.

In *The Republic* we get a mature version of the Platonic theory of the forms, and it is easier to say of it, than of the earlier works, that it does indeed represent Plato more and Socrates less. The earlier works, such as

---

[9] **This accords with the statement contained in Acts 17, the New Testament.**

The Meno and *Euthyphro* (which we have discussed already), leave one somewhat uncertain where Socrates and Plato located the forms, and it is not at all clear that we are to look for them in an invisible world-behind-the-world. But *The Republic* is fairly explicit in this regard. Socrates had been long dead by the time Plato penned this philosophical masterpiece, and by now Plato was certain that the forms were separated from the particulars, that they were non-spatial, non-temporal, invisible, yet actually existed.

> You are aware that students of geometry, arithmetic, and the kindred sciences assume the odd and the even and the figures and three kinds of angles and the like in their several branches of science. . .And do you not know also that although they make use of the visible forms and reason about them, they are thinking not of these, but of the ideals which they resemble; not of the figures which they draw, but of the absolute diameter, and so on - the forms which they draw or make, and which have have shadows and reflections in water of their own, are converted by them into images, but they are really seeking to behold the things themselves, which can only be seen with the eye of the mind?[10]

Again, we get this exchange between Socrates and Glaucon:

> Soc: There is a many beautiful and a many good, and so of other things which we describe and define; to all of them the term "many" is applied.
>
> Gla: True, he said.
>
> Soc: And there is an absolute beauty and an absolute good, and of other things to which the term "many" is applied there is an absolute; for they may be brought under a single idea, which is called the essence of each.
>
> Gla: Very true.
>
> Soc: The many, as we say, are seen but not known, and the ideas are known but not seen.[11]

---

10 Plato, *The Republic*, Book VI, trans. B. Jowett, New York: Doubleday, 1989, p. 203.

11 Ibid., p. 199.

In the above exchange, when Socrates says, "ideas," understand that he is talking about the "forms", and when he says "many," he is talking about particulars. Behind this particular circle, which is imperfect, stands the perfect form of circle, which I can know only with my mind. Later on, in Book X of The Republic, we get this:

> Soc: Whenever a number of individuals have a common name, we assume them to have also a corresponding idea or form: — do you understand me?
>
> Gla: I do.
>
> Soc: Let us take any common instance; there are beds and tables in the world — plenty of them, are there not?
>
> Gla: Yes.
>
> Soc: But there are only two ideas or forms of them — one the idea of a bed, the other of a table.[12]

Plato is a metaphysical dualist, as opposed to the earlier monists that we have considered, by which we mean that he believed in two levels of reality, a visible, material level, and an unseen level which may best be described as ideal or even spiritual. It is important to understand why we do not describe Plato as a pluralist, a term we saw applied to Empedocles. A pluralist may be a strict materialist who believes in only one level of reality, but who believes that that one level is made up of more than one element — earth, air, fire, and water in the case of Empedocles and, later, of Aristotle. A monist may also be a materialist, as were the pre-socratic philosophers we have considered, or he or she might even be an idealist; but in any case the monist believes that everything is composed of one, and only one, basic element — water, in the case of Thales, or fire, in Heraclitus's case. Plato is none of these. He is a dualist, holding that there are two levels of reality. The physical level may be composed of one or many elements; the non-physical level is, as its name implies, not composed of matter at all.

Notice also that Plato's metaphysical theory may be used to reconcile the positions of Heraclitus and Parmenides, by showing how all can be changing and yet not changing, and both at the same time. Change is apparent, even obvious, to anyone who is merely looking at the immediate

---

[12] **Ibid., Book X, p. 289.**

world of the material particulars; but on the deeper and more actual world of the ideal nothing is changing, all is eternally stable, truth is always truth, beauty, justice, and courage are forever equal to themselves. Democritus's answer to Heraclitus and Parmenides was a materialistic one, making use of the notion of indestructible atoms. Plato's is both materialistic and non-materialistic.

The perceptive student will have realized by now what Socrates and Plato saw and insisted upon long ago, that in order to know real truth (this assumes of course that Socrates and Plato were correct) one must turn away from the material world to the world of the invisible forms, for that world alone is able to sustain the meaning of truth as most of us wish to understand the word.

And there is more to be said.

In order to solve the epistemological problem raised by the question of how we are able to know these unseen forms, Plato postulates the existence of the undying soul and reincarnation. We shall consider these postulations later, when we take up epistemology in greater detail.

Now, how much stock ought we to put in all of this? The modern student, particularly the American raised in a society that is empirically, pragmatically orientated, is apt to see Plato's forms as a clever, if unconvincing, mind game that belongs in a science fiction novel. One would be well advised, however, not to dismiss Plato too hastily, for physicists and mathematicians, among others, have found his ideas particularly compelling and useful in explaining the strange microcosmic world of quantum physics. No less a light than Bertrand Russell has stated that it is very difficult to understand mathematics without appealing to the forms, and in attempting to understand the odd Mandelbrot set, Roger Penrose has said:

> I cannot help feeling that, with mathematics, the case for believing in some kind of etherial, eternal existence, at least for the more profound mathematical concepts, is a good deal stronger than in. . .other cases. . .The view that mathematical concepts could exist in such a timeless, etherial sense was put forward in ancient times (c. 360 B.C.) by the great Greek philosopher Plato. Consequently, this view is frequently referred to as mathematical Platonism.[13]

---

[13] **Penrose, Roger, *The Emperor's New Mind*, Oxford: Penguin Press, 1989, p. 97.**

We will look again, and with greater scrutiny, at Plato's theories of metaphysics, epistemology, and ethics. Indeed, the purpose of this book is to examine western philosophy by seeing precisely how subsequent philosophers dealt with the problems he raised in each of these areas. One of these, a gifted young man from the north, studied with Plato for about twenty years, disagreed with much that Plato had taught him, and established a rival system of epistemology that has been championed by scientists and empiricists ever since. Are you a Platonist or an Aristotelian? That is the question.

Aristotle the Stagirite (384-322 B.C.)

"All men are either Platonic or Aristotelian," said the English poet Samuel Taylor Coleridge. This sentiment is also reflected in Raphael's famous fresco "The School of Athens", painted in the Vatican during the period we call the High Renaissance. In that work we are looking at the interior of a Romanesque temple and a crowd of togaed men ranged on either side of two central figures, Plato and Aristotle. Everyone who is anyone (or at least was up to that time) is pictured, including Socrates, Heraclitus, Pythagoras, Diogenes the cynic, and (as statues) Apollo and Athena. Raphael brilliantly suggests the metaphysical differences between Plato and Aristotle by having the older Plato point upward to the heavens and a young, bearded Aristotle point downward to the earth.

Few people have ever been asked the question, but it is an important one and I ask it again: are you Platonic or are you Aristotelian? If you are Platonic you tend to be idealistic, rationalistic, reflective. If you are Aristotelian you are more of a materialist, empirical, logical. Perhaps most of us feel we are a combination of the two.

Aristotle was a student of Plato and an outsider in Athenian society, coming from the northern city of Stagira in Thrace. By common report he came to Athens when he was about 18 years old and stayed there for at least 20 years, studying with Plato at the famous Academy. He was in fact so brilliant that it was naturally assumed he would succeed to the position of scholarch when Plato died. He did not. Instead, a local Athenian of lesser ability was chosen, and Aristotle, in something of a huff one would imagine, left Athens to go back north to the court of King Philip of Macedonia where he became tutor to the heir apparent, a wild and undisciplined lad named Alexander. Some three years later Aristotle returned to Athens and founded a rival school to the Academy, the Lyceum.

What went on in the Lyceum is of some interest because it bears directly on what ultimately came down to us as the philosophy of Aristotle. The building that housed the school was surrounded by a park and well-kept walkways, and Aristotle's method of instruction was to walk outside, talking as he went, with his students following and taking notes. This method of teaching has come to be known as the Peripatetic method, and Aristotle, and those who followed him, are sometimes called peripatetic philosophers. But it is the note taking of the students that is of particular interest to succeeding generations of scholars (all students, please pay close attention). The written works of Aristotle, including the famous *Nicomachean Ethics*, were not written down by the Philosopher himself but were compiled after his death from the notes of his students.

Now to the rather dismal end. While Aristotle was philosophizing away in Athens his former student Alexander was out conquering the known world, including all of the Peloponesian Peninsula. After Alexander's death things began to fall apart, and Athens rebelled, not only against Macedonia but against all things considered Macedonian. Aristotle was charged with not respecting the gods of the state. He fled Athens rather than stand trial, and died in the island of Euboea at the age of 62. He had invented logic, formalized the laws of inference, established the rudiments of what would become the scientific methods of inquiry, established the world's first important library, been the world's first systematic botanist and biologist — and he was all but forgotten and, with the advent of Christianity, lost to the west for over a thousand years.

The problem, from Aristotle's point of view, appears to have been that he lacked a good Christian theologian to champion his cause. Plato had Augustine, and Neoplatonism became the philosophical foundation for Christian theology for hundreds of years until finally Aristotle came back to the intellectual scene, via Arabic translations of his work discovered as the Christians and the Moslems collided with one another. In the late twelfth and the thirteenth centuries Aristotle found his champion, a Dominican monk from Aquino, Italy, named Tomaso (alias, Thomas Aquinas), who proceeded to brilliantly synthesize Aristotelian thought with Christian theology. The impact of Aristotle on European intellectual development was simply transforming. It is no exaggeration to say that science, as a disciplined method of inquiry, was generated in the womb of Aristotle's philosophy.

Naturalism is the metaphysical position which holds that there is only one level of reality, that which we experience with the senses. This opposes the Platonic dualism, which holds that there are two levels of reality, the level of the material, and that of the unseen forms.

But what, precisely, did Aristotle believe and teach?

In the first place, he was a **naturalist**, which means that he believed in only one level of reality, and that was the level available to each of us through the use of our senses. This placed him at serious odds with his famous teacher, Plato, and left him to explain the forms or reject them as useless. It may seem strange, but Aristotle did *not* reject the forms, he merely rejected Plato's idea that the forms had ontological reality and existed in an invisible world-behind-the-world. According to Aristotle, the form of a thing actually exists in the thing, not apart from it. It is the very "essence" of what the thing is, what marks it out as human, for instance, rather than fish or fowl. Aristotle thought Plato's error was, among others, linguistic; he assumed that because we label like things with common terms (Aristotle called the terms "universals") we must grant them actual existence in order to have true knowledge of them. There was, Aristotle felt, a much more commonsensical explanation for our knowledge. We simply learn, by observation, and apply our words accordingly.

This disagreement will resurface over a thousand years later as the so-called "Battle of the Universals". Peter Abelard and Thomas Aquinas will both offer Aristotelian solutions to the problem. Abelard's solution will be rejected, Aquinas's accepted.

But more of this later.

By now the student ought to understand the point Raphael is making in his famous painting, "The School of Athens", by having Plato point upward to heaven and Aristotle point down to earth. The invisible (or, in Christian terms "heavenly") world was the real one for Plato, while for Aristotle there was no reality beyond that which we see around us; and because he held that the real world was the one we perceive through our senses, and that it was actually there even as we perceive it, he urged his students to be about the business of studying physical reality. Remember, Plato believed that to know only the world of the immediate particulars, what I have just called physical reality, was to have only the most superficial knowledge of things as they are, since the eternal and unchanging truth was to be found in the world of the invisible forms. It is easy to see why Plato's philosophy was so eagerly seized upon by the early Christians, and why Aristotle, after he was rediscovered, was initially resisted by Church authorities.

Aristotle's fruitful mind gave us much of lasting value. Metaphysically, for example, he gave us metaphysics. At least he gave us the material that gave rise to the term. When his works were being collected by a later generation of scholars there was one section they didn't quite know what to do with. The *Physics* was no problem; but there were other writings that had to do with first causes, being *qua* being, that seemed out of place in a treatment of the purely physical. So they appended these writings to the *Physics* and called them *metaphysics*, or "after" (*meta*) the *Physics*, and the name stuck.

Aristotle invented logic. This is not to say that no one was thinking logically prior to his advent, but rather that prior to him no one had bothered to formalize the rules for correct reasoning and thinking. The laws of inference, for example, were first set down by Aristotle, as well as the correct forms for deductive and inductive arguments. Earlier, while discussing Parmenides, I made reference to Aristotle's law of identification, the first of his laws of inference. This law simply states that a thing is equal to itself, or in symbolic terms A = A. Parmenides's assertion that was is, *is* and what is not, *is not* is a proposition warranted by the law of identification. The statement that a thing either is or it is not is warranted by the law of the excluded middle. And the statement that something cannot be and not be at the same time is warranted by the law of contradiction. These three laws of inference, simple as they may seem, are foundational to correct thinking and appear to be universally applicable. Suppose, for example, someone wishes to argue that these do not hold in his or her society but are merely a product of the mentally straight-jacketed West. Notice that it is impossible to make such an assertion without appealing to the law of contradiction itself; for if the law of contradiction does not hold, then one is left with the curious proposition that the laws of inference hold and do not hold, and the proposition is entangled in hopeless self-contradiction.

Deduction, another of Aristotle's formulations is also universally applicable and is used by scientists, mathematicians, stockbrokers and housewives. At its simplest, deduction is reasoning from the general to the particular, or from a universal ideally derived *a priori* to a particular conclusion. The classical example of deductive reasoning is the Aristotelian syllogism, to wit:

Major Premise: All humans are mortal.
Minor Premise: Socrates is human.
Conclusion: Socrates is mortal.

Notice the movement from the general "all" downward to the particular "Socrates", with the inescapable conclusion that, if our premises are correct, Socrates indeed is mortal. Do we all, in fact, use syllogistic logic everyday? Without a doubt. Notice the following:

> Major Premise: All red traffic lights mean stop.
> Minor Premise: This is a red traffic light.
> Conclusion: I must stop at this red traffic light.

With little effort the student may think of many examples of deductive reasoning that he or she uses, or sees being used, on a daily basis. But isn't there something odd about all this? Isn't it ridiculous to say that Aristotle invented deductive logic when this implies that people not familiar with Aristotle can't be expected to stop at red lights. Remember, Aristotle did not invent the process, rather he invented, formalized the proper procedure, which was a great leap forward, for in so doing he help us to understand when to use deduction and when not to use it, and he help to show how to use it properly.

Another of Aristotle's formulations, and one of his great contributions to the intellectual development of humankind, was what might be thought of as deduction's opposite, or induction. If deduction is reasoning from the general to the particular, then induction is reasoning from the particular to the general. This is the sort of reasoning we would expect to appeal to a man like Aristotle, who was committed to the proposition that the world as we see and experience it is the real world. Observing particulars was the way, he was certain, in which to learn about ourselves and the universe we inhabit. There must be, however, a great deal more to true knowledge than just observing particulars, for if we are unable to draw general conclusions from what we observe then with each particular we must start over at ground zero, as if we had learned nothing from experience. We do not do this, nor does anyone else. Rather, we have the mental capacity to abstract certain common elements from common things and make the general observation that like behaves as like. Fire, for example, burns. I do not have to touch every fire I see to reach this conclusion. One will do. And after that, supposing I possess normal intelligence, I am able inductively to make a general proposition: all fire burns.

Inductive reasoning is at the very heart of the scientific methods of inquiry, as it will be laid down many years after Aristotle's death by such luminaries as Francis Bacon and William of Ockham. Deduction, too, is a critical component of science. Notice that the general proposition, all fires burn, established inductively by observation of particulars, may now be used as a major premise in a deductive syllogism, and the two types of reasoning identified by Aristotle are built upon one another.

Aristotle did not confine himself to physics, metaphysics, and logic. He appears to have roamed the entire intellectual landscape, writing treatises on politics, poetics, tragedy, and ethics. We will examine more closely one of his most famous works, *The Nicomachean Ethics*, when we deal with ethics later. Let us for the time being close out this chapter with the reflection that the world we inhabit would scarcely be recognizable if Aristotle, or someone like him, had not come onto the scene to provide his rich and brilliant footnote to Plato.

Chapter 2
What Shall We Do Now?

Let us swing from time's roofbeam, you and me,
Cut the Gordian knot, dance with infinity.
Let us acknowledge what we have known from youth —
The gnostics simply failed to tell the truth,
And violated a universal rule of thumb:
In God's logic one requires a middle term.
Let us not worry about the simpler matter,
Squaring the circle for instance, we'll do that later.

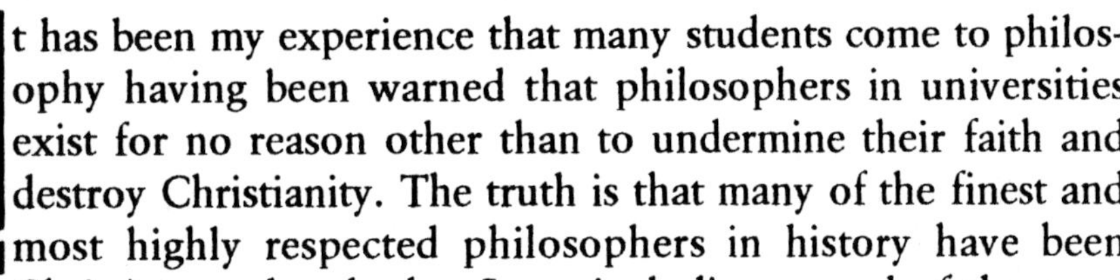

It has been my experience that many students come to philosophy having been warned that philosophers in universities exist for no reason other than to undermine their faith and destroy Christianity. The truth is that many of the finest and most highly respected philosophers in history have been Christians and orthodox Jews, including several of those we will be considering in this chapter. But it remains that during the period beginning with the fall of the Alexandrian empire, in 146 B.C., and extending for over a thousand years up to the eleventh century, philosophy did not fare particularly well. Part of the problem was that the Christians, who rose to power in the fourth century A.D., did not like the pagan Greeks or what they had been doing, no matter how brilliant they were. The classical Greeks, those we have been considering, were thorough **humanists**, whereas with Christianity we get a shift away from the human to the divine, and unless a Greek philosopher could survive this radical paradigm shift he was doomed to the dust bin. Plato survived, Aristotle did not. In an altered form Zeno and the stoics survived, Epicurus did not. There was no place in the theo-centric world of the middle ages for humanism and the pleasure principle. And even Plato had to undergo a rather strange metamorphosis to become palatable to the monks and priests who kept learning alive during what is sometimes called the Dark Ages.

Humanism, while heavy with philosophical implications, is not actually a school of philosophy. It is any philosophy which sets humans, rather than gods or non-humans, at the center, and which insists that the purpose of life, for humans, is to learn about and improve the position of humans.

The Epicureans & Stoics

The Epicureans and Stoics make an interesting appearance in the New Testament, Acts of the Apostles, Chapter 17. Paul is in Athens with no ostensible purpose other than to wait for Timothy and company and to travel on to Corinth. There he encounters philosophers identified as Epicureans and "Stoicks", who bring him up to the Areopagus for a confrontation that results in his famous sermon, now preserved in bronze and mounted at the base of the Areopagus in Athens. "Ye men of Athens," he began, "I perceive that in all things you are given to demon worship."[1] Actually, neither the Epicureans nor the Stoics can be said to have been given to demon worship, though generally the Athenians may have been. Gods and demons had little place in the thinking of either group. Epicurus held that the gods had no interest in humans whatever, for if they did, this would make them, to some degree, dependent upon human actions for their happiness and doom them to ungodlike misery. They ignored humans, which Epicurus felt was just as well. Humans, freed from any obligation to placate the gods, could pursue their own course and find their own fulfillment. Stoics, such as Epictetus, made reference to the gods and seeking the true nature of good and evil, but as the philosophy developed and was finally taken up by the Romans it became a sort of secular religion that promised the good life to those who concentrated their mental energy on those things that could actually be affected, namely the attitude and spirit.

Epicurus (341-270 B.C.)

Epicurean philosophy derives its name from Epicurus of Samos. He was a materialist, powerfully influenced by Democritus and Parmenides, who rejected the philosophies of both Plato and Aristotle as being too intellectual for anyone's good. Philosophy, he held, ought to make a difference to people:

> Vain is the word of a philosopher which does not heal any suffering of man. For just as there is no profit in medicine if it does not expel the diseases of the body, so there is no profit in philosophy if it does not expel the suffering of the mind.[2]

---

1 Acts, 17:22. King James: "Ye are given to superstition." Greek: "*deisidaimonesterous*," demon worship.

2 Epicurus, Fragment 221, in Giovanni Reale, *A History of Ancient Philosophy, vol. 3, The Systems of the Hellenistic Age*, ed. and trans. John R. Catan, Albany: State University of New York Press, 1985.

Epicurus lived in an age both cosmopolitan and, most would agree, rapidly tending toward decadence. It is not surprising that his concerns were not those of the golden-age Greeks, and that forms and first causes were not the sorts of things he gave a great deal of time to. He was a well-educated man, familiar with the philosophers who had preceded him, able to understand and comment upon various **cosmological** and metaphysical schemes and their subtle nuances, but his interest was on living the good life in the here and now. If one was miserable, what did it matter that he or she could deliver a brilliant discourse on Aristotle's four causes?

Epicurus and his followers have been traditionally associated with **hedonism**, the philosophy that says the highest good (some said the *only* good) is pleasure, and that one can do no better than to seek pleasure in whatever form one finds it.[3] In fact, he was a hedonist inasmuch as he believed and taught that the pleasure principle was fact and ought to be yielded to. But he was nothing like Aristippus of Cyrene, who believed that the physical pleasures are the highest and are always good, no matter what the source. This so-called Cyrenaic hedonism has unfortunately been laid at Epicurus's doorstep, and he and his followers have been pictured as the Greek version of Animal House. What he actually taught was that moderation in all things was the rule to follow, and that the simple pleasures of the mind were those to be sought by any who wished to find true happiness:

Hedonism: The pleasure principle, the belief that the pursuit of pleasure is what life ought to be about. In its strictest form, nothing that gives pleasure is wrong.

> My body exalts in living delicately on bread and water and it rejects the pleasures of luxury, not in themselves, but because of the trouble that follows upon them.[4]

Many years later John Stuart Mill, in *Utilitarianism*, came to the defense of Epicurus (and to his own as well) by stating that the followers of Epicurus, at a very early period, were contemptuously described as having no higher end than pleasure and desire, a "doctrine worthy only of swine". But, says Mill,

---

[3] There are, of course, a variety of schools clustered beneath the hedonistic penumbra, and how much pleasure one should seek, or what type, depended upon whom one chose to listen to.

[4] Stobaeus, *Anthology*, bk. 3, sec. 17, line 33, in Reale, *Systems of the Hellenistic Age*, p. 170.

> There is no known Epicurean theory of life which does not assign to the pleasures of the intellect, of the feelings and imagination, and of the moral sentiments a much higher value as pleasures than to those of mere sensation.[5]

The Epicureans survived into the Roman period, only to dwindle and die as the Christian tide swept in with its austere code of strict morality. The Stoics fared a good deal better, being sufficiently austere and moralistic to commend themselves to the church fathers. Founded by Zeno (c. 334-262 B.C.), the system took its name from the Greek *stoa*,[6] because Zeno was reputed to have done most of his teaching from the *stoa poikile*, the painted porch, of one of the temples. Stoicism appealed not only to the later Christians, but of more immediate importance, to the Romans who were even then in the process of taking over the known world; and stoicism has a certain attraction that has kept it alive and relevant to the present.

A stoic individual is typically pictured as one who shows no emotion, either sorrow or elation, pain or pleasure. This is not necessarily true, but it is close enough to the truth to be useful to the student. Ask yourself, "How free am I, and to what extent do I actually control my own destiny?" The answer must be, in both cases, not much. Did you, for example, choose where you would be born, to whom you would be born, what sex you would be, what race you would be, how rich or poor you would be? If you answered, "No," to all of the above, as I assume you did, then ask yourself how much of your life you currently control. Must we not all admit that we have very little control over our lives moment by moment, day by day? In fact, doesn't a great deal of our frustration and misery spring from the fact that we have little control over most things, but that we go about assuming that we do, and should? Perhaps we are all driven, as Friedrich Nietzsche held, by the will to power, but if this is the case, then we are doomed to defeat because we are virtually powerless to affect a major portion of the events in which we are caught up.

But there is one thing we can control, say the Stoics, and that is ourselves. At least we can control our own minds and our own attitudes, and if we can, by a personal act of the will, do this much, then we can be happy

---

[5] Mill, John Stuart, *Utilitarianism*, New York: Bobbs-Merrill, 1957.

[6] i.e. "a porch"

no matter what the external circumstances. Mental self-discipline then becomes the stoic key to the good life, because this is all we can hope for, and it is foolish to makes one's happiness dependent upon forces, events, other people, over which one can exert no control whatever.

It doesn't take a good deal of reflection to realize that this was a philosophy almost made to order for the Romans, a people who emphasized, above all else, doing one's duty regardless of the cost. It is revealing that one of the foremost stoic philosophers in history was the Roman emperor Marcus Aurelius Antoninus (A.D. 121-180), who wrote on an occasion:

> The ruling mind does not disturb itself; I mean, does not frighten itself or cause itself pain. . .Let the body take care, if it can, that it suffers nothing, but let it speak if it suffers. But the soul, the seat of fear and pain, has full power to form an opinion about these things and need suffer nothing, unless at times it deviates into an opinion. The mind itself wants nothing, unless it creates a want for itself; therefore it is both free from perturbation and unimpeded, if it does not perturb and impede itself.[7]

Herein we find the very heart and soul of stoicism, as it was understood and practiced by the Romans, as it was, in fact, understood and practiced by the Greeks. The Stoic seizes control of his or her mind and attitudes and thereby refuses to allow the uncontrollable events of life to dictate the terms of happiness. I have found that students usually have a good deal of fun with this one, as well as deriving a good deal of profit from it. It is immediately applicable to anyone's life, and one needn't be an advanced student of logic or metaphysics to put it to work. But it does take mental discipline.

Aside from Marcus Arelius, the greatest of the Stoics was probably Epictetus (c. A.D. 50-130), who began life as a Greek slave and became one of the most prominent philosophers of his day.[8] Think of the life of a slave, and you may understand why the philosophy of Zeno the Stoic would have been appealing to this man; for the slave owns nothing, not even his own

---

7 **Marcus Aurelius, *Meditations*, trans. George Long, Roslyn, New York: Walter J. Black, Inc., 1945, pg. 70.**

8 **Other famous stoics include Cicero, Cato, and Seneca, all in high places of Roman authority.**

life, but is constantly at the beck and call of the master. According to tradition, Epictetus's master broke his (Epictetus's) leg while punishing him for something he didn't do. "If you continue to twist my leg," he is supposed to have said, "you will break it." And when the leg snapped: "You see, I told you so."

Epictetus wrote a short work, *The Enchiridion*, which opens in words heavy with wisdom and from which we all can benefit:

> There are things which are within our power, and there are things which are beyond our power. Within our power are opinion, aim, desire, aversion, and, in one word, whatever affairs are our own. Beyond our power are body, property, reputation, office, and, in one word, whatever are not properly our own affairs.[9]

The Enchiridion became standard issue for Roman soldiers, and was carried into battle all over the Empire. Who, more than a soldier, understands the value of discipline, the necessity of steeling oneself against pain and hardship? But there is more than one kind of warfare, and there are those, the Apostle Paul among them, who used the figure of a soldier doing battle as symbolic of the Christian warring against the world, the flesh, and the devil. There was much in Stoic philosophy that appealed to the Christians, which is why Stoicism powerfully influenced those early believers. Stoics, for example, believed in Fate as the controlling force in one's external life. It was relatively easy for the Christians to substitute God for Fate, and, with their belief that all things that come from God must be good, to urge their brothers and sisters to rejoice in the face of incredible hardship and trial. Another feature of Stoicism that the early Christians found attractive was that the Stoics, unlike the Epicureans, were not pursuing pleasure, whether the higher or the lower type. Rather, if pleasure came, they rejoiced in it; if hardship came, they treated it like pleasure. Either was an imposter, fated to come into all lives, under the control of none, and bound to last only so long and then go away. This Stoic image of the philosopher has become something of a stereotype in the western world, so that all philosophers are pictured as being cool, in control, logical, somewhat above it all. My wife, who lives with a philosopher, probably has an earthier assessment.

---

[9] Epictetus, *The Enchiridion*, in *Discourses of Epictetus*, trans. Thomas Wentworth Higginson, Roslyn, New York: Walter J. Black, Inc., 1944, p. 331.

Stoicism as a philosophical system began about 200 years before the birth of Christ, and came to fruition during the first century of the Christian era. So did a renovated form of an earlier philosophy, Platonism. Both of these were powerfully influential on the intellectual formation of the new faith.

Augustine, Biship of Hippo (A.D. 354-430)

I have often thought it would be interesting to do a study of Protestantism and Catholism to determine to what extent, if any, the theological differences in the two can be traced back to the basic Plato/Aristotle split. Martin Luther, who led the Protestant reformation, was an Augustinian; Thomas Aquinas, the official philosopher of the Catholic Church, was Aristotelian. I doubt that I shall ever find the time to undertake such an enterprise, but perhaps one of my students will, and make glowing references to my inspirational suggestions in the foreword of her book, or his. Augustine was committed deeply to the Platonic world view, as deeply committed to it as Aquinas would later be to the Aristotelian view. But the Platonic philosophy Augustine took up, and which, along with the New Testament, became foundational to his theology, was not exactly the philosophy of Plato but Plato in a new form, or Neoplatonism.

By the time Augustine arrived, the new center of intellectual activity in the Greek world had become Alexandria, Egypt. Here Jew, Greek, Roman and Arab mingled, and the result was a true melting pot in which idea vied with idea for ascendancy. Many of the Alexandrian intellectuals were of a mystic bent, and Plato's thinking appealed to them. He had taught that the world we see around us — changing, temporal, ephemeral — was not the proper object for the attention of the philosopher. Rather, true thought was always about the forms, those eternal, non-spatial, invisible entities that exist in a world-behind-the-world, and give the material world such substance as it has. One can almost hear the Apostle Paul whispering in the background: "That which is seen is temporal, but that which is unseen is eternal."[10]

Two Alexandrians deserve to be mentioned as important to the formation of Neoplatonism, Philo (25 B.C.- A.D. 40) and Plotinus (A.D. 204-269). The differences in the two are many, and complex, (Philo, for example, is more often referred to as a Middle-Platonist rather than a Neoplatonist.), and both constructed complicated metaphysical systems which the student, at this point, need not worry about; but both are

---

[10] II Cor. 4:18.

important to an understanding of early Christianity, and Plotinus in particular was a critical factor in Augustine's being attracted away from Manicheanism and to the Christian faith.

Philo was a Jew who was staunchly orthodox, at least when it came to adhering to the Jewish ceremonial law, but who also was drawn to the philosophy of Plato, particularly to the metaphysics of the *Timaeus.* He seems to have been sincere in his belief that the Greek philosophers were influenced by the Hebrew prophets, though there is no evidence to support such a belief. Nonetheless, he took it upon himself to attempt a synthesis between the two, which he accomplished by allegorizing the scriptures. For our purposes, however, and to establish an intellectual link between Philo and the Christians, we need to direct our attention to a Greek notion that goes back at least to Heraclitus, was prominent in the teaching of the Pythagoreans, and was taken up by Plato when he came on the scene. This is the so-called *logos.*[11] "*En arche en ho logos,*" wrote the Apostle John. "*Kai ho logos en pros ton theon, kai theos en ho logos.*" Translated: In beginning was the Word, and the Word was toward the God, and God was the Word. Christians identified the *Logos* as the Christ, the Second Person of the Trinity. What did it mean to the Greeks, or more importantly, what did it mean to Philo, and later, to Plotinus?

Logos: a Greek word that may be translated "word, expression, concept."

Nous is the word that is usually translated "mind."

Within their very complex cosmologies, the Logos was something of a creative agent, sometimes identified with *Nous*, or mind, but clearly subordinate to God. It appears to have been thought of as the lodging place of the forms, which were ultimately expressed in the grosser materialistic particulars we see in creation. Notice what Philo and Plotinus did. They took Plato's metaphysics and made it, to some degree at least, palatable to Christians. This is a woefully oversimplified treatment of Neoplatonism, but it will do for now. The important thing is that Neoplatonism, in a variety of forms, swept the Mediterranean world in the early Christian era, and for awhile rivaled Christianity. It didn't prevail, according to Copleston, because it was so complicated that it left all but the philosophers in utter bewilderment.[12] But it certainly was not beyond the grasp of Augustine, the

---

[11] *Logos* is very difficult to translate into English, because it has multiple meanings, depending upon how it is used. It is translated (see below) in the first chapter of John in the New Testament; but it might mean concept, expression, or even idea. Clearly, it carries the connotation of something being communicated.

[12] Copleston, Frederick, *A History of Philosophy*: Vol. 1, Part II, Greece and Rome, Garden City, New York: Image Books, 1962.

bad boy turned saint, who was the first major theologian of the Christian Church, and who influenced Christianity far beyond what many today seem to realize.

Augustine was born in 354 in Thagaste, a city in North Africa. His mother, Monica, was Christian; his father, Patricius, was not. He was sent to study in Carthage, was well educated, and was introduced through his studies to current philosophies. Because he could, and did, think deeply in his search for the truth, he was quick to detect problems in the Christian position that seemed to him unresolvable. It was the old problem of evil, raised in its best known form by the Epicureans centuries before; to wit:

> Is God able to prevent evil, but not willing?
> Then He is not all-good.
> Is God willing to prevent evil, but not able?
> Then He is not all-powerful.
> Is He both willing and able?
> Then whence comes evil?

If either of the first two questions is answered in the affirmative, then the God of the Old and New Testaments, that is to say the God of the **theists**, is non-existent, for it is an article of faith with the theists (and this includes both Christians and orthodox Jews) that God is both all good and all powerful. And yet if God is both willing and able to prevent evil, then we are left to struggle with the final question — why is there evil in the world? One way to deal with the problem is to deny the existence of evil, and there have been some over the years who have taken that route. Others, such as Leibniz, have chosen a middle path, admitting that there are things in the world that certainly appear to be evil, but that we must admit, given an all-powerful God and infinity from which to draw, this must be the best of all possible worlds.

Theism is the belief that God is a person, all-wise, all-knowing, all-powerful, and actively involved in creation.

Augustine could not stand for such solutions. I applaud his honesty, for the first solution denies reality, and the solution of Leibniz begs the question rather than answering it.

Others say that the answer is obvious. God has neither created nor willed evil. Rather, he has given humans free choice, and they have used this marvelous gift to bring in all the misery we see around us. This might account for moral evil, but it does nothing to account for the multitude of natural evils, such as earthquakes, fires and floods. And it solves the problem

Omniscience & Omni-benevolence: just fancy Latin terms for all-knowing, and all-good. Both of these are necessary traits if the theists are correct about God's nature.

of moral evil only by sacrificing two of the attributes of God necessary to the Christian faith — God's **omniscience**, and His **omni-benevolence.**

Where could Augustine go?

It seemed to him that there must be two spiritual forces, equally powerful, struggling with one another for dominance of the cosmos. One of them must be good, and one must be evil, and neither could be omnipotent. Thus, Augustine was drawn to Manichaeanism, a religion founded by a third-century Persian named Mani. His adherence to this doctrine didn't last long, and he became a skeptic, wondering for a time whether or not he himself actually existed. It was through reading the *Enneads* of Plotinus that he finally found a way of solving, to his own satisfaction, the problem of evil that had kept him from Christianity. Plotinus had taught that evil was not a positive thing, but that it was rather a privation, an absence of the good. The student is apt to find this puzzling rather than satisfying, so let us think about it. Recall that the Manichaeans posited two forces of equal power, one good and one evil, struggling for supremacy. Certainly, in looking at the world, that seems to be the case. But suppose I hold up two cards, one black and the other — make it any color you wish — say white. I ask, how many colors do you see? Two, you would probably respond. Yes, I might say, I know it looks that way, but in fact one of these is not color at all but is merely the total absence of any color, and the other is a mixture of all the colors of the spectrum. One is positive, very positive, the other is very negative, so negative that it is actually nothing but total privation.

This seems to be of little help in resolving the problem, and at any rate it is a simple illustration of something which in Plotinus is much more complex, but combined with the Platonic teaching of a world of immaterial reality, it got Augustine out of his skepticism and started him on the road to conversion to Christianity. Ultimately he became, not only a Christian, but a bishop, a theologian, the most important philosopher of the early Middle Ages, and the author of three major books, *The Confessions*, *The City of God*, and his **theodicy,**[13] *On Free Choice of the Will.*

The Confessions and *The City of God* are by far the most widely read of the works of Augustine, but *On Free Choice of the Will*, while not as well known to the reading public, is in many ways the most influential of all, for

---

[13] A "theodicy" is a work which undertakes to justify the ways of God to men. Perhaps the best known theodicy is that of Leibniz, which he called (what else?) *Theodicy*. It was this work that Voltaire lampooned in *Candide*, with Dr. Pangloss's repeated assurance that we are living in the best of all possible worlds.

it is in this work that Augustine lays out many of the arguments one hears even today when people discuss God and the problems of theism. Free will, for instance, and whether or not there is such a thing, has troubled philosophers almost from the very beginning, but it has been particularly troubling to Christians. If God knows everything, and that is certainly one of His attributes according to theists, then He must know not only what has happened, but what is happening, and will happen. But what does this do for the idea of free will? If God already knows what we will do, then in what sense can we said to be truly free? Must we not be moving in the divine thought waves, carried along on a river from which there is no escape? Augustine's solution to this is at once Christian and Platonic. Time is something that exists in the physical sphere, and in that sphere it runs in only one direction; but God is outside the sphere of time altogether, seeing past, present and future as one eternal present. Seeing all, however, is not the same as controlling all, and in the temporal sphere we inhabit there is indeed freedom of will.

It is this freedom of will that also allows for the existence of evil in a world created by a good God. This adds something to Plotinus's conception of evil as a privation of good.

> The positive, existent quality is righteousness, and sin is a willful deviation into that which God never created and never intended. God gave humans free will, not so that they could do evil, but so that they could freely do good, and absent the possibility of sinful behavior righteous behavior is meaningless. . . Thus, to blame the fault of a creature is to praise his or her essential nature, that of a free, rational being created in the image of god.

This quotation is one of my own, from another book, and I think it expresses the Augustinian position as well as anything else I might have chosen.

When it came to the creative action of God, Augustine was an **exemplarist**, which means that the physical things of this universe exist in seminal form (as seeds) in the mind of God, and that they are then manifested forth as we see them all around us. Typically, students find this a bit strange, but they also find Plato's teaching of the forms strange. If one thinks about it a bit, however, and assuming the thinking one is a theist, it isn't quite so strange after all. Would it not be correct to say (once again, I assume I am addressing a theist) that everything we see sprang from the mind of God and may therefore be thought of as existing first as an idea in the mind of God? And if the answer to this is, "Yes," and if we have agreed with Augustine that God lives in a timeless eternity, then is it so difficult to imagine that all of the "ideas" are eternally existent with him? It almost seems, as many of the early Christians believed, that Plato, pagan that he was, had some sort of insight into divine matters. They probably had it backwards.[14] The truth is probably the other way around: Plato looks so Christian in so many ways because he was so influential on the development of early Christianity; and the more accurate statement would be that the Christians look very Platonic.

Very well, we now have a dualistic cosmology with the eternal God and the forms (ideas in God's mind) existing apart from the material world. The material world is, of course, temporal and passing away, and the unseen world is nontemporal and abides forever. Do we have access to the unseen world in any form? Augustine's answer is that we do, and he immediately cites the examples of what philosophers have come to call *a priori* truths, the self-evident truths such as the axioms of geometry. The shortest distance between two points on a plane surface is a straight line. The angles of a triangle total to 180°. These truths are also ideas in the mind of God, and we can know them and use them any day we choose; but though they are in the world they are, in an important sense, not of the world, and they actually exist in that eternal non-time with God. Thus, there are some truths that seem to occupy a position in both camps.

The dualism of Augustine shows itself in another important way as well. There were, for him, two cities, the City of God and the City of the World. Initially humans were members of the City of God, but with the loss of innocence in the Garden of Eden, and the fall, humans took up residence in the City of the World. After the coming of Christ, citizenship in the City of God was again made possible, and some have been saved and have moved into the heavenly city. His ideas in this regard are expressed in his famous work, *The City of God.* The important thing is to notice Augustine's strong resemblance to the Neoplatonics, and, backward through them, to Plato himself. One could deny this, of course. Some have said that Augustine was really influenced by the New Testament, from which he quotes so liberally so often. After all, mightn't one make most of Augustine's arguments about

---

[14] **I once had a psychology professor who remarked how confused some individuals get about the ancients. He had heard someone say how brilliant Sophokles was to have anticipated Freud. Wrong, said the professor. Better said — how clever Freud was to have hitched his wagon to Sophokles.**

creation using biblical texts for support rather than Plato? To a degree the answer is yes. There is no doubt that the New Testament, as well as the Old, were critical to the development of Augustine's philosophy and to his understanding of God, salvation, and escatology. But one cannot read Augustine without seeing the depth of his debt to Plotinus and Plato.

The importance of this indebtedness is two-fold, assuming that one wishes to understand the development of philosophy in the west. First, the notion that the period from the fall of the Rome Empire (A.D. 410 or A.D. 476, depending upon which historian one is consulting) to the onset of the High Middle Ages was some sort of "dark age" is simply not true. Learning did not cease, philosophy did not grind to a halt, and the Greeks did not disappear from the scene. Aristotle in fact went away, and with him went any hope for a viable science; but Plato, in a modified form, remained active. Second, the Platonic cosmology became the Christian cosmology, and because the Church was the center of learning and scholarship during this period, the Platonic cosmology became the cosmology of the West.[15]

The word **cosmology** is an interesting one, and is well worth the attention of the student of philosophy. Like so much of our intellectual vocabulary, it is a product of the Greeks. The word *logos* is one we have already discussed, but *cosmos*, while familiar to most students because of its use in such words as cosmonaut and cosmetic, may need some elucidation. It basically means an orderly arrangement, and it is interesting that the Greeks, specifically the Pythagoreans, were the first to use the word to signify the universe. This shows that, to the Greeks, this space in which we live is one that is ordered, that it follows rules, and that it may be understood. Cosmology, closely related to metaphysics, is the study of this supposed orderly arrangement.

Cosmos: a Greek word which carries the idea of an ordered arrangement. It is significant that the Greeks used this word to indicate the universe in which we live.

Now, when we speak of the Christian cosmology, or the Western cosmology, and of its having sprung from the Platonic cosmology, what ought that to tell us? If the proposition is true, then most Westerners ought to take a dualistic metaphysical position, whether or not they would actually state their case in these terms. You might try this the next time you are lounging about the home with family, or standing with drink in hand at a party, or sitting in the student center over cokes and french fries with

---

[15] **This is the sort of generalization that philosophers love to leap into the middle of, and I can almost hear the murmur of dissent issuing from universities across the land. I understand that anyone familiar with history can produce exceptions that give lie to the generalization, nonetheless I must hold with the truth of the generalization.**

academically challenged individuals. Engage them in a metaphysical discussion by asking whether or not they agree that there is a good deal more to the universe than meets the eye. They may initially consider you mad, but they will probably warm to the subject when they realize that you are merely a curious person attempting to expand your horizons. Press them. Do they agree that the universe we see is a mere portion of what is really there, and that there is an unseen world behind this world which houses a host of powerful beings who are both aware of, and exercise some control over, the world in which we move? Chances are that most will agree to your proposition, though they may disagree as to how the orderly arrangement is fine tuned.

This is Plato. And this is Plotinus. And this is Augustine. And, of course, this is Judeo-Christian. This is the dualistic universe of Western humanity, the world of particulars and forms, the world of flesh and spirit, of the temporal and the eternal. This is why the vast majority of those inhabiting the portion of our globe from Russia to San Francisco and from the North Cape to the Persian Gulf believe in life after death, or in some form of reincarnation. Ideas do indeed have consequences, and it would be difficult to find a philosopher whose ideas have had more of an impact on our collective psyche than the North African saint, Augustine of Hippo.

But there was also another saint.

Thomas Aquinas (1275-1274)

Brother Thomas Aquinas,
good Dominican, plus or minus
a few heterodox deviations,
leaves Cell and Meditations
to wander in the Garden,
ease the massive burden
of his body onto a bench
beneath an oak.

Brother Thomas excuses
himself from books, induces
God from the shadow
on a sundial. Meadow
and wood pulsate
with spring. Late
snow crests foothills
to the north. Daffodils
nod before him.

I like wind, mountain thunder.
I like rain. I wonder,
and wondering I am sad
that Aristotle never made
connection between spring
and One who will bring
life out of death,
and bring rebirth.

Brother Thomas Aquinas,
good Dominican, zealous
of truth and beauty,
rises, returns to duty,
seeking the infinite
in imagined debate
with unnamed adversaries,
sighs to himself, buries
his wondering soul
in ink and parchment scroll.
Brother Thomas,
the good Dominican.

Being a philosopher is not a prerequisite for sainthood, nor conversely does being a saint qualify one as a competent philosopher. But during the time we are considering, being a philosopher usually did imply that one was either a cleric or was somehow attached to the Church. Bonaventure was canonized. Most of the others had to be satisfied with more modest accolades.

From the death of Augustine until the rise of Christian Scholasticism philosophy crept forward in paths projected by Plato and his children. In 524 Boethius penned his stoical masterpiece, *The Consolation of Philosophy.* In the ninth century the Carolingian Renaissance under the tutelage of Alcuin stirred up the waters at Aachen. But in general things were rather quiet. After all, when one has the truth and has structured a nice, orderly universe, why would one bother to look farther, or tolerate those who wish to. Then events conspired to roll the stone away from Aristotle's tomb with results that I can only describe as explosive.

Aristotle had, it turned out, only been entombed in the West. In the Middle East he was alive and well, venerated by the philosophers of Islam such as Averoes and Avicenna, and Islam was on the march. The westward movement of Islam was one of the conspiring events that resurrected Aristotle in Europe. The eastward movement of Europeans, following the proclamation of the first Crusade by Urban II (1095) was another. At about this time the *Organon* (Aristotle's work on logic) became available in Latin translation under the title given it by Boethius, *Logica Vetus.* James of Venice translated a number of his works from the Greek into Latin, and there were also translations from Arabic into Latin in Moslem-controlled Spain. By the end of the twelfth century the *Nicomachean Ethics* was available in translation.

These works were not received with any degree of joy in the Christian west because they opened a whole new non-theological philosophical world, and challenged the Augustinian view of the universe.[16] But Aristotle could be held neither down, nor back. Europe, and with it the entire West, was about to be transformed. No one knew it at the time, but we were on our way outward to the moon and planets and inward to the quanta and the neutrino. We were going to create television, microwave ovens, internal combustion engines — and nuclear bombs.

By the middle of the eleventh century Europe had its first university, the University of Salerno. In the twelfth century the University of Bologna was chartered, and, not long after, Paris, Oxford and Cambridge. The universities became critical to the development of philosophy in the west, because it was here that philosophy became secularized, divorcing itself from the church. From Augustine to the beginning of the High Middle Ages the Church was the repository of philosophy, the haven of philosophers, and most of these could as easily have been called **theologians.**[17] From the twelfth century to roughly the fifteenth century philosophy was carried on almost exclusively within the walls of the universities. Beginning with René Descartes (seventeenth century), and for a period of about two-hundred years thereafter, the most important philosophers operated outside both university and church. The twentieth century has seen a return of philosophy to the universities. With a few exceptions, theology never left the seminary.

Thomas Aquinas was a university man, spending a great deal of his

---

[16] Frederick Copleston discusses the Church's early prohibitions of Aristotle at some length. See Copleston, Frederick, *A History of Philosophy, Mediaeval Philosophy*, Vol. 2, Part I, Garden City, New York: Image Books, 1962, pp. 232-38.

[17] Philosophy is not theology, though the two disciplines have traditionally been close to one another. Theology (literally "God talk") is the study of God and religion by individuals already committed to belief in both. Philosophy brings no such prior commitment with it, and also studies many things outside the scope of theology.

productive life at the University of Paris. Now, let us see how he came to be there.

He was born in 1225 near Naples, Italy to a wealthy family. His father was closely related to the Count of Aquino. In those days it was a good thing to place a family member as high up the Church's hierarchical ladder as possible, and young Thomas, because of his obvious mental ability, was groomed from the beginning for such a position. At the age of five he was enrolled in the Benedictine abbey school at Montecassino.[18]

In 1239 Thomas was sent to the Imperial University of Naples, and he began to deviate from family plans. He was befriended by Dominican monks, intellectuals under strict vows of poverty, and he announced he intended to join the order. His mother threw something of a fit and sent his brothers, who were army officers, to kidnap him until he came to his senses. According to the story, he was held captive for several months, during which time he was pressured to renounce his vows and come back to the original career outline. They even went so far (if one chooses to believe one sensational account[19]) as to send a provocatively dressed girl into his room one night Quote: "She tempted him to sin, using all the devices at her disposal, glances, caresses and gestures." He prayed until she left. Finally, his family relented, and back he went to the Dominicans, who sent him to the University of Cologne to study with Albertus Magnus, and eventually to the University of Paris.

Because the university life of the thirteenth century was so vital to the development of Aquinas as a philosopher, we need to see what this life entailed. In the first place, "university" comes from a Latin term that means a corporation, and the typical university of the time was chartered, much as a corporation is today. Receiving its charter from the Church, or the government, or both, the university was virtually independent of the community in which it was located, a fact which led, in many cases, to hostility between the students and the local citizens. "Town and gown" conflicts were insured by the law's having no jurisdiction on campus. Ah, me! The more things change, the more they stay the same.

---

[18] **Those my age and older will know the name. During World War II the Axis turned it into a fort. We bombed it, much to the distress of many, including General Eisenhower, who had to make the final decision to bomb.**

[19] **William of Tocco in Bourke, *Aquinas' Search for Wisdom*, p. 37.**

The degree program was basically the same then as it is now. Four years of study led to the bachelor's degree. Another two years got one a master's. Four more years, with dissertation orals, and public defense of thesis and the student became a doctor and could go forth and make students as miserable as he had been.[20]

The course of study for a bachelor's degree was the *trivium:* grammar, rhetoric, and logic. For the master's degree one took up the *quadrivium*: arithmetic, geometry, astronomy, and music, plus the works of Aristotle. Thus, the seven liberal arts.

Students seem to have done as much singing and drinking in those days as they did studying (Students today are much more serious), a typical student song running as follows:

Let us live then, and be glad
While young life's before us!
After youthful pastime had,
After old age, hard and sad,
Earth will slumber o'er us.

Live this university,
Men that learning nourish.
Live each member of the same
Long live all that bear its name.
Let them ever flourish![21]

Of particular interest is the debate, a forum held in public and governed by strict rules, in which the students vied with one another before panels of doctors. Many students have asked me why Aquinas's arguments take the form that they do. The answer is, it is the form of the medieval university debate. The proposition is stated, always in terms that Aquinas intends to disprove, with arguments for the proposition following, and Aquinas's arguments against the proposition at the end. Another thing noted by students and questioned: "Who is the 'Philosopher' he keeps referring

---

[20] **"...As miserable as he had been" is *not* sexist language. It is fact. No females were allowed in these universities.**

[21] **Quoted in Lamm, Robert C. & Neal M. Cross, *A Search for Human Values*, Vol. I, 9th Ed., Dubuque, Iowa: Brown & Benchmark, 1993.**

to?" It is Aristotle. By the time Aquinas was writing, Aristotle was so highly regarded that he was simply referred to as "the Philosopher", with no further identification needed. One cannot read Aquinas without realizing that Aristotle was second only to the Bible or earlier church fathers in authority. To cite Aristotle was to win the argument, or at least to badly cripple one's opponent, assuming he could not reply with something more authoritative (i.e., scripture or a Church Father). This will give some insight into why, when scientists such as Copernicus and Galileo began questioning Aristotle, they were treated by the Church as heretics. To illustrate, here is a sample of a Thomistic argument, from his monumental work, *The Summa Theologica.*

WHETHER VIOLENCE CAUSES INVOLUNTARINESS

We Proceed thus to the Fifth Article:--

Objection I. It would seem that violence does not cause involuntariness. For we speak of voluntariness and involuntariness in terms of the will. But violence cannot be done to the will, as was shown above. Therefore violence cannot cause involuntariness.

Obj. 2. Further, that which is done involuntarily is done with grief, as Damascene and the Philosopher say. But sometimes a man suffers compulsion without being grieved thereby. Therefore violence does not cause involuntariness.

Obj. 3. Further, what is from the will cannot be involuntary. But some violent actions proceed from the will. . .Therefore violence does not cause involuntariness.

On the contrary, The Philosopher *and* Damascene *say that things done under compulsion are involuntary. I answer that,* Violence is directly opposed to the voluntary, as likewise to the natural. For the voluntary and the natural have this in common, that both are from an intrinsic principle, whereas the violent is from an extrinsic principle. And for this reason, just as in things devoid of knowledge. . .it effects something against the will. . .

Reply Obj. 3. As the Philosopher says, the movement of an animal, whereby at times an animal is moved against the natural inclination of the body, although it is not natural to the body, is nevertheless in a way natural to

> the animal, to which it is natural to be moved according to the appetite. Accordingly this is violent, not absolutely, but relatively.[22]

The Battle of the Universals was a major debate that broke out in the universities of the High Middle Ages. It pitted the "realists", those who believed Plato's forms actually existed, against the "nominalists", those who thought these were only names, semantical devices used for purposes of communication.

One final observation I wish to make before we get to the actual philosophy of Thomas Aquinas. Instruction in the medieval universities was always and only in Latin. The Latin Quarter in Paris was so named because that is where the students lived, and all students uniformly spoke Latin to one another as a sort of initiates language. Thus, if someone claimed to be a student but could not speak Latin, he was lying. It would not be until the seventeenth century, with René Descartes, that philosophers would begin to write in the vernacular.

In the late eleventh century a philosophical battle erupted in the universities pitting Plato against Aristotle, and the **nominalists** against the **realists**, the so-called **Battle of the Universals**. The problem was suggested as early as the sixth century by Boethius, and as time went on philosophers began choosing sides, with Anselm of Canterbury among others lining up with the realists, and Roscelin siding with the nominalists.

To appreciate the argument the student will need to refresh his or her memory of Plato and Aristotle and their respective doctrines of the forms. Plato postulated the necessity of the forms, because without them there could be no ultimate truth about abstract qualities, and without truth in these areas we can have no real knowledge of things most important to the human enterprise. Aristotle agreed, but he did not agree that this necessitated giving the forms (remember, he called them universals) ontological existence in an invisible, eternal world-behind-the-world. Here the battle was joined. The realists argued that the forms were real, which was not only Platonic but was Augustinian, and seemed to be demanded by a literal understanding of the New Testament. The nominalists ("Come on, guys, they're only names.") felt that the realists were postulating the unnecessary, that the universals were certainly needed for purposes of communication, but that to give them actual existence was to move backward to the very sort of superstition and foolishness that they should all be struggling to get away from. Clearly the

---

[22] Thomas Aquinas, *The Summa Theologica*, in *Introduction to Saint Thomas Aquinas*, ed. Anton C. Pegis, New York: Random House, 1948, pp. 487-488.

This abbreviated quotation is given merely to show the format of Aquinas. The full argument is a good deal more complex.

nominalists were skirting the edge of heresy, at the least, and had plunged headlong into serious heresy at the worst.

This may seem on its face to be the sort of argument typical of those associated with medieval Scholastic philosophers (i.e. "Can God make a rock He cannot move? . . How many angels can dance on the head of pin?"), but philosophers understand that its metaphysical implications are weighty, and its resolution critical to the development of science in the west. There is no doubt about it — this was a pivotal moment in Western intellectual development. Were we to arm ourselves with Ockham's razor[23] or not?

In the twelfth century the rather brilliant Peter Abelard (University of Paris) attempted a compromise called Conceptualism, suggesting that both positions were correct to some degree, that form is real, but that it exists in the object itself and not apart from it. I have the uncomfortable feeling that the student is not sure what all this means, and it is certain that I cannot clear up in a few paragraphs what it took the best minds in Europe several centuries to untangle. It will have to suffice to say that Abelard's solution was basically Aristotelian, and that he was all but run out of town for his efforts. Actually, his real problem appears to be that he was about a hundred years ahead of his time.[24] This is odd as it turns out because his argument, rejected by the Church, is substantially the same one taken up, dusted off, and used in a more polished form by Aquinas a century later. But by then Aristotle's views were better known and philosophers had a more complete body of his thought to work from. Thus Aquinas came in at the end of the fight and helped to resolve it with a synthesis that has stood unchallenged by Catholics since that time.[25] Synthesizing Church theology with Aristotle's philosophy became Thomas Aquinas's specialty, and he did it as no one has been able to, before or since.

Thomas believed, as had others, that the human intellect, if properly

---

[23] **The principle named for William of Ockham, about whom more anon.**

[24] **The student who is simply dying to get into the Battle of the Universals and relive the thrilling experiences of yesteryear is directed to the work of Frederick Copleston, who produced one of the best-known histories of philosophy. But this is slow going for beginners. Bertrand Russell, *A History of Western Philosophy*, is much easier to read.**

[25] **Aquinas remains the official philosopher of the Catholic church, and Thomism the official Catholic philosophy.**

used, would not contradict revelation, for both were given by God. This is not to say that he thought intellect would bring one to the same place as revelation, because the human intellect was limited by the fact that it was human, thus finite, thus subject to sin and error; but there was a great deal that the intellect could tell one about the way the universe is structured and about the One who structured it. And what if rational thought were to produce conclusions that contradicted the faith? That would be proof, for Aquinas, that the thinker had erred in his thought processes. Aquinas is begging the question, of course, but we will overlook that for the time being.

There were few areas of human experience that did not come under the scrutiny of this remarkable man and are not treated of in his two tomes, *Summa Theologica* and *Summa Contra Gentiles.* We will look at two of his better known efforts here, and in greater detail later. First, his arguments for the existence of God. Second, his arguments concerning law and government.

It can scarcely surprise anyone that a Dominican monk would attempt to prove the existence of God, particularly if he believed, as Thomas did, that the human intellect was capable of arriving at some of the revelatory truths. Most everyone who was anyone, from Augustine up to and including the Scholastics, had arguments for God's existence, and it would have been a strange thing if one of these churchmen had said, as most contemporary philosophers believe, that God cannot be shown by rational argument either to exist or to not exist. Unconstrained by Hume and Immanuel Kant, neither of whom would be born for another five hundred years, Aquinas has a go at it. His proofs, famous the world over, are five-fold.

It is instructive to note the form in which the five proofs were framed; unlike the better known arguments that had been constructed earlier, by Anselm of Canterbury and Augustine, these are inductive and very Aristotelian.[26] Thomas reasons from particulars to general conclusions, inviting us to look at the world around us, and using our intellect, to ask how it all got there and how it is able to operate. He feels confident that if we do, we will agree that the truth of God's existence cannot be avoided.

I am powerfully tempted to lay out the five proofs here and now for

---

[26] The third argument, from necessity, and the fourth, from degree, look almost ontological, but closer examination shows that they begin with the things we see around us and reason toward the unseen. In short, they are *a posteriori*.

examination by all; but I will avoid the temptation with the promise that I will deal with them more fully when we come to the section on metaphysics.

Let us pass on to another of Aquinas's major contributions, his thoughts on justice and the law.

I trust that all students who have reached the college level in their studies have at some time read Dr. Martin Luther King's "Letter From a Birmingham Jail". In April of 1963 Dr. King was jailed in Birmingham for participating in a non-violent demonstration that involved disobedience of some of the Jim Crow laws of that city. Eight liberal white clergymen wrote an open letter to one of the newspapers in which they were critical of King's actions, asking him to desist, suggesting that it was not a good public testimony for a minister of the Gospel to be put in jail for breaking the law. "The Letter" is King's response. The letter shows the timelessness of good thinking and therefore the relevancy of philosophy to our day or any other.

To begin, King asks whether or not we ought to obey unjust laws, then, having answered that we should not, he takes up the question of how we can reasonably tell a just law from an unjust law. He begins with Augustine, who affirms in the *City of God* that "An unjust law is no law at all." He then proceeds to Aquinas and the *Summa Theologica*, and argues that an unjust law is one which is out of harmony with the moral law.

> To put it in the terms of Saint Thomas Aquinas, an unjust law is a human law that is not rooted in eternal and natural law.[27]

Aquinas states that there are three kinds of law, divine law, natural law, and human law. Divine law is God's eternal law which governs the universe in which we live. We know only a portion of the divine law, but whether or not we know it, it is unchanging and controlling. Natural law is that portion of the divine law which is directly applicable to humans, and which humans see in action around them. Aquinas often calls it moral law. Humans may break this law, and frequently do, to their own hurt and destruction, but they know it and indeed have access to it through their own experiences. Human laws are exactly what we would expect, they are laws created by and enforced by humans. Now, as to the question of injustice. Divine and natural law cannot be unjust, because they come from God, but

---

[27] King, Martin Luther, Jr., "Letter From a Birmingham Jail," in *Civil Disobedience: Theory and Practice*, ed. Hugo Adam Bedau, New York: Pegasus, 1969, pp. 77-78.

human laws are just only if they are in accord with the divine and the natural law. Aquinas states, in the *Summa Theologica*, that human laws may be unjust for one of three reasons. First, they may be contrary to the rights of humans. Second, they may be contrary to the rights of God. Third, they might distribute burdens unjustly.

> As Augustine says, that which is not just seems to be no law at all. Hence the force of a law depends on the extent of its justice. Now in human affairs a thing is said to be just from being right, according to the rule of reason. But the first rule of reason is the law of nature, as is clear from what has been stated above. Consequently, every human law has just so much of the nature of law as it is derived from the law of nature. But if in any point it departs from the law of nature, it is no longer a law but a perversion of law.[28]

Breaking the law is not something that ought to be done in a light and frivolous manner, but there are times, if Aquinas's arguments are cogent, when a particular law must be broken, because to obey it would be to denigrate both humans and God. As Dr. King put it, there are some laws (specifically the Jim Crow laws) that defile and degrade human nature, so that both the enforcer of the law, and those upon whom the law is enforced, are made the worse off.

This is perhaps the most controversial of Aquinas's teaching, and certainly the one that has been appealed to most often by individuals in rebellion against authority. The concept of "natural law" has had wide currency, particularly during the seventeenth and eighteenth centuries when political philosophers such as John Locke were formulating the principles which would undergird the new American Republic. It is not by accident that the philosophically-sophisticated Thomas Jefferson referred to the "law of nature and of nature's God" in his Declaration of Independence. The notion that all men are created equal is, he says, self evident, and based upon the opinions of mankind. Perhaps Aquinas was not critical to the success of the American Revolution, but it certainly did the revolutionaries no harm to have him around.

We will consider some of Aquinas's principles of logic shortly, but

---

[28] **Saint Thomas Aquinas, *Summa Theologica,* Q. 95, Art. 2, Obj. 4., ed. Anton C. Pegis, New York: Random House, 1948.**

first I want to take one last look at how he used the concept of natural law to argue for a just human law. Question: is it lawful for one to commit suicide?[29] In arguing that it is not, Aquinas cites a number of scriptures, as well as the Philosopher. His argument concerning natural law is rather simple, but also, in my opinion, rather appealing. Everything by nature loves itself and seeks life rather than death. If one doubt this, let him or her simply observe living creatures faced with something that threatens their lives, and let him or her note how those creatures will struggle to stay alive and avoid death. The desire to live is encoded in the living and is thus a natural law derived from the divine law; ergo; to kill oneself is to violate the natural law as well as divine law. By extension, those human laws making suicide a crime must be just and ought to be obeyed.

Formal logic, a gift of Aristotle to humankind, was Aquinas's logic because he participated in the rediscovery of Aristotle, because he mastered logic, and because he used it. I have chosen not to include a separate section on logic in this book because logic is properly a sub-field of epistemology (logicians would argue that it is not), and because it has become rather complex over the years and deserves a complete book all its own. But it occurs to me, reading over what I have written about Aquinas, that some might wonder why he went to such lengths to establish rational proofs for the existence of, and the character of, God, why he insisted that reason was not contrary to faith, that the two complemented one another. The earlier churchmen had few qualms, if any, about flaunting their faith in the face of reason. "I believe in order to understand," said Augustine. And one went so far as to say, "I believe because it is absurd." With Aristotle reborn, however, and occupying, as he did, such a lofty position, such attitudes were passe and probably caused Aquinas and his colleagues to wince.

As we saw in the first chapter, Aristotle formulated three laws of reasoning called the laws of inference: the law of identification, the law of the excluded middle, and the law of contradiction (or non-contradiction). They are universally applicable, and anyone who hopes to think clearly violates them at his or her own peril. The law of identification simply states that a thing is equal to itself. I am ________, and you may place your own name in the blank. By the law of identification, you are yourself. Now, if this is true, it must follow that you are not somebody else. Second, by the

---

[29] **The argument is contained in the *Summa Theologica*.**

law of the excluded middle, you are either yourself, or you are not. Finally, we get the very important law of contradiction. You are one or the other, but you cannot be both at the same time and under the same conditions. These laws, simple and obvious as they may seem, are foundational to all thinking and cannot be avoided. Suppose, for example, you wish to state that these laws do not hold. In making that statement, you are making use of the law of contradiction. For if the law of contradiction does not hold, then the statement that it does not becomes meaningless and self-contradictory, the implication clearly being that the law both holds and it does not.

The rediscovery of these laws, and their renewed application by the philosophers of the High Middle Ages, shook the older theology to its foundations. God must have established these laws, for they appear to be operative throughout the universe. Now if this is true, and if the natural law is a reflection of the divine law, then these foundational principles of logic must reflect God himself. The later investigations of Isaac Newton, Descartes, and Leibniz will be undertaken with the understanding that nature obeys and is an expression of God Himself. Therefore, the question of the nature of God, and whether or not He is operating by these same laws, becomes critical to the development of Newtonian physics and science. This consideration raised once again the old problem of evil with which Augustine struggled, as well as other questions which seem strange to us but which are actually very meaningful. Can God indeed make a rock which He cannot move?

If God can make a rock which He cannot move, and if one accepts the definition of the God of the theists, then there has been a violation of the law of identification and the law of contradiction; for we see at once that God is not omnipotent if there is something He cannot do, even if it is the result of divine action. Very well, then God cannot make a rock that he cannot move. The same two laws are violated; for there is still something which God cannot do, and this does violence to the definition of God, given once again theistic thought. And what about the problem of evil? God can either be all good, or He can be all powerful, but it is difficult to see how he can be both at the same time and still account for the existence of evil in the world. Perhaps the laws of inference simply do not hold where God is concerned, but if not then where else may they not hold? What an entangling and seemingly unresolvable problem.

I trust the student is able to see that all of this bears a striking familial resemblance to the Battle of the Universals. If the hardcore nominalists have taken the correct position, then the problem simply fades away, but, then, if they are right there is no compelling reason for anyone to attempt to sustain the argument for theism. If, on the other hand, the realists are correct, then the theistic God is saved but the problem remains unresolved. What is more, the theistic God is saved at the expense of the universality of the laws of inference.

This is giving me a headache! But no matter. Thomas Aquinas is about to come to my rescue.[30]

Aquinas successfully synthesized Aristotelian philosophy and Christian theology, making it possible to be both an intellectual and a Christian, and fulfilling the desire of Albert the Great that faith and philosophy complement one another. He did it, as Peter Abelard had attempted to do, by locating the universal (or the form) in the particular, arguing from Aristotle that matter has only potentiality until entered into by form. This will probably make little sense to those who do not have some familiarity with Aristotle's four causes, laid out in his *Metaphysics.* But imagine a piece of marble, and imagine someone saying, "I see the goddess Athena in the marble." Perhaps this is true, but the goddess is there only potentially until the artisan, using skill and labor, injects the idea of Athena into the matter.

Now, suppose we ask whether the form or idea existed before the particular, in the particular, or after the particular has ceased to exist. Aquinas answers that all three are correct. I will leave the student to think about this. There is no doubt, however, that both form and matter are necessary for there to be a particular, and the Battle of the Universals is resolved in a neat compromise that saves Plato, justifies Aristotle, and leaves the intellectual free to be a Christian and pursue his studies, with the assurance that there is no conflict between the faith and the intellect.

This does not, of course, resolve the questions about the nature of God and the existence of evil. In fact, these have never been satisfactorily resolved. For the Catholic, however, the Thomistic synthesis still stands and Thomism is the bedrock of philosophy. This is, in a sense, the beginning of modernism, for the way is now open for the Renaissance and subsequently

---

30 Students who have difficulty in keeping their grades up may take heart in the fact that when Thomas Aquinas first came to the University of Paris his fellows dubbed him "the Dumb Ox" because he was heavy, slow, and the equivalent of a rural hick. Albert the Great, seeing his brilliance, is supposed to have said, "We call this man the Dumb Ox, but someday his bellow will be heard throughout the whole world."

for the Enlightenment. Modern philosophical thought is generally conceded to have begun with Rene Descartes, whom we shall look at in the next chapter, but it is difficult to imagine how Descartes, who was a scientist as well as a philosopher, would have fared if Aquinas had not been on hand at the crucial moment to save Aristotle from the early medievalists.

And yet, there is a darker side to all of this, a side which has to be seen if we are really to understand the development of Western thought. For all of our glowing encomiums, Aristotle was only a man, and as a man he made some horrible, even laughable, mistakes. Most of us learned in elementary school that Aristotle believed rotting meat gave rise to maggots and frogs were produced by mud at the bottoms of ponds. This wasn't all. He thought that birds could fly because they were lighter than air, that clouds rested on the ground at night, that a ten pound weight, if dropped, would fall twice as fast as a five pound weight, that there were only four elements, and that the sun, moon and stars revolved around the earth. These are merely representative of some of his peculiar notions, not exhaustive.

The Medieval Synthesis did a great deal more than solve the Battle of the Universals; it incorporated Aristotle into Christian theology in such a way as to make it extremely hazardous to one's health to disagree with him. This Aristotelian world-view is the one which Copernicus and Galileo, and others, had to overcome when they were faced with growing evidence that the sun, not the earth, is the center of our immediate universe. The irony of it all! Aristotle and Aquinas, the very men who freed us from what would have appeared to have been the intellectual dead end of early medievalism gave us the materials to create the cosmological dead end of late medievalism.

Because the cosmology of the High Middle Ages was so troubling for so many of the new generation of scientists and philosophers, let us close this chapter out by examining it.

Atomic theory, they had none. But they did understand that the physical universe was composed of different elements. Thus, ignoring Democritus, medieval thinkers took up Empedocles and Aristotle and said that there were four elements and only four: earth, air, fire, and water. The chemical theory resulting from this simplistic configuration (it was alchemy, but never mind) was qualitative rather than quantitative and produced a host of fellows hell bent on turning lead into gold. This strange, qualitative pseudo-science would plague chemists until Antoine Lavoisier would show (eighteenth century France) that phlogiston, a truly Aristotelian concept, is not what causes things to burn.

Gravity was another theory waiting in the wings to push Aristotelian physics aside. For Aristotle, things fall to earth because heavier elements fall through lighter elements, toward the center of the earth, while the lighter elements naturally rise upward. Thus, if I drop my pen it will fall, proof that it is composed of earth and water, and not of air and fire.

Astronomy was, of course, a major problem for Aristotle, and for all his intellectual offspring, although during the time of Thomas Aquinas it is probable that nothing could have appeared more sure and certain than that the earth, unmoving, was the center of the universe. Bear in mind, the next time you hear someone appeal to common sense, that the Aristotelian cosmology is the very epitome of the common sensical. Bear in mind, also, the next time you hear someone attempt to construct scientific theory from the Bible, that for many generations it was held that the Aristotelian cosmology was perfectly in accord with the first chapter of Genesis.

The earth was flat and unmoving, surrounded by invisible canopies to which the various planets, the stars, the moon, and the sun were attached; and these were moving around the earth. Up was up, and down was down, and this became extremely important to the Christians of that day. Recall the Aristotelian theory that was used to explain what we today explain by the theory of gravity: something fell because of its weight, but its weight was a matter of quality rather than quantity. Earth and water were the heavier elements, therefore they fell through the lighter elements of air and fire. The heavier an element was, the faster it would fall. All very quaint and curious, one might say. But the act of synthesizing this with Christian theology produced something curious, scarcely quaint, and scarcely helpful to those who would follow and attempt to make sense of the universe.

Aristotle was force fitted not only to this life, but to the next as well, and heaven and hell became places physically located either up there or down there. A person went to hell, for example, because he or she died in sin, and sin had weight that pulled one downward. The person purged of his or her sins went upward with the lighter elements, just as a flame of fire licks upward. It is impossible to say just who among the intellectuals actually believed this and who did not, but this was how things were seen by most people in the west, and this is what the Church taught.

In the early fourteenth century a Florentine poet, Dante Alighieri, published a long work in the Tuscan dialect that stands as the finest thing produced in the period and one of the finest works of world literature. He called it *The Commedia,* but it was quickly given the additional appellation Divine, and it is as the *Divine Comedy* that it has come down to us. I know of no better example of how philosophy influences all it touches. Few people actually read Aristotle and Thomas Aquinas, but many went to churches where they were taught by those who did, and many read the Divine Comedy and absorbed its visions — sometimes wonderful, sometimes horrifying — of heaven, purgatory, and hell. Think of two equilateral triangles, set base to base, one pointing up and the other down, and imagine the souls of the dead going one direction or the other, or stuck between the two in purgatory. Those weighed down by sin plunge into hell, and the greater the sin, the farther down they go. The ninth and final level is reserved for Lucifer, Judas Iscariot, and Brutus. The lighter souls go up, and at the top of the seven story mountain are the purest and therefore lightest spirits of all. Those in purgatory, who have not committed mortal sin, are able to redeem themselves by working their sins off, and as they work they grow lighter, and up they go.

This work of incredible genius demonstrates how the thinkers of the High Middle Ages wedded the world view of the Classical Greeks with Christianity. The result was a system so stable, so comforting to live within, that one may easily imagine it lasting for a thousand years. In fact, it was already on its way out. Beautiful and satisfying as the universe of Aquinas and Dante may have been, the wrecking crew was already waiting in the wings.

William of Ockham (c. 1280-1349)

Pluralitas non est ponenda sine necessitate.

"Plurality is not to be posited without necessity." So reads the Latin statement beneath Ockham's name above. He did not always say it like this. On several occasions he wrote, "What can be explained by the assumption of fewer things is vainly explained by the assumption of more things."[31] This is the dreaded Ockham's Razor, a principle of parsimony first given out in seminal form by Duns Scotus, but brought to perfection and fame by the man whose name it bears. Put in laymen's terms, always begin any investigation by assuming that the simplest and most obvious explanation for something is the correct one.

---

[31] **William Ockham, *Philosophical Writings*, trans. Philotheus Boehner, Indianapolis: Bobbs-Merrill Co., 1976.**

Sooner or later, it seems, everyone finds himself or herself making use of Ockham's Razor. I recently saw Jody Foster make reference to it in the movie *Contact.* Even Lisa Simpson, the television cartoon character, cited Ockham in explaining to her little friends why strange occurrences should not be explained by appealing to ghosts.

It is clear that Ockham's intentions were theological, but his work resulted in this principle of general scientific applicability, and he laid the groundwork for what would become science and the empirical theory of knowledge.

> We are not allowed to affirm a statement to be true or to maintain that a certain thing exists, unless we are forced to do so either by its self-evidence or by revelation or by experience or by a logical deduction from either a revealed truth or a proposition verified by observation.[32]

John Locke and David Hume would not have written this in just this way, but the portions of the statement having to do with logic, self-evidence and observation might easily have come from the pen of an eighteenth century empiricist. But Ockham was not an eighteenth century empiricist; he was a fourteenth century Scholastic philosopher and an English Franciscan monk. I can think of no more appropriate philosopher with which to end this chapter, for in the next chapter we will be considering what I call the early modern period in philosophy, and William of Ockham stands as a man with a foot in both camps. He was in the High Middle Ages, but he truly was not of them, which is quite probably why his life ended the way it did. The world in which he was born and lived was not ready for him. The world of the following century would welcome him with open arms.

We know little of Ockham's early life, other than that he was born, probably at Ockham, probably about 1280, that he studied and taught at Oxford, and that in about 1323 he was hailed before Pope John XXII in Avignon to answer fifty-six articles of accusation brought against him by one Lutterell, a former chancellor of Oxford. The initial dispute, oddly enough, had nothing to do with science or philosophy, but was all about the Franciscan vow of poverty. For Ockham, things rapidly got worse rather than better, and he wound up fleeing for his life to Bavaria, where he begged the protection of King Louis, and where he was finally excommunicated. He

---

32 Ibid, p. xx.

died in Munich in about 1349.

He was a committed Christian, but he was also the foremost logician of his day, who believed, as had Aquinas, that the intellect ought to be respected as a gift from God.

> I consider it to be dangerous and temerarious to force anyone to fetter his mind and to believe something which his reason dictates to him to be false, unless it can be drawn from holy scripture or from a determination of the Roman Church or from the words of approved doctors.[33]

With the last part of this statement Ockham seems to be trying to cover all his bases, but what he is actually doing, whether or not he intended it, is setting up a dichotomy which will characterize the Renaissance battles between the Church and the intellectuals, and which will carry down to the present time. "*Die Gedanken sind frei,*" sang the Germans during the Enlightenment. "Thoughts are free." We have that very suggestion in the statement of Ockham, and the time will come, in the not too distant future, when intellectuals will refuse to have their minds fettered, even in the face of scripture or Papal dictate. If one knows, for example, as Galileo knew, that the earth orbits the sun, why should a thousand doctors of the Church swearing to the contrary cause him to recant?

In the Battle of the Universals Ockham was a nominalist, opposing Duns Scotus. This is not difficult to imagine, for his own principle, Ockham's razor, would seem to dictate against the postulation of invisible forms to explain what might be easily explained in a simpler way. The forms will not fare well in the period we are about to consider. In fact, it will take another generation of philosophers, the mathematician-philosophers of our own century, to revive the forms and given them something like the respectability they enjoyed in Classical Greece and in the early Middle Ages.

Ockham was followed by Francis Bacon and others, and a new age was ushered in, and age that had little use for Medieval problems. It was an age of exploration, discovery, changing values, intellectual daring, thinking that would change the rules and give us something of the modern world view.

---

[33] Quoted in Ockham, *Philosophical Writings*, trans. Philotheus Boehner, Indianapolis: Bobbs-Merrill Co., 1976.

Chapter 3
If It's Not Flat, Why Don't I Fall Off?

William, take your razor out
and lather up my mind;
It's overgrown with concepts that
are loose and ill defined.

Unnecessary entities
are cluttering my head.
The forest hides amid the trees.
I'm lost among the dead

And sterile thoughts of yesterday.
I need a clean, close shave.
Just name your fee. I'll gladly pay.
Sign me: your humble slave.

I thought this verse about Ockham's razor was more appropriate for the beginning of this chapter than it was for the last part of Chapter 2 because it wasn't until the fifteenth century that Ockham's razor began to be put to use, with startling, and sometimes painful, results. It ought to be noted that the use to which Ockham's Razor was ultimately put was neither that intended by Ockham, nor one of which he would have approved. Nevertheless, once a general principle is set loose in the world, and if it is shown to be sound, one cannot always control its application.

I have labored over the years to get my students to understand that hard and fast lines cannot be drawn between the various disciplines, particularly science and philosophy. And of course, neither science nor philosophy can be properly understood without some appreciation of what the Germans call ***Zeitgeist,*** the spirit of the times in which they were birthed. That there was a restlessness over the European scene as the fifteenth century got underway all agree, and most agree that it had something to do with a

Zeitgeist is a German word that means literally "time spirit." It is usually translated "spirit of the age." It is used to suggest that things intellectual and artistic grow out of the cultural background that prevails at the time.

shift in emphasis away from the divine and toward the human. If there is one word that describes the Classical period in Greece, that word is humanism. If there is one word that characterizes the time of the fall of the Roman Empire, that word is pessimism. If there is one word that characterizes both the early and late Middle Ages, that word is God. The Renaissance, however, is difficult to describe in one word. There was clearly a return to humanism, but it was also a time of chaos, of breaking down and building up, of expanded vision, and of great uncertainty. The Renaissance was far more than a rebirth, a resurrecting of the Greeks. It was more like a resurrection of the Greeks into a new world that the Greeks themselves would have found odd and out of control.

The Medieval world was a comfortable world, one of orderliness, circumscribed by God and the Church. The world of the Renaissance was a world in change. It must have been an exciting time to have been alive, but it must also have been a troubling time in many ways. The clean, well-lighted place of Aquinas and Dante turned out to be a place of limitless space, uncertain boundaries, and new rules and laws which simply did not make sense to ordinary people trying to get on with their lives. There was no up and no down. Heaven and hell had to be relocated, and no one seemed to know where. It wouldn't be long before René Descartes would be on the scene arguing that it was perfectly possible to doubt the existence of most anything one wished.

But I'll save Descartes for later.

I cannot trace the history of philosophy during this period without spending some time talking about men who were philosophers in only the broadest sense of the word. They were lovers of wisdom. But we call them other things, scientists usually, or astronomers.

The New Astronomers

How I see myself has something to do with the way I view the universe in which I live. If I believe the planet I occupy is the virtual center of everything, that God has made everything to revolve around me and others of my kind, that it was all made with me in mind — if this is my universe, then I see myself as very important indeed. Suppose however that I see myself as living on a speck of cosmic dust whirling through vast, empty spaces at immeasurable speed, one of millions who have come here by chance rather than design — if this is my universe, then I may be slightly humbled.

Copernicus, Galileo, and Kepler had no intention of foisting the latter view on humankind. Their sole motive was to explain what was becoming increasingly inexplicable. I have called the Medieval cosmology Aristotelian, for so it was. But most books refer to it, also correctly, as the Ptolemaic view. Ptolemy was a Greek astronomer and mathematician who lived in Alexandria, Egypt during the second century A.D, and in that early time, the very beginning of the Christian era, he constructed a cosmological theory that lasted for nearly fifteen-hundred years. Now the simplest definition of a theory is that it is a model, an educated guess about the way something works. It is used to generate hypotheses which are then tested in controlled experiments. The hypotheses, assuming they are confirmed, are then used to construct paradigms of whatever we have under study. In the case of the Ptolemaic theory, the thing under study was the universe, and the theory, a **geocentric** one, ought to have been able to generate accurate predictions about the movements of the stars, planets, moon and sun through the heavens. It did, up to a point, but as more data began to come in, and more accurate data at that, the Ptolemaic theory began to break down.[1] The theory was reconstructed, and reconstructed, and reconstructed, and with every reconstruction it became more cumbersome, more unwieldy. Something was wrong; but what?

Geocentric: The old theory of the solar system, which puts the earth at the center.

It couldn't possibly have been the Ptolemaic theory, because the Church was committed to the theory, had its theology tied into it, was teaching it in its universities and preaching it (in so many words) in its pulpits. Even William of Ockham had said, recall, that the free, inquiring mind could be fettered by scripture, the Church, or doctors of the Church, and all three were present to uphold the theory of Ptolemy (or Aristotle). But, surprise, the Church and its doctors were wrong, and against them, voices crying in the wilderness, were these renegade astronomers who began arguing for a **heliocentric** model.

Heliocentric: the Copernican theory of the solar system. It places the sun at the center and has the earth and other planets revolving around it.

Nicholas Copernicus (1473-1543), the Polish astronomer and mathematician who began the uproar and gave his name to the Copernican Revolution, did not actually advance the theory that the earth was not the

---

[1] **This is not unusual. In fact, it is pretty much the rule in science. Newtonian theory, for instance, worked well as long as we were looking only at the macrocosm; but as we began probing downward into the strange, sub-atomic world of the quanta, Newtonian theory started coming apart at the seams. Einstein was so troubled about this that he refused to accept Bohr's ideas about quantum physics. Einstein, by almost universal agreement, was wrong.**

center of the universe. What he argued was that calculations were more accurate, and problems generated by the Ptolemaic theory were more readily resolved, if we begin by using the sun as a fixed reference point. But this was enough to open the way for modern astronomy.

> Today we honor Copernicus not because he produced the modern view of the solar system (he didn't) or because his system was simpler than Ptolemy's (it wasn't), but because he was the first person in modern times who had the courage and perseverance to carry his idea beyond the realm of philosophical speculation. It was he who pointed out that the emperor's new clothes might be missing, so that after him everyone came to see geocentrism as just an assumption, one that could be challenged like any other.[2]

Copernicus was working in Rome as a professor when he began his research that would ultimately topple the Thomistic universe. He realized that he could not safely expound his principles there, so he returned to the relative security of his home town in Poland. And there he sat. In plain language, he was afraid to publish. Finally he screwed up his courage, wrote the work which became known throughout the world as *Revolutions of the Heavenly Bodies*, and respectfully dedicated it to the Pope. It was printed in May of 1543 when Copernicus was on his death bed. Death, as it turned out, was a good career move for Copernicus, for it put him beyond the reach of those who would have forced him to recant. The Pope, one may assume, was not the least flattered by Copernicus's dedication.

For over seventy years the Church did nothing with the Copernican blockbuster, thinking perhaps to kill it with silence, or by treating it as some sort of strange hypothesis.[3] Then the eventful year of 1616 dawned. What a year that was. The King James Bible made its appearance, Cervantes and Shakespeare died, *The Tempest* was staged, and Galileo burst out of obscurity with his telescope and the unequivocal announcement that Copernicus had been right. The Church could let it go no further. Coperni-

---

[2] Trefil, *The Dark Side of the Universe: A Scientist Explores the Cosmos*, New York: Macmillan Publishing Co., 1988.

[3] One of the contemporary professors, Calganini, was allowed to teach the view, but only as a sort of oddity. This is analogous to a fundamental Bible school teaching evolution, not for its value, but to show how it deviates from scripture.

cus was condemned, along with all who held to his teaching or propagated his new theory. But Rome was not alone in its condemnation. Martin Luther had already declared that, "This fool wishes to reverse the entire science of astronomy; but sacred Scripture tells us that Joshua commanded the sun to stand still, and not the earth."[4] Even the mild mannered Melanchthon spoke of certain men who either from love of novelty or to make a display of ingenuity, have "concluded that the earth moves," and "maintained that neither the eight spheres nor the sun revolves." Down in Geneva, Switzerland, John Calvin condemned all who asserted that the earth is not the center of the universe. And in England, as late as the eighteenth century, John Wesley stated that the Copernican theory tended toward infidelity.

The problem with all these attacks on Galileo and his supporters was that they were scriptural and not scientific; they were based, not upon empirical evidence, but upon what someone thought the Bible said. Today, having been raised in a Copernican universe, we look at the Bible and find ourselves amazed that anyone could come to such interpretations, and this proves (or ought to prove) to us all that what one gets out of any written text frequently depends upon what one goes into it looking for.

But Galileo was more of an upstart than what might be suggested even by his Copernican leanings. Almost as if he intended to call down anathemas upon himself, he took up the law of falling bodies and proceeded to demonstrate that Aristotle got that one wrong too. Everybody knew that the velocity with which any body fell to earth was a function of its weight, and that a heavy body fell faster than a lighter one. It was only common sense.[5] But apparently, over a period of some two-thousand years, no one had ever thought to try it out. Galileo did, and found much to his amazement, and everyone else's, that they fell at the same rate, which he calculated at thirty-two feet per second, per second.[6]

---

[4] Quoted in White, Andrew Dickson, *A History of the Warfare of Science and Theology*, Vol. I, Gloucester, Mass.: Peter Smith, 1978, p. 126.

[5] For many years I have tried this little experiment with my students. "If I drop a ten pound weight and a five pound weight," I ask them, "which will fall faster?" About half of my students think, in defiance of Galileo and Newton, that the heavier weight will fall faster.

[6] Tradition has him dropping these weights from the tower of Pisa. I have been unable to confirm this. What he did, for certain, was roll them down incline planks.

This was too much! First, Galileo said that the earth wasn't fixed and up and down were at best relative terms. Now he purported to show that even those plummeting into hell did so at a uniform rate. In 1632, at the behest of Pope Urban VIII, Galileo was haled before the Inquisition without the benefit of defender or advisor. It is not surprising that Galileo recanted, denounced his own work as heretical, though one story, probably apocryphal, has him muttering under his breath as he left the hall, "Nevertheless, it does move." It didn't matter, however, what anyone did at this point. The genie was out of the proverbial bottle and no one could force him back in. Humpty Dumpty had fallen and been irreparably smashed into a million pieces. And up in Regensburg, Germany, Johannes Kepler had shown, not just that the earth moves about the sun, but that the earth, and the other planets, orbit the sun in elliptical paths. Isaac Newton was only a whisper away. The Ptolemaic theory was down for the count.

I know it must seem that I am being unduly harsh on the Church, both Catholic and Protestant, and its many champions. This is not my intent. These men were having their world pulled down around their heads, were attempting to salvage something from the wreckage, and finally didn't know what they were to do. I am not at all certain that I would have known what to do had I been in their place. And to make matters worse, there were more problems for them than those generated by a few wayward astronomers.

Luther and Company

Most of us know the story of Martin Luther, and how in 1517 he nailed his 95 theses on the church door at Wittenburg in defiance of Rome and kicked off the Protestant Reformation. Many of us don't know however that Luther had no plans to break from Rome, no plans to get himself excommunicated, and no plans to start a Protestant anything. All he was doing with his 95 theses was issuing a challenge to debate the issue of Papal indulgences. Were he alive today there would be little, if anything, to debate, because many of the highest Roman authorities would agree with him, as some did even then. Today it is not at all uncommon to find Catholics in good standing disagreeing openly with the Pope on issues such as birth control or the ordination of women to the priesthood. But the twentieth century is not the sixteenth century, and the authority of the Pope today is not what it was then.

A massive building program was underway in Rome in those days, the most ambitious elements of which were concentrated on the great Basilica of St. Peter in the Vatican. But the work was only limping along because the builders were running short of cash, or at least of liquid cash. There were a number of possible solutions, the most obvious one being the extraction of money, in some form and by some means, from those under Papal control, *ergo* practically every human from the Adriatic to Finesterre and from Sicily to Scandinavia. A hundred years earlier people would simply have paid up, with a bit of grumbling perhaps, and that would have been that. Not so by 1517. There was a growing sense of national identity that would culminate in the development of the individual nations, and the French, English and German Christians were in no mood to have their resources drained away into Italy.

Enter: the indulgence salesmen.

These were individuals, sent out under Papal Authority and with all the requisite ecclesiastical blessings, to peddle what amounted to "get out of jail" cards. For "jail" read "purgatory." The whole thing seems so unlikely today that we are apt to think there must have been something more to it than that; but try as I might, I have never been able to confirm to my own satisfaction that there was anything more to it than that. You paid your money, you got an indulgence from the Pope, you didn't have to go to purgatory when you died. For those who already died there was an equally attractive plan: living relatives bought an indulgence in their loved one's names and they were freed from purgatory and went directly to heaven.

> As soon as the coin in the coffer rings,
> The soul flies out of purgatory and sings.[7]

The most ambitious and skillful of these indulgence salesmen was a Dominican named Tetzel. Martin Luther had already delivered sermons against the efficacy of indulgences, and the elector of the area, Frederick the Wise, had forbidden their sale. Matters came to a head when a group of people who had purchased them brought them to Dr. Luther and asked if they would do what the salesmen claimed. Luther pronounced them fraudulent, and then went forth to issue his 95 theses. Greater wisdom and

---

[7] **This little jingle was actually used by Tetzel. It rhymes in German as well as English. Quoted in Bainton, Roland, *Here I Stand: A Life of Martin Luther*, New York: Mentor Books, 1963.**

prudence on both sides might have kept the Church intact, but for every wise and prudent individual (Erasmus of Rotterdam, for instance) there appears to have been a dozen hot heads, and the ecclesiastical Roman Empire went the way of its political predecessor.

There followed one of the most traumatic events in the history of a continent fraught with trauma — the Thirty Years War. From 1618 to 1648 Catholic and Protestant armies fought over the area we now know as Germany, and by some estimates three-quarters of the population died, either directly, because of the fighting, or indirectly, as a result of plague and famine. When the war finally played out and the dust settled, nothing had changed, nothing had been resolved, and humans would never again be so certain of what they had thought of as true.

There were other events no less momentous and unsettling during the period at which we are looking. The voyages of exploration took place, with new methods of navigation and a new scrambling for empire. Gunpowder was introduced into Europe, feudalism broke down, and the day of the armed warrior on horseback was over. The first books were printed by moveable type, the Bible was translated into languages other than Latin, and there was a growing, literate middle class with access to the written ideas of the best minds of the day. Capitalism began to rise, and nationalism, and trade flourished as never before.

I have spent a good deal of time in this chapter talking about everything but philosophy. This is because the history of philosophy is a history of ideas, and ideas are not generated out of thin air. They can only be understood as a product of the total environment from whence they spring. If some remarkable genius comes to give form and voice to the ideas, he or she must nevertheless utilize the raw material at hand, must be, to some extent, driven by the prevailing winds. We come now to one such genius.

René Descartes (1596-1650)

He is called the Father of Modern Rationalism, and the title is appropriate, for most any modern day rationalist will in one way or another pay tribute to Descartes and acknowledge his influence. He was far more than this, however. One may reasonably assert that the modern era of philosophy began with René Descartes, along with the modern attitude toward human consciousness and self-awareness.

Born in the French province of Touraine, Descartes lived at home with his father, a famous lawyer (his mother died when he was one), until he was nine years old. He was then sent away to the Jesuit college at La Fleche where he studied Greek, Latin, history, liberal arts, science, mathematics, and philosophy. He also became something of a dandy — dancing, fencing, gambling. He later studied law at the University of Poitiers. When he was twenty-two years old the Thirty Years War broke out, and Descartes enlisted, though it is not clear that he was ever in combat.[8]

On November 10, 1619, while staying alone in Germany, Descartes had what he called a revelation, and he makes it clear that he believed its source to be God. It was a revelation that was to transform philosophy. No one can tell the story better than Descartes himself.

> There was no conversation to occupy me, and being untroubled by any cares or passions, I remained all day alone in a warm room. There I had plenty of leisure to examine my ideas.[9]

He goes on to speak of the opinions of men that he had received all of his life, and how he decided he must reject them and begin anew. He was particularly impressed with the necessity for the establishment of some method with which to undertake the investigation. He enumerates four rules which he thinks must underlie his method, whatever he ultimately decides it will be: (1) never to accept anything as true until he recognizes it certainly and evidently such; (2) to divide as many difficulties as he might encounter into as many parts as might be required for proper solution; (3) to think in an orderly fashion, beginning with the simplest things; and (4) to thoroughly review his work so as to make sure there are no errors.

All of this is embodied in one of the most famous works on philosophy ever written, *The Discourse on Method* (herein after referred to simply as *The Discourse*). This remarkable book ought to be recommended by every philosophy teacher to every student in every college or university in the country. Unlike many works on philosophy, it is very readable, since Descartes wrote it in the form of an autobiography or an intellectual journal.

---

[8] For biographical information on René Descartes I am indebted to Laurence Lafleur, whose translation of Descartes's *Discourse on Method* is one of the best, and to Douglas Soccio, *Archetypes in Wisdom*.

[9] Descartes, René, *Discourse on Method*, trans. Laurence J. Lafluer, Indianapolis: Bobbs-Merrill Co., 1960.

Further, Descartes wrote *The Discourse* in French rather than Latin, something scholars up to his time rarely did. The result was that it was widely read, not only by philosophers and pedants, but by nonacademic types, and Descartes quickly became famous throughout Europe.

Now, precisely what is in this revolutionary book that caused such a stir? Obviously, based upon the title alone, it must have something to do with method. Indeed it does, for Descartes was convinced that if he were to come to any truth concerning matters philosophical and metaphysical, he must begin all over again using the right sort of method. But, one might ask, given the rich philosophical heritage from which Descartes had to draw, why did he feel the need to start over from scratch? Simply because he was convinced that philosophy had come to a sort of dead end and had bogged down in confusion and contradiction. As a matter of fact, confusion and contradiction were everywhere Descartes looked. The Church had broken up into warring parties, the world he knew was at war, astronomers had shown to his satisfaction that nothing was what it seemed, and some of the main problems that had occupied philosophers for over a thousand years (the existence of God, for example) had been abandoned as unsolvable.

Was nothing certain?

Descartes felt something was, and this was the world of mathematics, particularly geometry. Geometry is probably our oldest form of mathematics, having been used by the Egyptians, the Babylonians, the early Greeks, and most everyone since; and most would agree with Descartes that, within obvious limits, it is amazingly accurate in the answers it provides. Think back, if you will, to the time you were in high school and had to take geometry, assuming there was ever such a time in your life, and assuming you can actually remember what you were taught. You had to learn certain axioms, such as the one which says that the shortest distance between two points is a straight line, and you then used these axioms to solve problems.[10] Fine; but where did the axioms come from? That is, how do we know that the shortest distance between two points is a straight line? If you answered that we lay a straight edged ruler between the two points and measure, go to the back of the class. You are wrong. The answer is that the axiom is self-evident. All one has to do is think about it; and this is equally true of any of Euclid's geometric axioms.

---

[10] I am obviously talking about Euclidean, or plane, geometry. Non-Euclidean geometry has a different set of axioms owing to the fact that it does not deal with flat surfaces.

Suppose now that we could do philosophy the way we do geometry; suppose we had certain axioms, simple self-evident truths, that we could use to solve more difficult problems the way we solve geometric ones. If we did, then the confusion of philosophy would vanish away, and we would have answers that would be clear, convincing, and incontrovertible. Descartes was convinced that he was onto something revolutionary, something that would make all philosophers that went before him effectively obsolete. You may think so too, but you have probably been thinking, even as you have been reading this, "But where are we to get our self-evident philosophical axioms?" Let's go to *The Discourse* and see what Descartes says on the subject. I return again to his first rule, cited above.

> . . .Never accept anything as true unless I recognized it to be certainly and evidently such; that is, carefully to avoid all precipitation and prejudgment, and to include nothing in my conclusions unless it presented itself so clearly and distinctly to my mind that there was no reason or occasion to doubt it.[11]

And a bit farther on we get:

> I thought that I should. . . reject as absolutely false anything of which I could have the least doubt, in order to see whether anything would be left after this procedure which could be called wholly certain.[12]

Very well. Here is how he establishes his axioms. In order to qualify an idea must be clearly and distinctly known to him, firsthand. The revolutionary aspect of this method is probably less than obvious to the twentieth century American student, for individualism, particularly in thought, is something we tend to take for granted -- or at least we say we do. But at the time Descartes was formulating his philosophy the notion that someone could think for himself or herself, or even that they ought to, was only beginning to receive grudging acceptance. Martin Luther had taught

---

11 Descartes, René, *Discourse on Method,* trans. Laurence J. Lafleur, Indianapolis: Bobbs-Merrill Co., 1960, p. 15.

12 Ibid., p. 24.

that an individual could go directly to God, without the mediation of a priest, and Ockham had barely suggested that people ought to be able to think for themselves, but most responsible souls feared this would lead to heresy and anarchy.

Descartes's method, however, is much more radical than this. He wants to throw out everything he has ever learned, to put everything into doubt, and to begin anew by seeing if there is anything of which he can be absolutely certain. This "methodic" doubt of his has sometimes been misunderstood. It is not that he really doubted the existence of the world around him and wound up trying to walk through walls. Rather, the doubting is purely methodical, purely a philosophical ploy that he uses to establish his axioms.

So Descartes starts to clean house. Out goes the external world, for he might be dreaming or he might be a victim of deception by some evil spirit. His own body has to go for the same reason. Finally, he reaches a truth which he cannot doubt, and he states it in terms that have become famous and that ring across the centuries. He could not, after all, doubt his own existence, for he was the very one doing the doubting, and unless he existed there would be no doubter at all. *Ergo*: I think, therefore I am. Many students have heard this famous proposition in Latin — *cogito ergo sum* — but it was actually written first in French, and was translated into Latin only later.

This, Descartes's "cogito", was to become the corner stone of his philosophy, and because it is so important, and because he is the father of modern rationalism and indeed the father of modern philosophy, it would serve us well to spend a bit of time with it.

First, it is important to understand that the "I" of which Descartes speaks is not the body in which the "I" is housed. He makes this clear in *The Discourse*, and in so doing proves, he feels, the existence of the immortal soul.

> I then examined closely what I was, and saw that I could imagine that I had no body, and that there was no world nor any place that I occupied, but that I could not imagine for a moment that I did not exist. On the contrary, from the fact that I doubted the truth of other things, or had any other thought, it followed very evidently and very certainly that I existed. On the other hand, if I had ceased to think while my body and the world and all the rest of what I had ever imagined remained true,I would have had no reason to believe that I existed during that time; therefore I concluded that I was a thing or substance whose whole essence or nature

> was only to think, and which, to exist, has no need of space nor of any material or body. Thus it follows that this ego, this mind, this soul, by which I am what I am, is entirely distinct from the body and is easier to know than the latter, and that even if the body were not, the soul would not cease to be all that it now is.[13]

Descartes is thus a **dualist**, a term with which we are familiar from our study of Plato, and he is also an **essentialist**, a term which we have not yet discussed. Notice that he does not disbelieve in the material world, including his body, but that he says it is perfectly possible to doubt the existence of the world of matter. But it is *not* possible, he says, to doubt that he exists as a thinking being, and for him this means that the material and the ideal[14] are separate entities, and that the ideal is the more certain, the more real, of the two. When Descartes says he is a being "whose whole essence" is to think, he marks himself as an essentialist, as were most of the philosophers who had gone before him.

Dualism. Remember that Plato was a dualist, holding that there are two levels of reality. Descartes too is a dualist, believing in a physical and a mental reality, separate from one another.

Essence may be defined as that core *something* which makes a thing what it is, as distinguished from other things. An essentialist believes that humans are human because they possess some inborn quality which sets them apart from non-humans. For Aristotle the human essence was the ability to reason, the human was the reasoning animal. For the Judeo-Christians the human essence is godlikeness, they possess immortal souls created in the image of God. Descartes, as essentialist, seems almost like a hybrid of Aristotle and the Christians: essentially, the human is an immortal, non-material being who thinks. The existentialists, particularly Jean Paul Sartre, thought that Descartes had it backward. We shall examine the existential position in the next chapter.

We will see more of essentialism when we come to theories of what it is to be human. The essentialist — and Descartes was one — believes that there is something inborn that sets the human apart from other creatures. For Descartes it is the conscious, thinking soul.

Now, having established his own existence to his satisfaction, Descartes proceeds to prove the existence of God. His argument is **ontological**, and the student may not find it convincing. Certainly Immanuel Kant didn't.

---

[13] Ibid., p. 25

[14] In order to understand Descartes it is necessary to say something about his metaphysics. There are basically only three metaphysical positions: materialism, idealism, and dualism. In the idealistic position, one affirms that reality is idea or spirit. This must not be confused with the word "ideal" as it is typically used in a non-philosophical context.

Remember, now, what Descartes is attempting to do. He is trying to create a philosophy that will be like geometry, proceeding deductively from *a priori* axioms to particular conclusions, assured that if his premises are correct and his reasoning is correct his conclusions must be incontrovertible. His first self-evident *a priori* is that he, a thinking being, exists. From this position, he undertakes to prove that God exists as a perfect being.[15] His proof is vaguely reminiscent of Anselm, and also smacks a bit of Aquinas's fourth argument for God's existence, the argument from Degree.

I clearly have an idea of a perfect Being, says Descartes, one lacking nothing. Now, since the idea is there, from whence did it come? I have no experience of perfection. I have never seen a perfect thing, and I am certainly not perfect. But I have this clear idea of perfection embodied in one Being. Where did I come by such a notion? It did not come from within myself, since I have no experience from which to draw such a conception. But I also have a conception of a perfect triangle, the angles of which equal two right angles, and that conception persists without my having seen or experienced such a thing. Critical to Descartes's argument is the assumption that perfection includes existence, or that to be non-existent is somehow to be less than perfect. It follows then, Descartes believes, that his very conception of such a Being is proof of that Being's existence in fact.

Ontological arguments like this one, or the earlier argument of Anselm, or the later one of Spinoza, usually seem very odd to students, especially to Americans raised in a rigidly empirical milieu. Europeans, in my experience, are much more at home with this sort of thing. Is conception sufficient to prove existence? Initially, most students I have known have answered that it is not; but I will leave you to think about it. Kant, as I have already indicated, found Descartes's ontological argument unconvincing because existence alone is not a predicate but only a relational noun establishing a conditional. Let us leave this one alone for the time being and return to it later when we come to the section on metaphysics. Descartes, at any rate, felt confident that he had proved his own existence, and that of God, and he then went on to show that the external world existed. But his dualism raised all sorts of problems, some of which have yet to be resolved. In fact, some of the Cartesian[16] problems were present, and left hanging, in

---

15 The argument is contained in *The Discourse*, pp. 27-29.

16 When you see the word "Cartesian", realize that it always refers to René Descartes. Descartes was one of the greatest mathematicians of his day, the inventor of analytical geometry, and many of his formulae are still with us. More often than not, "Cartesian" will crop up in mathematic courses.

the philosophy of Plato, another well known dualist. For example, Aristotle understood that Plato had left an unresolved difficulty by suggesting that somehow the ideals gave existence and substance to the material particulars. Aristotle, in the *Metaphysics*, asked a simple question: how? Plato never seems to have dealt with this adequately. Now, it rises up to plague his seventeenth century successor, René Descartes.

Look at it like this. We have a material world that most will agree is real and has to be accounted for. Perhaps we also have an ideal world. Descartes and many others, both before and after him, think so, although those who take a materialistic metaphysical position deny it. Now, where does my mind fit in? If it is separate from the brain,[17] then it must be located in the ideal world, as Descartes said it was, but this only confounds the issue and settles nothing. To prove this to yourself, try this little experiment. Stop what you are doing, lay the book aside, hold your right hand up before you, and make your little finger wiggle. Were you able to do it? Can we agree that your little finger wiggled because your mind (or your brain, if that suits you better) somehow told your finger to move? Yes, but how did this occur? That is, how did something immaterial cross over into the material realm and cause it to change in some way. To put it in laymen's terms, can mind influence matter, is psychokinesis possible, and if not then why do we seem to see it happening all the time? One way to solve the problem is to deny the existence of mind, as the materialists have done, to say that "mind" is a primitive holdover from the Greeks, that we have no "mind" but only a "brain." It they are right, then the problem is no problem at all, but an instructive example of sloppy thinking.

I wish the problem could be resolved in this simple manner, but it cannot. Descartes thought that there was a place in the human body where mind and body met, and he said that it was the pineal gland, the seat of the soul. Sorry, René, this won't work.

The problem remains unresolved. Perhaps one of my students can work on this one over summer vacation.

I have said that Descartes is called the father of modern rationalism. Rationalism is not a synonym for sanity, or for clear thinking. In philosophy, rationalism is the epistemological theory that knowledge is

---

[17] **Is the "mind" identical with the "brain"? This is a good, metaphysical question. Many would say yes. But this raises other questions that are entangling to say the least. We will look at some of these when we come to the section on metaphysics.**

inborn. The opposing theory, empiricism, holds that all knowledge comes as a result of experience. Now a rationalist such as Descartes would not deny that some knowledge comes to us through experience,[18] but he would say that the important truths, those truths which stand as axioms from which we deduce answers to the greatest questions we have, are not experiential truths, but are innate. This sort of knowledge is certain and universal, and is called *a priori* by philosophers. Why *a priori*? Because it is knowledge that exists prior to experience. Empirical knowledge, on the other hand, is called *a posteriori*, because it exists following, and as a result of, experience. I have given an entire section to epistemology later in the book, and we will be able to discuss the problems implicit in these two positions then. Perhaps you can prep yourselves for that by asking a couple of simple questions. First, is some knowledge inborn? Second, if so, what are some examples of inborn knowledge. Hint: instinct is not a good example, because it is not clear that instinctive knowledge is something that humans possess. Second hint: intuition may not be a very good example either, although I know people, both men and women, who claim to have solved major problems through intuitive flashes.

Science Comes of Age

Science is the gift of the West to the world. Some see this sort of assertion as chauvinistic and belittling to eastern peoples. Orientals, they say, are able to think just as well as anyone. True, and frequently they think better than others, but it remains that science, as a method of inquiry, developed in the West, and came about as a result of the philosophical efforts of western thinkers. Science in fact came of age in the period we are now considering.

It began with Aristotle, but the scientific method of inquiry was not developed by Aristotle. Allow me to explain, or rather, allow me to give my version of what occurred without presuming to possess the only version worthy of consideration. In my opinion, the most important initial step toward science, as we understand it, was taken by Duns Scotus, when he floated, however feebly, the principle that William of Ockham later formalized. The principle, as we have seen, was one of parsimony, and we call it Ockham's Razor. Never postulate the unnecessary. Always begin an

---

[18] This is not a two-way street. I have never yet met an empiricist who felt that some knowledge is inborn. Empiricists think that all knowledge comes as a result of experience.

investigation into the cause of something with the assumption that the simplest and most obvious explanation, all other things being equal, is most probably the correct one.

The second step toward science was taken by Francis Bacon (1561-1626) when he outlined the method that one ought to use in solving problems. In 1620 he published *Novum Organum*, in which he stated that science should follow an inductive method of investigation. All of this can get fairly entangled in the minds of those who have never been exposed to philosophy, and that means most of us whether or not we have darkened the doors of universities. So let me explain. Aristotle identified two types of reasoning processes, deductive and inductive. You may have heard deductive reasoning called reasoning *a priori*, and you may have heard inductive reasoning called reasoning *a posteriori*; and if you paid attention earlier when I was discussing Descartes's rationalism and comparing it to empiricism you will remember that rationalism posits the existence of knowledge, both universal and necessary, which is inborn. It was these inborn, universal truths that Descartes was after, hoping to use them as premises from which to reason deductively to clear and incontrovertible conclusions about the particulars in the material world all about us.

How would this work in practice? Suppose I wish to travel from Dallas to Fort Worth in the quickest way possible. I begin with the *a priori* which says that the shortest distance between two points is a straight line. I then take a map, draw a straight line between Dallas and Fort Worth, and I conclude that there is no way I could travel which would be shorter. This is deductive reasoning in its most classical sense. It takes a universal principle, applies it to a particular situation, and comes up with a solution that must be true.[19] I don't have to actually travel from one point to another to check this out. Pure reason alone will convince me that the straight line is the shortest way to get there. Old timers call it traveling, "As the crow flies."

Now I have expended some 250 words explaining deductive reasoning only to say that this is not the method Francis Bacon insisted must be used in science. He said *inductive* reasoning, but sometimes the best way to understand something is by beginning with what it is *not*. Inductive

---

[19] **Yes, all you non-Euclidian geometricians, I heard you. Because we are not actually traveling on a plane, but are on a globe, the straight line is technically not the shortest way. But for all practical purposes, and given the short distance between Dallas and Fort Worth, Euclid will work fine.**

reasoning goes in the opposite direction from deductive reasoning, that is, not from the general or universal to the particular, but from the particular toward the universal. To reason inductively is to reason from experience, *a posteriori*, and to establish universal principles that can then be used in a deductive process. Does it sound as if it all goes around in a big circle? Actually, it does.

The scientific method, then, involves observing particulars until we are able to make general statements about the way they behave. We also set up experiments under controlled situations, and these aid us in establishing our universal principles. And always, we observe and record our results. Let us take another example. I observe that my father grew old and died, that his father before him grew old and died, that his father before him, *etcetera*. . . No matter how many particular humans I observe, I notice that they all follow the same trend, aging and death. From this I establish the principle that humans are mortal. The process is inductive, involves observation, and is even experimental in the sense that no matter how I vary the conditions the result remains the same.

But this is an oversimplified account, for regardless of what some scientists who lack a solid background in philosophy may think, science involves as much deduction at the foundational level as induction. And there is also a major flaw in induction which David Hume will identify and which renders any inductive conclusion at least suspect. Nevertheless, the scientific method is useful and has done more perhaps than any other single philosophical tool to create the world as we know it.

Deus ex machina. **Literally, "God in a machine." It goes back to the days of Greek drama and the use of machinery to swing gods onto the stage. A god has to be able to fly after all. The meaning expanded to its present use — God explained in a mechanistic fashion.**

During the seventeenth and eighteenth centuries science grew and humankind began with what seemed growing acceleration to push back the darkness. René Descartes and Isaac Newton were two of the scientist-philosophers in the vanguard of this movement. They in particular are responsible for the idea that the universe, and all that it holds, are analogous to machinery and run on purely mechanistic principles. This ***deus ex machina*** explanation has been so widely used in the West that many people never stop to think that it is, after all, only an analog, and may not even be a very good one. David Hume didn't think so.

The British Empiricists

On the Continent, Cartesian rationalism carried the day and became so deeply entrenched in intellectual circles that it would not be even partially dislodged until the end of the nineteenth century with the advent of a group we call logical positivists. But in the British Isles philosophy went in different direction, toward empiricism. In fact, empiricism has become so connected to the British in particular, and to the English speaking world in general, that one has to often remind oneself that empiricism really had its beginnings with Aristotle and other Greeks. Most American students have some trouble understanding rationalism, but they take to empiricism like they were born to it. And in a sense they were. America's intellectual heritage is largely British, and at the time America was becoming a nation empiricism was becoming a major factor in epistemology.

When we speak of the British empiricists, three men come to mind immediately — John Locke (1632-1704), George Berkeley (1685-1753), and David Hume (1711-1776). Metaphysically, one was an idealist (Berkeley), one (Locke) appears to have been a dualist, and the third (Hume) is rather hard to classify, though he was probably an idealist who wound up a thorough skeptic. To further underscore their differences, Locke was English, Berkeley was Irish, and Hume was Scottish. But on one thing they were all agreed — rationalism could not account for knowledge. The only thing that could was experience, which is precisely the meaning of the word empiricism in Greek. Because Locke was the first of the three to commit his thoughts to writing, and because he is the one with which most Americans are familiar, we will deal with him first.

John Locke, whom Louis XIV was supposed to have characterized as a dangerous man, came to his epistemology by a circuitous route via his theories on government. He was deeply committed to government principles that placed him on the wrong side of those in power, and when he was about fifty years old Locke wound up fleeing for his life to Holland. There he wrote some of his most important philosophical works. In the seventeenth century, the most common theory of government was that of absolutism, with all authority being vested in a ruler placed on the throne by God. It was the so-called "divine right of kings" which Louis and Peter the Great and others of their ilk were exercising. To Locke, the rationalism of Descartes played right into the hands of autocrats by suggesting that certain individuals were born to reign over others and that this could be known with certainty and clarity just as could other eternal truths. Locke had other notions. He believed that there was no such thing as *a priori* truth. If people believed in the divine right of kings, it was not because they had some inborn idea of such a thing, but because someone had taught it to them. It was all a matter of learning, and we all start from ground zero.

> Let us then suppose the mind to be, as we say, white paper, void of all characters, without any ideas; how comes it to be furnished? Whence comes it by that vast store, which the busy and boundless fancy of man has painted on it with an almost endless variety? Whence has it all the materials of reason and knowledge? To this I answer, in one word, From experience; in that all our knowledge is founded and from that it ultimately derives itself.[20]

In this famous passage John Locke presents his theory that the mind, at birth, is like a blank slate, or, in the Latin, *Tabula Rasa.* This is a very apt metaphor, if one wishes to illustrate what empiricism is all about, for the obvious question is (and Locke asks it in the passage we have just considered), how then does the blank get filled up? It is written on by the finger of experience. Locke is not only attacking Continental rationalism, but the time-honored philosophies of Socrates and Plato. If he (Locke) is right, then education cannot be a drawing out, as Socrates supposed, but must be just the opposite, a putting in; and what one puts in will be what one is subsequently able to draw out. Take European peasants, for example, and tell them from the mother's knee that the man in the big castle with the crown on his head is there because God put him there, and that to oppose him is to oppose God, and no one should be surprised to find them bowing the knee to the king. This is not *a priori* knowledge; it is bad teaching. Locke wished to write a different political philosophy onto the blank slate of human minds. According to Locke, the man in the castle was not there because God put him there, but because the people did. And the people could just as easily take him out and put in someone else.

John Locke was not the originator of what we call the contract theory of government. As early as the fourth century B.C. Plato, in *The Republic*, has Glaucon arguing for something like contract government, only to have the idea rejected by Socrates. Locke seems however to have taken his ideas for contract government from Thomas Hobbes, who in his classic *Leviathan*, states that governments are instituted by humans, generally to avoid killing one another.

---

[20] Locke, John, *Essay Concerning Human Understanding*, ed. Mary Whiton Calkins, La Salle, Illinois: Open Court, 1905, pp. 25-26.

> Hereby it is manifest, that during the time men live without a common Power to keep them all in awe, they are in that condition which is called Warre; and such a warre, as is every man, against every man. . .(There is) no Knowledge of the face of the Earth; no account of Time; no Arts; no Letters; no Society; and which is worst of all, continuall feare, and danger of violent death; And the life of man, solitary, poore, nasty, brutish, and short. . .[21]

Hobbes goes on to explain that it is precisely to escape this miserable situation that men come together and voluntarily yield up some of their rights in order to establish a government that will both restrain some and protect others. If greatness is measured by the influence one exerts on others, then Thomas Hobbes is our greatest political philosopher. But few of us would wish to live in a society under the control of his Leviathan (his term for the government), because he makes no concrete provision for removing a bad government once it is put in control.

Locke, on the other hand, has a more optimistic view of things, and a much better opinion of humankind in general. Further, he was much more committed to individual freedom than Hobbes ever was, and it is this in Locke that got hold of the new men of the Enlightenment, including Americans such as Thomas Jefferson.

> Men being, as has been said, by Nature, all free, equal and independent, no one can be put out of this Estate, and subjected to the Political Power of another, without his own Consent. The only way whereby any one divests himself of his Natural Liberty, and puts on the bonds of Civil Society is by agreeing with other Men to joyn and unite into a Community, for their comfortable, safe, and peaceable living one amongst another.[22]

This is the contract, and it was radical stuff for its day, the kind of which revolutions were made.

> We hold these truths to be self evident that all men are created equal, that they are endowed by their Creator

---

[21] **Hobbes, Thomas, *Leviathan*, ed. Francis B. Randall, New York: Washington Square Press, pp. 84-85.**

[22] **Locke, John, *Two Treatises of Government*, ed. Peter Laslett, New York: New American Library, 1965, pp. 374-375.**

> with certain inalienable Rights, that among these are Life, Liberty and the pursuit of Happiness. that to secure these rights, Governments are instituted among men, deriving their just powers from the consent of the governed.

Most Americans, and indeed most educated people no matter where they live, are familiar with these words, written by Thomas Jefferson in 1776. Many of these also know that John Locke was the philosopher who provided the inspiration for much of what Jefferson wrote. Few, however, understand just how fundamental Locke's epistemological position was to his position on justice and good government. Locke was rejecting, not only the way people on the Continent were governed, but the ways in which their greatest philosophers thought about learning and knowledge. The break was permanent. The British, and subsequently the Americans, Canadians, Australians, all, in short, who came under British influence, do not to this day feel comfortable with rationalism, nor with government that does not substantially line up with Locke's theory. This sweeping generalization, false in some particulars, is nevertheless true enough in general.

The egocentric predicament takes a number of forms. Mainly, it is the problem that arises from my being ostensibly the center of the universe. I know, of course, that I am not; but unfortunately this is the only way I can perceive the world.

Now, to return briefly to Locke's epistemology and to some of the problems raised by his empiricism. Without intending to, Locke created what philosophers call the **egocentric predicament,** and it is this predicament, and Locke's failure to resolve it, that gives rise to our next major empiricist, George Berkeley. The egocentric predicament is this. If there are no universal, innate truths, and if all learning comes about as a result of experience, then clearly the individual human mind is at the very center of the process. In other words, what I take in via my senses becomes reality for me. But is my reality, which is the only reality I know, the same as your reality? We see, as we saw with Plato, that epistemology, or what I can know, is closely bound up with metaphysics, what is really there.

The coherence and the correspondence theories are theories of truth. We will deal with them more fully when we get to the section on epistemology. In "coherence" a proposition is true if it hangs together with other known truths. In "correspondence" a proposition is true if it corresponds with the facts.

Later we will look at the various theories of truth, and what we intend to convey when we say of something, That is true. But even now it will help us to differentiate between Descartes's truth and the truth of the empiricists. Rationalism lends itself to a theory of truth called the **coherence theory**, which holds that a proposition is true if it "coheres" or hangs together with other propositions. Empiricism leads to the **correspondence theory** of truth, which says that a proposition is true if it corresponds with the facts as we have them before us. But, once again, this can be troublesome. Let me show you why. I sit before us an empty can which recently held a well-known brand of soft drink. I say, "The can is obviously red." You say, just as confidently, "The can is a sort of orange-pink." Which one of us has told the truth? Or, applying the correspondence theory, Which proposition is in agreement with the facts?

Anticipating this problem, John Locke held that all things have primary and secondary qualities. A primary quality is a quality that is in the thing itself, whereas a secondary quality is one that is supplied by the mind of the beholder. Examples of primary qualities are weight and dimension, or things that we can measure and agree upon independent of ourselves. Secondary qualities include color, taste, sound, or things that, according to Locke at any rate, are products of the individual mind. If I see red and you see orange-pink it is because each of us is applying a different set of secondary qualities to our perception of the can before us. Now this is interesting, but does it really solve anything, or does it leave us in a state of confusion? Our next empirical philosopher will confuse things even more.

Primary qualities: qualities that supposedly are a part of the object itself, such as height, weight. Secondary qualities: those qualities which we supply from our own minds, such as color, taste, sound. This is Lockean and many have disagreed.

George Berkeley, Irish and bishop in the Anglican Church, took up the problem of perception from John Locke and pushed it in even farther. One witty individual characterized Berkeley's philosophy as "utterly absurd, and utterly irrefutable." In fact, Berkeley is neither absurd nor irrefutable, but he can appear that way unless we see what he was doing and why. The bottom line was that Berkeley intended to prove the existence, even the necessity of God, and he felt that John Locke had left him the perfect opportunity. Berkeley was essentially in agreement with Locke's empiricism, but he felt that Locke had gotten to the abyss, as it were, and then pulled back for fear of what he had seen there. Why postulate the existence of primary and secondary qualities? Why not admit the obvious? There are no such things as primary qualities; all qualities are secondary, that is supplied by the mind, which leaves us in a universe totally created and sustained by mind. Berkeley was thus a **metaphysical idealist**, reducing Locke to the seemingly absurd position of denial of material reality. "If a tree falls in the forest," Berkeley asked (one of his most oft-quoted questions), "and no one is there to hear it, does it make a sound?" He answered that it does not. Whether or not she realized it, Sylvia Plath got to the heart of the matter in one of her poems:

> I close my eyes, and all the world drops dead.
> I think I made you up inside my head.

When in 1710 Berkeley published his views in his most famous book, *Principles of Human Knowledge*, the entire intellectual world seems to have dismissed him as some sort of lunatic. His friend Dean Swift reportedly left him standing on his doorstep when he came to call, saying that if his (Berkeley's) views were correct he could just has easily have walked through a closed door as an open one.[23] And when James Boswell asked the celebrated Samuel Johnson how he would refute Berkeley, Johnson is supposed to have kicked a stone and replied, "Sir, I refute him thusly."

I urge the student not to be so hasty in dismissing George Berkeley, but rather to think carefully about what he is saying. Would we not agree that to some extent at least our minds are involved in the business of establishing reality? Take the tree falling in the forest for example. Clearly the falling tree creates sound waves; but does it not take an ear, nerves, and mind to translate all of this into sound? Besides there is, as the Bard has said, a method to Berkeley's madness. What he really wishes to show is not that reality does not exist if I am not about to perceive it, but rather that reality does not exist if Mind, some sort of mind, is not about to perceive it. And this brings in the necessity of God. All the world does not drop dead when I close my eyes because God is there, eyes eternally open, mind eternally awake and vigilant, to assure the stability of the universe which He has created. Without the mind of God, there can be no assurance of reality, as Berkeley sees it.

But perhaps Berkeley was right in his identification of the problem left unwittingly by Locke but wrong in his proposed solution. Perhaps there is no God. If there is not, then we are left in a dire predicament indeed. We are left to admit that we cannot know reality, that there may be no reality to know. Surely no one would have the temerity to argue such nonsense. Ah, but one did — a Scotsman named David Hume. Hume quite simply left philosophy in a shambles.

Born in 1711 to strict Presbyterians, Hume was for a time home schooled by his mother, who reportedly said of him, "Davey is a well-meanin' critter, but uncommon weakminded."[24] When he was twelve years old he was sent off to the University of Edinburgh, where he was supposed

---

[23] Reported in Warnock, G.J., *Berkley*, London: Penguin Books, 1953, p. 13.

[24] This interesting account is given in Velasquez, Manuel, *Philosophy*, 6th ed., Belmont, Ca.: Wadsworth Publishing Co., 1997. One feels moved to ask, if Hume was weakminded, where does that leave the rest of us?

to study for the law. Instead, loathing the law, he took up literature and philosophy, and spent a great deal of time in what his strict mother could only have seen as loafing around the house. He was finally forced out when a local lady accused him of fathering her child, and he ultimately wound up in France, where he wrote *A Treatise of Human Nature.* He was twenty six years old, and had written, though it was not well received, one of the classics of western philosophy.

He appears to have been, as I have indicated, an idealist who somehow lost his ideals, for he pushed beyond both Locke and Berkeley. I am reminded in this regard that Jean Paul Sartre decried those atheists who do not have the courage to push on to the ultimate conclusions of their atheism. They wish to hold that the non-existence of God changes nothing, that we can continue with our same norms of honesty, etc. On the contrary, says Sartre, if God does not exist everything is changed, and all *a priori* values disappear along with Him. Hume did not say this, or anything like this, of his empirical predecessors; but he might have. It was clear to him that neither Locke nor Berkeley followed their thoughts on to their inevitable conclusions, probably because those conclusions would have been unthinkable. But Hume, unconstrained by Locke's and Berkeley's presuppositions, rode the current to where it took him, to a hard skepticism.

He began by denying that we have knowledge of either mind or matter, showed that we cannot know whether or not there is a God or personal immortality, denied the possibility of miracles, and argued that there is no demonstrable link between cause and effect. No matter how often two things have been observed to relate to one another in a cause-effect fashion, one can never know with certainty that they will continue to do so, and thus it is impossible to formulate universal laws based upon one's observations.

> First we may observe, that the supposition, that the future resembles the past, is not founded on arguments of any kind, but is derived entirely from habit, by which we are determined to expect for the future the same train of objects to which we have been accustomed. This habit or determination to transfer the past to the future is full and perfect; and consequently the first impulse of the imagination in this species of reasoning is endowed with the same qualities. . .(But) every past experiment may be considered as a kind of chance; it being uncertain to us, whether the object will exist conformable to one experiment or another. . .We may observe (however) that there is no probability so great as not to allow of a contrary possibility.[25]

---

[25] **Hume, David, *A Treatise of Human Nature*, ed. D.G.C. Macnabb, New York: World Publishing Co., 1962, pp. 185-186.**

Later, in his *Enquiry Concerning Human Understanding,* he takes up the argument again:

> The contrary of every matter of fact is still possible; because it can never imply a contradiction, and is conceived by the mind with the same facility and distinctness as if ever so conformable to reality. *That the sun will not rise to-morrow* is no less intelligible a proposition, and implies no more contradiction that the affirmation, *that it will rise.* We should in vain, therefore, attempt to demonstrate its falsehood. Were it demonstratively false, it would imply a contradiction, and could never be distinctly conceived by the mind. All reasonings concerning matter of fact seem to be founded on the relation of Cause and Effect. . . If we would satisfy ourselves, therefore, concerning the nature of that evidence, which assures us of matters of fact, we must enquire how we arrive at the knowledge of cause and effect. . . (It) is not, in any instance, attained by reasonings *a priori*; but arises entirely from experience, when we find that any particular objects are constantly conjoined with each other.[26]

Those who have taken science courses may recall that scientists do not claim to have proven things by their experiments, but rather to show only a significant probability of relationship. This goes back to David Hume, and to his very first published work. At age twenty-six he pulled down many an imposing philosophical edifice. But he wasn't through yet.

Descartes was a man revered throughout the West, and his "I think therefore I am" had passed into the philosophical lexicon as a sort of pillar of the rationalistic position. Hume, predictably, wasn't buying any of it. What was this "I", this "self", of which Descartes spoke? Hume, a convinced empiricist, had only his experience, his perceptions, to go on, and search himself though he might, he could find no one thing that he could identify as the self.

> There are some philosophers who imagine we are every moment intimately conscious of what we call our self; that we feel its existence and its continuance in existence; and are certain, beyond the evidence of a demonstration,

---

[26] Hume, David, *An Enquiry Concerning Human Understanding,* LaSalle, Illinois: Open Court Publishing Co., 1956, pp. 24-26.

> both of its perfect identity and simplicity. . .For my part, when I enter most intimately into what I call myself, I always stumble on some particular perception or other, of heat or cold, light or shade, love or hatred, pain or pleasure. I never can catch myself at any time without a perception, and never can observe anything but the perception.. . .If any one, upon serious and unprejudiced reflection, thinks he has a different notion of himself, I must confess I can reason no longer with him.[27]

Hume establishes here what has come to be known as the "bundle theory" of the self. It is not, as Douglas Soccio has noted, that Hume doubts there is something that gives unity and continuity to what we call the self, and to our history, but rather that he doesn't believe we can know what that something is. Now recall that Descartes began with an *a priori* assumption that he existed as a thinking entity, and that he went on from this point to prove the existence of God. Hume sees matters from exactly the opposite point of view: if he cannot know for certain that his self exists, God's existence becomes doubly uncertain. He doesn't doubt the existence of God, but neither does he affirm His existence. He simply says that he doesn't know, that it is impossible to know, and that those who claim to know[28] cannot have thought carefully about what they are saying. Once again, Hume is being entirely consistent with the position he has taken. To say, "I believe that God exists," is another matter. One may freely believe what one wishes. But this, if you will recall, is not what Descartes and Berkeley had done. Descartes claimed to have proven the existence of God, *a priori*, and Berkeley had brought God into the philosophical dialectic by using Him to assure that what we experience is really there and remains there, even when we are not actively perceiving it.

Hume will have none of it.

All knowledge is *a posteriori*, based upon experience, and none of us has ever had the experience of God. That is, we have no sensual perception

---

27 Hume, David, *Treatise*, pp. 300-302.

28 The operative language is "know," and it is clear we are talking about epistemological problems. How do we know anything? If the empirical theory of knowledge is the correct one, then Hume's position appears to be unassailable. Is he, in this, taking a position so different from that of Jesus, who is recorded in John 3:11 as having said to Nicodemus, "Amen, amen, I say to you, the thing we know (Greek, *oidamen*, frequently translated "see"), we speak, and give witness to that which we see."?

of Him, *ergo* we cannot say that we know that God exists.

It seems hardly necessary to point out that David Hume upset many people, irritated others, infuriated some, and gained the admiration and respect of others. Perhaps the most irritating thing about him, to those who saw him as an enemy, was that he was such a charming fellow, so genuinely likeable, the ideal companion. He was never rude or argumentative, he loved pretty women, though he never married, and he was something of an epicure when it came to food and drink. He frequently referred to "The Deity" in his writings, and one might suppose that he was a deist, as were many of the philosophers of his day; but the deistic position would have been inconsistent with his philosophy, and he was nothing if not rigorously consistent. He was an agnostic, pure and simple.

Many of his opponents waited for him to come to his senses, claiming that he would repent on his death bed. He never did. In 1776, shortly after the Americans declared their independence, he died quietly and, according to witnesses, with calm and dignity.

Immanuel Kant (1724-1804)

David Hume lived during the period known to historians and literati as the Enlightenment. The term implies much, and in many ways it is well chosen. It was a time of tremendous optimism, of great confidence in the abilities of humans to think, and by thinking to resolve problems. Science expanded during this time. Descartes, Newton and Leibniz mapped out the universe in ways that no one ever had, and Alexander Pope wrote his famous couplet:

> Nature and nature's laws lay hid in night.
> God said, "Let Newton be," and all was light.

But all was not light, poetic hubris notwithstanding. In philosophy, for those who really understood it, darkness lay all about, for Hume had effectively driven matters into a cul-de-sac from which there seemed to be no means of escape. There seemed to be no problem that science couldn't solve, and no problem that philosophy could. One would think that reasonable people would have, at this point, abandoned philosophy as a meaningless wrangling about nothing in particular. Why should anyone give his or her time to a discipline that had finally proved that no one could prove anything, that nothing could be known, that the best anyone could do was ask questions, and that perhaps even the questions couldn't be formulated with confidence? On the other hand, to abandon philosophy was to abandon the search for

God, morality, beauty, justice -- all the things that matter most to humans in a troubling world. Not all were willing to do this. Immanuel Kant was one of these. He knew, however, as few did, that if philosophy was to be saved David Hume had to be answered.

He was born in Königsburg (now Kaliningrad), a city on the bleak, Baltic coast, in the German province of East Prussia, and was raised a Protestant fundamentalist[29] by strict parents of Scottish descent. His schooling took place in Königsburg, and he eventually wound up as a lecturer in the university there. In fact, he rarely travelled beyond the borders of his hometown, but he impacted philosophers around the world.

People called him "the Little Professor," and housewives in Königsburg reportedly set their clocks by his punctual comings and goings. One of the better known descriptions of Kant and his strict adherence to routine is given by the German Poet Heinrich Heine:

> I do not believe that the great cathedral clock of this city accomplished its day's work in a less passionate and more regular way than its countryman, Immanuel Kant. Rising from bed, coffee-drinking, writing, lecturing, eating, walking ,everything had its fixed time: and the neighbors knew that it must be exactly half past four when they saw Professor Kant, in his gray coat, with his cane in his hand, step out of his housedoor, and move toward the little lime tree avenue, which is named after him, the Philosopher's Walk. Eight times he walked up and down that walk at every season of the year, and when the weather was bad, or the gray clouds threatened rain, his servant, old Lampe, was seen anxiously following him with a large umbrella under his arm like an image of providence. [30]

It would be difficult to imagine a less likely person than the Little Professor from Königsburg as the one to leap into the breach, as it were, and defend metaphysics and epistemology against the near fatal onslaught of David Hume. But he did, and in so doing he became arguably the greatest of all modern philosophers. In the beginning he was merely another

---

[29] His denominational affiliation was with the Pietists.

[30] Royce, Josiah, *The Spirit of Modern Philosophy*, Boston: Houghton Mifflin, 1892, p. 108.

Continental rationalist, following along quietly in the well-worn path of Descartes and Leibniz, until Hume brought him up short. Kant tells of his awakening in a passage that is justly famous.

> I openly confess my recollection of David Hume was the very thing which many years ago first interrupted my dogmatic slumber and gave my investigations in the field of speculative philosophy a quite new direction. I was far from following him in the conclusions at which he arrived by regarding, not the whole of his problem, but a part, which by itself can give us no information. . . I therefore first tried whether Hume's objection could not be put into a general form, and soon found that the concept of the connection of cause and effect was by no means the only concept by which the understanding thinks the connection of things *a priori*, but rather that metaphysics consists altogether of such concepts.[31]

Interrupted my dogmatic slumber. I love it! One can almost see the furrowed brow of Kant as he reads through *The Treatise* and *The Enquiry* and realizes that things are not what they seem to be.

I must ask the student now to think, to think hard and persistently, and to learn about problems he or she has probably never imagined existed. To those who are willing to do this, I can promise a rewarding, mind-expanding experience. To those who are not, I can guarantee confusion and headaches. Philosophy is notoriously difficult, and Immanuel Kant is (Hegel aside) as difficult a philosopher as ever lived. One of my teachers, a more brilliant man I never met, used to say of Kant's philosophy, "It hard!" One of my students undertook to read Kant, but later told me he had given it up. When I asked why, he replied, "It was like jumping face first into an angry alligator." In all fairness, Kant is difficult, but nothing like an angry alligator. He can be understood if one gets one's bearings by first getting clear on some of the terms that he uses, how he uses them, where he begins, and where he intends to go. In what follows we will be looking at one of his most famous works, the *Critique of Pure Reason.* I will refer to it simply as the *Critique.*

First, think back to Plato and how he dealt with two conflicting schools that had come down from pre-Socratic times, the Heraclitians and the Parmenideans. The one group held that all was in a constant state of

---

[31] **Kant, Immanuel, *Prolegomena to Any Future Metaphysics,* trans. Lewis White Beck, Indianapolis: Bobbs-Merrill Co., 1976, p. 8.**

change, and the other said that change was impossible and that nothing was changing. Plato understood that, to a degree, both were wrong and both were right, and his dualistic system was able to resolve the issue by uniting them. Kant was faced with a similar situation as he stood between the rationalists and the empiricists. Was it possible that both were partially right and that the truth lay somewhere between the two positions? Kant dearly wished to salvage something for rationalism, for if he (or someone) did not, and if epistemology were left to the empiricists, then the last word belonged to David Hume, and the philosophers may as well fold their tents and steal quietly away into oblivion. In the opening lines of the *Critique*, some of the most famous ever written by a philosopher, Kant throws down the gauntlet to Hume.

> There can be no doubt that all our knowledge begins with experience. For how should our faculty of knowledge be awakened into action did not objects affecting our senses partly of themselves produce representations, partly arouse the activity of our understanding to compare these representations. . . *But though all our knowledge begins with experience, it does not follow that it all arises out of experience.* For it may well be that even our empirical knowledge is made up of what we receive through impressions and of what our own faculty of knowledge (sensible impressions serving merely as the occasion) supplies from itself.[32]

Note particularly what I have italicized and also what follows. What Kant is saying is that Locke, Berkeley, and Hume are correct in saying that all knowledge begins with incoming sense data. But that is only the beginning. Something happens to those data once they get into us, or inside our minds. We supply something, and the something we provide takes this mass of incoming, raw data, arranges it, puts it into order, makes sense of it. Otherwise, we would have only a mass of data.

Kant states that if there is such a thing as innate knowledge, knowledge which we possess apart from experience, it is *a priori* knowledge; and knowledge we have as a result of experience is *a posteriori* knowledge. In this, Kant merely uses the terms that his predecessors have used, and with which we are by now familiar. But he quickly follows with

---

32 **Kant, Immanuel, *Critique of Pure Reason*, trans. Norman Kemp Smith, New York: The Modern Library, 1958, p. 25.**

A tautology is a self-evident, and sometimes even empty, truism. An example is "A = A." This is tautologically true, and not too terribly interesting by itself; but it leads to profound truth.

some new terms with which we have not yet dealt, and this will require some serious thinking.[33] There are two types of propositions (Kant calls them judgments) one may use in making positive statements about the universe in which he or she lives. The first type Kant calls an analytic proposition, and he defines it as one in which the predicate is contained in the subject. An example would be, my brother is a male. Now this is universally and necessarily true, but it is also not particularly helpful. It is what philosophers and mathematicians call a **tautology** or a truism, a proposition that is undeniable but that really gives one no information. But it is *a priori.* I do not need to verify the truth of the statement by appealing to experience; I only have to understand the meanings of the words.

Kant calls the second type a synthetic proposition. This must be empirically warranted, and is therefore *a posteriori.* An example would be, my shirt is blue. This proposition indeed gives one information, but it is limited in that it is neither universal nor necessary, and it is confined to only one object out of a world of similar objects.

Very well, we have then the analytic *a priori*, warranted both semantically and by the law of identification, and we have the synthetic *a posteriori*, warranted by empirical observation. There can be no analytic *a posteriori*, since by definition *a posteriori* propositions can be neither universal nor necessary. That brings us to the final class, synthetic *a priori*, and it is this type proposition which intrigues Kant, and which he spends a good deal of time discussing. Question: can there be such a thing. That is, are there synthetic propositions that are both universal and necessary.[34] Kant sets out to show that there are, and that the synthetic *a priori* is the meeting place of the rationalists and the empiricists.

Imagine that you are watching two baseball players, A and B, throwing a ball back and forth. Player A throws the ball, and you watch it as it travels along on a path to the glove of Player B. Now, what did you see? Did you see a series of balls strung between the two points, or did you see one ball, moving through both time and space, from one point to the other? You saw, of course, the one ball, and it is difficult for the strict empiricist to

---

[33] I am not going to quote directly from the *Critique* for fear that the long, convoluted sentences will only obscure what is difficult enough as it is. Instead I will paraphrase. The interested student is referred to Section IV of the introductory portion of the *Critique*.

[34] I am indebted to W.T. Jones, for the excellent coverage he gives this subject in his *Kant to Wittgenstein and Sartre*, New York: Harcourt, Brace & World, 1952.

account for this, for if your mind is nothing more than a passive receptacle there is no reason why you shouldn't have experienced this as many rather than one. But more than this. Since both space and time are involved, and they must be, how did they get into the mix? You didn't perceive them, for they are non-perceptible, invisible entities, but very real and very necessary if any sense is to be made of this. Further, do you imagine that this was only your perception, or would you agree that all those viewing the action, including the two players, saw the same thing? If they did not, then no one would go to baseball games, because no one would be able to make any sense of what was going on. Thus, the perception of space and time must be universal and necessary, must also be something perceptible in experience, and must represent a synthetic *a priori.*

This is astounding and truly revolutionary. Kant actually called it the Copernican Revolution. He had shown that the human mind is an active participant in the creation of reality, not in the way that Berkeley imagined, but in the fact that it takes in raw data and makes it intelligible using inborn, *a priori* knowledge. Among the synthetic *a priori* truths (Kant's term for them is "categories") are time-space and cause-effect. The others — there are twelve of them — are a bit more complicated and needn't trouble us just now. The important thing is that they have a unifying effect on all incoming sense data. They give coherence to our experience of the world around us, shaping things in the only way they can be shaped, and are, Kant says, "transcendental."

> There can be in us no modes of knowledge, no connection or unity of one mode of knowledge with another, without that unity of consciousness which precedes all data of intuitions. . .This pure original unchangeable consciousness I shall name *transcendental apperception.* That it deserves this name is clear from the fact that even the purest objective unity, namely, that of the *a priori* concepts (space and time), is only possible through relation of the intuitions to such unity of consciousness. The numerical unity of this apperception is thus the *a priori* ground of all concepts, just as the manifoldness of space and time is the *a priori* ground of the intuitions of sensibility.[35]

---

[35] **Kant, Immanuel, *Critique,* p. 86.**

Phenomenal reality is Immanuel Kant's term for reality as it appears to us. Noumenal reality is reality as it actually is. Phenomenal reality we know. Noumenal reality we can never actually know, if by "know" we mean directly experience.

This is brilliant and original, but it does raise certain problems. If my mind transcends and unifies material reality, taking the mass of incoming sense data and putting it together in patterns predetermined by these innate *a priori* categories, then what can I know of the real world? Kant answers, nothing! The real world, what he calls the **noumenal** world, I can never know. I can only know the **phenomenal** world, the world as I create it in my own mind. Of course, my phenomenal world doesn't differ substantially from yours, for the categories are the same for all of us; but for all of us the things-as-they-are remain forever beyond us, hidden beyond a curtain that we can't penetrate.

This, however, did not trouble Kant a great deal, because it means that in the real world, the noumenal world, time-space and cause-effect do not exist, and this frees us from the rigid determinism of the empiricists and leaves us as free moral agents, able to choose and act, and responsible for our choices and our actions. As is always the case when studying Kant, serious, sustained thought is called for here. In the phenomenal world, the world-as-I-see-it, the baseball players throw the ball back and forth and I see this as occurring in time and space and ruled over by cause and effect because that is the way my transcendent mind orders it. But behind the curtain, in the noumenal world-as-it-really-is, no such categories are in operation; and it is in the noumenal world that God, morality, and metaphysics reside. He has done what he wished to do: he has saved metaphysics from the meddling David Hume by pushing it beyond his reach, behind the curtain. But he has sacrificed something in the bargain. Since the time of Kant very few philosophers have attempted to prove the existence of God, since Kant, who himself did not doubt God's existence, has effectively shown that proofs cannot be given. Now the perceptive student may say at this point that he or she can understand how, if Kant is correct, the sorts of proofs Aquinas constructed cannot work because they are empirical and *a posteriori.* But what about the ontological arguments of Anselm, Descartes and Spinoza? Mightn't these arguments, which are all *a priori,* be sound? Unfortunately Kant also deals what may be lethal blows to the ontological argument for the existence of God. We will discuss this at greater length in the section on metaphysics.

There is a great deal more to be said about Kant, for he impacted the moral dialectic with a monumental contribution, *The Foundation of the Metaphysics of Morals,* which we will take up when we come to ethics.

With the death of Kant, in 1804, philosophy moves into a new era, the modern era, a troubling and yet an exciting time.

Chapter 4
Leaping to Infinity

This fellow Hegel drives me up a wall.
I just can't understand the man at all.
Why even Bertrand Russell, let's admit it,
Tossed him aside and muttered, "I don't get it."
I'd say this emperor is lacking clothes,
If I could understand him; but who knows?

Said Hegel unto Kierkegaard,
"Kindly stay out of my backyard."
To which the daunty Dane replied,
"If it's your yard, then Buddha lied."

In this chapter I intend to bring philosophy up to date, at least from an American point of view. I am not going to deal with Jeremy Bentham and John Stuart Mill because their major contribution was in the area of ethics and, as with Kant's *Foundation of the Metaphysic of Morals*, I wish to save them for another day. Let me say in passing however that their influence on contemporary thought cannot be minimized. Some have suggested that ethically we live in the utilitarian era. This was certainly true of Great Britain during the nineteenth century, and the nineteenth century was the British century worldwide. On the Continent, however, a non-British storm was brewing, and out of it would come a system and, in reaction to the system, a compelling, subjective thinker who was defiantly unsystematic. As Sartre said in *Being and Nothingness*, "Against Hegel one ought always to oppose Kierkegaard." Kierkegaard couldn't have said it better himself. "The System," Kierkegaard's sarcastic way of referring to Hegel, gave rise to Communism, and Kierkegaard gave rise to individuals who refuse to be a part of any system, who sit alone thinking about troubling things such as absurdity, inauthenticity, forlorness. We call them existentialists.

Georg Friedrich Hegel (1770-1831)

The term "system" was well chosen, and regardless of how Kierkegaard intended it, Hegel no doubt would have been pleased, for a system is precisely what he intended to create. And what a system! He would begin with "Being" (which is God) and conclude with God in an unfolded and fulfilled form, which he defined as "pure thought thinking itself." And in between he would take us on one of the most amazing, some would say most confusing, intellectual trips that ever sprang from a western mind.

It is not at all uncommon for contemporary philosophy texts to skip Hegel altogether, or to make reference to him only in passing, for though he was widely discussed in his day few today are certain how seriously he ought to be taken. The German philosopher Schopenhauer referred to his work as, "This sickening humbug," while Kierkegaard indicated that Hegel's greatest sin was that he apparently took himself seriously. It wasn't that Hegel was stupid, but rather that he lacked a sense of humor. All Hegel had to do to be the greatest thinker in history, according to Kierkegaard, was to come to the end of his "system" and say with his final sentence, "This has all been a colossal joke," or words to that effect. But he didn't, because he apparently didn't realize he had been joking.

Kierkegaard was wrong, and probably knew he was wrong when he said it. Any man whose thinking gave rise to an economic theory that has dominated a good part of the world during our century, who influenced even those philosophers who loved to denigrate him (such as Kierkegaard and Schopenhauer), and who is being widely studied and written about even as I speak, deserves to be looked at.[1] The twin problems in giving coverage to Hegel in a book of this type are first to do justice to him, and second to avoid leaving the student in a state of advanced confusion. To this end, I shall take up only one aspect of his philosophy, that portion that has been the most influential in the world, his metaphysics, more specifically his famed dialectic. First, a bit about his life.

He was born in 1770, as the Age of Enlightenment was coming to a close, and he died some 61 years later, when Romanticism was in its

---

[1] **I urge the student, for his or her own information, to check the current literature to see how many journal articles have something to do with the work of Hegel. Compare this number with those dealing with any other nineteenth century philosopher. I will wager that Hegel will win handily.**

ascendancy. Remember that the Romantic period produced poets such as Schiller in Germany and Wordsworth in England who were urging anyone who would listen to simply lay aside their books, go out into the woods, and drink in all the truths of nature.

> And bring no books; for this one day
> We'll give to idleness.
>
> Books! 'Tis a dull and endless strife:
> Come hear the woodland linnet,
> How sweet his music!
>
> One impulse from a vernal wood
> May teach you more of man,
> Of moral evil and of good,
> Than all the sages can . . .
>
> Enough of Science and of Art,
> Close up those barren leaves;
> Come forth, and bring with you a heart
> That watches and receives.[2]

This was clearly in reaction to the rigidly logical approach of the Enlightenment, but it was just as clearly an over reaction. Hegel, though he admired Schiller, would have none of it.

Hegel was, by training, a theologian. He went to the Protestant seminary at Tuebingen, where he came under the influence of Rousseau, Goethe, and Immanuel Kant. Between 1801 and 1806 he was a professor at the University of Jena, and it was during this time that he formulated the ideas that he would present in his most famous book, *The Phenomenology of the Spirit*, a complex, difficult work in which he purports to show nothing less than how history must unfold. It will follow a dialectical process in which a thesis is negated and yet both the thesis and its negation are preserved in a synthesis, which will then itself become a thesis for a negation (antithesis). I doubt very much that any one reading this has even the remotest idea what I am talking about, so I will try to explain.

---

2 These lines, from William Wordsworth, are an admirable example of the romantic attitude toward science and philosophy. Hegel loved the poetry, but rejected the underlying sentiment.

Immanuel Kant was the prime mover among German philosophers at the time Hegel was coming to maturity, and it is not surprising to find Hegel taken up with, and responding to, Kant. He rejected the Kantian notion that the noumena are unknowable, for he reasoned that if we know they exist we must know them, and anything that exists must be knowable, because (one of his more famous quotables) "the rational is real and the real is rational." He then went on to state that the Kantian categories (time, space, etc.) actually exist independent of individual human minds; but not independent of Mind. This is the point at which Hegel loses many of his readers, particularly those in the English speaking world. His philosophy takes on an almost eastern cast. He seems in some ways to be anticipating the work of Carl Jung.

Reality, according to Hegel, is Mind, or Spirit. This makes him an idealist, of course, and he is a monist to boot, because Mind is everything — and everything is Mind. Sometimes he refers to reality as Absolute Spirit, and his philosophy is thus called absolute idealism. Now, what is this great Mind doing, just sort of hovering about being a mind? Not actually. Mind is revealing itself in a magnificent unfolding that is sweeping up everything in its path, engulfing all that is, and the process by which this is being accomplished is a dialectical one.

We have used the term dialectic already, but the use to which we have put it is not at all suggestive of what Hegel had in mind. Dialectic, as it pertained to Socrates, involved two or more people talking back and forth, placing idea alongside idea to see which was more likely to be valid. This is, more or less, the way philosophers had used the term from Socrates until the advent of Hegel. Hegel had a very different notion. Notice that the Socratic dialectic is one of thesis and antithesis with one or the other being rejected as false. By the law of the excluded middle, Euthyphro's definition of holiness is either true, or it is not true, but it cannot be both true and not true at the same time as this would violate the law of contradiction; and as the dialectic between Euthyphro and Socrates unfolds Plato hopes to show that Euthyphro is simply wrong. His definition of holiness is wanting and must be rejected. In the Hegelian dialectic nothing is rejected, but everything gets changed.

The Hegelian Dialectic: named for the German philosopher who proposed it. A process by which history supposedly unfolds. It is triadic, beginning with thesis, which gives rise to antithesis, finally resulting in synthesis.

Hegel's process is triadic: it moves forward in groups of threes. Thesis automatically gives rises to its antithesis (or its opposite), and the two merge into a synthesis, which itself becomes a thesis that generates another antithesis, and so it goes. This is the so-called **Hegelian dialectic.**

But what, precisely, does it mean?

Suppose we look at it like this. If I say to you that it is impossible to understand what a thing is unless and until you have understood what it is not — would this excite your interest? For example, would it make any sense to talk of truth if we had no conception of falsehood? The answer appears obvious to me, and I trust it will to the student as well. In fact, with very little effort we can think of all sorts of things that we understand that would be totally incomprehensible to us if we did not have some understanding of their opposites. Hot and cold, for example, or tall and short. And suppose all women looked like the young Marilyn Monroe?[3] Wouldn't feminine beauty under those circumstances be impossible to define. We couldn't say Miss Monroe was beautiful, just that she was what she was and that everyone else is the same way. Perhaps this will illustrate what Hegel means when he says that a thing gives rise to its opposite.

But what happens to the two things once they have risen up in opposition to one another? In the Hegelian dialectic they merge to form a synthesis. Neither is lost, but both are changed, and the resultant synthesis, for Hegel, is higher, better than either the thesis or the antithesis from which it was developed. Let us try another example. Let Hot be our thesis. Over against it we will get Cold. The two will then merge to form Lukewarm, which will then become a thesis for another antithesis. But these are only examples, and examples of the simplest types, used to facilitate some understanding of what Hegel is about. He is, I assure you, frying much bigger fish than "hot," or "cold," or even Marilyn Monroe. He begins his triadic dialectic with the most obvious of theses: God, or Pure Being. Now what can the "Other" be, that thing which arises over against Being to define being by showing us what it is not. It can only be one thing; thus we see Being generating Nothingness. The two then merge to the synthesis of Becoming. And Hegel is off and running, moving toward the ultimate synthesis, Pure thought (Mind or Spirit) thinking itself, which is God again, but God in a new, completed form. Nothing is lost in the process. Everything is included in the final product. So what about you and me? Are we there too? As I understand Hegel, we are, but it is impossible to think that we are there as conscious individuals, and it is equally impossible to see that human volition has anything to do with any of this. It seems, supposing I

---

3 I speak from the point of view of an aging heterosexual who spent his youth in the mid-Fifties in love with Miss Monroe. If she doesn't do it for you, cross her name out and fill in the blank with someone else.

have understood Hegel correctly, that the end will come about in spite of anything any individual says or does. We are on a great, cosmic ride to Nirvana.

But enough of my examples. Let us hear from Hegel on the subject.

> There are three aspects in every thought which is logically real or true: The abstract or rational form, which says what something is; the dialectical negation, which says what something is not; the speculative — concrete comprehension: A is also that which it is not, A is non-A. These three aspects do not constitute three parts of logic, but are moments of everything that is logically real or true. They belong to every philosophical Concept. Every Concept is rational, is abstractly opposed to another, and is united in comprehension together with its opposites. This is the definition of dialectic.[4]

If you do not understand this, don't worry a good deal about it, for seasoned philosophers have a great deal of trouble with Hegel. You should, however, have the general idea by now of the Hegelian dialectic and the form it takes. Understand also that Hegel has not created just a system, in the same way that Aristotle created a system. Aristotle's logic is merely a framework on which Aristotle invites you to hang anything you like. If you understand the form of the classical syllogism then you needn't be bothered with what you use as a major premise and a minor premise. You only need to be bothered with assuring yourself that you have used the form properly. If you understand Hegel's dialectical form, however, it does not follow that you may put anything into it that you wish, for Hegel is very insistent on the way in which the dialectic must unfold.

Strange as all this may seem to today's student, Hegel was the most widely-discussed philosopher of the first half of the nineteenth century. He wound up in Berlin, where he occupied the chair of philosophy, and from whence he dominated metaphysical thought on the Continent. His dialectical method, put to other uses, has dominated much of the world down to the present day, for he gave rise to a group of thinkers who agreed with him as to form but disagreed as to substance. The dialectic will work, they believed, but only if we reject Spirit and substitute Matter. Thus was

---

[4] Hegel, G.W. *Encyclopedia of Philosophy,* trans. Gustav Emil Mueller, New York: Philosophical Library, 1959, p. 82.

born **dialectical materialism** which provided the philosophical basis for communism.

Communism

Dialectic materialism: an economic theory of Karl Marx which weds the form of the Hegelian Dialectic to the idea that history is unfolding along economic rather than spiritual lines.

Karl Marx (1818-1883)

Communism begins with an assumption that reality is matter and not spirit, and continues with an assumption that the human is an economical creature and that all history is thus economically determined. Grant communists these propositions and they will proceed to apply the dialectic to history and show you why capitalism is doomed and communism must triumph. No one ever did this better than Karl Marx, and it is probable that no one was more convinced than he that his system would lead to a golden age in which peace, love, and brotherhood are something more than mere words.

Marx was born in Trier, Germany, the son of Jewish parents who had left the synagogue and converted to Christianity. The family name was Levi, but Marx's father, who was a lawyer, changed it to Marx for what appear to have been social and business reasons. When he was seventeen Marx entered the University of Bonn, but at his father's insistence he later transferred to the University of Berlin. Here he fell under the influence of Hegel, and of radical freethinkers. When he left the university, he was unable to find employment as a teacher, and he went to work for one Moses Hess editing a journal called *Rheinische Zeitung*. But by 1843, the same year Marx was married, the journal was closed down because of Marx's radical writing, and Marx moved on to Paris. He managed to get thrown out of that city within a year, moved to Brussels, and from thence to London, where he met young Friedrich Engles. Together they wrote and published what was to become one of the most famous revolutionary documents of history, *The Manifesto of the Communist Party*. In 1848 *The Manifesto* was published in all major European languages, and that same year revolution broke out in Europe. Marx and Engles did not cause the revolution with *The Manifesto*, but one must admit that their timing was excellent, and their work was certainly used after the fact to justify the actions of the revolutionaries. "A specter is haunting Europe," Marx and Engles wrote. "The specter of communism."

> The history of all hitherto existing society is the history of class struggles. Freeman and slave, patrician and plebeian, lord and serf, guildmaster and journeyman, in a word, oppressor and oppressed, stood in constant opposition to one another, carried on an uninterrupted, now hidden, now open fight, a fight that each time ended, either in a revolutionary reconstitution of society

> at large, or in the common ruin of the contending classes.
>
> Our epoch, the epoch of the bourgeoisie, possesses this distinct feature. It has simplified the class antagonisms. Society as a whole is more and more splitting up into two great classes directly facing each other -- bourgeoisie and proletariat. . .
>
> The Communists disdain to conceal their views and aims. They openly declare that their ends can be attained only by the forcible overthrow of all existing social conditions. Let the ruling classes tremble at a Communist revolution. The proletarians have nothing to lose but their chains. They have a world to win.
>
> Workingmen of all countries, unite!

After the barricades were cleared and the revolution was put down, many of the participants fled to America to become seed corn for American socialism in its manifold forms.

The Manifesto is the most famous and widely-read piece of literature to come out of the communist camp. It is to communism what the opening section of the Declaration of Independence was, and has been, to Americans — a statement of what the movement is about at its heart. But while it contains philosophical undertones, as did Thomas Jefferson's famed proclamation, it is not philosophy but polemic. To get to communist philosophy one must be willing to dive into *Das Kapital*, the three-volume work which Marx began when he was forty-two years old and living in exile in London. Here Marx has a go at wedding Hegelian dialectic to economic history and comes up with the peculiar offspring that all communists have held dear and proclaimed with evangelistic fervency — dialectic materialism. In calling dialectic materialism the "peculiar offspring" of Hegel and Marx I am not, I trust, dismissing them with a quick *ad hominem*. Rather, I use the word "peculiar" to describe Marxism because it is the best one I can think of. Marx has taken a questionable metaphysical system, a questionable theory of economical development, put the two together, and announced that this is the way history will unfold because it must unfold this way. History, however, appears to have its own agenda.

***Ad hominem*: literally, to the man. A false argument in which one attacks another's position by insulting the person rather than by dealing with the argument.**

According to Marx, history is an ongoing process of dialectical tension between two classes, always two, an upper class and a lower class. Already we see the influence of Hegel as the thesis of "upper class" gives rise to the antithesis of "lower class"; and we are not surprised to see these coming together in a synthesis. There are five historical epochs, primitive/communal, slave, feudal, capitalist, socialist/communist. Notice that capitalism grew out of feudalism, and that the final stage, the one which will succeed capitalism, is the communist stage. Notice also that like Hegel, who begins and ends with God, Marx begins and ends with something communal, but that the two are different and the final form is more complex, more fully developed.

Marx was a product of the period we know as the Industrial Revolution, during which whole populations were displaced from rural environments to the slums of great cities, where they worked in mills, mines and factories under harsh and often dangerous conditions. The material means of production were held exclusively by the capitalists, whom Marx identifies as bourgeoisie, while the labor was provided by the lower class, or the proletariat. The result was an entire class (the proletariat) alienated from the product of its labor, paid in money which was only a fraction of the value their labor had helped to create, and consigned to the margin of society to exist as something not quite animal but certainly sub-human. This would continue, Marx believed, until the revolution, which would arise naturally from the conditions themselves as capitalism played slowly out and was swallowed up by the proletariat in a new synthesis, and the dictatorship of the proletariat would come in.

But where, one might ask, is all this going? It is going toward a classless society in which all things are owned in common, each works to fulfill his or her own ambition, and all are taken care of. Then comes another question: why should the classless society itself not become a thesis for another antithesis, then be swallowed up in further synthesis? To ask such a question is to reveal that you have not paid strict attention to Hegel. The dialectical process does not run on to infinity, but must stop when the logical end is reached, the end being God. For Marx, the logical end, what he (an avowed atheist) possessed in lieu of God, is the classless society. From here there is nowhere else to go. Perhaps this must be taken on faith. I don't believe it, but if others do, what can I say. My experience is that faith is difficult to argue against.

Few things that Marx said must happen actually happened. The communist revolution, for example, could only occur in a society ripe for revolution, one in which the capitalistic system was well established, had absorbed all it could, and was beginning to totter with age. That meant Germany and the industrialized West. In fact, when the revolution came it came in a nation that was backward and unindustrialized by western standards — czarist Russia. Few of the western nations ever fell to communism, and where communism was tried it quite simply failed, leaving misery and disillusionment in its wake. For the few, diehard ideologues, this only proves that true Marxian principles were never actually instituted or adhered to; but the fatal flaw in this line of reasoning is that it deviates from Hegelianism and the dialectic. The dialectic, recall, *must* work. It is unfolding irresistibly and carrying all along with it. Actually, it is not, for between theory and reality a great gulf sometimes yawns, as in this case. History has been considerably kinder to Adam Smith than it has to Karl Marx.[5]

History has also, in an odd way, been kinder to Søren Kierkegaard, who opposed Hegel, than it has to Hegel. In the renegade Dane we see a man who asserted his individualism, who refused to be a part of the system, and who, in his rebellion against the dominant philosophy of his day set the stage for the twentieth century, the so-called existential age.

Søren Kierkegaard (1813-1855)

"A man" Miguel de Unomuno says of Kierkegaard, "and what a man."[6] He was, let us admit, a different sort of man, one who wrote of himself, "Had I to carve an inscription on my grave I would ask for none other than 'the individual.'"

He stood in opposition to Hegel, and still does, as I have indicated by the quote from Jean Paul Sartre in *Being and Nothingness*; and in this we find one of those delicious examples of irony which excite the poets. In the Hegelian system thesis gives rise to antithesis. In the real world of philosophical exchange the thesis of Hegel gives rise to the antithesis of Kierkegaard, who negates the whole process by refusing to take part in a synthetical arrangement. Kierkegaard, the individual, remains ever the individual, alone and defiant, refusing to be swallowed up in the great abstraction of thought thinking itself.

He was born in Copenhagen, Denmark, the youngest of seven children. His father, Michael, was an interesting soul, one who had a marked influence on his precocious young son. He (Michael) had begun life on the lonely moors of the Jutland peninsula herding sheep, miserable to the point that one day he cursed God for his condition. He later went to

---

[5] **I have had nothing to say about Adam Smith, though he is arguably the most important of the eighteenth-century economic philosophers. His monumental *Wealth of Nations* remains, for all free-marketers, a text only slightly less authoritative than scripture.**

[6] **He makes the statement in his famous existential work, *The Tragic Sense of Life*.**

Copenhagen and became a wealthy merchant; but he was dogged by the conviction that in cursing God he had committed the unpardonable sin. Later, shortly after the birth of his youngest son, Michael's wife died, and he quickly fell into a sexual affair with a housemaid. This only confirmed to him that he was something of an incurrable sinner. He managed to convey all of this to Soren, who was nothing if not impressionable.

In 1830 Søren entered the University of Copenhagen to study, at his father's insistence, theology. One can easily imagine that Michael, devout and sin-ridden Lutheran that he was, felt that in handing his favorite son over to God he would somehow atone for his past. But it didn't work. Søren was not interested in theology, but instead gave his time to literature, philosophy, drinking, partying, in short to living the collegiate life. He and his father had a serious falling-out at this time. But they managed to make up before Michael died in 1838, and Søren returned to the study of theology, passed his exams with honors, and submitted his thesis on Socratic irony.

He was twenty-seven years old.

In this same year he met a woman who was to change his life, give direction to his philosophy, and whose name will be forever linked with his, in spite of the ironic fact (Søren would like that) that they were never physically linked. Her name was Regine (pronounced *Regina*) Olsen.

She was upper-class, wealthy, beautiful, and she was only fourteen years old when she and Søren met. As one has noted, compared to the cynical, witty Kierkegaard, she was a guileless child. But they fell in love, and when she was seventeen they became formally engaged. It didn't last long; within weeks Kierkegaard broke the engagement — then spent the rest of his life trying to explain why, affirming with, almost literally, his dying breath his love for Regine Olsen. Kierkegaard's explanation for his action, whether or not one chooses to believe him, is interesting.

He had been deeply moved by the biblical account of Abraham's sacrifice of Isaac, so moved in fact that he later wrote a major book about it, *Fear and Trembling*. As he tells it, he became convinced, based on the story of Abraham and Isaac, of a principle by which one ought to order one's life: if one sacrifices what one loves to God, then God will give it back, with added blessing. So he took Regine up to Mount Moriah, figuratively speaking, bound her, laid her on the alter, and plunged in the flint knife.

He then went off to the University of Berlin and wrote *Either/Or*. When he returned to Copenhagen he found that he had *either* not understood the biblical account, *or* the principle that had worked for

Abraham was not a principle that would work for Søren Kierkegaard. Regine had become engaged to one of their mutual friends, whom she quickly married, and Søren Kierkegaard was left to spend the rest of his life as a bachelor, meditating on what had gone wrong.

So runs the analysis as provided by Kierkegaard. I never put much stock in this myself, but why quibble about it at this late date. Kierkegaard believed it, and his analysis becomes the important one because it is from this foundation that much of the important work that followed was launched.

Let's go back to Berlin and to the few months that Kierkegaard was there after he broke the engagement to Regine. It was there that he wrote *Either/Or* and positioned himself as the everlasting opponent of Hegel. In 1843, with Hegel dead, the Chair of Philosophy at the University of Berlin was occupied by Friedrich Wilhelm von Schelling, an aging idealist who spent his waning years fighting what then appeared to be a rearguard action against Hegel. In retrospect the fight was more successful than anyone at the time could have realized, for among those who heard Schelling's lectures was Søren Kierkegaard, destined to become Hegel's most illustrious opponent. It wasn't that Kierkegaard had no respect for Hegel's intelligence. Quite the opposite. He felt that Hegel had pulled off a brilliant *tour de force*, one of the great achievements in the history of Western Philosophy. The problem was that, when all was said and done, he didn't think it really mattered to anyone, other than those ensconced behind ivy-covered walls or wandering through the hallowed corridors of higher learning. Kierkegaard's cry, in the face of Hegelianism, rings across the years: What about me?

I am not a particle in the whirling galaxy of thought. I am an individual, shut up for better or worse at solitary confinement within myself, forced to make decisions that will affect me all of my live, with no way to tell whether I am right or wrong. Every decision I make is a leap into the dark. I am well aware of my smallness, my weakness, and well aware of my impending death. And yet, as I stand here I think, I feel, I know passion and loneliness, and I intend to affirm myself as having value in spite of the sense of absurdity that such affirmation calls forth. I am here. I exist.

Kierkegaard wasn't the first human to express himself in these terms. One hears existential anxiety in the voice of the psalmist of ancient Israel:

> When I consider thy heavens, the work of thy fingers, the moon and the stars, which thou has ordained; What is man that thou art mindful of him? and the son of man, that thou visitest him? For thou hast made him a little lower than the angels, and. . .madest him to have dominion over the works of thy hands. (Psalms 8:3-6).

Another pre-Kierkegaardian who talked in existential terms was the troubled mathematician-philosopher Blaise Pascal.

> I know not who put me into the world, nor what the world is, nor what I myself am. I am in terrible ignorance of everything. I know not what my body is, nor my sense, nor my soul, not even that part of me which thinks what I say, which reflects on all and on itself. . .I see those frightful spaces of the universe which surround me, and I find myself tied to one corner of this vast expanse, without knowing why I am put in this place. . .I see infinities on all sides. . .I know that I must soon die.[7]

I, I, I. . .Me, me, me. Is that all these existentialists can think about? Why can't they forget themselves and go along on the great Hegelian ride. Because the human, in his or her self-awareness, is shut up at solitary confinement within the human body, eternally alone and seeking to make contact with some outside reality, but doomed to failure. Now what can be done about this? The right action, indeed the only action for the authentic person, is to accept one's individuality, one's solitude, and take responsibility for oneself. But this is, as Pascal has said, terribly frightening, so most people try to lose themselves and their individuality by merging with the group, or, as Kierkegaard called them, the crowd. Nietzsche would say "the herd." It's all the same thing, and it leads to inauthenticity.

The term "existentialism" is itself instructive in this regard. Think back to the Greeks and the Christians. On the subject of human nature they were "essentialists," believing that there is some inward core of being that all humans share in common and that defines what it is to be human. For Aristotle, the human essence is rationality, Man is the thinking animal. For the Christians, the defining quality is the human soul, created in the image of God. The existentialists deny that there is a human essence. Put another way, essence does not precede existence, but rather existence precedes essence, and the human is not defined by what he or she *is*, but by what he or she *does*. We will see this idea more fully worked out when we come to the twentieth-century existentialists, particularly Jean Paul Sartre. But we see it already in seminal form in the writing of Søren Kierkegaard. "The

---

[7] Pascal, Blaise, *Pensees*, trans. William F. Trotter, ed. H.S. Thayer and Elizabeth Thayer, New York: Washington Square Press, 1965, p. 61.

question is not what am I to *believe*," he wrote in his journals, "but what am I to *do*."[8]

But what can I do? The answer is, whatever I choose. The existentialists are absolutely convinced that the human is free, totally free, and responsible for his or her choices. The metaphysical justification for this will be worked out more fully by Jean Paul Sartre. Kierkegaard simply takes it as a given. If you don't like what you are and wish to confront the responsible party, look in the mirror. If you can't deal with the awesome weight of individual responsibility and attempt to excuse yourself by blaming your heredity or your parenting, the existentialists will accuse you of inauthenticity and cowardice. Suppose that I look about me, as did Pascal, see the big, scary universe, and decide that I do not wish to pursue a lone course. It makes no difference; I am still alone and responsible for myself. Suppose that I seek out a guru who seems to have all the answers, beg him to allow me to sit at his feet, tell him that I will follow his instructions, do whatever he says. That too is a choice for which I am responsible, and I have lost my identity and become inauthentic in the bargain. I must take responsibility for myself, live in the moment without excuses, refuse to look to groups or other individuals for meaning and purpose.

Kierkegaard was a Christian, and he was particularly interested in how one gets to God. To him, the institutional Christians who merely went through the motions of being believers without actually risking anything were the living pictures of lost, inauthentic souls. And this meant most everyone. Getting to God required passion and the willingness to go forward on faith in the face of the overwhelming fact that the whole thing is an absurdity. You are standing, for example, on the edge of a cliff at night, and you hear a voice out in the darkness that whispers, "This is God speaking. Jump, and I'll catch you." Do you jump? But this is absurd. Nevertheless, you will either jump or you won't; and having jumped (if you choose to), you will either plummet to your death on the rocks below or you will tumble into the arms of a loving God. Whatever you do, this is your experience and cannot in the most important sense be shared with anyone else.

The term "leap of faith" was coined by Kierkegaard to express, not only coming to God, but to show how one makes any major decision that

---

[8] Kierkegaard, Søren, *Søren Kirkegaard's Journal and Papers*, trans, & ed. Howard V. Hong and Edna H. Hong, Bloomington, Indiana: Indiana University Press, 1967, p. 44.

takes one from one stage of life to the next. Life was, he held, lived in three different stages, each higher than the one that goes before it,[9] but the passage from one of these stages to the next was not automatic, did not come with growth or maturity. In each case "the leap" was called for.

It is not surprising that Kierkegaard was unknown during his life time outside his native Copenhagen. Not only did he not travel widely, but he wrote in a language (Danish) which few were able to read. To complicate matters — assuming fame was what he was after — he was swimming against the philosophical current, talking about things that no one wished to hear, holding up Hegel to ridicule while at the same time championing the idea that subjectivity is truth. Like so many important thinkers, he was ahead of his time. His ideas would resonate well in the twentieth century, but by then he would have been in his grave over fifty years.

Another nineteenth century existentialist who got no hearing during his life but became posthumously famous was the German, Friedrich Nietzsche.

Friedrich Nietzsche (1844-1900)

I actually hesitated before calling Nietzsche an existentialist, because I know that if such a thing is possible I just caused him to turn over in his grave. Neither he nor Kierkegaard would take kindly to having labels put on them. Individualists are funny like that. Still, they are both considered existentialists, not because they can be comfortably placed within a philosophical system — they cannot — but because the themes with which both of them dealt, and the direction in which they wished to take us, are typically existential.

In a class of twenty-five students I can usually count on about three who have heard of Nietzsche, which is about three more than the number who have heard of Kierkegaard. This is a bit puzzling, for both are widely read, widely translated, and their works may be found in any decent bookstore. For those who know Nietzsche, I always have a question: What do you know about him? "Oh," the response will be, "he's the guy who said God is dead." Yes, he did. And I suppose if one makes such an announcement he can at least expect some raised eyebrows. But why, I then ask my

---

[9] **The three stages are the aesthetic, in which one lives for pleasure, the ethical, in which one's life is guided by adherence to ethical principles, and the religious, the highest stage, which may actually require what Kierkegaard calls a "teleological suspension of morals."**

students, would he say such a thing? What was he trying to convey? My answer: blank stares. Suppose we read exactly what Nietzsche said, then we shall ask why he said it, and finally we will see why he is classed with the existentialists.

> Have you heard of the mad man who on a bright morning lighted a lantern, ran to the market, and began to cry, "I am seeking God! I am seeking God!" There were many standing about who did not believe in God, and they began to laugh. "Did he get lost?" said one. "Did he run away like a child?""said another. "Or did he hide? Is he afraid of us? Did he get on a ship and immigrate?" So they shouted and laughed among themselves. But the mad man sprang into their midst, and His eyes bored into them.
>
> "Where is God?" he cried. "I will tell you. We murdered him, you and I. We are all his murderers. . God is dead. God will stay dead. And we have killed him. The holiest and mightiest being that ever lived has bled to death under our knives -- who will wash this blood from us? . .We must ourselves become gods to be worthy of such a deed."[10]

In this remarkable passage there is much to be discussed. First, notice that this is not the statement of an atheist, though it is clear enough that Nietzsche was an atheist. Second, there is a wonderful irony in Nietzsche's putting these words in the mouth of a mad man, for he is clearly the most sane one in the crowd. Third, it is we who have killed God, we who are to be condemned. Fourth, God will not be coming back from the dead; already the smell of divine putrefaction has reached our nostrils. And finally, we must now become gods ourselves and step into the place which God once occupied.

Nietzsche claimed that he discovered, and was the first to announce, the death of God. Truth is, Kierkegaard beat him to it, but he didn't make the announcement in just these terms. Both men understood, long before anyone else, that beneath the seeming stability of civilized Europe there were rotten foundation timbers. God had been the center of human society in the West for hundreds of years, but something happened, and God's hold on people began to weaken. Perhaps Copernicus was the real mischief maker.

Same as killing God

---

[10] **The passage is from Nietzsche's "*Die Froehliche Wissenschaft*." The translation is my own.**

"Ever since Copernicus," said Kierkegaard, "we have been rolling toward X." But Nietzsche does not blame Copernicus, nor would Kierkegaard. The charge is that we all have taken part in the murder, and it is all of us who must now live in a universe from which the divine is absent.

When we look at his early life, Nietzsche seems an unlikely source of such ideas. He was the son of a Lutheran minister, who died when Nietzsche was a small child. Raised in a household of doting women, the young Nietzsche was so pious that his school companions called him, "the little pastor," and everyone assumed he would follow in his father's footsteps. Had he done so he would without a doubt have been much happier, but we would have been bereft of one of the most original European thinkers. Instead, as he grew up he began to question the existence of God, and by the time he had turned twenty and had gone away to the University of Bonn he was in full and open rebellion. Well. . .sort of.

Truth is, he was never able to be an open rebel and like it, and he found the other students coarse and disgusting. Still, he tried his hand at drinking, fighting, and whoring, only to come down with a case of syphilis and a nervous collapse. As Frederick Copleston has insightfully said, "How he longed to be a sinner, this incorrigible saint." What was left for him to do, now that his faith was gone, his health was ruined, and he had already set the pattern for what he was to be for the rest of his life? He was a loner, the eternal outsider, destined to wander the earth and never have a home.

He transferred to the University of Leipzig, where he found a new direction of study and a mentor. Professor Friedrich Ritschl recognized Nietzsche's brilliance and encouraged him to study philology, philosophy and literature. Here also Nietzsche encountered a philosopher that gave a new direction to his thinking, Arthur Schopenhauer, the pessimist and anti-Hegelian. In his most famous work *The World as Will and Idea*, Schopenhauer had argued that life is nothing more than the will to survive, and that such happiness as we can garner must come from eliminating our wants and desires.[11] Nietzsche eventually worked the "will to survive" into one of his more famous, if grossly misunderstood, doctrines — the will to power.

Having graduated from Leipzig, Nietzsche took a position as a professor of classical philology at the University of Basel, and as *Doctor*

---

11 He must have been reading over the Buddha's shoulder. Those familiar with eastern philosophy, particularly Buddhism and Hinduism, cannot help but see certain superficial similarities between some of the nineteenth century idealists and the eastern sages.

Nietzsche, he plunged headlong into the academic life from the other side of the podium. It didn't work. He was not a good lecturer, did not get along well with students or colleagues, and to complicate matters even further was in poor health. What to do? In 1870 the Franco-Prussian War broke out, and he volunteered as a medic, served awhile, then returned broken and discouraged to Leipzig, from whence he began the gypsy existence that he would follow for the rest of his life. He drifted down to Italy, up to Switzerland, over the Germany, back down to Italy, and he wrote, telling out his poetic vision to a world that didn't want it. His eyes began to fail, his mind began to go, affected by the syphilis that was, in those days, incurable, and he went home to be cared for by his sister Elisabeth. In Weimar, hopelessly insane, he died unknown. The year was 1900.

He was hardly laid away when his star began to rise, or perhaps, more accurately, he exploded into public view. Everyone who was anyone began reading and commenting on Nietzsche. Those who had ignored him while he was alive came forward to claim that they were his most intimate and beloved of associates. He was lionized, rhapsodized,[12] praised, condemned — but mostly he was misunderstood. In a poetic self-evaluation he had written:

Ja, ich weiss woher ich stamme!
Ungesättigt gleich der Flamme
glühe und versehr ich mich.
Licht wird alles, was ich fasse,
Kohle alles, was ich lasse:
Flamme bin ich sicherlich![13]

An iconoclast, philosophizing (as he himself said) with a hammer, he

---

[12] Richard Strauss wrote one of his best known symphonies, *Also Sprach Zarathustra*, on Nietzsche's book by that name.

[13]
Yes, I know from whence I spring!
Insatiable, like the flame
I glow and consume myself.
All that I grasp becomes light,
All that I leave becomes ashes:
I am certainly a flame.

(The translation is mine.)

came to destroy all that had gone before and raise up something new from the rubble. Though there is no evidence that he had actually read Kierkegaard, he had come to many of the same conclusions, the difference being that, unlike Kierkegaard, he had no God to which to leap. Humankind had murdered God, and Nietzsche was not about to let us off the hook. But neither was he about to allow himself to sink into the pessimism characteristic of Schopenhauer. Happiness was possible for the individual who was willing to cut loose from all the old ways associated with the God-centered world, and go forward into the darkness armed only with courage and the will to power. For those who wished to ignore truth, who refused to face God's death and their complicity in His murder, who sought the comfort of "the herd" with its ready-made values and slave morality, Nietzsche had only contempt. He was Kierkegaard with a spiked club, Schopenhauer with joy, Prometheus with a blow torch.

In 1885, while living in the Swiss Alps, he produced his most famous creation, and his most controversial and perhaps least understood, Zarathustra the prophet. Zarathustra was an actual person, the prophet of the Persian religion we call Zoroastrianism; but what Nietzsche created was a new prophet altogether, the announcer of the death of God, the bringer of the superman.[14] Superman is not, for Nietzsche, a figure in a comic book, not a Nazi or a sword wielding Viking, but rather the next step in human development. With the death of God something new is called for, because with God's death all the old values have died and will not be coming back. The human is no end, but merely a way station, a point along a continuum, something to be surpassed. But before there can be superman, God's death must be reckoned with, and He must be forever laid away. Thus, early in *Thus Spake Zarathustra,* Nietzsche has the prophet encountering a holy man in a forest who tells Zarathustra that he spends his time praising God. After he and the holy man have parted company, Zarathustra says in his heart: "Can it be possible that this holy man in his forest has not heard that God is dead?"[15] He then proceeds to the nearest town to preach to the people.

---

[14] The German word is *übermensch*. A literal translation: *overhuman*. *Superman* is a much better way to render it, though I will admit it has gathered up some troubling connotative baggage over the years.

[15] Nietzsche, Friedrich, *Also Sprach Zarathustra,* Munich: Wilhelm Goldmann Verlag, p. 11. The translation is my own.

> I teach you of the superman. The human is something that must be surpassed. What have you done to surpass him? All before have created something greater than themselves. Would you rather be an ebb tide, going back to the animals, than to surpass the human? What is the ape to the human but a joke, a shame? So shall the human be to the superman.[16]

But the listeners predictably do not understand him and go on with their fun and games.

> When Zarathustra had spoken thus he looked at the people and was silent. "There they stand," he said in his heart. "They laugh. They don't understand me. I am not the mouth for these ears."[17]

Indeed *they* did not, and he *was* not. Nietzsche remains misunderstood to this day, for reasons that are both puzzling and instructive. In the seventeenth century Alexander Pope wrote that a "little learning is a dangerous thing." This saying seems to have been tailor made for anyone who wishes to study Nietzsche. He is not, like Hegel or Kant, misunderstood because his language is difficult or his sentences hard to follow. He is misunderstood because his teaching is given in poetry and is highly symbolical, and sometimes this is the most difficult language of all. The death of God, for example, is not something he initially greeted with joy, as is evident from the passage of the mad man quoted above. He found it very depressing. The joy that he gains from this horrible murder is not in the murder itself, but rather that, terrible as it is, it has opened the way for the coming of the superman; and even that joy is dampened by the realization that humans are not ready for the superman's arrival. They must first be bludgeoned into understanding. Nietzsche predicted what finally occurred, that Europe would be swept by convulsive and destructive wars.

Nihilism is something all existentialists talk about. It means "nothing," and is used to indicate that the universe in which we live is ultimately meaningless.

According to Nietzsche, God's death has led to **nihilism**, the Latin for "nothing." He is thus, along with a Kierkegaard, a forerunner of the twentieth-century existentialists, teaching that any meaning humans can gain about life must come from themselves, for the absolute and transcendent values of an earlier age no longer exist, having died along with the only one

---

16 Ibid., p. 11.

17 Ibid., p. 14.

who could give them reality, God. We must, therefore, create our own values. This leads, as well, to such ideas as **absurdity** and existential ***angst.*** The cowards (which he seems to think is the proper designation for most of humanity) will shrink back from this, back into the anonymity and comfort of "the herd." But the brave souls, the supermen, will go joyously forward, willingly accepting their lot, determined to seize the day and create their own world in the face of nihilism and ultimate annihilation.

But perhaps annihilation is not the proper word, for Nietzsche introduces a strange metaphysical mechanism, also widely misunderstood and frequently dismissed as nonsensical, that of eternal recurrence. As Rudyard Kipling once wrote:

> *They will come back— come back again —*
> *As long as the red earth rolls.*
> *He never wasted a leaf or a tree.*
> *Do you think he would squander souls?*[18]

When Nietzsche says "eternal recurrence" he means just that. All that is happening has happened many times before and will happen again, over and over. We are trapped on a great, metaphysical carrousel, with no exit, doomed to ride round and round, forever and ever. This sounds so much like some form of Hinduism that when we first encounter it we are apt to be jolted backward (so to speak), amazed that an atheist could believe in such a thing. Do not be fooled by appearances. This is not Hinduism, and may even have some basis in physical reality. Or it may be nonsense. It all depends upon what one wishes to assume about the universe in which we live. If we begin with the assumption that all things have a beginning and an ending, then there can be no eternal recurrence. If, however, we assume that we live in a universe made up of a finite amount of indestructible matter, converging in patterns, breaking apart, coming back in new patterns, all within a finite framework but an infinity of time, then perhaps there is no good reason to suppose that the material pattern we are living in at this moment will not, at some time in the distant future, repeat itself. Nietzsche, at any rate, believed it, and not everyone has thought him wrong.

---

18 "The Sack of the Gods," from *Rudyard Kipling's Verse,* Definite Edition, Garden City, New York: Doubleday, 1940.

> The attempt by the German philosopher Friedrich Nietzsche to prove recurrence is interesting because it is *almost* a valid argument, given certain (untrue) presuppositions about the nature of the physical universe. That is, Nietzsche's proof contains all the essential ideas needed for a rigorous proof of recurrence of a finite physical system evolving in a particular chance like way. Nietzsche. . .argues for the finiteness of energy of the universal system. This is indeed an essential assumption in any valid proof of recurrence.[19]

The quote is by Frank Tipler, a physicist. Without presuming to argue either for or against Tipler's position, I merely note that it is interesting to find a physicist commenting upon Nietzsche's argument and finding it "almost" persuasive. For our purposes, it is important to see that Nietzsche uses this metaphysical argument to underscore his belief that life has no meaning. It is absurd, and there is nothing we can do about it.

A Brief Interlude

We have now come to the twentieth century, our century, called by Winston Churchill "the terrible twentieth" and by the *Cambridge Modern History* "the era of violence."[20] Or it is sometimes called the existential century, for in our time many of the themes with which Kierkegaard and Nietzsche dealt have become grist for the mills of contemporary philosophers. Existentialism is not, as I have noted, a system of philosophy, but is better described as a group of philosophers, novels, poets, dealing with problems common to a generation left somewhat dazed and confused by all that has transpired. The century has indeed seen its share of systems, but none of these has been able to gain the attention of ordinary people in the way that existentialism has.

Logical positivism came on strongly in the early part of the century, championed by Bertrand Russell, Alfred Whitehead, A.J. Ayre, Ludwig Wittgenstein. In fact, as late as the sixties I was told by one of my professors that logical positivism was probably here to stay. Wrong, professor. It

---

[19] Tipler, Frank J., *The Physics of Immortality*, New York: Doubleday, 1994, p. 77.

[20] Quoted by Barbara Tuchman in the introduction to Gideon Hausner's *Justice in Jerusalem*.

already rocks with age.

Phenomenology, an epistemological system created by Edmund Husserl, looked promising enough in the thirties that young Jean Paul Sartre went to Berlin to study with the master himself. Today it is interesting primarily because of its contribution to twentieth century existentialism, and to the development of Sartre and Martin Heidegger.

Structuralism and Poststructuralism are movements of the latter twentieth century that have stirred some interest. This is particularly true of that movement within poststructuralism that has come to be called deconstructionism. I will have more to say about the deconstructionists and their best known spokesman Derrida, when I deal with the feminists.

Very well, enough for our interlude. Let us return to the philosophers and see how they are faring in the turbulent twentieth century.

Jean Paul Sartre (1905-1980)

Perhaps it is true, as some scholars have said, that human societies, as they develop, cycle through periods of chaos, adjustment, stability, then back to chaos again. Our recent experience seems to confirm this, in a vague way, for it would be difficult to imagine a more stable period than the nineteenth century, and difficult to imagine a more chaotic one than the twentieth. As the nineteenth century closed, it must have seemed to most informed observers that humans had finally solved most of the big problems that had plagued them for the five thousand years or so of recorded history. Oh, there were a few isolated pockets of problems, but by and large it was a marvelous time to be alive. The Kingdom of God was just around the corner. They didn't know it, but Armageddon was just around the corner for an entire generation of young Englishmen, Frenchmen and Germans. And that was only the beginning. Within 45 years of the beginning of the new century well over 100 million[21] people would have died as a result of wars, and there would be no end in sight. Gentlemen cried, "Peace, peace," but there was no peace. It was into this maelstrom that Jean Paul Sartre was thrown.

Born in 1905, seven years before the Titanic sank, and nine years before the guns erupted on the Western Front, Sartre was raised in the home of his maternal grandfather. He was a cousin to the famous missionary

---

21 **Who actually knows how many? If someone has a more accurate figure, let him or her produce it. If not, then accept my figure. To tell the truth, I think I am being conservative.**

Albert Schweitzer. He grew up in a warring world bounded by his mother's Catholicism and his grandfather's Lutheranism. But he was precocious, learned to read at an early age, and he escaped, as have so many others, into a world of books.

Sartre was too young to experience the First World War directly, although one can imagine that he and his family had their home lives seriously disrupted as the armies fought back and forth over what politicians were pleased to call No Man's Land. Nevertheless, by the age of ten he was convinced that he would be a writer. He did well in school, graduated in 1929 from the highly regarded *Ecole Normale Superieure*, and for the next ten years he was a philosophy teacher.

Phenomenology: an epistemological philosophy of the early twentieth-century that purports to study perceptions as they are actually experienced, not merely as theories of experience.

But he found philosophy disappointing, for reasons that Søren Kierkegaard would have understood perfectly: it dealt largely in abstractions, whereas life, with all its problems and difficult decisions, was lived in the concrete. During the thirties he discovered the philosophy of Edmund Husserl, phenomenology, and it seemed to him to answer some of his problems. No one can hope to explain **phenomenology** in a few sentences, but I will give it a try, if only for my own satisfaction. Husserl was interested in producing a descriptive analysis of consciousness, one that dealt with concrete, experienced facts, and not with abstract theory. He was convinced that by concentrating on experience and using descriptive statements he could get to pure consciousness itself. For two years, 1933-34, Sartre studied with Husserl in Berlin. It is this experience which provided him with the basis for his existential epistemology.

But just as he was getting a handle on things World War Two blew in, and he found himself in uniform and a prisoner of war in what must have seemed a record time. Released after France had capitulated to Germany, Sartre returned to Paris to live out the occupation under other than ideal conditions. At some point he met Albert Camus, who was editing an underground newspaper for the Resistance, and both of them involved themselves to some measure in anti-Nazi activity. More has been made of this by Sartre enthusiasts than is warranted. The idea persists of Sartre and Camus as partisans, passing secret messages and blowing up bridges, while somewhere in the background Edith Piaf sings *La vie en Rose*. This is purely fanciful. But at the least they didn't collaborate with the enemy, and they survived the war with reputations intact, ready to do battle on another front.[22] The other front was purely intellectual, existed in the realm of ideas,

---

[22] Both Sartre and Camus are classified as existentialists. Both won the Nobel Prize for literature (Sartre refused to accept his). Sadly, they had a falling out, and the friendship was over for good. Camus died in an automobile accident in the south of France in 1960.

and everyone involved, even those who were only onlookers, must have been surprised at what they saw happening. At the end of the War the existentialists caught the imagination of the public in a way that philosophers seldom have, and there were actually small scale riots as people fought to get into Sartre's lectures. All over the world the existentialists were talked about, their ideas discussed. In America, in the North Beach area of San Francisco, individuals who came to be called "beatniks" wallowed in existential boredom while outlandishly asserting their authenticity. The same crowd in the Scandinavian countries were known as "*existentialister.*"

Clearly, there was something in existentialism that spoke to the post-War generation, a generation attempting to make sense of that which gave every appearance of being senseless. Twice in thirty years those raised on idealism, rationalism, empiricism had chosen up sides and slaughtered one another. Something was clearly missing from the philosophical equation, or perhaps philosophy itself needed to be overhauled. Individuals could understand all about the categorical imperative, then build killing machines; could argue utilitarianism's merits over deontological ethics, then bomb cities to rubble; could then rid themselves of guilt by fading into the group and claiming to be following orders.

Evil was real, and had gone nowhere in the intervening ten-thousand years, except underground for brief periods. But where had God been when all this had been going on? Existentialism, and its main spokesman Jean Paul Sartre, had answers that seemed to go to the heart of the rootless, anxiety-ridden, twentieth-century human.

There is no God, Sartre said, and the result of this simple fact, among others, is that he must reject human essence as an *a priori* given. Rather, the individual is creating his or her essence moment by moment as he or she exists and makes decisions. Descartes, the essentialist, had it backwards: not, "I think, therefore I am," but "I am, therefore I think." So only at the end of one's life can we say what that individual *essentially* was.

> If God does not exist, there is at least one being in which existence precedes essence, a being who exists before he can be defined by any concept, and. . . this being is man. . .Man exists, turns up, appears on the scene, and, only afterwards, defines himself. . .There is no human nature, since there is no God to conceive it. . .Man is nothing else but what he makes of himself. Such is the first principle of existentialism.[23]

---

[23] Sartre, Jean Paul, *The Humanism of Existentialism,* trans. Bernard Frechtman, *The Fabric of Existentialism: Philosophical and Literary Sources,* ed. Richard Gill and Ernest Sherman, Englewood Cliffs: N.J.: Prentice-Hall, 1973.

Second, there are no eternal values, no transcendent truths to guide one, because all of these died with God. This leads to forlorness. As Sartre said, "God does not exist and. . .we have to face all the consequences of this."

> The existentialist. . .thinks it very distressing that God does not exist, because all possibility of finding values in a heaven of ideas disappears along with Him; there can no longer be an *a priori* Good, since there is no infinite and perfect consciousness to think it.
>
> There is no determinism, man is free, man is freedom. On the other hand, if God does not exist, we find no values or commands to turn to which legitimize our conduct. So, in the bright realm of values, we have no excuse behind us, nor justification before us. We are alone, with no excuses.[24]

Like it or not, you are condemned to be free. The only way in which you are not free is that you are not free not to be free.

> Man is condemned to be free. Condemned, because he did not create himself, yet, in other respects is free; because, once thrown into the world, he is responsible for everything he does. The existentialist does not believe in the power of passion. He will never agree that a sweeping passion is a ravaging torrent which fatally leads a man to certain acts and is therefore an excuse. He thinks that man is responsible for his passion. . .Man, with no support and no aid, is condemned every moment to invent man.[25]

But how would one support the idea of freedom for the human, especially when so many others, particularly among the scientific community, are committed to some form of determinism?[26] Sartre does it at length in his most famous philosophical work, *Being and Nothingness*, but he does it in terms difficult for a beginning student to follow. I shall attempt to paraphrase and simplify.

---

[24] Ibid., p. 523.

[25] Ibid., p. 573.

[26] This is certainly true in psychology. Both Freudians and Behaviorists adhere to systems predicated on deterministic models.

Look at the world, as it spreads out around you, and you will immediately note that it presents itself in two essential forms: that which is you, and that which is not you. Let us call it *self* and *other.* This is hardly a novel reflection. Sartre picked it up from Fichte, Schelling, Kant, Hegel, Kirkegaard, Heidegger, and others who went before him. Now, take a portion of this "other" that presents itself to you, say the wall across the room, and ask yourself what it is as opposed to yourself. Clearly it is being, but it is not being the way you are. Sartre calls it *being-in-itself,* and gives it such defining characteristics as massiveness, inertness, isolation from what it is not, and unconscious.

> Being-in-itself is never either possible or impossible. *It is.* This is what consciousness expresses in anthropomorphic terms by saying that being is superfluous (*de trop*) — that is, that consciousness absolutely can not derive being from anything, either from another being, or from a possibility, or from a necessary law. Uncreated, without reason for being, without any connection with another being, being-in-itself, is *de trop* for eternity.[27]

Got it? Good! Let us go forward.

Having defined the "other" as being-in-itself, Sartre now defines another type of being, being-for-itself, which he equates with conscious being. This brings the human in, and this accounts for the "nothingness" which appears in the book's title.

> Human consciousness, nothingness, and being-for-itself are equivalent terms in Sartre's vocabulary. Each term represents merely a different aspect of the same phenomenon, which is called human consciousness because it is a characteristic of the individual human being, nothingness because it is a translucent awareness of something it is not, and being-for-itself because through it being becomes aware of itself. From a still different point of view it is freedom, because as nothingness it cannot be the object of determination through outside influence. Consciousness of oneself as freedom comes with the experience of anguish.[28]

---

[27] Sartre, Jean Paul, *Being and Nothingness,* trans. Hazel E. Barnes, New York: Washington Square Press, 1992, p. 29.

[28] Greene, Norman N., *The Existentialist Ethic,* Ann Arbor: University of Michigan Press, 1966, p. 17.

This is important to the case Sartre is attempting to make. If there is only one type of being, and if the human is only being-in-itself, as is the wall before or the floor beneath, then he or she is acted upon by the forces of the universe just as anything else is, determinism becomes a fact, and the idea of freedom is just that, a mere idea. But Sartre argues that the human is different. The human, *being-for-itself*, is the negating factor in the universe, and because the human is nothingness, he or she is free from the laws which bind other things and is compelled to create himself or herself by making choices. Sartre is not denying that the human body is subject to cause and effect, nor is he saying that there are no physical constraints placed upon us. The fact that we are at least partially physical and thrust into physical surroundings means that we must obey certain laws that govern the interactions of material things. It is in the mental sphere, the sphere of consciousness and volition, that we are nothingness and are thus free.

This poses interesting problems for human relations, for though I am free, you stand over against me in an interesting position. Are you, as I perceive you, being-for-itself, or are you being-in-itself? Are you a free, morally responsible, self-determining being, or are you a thing, to be taken in, devoured, used? Sartre suggests that our tendency is always toward treating the "other," even if the other is another human, as a mere thing, and this attitude (whether or not he realized it) is suggestive of Nietzsche's will to power. We move through life, so these existentialists suggest, with nothing to guide us but ourselves, with no meaning other than the meaning we choose to assign, free and responsible for all that we do, but terribly alone in a universe which cares for us not a whit. Stephen Crane expresses this ultimate existential absurdity in a short poem which he, with shrewd poetic insight, did not give a title.

> A man said to the universe:
> "Sir, I exist!"
> "However," replied the universe,
> "The fact has not created in me
> A sense of obligation."

I have said several times, and many others have noted as well, that existentialism is not a philosophical system in the strictest sense. Sartre came as close as anyone to giving some sort of systematic unity to it, or at least to giving it some connection to philosophical systems that had gone before. Those who consider themselves existentialists, and those who do not but whose work clearly places them within that circle, are typically too individualistic, too rebellious to allow themselves to be classified and pigeon holed. One is made to wonder then how this anti-systematic non-philosophy came to such a dominant position among twentieth century intellectuals, and even to filter down to affect the lives of people who rarely pick up books. Perhaps the existentialists are not creating the **zeitgeist** but are merely reflecting and giving voice to it.

Zeitgeist (German), is literally translated "time spirit." It means the spirit of the age and suggests some intangible something which influence art, science and philosophy in any given period.

More perhaps than any other intellectual movement, existentialism has been picked up by non-philosophers and used as a vehicle. Poets, novelists, playwrights, cinematographers have repeatedly dealt with existential themes. And, of course, both Sartre and Camus were creative writers who worked existential themes into their novels, plays, and short stories. An example is Sartre's famous play, *No Exit*, in which three dead persons meet in hell, hell being a small room where they are condemned to spend eternity together. The hell of it is that, in each case, the people involved are not authentic people, but are mere caricatures. Each spent his or her life in inauthenticity, attempting to be what they thought others expected, and every choice they made served to solidify the caricature. Now they are fixed for eternity (their essence is now established) and must go on this way. They have lost all sense of what it is to be individual and human. They are not only in hell, but they contribute to the hell of those with whom they must suffer. It is Sartre who passes the final judgment.

> Therefore, in the name of this will for freedom, which freedom itself implies, I may pass judgment on those who seek to hide from themselves the complete arbitrariness and the complete freedom of their existence. Those who hide their complete freedom from themselves out of a spirit of seriousness or by means of deterministic excuses, I shall call cowards; those who try to show that their existence was necessary, when it is the very contingency of man's appearance on earth, I shall call stinkers. But cowards or stinkers can be judged only from a strictly unbiased point of view.[29]

One needn't, of course, be either a coward or a stinker. One can be what Kierkegaard and Nietzsche, and now Sartre and Camus, urge one to be — authentic, self-creating, self-fulfilling and human. But it will take courage, and the willingness to walk forward into the darkness without excuses and

---

29 Sartre, *The Humanism of Existentialism*, p. 594

without regret. Frankly, I am not certain that I am up to it. If you are, I salute you.

The Feminists & Poststructuralism

You have probably noticed that in the history of philosophy women have been conspicuously absent. This fact is easily explained but not easily justified. Women did little to contribute to the development of philosophy because they weren't allowed to, were scarcely allowed outside the home, were looked upon as suspect if they aspired to anything beyond cooking meals and having babies. This is tragic, because if the late twentieth-century has taught philosophers anything, it is that women are capable and competent, well up to any standard of clear and cogent thinking that one wishes to set. But for over two thousand years philosophy was robbed of the input of half of the potential philosophers on earth because their gender rendered them non-participants. We are the poorer for this, and nothing can be done about it. It does no good, in my opinion, to attempt to rewrite history by talking about Hildegarde, Heloise, Perictione, Anne Conway as if they were major contributors. They were not. They were not allowed to be. But in the late eighteenth century a woman came on the scene who refused to sit quietly at home, who insisted on being heard, and who wrote two books that became internationally famous and made her a prime player. The woman was Mary Wollstonecraft, and the books were *A Vindication of the Rights of Men* and *A Vindication of the Rights of Women*.[30]

A feminist, in the broadest sense, is anyone, male or female, who believes in the equality of women and works to achieve such equality.

Let us, before we go further, define **feminist**. A feminist, by the simplest definition, is anyone, woman or man, who believes that no one ought to be discriminated against because of sex, that women are equal to men, ought to be treated as equals, and ought to be allowed to go as high and as far as their abilities will carry them in any field which they choose.

Mary Wollstonecraft is a classical feminist, as was her husband William Godwin, and John Stuart Mill, who came after them. Women are different, in the classical view, because they are raised to be different. In *A Vindication of the Rights of Women*, Wollstonecraft says:

> Men who, considering females rather as women than human creatures, have been more anxious to make them

---

[30] Mary Wollstonecraft is, ironically, best known, not for her philosophy, but as the mother of Mary Godwin Shelly, author of *Frankenstein*.

> alluring mistresses than affectionate wives and rational mothers; and the understanding of the sex has been so bubbled by this specious homage, that the civilized women of the present century, with a few exceptions, are only anxious to inspire love, when they ought to cherish a nobler ambition, and by their abilities and virtues exact respect.[31]

Women, however, are a part of the problem, as Wollstonecraft sees it, and she urges them in another direction.

> I wish to persuade women to endeavour to acquire strength, both of mind and body, and to convince them that the soft phrases, susceptibility of heart, delicacy of sentiment, and refinement of taste, are almost synonymous with epithets of weakness. . .Besides, the woman who strengthens her body and exercises her mind will, by managing her family and practicing various virtues, become the friend, and not the humble dependent of her husband.[32]

John Stuart Mill, another of the classical feminists, is in agreement with Wollstonecraft.

> As I have already said more than once, I consider it presumption in anyone to pretend to decide what women are or are not, can or cannot be, by natural constitution. They have always hitherto been kept, as far as regards spontaneous development, in so unnatural a state that their nature cannot but have been greatly distorted and disguised; and no one can safely pronounce that if women's nature were left to choose its direction as freely as men's, and if no artificial bent were attempted to be given to it except that required by the conditions of human society, and given to both sexes alike, there would be any material difference, or perhaps any difference at all, in the character and capacities which would unfold themselves.[33]

---

[31] **Wollstonecraft, Mary, *A Vindication of the Rights of Women*, in *A Wollstonecraft Anthology*, ed. Janet M. Todd, Bloomington, IN: Indiana University Press, 1977, p. 85.**

[32] **Ibid.**

[33] **Mill, John Stuart, *Human Worth*, eds. Richard Paul Janaro and Darwin E. Gearhart, New York: Holt, Rinehart & Winston, 1972, p. 53.**

Thus classical feminism has sought, among other things, to do away with what it considers the artificial distinctions between men and women, under the assumption that nurture, not nature, has made the genders different, with the women getting the worst of things.

In 1949 Simone de Beauvoir, Sartre's friend and collaborator, published a book in Paris that was destined to become the seminal work of modern feminism, *The Second Sex.* The book is long, covers a great deal of ground, and I cannot do more in the brief space remaining to this chapter than touch on some of its salient points.

Simone presents the female as the "other," and she thinks the male reacts toward the female much as a being-for-itself would react toward a being-in-itself. The male is the human, as the male sees things, and the female is a sort of thing, like a human in some ways but different to the point of being offensive. Aristotle thought that women were deformed men, and Freud thought that all women secretly imagine themselves to have been mutilated because they don't have penises. This is how women have been treated throughout history, and they have even come to see themselves in this unflattering light.

Moreover, women have never had the sort of freedom men have had. This is an obvious truth, and there are many examples of inequity between the sexes. One of these is childbearing. Men do not have children, do not generally do much to take care of children once they are born, and are free to go outside the home and be what they wish. According to Simone, women will never be free, politically or otherwise, until they are able to assume control over their own bodies. This means the right to choose for or against pregnancy, the right to make the choice for themselves whether to carry a child to term or to abort. Those caught up in the abortion debate that has raged through the latter years of this century often fail to realize that for Simone de Beauvoir, and for the many millions of women whom she has influenced, the question of whether or not a woman must carry a pregnancy to term is only one of a series of questions at the heart of the true issue — what must women do to be freed from the domination of males?

But not all feminists agree with Simone. The so-called new feminists, of whom Carol Gilligan is a prime example, are not so sure that nurture is the critical factor in the way women and men develop. Men and women are different by nature, Gilligan says, and the difference is worth preserving. In her landmark book, *In a Different Voice,* she argues that women are fundamentally different, but equal, and that the real problem is that women are seen as inferior because they deviate from certain norms. But the norms are masculine, created by men, and based on male behavior. The classical feminists, in this view, have made matters worse by accepting male established norms and attempting to force women, against their nature, to live up to them.

Men, for example, excel in setting up laws and regulations. Masculine ethics are apt to be absolutist, rule oriented, and those who step over the wrong lines are declared immoral or illegal. Men prize logic, thus they have set up the Greek philosophers as ideals, and have come to prize detached, objective thought while denouncing emotionalism as non-philosophical. Then, having established male characteristics as norms, they deride women as too emotional to engage in serious thought. But who, the new feminists wish to know, has said that emotionalism is out of place in philosophy? Gilligan for one says that there is such a thing as feminist ethics, and that rather than emphasizing rules and logic, it centers on such feminine qualities as maintaining relationships, caring, nurturing.

Perhaps this discussion could be broadened to take in more than ethics and the development of moral sensitivity. Perhaps the entire world has been dominated by men so long ("phallocentric" is the term used by some feminists) that in order to gain an objective hold on truth we must tear it down (or deconstruct it) and rebuild it from the foundation up. And perhaps, if one takes the position that all human thought is linguistically determined, the first thing that needs to be deconstructed is language. These considerations have led some French feminists to connect to the poststructuralism of Jacques Derrida and others, and to attempt to apply deconstructionism (which mainly has to do with literary criticism) to the ongoing feminist dialectic. These efforts begin with René Descartes, the prime creator, say the deconstructionists, of the modern world view, a world view that is masculine and oppressive. One of the better known of the deconstructionists is Luce Irigaray, whose *Speculum of the Other Woman* was translated and published in this country in 1977. It is — need I say it? — very difficult reading.

The deconstructionists, however, in spite of the difficult ways in which they express themselves, have already made their mark. This is particularly true in education. The next time you write a theme and use the word "spokesman" your teacher is apt to draw a line through it and substitute "spokesperson." If you say, "We need to man the barricades," someone is apt to ask you whether or not women are invited to participate. Politically correct language, as it is called, has its detractors as well as its supporters. It is an interesting example of how philosophy continues to influence all of us, even those of us who have never bothered to ask what it's all about.

A Quick Review of Section I

1. We began with the Greeks in 500 B.C., and we have ended in the twentieth century, in the American classroom, where the students are struggling to make sure they use gender-neutral language in writing their themes. We followed history, and we found that our history is, as much as anything, a history of ideas and their development. Ideas, we have found, have consequences.

2. The Greeks hammered out an atomic theory, established philosophy as an academic discipline, and in so doing formed the western mind. Today all of us in the West tend to think like Greeks; that is, we lay proposition alongside proposition and reason toward conclusions in a linear fashion. Intuition and flashes of insight, while not alien to westerners, are generally left to poets and prophets. Science, a product of the West, is empirical and inductive.

3. Plato and Socrates fathered western philosophy by asking the questions that all philosophers have tried to answer since. Those questions include (1) what is the truth and how can one know it? (epistemology); (2) what is really there? (metaphysics); and (3) what ought one to do? (ethics).

4. During the Middle Ages philosophy was carried on by churchmen such as Augustine, and by scholars such as Aquinas. Predictably, much of their effort was theological in nature. Aristotle, who had been lost to the West after the rise of Christianity, was rediscovered in the late Middle Ages, and with his rediscovery philosophers gained a new interest in logic and correct thinking, which eventually led to the Renaissance and to the development of science.

5. With René Descartes modern philosophy began. Descartes was a rationalist, who attempted to ground philosophy to a deductive methods modelled on geometry. His epistemological theories were rationalistic, thus he is called the father of modern rationalism. He is most widely known for his statement, "I think, therefore I am."

6. In the British Isles, Cartesian rationalism ran up against a different epistemological school, that of empiricism. The British empiricists, Locke, Berkeley, and Hume, argued that knowledge is not inborn, as Descartes had supposed, but comes from experience. Whether or not they intended it, they left philosophy in a profound skepticism.

7. Immanuel Kant came to philosophy's rescue with his transcendental idealism. In an important sense he wedded rationalism and empiricism, and in so doing he showed that the human mind is the active agent in creating reality, as we perceive it, from the incoming raw material of pure sense data. However, he left an uncrossable gap between phenomena, things as we know them, and noumena, things as they really are.

8. In the nineteenth century Hegel appeared, and for many years dominated Continental philosophy with his idealism. In explaining how history unfolds, he created the "dialectic," a three-part process in which thesis and antithesis combine to synthesis. His philosophy became the foundation for Karl Marx's dialectic materialism, the philosophical position of communism.

9. In response to Hegel, Kierkegaard rose up. He stood in opposition to Hegel's system by affirming the importance of the individual, and in so doing he became the father of existentialism. Existential themes include authenticity, inautheticity, anxiety, the necessity of making choices and of moving from one stage of life to the other by means of "the leap," an act of faith based upon subjective truth. Unlike many of those who followed him, Kierkegaard was a Christian. Nietzsche, however, was an atheist and declared the death of God.

10. Atheistic existentialism dominated the middle years of the twentieth century, and existential themes became common fodder for poets, novelists, and movie makers. Jean Paul Sartre declared that existence precedes essence, emphasizing the utter freedom of humans. "Condemned to be free" are the words he used to indicate the human condition. With this, and the death of God, humans are faced with anxiety, dread, absurdity.

11. The latter part of the century has seen the rise of feminism. Grounded in the writings of earlier philosophers, particularly Mary Wollstonecraft and John Stuart Mill, feminism has sought, among other things, to free women from masculine domination so that they may pursue their lives as equals among equals.

Section II
Metaphysics

Imagine, if you will, some physical entity
Multiplied by itself from here to infinity.
Imagine Aristotle's Third Man drawn in space,
And regressed to the vanishing point of the race.
Imagine yourself caught on a carrousel,
And doomed to ride forever. I think that hell
Must be like this: eternal entrapment in time,
Like facing mirrors imaging an endless room.

Chapter 5
No Matter — Never Mind

Eternally imploding, tumbling toward
some infinite black hole,
I seek that basic substance
of which all things are made;

then rebound ever outward,
light years beyond
galaxies and dying suns,
constrained only by
imagination.

One day my wife and I were wandering among the shops at an arts and crafts show when we came to one that particularly caught my attention. "Metaphysical rings," read the sign above the door. This I had to see, so we went in. When I asked the artisan what a metaphysical ring was, he told me it was a ring with some sort of spiritual message. He specialized in these, and he was good, and I bought one of his rings. In the course of our exchange he asked what I did, and when I told him that I taught philosophy he brightened up and said that I ought to understand what he was doing. I assured him that I did, and I might have said (but didn't) that unless he was particularly well-read *he* might not have understood what he was doing.

Metaphysics is another philosophical term which has managed over the years to pass into general usage and take on connotations not given to it by philosophers. Laymen have tended to narrow its meaning, so that when they say metaphysics they suggest something unseen, spiritual, transcendent. Philosophers would not disagree with this definition, but they would insist that the word means a great deal more. It might just as easily connote

Metaphysics: The study of reality, or what is actually there.

something that is seen, material, bound in both space and time, concrete. **Metaphysics** is simply the study of reality. It seeks to answer the question, "What is actually there." Aristotle, though he didn't used the term, identified the area of inquiry as that of *being qua being.*

I am now about to repeat myself, something which I often do, and something that is sometimes necessary if one wishes to get difficult concepts to stick in the minds of those being addressed. When Aristotle's work was being compiled into book form, largely from notes taken by students, some of the material didn't fit easily into the established categories. It wasn't logic. It wasn't botany nor biology. Nor was it physics, though it had some physical overtones. The compilers, because they didn't know exactly what to do with it, placed it at the end of the *Physics,* and called it *meta* (after) physics. This, as it turned out, was a good choice for a name, because it suggests something more than what was initially intended. It is not just that the material was placed in a book after the *Physics,* but that its subject goes beyond the purely physical to larger questions. .

You may not yet see the full implications of these larger questions, so let me ask you to engage in some mind-expanding exercises. Stop what you are doing and look around you. Certainly this is something you have done many times before, and certainly you have noticed that the things around you give the appearance of solidity and extension in space. You are, after all, sitting on something that you do not sink through, and you haven't yet figured out how to walk through walls, nor have you been beamed up to the starship Enterprise. Suppose you say all evidence suggests that we live in a universe composed of matter, that regardless of how we break it down or how small the parts may be into which we divide it, it will still be matter and nothing but matter. This matter, you might say, must obey the physical laws of cause and effect, of space and time, and these laws must hold throughout the universe. You may even say that there is no good reason to postulate anything unseen and immaterial standing over and above matter, as such postulations are unnecessary and violate the principle of Ockham's Razor. If you said this, or something like this, you are a metaphysical **materialist.**

Materialism is the metaphysical position that all of reality is ultimately reducible to matter.

But you needn't have said any of this. You might just as plausibly have argued that mere appearance is not reality, that there is an ultimate truth and reality that transcends the apparent and gives it substance, and without which there would be nothing. What you see is not always what you get. Very well, but this position is far from obvious on its face, and if you wish to be taken seriously you have some explaining to do, especially to the pragmatic materialist we just heard from. What keeps him or her from seizing Ockham's Razor and slicing your theory to bits? The problem with materialism, you might say, is that the materialist has leaped to a superficial explanation without stopping to ask some very basic questions. How can we make any statement about what is really there unless we have made some sort of observation? How could we observe anything without having the means to observe? And how could the observations make sense, supposing we have the means, unless there is a mind able to process and interpret them. All percepts are ultimately products of the mind, which means that reality is not material but mental. If you think along these lines, you are a metaphysical **idealist.**

Idealism is the metaphysical position that all of reality is reducible to idea or mind.

Perhaps, however, you listened to the materialist and the idealist at length, and you finally intervene with some thoughts of your own. Both of them, you might say, are wrong. They have each grasped a portion of the truth but failed to see the larger picture. Surely there is a physical universe composed of matter, and evidence suggests that it exists in reality regardless of any individual's perceptions of it. But there are just as surely such things as minds, and these minds, which are non-physical, are as much a part of the make-up of reality as is matter. In fact, the idealist is correct in ascribing a creative function to minds. You may even go farther, postulating the existence of God, or other non-physical mental beings, who, though unseen, created and ultimately uphold the material universe. You, my friend, are a metaphysical **dualist.**

Dualism is a mixture of materialism and idealism. For the dualist there are two realities— one of matter and another of idea.

Materialism, idealism, dualism. These are basically the three metaphysical positions one may take, and it is unlikely you will ever meet anyone who thinks at all who does not ascribe to one of them. Materialism and idealism are, for obvious reasons, mutually exclusive; that is, one cannot be exclusively one and the other at the same time. If one attempts to do so, he or she has become a dualist. When we look back at the history of philosophy, we find that each of these metaphysical positions has its roots deeply embedded in Greek attempts to come to some understanding of the universe in which we live.

The Materialists

> The Universe, that is the whole mass of things that are, is corporeal, that is to say body; and has the dimensions of magnitude, namely, length, breadth, and depth. Also every part of body is likewise body, and has the like dimensions. And, consequently, every part of the Universe is body, and that which is not body is no part of

> the Universe. And because the Universe is all, that which is no part of it is nothing, and consequently, nowhere.[1]

Thus said Thomas Hobbes in 1651. And in this statement we see a critical component of materialism. Because the materialists feel that all is matter, it must follow that it obeys the laws of matter. If one shoots a billiard ball into another billiard ball there will be a reaction. The balls will obey Newton's first and third laws of motion. Being bound in both space and time, neither will suddenly disappear and come up again in another place, and neither will move backward into an earlier time. The way in which the balls will react is rigidly determined by physical law. Now, if this is true of billiard balls, it must also be true of any other material, and according to the materialist this is everything, and must also include the human. In 1795 Baron D'Holback wrote:

> Man, then, is not a free agent in any one instant of his life; he is necessarily guided in each step by those advantages, whether real or fictitious, that he attaches to the objects by which his passions are roused: these passions themselves are necessary in a being who unceasingly tends towards his own happiness.[2]

Here we have another feature of materialism: it is deterministic. One of the great metaphysical questions with which philsophers and theologians have wrestled for centuries is this: are humans free to choose what they will or will not do? Materialists must answer that they are not, they are determined. The human may imagine himself or herself free, may believe that he or she is making choices about the course of life, but this is purely illusion. There can be no such freedom in a world of matter that obeys physical law.

What about thoughts, however? The idealist, as you will recall, talks in terms of mind, and mental images. How can these be material? The materialist has an answer. All of this may be explained in purely physical terms. Properly speaking, there is no such thing as mind; there is only a physical brain, and this brain, composed of matter, is the source of all

---

[1] Hobbes, Thomas, *Leviathan*, Oxford: The Clarendon Press, 1909, p. 524.

[2] Holbach, P., Baron d', *The System of Nature*, London, 1795.

thought and mental images. This physical explanation of mental activity is a reductionistic one; and here we have a third feature of materialism. **Reductionism,** the theory that one type of reality may be explained in terms of another type, has become an important part of materialism over the years.

Reductionism is the belief that one reality may be explained in terms of another, for example, the belief that the universe is actually a machine running on purely mechanistic principles.

In the preceding paragraph we see a perfect example of how a materialist might explain mental events in terms of physical ones. Newton and Descartes used reductionism when they used mechanical laws to explain the way the universe operates. And in the quotation above we see Thomas Hobbes appealing to reductionism as he explains the human being in mechanical terms.

Put materialism, determinism, and reductionism together, add in an empirical theory of knowledge and a commitment to inductive reasoning, and you have the metaphysical basis of science, at least in a skeletal form.[3] The entire enterprise was developed by philosophers and sprang from philosophy, though many who call themselves scientists don't appear to understand this. All science from the Enlightenment up to the twentieth century was grounded in materialism. The twentieth century, as we shall see, has not been kind to the materialists. But that comes much later.

The Idealists

On its face, idealism seems very strange, for it seems to belie human experience. Surely no one can deny the reality of the physical universe, the solidity of the ground upon which we stand, the permanence of the earth and sun. But to approach the problem in this way is to miss the point the idealists are trying to make. They are not denying reality, nor are they saying there is nothing there. Rather, they are saying that reality, while it may appear to be material, is actually mental, has its genesis in, and is upheld by, that which is non-corporeal.[4]

One of the most famous of the idealists is George Berkeley, the eighteenth century Irish bishop who was also an empiricist. He is famous for having said *esse est percipi*, Latin for "to be is to be perceived."

---

[3] This definition of science is a rudimentary one. In fact, science is a good deal more complex. Some of our greatest scientists have not been materialists, and most of the great scientific theories have not been grounded in empiricism. Still, as a general definition of science, this will work.

[4] The actual words which idealists use to identify the basis of reality are not always the same. Some talk of "idea" and some of "mind." Some use the term "energy."

> It is evident to anyone who takes a survey of the objects of human knowledge that they are either ideas actually imprinted on the senses, or else such as are perceived by attending to the passions and operations of the mind, or lastly, ideas formed by help of memory and imagination. . .
>
> This perceiving, active being is what I call "mind," "spirit," "soul," or "myself." By which words I do not denote any one of my ideas, but a thing entirely distinct from them, wherein they exist or, which is the same thing, whereby they are perceived — for the existence of an idea consists in being perceived. That neither our thoughts, nor passions, nor ideas formed by the imagination exist without the mind is what everybody will allow. And it seems no less evident that the various sensations or ideas imprinted on the sense, however blended or combined together. . .cannot exist otherwise than in a mind perceiving them. . .The table I write on I say exists, that is, I see and feel it; and if I were out of my study I should say it existed — meaning thereby that if I was in my study I might perceive it, or that some other spirit actually does perceive it. . .
>
> [It is not] possible that they [unthinking things] should have any existence out of the minds of thinking things which perceive them.[5]

Can he possibly be saying that if something is not perceived then it doesn't exist? That is precisely what he is saying, and in further illustration of this rather odd contention he asks one of the most famous of the questions of philosophy: If a tree falls in the forest, and if no one is there to hear it, does it make a sound? He answers that it does not. Of course, you have already seen the fuller implications of the question. If to be is to be perceived, and if a tree falls in the forest and no one is there to perceive it, mustn't it be true that there is no tree to fall and no forest for it to fall in?

As we have already seen, Berkeley got around this apparent difficulty by positing the existence of God, who is ever awake and ever perceptive, and who therefore assures the ongoing stability of creation. Not all philosophers, however, are willing to make the leap of faith with Berkeley.

---

[5] Berkeley, George, *A Treatise Concerning the Princples of Human Knowledge*, in *The Works of George Berkeley*, vol. I, ed. George Sampson, London: George Bell & Sons, 1897, 179-180.

They are obviously more comfortable with absurdity than they are with Berkeley's solution.

For our own edification, let us play the game by George Berkeley's rules, assuming what he assumes,[6] and let us see where this takes us. If all I can know is what I perceive; if all perception is solely by means of the five senses; if mind is the active agent in all perception; then reality must be mental, idealism, as a metaphysical position, must be sound, and Berkeley has taken an irrefutable position. The problem is that he has dug a hole, so to speak, jumped in, then pulled the hole in after him. Positing the existence of God as a way to assure the ongoing stability of the universe will not work, since God is not perceivable by any of the five senses, to be is to be perceived (Berkeley said it, I did not), *ergo* God does not exist.

George Berkeley's idealism leads straight to skepticism, at best, **solipsism**, at worst, and these are the very things he thought he was avoiding. Nevertheless, we would be very foolish to abandon idealism outright, for the discoveries of twentieth century physicists have corresponded to the metaphysical pattern of idealism much more closely than that of materialism. Odd as it may seem, we do not live in a universe of matter, and what exists does not obey the physical laws discovered by Descartes and Newton. Berkeley may not have been absolutely correct, but neither was he totally wrong. In fact, given what we now know, Berkeley and the idealists may turn out to have had a sounder metaphysical stance than their opponents in the materialism camp.

Solipsism is the belief that only I exist, and that everything else is merely a figment of my own imagination.

Suppose we return to the fifth century B.C. where this all started, and see who held to what, and why. You should be able, at this point, to follow metaphysical arguments, and to distinguish them from some of the other philosophical concerns raised by the Greeks. And, as always, you will find them amazingly up-to-date.

The Greeks Monists

If we go back to Thales of Miletus we find the beginnings of materialism, for you will recall that he believed everything in the universe was composed of water. The reasons he gave, preserved for us by Aristotle in the *Metaphysics*, are plausible in the sense that we can understand how

---

6 He assumes, of course, that empiricism is the correct approach, the only approach, to the question of how we know anything. This assumption will get him into a great deal of trouble once David Hume comes on the scene.

he reached this conclusion, and we can see that his assigned causes are natural rather than mythological. In this, there is no indication that he is anything other than a materialist.

With Anaximander, also a Miletian, and a student of Thales, we go over to the other side and meet what appears to be an idealist. Certainly the things about which he talks, and the way in which he frames his argument, lead to this conclusion. His first principle is nothing physical but is what he called *apeiron*, a word somewhat difficult to translate, but suggestive of something without boundaries or qualities, a vast indefinite-infinite. It is interesting that out of this infinite nothingness arose, according to Anaximander, all four of the elements that Empedocles would later identify as making up everything that we see — earth, air, fire and water. But because these all spring from the one, *apeiron*, and return to it, Anaximander must have been a monist, and if not an outright idealist certainly tilted in that direction.

Anaximenes (c. 500 B.C.), another of the Presocratic Miletians, argued that the universal matter was air — or did he? He actually said that the basic thing from which all was generated, and to which all returned, was ***pneuma*** a Greek word which can have multiple meanings. It certainly means the wind or air that is circulating around us, but it can just as easily be translated "spirit," as it typically is in English versions of the Greek New Testament.[7] Anaximenes does not clearly specify whether he means "air" or "spirit," and it is probable he meant both, seeing the air as some sort of spiritual force. Thus, though succeeding generations of philosophers tended to make air a physical thing, and Axaximenes a materialist, he may actually have been an early idealist.

The Ephesian philosopher Heraclitus is another who is metaphysically ambiguous. He believed that the basic matter was fire, and that the entire process of existence was one of change, aptly represented by a fire which consumes fuel and changes it into heat and smoke. Today's scientists can explain all of this in purely materialistic terms, and given our present state of knowledge we would have no difficulty classifying Heraclitus as a materialist; but he may have intended something very

---

[7] ***To* pneuma *opou thelei pnei. . .Outos estin pas ho gegennemenos ek tou* pneumatos. Tran. The wind bloweth where it listeth. . .So is everyone who is born of the spirit. John 3:8. This is an interesting play on the Greek word *pneuma* which a translation cannot catch.**

different. It was Heraclitus who introduced the *logos* into the philosophical dialectic, and logos is certainly an idealistic concept.

> The Logos is eternal
> but men have not heard it
> and men have heard it and not understood.
>
> Through the Logos all things are understood yet men do not understand as you shall see when you put acts and words to the test I am going to propose.
>
> One must talk about everything according to its nature, how it comes to be and how it grows. Men have talked about the world without paying attention to the world or to their own minds, as if they were asleep or absent-minded.
>
> Man, who is an organic continuation of the Logos, thinks he can sever that continuity and exist apart from it.
>
> How can you hide from what never goes away?
>
> To God all is beautiful, good, and as it should be. Man must see things as either good or bad.
>
> Not I but the world says it; All is one.
>
> God is day night winter summer war peace enough too little, but disguised in each and known in each by a separate flavor.[8]

Logos is both spiritual and mental, both mind and creative force; and Heraclitus closely identified fire with *logos*. So he was probably a metaphysical dualist. This is strongly suggested by his statement, in the fragment above, that man is an organic continuation of the *logos*. But, as with Anaximenes, succeeding generations would not see fire as spirit, and would group it, along with water and air, as one of the four physical elements.

In the Pythagoreans (6th century B.C.) we encounter the purest idealists of all the pre-Socratic philosophers. Though we do not know

---

[8] Fragments 1, 64, 73, 106, 118, and 121 in *Herakleitos and Diogenes*.

exactly what Pythagoras taught, we do know that he was an actual man, and we have enough writings from his students to come to some comfortable conclusions. Those of you who took geometry in high school will no doubt remember the Pythagorean Theorem for finding the hypotenuse of a right triangle: $a^2 + b^2 = c^2$. Pythagoras of Samos left the Greek mainland sometime in the sixth century B.C. to set up a religious community in southern Italy at Crotona. For several hundred years the community continued, and during this time, attempting to purify the psyche,[9] they developed the first systematic mathematics. But they went far beyond this. They were convinced that reality was number, and that numbers were real things and not just mental constructs. Everything was associated with a number. A point was one. A line was two. A surface was three. Earth was associated with the cube, and fire with the pyramid. The Pythagoreans also believed in the principle of *logos*, but they assigned it numbers and rational qualities. These Presocratics cast a long shadow, not only because of their contributions to mathematics, but because of their emphasis on form rather than matter. Among those whom they strongly influenced was Plato, a man who also ascribed ontological reality to the forms.

Now all of the philosophers we have been considering had one thing in common metaphysically — they were all *monists*, which is to say they all believed that reality was ultimately reducible to some one substance, whatever it was. For some it was fire, for some water, for some number. At least one of them (Thales) appears to have been a materialist, one (Pythagoras) was a pure idealist, and the others may have been dualists, though in some cases (Anaximander, for example) this is arguable. Empedocles, however, made a radical departure from the group. He was a **pluralist**, and he gave to philosophy the idea of the basic four elements, an idea that carried well into the modern era.

The pluralist believes that reality is composed of more than one element. Not to be confused with a dualist, who believes in two separate levels of reality.

Metaphysical Pluralism

No one knows better than a teacher of philosophy that one of the most difficult things for students, no matter what field they are attempting to master, is to learn new terms and to avoid getting them entangled one

---

[9] From the Greek *psuche*, usually translated "soul," but not to be confused with the Christian idea of soul. For the Greeks, soul was more of a mental thing, less of a spirit. When the Greeks wanted to say spirit, they used a word with which we are already familiar from Anaximenes, *pneuma*.

with another. The new terms we have been learning for the last several pages all have to do with the field of metaphysics, and are terms philosophers have developed over the centuries to describe various metaphysical theories. I said earlier one cannot be both a strict materialist and a strict idealist, for the two are mutually exclusive. If one holds to both positions he or she becomes a hybrid, a dualist. We now come to another metaphysical position, and it stands in opposition to monism the way idealism stands in opposition to materialism. One can be a monist, believing that everything is basically one substance, or one can be a pluralist, believing that there is more than one substance, but one cannot be both; and between these two there is no hybrid. Monism has long since had its day and gone the way of nickel candy and Tom Swift. Pluralism, on the other hand, is alive and well, and is flourishing in chemistry and physics. There seems to be no doubt that there are different kinds of basic elements, though they are not the ones Empedocles postulated. The question is, why did he become a pluralist when all of his brilliant predecessors and contemporaries were monists?

Do you remember Parmenides, Heraclitus's adversary, who said, in defiance of Heraclitus, that change was an illusion and that nothing was changing? If you have already forgotten about him it might be well to go back to the first part of the book and do some reviewing, for his arguments are critical to Empedocles and metaphysical pluralism. Moreover, Parmenides was important to the development of western philosophy because he was the first philosopher to reject apparent reality and base his theory on pure reasoning. No matter how things may look, he said, change cannot be taking place, and he attempted to prove this by structuring an argument on the concepts of being and nothingness. If he were correct, his argument has extremely interesting implications.

Being *is*. Non-being *is not*, is non-existent, is therefore illusion. All that *is* equates with being. Being must therefore be eternal, unchanging, a perfect and complete "whole," immobile and pure. Empedocles agreed with Parmenides, presumably because he thought Parmenides's argument was logically sound, and if logically sound then unavoidably true. But Empedocles was not willing to leave it at that, because Parmenides left so many questions unanswered. The problem of the one-and-the-many was one with which the Greeks had been wrestling from the outset of their philosophical enterprise: how are the many individual things that we see generated out of the one basic substance? Empedocles was not willing to deny reality to the point of saying he was not in the midst of many changing individual things. Now, how was he able to reconcile himself with

Parmenides, whom he credited with having taken the correct position? He did it by saying that such changes as take place do so within the whole of being and not by going outside it.

It is difficult to imagine exactly what he was talking about, so let us look at a simple example. Suppose we write down the numbers 1, 2, 3, 4, and then we draw a circle around them and let this represent our universe. Everything that is exists within the circle and is comprehended in the four numbers, the circle, the space within the circle. This is the Parmenidean cosmos as Empedocles pictures it. Now, we can rearrange the numbers in any sequence we choose, 2, 1, 4, 3 for example, moving through sixteen possible permutations, without doing harm to Parmenides's principle, for nothing has gone out of existence, nothing has come into existence, such change as has taken place is nothing more than a shuffling of existents within the circle of being.

For the numbers, let us substitute four elements — earth, air, fire, water — and we have what Empedocles called the four basic "roots."[10] To these he added two basic motions, love and strife, using these to explain how change actually occurs. It is love that brings the elements together in their various combinations, and it is strife that separates them, and these actions take place during world cycles.

Empedocles was a materialist, for though he seems to have anthropomorphized love and strife and to have given them a sort of life of their own, it is clear that he is utilizing, shall we say, poetic license to make his case. Empedocles saw no intelligent action behind this breaking apart and coming together. It was purely chance and random combination that produced the things we see all around us.

Anaxagoras, another pluralist (remember, tiny seeds, hot dogs become fingernails), held to a sort of primitive dualism. He brought in the idea of Mind (Greek: *nous*) as the guiding principle behind creation because it seemed obvious to him one needed to account for what appeared to be an intelligible pattern to another otherwise unintelligible universe. Over the years *nous* and *logos* stood in an interesting relationship to one another. *Nous* was as close as these Greeks came to the God of the Hebrews, whereas

---

[10] Empedocles was not the first Greek to think of these four as the basic elements, but he appears to have been the first philosopher to do so. Remember that the philosophers that went before him were monists. The poets had talked about earth, air, fire and water as the basic elements for years prior to Empedocles's arrival.

logos seems to have been the subordinate, active force, a demiurge that moved, changed, broke down, built up.[11]

With Democritus of Abdera we come to the last pre-Socratic metaphysician with whom I wish to deal. A materialist who rejected both the *nous* of Anaxagoras and the *logos* of Heraclitus and Pythagoras, Democritus postulated the existence of atoms, tiny, indivisible bits of matter, indestructible and fixed in number, that combine in accordance with mechanical laws of motion to form all the individual things in the universe. As Empedocles before him, Democritus accepted the Parmenidean position of being and non-being. What he did not accept was the idea that empty space was the same as non-being. Thus, Democritus split being into two things, atoms and the void, or things and empty space, giving ontological reality to space, even when it is empty of matter. This was necessary to his theory, for that which appears to us as solid is in reality composed as much of empty space as anything. Atoms, the tiny, indestructible, indivisible building blocks of which all things are composed, are for Democritus the ultimate reality. There is nothing more. If one asks how these bits of matter come together to compose things, Democritus answers, in the spirit of Empedocles, that it is purely by chance. They whirl through the void, bump into one another, and some of them stick together. Why one atom should stick to another is a question reserved for twentieth century physicists.

Because we have followed in the footsteps of the Greeks, and because we too have an atomic theory that, for all practical purposes, is a great deal like that of Democritus, most of us probably find Democritus much easier to understand than did his own contemporaries.

A Brief Interlude

For those of you who have come this far, and feel like throwing up your hands in utter dismay and bewilderment, I can almost sympathize with you. Almost — but not quite. If you have actually lived as long as you have and never once exercised sufficient curiosity to generate a sense of wonder about the world around you, I confess that I do not understand you. Plato said that wonder is the mark of the philosopher, and that philosophy has its origins in wonder. The sense of wonder is present in all children, as any parent can affirm, and as some of you can still remember from your own

---

[11] **This interpretation is mine, not necessarily that of other philosophers, and I am not so committed to it that I couldn't be persuaded otherwise.**

childhood. Those of you who have retained the sense of wonder ought to be happy, for you are the philosophers and poets of the world. Those of you who have lost it ought to make an attempt to get it back.

The Greeks created western philosophy, and the western intellect along with it, because they were imbued with a sense of wonder. Those whom we have been considering are doing nothing more than attempting to answer questions generated by the sense of wonder. I wonder why things are the way they are. I wonder if they are really the way they seem. I wonder what things are composed of, if it is one thing or many. And I wonder, if there is one basic thing, why and how it manifests itself in so many different things. When something comes into existence, where does it come from? When it goes out of existence, where does it go? These are the questions that any child might ask, and it is in attempting to answer them that humans have dived down to sub-atomic quanta and soared out to the stars. If none of this interests you, then open a beer, sit in front of the television, and watch the football game. And you will have my sympathy. Well. . .almost, but not quite.

The Metaphysics of Plato

You may have noticed the curious absence of the human in the speculations of the philosophers we have been considering. Actually, the human is not totally absent, but is sort of pushed out to the periphery. Plato, on the other hand, sits the human squarely in the middle of his system, and there he and she will stay until the Christians come along to put God in the central place. Not only is Plato a humanist, he is also a dualist, but a dualist who clearly gives idea (or form) the prime emphasis. Pure materialism, such as that espoused by Democritus and Empedocles, will scarcely be seen again in the West until the period we call the Enlightment. With Plato the dualists are in, and they remain very much so to the present.

Remember, dualism and pluralism are not the same thing. A pluralist is a person such as Empedocles who said that material reality is composed of more than one element. A dualist says that reality exists on two levels, material and ideal or spiritual. A dualist may well agree that on the material level there are a number of elements that combine to make up the things that are there. But he or she would say that there is another, unseen level of reality that is not matter and probably not pluralistic. Further, like Plato, most dualists assign greater importance to the unseen than to the seen.

Based on interaction with students over the years, I would guess that upwards of ninety percent are metaphysical dualists, not because they have thought a great deal about it and worked it out for themselves, but because this is what they have been taught in Sunday School, the mosque, and synagogue. It is the dominant metaphysical position of the West, with materialism following a distant second.

Welcome to the world of Plato!

Plato did not develop his metaphysics by observing the world around him, as did most of those we have been discussing, but rather as a result of pure thought. In this, he resembles Parmenides and Pythagoras more than any of the others. He postulated the world of the immaterial forms as an epistemological necessity, and this led him, once again as a matter of necessity, to postulate the immortality of the human soul and reincarnation. It is quite impossible to separate Plato's metaphysics from his epistemology, therefore I cannot avoid repeating some of what I have already said about him, both here, and in the following section.

Plato, you will recall, disagreed heatedly with Protagoras and the Sophists. For him, truth was truth. It did not change and vary, and in holding that truth was relative to the person or to the culture in which a person lived, the Sophists were denying the very idea of truth as Plato understood it. But this caused real problems. Some of the most important questions we can ask have to do with abstract things such as justice and beauty. Are these not largely matters of opinion, true only for the individual who holds them?

Truth, particularly truth about abstract things, might be relative, not only to individual or to culture, but to time period. Have you ever heard a person from your parents's generation decrying the morals of today's young people? And did you perhaps tell them that things have changed, that what was considered wrong thirty years ago is no longer considered wrong? You may have been convinced by this argument, and maybe you convinced your parents, but you would not have convinced Plato. He would say that either you or your parents (or perhaps all of you) are seriously confused and ought to give the matter more thought. Something that was wrong thirty years ago cannot be right today simply because time has passed.

Suppose that you were arguing directly with Plato, and you responded that there is an important difference between the truth of, say, moral values and the truth about the color of the shirt the professor is wearing today. He might agree with you, but then ask what point you are trying to make. You would probably reply that the truth of the professor's shirt color is easily determined by simply looking at it, whereas the truths about moral issues, beauty, justice, *etcetera*, are not because one can see none of those things. Plato would say that you have got it exactly backwards. It is the truth about the world of things (Plato called them particulars) that is difficult, in fact impossible, to establish, because material things are changing just as Heraclitus said they were. There is no fixed, permanent truth in the material world. The professor's shirt may appear to be red, but the truth is that even as you speak that shirt is fading to pink or orange. This is precisely why those of you who think moral standards have changed over the years are involved in major confusion. You see no difference in the world of the perishing particulars and that of the eternal ideals. In the ideal world, where true moral value is to be found, nothing ever changes or goes out of existence, and the only way any abstract quality can be known is by coming to know its **form**.

By now the student should be somewhat familiar with the "forms" of Plato. These are non-spatial, non-temporal entities that stand behind the particulars of the world and give them substance.

But how can we know something that we cannot apprehend with at least one of our senses? The question is epistemological, and Plato's answer is metaphysical.

> What about the actual acquiring of knowledge? Is the body an obstacle when one associates it in the search for knowledge? I mean, for example, do men find any truth in sight or hearing, or are not even the poets forever telling us that we do not see or hear anything accurately, and surely if those two physical senses are not clear or precise, our other senses can hardly be accurate, as they are all inferior to these. Do you not think so?
>
> I certainly do, he said.
>
> When then, he asked, does the soul grasp the truth? For whenever it attempts to examine anything with the body, it is clearly deceived by it.[12]

Very well. Plato has identified the problem. But what is the answer? He gets to it immediately.

> Is it not in reasoning if anywhere that any reality becomes clear to the soul?
>
> Yes.
>
> And indeed the soul reasons best when none of these senses troubles it, neither hearing nor sight, nor pain nor pleasure, but when it is most by itself, taking leave of the body and as far as possible having no contact or association with it in its search for reality.[13]

---

[12] Plato, *Phaedo,* In *Plato: Five Dialogues,* trans. G.M.A. Grube, Indianapolis, IN: Hackett Publishing Co., 1981, p. 101.

[13] Ibid., p. 102.

But the simple truth is that I am a physical being, and that my body is a part of me so that I cannot simply lay it aside and give myself to pure thought. Plato does not agree. A little further on we read this:

> If we are ever to have pure knowledge, we must escape from the body and observe matters in themselves with the soul by itself. It seems likely that we shall, only then, when we are dead, attain that which we desire and of which we claim to be lovers, namely, wisdom, as our argument shows, not while we live. . .Then and not before, the soul is by itself apart from the body. While we live, we shall be closest to knowledge if we refrain as much as possible from association with the body or join with it more than we must, if we are not infected with its nature but purify ourselves from it until the god himself frees us.[14]

Notice what Plato has done. Not only does he believe that reality exists on two levels; he believes as well that the ideal level is the greater reality of the two because it is the only level which is stable and eternal. Thus, if we are to know the real eternal truth, we can do so only by reasoning. Physical experience will only confuse us. But there is yet a greater and more certain way to know the truth, according to Plato, and that is to die and leave the body. Plato thus argues that if we are to know truth, the soul must be immortal.

Would it not be possible, however, for one to respond that Plato's argument for the immortality of the soul is merely one of expedience? All he has shown is that in order to come to full and complete knowledge we must be able to leave the body and journey to the realm of eternal, unchanging things. This is not to say, however, that such a thing can happen. Perhaps we must simply admit that ultimate knowledge of truth is not possible. In the *Meno* Plato raises the issue, and at the same time identifies a problem that has never been fully resolved.

> Meno: How will you look for it (the truth), Socrates, when you do not know at all what it is? How will you aim to search for something you do not know at all? If you should meet with it, how will you know that this is the thing that you did not know?
>
> Socrates: I know what you want to say, Meno. Do you realize what a debater's argument you are

---

[14] **Ibid., p. 103.**

> bringing up, that a man cannot search either for what he knows or for what he does not know? He cannot search for what he knows — since he knows it, there is no need to search — nor for what he does not know, for he does not know what to look for.[15]

This is, believe it or not, a major problem for epistemology and science. It is sometimes called the Socratic paradox. How can one set out to discover anything. If one were ignorant, then he or she would not know what to look for. As a matter of fact, if one were ignorant, there would be no reason to undertake the search because there would be no sense of anything lacking. But even if the search for truth is begun, given the state of ignorance of the seeker, how is he or she to know the truth if it is found? We will take up the Socratic Paradox again when we come to epistemology. At this point, however, the subject is metaphysics, and Plato has Socrates reply to *Meno* in a way that, he believes, clearly establishes both the necessity of, and the truth of, the immortality of the soul.

> They (the wise ones) say that the human soul is immortal; at times it comes to an end, which they call dying, at times it is reborn, but it is never destroyed, and one must therefore live one's life piously as possible.
>
> As the soul is immortal, has been born often and has seen all things here and in the underworld, there is nothing which it has not learned; so it is in no way surprising that it can recollect the things it knew before, both about virtue and other things. As the whole of nature is akin, and the soul has learned everything, nothing prevents a man, after recalling one thing only — a process men call learning — discovering everything else for himself.[16]

Here we are at the heart of Plato's metaphysics as well as his epistemology. Strange as it may seem, he holds that we all know the truth about virtue, beauty, justice, mathematics because we learned about them when we were in a disembodied state before we were born; and when we die

---

15 Plato, *The Meno*, in *Plato: Five Dialogues*, trans. G.M.A. Grube, Indianapolis, IN: Hackett Publishing Co., 1981, p. 69.

16 Ibid., p. 70.

we will go back to the same state and place and abide there until we are reborn. As disembodied souls we have seen the forms of truth, beauty, and so on, and so learning is not a matter of having knowledge put into us, but rather of remembering that which we already know.

As with the Socratic paradox, we will look more closely at this theory of knowledge when we come to the section on epistemology. It is impossible, however, to discuss Plato's metaphysics without discussing his epistemology as well, because as you have readily seen from the line he took in both the *Phaedo* and the *Meno*, his epistemology depends upon his metaphysics, and his metaphysics is, in turn, fed by his epistemology. What we can know and how we can know it depends, for Plato, upon the very structure of reality.

You probably remain unconvinced and unsatisfied. It probably still seems to you that Plato is merely being expedient, and that the fact that true knowledge demands a metaphysics something like the one he has postulated does not make the postulation true. Very well, so you are a hardened skeptic. What would it take to convince you? Would you be satisfied if Plato were to demonstrate before your very eyes that knowledge is inborn? This is precisely what he attempts to do.

First, why should Plato go to the trouble to demonstrate anything? Isn't his theory absurd on its face, and isn't he simply wasting his time and ours? It is very obvious to anyone who will reflect a moment that there are many things he or she doesn't know; and if we learned all in a disembodied state, and if all knowledge is inborn, how is our demonstrable lack of knowledge to be explained? The trauma of birth is Plato's explanation. In the course of birth trauma, we forgot what we knew. Nevertheless it is still there, buried somewhere in our minds, and a good teacher will help us to draw it out.[17]

All right, let's get to the demonstration. It takes place a little over half way through the *Meno* when Meno, unwilling to buy into Socrates ideas sight unseen, asks for a demonstration. Socrates is more than willing to oblige him. He (Socrates) brings in a slave boy who is obviously uneducated, but who is rather intelligent, and proceeds to put to him a series of questions about a square, its division and size.[18] The boy is able to answer all of

---

17 **For those of you who think this sounds a great deal like Sigmund Freud, your insightfulness is to be commended. Freud was very obviously influenced by Plato, unless perhaps both of them met during a disembodied state and Freud actually influenced Plato.**

18 The exchange is in the *Meno*, p. 70.

Socrates's questions, much to the amazement, one would imagine, of the bystanders. Socrates may as well shout, "*Quod erat demonstrandum*," for he considers his case made. No one had taught the lad any of this, and yet he knew it all. From whence came this knowledge if not from the lad's own mind; and where did he get this learning if he was not born with it; and how could he have been born with it unless he had learned it at some time; and when would this have occurred unless he were alive and conscious somewhere prior to his birth?

I highly recommend that the student get hold of the *Meno* and read this exchange, for it is one of the most brilliant and engaging pieces of writing in western literature, whether or not the reader winds up subscribing to Plato's metaphysical position.

As in every intellectual field, Plato casts a long shadow in the area of metaphysics. Our word "education" is derived from the Latin, *educere*, which means "to draw out." Thus, every time we use the word we are paying tacit tribute to the Platonic theory of knowledge, and to Platonic metaphysics.

You have probably heard someone say that Jim or Susan is the ideal such-and-such. Assuming you have, did you understand what was being said? And whence comes such language? Once again, every time someone says something like this he or she is admitting, whether or not the speaker or listeners realize it, to the tremendous influence of Plato and his metaphysics. Jim, or Susan, is being compared favorably with the ideal or form, which is assumed to exist beyond the material realm and to embody perfection.

Perhaps you have two friends, a male and a female, who spend a great deal of time together, and you may have asked one of them (in so many words) what sort of relationship they have. "We are not lovers," might have been the response. "It's purely Platonic." Score another one for Plato's metaphysics. What you were just told is that the relationship conforms to the ideal of love which exists beyond the low, crass level of the purely physical.

Suppose you just learned that the Internal Revenue Service has called you in for an audit on your 1996 income tax return, and in response you proceeded to turn over a table, knock out your front windows, and are standing in the middle of your living room screaming obscenities. Your significant other comes into the room, watches you for a moment, then says, loud enough to be heard over your screams, "Get control of yourself!" Plato is in your face again.[19] Who did your significant other address? You. Then whom are you to get under control? You. Then there must be two yous, the rational, soulish you to whom your significant other spoke, and the lower, out-of-control you who has got to be reined in. This brings us to another of Plato's theories of reality: human reality. Put as a question: how is the human being actually structured?

Plato believed that humans are tripartite, composed of reason, willpower, and appetite. In his dialogue *Phaedrus* he has Socrates illustrating this with the analogy of a chariot pulled by two spirited horses and guided by a charioteer. The charioteer corresponds to reason, while the two horses are willpower (or spirit) and appetite. Both horses must be controlled, for they are plunging away in opposite directions, and neither puts any restraint on its desires. The appetites are constantly after the things of the flesh, things that may be good in themselves but that spell ruin to the individual if too freely indulged in. The spirit leads in the other direction, but it is not able by itself to control the appetites. Reason, however, if it is functioning properly, can keep both horses pulling together and can set the chariot on its proper course, straight down the road.

The idea that the human is composed of three parts is a common one in the West. The Christians believe it (spirit, soul, body), as do the Freudians (id, ego, superego), but Plato was on the scene first, and there is little doubt that he strongly influenced those who followed him, particularly Sigmund Freud. Plato pushed this even farther, however, arguing that society as a whole, ought to be a collective reflection of the individual, and that a well-balanced society is merely the well-balanced human writ large. In Book IV of the *Republic* he divides society into three classes, each class corresponding to one of the three parts of the human soul we have just been considering. The guardian class corresponds to the charioteer, or the rational part of the soul, and it is this class that ought to rule in a well-balanced society. The warrior class, composed of soldiers and what we might think of as police, correspond to the spirit or willpower. And the workers are appetitive. In the well balanced society each will be in his or her proper place, functioning in his or her intended manner, all with an eye to the common good. Few people I know would care to live in Plato's so-called ideal society; but the important thing is to note how his social organization

---

19 Actually, it's more Cartesian than Platonic, but because Descartes was so strongly influenced by Plato, we may as well give this one to Plato too.

grew out of his metaphysics, and how both were arrived at by means of pure reason and dialectic with little appeal to empirical observation. This may be the fundamental weakness in Plato, for in practical fact it is not at all clear that his ideal society would work well.

There is another illustration Plato used in the *Republic* and which is important to any discussion of metaphysics — the well-known parable of the cave. Because it figures prominently in Plato's epistemology, I will save it for that section.

Aristotle's Metaphysics

As we have seen, the word metaphysics came to us from Aristotle. But though we took the term from him, his view of reality has, over the long run, been considerably less influential than that of some of the other philosophers we have discussed. One reason is that, as we have seen, his metaphysical position was not compatible with the position of the early Christians, and for many centuries he was effectively buried and forgotten. Then, once he had been rediscovered, his systems were synthesized with medieval Christian theology to create a world view which was subsequently overthrown by the scientists and astronomers of the Renaissance. We know, for example, that the earth is not the center of the universe; that objects do not fall downward at a certain velocity because of their weight; that there are more than four elements; that spontaneous generation is not possible. All things considered, Aristotle's epistemology has been much more important to succeeding generations than his metaphysics. Still, there are things that we can learn from his metaphysics. At the very least we can witness the thought processes of one of the greatest thinkers of western history.

Metaphysically, Aristotle is sometimes called a **naturalist**, which means that he believed in only one level of reality, the level that we experience and are able to take in by means of our five senses. This particular designation has always troubled me a bit, because there is some indication that Aristotle believed in a world of unseen beings, and it is not clear (to me at least) whether or not he believed the soul is immortal.[20] Clearly, however, he was a pluralist, not altogether different than Empedocles, and he believed that the universe, as we see it, has always been and always will be.

---

[20] I am in the minority on this one. Most scholars feel the evidence is that Aristotle believed there is no part of the individual that survives death.

In the *Metaphysics*, Aristotle had a great deal to say about cause, and about being as such. Much of this was foundational to Thomas Aquinas when he began putting together arguments for the existence of God. It troubled Aristotle that the philosophers who went before him had gone to great lengths to attempt to answer questions about the basic "stuff" of which the universe was composed, but that they were unable to give the actual mechanism whereby the individual things we see about us are generated out of this basic stuff.

> If it is really true that all generation and destruction is out of some one entity or even more than one, why does this happen, and what is the cause? It is surely not the substrate itself which causes itself to change.[21]

In his search for cause Aristotle, with his practical and analytical mind, identifies four causes that can be used to explain the existence of anything. The four are the material, the formal, the efficient, and the final. Suppose, for example, we are looking at a statue of Pallas Athena and we ask how the statue came to be — in other words, what caused it. Aristotle would answer that there are four causes. One is the material, marble no doubt, from which the statue is made, and this is the **material cause**. Another is the artisan who actually made the statue, **the efficient cause**. But this would not be enough, for there must also have been a **formal cause**, the idea which the artisan had in mind when he first viewed the block of marble and saw what he would do with it. And finally, the purpose which the statue serves is what Aristotle called the **final cause**. With these four, Aristotle feels that he has exhausted the topic and has fully explained cause in all its aspects.

The four Aristotelean causes: material, efficient, formal, final. These account for all changes in the cosmos.

The final cause, that which deals with the purpose for which a thing was made, was much more important to Aristotle than it is for most of us, particularly when we are discussing things that are not artificial (that is made by humans). He thought that all living things had their purpose within themselves, and that their development could be explained as a function of this innate purpose. The Greek word is ***entelechy***, from *en* (in or within) and *teleos*, a word that is a bit difficult to define, but that suggests an end or a goal. *Teleos* appears in many of our words, including telephone (literally, to complete a sound), telegraphy (to complete, or send a message), and

Entelechy, the force within that drives a thing toward its goal. Aristotle believed that everything was goal directed, and that the direction was given by that which was innate.

---

21 Aristotle, the *Metaphysics*, trans. Hugh Tredennick, Cambridge, Mass.: Harvard University Press, 1980, p. 23.

television (to complete something visual). Aristotle believed that there was purpose behind everything, and that this purpose was innate. Potential is another word that he used to explain *entelechy.* An acorn, for instance, is a potential oak, it has "oakness" in it, and its purpose, expressed metaphysically as its final cause, is to become an oak.

The human also has *entelechy.* Within the human, even while it is a mere conceptus in its mother's womb, is the potential to become a mature, rational human; and it is being driven by its *entelechy* in that direction. A thing, whatever it is, can do no better than to reach its potential, that for which it was intended as determined by this inborn force driving it toward its goal.

I hope you remember that when we were talking about philosophy as it developed during the late Middle Ages, we saw that Peter Abelard and Thomas Aquinas synthesized Aristotle and Christian theology by suggesting a way in which Aristotle's theory of form could be made to agree, somewhat, with Plato. In fact, Aristotle disagreed with Plato. Though he agreed that there are forms, he did not believe that the forms had ontological existence in a world behind this world. Rather, he thought that form was a part of the particular and could not exist apart from it, which leads us to his understanding of "soul."

The confusion that arises among today's students over the Greek concept of the soul probably has to do with ideas they absorbed as they have travelled through the Judeo-Christian West. Soul is assumed to be synonymous with spirit, and is held to be that invisible part of us, created in God's image, that survives death in some form.

The Christian soul would scarcely be recognizable to the Greeks, especially to Aristotle. To him, just as form was present in particular and could not exist apart from it, soul was a part of the thing which it animated, and is more to be identified (in the case of humans) with the rational principle than with anything spiritual. Aristotle taught that there are a hierarchy of souls, beginning with the lowest type, the vegetative soul, and moving upward through the highest type, the human or rational soul. All living things have souls, but not all have rational souls.

Vegetative soul — for Aristotle, the lowest type of soul, that which is possessed by all living things, including plants.

Take, for example, the potted plant on by desk. Does it have soul? Yes, but only the lowest type, the **vegetative soul**. This soul contains the *entelechy* of the plant and provides it with the impetus to live up to its full potential. It will never perform brain surgery, but it will grow into a lush, green plant and do whatever it is that plants do.

Now let us move up the ladder to a higher type of soul, the soul of the animal, or what Aristotle calls the **sentient soul.** This is the soul possessed by my cats and my neighbor's dogs. It is sentient because the creatures who possess it have self-awareness as well as the ability to function vegetatively. Thus, while the cat and dog have both a sentient and a vegetative soul, the lower forms of life lack sentience. It is clear that sentient beings are more complex, have greater potential and a greater distance to go to fulfil their *entelechy* than does the plant on my desk.

The next step up the ladder in Aristotle's hierarchy of souls is the sentient soul. This type of soul is possessed by animals and humans, but not plants. Self aware

Finally we come to the highest and most complex being of all, the human. The human has the first two types of soul, vegetative and sentient, but adds to this another, higher type, the **rational soul.** This becomes very important when Aristotle begins to put together his ethical theory and his theory about what constitutes virtuous behavior. Humans can choose to live on the purely vegetative and animal level if they wish; but they can find no satisfaction in this because their purpose as humans is being thwarted. They will always feel unfulfilled, as if there is something missing. There is, Aristotle would say; their souls are being slowly starved.

Finally we reach the highest type of soul, the rational soul. This soul is possessed only by the human, the rational animal.

A Second Brief Interlude

As with Plato, so with Aristotle, his ethics as well as his epistemology arose from his metaphysical assumptions. If you give the matter some thought, you will probably be able to see that this is true of yourself as well as these pre-Christian Greeks. If you are a dualist, believing in God, convinced that you possess an immortal soul that will survive death, then you probably believe that God has created not only the universe, but is also responsible for judging between right and wrong. You are much more likely to hold to some form of rationalism and to believe in ethical absolutes, than is someone who is an atheist or an agnostic. If your metaphysical position is closer to that of Aristotle, and if you believe that what we see is what we get, then you are probably an empiricist who leans toward some form of ethical consequentialism. Either way, it seems certain that your ethics, your ideas about learning, your very concept of truth — all depend strongly on your metaphysical position. For this reason, it is important that you give some serious thought to the question of what is really there, and that you at least attempt to support your beliefs with logic. That is what education ought to be about, and that is what educated people ought to do.

As It Unfolded

Dualism became the dominant metaphysical position in the West because it agreed so well with the writings of the Apostle Paul, to the extent that he expressed himself on the subject. For over a thousand years there was scarcely a philosopher in operation who wasn't also a theologian, and there were no theologians who did not believe in the existence of, the primacy of, the unseen spirit world. Anything less would have been heresy. I haven't taken a poll on the subject, but I feel comfortable in saying that dualism remains the dominant metaphysical position in the West, in spite of the conceptual changes wrought by Galileo and Isaac Newton. This is true, however, only if one samples the entire population. Narrow the field to philosophers and scientists, and strange as it may seem many of them, if not the majority, will argue for some form of idealism. I said earlier that the twentieth century has not been kind to materialism. Allow me to show you why.

Suppose we go back to one of the early Greek materialists, Democritus, dust off his atomic theory, and revise it to include what we now know that he and his contemporaries did not. First, we can agree that the Greek atomic theory was a stupendous intellectual achievement, made all the more impressive by the fact that, in its general outline, it is the same as ours. We have had to add virtually nothing to Democritus in order to make use of what he gave us four hundred years before the birth of Christ. All of reality, he said, is reducible to tiny, indivisible bits of matter. These bits of matter are finite in number and are indestructible. They are drawn together by a process of mutual attraction, and what they become (tree, cloud, flame, etc.) depends on how many there are and the way in which they are structured. Over time they break apart, the thing they formed ceases to be, they come together in new formations to form new things, and so on, over and over. Solids only appear solid. Actually, they are composed largely of empty space.

Pure materialism? Yes, until we comes to the twentieth century and meet an interesting German physicist named Albert Einstein, who presents us with the unsettling notion that material and energy are the same thing, or, as he elegantly put it, $e=mc^2$. Take any matter, multiply it by the speed of light, square the result, and you have pure energy. Turn it around. Take pure energy, find its square root, divide it by the speed of light, and you have mass. Push any particle to the speed of light and its mass becomes infinite. For the first time we can begin to understand why the solid table upon which you are leaning is really a composite of particles and empty space, for the particles, whirling at the speed of light, assume solidity.

Materialism, in its classical form, is over and done with.

> Matter has been dematerialized, not just as a concept of the philosophically real, but now as an idea of modern physics. Matter can be analyzed down to the level of the fundamental particles. But at that depth the direction of analysis changes, and this constitutes a major conceptual surprise in the history of science. The things which for Newton typified matter — e.g., an exactly determinable state, a point shape, absolute solidity — these are now the properties electrons do not, because theoretically they cannot, have . . .
>
> The dematerialization of matter. . .has rocked mechanics at its foundations. . .The 20th century's dematerialization of matter has made it conceptually impossible to accept a Newtonian picture of the properties of matter and still do a consistent physics.[22]

But things have gotten considerably more complicated than even Einstein made them. In the strange world of quantum physics, as Niels Bohr and Werner Heisenberg have delineated it, reality is actually changed by our observing it.

> The new physics, quantum mechanics, tells us clearly that it is not possible to observe reality without changing it. If we observe a certain particle collision experiment, not only do we have no way of proving that the result would have been the same if we had not been watching it, all that we know indicates that it would not have been the same, because the result that we got was affected by the fact that we were looking for it.[23]

The implications of this, for any metaphysical theory, are simply staggering. Reality is not merely energy (whatever that is), but it is actually a function of our observation; or, to put it another way, we create reality by choosing to look at it a certain way.

How does this differ substantially, if at all, from what George Berkeley said in the eighteenth century — and for which he was put down

---

[22] Hanson, N.R., "The Dematerialization of Matter," in *The Concept of Matter*, ed. Ernan McMillin, Notre Dame, IN: University of Notre Dam,e Press, 1963, pp. 556-557. Quoted in Manuel Velasquez, *Philosophy*.

[23] Zukav, Gary, *The Dancing Wu Li Masters*, New York: Bantam Books, 1980, pp. 30-31.

as a raving lunatic by at least some of those in the intellectual community? Twentieth century physicists have altered Berkeley's motto somewhat, however. It is no longer, *to be is to be perceived*, but rather, *what something is depends upon how it is perceived.* If this sounds to you like wild and crazy fantasy, imagine the surprise of the hardheaded physicists who made these discoveries, and who have had to live with the metaphysical ambiguity of what they have learned.

A Closing Thought

I imagine that metaphysics did not turn out to be exactly what most of my students thought it would be. Most, no doubt, were expecting angels, demons, spirits of various sorts, and God in particular. I am sure this is what the maker of my metaphysical ring had in mind. This is not altogether wrong, for whether or not angels, spirits, and God exist is certainly a question that falls within the metaphysical area of inquiry. But the area is much broader than this, as we have just seen.

In this Chapter I have attempted to give the student a broad introduction to metaphysics by showing the ways in which philosophers have sought to deal with the overall question of what is really there. In Chapters 6 and 7 I will take up some of the more narrow and specific questions metaphysicians have raised, including whether or not there is a God, whether or not humans have free will, if mind exists apart from brain, and if we can expect to survive death in some form.

Chapter 6
All about God

I have always considered that God
Must find it exceedingly odd
To think that his tree
Won't continue to be
When there's no one about in the quad.

Dear Sir:
Your astonishment's odd.
For I'm always about in the quad.
And so my tree will continue to be,
Since observed by
  Yours faithfully,
  God.

Most of the verses that head up chapters and sections in this book are my own. The two limericks above are not. In fact, though they have been around for years, and are known to most everyone who teaches philosophy, no one has ever come forward to claim authorship. So I suppose they are in the public domain and may be used by anyone who wants them. I must say that they bear a distinct English flavor and were probably produced by some wit at either Oxford or Cambridge to demonstrate familiarity with the metaphysics of George Berkeley. I use them, however, to alert the student that we are about to talk about God, whether or not God exists, and whether or not we can construct rational arguments that prove his[1] existence.

---

1 It has become fashionable in this era that strains for political correctness to mix one's pronouns when referring to God so that everyone, regardless of gender, feels included. With apologies to all my female students, I think I'll avoid this entanglement and just go on referring to God (assuming there is a God) as "he."

2 The word literally means "god talk," and that may be the best definition we have. Theologians talk about God.

We need to distinguish at the outset between **theology**[2] and philosophy. Both of these academic disciplines deal with the existence and attributes of God, but theologians begin their study with a basic commitment to the belief that God exists. Philosophers have no such initial commitment. Instead, they take the position that we ought to examine the available evidence as objectively as possible, and make our decision to believe or not to believe based on that examination.

Theism vs. deism: the belief that God is a person as opposed to the belief that God is an impersonal force.

With regard to God, there are only so many positions one can take. Suppose you hold that there is a God. You might be either a **deist** or a **theist**. You might, on the other hand, be an **atheist**, believing that there is no God. And finally, you might be an **agnostic**, one who says that there is not enough information available to say one way or the other, thus we simply cannot know whether or not there is a God.[3]

Atheism literally means "no God." Agnosticism literally means, "no knowledge." For some, there is no basic difference.

So much for the atheists and agnostics. What about the others?

In the West, most of those who believe in God have been theists. A theist believes that God is a person, possessed of intellect, will and emotion, who is directly involved in his creation, responds to prayer, knows all that occurs, is omniscient, omnipotent, omnipresent, and, above all, omnibenevolent. This clearly describes the God of Abraham, Isaac, Jacob, Jesus of Nazareth, Mohammed, and most of those who claim to be their followers.

A deist believes that there is some higher force or power that one may designate as "God," but that this higher power lacks the attributes assigned to God by the theists. Is God a he or a she? To the deist, God is more often than not described as an "it," for God is not necessarily a person, has no interest in particular individuals, and has not, for ages upon ages, intervened directly in creation. God was present at the beginning to get things started, to set up the rules by which the universe would operate; and, having done this, God has now withdrawn and left things to run on their own. Deism was a popular position during the period we call the Enlightenment, and many of the famous philosophers and intellectuals of that time were deists, including Voltaire, Thomas Jefferson, and (probably) Benjamin Franklin. Deism has also fared well in the Orient, among the Buddhists and some of the

---

[3] There are those today who hold that agnosticism is no longer a viable designation, and that anyone who says there is not enough evidence to affirm or disaffirm God's existence must be counted an atheist. This position turns on the argument that one cannot prove a negative, that the one affirming the existence of something (or someone) bears the burden of proof, and that those arguing for God have not met that burden.

Hindus. Those early Greek philosophers who believed in God (and most of them used the term from time to time) would probably have to be put down as deists.

Proving God

Some of you may be uncomfortable with a human attempt to prove God's existence. You may even have been taught that to so much as question the existence of God is to show a lack of faith; and of course without faith it is impossible to please God. Therefore, away with all such stuff!

Before any of you reject, as an exercise in blasphemy, the attempt to prove, or disprove, God, may I direct your attention to the New Testament letter to the Romans, penned by the Apostle Paul in about 60 A.D.? In the opening chapter of that letter, beginning with verse 18 and running through verse 20, Paul writes as follows:

> For the wrath of God is revealed from heaven against all ungodliness and unrighteousness of men, who hold the truth in unrighteousness; because that which may be known of God is manifest in them; for God hath shewed it unto them. For the invisible things of him from the creation of the world are clearly seen, being understood by the things that are made, even his eternal power and Godhead; so that they are without excuse: because that when they knew God, they glorified him not as God, neither were thankful; but became vain in their imaginations, and their foolish heart was darkened.

Laypersons may not recognize it, but all philosophers see immediately that the Apostle has framed a variation of the teleological argument for the existence of God. Look at it again. He is arguing from visible things to things invisible, saying that the visible or created things reveal something about the character of God, namely his eternal power and his deity (Godhead in the King James). Finally, Paul says that everyone knows this, the implication being that those who deny God's existence are being willfully ignorant.

If you do not care for the Apostle Paul and would feel more comfortable with an Old Testament point of view, then kindly direct your attention to the Book of Psalms:

> The heavens declare the glory and God, and the firmament sheweth his handiwork. (Psm. 19:1)

Once again, we have here in embryonic form a teleological argument for the existence of God. The teleological argument attempts to demonstrate the existence of an intelligent creator by pointing to the apparent purposefulness of the physical world, the intricate way in which it is constructed, and the fact that the builder seems to have had certain ends in mind. Aquinas used this argument, as did William Paley; and even Charles Darwin found it interesting.

Now, if the Psalmist (presumably David, a man after God's own heart), and Paul, and Thomas Aquinas felt, at some point, the need to rationally argue for the existence of God, I feel justified in doing the same thing. But feeling justified and knowing what to do are two different things. If I wish to prove that God exists, how shall I go about it? I frequently ask my students this question, and usually find them rather puzzled. Perhaps it is because, though they have been taught all of their lives that there is a God, no one has ever asked them how they know it.

For philosophers, for whom anything and anyone is fair game, the proofs for God's existence have taken two forms, inductive arguments and deductive arguments. The earlier arguments, those of Augustine and Anselm of Canterbury, were deductive or *a priori*, whereas with Thomas Aquinas, the Aristotelian, we get a series of arguments that are, for the most part, inductive, that is they move from the particular and observable toward the general and the unseen. We shall look at some of these, not only to see how the arguments are structured, but to see whether they succeed or fail. Remember, we are talking about metaphysics, the study of reality, and we are attempting to see whether or not reality includes an unseen realm that somehow interacts with and influences that which is seen. If we can successfully demonstrate the existence of God, then dualism is probably the correct metaphysical position,[4] and we should probably all throw in with Plato, Augustine, and Aquinas.

But once again, and at the risk of being redundant, how are we to prove God exists? Suppose you were given this as a problem to solve and you were told that you were to be given a grade in class depending upon how successful you are in solving it. How would you go about it? Oh, and to make things even more interesting, suppose the problem were set in this

---

[4] **Probably, but not certainly. One might prove God and be an idealist rather than a dualist. But it would be very difficult, if not impossible, to believe in the God of the theists and be a materialist.**

fashion: your solution must be *a priori.* You cannot appeal to anything you can see in this universe. You are to imagine that you are pure mind and nothing else, and that you have no access to the world external to yourself. Simply sit down, close your eyes, and think of something that any rational person would agree proves God is, and that God is something like the one presented in the Bible. You might say this is impossible. You would be wrong. Some of the more well known, and more resilient, of the proofs for God's existence are of this type.

Augustine Argues for God

One must always remember that Augustine did not come to Christianity as did the Apostle Paul, via a dramatic and supernatural conversion. Rather, he was an intellectual from the outset, a man who read and considered a number of metaphysical positions, and who had to be convinced that Christianity was philosophically viable before he walked to the baptismal font. It isn't strange that such a man would feel the need to argue for God's existence. Rather, it would be strange if he did not do so. His favored proof for God begins with a belief that there are certain ideas of changeless and necessary truth within each human mind. He supposes that these ideas are common to all, and provide structural stability to mental life. If there is such a thing as truth, this must transcend the individual human mind. If not, then how would anyone claim to know anything, or to communicate that knowledge to another person, or how would he or she frame any proposition of any transcendent value?

So far, Augustine has only been talking about the human mind, and the ideas that exist there; but he will leap shortly to the existence of God. His argument works like this: there are eternal ideas in the human mind, ideas that go beyond the merely immediate and particular, for we not only hold such ideas, but we are able to communicate them meaningfully to others. Now where do such ideas come from? It cannot be that we generate them from within ourselves, for we are finite and in ourselves we have no concept of the eternal and transcendent. They must have their source in another, one that possesses both mind and concepts, but also knowledge of the eternal. Augustine holds this to be God, and he holds the existence within us of eternal and transcendent ideas as proof for the existence of God.[5]

---

[5] **For the full arguments see *The Basic Writings of Saint Augustine*, Grand Rapids, MI: The Baker Publishing Co., 1980. Also see, Copleston, Frederick, *A History of Philosophy*, Vol. 2, Part I, *Mediaeval Philosophy: Augustine to Bonaventure*, Garden City, NY: Image Books, 1962, pp. 84-85.**

Augustine does not stop here. He goes on to argue the existence of God much as we saw Paul the Apostle arguing. But it is significant that these are the least important of Augustine's arguments, and he seems to put them in as a sort of after thought. His most important and, he feels, most convincing argument is the one from the structure of human mentality. But how convincing was he? Am I to take my ability to conceive of truths that are eternal, or that at the very least transcend my time, place and person, as proof of the existence of one outside myself that I can comfortably identify as God? Frankly, I think I would like to hear something more on the subject. And there is a great deal more to be heard.

Anselm's Ontological Argument

Bertrand Russell tells of a time when he, a young student of philosophy, was walking along one Sunday morning when suddenly he stopped dead in his tracks, clapped his hand to his head, and muttered, "My God, the ontological argument is sound." He did not, of course, feel that way in later years, but one can imagine how that experience must have affected him at the time; and anyone who has ever, in an intuitive flash, clearly seen the solution to a philosophical problem, can share Russell's sense of wonder and amazement.

My own experience with the ontological argument is somewhat different. I remember where I was when I first read it, much as my parents remember exactly where they were when they heard that Pearl Harbor had been attacked. I was sitting in my room at home, reading a book about medieval philosophers and their intellectual search for God, and I came to Anselm and his *Proslogium.*

Anselm was a Benedictine, but his philosophical leanings were clearly Augustinian. He was born in 1033, was appointed Archbishop of Canterbury in 1078, and died at that post in 1109. His first important work was the *Monologium,* in which he argues *a posteriori* for the existence of God. This, however, did not satisfy him, and he continued to seek a proof for God's existence that would be strictly mental and subjective, in no way dependent upon factors outside the one doing the thinking. In other words, can one close one eyes, draw into oneself, and there, in introspective isolation, think of God in such a way as to make his existence a certainty? Anselm, after a good deal of thought, believed that he had found the solution, and he wrote the *Proslogium* to share his solution with the world.

God is that being greater than which none can be conceived, ergo, God exists. [6]

If you were waiting for something more, you may cease and desist. The *Proslogium* is a bit more complicated, with language that not even a good translation from the Latin can fully elucidate; but what you see above is Anselm's ontological argument in a nutshell. Could he have been serious? He could have been, and he was. There is no doubt that Anselm felt he had solved the problem of proving God's existence, and that any honest seeker must necessarily come to the same conclusion he did.

My initial reaction to the ontological argument was that Anselm had simply defined God into existence, that if one accepted Anselm's definition of God (i.e. the one greater than which none could be conceived), then one would be forced to admit that God existed. But, then, if one accepted Anselm's definition, there would be no need for the ontological argument, for the statement "God is that being. . ." carries with it the clear statement of God's existence. Quite frankly, I blew the whole thing off. I now realize that I acted rashly.

The truth is that the ontological argument of Anselm[7] is one of the most resilient and compelling of all the arguments for God. I have noticed that philosophers have an almost fatal attraction to it, as if it were a knotty chess problem (from this position white sets mate in one move). Perhaps we ought to look at it closer.

Frederick Copleston suggests that it can be written as a syllogism, thusly:

> God is that than which no greater can be thought: But that than which no greater can be thought must exist, not only mentally, in idea, but also extramentally:
>
> Therefore God exists, not only in idea, mentally,

---

[6] The student who wishes to read the Proslogium will find it in *Saint Anselm: Basic Writings*, trans. S.N. Deane, La Salle, IL: Open Court Publishing Co., 1962. It is contained in other works as well, but all of them reference the work cited here.

[7] I specify "of Anselm" because there are other ontological arguments. Both Descartes and Spinoza argued for God's existence in a similar fashion, and it was specifically to Descartes that Kant was responding when he attacked the ontological argument. But Anselm's argument remains the most well-known and popular with philosophers.

> but also extramentally.
>
> The Major Premiss simply gives the idea of God, the idea which a man has of God, even if he denies His existence.
>
> The Minor Premise is clear, since if that than which no greater can be thought existed only in the mind, it would not be that than which no greater can be thought. A greater could be thought, i.e. a being that existed in extramental reality as well as in idea.[8]

Go back to the major premise, God is that than which no greater can be thought. Does this not, in fact, beg the question by assuming as evidence that very thing we are trying to prove? Immanuel Kant certainly thought so, although his case against the ontological argument is not couched in just these terms. In Book II, Chapter III, Section 4 of his celebrated *Critique of Pure Reason* he undertakes to refute the ontological argument by showing that it does nothing more than define God into existence then invites us to accept the definition. But suppose we reject the definition, then what? Then, says Kant, in language that can be rather confusing, we are left with what amounts to nothing more than a conditional. *If* God exists, *then* God is that being greater than which none can be conceived. But nothing in this conditional statement can be taken to show that God actually exists, nor are we involved in self-contradiction (as Anselm suggests) if we reject the definition and God along with it.

Further, it is clear that for the ontological argument to work, existence in reality must be greater than existence in mere imagination. In fact, the argument turns upon this assumption. In the first major attack upon the ontological proof, Gaunilon, a monk of Marmoutier asks us to imagine an island, "the lost island," somewhere in the ocean.

> Somewhere in the ocean is an island, which, because of the difficulty, or rather the impossibility, of discovering what does not exist, is called the lost island. And say that this island has an inestimable wealth of all manner of riches and delicacies in greater abundance than is told of the Islands of the Blest; and that having no owner or inhabitant, it is more excellent than all other countries, which are inhabited by mankind, in the

---

[8] **Copleston, Frederick, *A History of Western Philosophy*, Vol. 2, Part I, *Mediaeval Philosophy, Augustine to Bonaventure*, Garden City, NY: Image Books, 1962, p. 183.**

> abundance with which it is stored.
>
> Now if some one should tell me that there is such an island, I should easily understand his words, in which there is no difficulty. But suppose that he went on to say, as if by a logical inference: "You can no longer doubt that this island which is more excellent than all lands exists somewhere, since you have no doubt that it is in your understanding. . ."
>
> If a man should try to prove to me by such reasoning that this island truly exists, and that its existence should no longer be doubted, either I should believe that he was jesting, or I know not which I ought to regard as the greater fool: myself supposing that I should allow this proof; or him, if he should suppose that he had established with any certainty the existence of this island.[9]

Anselm's reply to Gaunilon's criticism is instructive in that it raises the very question asked earlier: is existence in reality greater than existence in imagination? Anselm says that, in the case of Gaunilon's lost island, one might easily conceive a greater island than the one Gaunilon has posited, and that this is proof positive that the island exists only in the imagination and not in reality, for that which is imagined may always be exceeded by a greater imagination. But that which is in reality so great that a greater cannot be imagined must actually exist.

Now this is troubling. I feel as if I am on a wild goose chase. There is clearly something wrong with the ontological argument, but I am not sure exactly what it is. Perhaps Immanuel Kant can shed some light on the matter. Returning to the *Critique of Pure Reason*, Book II, Chapter III, Section 4, we find Kant denying that existence in reality is in fact greater than existence in mere imagination.

> A hundred real thalers do not contain the least coin more than a hundred possible thalers. For as the latter signify the concept, and the former the object and the positing of the object, should the former contain more than the latter, my concept would not, in that case, express the whole object, and would not therefore be anadequate concept of it.[10]

---

9 *Gaunilon in Behalf of the Fool*, in *Medieval Philosophy*, ed. Herman Shapiro, New York: The Modern Library, 1964, pp. 117-118.

10 Kant, Immanuel, *The Critique of Pure Reason*, trans. Norman Kemp Smith, New York: The Modern Library, 1958, p. 183.

Kant's point is that existence is not a property but a relationship between the thing conceived and the world. By saying that something exists we have predicated nothing positive about it, we have merely related it to other things. This is not easy to follow, but look at it in this way. Conceive of a beautiful city. Give it every quality, in your imagination, that you think the city ought to have. Spare nothing in creating your imaginary city. Do you have it? Fine, now add existence to it. By saying that it actually exists, have you added anything to the concept? Kant, for one, says that you have not.

Somehow I remain troubled by the ontological argument for the existence of God, and I am not alone. As I said earlier, odd as it may seem when one first hears it, it is one of the most resilient of all the arguments, one that most philosophers, sooner or later, are tempted to toy with. Perhaps it is the pristine, mental nature of the thing that is so alluring. There is no need to dirty one's hands in the rough-and-tumble world of empirical thought. Indeed, it almost seems fitting that a cloistered monk is the one who first came up with the argument. Let us go back over it from a bit of a different angle.

Do you have a conception of God? Of course you do. Now notice, I did not ask if you believe in God, nor did I ask if you have an understanding of God. Both of those are far different matters. I only asked if you have a conception of God, and you must answer that you do, or else there would be no point in our discussing these matters, since you would have no idea what I mean when I say, "God."

Very well, next question. Does your conception of God include the proposition that there is no higher being, that is that God is the being than which none greater can be conceived? I did not ask whether or not you can comprehend infinity or perfection; I merely asked if your conception of God includes the idea that there is nothing higher. If you say no, Anselm will answer that there is something wrong with your conception of God. If you say yes, Anselm will reply that you have just demonstrated the existence of God in reality. If you respond that you don't get it, Anselm will ask you whether or not you agree that existence in fact is greater than existence in mere imagination. Unless you wish to follow Bertrand Russell, clap your hand to your forehead and shout, "My God, the ontological argument is sound," you must now do one of two things. First, you must deny that existence in fact is greater than existence in mere conception. Second, you must hold that conception alone is not sufficient to prove ontological existence.

I will leave you to think about Anselm for yourself, and to wonder what he saw that you are missing (if anything), and I will move forward in time some six-hundred years. In the seventeenth century René Descartes, as we saw in the first section, floated a variation of the ontological argument, one which depended, not upon the definition of God, but upon the conception of the perfect.

Descartes's Ontological Argument

René Descartes was, epistemologically, a rationalist, as were Plato, Augustine, and Anselm of Canterbury. So, judging from what he wrote on more than one occasion, was the Apostle Paul. In his letter to the Romans (from which I have already quoted to show Paul's teleological argument) we get the following:

> When the gentiles, which have not the law, do by nature the things contained in the law, these, having not the law, are a law unto themselves: which shew the work of the law written in their hearts, their conscience also bearing witness, and their thoughts the meanwhile accusing or else excusing one another. (Rom. 2:14-16).

Clearly the Apostle believed that some knowledge — in this case a knowledge of right and wrong — is inborn, which is precisely what all rationalists believe. For Descartes, the truest, most certain knowledge that there is is that with which we are born. It is universal, certain, necessary, and Descartes called it, as we have seen, *a priori.* His test of the truthfulness of a given proposition was whether or not he could see it clearly and certainly. Thus: *cogito ergo sum.* He clearly and certainly saw himself as an existing, thinking entity, therefore there was no question but that his own existence was established.

His argument for the existence of God follows along much the same lines, and along the lines that the Apostle Paul might have used; but it has to do with a concept of perfection, and it has to do with answering the question of how we could come by such a concept. It is contained in Part Four of his *Discourse on Method.*[11] To understand Descartes's argument, ask yourself whether or not you have a conception of perfection. If you respond that you do, Descartes would ask where you came by such a conception. Clearly it was not empirical, that is, you did not gain it through

---

[11] Descartes, Rene, *Discourse on Method,* trans Laurence J. Lafleur, Indianapolis, IN: Bobbs-Merrill, 1960, pp. 24-27.

experience, since you have never seen nor in any way experienced the perfect. The concept must be inborn, but Descartes does not stop there. To have an inborn concept of perfection is to demonstrate that the source of the concept must come from somewhere other than ourselves, since we easily recognize ourselves as being less than perfect. So, whence comes the concept? Descartes argues that it comes from God, its only possible source. This is substantially the same argument Baruch Spinoza used (except Descartes beat him to it), to wit:

> Whatever perfection substance has is due to no external cause. *Therefore, its existence must follow from its nature alone*, and is, therefore, nothing else than its essence. Perfection consequently does not prevent the existence of a thing but establishes it; imperfection, on the other hand, prevents existence, and so of no existence can we be more sure than of the existence of the Being absolutely infinite or perfect, that is to say, God.[12]

An ontological argument is an argument that attempts to prove God's existence based upon the meaning of the word "God."

The italicized words in the above quote are mine. This is the very essence of an **ontological argument.** Existence follows from the nature of the thing alone. In the case of Anselm, the existence of God flows from the fact that he is that being greater than which none can be conceived. In the cases of Descartes and Spinoza, substitute the term "perfection" for "greater than which none can be conceived," and it becomes clear that their ontological arguments are not so very different from that of the eleventh century saint. The problem with saying that the existence of a thing follows from the thing's nature is that, in the case of God, we are the ones defining or describing the nature, and this leads directly to the criticism of Immanuel Kant (and others) that all of the ontological arguments effectively define God into existence, and that refusing to accept the definition takes the wind out of their sails.

To be fair to Anselm and others, I ought to point out that they say refusing to accept the definition lands one in self-contradiction; one cannot hold to the concept of God as the being greater than which none can be conceived, then say God does not exist. Kant asks, in so many words, why I must have the concept at all, as anything other than a conditional.

---

[12] Spinoza, Baruch, *Ethics*, New York: Hafner Press, 1974, p.50.

The ontological argument is troublesome, and it has not become clearer over the years. Perhaps we would be well off to lay it aside and ask if there is not a simpler way to prove that God exists, one that would appeal, as Saint Paul did, to the world around us. Such an argument would be inductive, empirical, *a posteriori*, and it would probably be much simpler to follow than the rather difficult deductive argument of Anselm. There are, of course, such arguments, and we shall turn to them now.

The Five Proofs of Aquinas

Those who know very little about philosophy are apt to have read enough history and humanities to know that Thomas Aquinas had five proofs for the existence of God, and that he put these proofs down for all the world to see in his philosophical classic, *Summma Theologica.*[13] It is worth noting that Aquinas did not think well of Anselm's argument, and that he in fact argued that the existence of God is not self-evident, that it must be proved. He then proceeded to prove it by five arguments: the argument from motion, the argument from cause, the argument from necessity, the argument from degree, the argument from design. Each of these is inductive, is based upon empirical observation, and is well suited for the man who wed Christian theology to Aristotle's philosophy.

The Argument from Motion

The first of the arguments is almost pure Aristotle.[14]

> Therefore, whatever is moved must be moved by another. If that by which it is moved be itself moved, then this also must needs be moved by another, and that by another again. But this cannot go on to infinity, because then there would be no first mover, and, consequently, no other mover, seeing that subsequent movers move only inasmuch as they are moved by the first mover; as the staff moves only because it is moved

---

[13] The five arguments may be found in *Summa Theologica*. This is contained, in part and in whole, in a number of collections. One of the better and more easily accessed is *Introduction to Saint Thomas Aquinas*, ed. Anton C. Pegis, New York: The Modern Library, 1948.

[14] Aristotle, *The Metaphysics*, Book XII, Chapter 6. A simple version is the *Pocket Aristotle*, ed. Justin D. Kaplan, New York: Washington Square Press, 1966.

> by the hand. Therefore it is necessary to arrive at a first mover, moved by no other; and this everyone understands to be God.[15]

Aristotle called God, in the course of his argument, the Prime Mover, and stated that God moved not by pushing or shoving, but by drawing things to himself. He also assumed, as does Aquinas, that there can be no infinite regress, and in fact one doesn't need to be particularly insightful to realize that this assumption is critical to the whole argument. If infinite regress is possible, then the argument fails because, for all we know, this business of one thing moving another has gone on and will go on from everlasting to everlasting. Aquinas's reasons for denying infinite regress, as seen above, are interesting and somewhat strange. Go back and re-read and see if you can follow what he is getting at. If the chain goes back to infinity, then there can be no first mover, and if there is no first mover then there cannot be a (let us say) fourteenth mover, and if any of the links fall out, then the entire chain must fall apart. This rather odd way of looking at things was probably more convincing to the Medieval scholars who first read it than it is to us today. It seems that he is juggling the concept of number, saying that fourteen (since I arbitrarily pulled that number out of the hat) is dependent upon the numbers before it, and all are dependent upon number one.

Nevertheless, forgetting the problem with infinite regress, the argument is clear enough. Things are indeed in motion. Nothing that is moving set itself in motion. All moving things were set in motion by something that preceded them, in the sense that it was in motion before it could set them in motion. But if (Aquinas and Aristotle would say "because") this chain cannot go backward to infinity, then there must be a first mover, itself unmoved. And this, says Aquinas, everyone understands to be God.

The argument fails.

If fails, in the first place, precisely because it is not clear that there cannot be an infinite regress. It fails, in the second place, because it is refuted by one of its main premises. If everything that is in motion must have been set in motion by something preceding it, then God must have been set in motion by something preceding him, *ergo* God cannot be the first mover, and there can be no unmoved mover.

---

[15] **Aquinas, p. 25.**

The Cosmological Argument

This is the argument from cause, or some would say the cause and effect argument. To understand why philosophers call it the cosmological argument, go back and review the information we have covered on the Pythagoreans, who were the first to refer to the universe as the *cosmos.* Remember, the word means an orderly arrangement, and as they applied it to the universe the Pythagoreans underscored their belief that we are a part of a system that is ordered, that follows rule (the rule of number, as they saw it), and that can be understood.

The rule, or law, of the universe that undergirds the cosmological argument is that every effect has a cause that precedes it. Stop and think a moment. Would you agree there is nothing in your experience as a human that suggests there can be an effect without a cause? Is there anything to which you could point and say, "It just happened; it is self-generating?" Is there a scientist we know of worth his or her salt who does not subscribe to the idea, in defiance of David Hume, of a connection between cause and effect?

Once you have granted Aquinas this point he will take you through the same line of reasoning we saw in the argument from motion. Once again, we see Aristotle's influence, as Aquinas refers to this argument as the argument from efficient cause.[16]

> The second way [to prove the existence of God] is from the nature of efficient cause. In the world of sensible things we find there is an order of efficient causes. There is no case known (neither is it, indeed, possible) in which a thing is found to be the efficient cause of itself; for so it would be prior to itself, which is impossible. Now in efficient causes it is not possible to go on to infinity, because in all efficient causes following in order, the first is the cause of the intermediate cause, and the intermediate is the cause of the ultimate cause, whether the intermediate cause be several, or one only. Now to take away the cause is to take away the effect. Therefore, if there be no first cause among efficient causes, there will be no ultimate, nor any intermediate cause. But if in efficient causes it is possible to go on to infinity, there will be no first efficient cause, neither will there be an

---

16 Remember that in the *Metaphysics* Aristotle identified four kinds of causes, the material, the efficient, the formal, and the final.

> ultimate effect, nor any intermediate efficient causes; all of which is plainly false. Therefore it is necessary to admit a first efficient cause, to which everyone gives the name of God.[17]

The argument fails!

It fails for the same reasons the argument from motion fails. First, there is no clear evidence that there cannot be an infinite regress, and Aquinas's strange line about intermediate and ultimate causes cannot salvage it. Second, it fails because its conclusion is contradicted by its premise. If every effect must have a cause, then one can hardly be justified in excluding God. Finally, if not fatal to the cosmological argument, David Hume's withering attack on the cause/effect connection certainly gives it a sound pummelling.

The Argument from Necessity

> We find in nature things that are possible to be and not to be, since they are found to be generated, and to be corrupted, and consequently, it is possible for them to be and not to be. But it is impossible for them always to exist, for that which can not-be at some time is not. Therefore, if everything can not-be, then at one time there was nothing in existence. Now if this were true, even now there would be nothing in existence, because that which does not exist begins to exist only through something already existing. Therefore, if at one time nothing was in existence, it would have been impossible for anything to have begun to exist; and thus even now nothing would be in existence — which is absurd. Therefore, not all beings are merely possible, but there must exist something the existence of which is necessary. But every necessary thing either has its necessity caused by another, or not. Now it is impossible to go on to infinity in necessary things which have their necessity caused by another, as has been already proved in regard to efficient causes. Therefore, we cannot but admit the existence of some being having of itself its own necessity, and not receiving it from another, but rather causing in others their necessity. This all men speak of as God.[18]

---

[17] Ibid., pp. 25-26.

[18] Ibid., p. 26.

I have always thought that of Aquinas's five arguments, three are weak and two are, if not strong, at least stronger than the others. The argument from necessity seems to me to be one of his better arguments, though it suffers, as do the first two, from the infinite-regress problem. The argument comes down to this: if it is possible for something not to exist, then sooner or later it will not; or, tracing backward, there was a time when it did not. Take yourself, for example. Is it possible for you not to exist? If you answer that it is possible, then be assured that there was a time, in the past, when you did not exist, and that there will be a time in the future when you will not exist. Now if this is true of you, then it is true of every other human, every animal, and of every physical thing you wish to consider.

Now, let us push matters further. Beings for whom non-existence is a possibility we will call contingent beings. Those for whom non-existence is not a possibility we will call necessary beings. There must have been a time when there were no contingent beings, because their non-existence, a clear possibility, must also at some time have been a certainty.

Are you following this? I profoundly hope so, though I confess that when I was an undergraduate, I probably would have had a great deal of difficulty with this matter.

Moving right along then. . .There must have been a time when no contingent beings existed, and there was a big, blank where the universe now stands. Thus, we must face the problem, not of nothing existing, but of the obvious fact that many things do exist, and it is impossible for something to have come out of nothing. Score one for Parmenides. According to Aquinas, there is only one way to account for the obvious existence of all the contingent beings in the universe. There must be necessary being(s) not dependent upon others for existence, who do/does not share, with contingent beings, the possibility of non-existence, and who caused the existence of all other things. This being we call God.

Did you notice the clever way in which I was talking about beings/being, then quickly shifted to the singular: this "being" we call God? I hope that you did, and that a warning siren went off in your brain, just as I hope that when you read the direct quote from the *Summa Theologica* you felt a bit uncomfortable. Perhaps you said to yourself something like this: "Thomas has proved more than he wished to, because I can use this argument to show the necessity of Zeus, Poseidon, Hades, Ares, and a whole pantheon of gods and goddesses."

Too, I would like to know from Aquinas how some necessary being needs to be caused by another. It seems to me that a necessary being, by definition, has to exist, does not have the option of not existing. If I am correct, then arguing (as Thomas does) for the impossibility of infinite regress is something like carrying coals to Newcastle. A necessary being is dependent upon nothing or no one for its existence, must exist, therefore cannot not exist. Once the necessity for such a being is established — and Aquinas attempts to do that by showing that such a one must be in order to account for the existence of anything — the question of infinite regress becomes irrelevant because such a being must have always been.

I have said that I think this is one of the stronger of Aquinas's five arguments for the existence of God. I don't happen to think that he gets as much mileage out of it as he might have. Its weakness is that it actually proves too much, and rather than establishing the existence of the God of Abraham, Isaac and Jacob, as Aquinas intended, leaves the cosmos potentially populated by millions of necessary beings.

The Argument from Degree

You may have noticed that not one of the arguments we have been considering has done anything to strengthen the hand of the theists. Even if Aquinas has proved the existence of God, he has not proved that God is an omniscient, omnipotent, omnibenevolent person, directly concerned with and directly intervening in his creation. The next two arguments, if they are successful, will remedy this problem in some measure. But I will warn all students in advance: the fourth argument, the so-called argument from degree, is the most Aristotelian (or Medieval) of all, and thus falls upon modern ears in strange and discordant tones.

> Among beings there are some more and some less good, true, noble, and the like. But more and less are predicted of different things according as they resemble in their different ways something which is the maximum, as a thing is said to be hotter according as it more nearly resembles that which is hottest; so that there is something which is truest, something best, something noblest, and, consequently, something which is most being, for those things that are greatest in truth are greatest in being, as it is written in *Metaph.ii.* Now the maximum in any genus is the cause of all in that genus, as fire, which is the maximum of heat, is the cause of all hot things, as is said in the same book. Therefore there must also be something which is to all beings the cause of their being, goodness, and every other perfection; and this we call God.[19]

[19] Ibid., pp. 26-27.

This argument is based upon Aristotle's idea of a hierarchy of souls, going upward from the simplest to the most complex, from the vegetative to the rational. Of all five, this appears to be Aquinas's least plausible argument for the existence of God; and yet it may be his most critical if he intends to prove the God of theism. Because Aristotle said something, it does not always follow that this is true.[20] I for one would be much more comfortable with Aquinas's fourth proof if he had done something nearer to what Descartes did in his ontological argument. In fact, it seems as if this is the direction he is going, but his commitment to rational, empirical argument will not let him. Therefore we are left to take, on faith so far as I can tell, that the maximum of any genus as the cause of everything else in the genus.

How are we to understand cause within this context? Suppose Aquinas had used the word defines instead of the more Aristotelian cause —the maximum of any genus defines everything else in the genus? Would this clear things up? Perhaps, perhaps not, but certainly it would give a different ontological[21] flavor to the fourth argument. The most that I could say, were I called upon to frame a case from degree, is that we have a concept of the perfect thing in any given genus, and that the concept must arise from something other than pure, empirical experience. But this, of course, is Cartesian and not Thomistic.

The Argument from Design

The argument from design is also called the teleological argument, and is probably the most popular and durable of all the arguments for the existence of God. This argument is implicit in the work of the Apostle Paul, as is the cosmological argument, and it has shown up across the years in theology and science, as well as philosophy. To understand it, let us begin by defining the word teleology. As we have seen when looking at the metaphysics of Aristotle, its root, *teleos*, suggests a goal, an end, or a purpose. If purpose can be seen in the universe, this would seem to imply the existence of intelligence standing behind and guiding it, and a certain

---

20 Aquinas appears to be referring to that part of Book II of the *Metaphysics* in which Aristotle opines that in every case the first principles of things must necessarily be true above everything else.

21 Remember, from Chapter 1, that ontology is the study of being. What I am suggesting by using the word here is that if we change "cause" to "define" we might well prove less than what Aquinas intends. To define something is not necessarily to bring it into being.

benevolence, since the sustenance of life is a part of the implied design. In the words of Aquinas:

> We see that things which lack knowledge, such as natural bodies, act for an end, and this is evident from their acting always, or nearly always, in the same way, so as to obtain the best result. Hence it is plain that they achieve their end, not fortuitously, but designedly. Now whatever lacks knowledge cannot move towards an end, unless it be directed by some being endowed with knowledge and intelligence; as the arrow is directed by the archer. Therefore some intelligent being exists by whom all natural things are directed to their end; and this being we call God.[22]

While this may be one of the oldest and best known statements of the teleological argument, it is far from the most cogent. In 1802 William Paley, a theologian, published a book called *Natural Theology,* in which he gave a more modern version, a version which no less a light than Charles Darwin greatly admired.

> In crossing a heath, suppose I pitched my foot against a *stone*, and were asked how the stone came to be there. I might possibly answer, that for anything I knew to the contrary, it had lain there for ever: nor would it perhaps be very easy to show the absurdity of this answer. But suppose I had found a *watch* upon the ground, and it should be inquired how the watch happened to be in that place; I should hardly think of the answer which I had before given, that for anything I knew the watch might have always been there. Yet why should not this answer serve for the watch as well as for the stone? Why is it not as admissible in the second case as in the first? For this reason, and for no other, viz. that when we come to inspect the watch, we perceive (what we could not discover in the stone) that its several parts are framed and put together for a purpose, e.g., that they are so formed and adjusted as to produce motion, and that motion so regulated as to point out the hour of the day; that if the different parts had been differently shaped from what they are, of a different size from what they are, or placed after any other manner, or in any other

---

[22] Ibid., p. 27.

> order, than that in which they are placed, either no motion at all would have been carried on in the machine, or none which would have answered the use that is now served by it. . .This mechanism being observed. . .the inference, we think, is inevitable, that the watch must have had a maker; that there must have existed, at some time, and at some place or other, an artificer or artificers, who formed it for the purpose which we find it actually to answer; who comprehended its construction and designed its use. . .
>
> [E]very indication of contrivance, every manifestation of design, which existed in the watch, exists in the works of nature; with the difference, on the side of nature, of being greater and more, and that in a degree which exceeds all computation. I mean, that the contrivances of nature surpass the contrivances of art, in the complexity, subtlety, and curiosity, of the mechanism; and still more, if possible, do they go beyond them in number and variety; yet, in a multitude of cases, are not less evidently mechanical, not less evidently contrivances, not less evidently accommodated to their end, or suited to their office, than are the most perfect productions of human ingenuity. . .
>
> Every observation which was made [above] concerning the watch, may be repeated with strict propriety concerning the eye, concerning animals, concerning plants, concerning, indeed, all the organized parts of the works of nature. . .
>
> Were there no example in the world of contrivance, except that of the *eye*, it would be alone sufficient to support the conclusion which we draw from it, as to the necessity of an intelligent Creator. . .If there were but one watch in the world, it would not be less certain that it had a maker. . .So it is with the evidences of a Divine Agency.[23]

I have quoted this at some length to give the full force of Paley's argument. Here, in the fifth and final of Aquinas's arguments for the existence of God, we have another that I find, if not persuasive, at least potent. I have no doubt that the student has encountered many variations of the teleological argument, and has even perhaps framed some variation of it

---

[23] Paley, William, *Natural Theology*, in *The Works of William Paley*, Philadelphia: Crissy & Markley, 1857, pp. 387-485.

on his or her own. If the earth were a little further from the sun we would all freeze to death. If it were a little closer we would all burn up. If the ozone layer, thin as it is, were not in place we would be destroyed by cosmic rays. There is a very thin envelope of atmosphere which will support life — a few miles down in the ocean, a few miles up into space — and outside of this no life is possible.

Move from the cosmos to the animal world, to the way in which the eye (as Paley says) is constructed, to the way in which bees gather pollen and produce honey. Isn't purpose written into the universe all around us, and doesn't this in fact demonstrate a purposeful creator?

Well, say the critics, not necessarily. In his famous *Dialogues Concerning Natural Religion*, David Hume, as we might suspect, makes it clear that he for one is not convinced by the teleological argument. Cleanthes states his version of the teleological argument as follows:

> Look round the world, contemplate the whole and every part of it: you will find it to be nothing but one great machine, subdivided into an infinite number of lesser machines, which again admit of subdivisions to a degree beyond what human senses and faculties can trace and explain. . .The curious adapting of means to ends, throughout all nature, resembles exactly, though it much exceeds, the productions of human contrivance — of human design, thought, wisdom, and intelligence. Since therefore the effects resemble each other, we are led to infer, by all the rules of analogy, that the causes also resemble, and that the Author of nature is somewhat similar to the mind of man, though possessed of much larger faculties, proportioned to the grandeur of the work which he has executed. By this argument *a posteriori*, and by this argument alone, do we prove at once the existence of a Deity and his similarity to human mind and intelligence.[24]

But Philo (read David Hume) will have none of it.

> If we see a house, Cleanthes, we conclude, with the greatest certainty, that it had an architect or builder because this is precisely that species of effect which we have experienced to proceed from that species of cause.

---

[24] **Hume, David, *Dialogues Concerning Natural Religion*, ed. Henry D. Aiken, New York: Hafner Press, 1977, p. 17**

> But surely you will not affirm that the universe bears such a resemblance to a house that we can with the same certainty infer a similar cause, or that the analogy is here entire and perfect. The dissimilitude is so striking that the utmost you can here pretend to is a guess, a conjecture, a presumption concerning a similar cause; and how that pretension will be received in the world, I leave you to consider.[25]

Hume is correct in characterizing the teleological argument as an argument from **analogy**. An analogical argument is one in which one attempts to clarify something unknown by comparing it to something known. In this case, the universe is compared to a machine, and the inference is taken that because a machine has a designer so must the universe. In the Paley argument, the analogy is with a watch. The weakness of any analogical argument is in the analogy itself, for there is nothing that can be compared to something else with a perfect, one-for-one correspondence. The more completely two things may be compared, the better we may draw inferences about the one we do not know from looking at the one we do. In the dialogue above, Philo tells Cleanthes that his analogy is weak, therefore his conclusions are weak. There is too much dissimilarity between a human-made machine and the world around us for any of us to leap to the conclusion that because the one bespeaks intelligent design so must the other as well.

An analogical argument is an argument by comparison. One argues from the thing that is known to clarify the thing that is not known by showing that the one is essentially like the other.

Another way of looking at the apparent design in creation is to see it in an evolutionary light. For example, the ozone layer has nothing to do with protecting life, according to critics of the teleological argument; rather, such life as exists on the earth is that which has evolved and fitted itself to the existent conditions. This explanation, however, begs the question as much as do any of the arguments of the theists. Clearly, the very thing we are seeking to discover is how the earth and the living things on it got here, and to say that life as we know it is a result of an evolutionary process, therefore the teleological argument must be false, is as good an example of *petitio principii*[26] as one could hope for.

---

[25] Ibid., p. 18.

[26] *Petitio principii* is just a fancy Latin term for begging the question, assuming as a premise in an argument something that one cannot know unless the very thing one is seeking to prove is in fact already known to be true.

A Brief Interlude

Perhaps we should stop at this point, catch our breath, and review a bit. We have looked at a number of the very well-known arguments for God's existence, including the deductive, ontological arguments of Anselm, Descartes, and Spinoza, and the five inductive arguments of Thomas Aquinas. How do you feel? Have any of these theistic philosophers made the case for God? And, perhaps just as important, have they made the case for the God of theism?

The accepted wisdom among philosophers is that no one has yet constructed a conclusive argument for God's existence, though many have found Aquinas and others persuasive. I suppose I ought to have the fortitude to get on record with a qualified opinion. I have already said that of Aquinas's arguments, I find the arguments from necessity and design the most potent. If one could show that an infinite regress is in fact impossible, then the argument from motion and the cosmological argument would both be strengthened considerably, though it would still be true that the major premise of each argument is contradicted by the conclusion. Contradiction or not, if we are dealing with a finite amount of time and space, the necessity to postulate an unmoved mover and an uncaused cause seems unavoidable.

Does any of this, however, get us any closer to the God of Abraham, Isaac and Jacob, in other words to the God of the theists? Unfortunately, it does not. And there are many who say the impersonal God of the deists (As in: "May the force be with you.") amounts to no God at all.

My guess is that if anyone ever solves the problem of God to the satisfaction of all, or even most, the solution will turn out to be some variation of the ontological argument. I'll show you why later, when we get to Immanuel Kant and how he dealt with the problem of God.

Unresolved Issues

There are a number of issues, unresolved the last time I checked, which have bedeviled philosophers over the centuries when the question of God has come up. Two of these are major enough to engage our interest, they are the problem of evil and the more complex problem of the nature of God. How can a being with the attributes God must have to meet theistic qualifications for deity interact with finite, material, time-bound creatures such as us.

First, the problem of evil.

You will recall that we talked about this in the first section when we were looking at the philosophy of Augustine. But there is no compelling reason why we can't look at it again, in the light of metaphysics and one of our major metaphysical questions. The Epicureans were some of the first to raise the issue of evil as a problem that reaches up to the heavens and threatens the position of God (or the gods, as Epicurus saw it). But even the Apostle Paul, who had some familiarity with the Epicureans, understood the nature of the problem and made an attempt to deal with it. Let us lay it out in its simplest form.

1. There appears to be evil in the world.

2. God is presented as being all powerful, all knowing and all good.

3. Whence, therefore, comes this evil?

If you do not immediately see the problem presented by these three propositions, then you are either mentally slow, or you are deliberately ducking the issue. Now there are a variety of ways of ducking the issue, but the main one is by taking the first proposition, placing emphasis on the word "appears," and saying that there is not actually evil but only the appearance of evil. In fact, everything is good, but we just do not have the total picture. Once the picture is complete — presumably at some future date in eternity — we will see that everything was good and all was for the best. This is basically the line taken by Leibniz in his Theodicy:

> [E]vil, or the mixture of goods and evils wherein the evil prevails happens only by concomitance, because it is connected with greater goods that are outside this mixture.[27]

Leibniz holds that, given infinity from which to choose, this must be the best of all possible worlds. But why must it be? Because God made it, and all agree that God is omnibenevolent, therefore whatever God has made must be the best.

This is also the line of Aloysha Karamazov, and, to some extent, of Paul, who does not say exactly that everything is good, but does say that all things work together for good.[28] This entire line, from Paul, through

---

27 Leibniz, G.W., *Theodicy*, Ontario: J.W. Dent & Sons, 1966, p. 76.

28 But only for those who are the called of God. Paul makes this statement in Romans, chapter 8.

Leibniz, to Dostoyevski, begs the question rather than answering it.

Then, of course, there is a minor problem of semantic ambiguity. What is meant by the word "evil"? A tornado that wipes out my home is not the same sort of evil as a Hitler who attempts to wipe out an entire generation of people. But if one considers that an all-powerful God could prevent either, then the difference becomes, for the purposes of our discussion, negligible.

Assuming that we can agree that there is evil in the world, both natural and moral, and that this evil is hurtful to innocent people, and assuming that God is aware of this and is able to do something about it, the natural question is, why doesn't he? This is the very essence of the problem of evil. One of my associates has said that the only way to solve the problem is to give up one of the "O's". If he is correct, then we must sacrifice either God's omniscience, his omnipotence, or his omnibenevolence in order to explain the presence of evil in the world. The Epicureans did just this, holding that the gods were not involved in the affairs of men, didn't know what men were doing, and didn't care. This was also David Hume's response in *Dialogues Concerning Natural Religion.* There, he has Philo saying:

> It must, I think, be allowed that, if a very limited intelligence whom we shall suppose utterly unacquainted with the universe were assured that it were the production of a very good, wise, and powerful being, however finite, he would, from his conjectures, form beforehand a different notion of it from what we find it to be by experience; nor would he ever imagine, merely from these attributes of the cause of which he is informed, that the effect could be so full of vice and misery and disorder, as it appears in this life. Supposing now that this person were brought into the world, still assured that it was the workmanship of such a sublime and benevolent being, he might, perhaps, be surprised at the disappointment, but would never retract his former belief if founded on any very solid argument, since such a limited intelligence must be sensible of his own blindness and ignorance, and must allow that there may be many solutions of those phenomena which will forever escape his comprehension. But supposing, which is the real case with regard to man, that this creature is not antecedently convinced of a supreme intelligence, benevolent, and powerful, but is left to gather such a belief from the appearances of things — this entirely alters the case, nor will he ever find any reason for such a conclusion. He may be fully convinced of the narrow limits of his

> understanding, but this will not help him in forming an inference concerning the goodness of superior powers, since he must form that inference from what he knows, not from what he is ignorant of. The more you exaggerate his weakness and ignorance, the more diffident you render him, and give him the greater suspicion that such subjects are beyond the reach of his faculties. You are obliged, therefore, to reason with him merely from the known phenomena, and to drop every arbitrary supposition or conjecture.[29]

In other words, what one gets out of the examination of the world depends upon what one goes in looking for. If one begins with the supposition that all is the work of a benevolent God, then all of the evil is explained in a such a way as to leave that presupposition intact. But if one begins with no presuppositions, then there is nothing in the world to lead one to such a belief.

Attempts to deal with the problem of evil have been going on since long before the birth of Christ. One of the best known of these, found in the Old Testament, is the book of Job, a favorite of philosophers because it raises the question of why bad things happen to good people. Job is presented at the outset of the story as the most righteous man on earth, a God-fearing man who avoids evil. Then we get a curious scene in heaven in which God and Satan make a sort of bet. Satan's challenge: why shouldn't Job be righteous when he has everything he could wish for and the protection of God as well; but quit protecting Job and let me at him and I'll make him curse you to your face. God accedes to these terms, and off goes Satan to ruin Job's life by taking away everything he has (except a nagging wife), and smiting him with boils from the crown of his head to the sole of his foot. Throughout the book Job continues to seek the answer to the simple question, why? In fact, he never exactly knows. God answers him at the end of the book, but the answer is, in so many words, that there are mysteries in life that go beyond the understanding of mere mortals. Job is satisfied with this. Most philosophers are not.

The most-widely used explanation for evil is that humans are its cause, not God. God gave humans freedom of will because he desired

---

[29] Hume, David, *Dialogues Concerning Natural Religion*, New York: Hafner Press, 1977, pp. 71-72.

creatures who could relate to him as something other than automatons. Give any creature absolute freedom, and you are giving them the right to do with this gift what they will, including using it for bad purposes. This is precisely what has happened. This argument falls prey, however, to another one of the O's, God's omniscience. If God knows everything, then he certainly knew what was going to happen long before he ever created humans and gave them the gift of free will. So if he created knowing what the results would be, doesn't that make God responsible for the evil? There seems to be no way out of this difficulty unless, as my colleague has said, we give up one of the O's.

Suppose instead of apologizing for the existence of evil we embrace it as a necessary thing, one without which we could not know good, and without which a world such as ours would be impossible. Imagine a world, if you can, in which there is no evil, nothing bad, no problems of any type. In such a world there would also be no such thing as good, for good would have lost its meaning. There would be no real joy, for joy could not be understood if every moment were lived without the possibility of sadness. You would have no idea when you were feeling fit, for the possibility of sickness would be non-existent. Clearly, such a world would be totally alien from the world we know, and it might not be at all worth living in. This is the position taken by John Hick in *Philosophy of Religion.* It is not a new argument; but Hick invigorates it with a freshness that makes it compelling and up to date.

The problem of evil and the existence of a good, all-powerful God has no solution. Faith either takes over or it does not. If it does, the problem melts away. If it does not, the problem will always be there.

Finally, there is the problem of the nature of God. I will not deal with this at length, but only say that the question of how God can be both inside and outside of time, both infinite and finite, both qualitatively different from creatures and at the same time interact with them, has caused philosophers and theologians a few sleepless nights. Attempts to deal with this problem are at the roots of the gnostic heresy of the first century, and led to the long war between Athanasius and Arius, and their followers. If you are an orthodox Jew or a Moslem you have not thereby escaped the problem. As long as you hold that God interacts with humans, this problem is with you.

Perhaps the only solution is atheism. But is this an acceptable solution?

I will close out this chapter by making reference to Blaise Pascal, a French philosopher and mathematician of the seventeenth century. Pascal was interested in probability theory, and he brought this to bear on the problem of God. He knew that there was no clear proof for the existence of God, so he came up with his by now well-known wager. "Let us weight the gain and loss in betting that God exists: if you win, you win everything; if you lose, you lose nothing. You should unhesitatingly bet that he exists." I will leave you to think about this.

Chapter 7
Some Other Metaphysical Questions

Open pawn to white king four,
give king's bishop open door.

Hold your queen and do not use her
Early, or you'll surely lose her.

Castle quickly to the right
Once you've moved the white king's knight.

At all costs, control the center,
If you plan to wind up winner.

Guard this truth without debate:
Two knights can't deliver mate.

Swapping pieces? Have no doubt,
Two rooks give you end-game clout.

If you're playing Aljechin,
Close all files, and guard your queen.

If you lose, don't mourn the loss.
That, as Chinese say, is joss.

Set the board up, play once more.
Open pawn to white king four.

Cyclical and pointless:
Life is like a game of chess.

In Chapter 6 we considered what is perhaps the major metaphysical question with which philosophers over the years have dealt: is there a God? A second question flows from this one: if yes, what is his nature? But while these are important metaphysical questions, they are not the only ones. In this chapter we shall examine some of the others, and I think you will agree that they are all important, even critical, to the human enterprise, for they go to the very heart of what it is to be human.

1. Am I free or determined?
2. Do I have a mind or only a brain?
3. Do I have an essence that makes me different from other living creatures, or am I merely a thing, an aggregation of matter, not qualitatively different from an earthworm or a stone?

In the last chapter we saw how philosophers over the years have struggled to prove the existence of an intelligent force above and beyond humans. In this chapter we shall be looking at the human and asking, "What manner of creature is this?" Pursuing the answers to this question, the honest seeker may find himself or herself tangled in loose ends and fascinating riddles.

Tin Soldiers and Nixon Coming

In the spring of 1970 I was at Midwestern University in Wichita Falls, Texas. One fine morning we awoke to the news that the day before, on the campus of Kent State University, four students had been shot dead by members of the Ohio State National Guard. The Guard had been called out to quell rioting that had begun the night before when a mob of students had burned the ROTC building on campus, then had gone into town and destroyed some property there. All of this is difficult, no doubt, for students today to imagine, but it grew out of the anger then raging across the land because of American involvement in Vietnam. The Guard, armed with rifles and tear gas, went onto the campus, the students lined up shouting insults at them, the Guard fired, down went four students.

About a week later one of my friends, a psychology teacher, gave a party at her home. The place was wall to wall with students and teachers, and we were all angry, still smarting from the news of Kent State. Our hostess was a hardcore follower of B.F. Skinner, the **behaviorist**, and she and I had an ongoing, if civil, disagreement about human behavior. On this particular evening she was as angry as anyone and stated that the commanding officer and the men who fired the shots ought to all be locked up.[1] I stepped in to complicate matters by telling her that if she actually

Behaviorism is a school of psychology which says that the proper area of psychological study is behavior, and not inner "states of mind."

---

1 I ought to emphasize, in the interest of fairness to all parties, that not all of us see the Kent State incident today the way we did then. We did not know everything that had led to the shootings. We simply knew that students were protesting against the War, and that they had been gunned down.

believed what she was teaching at the university, she could not possibly hold any of these men accountable for their actions. The disagreement continued late into the night. She held that the men were certainly accountable. I insisted, and still insist, that if B.F. Skinner and J.B. Watson were correct, not one of the Guardsmen who fired the shots that day can be held accountable for his actions, for they are all determined by events outside their control, are not free moral agents, and are simply not responsible.

Free or not Free

Think back to our discussion about God and how the great medieval philosopher Thomas Aquinas sought to prove his existence. You will recall, I trust, that the first two of his five arguments were the argument from motion and the cosmological argument. Both arguments ran into problems, one of which was that the conclusions were contradicted by the premises. If I begin with the assertion that everything must have a cause or that everything that is in motion must have been set in motion by another, then it becomes somewhat problematic if I reach a conclusion which says that there is an uncaused cause and an unmoved mover.

The whole idea of something being self-generating is, in fact, troubling. Think about it in light of Aquinas's argument from motion and his cosmological argument. Do you know of anything in the universe to which this would apply? Did the house you live in, for example, build itself, or did the car you drove to school suddenly appear on your driveway with a note attached saying, "Here I am, courtesy of myself?" You might say that these are not fair examples, for in both cases we are talking about inanimate matter which cannot possibly move itself or make choices. Very well, let's talk about living creatures.

Which living creature, the human included, produced itself? And remember, Aquinas's arguments are based upon your answering that there are none. You might say that, of course, there are none, but that this does not get us to the heart of the matter. In deciding whether humans are free or determined, you would probably say, we ought not to be asking how we as physical creatures came to be, but if the decisions we reach are those we came to on our own and for which we are thus responsible. Isn't this, after all, what freedom of the will means?

You are both right and wrong. Or rather, you may be right, but an as-yet-unproven assumption lies behind your use of the word "will." The assumption is that the thing we call will is itself an immaterial entity not subject to the law of cause and effect, and that it springs from an immaterial mind, for only from such a mind can free decisions be generated. Suppose that there is no such thing as mind, that there is only brain, a purely physical thing functioning in a purely physical way, with rigidly predictable results. Can there be room in such a material mass for such a thing as your will? Many scientists, and many philosophers, do not think so, and say that the sooner we get over such medieval notions the better off we all will be. One of the scientists who felt this way was the late B.F. Skinner, the apostle of behaviorism, whom my teacher friend in the Kent State controversy followed so faithfully. This gets us back to the shootings and the question we were arguing that night many years ago. Were the guardsmen who shot the students responsible for their actions? Were the students who burned the ROTC building and trashed the town responsible for theirs? Am I, as I sit writing this sentence, doing so of my own free will, or is it because events over which I had no control conspired to lead me step by step to this time and place?

Skinner said on an occasion that the hypothesis that man is *not* free is essential to the application of scientific method to the study of human behavior. He said this because the scientific method of inquiry is predicated upon the assumption that there are inviolable laws governing the universe, and that all things in the universe obey these laws. If this is not the case, if some things do not obey these laws, then the inductive method of reasoning so foundational to scientific examination becomes useless in attempting to examine these things.

Human behavior is one of the things that has traditionally been thought to spring from the human mind, store house of the will, and immaterial unmoved mover. But if this is so, if we exempt humans, in part or in whole, from obedience to natural laws, then to that extent Skinner was correct, and we cannot study them scientifically.

But Skinner and others believe there is no good reason why we should exempt humans. They are no different from any other animal, or from any other physical thing. They obey the irresistible law of cause and effect in every aspect of their being. As John B. Watson, founder of behaviorism, put it: "A human being is simply an assembled organic machine ready to run."

Unless you have taken a course in psychology and have encountered Skinner and the behaviorists, you probably have no idea what all this means. Further, you are probably used to the idea of yourself as a free moral agent. If you were asked whether you came to school today as a result of a decision you made, you would doubtless say that you did. You might easily have stayed at home and slept in, but you chose to.get up, chose to get dressed, and moment by moment moved in this direction. At any of dozens of different times you might have turned in another direction of your own free will; but you did not, and here you are.

Yes, Dr. Skinner would say, were he alive to say it, yes, it certainly seems this way to you, but it is pure illusion. You came to class today because you have been conditioned to be here. Everything in your past has conspired to lead you to this place and time. The reason you think you have free will is because we cannot be sure of all the events controlling your behavior. But the one thing we can be sure of is that you are just as rigidly controlled, just as surely determined, as any other physical thing in the universe. To assume that you are not would be to insult our collective common sense by saying that one thing in the universe (the human mind, or will, or spirit, call it what you wish), does not obey known physical laws because. . .well, just because.

This, however, lands us in a terrible predicament. For if we allow no more freedom to human will than we do to the billiard balls rebounding off the cushion of the billiard table, then there is no way we can logically hold anyone accountable for his or her actions. You blow up buildings, rape and murder, pillage and plunder, and you are both legally and ethically innocent of any wrong doing because you didn't choose to do any of it. You were simply reacting to whatever forces were moving on you at the time.

We are faced here with a metaphysical question for which we dearly need an answer. As C.A. Campbell has said:

> [T]he kind of freedom in question is the freedom which is commonly recognised to be in some sense a precondition of moral responsibility. Clearly, it is on account of this integral connection with moral responsibility that such exceptional importance has always been felt to attach to the Free Will problem.[2]

Free Will and the Greeks

The Greeks were well aware of the problem. In fact, one of their most famous authors, Sophokles, wrote one of his most famous tragedies to dramatize, among other things, the clash of free will and fate in the person of Oedipus, King of Thebes. Aristotle, in his *Poetics*, uses this play as one of his main examples.

---

2 Campbell, C.A., *On Selfhood and Godhood*, New York: Macmillan, 1957.

The story, familiar no doubt to all college students, is of a boy child, born to the king and queen of Thebes, and born under a curse. A prophecy, given at his birth, foretells that he will grow up to murder his father and marry his mother. His father, to thwart the prophet, takes the infant, drives a wooden pin through his heels, and leaves him naked on a mountain side to die. But death by exposure is not in the child's future. He is found by a shepherd, who takes him to Corinth, where he is named Oedipus (i.e. Swollen Foot), and raised by the king and queen of Corinth as their own. Thus he grows up thinking that he is the actual son of Polybos and Merope.

Meanwhile, back in Thebes, Laios and Iocaste, Oedipus's true parents, think they have escaped their prophesied fate. In fact, they are moving toward it moment by moment. When he reaches manhood, Oedipus hears of the thing told of him by the oracle, and he leaves Corinth so as not to fulfill it. Remember, he thinks that the king and queen of Corinth are his parents. Off he goes, running straight to (where else?) Thebes, where he proceeds to do precisely what the oracle said he would. After Oedipus has married his mother and settled down to a life as the king of Thebes, a plague strikes the town because of a great, unpunished sin.

It is time for Oedipus to learn the truth. He goes looking for the man who has killed the king and brought this misery upon the city of Thebes, only to find that it is himself. He comes to the end, ruined and cast out, blinded by his own hand, doomed to wander the roads of Greece as a beggar.

> Men of Thebes: look upon Oedipus. This is the king who solved the famous riddle and towered up, most powerful of men. No mortal eyes but looked on him with envy. Yet in the end ruin swept over him. Let every man in mankind's frailty consider his last day; and let none presume on his good fortune until he find life, at his death, a memory without pain.

There is a lesson in this, as there always is in great literature, but it is not an easy one to learn. It begins with a question, one which plays well in the metaphysical discussion we are having. To what extent can Oedipus be considered a free man? In trying to escape his fate, he ran directly into it.[3] Exercising what he thought was freedom, he was actually spiraling

---

3 The same story is told in a more modern form by John O'Hara in *Appointment in Samara.*

downward in ever tightening circles to the pit. When looked at in one way, Oedipus has no freedom at all. He is fated to live out the prophecy of the oracle, and his attempts to avoid it only drive him toward its ultimate fulfillment. But when looked at in another way, Oedipus is as free as any man could ever want to be, and it is his freedom and the way in which he uses it that marks him as one of the most tragic, and at the same time one of the most noble, of the Greeks.

To demonstrate this to yourself, and to see how it applies directly to you, begin by asking yourself to what extent much of your life was determined for you by circumstances outside your control. Did you choose, for example, where you would be born, to whom you would be born, what race or sex you would be, whether you would be rich or poor? Further, did you choose what kind of parents you would have? Perhaps you have the very best of parents, or perhaps your parents are abusive and neglectful. Either way, you did not choose this and have had no control over it.

How much of your life do you actually control. The answer, of course, is that you control very little. You have virtually no control over other people with whom you work or go to school. In fact, when looked at in this way, it is difficult to see that any of us is any freer than was Oedipus. It seems that much of our life was determined for us before our births and that there is little we can do to alter it.

On the other hand, Oedipus was free to do at least one thing, and this may have been the most important thing of all. He was free to seek the truth about himself and to find it, and having found it he was free to choose how he would react to his new-found knowledge. No one told him to put out his eyes. That was his choice.

In the story of Oedipus we have perhaps the best illustration of the Greek attitude toward freedom of the will. There was clearly a dark side to the Greek character, one which looks at humans as something like pawns of dark, irrational forces. But there was the other side of the Greek character as well, one that was optimistic, daring, sure of the ability to seek the truth and find it. This is almost like the two sides of Greek nature emphasized by Friedrich Nietzsche in *The Birth of Tragedy*. There is the dark and uncontrollable side represented by Dionysus, and the controlled, rational side represented by Apollo. According to Nietzsche, the Greeks owed their magnificent Golden Age, with its creativity and high civilization, to the balancing of both these forces. It was only when they were out of balance, with the one side gaining ascendancy over the other, that human kind became threatened with ruin.

One might argue that in the case of Oedipus, the forces of light and darkness got out of balance, with the dark, Dionysian force taking control and submerging the rational, restraining force of Apollos.

> Oedipus, murderer of his father, husband of his mother, solver of the riddle of the Sphinx! What is the significance of the mysterious triad of these deeds of destiny? . . With the riddle-solving and mother-marrying Oedipus in mind, we must immediately interpret this to the effect that wherever by some prophetic and magical power the boundary of the present and future, the inflexible law of individuation and, in general, the intrinsic spell of nature, are broken, an extraordinary counter-naturalness. . .must have preceded as a cause. . .[I]t seems as if the myth were trying to whisper into our ears the fact that wisdom, especially Dionysian wisdom, is an unnatural abomination; that whoever, through his own knowledge, plunges nature into an abyss of annihilation, must also expect to experience the dissolution of nature in himself.[4]

So what destroyed Oedipus? Was it his fate? Or was it himself trying to understand, and even to circumvent, his fate? Perhaps the message is that we are not free, can never be free, and that any attempt to achieve freedom is doomed to failure. But isn't the attempt to be free itself the free act of a free and undetermined human?

There is no doubt about what Aristotle thought. In Book III of the famous *Nicomachean Ethics* he talks about voluntary and involuntary[5] actions at length, and he makes it clear in Part 2 of Book III that moral choice must be a voluntary action.

> It is of course generally recognized that actions done under constraint or due to ignorance are involuntary. An act is done under constraint when the initiative or source of motion comes from without. It is the kind of action in which the agent or the person acted upon contributes nothing. . .[T]he agent acts voluntarily [when] the

---

[4] Nietzsche, Friedrich, *The Birth of Tragedy* in *The Philosophy of Nietzsche*, New York: Modern Library, 1927, p. 995.

[5] The Greek word translated voluntary is *hekousion*. Its opposite, involuntary, is *akousion*. These are very difficult words to translate into English. Voluntary and non-voluntary will have to do.

> initiative in moving the parts of the body which act as instruments rests with the agent himself; and where the source of motion is within oneself, it is in one's power to act or not to act.[6]

There is no clear solution to the problem of the free will in any of this, for while Aristotle seems to assume the power of any individual to act freely, the assumption runs into the problem of determinism in the person of Oedipus, whom we may clearly see as being a great deal like ourselves.[7] None of us has to operate under the dark cloud of patricide and incest, but our environment and circumstances have dealt us our own cards which we must play, and if B.F. Skinner and others are correct, natural law will determine how we will play them.

In Part 2 of Book III of the *Nicomachean Ethics*, Aristotle has another go at it, this time taking up the subject of choice.[8]

> After this definition of voluntary and involuntary actions, our next task is to discuss choice. For choice seems to be very closely related to virtue and to be a more reliable criterion for judging character than actions are. Choice clearly seems to be something voluntary, but it is not the same as voluntariness; voluntariness is a wider term.[9]

The narrower, "choice," equates to something that is freely chosen after careful thought and consideration, as opposed to other voluntary actions, which may be a result of passion or emotion. To act on passion or emotion would nevertheless be, for Aristotle, voluntary, because these are things that come from within. Only those things that come from without

---

[6] **Aristotle, *The Nicomachean Ethics*, Book III, Indianapolis: Bobbs-Merrill Co., 1962, pp. 52-53.**

[7] **In fact, if he is not like all of us, a sort of Greek "Everyman," then according to Aristotle he cannot be a truly tragic figure. His argument for the tragic as the universal is found in the *Poetics*.**

[8] **Greek: *proairesis*, literally a choosing ahead, and a key to understanding Aristotle on the subject of morals. Simply put, without *proairesis* there can be no true morals.**

[9] **Ibid., p. 58.**

and dictate our actions can be said to result in involuntary actions. Thus, one's actions might be determined by outside events, or they might be free. But even the free action cannot be called choice unless it is the result of rational thought.

How utterly Aristotelian! The pinnacle of human behavior is reached when one is freely using one's intellect. At this point the human soul is truly engaged, whereas being driven by emotion and passion is somehow subhuman, worthy of animals.[10] As it applies to Oedipus, he is never more human than when he shows his determination to know the truth even when his wife/mother is urging him to forget the whole thing.

If Oedipus is truly a universal as Aristotle says he is, and as he must be if he is to arouse within us the fear and pity that leads to catharsis, what is the Greek view of the human that we are to take away from all this? The Greeks clearly saw the problem of freedom of the will versus determinism (or fate), and their solution, at least the one proffered by Aristotle, was that the only freedom humans have is to engage their highest soul, the rational, in making choices. Notice, however, the assumption behind this solution — that the soul, the rational part of the human, is somehow separate from the physical, fate-driven, passion-hounded part. This is not an assumption that twentieth century behaviorists are willing to grant.

Free Will and the Christians

The Christians have a book. They got part of it from the Jews who went before them, and they produced part of it themselves. They agree that this book, the Bible (Greek: *ta biblia*, the books), is God-breathed and therefore true. But time and again, throughout the Bible, we see a clashing of free will and fate, with humans doing no more than what God said they would do, and then God holding them responsible and visiting the direst of consequences upon them. Two examples will suffice. In the Old Testament Book of Exodus, when the Children of Israel were being held in slavery by Pharaoh, Moses and his brother Aaron went in to Pharaoh repeatedly and said, "Thus saith the Lord, 'Let my people go, that they may serve me.'" But Pharaoh would not let the people go because, oddly enough, God hardened his (Pharaoh's) heart.

In the New Testament we have the sad and sordid story of the most

---

10 **To understand why this is so, go back and review what we studied about Aristotle and his hierarchy of souls.**

notorious of all sinners, the man who betrayed Jesus, Judas Iscariot. But the Bible says that Jesus knew who would betray him, and that he foretold it. Now, once Jesus had said to Judas, "You are the one who will betray me," what choice did Judas have in the matter? Could he go against God in the flesh, of whom it was said that he could not lie?

There would be no particular problem with either Pharaoh or Judas if neither were held morally accountable for his actions; but the Bible records that both were, and here we go again. How can anyone be rightly held accountable for his or her actions if he or she has no choice in the matter? We see once again the close connection between freedom of the will and morality. The Apostle Paul, keenly aware of this implied difficulty, takes up the case of Pharaoh in chapter 9 of the letter to the Romans.

> For he saith to Moses, "I will have mercy on whom I will have mercy and I will have compassion on whom I will have compassion." So then it is not of him that willeth, nor of him that runneth, but of God that sheweth mercy. For the scripture saith unto Pharaoh, "Even for this same purpose have I raised thee up, that I might shew my power in thee, and that my name might be declared throughout all the earth." Therefore hath he mercy on whom he will have mercy, and whom he will he hardeneth.
>
> Thou wilt say then unto me, "Why doth he yet find fault? For who hath resisted his will?" Nay but, O man, who art thou that repliest against God? Shall the thing formed say to him that formed it, "Why hast thou made me thus?" Hath not the potter power over the clay, of the same lump to make one vessel unto honour, and another unto dishonour? (vss. 15-21).

This line may be acceptable to believers, but the general philosophical population is apt to find it puzzling to say the least. It seems as if the only response possible to the individual who says that Pharaoh has been found guilty of what someone else (in this case, God) did is, "Shutup."

But the Christians have more of a problem with free will than how one can be held morally accountable with it. As we saw in the last chapter, there is another problem that threatens to undermine the very nature of God as all-wise, all-knowing, and all-good. It is the problem of evil. The most popular solution to this problem, the one that has been offered by more Christians under more circumstances than any other, is what we might call the freewill solution. Evil is not in the world because God wills it, but because he created humans with free will and they, utilizing this freedom, have brought in the evil. Humans, not God, are responsible. Obviously, however, if there is no such thing as free will, this solution becomes, as the saying goes, not worth the reams of paper it has been inscribed on, or the theological ink with which it has been written. Christians have good reason to show that freedom of the will is fact, not fancy.

But matters are even more complicated by the foreknowledge of God, as seen in the case of Judas Iscariot. If God already knows all that will happen, are we not, in fact, simply moving in his thought waves, and can we in any sense be free?

There are basically two schools of thought among Christians on the question of freedom of the will. One is associated with John Calvin and Martin Luther, and emphasizes the sovereignty of God and the inability of humans to choose. The other, taking its name from Arminius, makes of humans totally free moral agents, responsible for their choices and accountable before God. In arguing for the Arminian position, Thomas Aquinas goes back as usual to Aristotle, and constructs an argument based on the ideas of motion, matter, and brute and human intelligence.

> Man has free choice, or otherwise counsels, exhortations, commands, prohibitions, rewards and punishments would be in vain. In order to make this evident, we must observe that some things act with judgment, as a stone moves downwards; and in like manner all things which lack knowledge. And some act from judgment, but not a free judgment; as brute animals. For the sheep, seeing the wolf, judges it a thing to be shunned, from a natural and not a free judgment. . .And the same thing is to be said of any judgment in brute animals. But man acts from judgment, because by his apprehensive power he judges that something should be avoided or sought. But because this judgement. . .is not from a natural instinct, but from some act of comparison in the reason, therefore he acts from free judgment.[11]

Very well, he said it, and he believed it, and it seems true enough, as he said in the opening part of the passage above, that without free will

---

11 Aquinas, Thomas, *Summa Theologica* in *Introduction to St. Thomas Aquinas*, ed. Anton C. Pegis, New York: Modern Library, 1948, p. 369.

exhortation, rewards, punishments, etc., would all be in vain, but the argument is not particularly cogent. It gets less so. A few lines later, in the same section of the *Summa Theologica*, we get this:

> Free choice is the cause of its own movement, because by his free choice man moves himself to act. But it does not of necessity belong to liberty that what is free should be the first cause of itself, as neither for one thing to be cause of another need it be the first cause. God, therefore, is the first cause, Who moves causes both natural and voluntary. And just as by moving natural causes He does not prevent their actions from being natural, so by moving voluntary causes He does not deprive their actions of being voluntary; but rather is He the cause of this very thing in them, for He operates in each thing according to its own nature.[12]

"Free choice is the cause of its own movement, because by his free choice man moves himself to act." Very true, this is precisely what we were discussing at the beginning of this chapter. The next sentence in the above statement, however, is troubling. Free choice, if it is indeed the cause of its own movement, must of necessity be a first cause of sorts. God as creator must be the ultimate first cause, as Aquinas states, but the individual with free choice does indeed become the first cause of its own actions and is thus cut loose in a sense from God. Only in this way can one be held responsible for his or her acts, and only in this way can we avoid assigning final responsibility for whatever happens in creation to God as first cause.

Aquinas is not to be charged with sloppy thinking. Whatever other problems he had, this was not one of them. He surely sees the trouble he is in here, but probably knows of no way to avoid it. Either God is sovereign or he is not God. Either humans are free and thus responsible for their actions or there is no just way to pronounce judgment on them when they do things they shouldn't (Remember Kent State?). Therefore God is sovereign, and humans are responsible, and the two positions appear to be logically incompatible, but each appears to be theologically necessary.

Are we left, then, with atheism and hardcore Skinnerianism as our only logical choice? This seems to leave us in a great deal of trouble too. Now we find ourselves facing the guardsmen who fired the shots at Kent State, or the most vicious of serial killers, and there is nothing we can say

---

[12] **Ibid., p. 370.**

but, here is an example of improper reinforcement contingencies. This too is unacceptable, however, for the word improper implies clearly that something is wrong, and no such judgment is possible. It is the old problem of "is and ought,"[13] and the attempt to extract values from facts.

The "is-ought" problem is one of those standard things that philosophers have been discussing since David Hume came on the scene. It is the ethical question of whether values can be extracted from facts.

Immanuel Kant Argues for Freedom

> Is pure reason sufficient of itself to determine the will, or is it only as empirically conditioned that it can do so? At this point there appears a concept of causality which is justified by the *Critique of Pure Reason,* though subject to no empirical exhibition. That is the concept of freedom, and if we now can discover means to show that freedom does in fact belong to the human will (and thus to the will of all rational beings), then it will have been proved not only that pure reason can be practical but also that it alone and not the empirically conditioned reason, is unconditionally practical. Consequently, we shall have to make a critical examination, not of the *pure* practical reason, but only of practical reason *as such.*[14]

Thus Kant begins his *Critique of Practical Reason,* a work not as famous as the *Critique of Pure Reason,* but one which is important to the subject under discussion; for if he has succeeded in doing what he set out to do, he may well have solved the freewill riddle. The question is, did he? I will quote a portion of Problem I from the *Critique of Practical Reason,* but I warn you ahead of time that you probably will not understand it. Never mind. I will clear it up with my usual over-simplifications.

> Since the mere form of a law can be thought only by reason and is consequently not an object of the senses and therefore does not belong among appearances, the conception of this form as the determining ground of the will is distinct from all determining grounds of events in nature according to the law of causality, for these grounds must themselves be appearances. Now, as no

---

13 This is the so-called naturalistic fallacy, which we will discuss when we come to the section on Ethics.

14 Kant, Immanuel, *Critique of Practical Reason,* New York: Liberal Arts Press, 1956, p. 15.

> determining ground of the will except the universal legislative form can serve as a law for it, such a will must be conceived as wholly independent of then natural law of appearances in their mutual relations, i.e., the law of causality. Such independence is called freedom in the strictest, i.e., transcendental sense. Therefore, a will to which only the legislative form of the maxim can serve as a law is a free will.[15]

Wow! How did he do that? I have always stood in awe of these German philosophers, and their ability to construct sentences that run on and on, yet somehow wind up being actual sentences. At any rate, what he is getting at is not easily grasped unless one comprehends his earlier work, *Critique of Pure Reason.* We looked at this in the first section. Remember that in that book he was attempting to answer David Hume, to demonstrate that knowledge was actually possible, and that cause and effect were reliable laws. He also, if you will recall, attempted to bring rationalism and empiricism together into some sort of whole. He did this by arguing that cause and effect, space and time, are *a priori,* synthetic categories which are inborn in the human mind, and which humans bring to their perception of the world around them. We take the mass of incoming raw sense data, and we organize it in the way we have been given to organize it, by applying these categories. In other words, according to Kant, cause and effect are not in the world outside of us, but are in our own minds.

Now, follow carefully. If the categories operate only to organize incoming sense data, what do they do with those things which are not incoming sense data but spring from within the mind just as the categories do? Kant says that they do not work on them at all, presumably because the purely mental stands on equal ground with the purely mental, and the two are independent of one another. The human will, because it is purely mental, is not subject to the law of cause and effect. It resides in that transcendental world apart from the purely physical.

I applaud Kant's genius, but I have never felt comfortable with this. Surely such things as will and desire are non-physical, but they are no more so than are any other conscious experience. This is precisely why Berkeley is able to ask his famous question: If a tree falls in the forest, and no one is there to hear it, does it makes a sound? If you answer that it does not, it is

---

[15] Ibid., p. 28.

because you recognize that all events that occur outside of us come to our awareness in the form of non-physical events which we must give physical reality by a mental act. So why should the falling tree be subject to the cause/effect category and the will not be? And besides, B.F. Skinner says that the whole notion of will and desire are just holdovers from an earlier and more ignorant time, and that we need to jettison them.

> Almost everyone who is concerned with human affairs. ..continues to talk about human behavior in this prescientific way. . .We are told that to control the number of people in the world we need to change *attitudes* toward children, overcome *pride* in size of family or in sexual potency, build some *sense of responsibility* toward offspring. . .To work for peace we must deal with the *will to power* or the *paranoid delusions* of leaders; we must remember that wars begin in the *minds* of men, that there is something suicidal in man — a *death instinct* perhaps — which leads to war. . .This is staple fare. Almost no one questions it. Yet there is nothing like it in modern physics or most of biology, and the fact may well explain why a science and a technology of behavior have been so long delayed. [The italics are Skinner's][16]

Skinner was after getting us to drop all reference to any sort of interior mental life. He held that to do anything less was to be unscientific and to return to the days of the Greeks when behavior was attributed to demons and spirits. I understand this. I understood it very well when the students at Kent State were gunned down. My problem, then and now, is not only that this relieves all humans of all moral responsibility, but that it actually falsifies human behavior, at least as it is experienced by humans. Perhaps for the sake of experiments within laboratories we can dispense with all references to will and desire, and simply measure and record observed behavior; but the picture of the human, as crafted by Skinner, is one that few of us will recognize.

Like it or not, the inner life is here to stay, and holding people responsible for their actions is needful if we intend to live together as anything other than a mob or an assembly of robots. So where do we go from here?

---

16 Skinner, B.F., *Beyond Freedom and Dignity,* New York: Alfred A. Knopf, 1971, p. 10.

Free Will and the Existentialists

From the very outset the existentialists, in the person of Søren Kierkegaard, have emphasized individual responsibility and human freedom. The problem is that Kierkegaard, while making it clear that he believes in freedom of the will, does not go to any great lengths (as does Kant) to prove that such a thing has actual existence. It is Jean Paul Sartre the twentieth-century existentialist, who attempts to make the case for freedom, and he does it, as we have seen, by arguing that the human is being-for-itself, which equates to nothingness. Because it is nothingness, it cannot be acted upon by physical forces. The human is therefore generating himself or herself out of the ongoing nothingness of human existence.

To Sartre we are condemned to be free. We must make choices. Even choosing not to choose is a choice for which we are responsible, and in our choices, and all that results from them, we are ultimately creating the meaning of our own lives.

This is as good a time as any to take up the next of the metaphysical questions I listed at the start of this chapter: do I have a mind separate from the physical brain, or is mind merely an antiquated term left over from early superstition, and one that we would be well rid of? This question rises out of the question of freedom of the will (or perhaps the reverse is true), for it is critical to Skinner and those who oppose the idea of freedom of the will that they be able to show that there is only a brain, subject to the same physical laws as any other matter in the universe. On the other hand, if it can be shown that there is such a thing as human mind, distinct from that which is purely physical, then perhaps Kant and Sartre are correct. Non-physical mind could very well generate will from within itself. In fact, it might have to do so, for it is not clear how, if at all, something physical can work on and move something non-physical, and vice versa.

The Mind/Brain Problem

Socrates said, "Know thyself." Good. Now whom is it that I am being urged to get to know? You might say the question is stupid or that the answer is self-evident. I am obviously being urged to get to know myself. But kindly note that there is a certain duality implicit in this exhortation. For though the exhortation is addressed to me, the me to whom it is addressed is being urged to get to know another me, namely myself. The reason this sounds so strange when I put in these terms is that most of us have never stopped to analyze it. The subject is "you," and the object is "yourself," and they are separated by a predicate in an imperative voice.

Let's try another one. Suppose I suddenly leap up and begin screaming and turning over desks. Someone might say to me, "Get yourself under control." Once again, there is a duality implied in this command. Someone is being addressed, and someone else is out of control. The rational me is being urged to control the irrational myself.

Our language is loaded with these sorts of references, a clear sign that we believe, or at least we indicate, that there is within me another man, an inner man, separate from the physical body I occupy. Skinner calls this "the homunculus, the possessing demon, the man defended by the literatures of freedom and dignity," and he opines that "His abolition has long been overdue."[17] The idea of the homunculus as a little human within the human goes back at least as far as Paracelsus;[18] but the idea of the self as an inner being, separated from the physical self goes back much further. So does the idea that I have a mind that is immaterial and distinct from my physical body.

Today, this very day, I tried an experiment with three different groups of students in three different classes. I simply asked a question: do you have a mind that is something distinct from the brain, or is the mind simply another word for the brain? Of the nearly sixty students I asked this, not one said that he or she had a brain and nothing more. All said that they have minds, and that these are not the same as the brain.

Where would anyone get an idea of this type? Speaking for myself, it seems to be suggested by my own experience of what it is to be a human. Do I not, after all, have feelings that do not seem to be physical? Can I not feel anger, love, rage, pity, sorrow? Can I not close my eyes and visualize, let us say, a rich, red apple in three dimensions, complete with smell, texture, and taste? Yet where, in my physical brain, would one find this apple, assuming one were to cut into my brain. The image seems real enough, yet it clearly is not physical.

René Descartes, you will recall, believed he had proved the existence of the mind as an immaterial entity, and that he had done so by clearly and

---

17 Skinner, B.F., *Beyond Freedom and Dignity*, New York: Alfred A. Knopf, 1971, p. 200.

18 For an amusing account of the history of the homunculus see Tabori, Paul, *The Natural History of Stupidity*, New York: Barnes & Noble Books, 1993.

distinctly seeing himself as a thinking being. He could, he said, imagine himself without a body, but he could not imagine himself without a thinking mind, proof positive, he felt, that the body and the mind were distinct and separate things, and that the immaterial mind was actually the more real and certain of the two.

But Cartesian dualism, any dualism in fact, runs into serious problems. The main one is that it is difficult to see how an immaterial mind can assert any sort of control over a material body, for to do so would be, in effect, psychokinesis. If my mind can make my body move, why can't it make the chair across the room move. There are those who assert that this can be done, and some who even claim to be able to do it, but to my knowledge it has never been shown to be possible in a laboratory, with scientists, and under controlled conditions.

Occasionalists: Cartesians who attempted to solve the mind/body problem by arguing that God is able to coordinate mental events and physical events.

How mind and body work together was something René Descartes and his followers discussed for years without ever coming to an agreement. Some philosophers, called **occasionalists**, felt that God was actually the answer to the whole thing. God was able to cause the body and the mind to move in concert one with another even though there is no demonstrable connection between the two. That is, when you think, "Move, little finger," God causes the body to move in response.

The problem with this explanation is that it is so cumbersome and complicated as to be ridiculous. Most philosophers and scientists have long since abandoned any such notions, but the question of how mind interacts with body is still around and still troubling. As late as 1965 Karl Popper said, "What we want is to understand how such nonphysical things as purposes, deliberations, plans, decisions, theories, tensions, and values can play a part in bringing about physical changes in the physical world."[19]

An obvious answer to the problem is to deny either one or the other of the two substances (mind and matter) that have created the dichotomy. Another is to merge them into one and say that both really describe the same thing. Gilbert Ryle suggested that the mind/body problem arises when we mistakenly create an entity by bringing together many things, and then saying the whole somehow has being all its own. He calls it a category-mistake.

> A foreigner visiting Oxford of Cambridge for the first time is shown a number of colleges, libraries, playing

---

[19] Quoted by B.F. Skinner in *Beyond Freedom and Dignity, op. cit.* p. 10.

> fields, museums, scientific departments and administrative offices. He then asks, "But where is the University? I have seen where the members of the Colleges live, where the Registrar works, where the scientists experiment and the rest. But I have not yet seen the University in which reside and work the members of your university." It has then to be explained to him that the University is not another collateral institution, some ulterior counterpart to the colleges, laboratories and offices which he has seen. The University is just the way in which all that he has already seen is organized. When they are seen and when their coordination is understood, the university has been seen.[20]

Ryle further opines that this is exactly what has happened with the human. That is, those who believe in the mind, what Ryle calls the "ghost in the machine" are committing the category-mistake.

> The representation of a person as a ghost mysteriously ensconced in a machine derives from this argument. Because, as is true, a person's thinking, feeling and purposive doing cannot be described solely in the idioms of physics, chemistry and physiology, therefore they must be described in counterpart idioms. As the human body is a complex organised unit, so the human mind must be another complex organised unit, though one made of a different sort of stuff and with a different sort of structure. Or, again, as the human body, like any other parcel of matter, is a field of causes and effects, so the mind must be another field of causes and effects, though not (Heaven be praised) mechanical causes and effects.[21]

B.F. Skinner has another explanation, albeit a much simpler one. To him, there is no good reason to go delving into the interior of the human at all. We ought to get rid of all these mental terms that describe inner states and simply concentrate on the behavior of the human, that which is observable to all and obviously material. How then do we explain the human thinking process, assuming we wish to do so? Skinner's answer, and

---

20 **Ryle, Gilbert, *The Concept of Mind*, in *Twenty Questions: an Introduction to Philosophy*, New York: Harcourt Brace, 1996.**

21 **Ibid., p. 197.**

that of many other scientists, is couched in reductionistic terms. Remember the definition of reductionism? It is the belief that one type of reality may be completely explained in terms of another type. What follows is Thomas Hobbes's reductionistic explanation of the human body, from his classic *Leviathan.*

> [L]ife is but a motion of Limbs, the beginning whereof is in some principall part within; why may we not say, that all Automata (Engines that move themselves by springs and wheeles as doth a watch) have an artificiall life? For what is the Heart, but a spring; and the Nerves, but so many Strings; and Joynts, but so many Wheeles, giving motion to the whole Body, such as was intended by the Artificer?[22]

In this reductionistic treatment of the human body, the explanation offered is that of a machine, a rather common thing in that day. Both Newton and Descartes had explained the universe and its movements in purely mechanistic terms.

How might reductionism be used to explain mental phenomena? Generally, the explanation runs like this. Mental events are reduced to, explained in terms of, material events. What most people call mind is in reality nothing more than brain, a mass of matter, filled with ganglia. It is true that there is a great deal of mystery about how this thing actually operates, but we are learning more and more, pushing back the curtains bit by bit, and when we have finally come to a full understanding of how it all works we shall see that there is no immaterial reality at all, no ghost in the machine.

This explanation leaves a great deal to be desired. Matter, whatever else it is, has extension in space and existence in time. It is therefore divisible. As René Descartes, our most famous recent dualist, put it:

> There is a great difference between mind and body, inasmuch as body is by nature always divisible, and the mind is entirely indivisible.[23]

---

[22] **Hobbes, Thomas, *Leviathan*, New York: Washington Square Press, 1976, p. xxvii.**

[23] **Descartes, René, *Mind as Distinct from Body*, in *Twenty Questions, an Introduction to Philosophy*, *op. cit.*, pg. 187.**

Idea has no extension in space and no existence in time. It is not divisible, at least not in physical terms. To prove this to yourself, close your eyes and imagine a great oak tree on the crest of a hill, with a trunk so large that ten men holding hands could not reach around it. Its bark is rough and dark. Its leaves whisper in the wind.

Were you able to do this? I'm sure you had no problem with it at all. Now, ask yourself this: the tree that you imagined, was it real? You would probably reply that it was not real, it was imaginary. Let's examine this a little more closely. We can certainly agree that it was not real in the physical sense; but was the image real? Perhaps I am losing you at this point, so I will try it like this. The image of the tree that you had, was it "something," or was it non-existent? You cannot say that it was non-existent, because it clearly existed in your own mind (or call it brain if you have Skinnerian leanings). The image of the oak was just as existent as are any of your thoughts, and you would probably protest, if someone denied the truth of this, that you know very well what was going on in your mind when you thought of the oak, and that the fact that someone else could not see it certainly does not mean that it was not real.

This brings us to the very heart of the mind/body problem. The oak did not have physical or material reality, but it had some sort of reality; so what sort did it have? If you say, as I think you must, that it had mental reality, and that this was non-physical, then you have demonstrated that the reductionistic explanation of mental phenomena does not work. Mental phenomena simply cannot be explained in purely physical terms. While you are imagining the great tree, suppose we could look into your brain. Does anyone think that we will see a tree of some sort in there?

Think now of the many emotions to which you are subject. Have you ever been in love? Have you ever hated someone? Have you ever felt fear? Are these feelings real to you? No doubt you would say that they are, but you would probably also say that it is very difficult to equate them with the purely physical, even though they might result in certain physical reactions.

The inner life of humans is something we all know about and understand, for it is a part of what it is to be human. But if this inner life is mental, and if the mental cannot be reduced to the physical, then it becomes difficult to see how the purely physical can control or define it. It may very well be that physical events can strongly influence the mental, just as the mental can strongly influence the physical; but to admit to this is not to give a reductionistic explanation for the mental — or the physical.

The purely physical explanation of human life has run into another problem in this century, one which has caused a great deal of consternation for many materialists. I said earlier that twentieth century physicists have not been kind to materialism. We shall look further into the strange world of quantum physics in the next chapter. For the time being, however, suppose we take a trip into the amazing human brain. A neural impulse, for example, may be considered as something like an electrical charge. But what does that mean? Is electricity energy or mass? It isn't mass, therefore it must be energy. And then along comes Einstein to show that mass and energy, with the square of the speed of light factored in, are the same thing. Now, if the image of the tree that you conjured up in your mind was composed of neural impulses moving at or near the speed of light, then it may not be far fetched to think that somehow there can be a meeting between mind and matter, or the mental and the physical, and that they may indeed, on some level, be identical. There was a time when I would have been very hesitant to write something like this, but, given what physicists have been discovering about what is really there, I feel positively sane.

Let us move ahead to the third of the questions I posed at the beginning of this chapter. What manner of creature am I? Is there some inborn essence that separates me qualitatively from the rest of the universe, or am I merely quantitatively different. I assume that all college students know the difference between qualitative and quantitative, but on the outside shot that there may be someone who does not, allow me to explain. Qualitative is related to the word "quality" and indicates the fundamental, the essential. Quantitative relates to "quantity" and has to do with mere number or physical amount. If I am only quantitatively different from the earthworm, then I am different only because there is more of me — more brain, more size, more muscle. But if I am qualitatively different, then there is some essential something I possess and which the earthworm does not, that makes me different.

I believe that the difference between the two positions will become clear once we have gotten into the discussion.

Essentialism, as it concerns humans, is the belief that the human has some essence— for Christians the soul— that separates him and her from all other creatures.

Christian Essentialism

Most philosophers in the western world have been **essentialists**. This means they think there is a certain human essence, something humans possess that no other thing in all creation does, that separates between that which is human and that which is non-human. As a matter of fact, even non-philosophers in the west tend to be essentialists, but most don't know why. The Judeo-Christian position is unequivocally essentialist. But what is this essence? According to the Jews and the Christians, it is the human soul, made in the image of God. This notion goes back to the earliest days of the Hebrew peoples, and it is recorded in the first book of the *Bible,* Genesis.

> But there went up a mist from the earth, and watered the whole face of the ground. And the Lord God formed man of the dust of the ground, and breathed into his nostrils the breath of life; and man became a living soul. (Genesis 2:7-8).

This is the first time the word "soul" is used in the Bible, though earlier, in the first chapter of Genesis, the statement is made that God created man in his image. Neither of these things is said of any other animal, and the implication is that the human stands in some sort of special relationship with God. There is a way in which humans are different from all other beings, and this difference has to do with the presence of the human soul. This is the most well known and widely held of the essentialist theories in the west.

The Christian belief in eternal life is associated with the essentialist position, and is closely connected to the question of mind versus matter. The soul is seen as an eternal thing, undying, something which returns to God who gave it even though the body may die and decompose. Most of us are familiar with so-called near-death experiences. The person having the experience may have had a cardiac arrest, lost consciousness, and suddenly found himself standing outside his body and looking down at himself and those who are frantically trying to save him. He will then, as often as not, find himself traveling down a long tunnel toward a light, and he may hear music or sense the presence of another being from whom great love emanates. Those who have had these experiences, and others, see this as powerful proof for the existence of the soul and for life after death. If they are right, this is also proof that the essentialists have been right all along, and that the human is actually a dual being, body and soul. But there are other explanations. There is no evidence that death actually occurred in these cases. In fact, we call them "near-death" experiences. Perhaps these experiences are nothing more than hallucinations triggered by the lack of oxygen to the brain because the heart has stopped beating. Further, not everyone who has had a near-death experience reports anything upon being resuscitated other than a lost of consciousness and waking up subsequently with no sense of a passage of time.

Tempting as it may be to believe these accounts, there is to date no solid empirical evidence of life after death. Judeo-Christian essentialism must remain a metaphysical theory of human life, not a fact upon which we may confidently lean.

And yet, isn't there something in me that stays the same and never changes, even though my body begins to break down and to fall apart? We might illustrate this sense of continuity in this way. Suppose you are an excellent automobile mechanic. Moreover, suppose you are able to fix most anything on an automobile, from a dented fender to a blown head gasket. Now, suppose in 1965 you were given a new Mustang by your father for your birthday, and suppose over the years you kept this car up so that thirty years later it looked exactly the way it did when it was driven off the showroom floor. But in fact it is not the same car. Over a thirty year period, bit by bit, you have changed every part of the car for a new one. There is no single part, not so much as one bolt, that was on the original. In what sense is this the same car that came off the showroom floor in 1965? In no sense, you would probably say. It may look the same, but it is not.

Very well. Now think of your own body. I am told that every seven years you get a whole new one. There is not one cell, not one atom in your body now that was there seven years ago. In what sense, then, are you the same person now that you were then? If you, like your Mustang, are a purely physical being, then you must admit that you are a completely different being now than you were then. But are you? Something has given continuity to your experience of yourself, and this sense of continuity may be the thing that makes you believe in an eternal self resident in your temporal body.

Now, go back to the car. Suppose I asked you, "In what sense is the car you own today the same car your father gave you in 1965?" And suppose you thought for a moment, and that you replied, "It is the same type." If you said something like this, you might be invited to occupy the chair of philosophy in Plato's Academy, for you would be thinking like a Socratic Greek.

Platonic Essentialism

The Greeks were also essentialists, and they also believed in the soul, but their conception of soul differed from that of the Jews and Christians. The Greek word typically translated soul is *psuche.* It has come into our language as *psyche*, and we find it in such words as psychological, psychic, psychotic. There were no theological connotations to the word as Plato and Aristotle used it. For Plato, the *psuche* was the inner self, that part of the human that survives death, that is in touch with the world of the forms, that is therefore rational, appetitive and spirited. We saw in the first section the way in which Plato divided the human soul into three parts. In part IV of the Republic we again see the tripartite *psuche* in operation.

> Socrates: Might a man be thirsty, and yet unwilling to drink?
>
> Glaucon: Yes. It constantly happens.
>
> Soc: And in such a case what is one to say? Would you not say that there was something in the soul bidding a man to drink and something else forbidding him, which is other and stronger than the principle which bids him?
>
> Gla: I should say so.
>
> Soc: And the forbidding principle is derived from reason, and that which bids and attracts proceeds from passion and disease?
>
> Gla: Clearly.
>
> Soc: Then we may fairly assume that they are two, and that they differ from one another; the one with which a man reasons, we may call the rational principle of the soul, the other ,with which he loves and hungers and thirsts and feels the flutterings of any other desire, may be termed the irrational or appetitive, the ally of sundry pleasures and satisfactions?
>
> Gla: Yes, we may fairly assume them to be different.
>
> Soc: Then let us finally determine that there are two principles existing in the soul. And what of passion, or spirit? Is it a third, or akin to one of the preceding?
>
> Gla: I should be inclined to say — akin to desire.[24]

But in a bit Socrates proves to Glaucon that passion or spirit is a third part of the soul, separate and occupying its own space, not to be confused

---

24 Plato, *The Republic*, Book IV, trans. B. Jowett, New York: Doubleday, 1973, pp. 129-

with desire.

> Soc: But a further question arises: Is passion different from reason also, or only a kind of reason; in which latter case, instead of three principles in the soul, there will be only two, the rational and the concupiscent; or rather, as the State was composed of three classes, traders, auxiliaries, counsellors, so may there not be in the individual soul a third element which is passion or spirit, and when not corrupted by bad education is the natural auxiliary of reason?
>
> Gla: Yes, there must be a third.
>
> Soc: Yes. If passion, which has already been shown to be different from desire, turn out also to be different from reason.[25]

Socrates and Glaucon conclude that the human soul is tripartite; just as is the just society; and as the just society is characterized by a proper balancing of the three types of citizens, each in his own place doing well at what he does best, so the just human is a being with his tripartite soul functioning in a balanced fashion.

Notice that the three parts of the soul are all non-material. Appetite, spirit, rationality — each drives the body to seek things commensurate with its own needs and desires, but none is to be identified with the body itself. Think back to the figure of the chariot driver that Plato used in the *Phaedrus.* The chariot driver, representing the rational part of the soul, is in control of two spirited horses, one (spirit) plunging upward, and the other (appetite), pulling downward. The business of the charioteer is to keep the two horses pulling forward together on a level plane. In this illustration, the chariot itself is representative of the human body.

Freudian Essentialism

The tripartite human soul crops up again in Sigmund Freud's view of the human psychological dynamic. In fact, Freud is so very Platonic that it is sometimes difficult to tell the two apart. Freud, if you will recall, felt that the human psyche[26] is divisible into id, ego and superego. The id equates to the

---

[25] Ibid., p. 131.

[26] For "psyche" read "*psuche*" and you immediately understand just how close to the Greek Freud was.

appetitive part of the soul; the superego equates to the spirit; and the ego, or the self, equates to the rational, that which is in touch with the actual world and ought to have control over the other two. Freud differed from Plato in believing that the ego does not have direct access to the id, whereas Plato felt that the rational part of the soul could understand the appetitive soul perfectly. Otherwise, one may see Freud as a direct descendant of the classical Greeks.

Aristotle's Essentialism

> The formal nature [of anything] is of much greater importance than the material nature. . .
>
> If now this something that makes up the form of a living being be the soul, or part of the soul, or something that without the soul cannot exist (as would seem to be the case, seeing at any rate that when the soul departs, what is left is no longer a living animal, and that none of the parts remain what they were before, excepting in mere shape, like the animals that in the fable are turned into stone); if, I say, this be so, then it will come within the province of the natural philosopher to inform himself concerning the soul, and to treat of it, either in its entirety, or, at any rate, of that part of it which constitutes the essential character of an animal; and it will be his duty to say what this soul or this part of a soul is; and to discuss the attributes that attach to this essential character. . .for just as human creations are the product of art, so living objects are manifestly the products of an analogous cause or principle, not external but internal, derived like the hot and the cold [and the other material elements of our bodies] from the environing universe.[27]

And I thought the Germans wrote long sentences! Still, difficult as it may be to wade through, Aristotle gives us in this passage a good definition of essentialism. Notice that he equates the soul with that essential character of the (in this case) animal, and he feels that this essential character, which is inborn, determines what the creature, man or otherwise, will become. In fact, for Aristotle, the highest type of behavior in which a being, human or

---

[27] **Aristotle, *Parts of Animals*, in *Aristotle: On Man in the Universe*, trans. William Ogle, ed. Louise Ropes Loomis, New York: Walter J. Black, 1943, p. 46.**

otherwise, can engage, the most virtuous, is the completing of its purpose. This is what Aristotelian ***entelechy*** is all about. The soul drives one toward his or her final purpose. If happiness is your goal, you might be interested to know that according to Aristotle you can never really be happy until you have achieved your goal. Failing that, you will always have a sense of incompletion. As a twentieth-century Aristotelian has put it:

> Living things develop from an immature to a mature stage: at any given point they can be healthy or unhealthy: some of their activities involve striving for something needed, in the main unconsciously. . .Try to understand [the process of maturation] only in terms of itself or its preceding conditions at any given moment, and you will miss the main feature of the development. . .With the proper sustenance, internal causes proceed to guide the organism's growth according to the kind of thing it is. Such biological development is analogous to purposive human action toward some end, except that it is lacking in conscious awareness.[28]

Think of it like this. An acorn will become an oak because it contains, as its very essence "oakness," and this essence drives it unerringly toward its final goal. All life is goal directed, according to Aristotle, and the goal of any life is determined by its essence, that inborn quality which lies at its very core and separates it from other things.

Now what is the human essence? The Christians have said that it is its godlikeness, its identification with its creator in whose image it was made. To Plato and Socrates the human essence is a bit harder to define, but it is tripartite — appetitive, spiritual, and rational — and can only be healthy when it is in balance and the three parts are working together in harmony. To Aristotle the human essence may be expressed in one word: rational. The human is the thinking being, the being that is capable of reasoning. Therefore humans are never happier, never more fulfilled that when they are using their intellect to full capacity. Some Aristotelians, Ayn Rand for example, take it even further and argue that it is not just happiness we are talking about, but our survival as a species.

---

[28] Lowenthal, David, "The Case for Teleology," *Independent Journal of Philosophy* 2 (1978): 97. Quoted in Uyl, Douglas J. Den and Douglas B. Rasmussen, *The Philosophic Thought of Any Rand*, Chicago: University of Illinois Press, 1986.

> [T]o integrate perceptions into conceptions by a process of abstraction, is a feat that man alone has the power to perform — and he has to perform it by choice. The process of abstraction, and of concept-formation is a process of reason, of thought; it is not automatic nor instinctive nor involuntary nor infallible. . .Man has the choice to think or to evade — to maintain a state of full awareness or to drift from moment to moment, in a semi-conscious daze, at the mercy of whatever associational whims the unfocused mechanism of his consciousness produces. . .
>
> An animal's consciousness functions automatically; an animal perceives what it is able to perceive and survives accordingly, no further than the perceptual level permits and not better. Man cannot survive on the perceptual level of his consciousness; his senses do not provide him with an automatic guidance, they do not give him the knowledge he needs, or the material of knowledge, which his mind has to integrate. Man is the only living species who has to perceive reality — which means: to be conscious — by choice. But he shares with other species the penalty of unconsciousness: destruction. For an animal, the question of survival is primarily physical; for man, primarily epistemological. . . Man's unique reward, however, is that while animals survive by adjusting themselves to their background, man survives by adjusting his background to himself.[29]

Rand makes the point, and it is very Aristotelian, that the mind is the thing that the human has been given that allows him or her to cope with the world and to survive. He cannot outrun a horse. The elephant is many times stronger. The dog has a keener sense of smell; the eagle keener vision. Human superiority over other creatures is purely mental. In short, the human is never being more human than when he or she is thinking rationally. This is the very essence of the human.

Cartesian Essence

Self-consciousness is an interesting concept, for it implies a dualism: if there were not two there would be nothing to be conscious and nothing to be conscious of. René Descartes, the father of modern rationalism, is also

---

[29] Rand, Ayn, *For the New Intellectual*, New York: Signet Books, 1964, pp. 14-15.

the father of the modern concept of self-consciousness. I quote the following passage earlier, but I shall quote it again, for it bears directly upon the subject under discussion.

> I then examined closely what I was, and saw that I could imagine that I had no body, and that there was no world nor any place that I occupied, but that I could not imagine for a moment that I did not exist. On the contrary, from the very fact that I doubted the truth of other things, (or had any other thought) it followed [very] evidently [and very certainly] that I existed. On the other hand, if I had ceased to think while my body and the world and all the rest of what I had ever imagined remained true, I would have had no reason to believe that I existed during that time; therefore I concluded that I was a thing or substance whose whole essence or nature was only to think, and which, to exist, has no need of space nor of any material thing or body. Thus it follows that this ego, this mind, this soul, by which I am what I am, is entirely distinct from the body and is easier to know than the latter, and that even if the body were not, the soul would not cease to be all that it now is.[30]

This very interesting passage has the ring of Aristotle cleaned up and dressed in Christian clothing. "I was a thing or substance whose whole essence or nature was only to think. . ." Now notice the two assumptions lying at the very base of Descartes's reasoning. First, if I can conceive of something as not existing, then it is possible that it does not in fact exist. Second, if I can conceive of two things that exist apart from one another (in this case body and soul), then they are in fact two separate entities. The first of these assumptions gets washed away by the second, for Descartes is not after showing that there is no such thing as the body. What he really wants to show is that soul exists apart from body, and that soul is the eternal, essential thing that makes the human what the human is.

You will notice, once again, that the metaphysical assumptions inherent in the Cartesian position are bound up with everything else we have been discussing in this chapter. If my ego, my self, is a non-material, thinking entity, then it is probably true that I have freedom of thought and will, that I am to some degree self-generating, that I am therefore morally

---

[30] Descartes, René, *Discourse on Method,* trans. Laurence J. Lafleur, Indianapolis: Bobbs-Merrill, Co., 1960, p. 25.

responsible for all that I do, say and think. Also, if the position of the essentialists is the correct one, then it follows almost as a matter of course that I have mind over and above my merely physical brain. Finally, if René Descartes is correct, then it is at least possible that the real me, the ego which dwells within, survives death in some form. It is at least arguable that it is not dependent upon my body for its ongoing existence.

There are all sorts of unresolved problems that spring from the Cartesian position. We have already discussed these. From the point of view of B.F. Skinner and many other scientists, the main problem is that it leaves us with the "homunculus," the man within, the invisible ghost in the machine, an uncontrollable entity which can never be brought under the scrutiny of the scientist and never studied within the context of the laboratory. Perhaps the problem is unresolvable and we simply have to decide which position is the most fruitful, the most necessary for the ongoing benefit of the human race. But isn't this a sort of cop-out? If we go this route, haven't we abandoned the search for the truth and thereby sacrificed philosophy on the alter of expediency? Perhaps it depends on what we mean by truth. In the remaining pages of this chapter we shall look at two other metaphysical positions which may offer some help in resolving the problem.

The Pragmatic Answer

Pragmatism is the only school of philosophy associated with America. It three major lights are Charles Peirce, John Dewey, and William James. As is suggested by its name, **Pragmatism** is concerned with the practical, or perhaps better said, with what works. If my particular beliefs lead to no important consequences, then the beliefs themselves must, to the pragmatists, be inconsequential. This, they say, is precisely where much of the philosophical enterprize has gone astray. What practical difference would it make, for example, if materialism or idealism is true?

Pragmatism: from the Greek, *pragma,* meaning "deed." This school of philosophy is the only one that is native to America. The emphasis is on practicality, or what actually works.

We will have more to say about the pragmatic position when we come to epistemology, and particularly when we come to the section that deals with the concept of truth. But there is this to be said about the mind/body debate. The pragmatist would begin by asking the debaters what difference it would make if one position was true rather than the other? If no practical consequence follows, then the debate itself is meaningless, a mere philosophical exercise. Very well, let us ask the question. Does it make any difference?

It seems to me that it does, and that the difference is critically important for humans and for the society which we have formed. The pragmatic test of truth is not does the proposition correspond with reality, nor does the proposition cohere with other propositions which we know to be true, but what practical difference does it make if the proposition is true? Put in simpler terms — does it work? Let us apply the pragmatic test to the debate between Skinner and Descartes (or any other essentialist you wish to name).

Suppose Skinner is correct: we are totally determined, a mere physical machine up and ready to run, and we will run as we are programmed.[31] In such a world moral responsibility is non-existent. One can talk of morals and being held accountable, but in truth there is nothing behind such talk. It is, to use the argument of Dr. Skinner, a result of ideas that have somehow hung on long after the demise of the pre-scientific age in which they were spawned. Can our society, or any society, function for long if it is based upon such philosophical premises? The answer seems to be that it cannot. Holding people responsible for their actions seems to be an absolute necessity, both morally and legally. Otherwise words such as guilt, or if you are more comfortable with the Latin, culpability, become meaningless, and we wind up putting people behind bars not because they deserve to be there (words like deserve, in the sense of earning something, are also out), but because we want to.

In short, by the pragmatic test, the position of Dr. Skinner does not seem to be workable.

The Existential Self

Since they are perhaps the newest of the newcomers to the debate, we will allow the existentialists to have the final word, and we will allow its most famous spokesman to do the talking. Jean Paul Sartre does not say that humans do not have an essence, but he does say that there is no essence in the Greek or Christian sense. That is to say, there is no human essence inborn and common to all humans which somehow determines what they will become. Rather — and this is important — **existence precedes essence.** Put in its simplest terms, the human exists as an individual first, then creates his or her own essence moment by moment by choices made and actions taken. In one of his best known short compositions, *The Humanism of Existentialism,* Sartre undertakes to make his point.

Existence precedes essence is the heart of Sartre's existentialism. First we exist, and from this existence we each create our own essence.

---

[31] In Skinnerian terms, "programmed" ought to read "reinforced."

> Let us consider some object that is manufactured, for example, a book or a paper-cutter. . .[T]he paper-cutter is at once an object produced in a certain way and, on the other hand, one having a specific use; and one can not postulate a man who produces a paper-cutter but does not know what it is used for. Therefore, let us say that, for the paper-cutter, essence — that is, the ensemble of both the production routines and the properties which enable it to be both produced and defined — precedes existence. Thus, the presence of the paper-cutter or book in front of me is determined.[32]

If you have followed him in this, then you will have no difficulty following him as he moves on to the idea of God as the artisan who has created the human.

> When we conceive God as the Creator, He is generally thought of as a superior sort of artisan. . .Thus, the concept of man in the mind of God is comparable to the concept of a paper-cutter in the mind of the manufacturer [and] the individual man is the realization of a certain concept in the divine intelligence.[33]

But take God out of the picture, and you are left, according to Sartre, with a being, the human, with no essence but only existence and a life stretching out before.

> Atheistic existentialism. . .states that if God does not exist, there is at least one being in whom existence precedes essence, a being who exists before he can be defined by any concept, and that this being is man. . .[M]an exists, turns up, appears on the scene, and, only afterwards, defines himself. . .[T]here is no human nature, since there is no God to conceive it.[34]

Actually, even the non-atheistic existentialists, such as Kierkegaard and Jaspers, are in agreement with Sartre on this point. Not that there is no

---

[32] Sartre, Jean Paul, *The Humanism of Existentialism*, p. 34.

[33] Ibid., pp. 34-35.

[34] Ibid., pp. 35-36.

human essence because there is no God to conceive it, but rather that there is no human essence properly speaking because that is the way God has created the human. One cannot be human, have freedom as a human, and be bound down by the sort of essentialism that dictates what one must become. Being free can be a very frightening thing, but that is what being a human is all about. In an odd sense, for these existentialists, the only thing that all humans have essentially in common is freedom. "Condemned to be free," Sartre has said of the human in an oft-quoted passage.

Now this has very interesting consequences when the existentialists get hold of it. B.F. Skinner was not an essentialist because he did not believe in an inner man, a ghost in the machine; and the result, for him, was a completely determined being that obeys the physical laws of the universe just as any other physical thing must. There is no freedom in this. Sartre and the existentialists are also not essentialists because they believe there is no inner essence that all humans have in common; but for them this results in a being that is totally free, being-for-itself, nothingness, creating itself as it goes along.

Am I free or determined. "You are determined," says Skinner, a scientific non-essentialist. "You are totally free, and condemned to be so," says Sartre, an existential non-essentialist. As to which of them is correct, philosophers over the years have been in closer agreement with Sartre than with Skinner. The debate goes on. But as we shall see in the next chapter, and as I have said before, the materialism of Skinner, Hobbes, D'Holbach and others has been left reeling from the discoveries of twentieth century physicists. To be quite frank, few of us at this point would be willing to go out on a limb and risk saying exactly what reality is.

Chapter 8
Into the Abyss

On Non-Locality

Now having heard, I trust, the full debate,
I'd like to think I've got this business straight.
We pluck some matter from infinity,
And split it into two parts, "A" and "B";
And "A" beings to gyrate to the right
At something very near the speed of light,
While "B" turns left at the same hectic pace.
But now, my friends, let us confound the case.
We stop "A" in its tracks, reverse its course,
And "B" reverses with an equal force;
And Einstein smites his breast in mortal shame
For the abuse he heaped on Bohr's good name.
Spinoza-like, I close my thoughts at random
with these three words: Quod erat demonstrandum.

he farther along we go, the more blurred the line between the physical and the metaphysical becomes. Or, perhaps better said, the more we know about the purely physical, the more the lines between the various metaphysical theories are blurred. The ongoing debate between the materialists and the idealists is a good example of this blurring.

At the closing of the nineteenth century humans inhabited a very comfortable world, comfortable in just about every sense of the word. The British stood across the sea lanes of the world, and governed a good portion of the world's peoples, insuring what has been called the *Pax Brittanica.* Science was forging ahead, producing what seemed to be miracle upon miracle. Pasteur, to name just one, had opened up the world of microbiology. On a more mundane level, the internal combustion engine would soon replace the horse as the most common means of transportation, and in a short time men would demonstrate the practicability of heavier-than-air flying machines. There probably seemed to be no problem that could not be solved just by careful application of rational thought; the Kingdom of God must have seemed just around the corner.

We now know that all of this was only partially true. Yes, many problems fell before scientific onslaught; yes, humans travelled farther and faster than they ever had; yes, we lived lives that, in material terms, were beyond the wildest dreams of our ancestors. But the Kingdom of God has not yet come, and in our century we have slaughtered more humans in wars than in all the previous centuries combined.

We have also seen troubling times intellectually. It must have appeared to the philosophers and scientists at the end of the nineteenth century that most of the important things that were going to be discovered had, in fact, been discovered. The universe was still comfortably Newtonian, a machine that ran according to well known laws. And philosophy, in spite of the rantings of Nietzsche and Schopenhaur, was a quaint and curious pastime for those who had the leisure to speculate about the Greeks and problems that never actually intruded into the world of waking reality.

All has been changed, changed utterly, to borrow the words of W.B. Yeats. And, to borrow more of his words, things seem to have fallen apart; the center cannot seem to hold.

The great Titanic sank, the world erupted in war, Newtonian physics has been shown to work only under certain narrow conditions, and down on the sub-atomic level nothing is what it appears to be. In philosophy, the world of metaphysics has been turned upside down by new discoveries in the mother of all the sciences — physics. You must believe me when I tell you that matter, as we think we know it, is not at the foundational level of the universe. And neither is idea. Push down and down, and you come to a point that seems to be a curious blending of matter and energy, pulsing back and forth in a curious dance in which one becomes the other then goes back again.

Welcome to the wonderful physical/metaphysical world of the twentieth century!

I never talk to students about physics and the things that have been, and are being, discovered without warning them ahead of time that they will find much of it hard to believe. So consider yourselves warned. The truth can indeed be stranger than fiction, so the next time you watch a *Startrek* episode, remember that what you are seeing is not nearly so strange as the truth of the reality underlying the universe which seems *prima facie* so very ordinary and easily understood. Just remember that common sense would tell us that we live on a flat, fixed earth and that the moon, sun, stars are revolving around us. The truth boggled the minds of those to whom it was first presented, but that did not keep it from being truth.

Very well. Shall we begin?

Einstein's Space/Time

You may have heard that Einstein was not a particularly good student, that he had trouble in high school, and that he was never very good at mathematics. If you heard this, you heard the truth. In fact, when Einstein's father asked the headmaster of the school young Albert was attending what career his son should follow, the headmaster replied, "It doesn't matter; he will never make a success of anything." His father probably believed this, for Einstein had given him little reason at the time to believe anything else. Nevertheless, after first failing the entrance examination, and after passing it on his second try, Albert was admitted to the highly reputed Swiss Federal Polytechnic School in Zurich, Switzerland. His plan was to become an electrical engineer.

He eventually graduated, but during his time at the polytechnical school Einstein became increasingly interested in physics and less and less interested in electrical engineering. He hoped, after graduation, for a university post. He got none. Instead, he went to work for the Swiss Patent Office in Berne, and stayed for the next seven years, working as a patent clerk. And there he completed and published the paper on **special relativity**[1] that was to gain him international fame, and change the way we now look at the universe.

Special relativity is Einstein's theory concerning the relativity of time and space, or what he referred to as space/time.

Space and time — there can be no more basic concepts to scientific observations, and certainly there can be no concepts more basic to the cosmological theories of Galileo, Isaac Newton, and René Descartes. In other words, the world view that was taken as a given at the turn of the century depended upon the underlying supposition that space and time were fixed, set in some sort of metaphysical concrete as it were. If I am moving from one point to another, for example, and if my beginning and ending points are known, along with the speed I am traveling, it is easy to determine

---

[1] Special relativity and general relativity are two different things, although they are closely related. In his theory of special relativity Einstein explains how time and space are relative things and the speed of light is the constant. In his theory of general relativity he gets into the problem of what gravity actually is.

how much time I will take in transit. But what if the very act of motion causes time to change? What if time is not the same for two people if one of them is moving and one is standing still?

This is ridiculous on its face. So what would cause an intelligent person to postulate such a thing? Suppose we allow Einstein to tell us.

> I stand at the window of a railway carriage which is travelling uniformly, and drop a stone on the embankment, without throwing it. Then, disregarding the influence of the air resistance, I see the stone descend in a straight line. A pedestrian who observes the misdeed from the footpath notices that the stone falls to earth in a parabolic curve. I now ask: Do the "positions" traversed by the stone lie "in reality" on a straight line or on a parabola? Moreover, what is meant here by motion "in space."[2]

Here we have the beginning of Einstein's speculations, the simple reflection that "reality" for one person may not be "reality" for the other. What is real depends upon what one observes, and this may depend upon how the observer is positioned. There is nothing particularly earth-shattering about this. In fact, it may be nothing more that the sort of sophistry that we saw in Protagoras and against which Socrates and Plato fought so vigorously.

But Einstein doesn't stop here. The railway car comes up again, and in an even more startling manner. He asks you to imagine a train going down a track, with a passenger in one of the cars and an observer standing along the track. When the train reaches the point where the passenger and the observer are opposite one another two lightning bolts hit simultaneously at two points along the tracks, points "A" and "B." Now assuming point "A" is ahead of the train and point "B" is behind it, the passenger on the train, because he is traveling toward "A" and away from "B," will see the lightning at "A" as striking first; and because he is traveling away from "B" he will see that lightning bolt as striking after the bolt at "A." The observer along the track, because he is stationary relative to the two strikes will see them as simultaneous.[3]

---

[2] **Einstein, Albert, *Relativity, the Special and General Theory*, trans. Robert W. Lawson, New York: Crown Publishers, 1961, pg. 9.**

[3] **Ibid., Chapter IX.**

If you, having read the above account, say, "Sure, that's obvious," or words to that effect without really thinking about all that this implies, please think again, or, better, listen to Einstein.

> [B]efore the advent of the theory of relativity it had always tacitly been assumed in physics that the statement of time had an absolute significance, i.e. that it is independent of the state of motion of the body of reference. But we have just seen that this assumption is incompatible with the most natural definition of simultaneity; if we discard this assumption, then the conflict between the law of the propagation of light *in vacuo* and the principle of relativity. . .disappears.[4]

Now kindly stop a moment and give some thought to this. We have just seen two individuals, one on a railway car and the other on an embankment beside the track. Both have witnessed the same event, lightning striking at two points along the track. The man on the embankment has seen the strikes as occurring simultaneously, whereas the man on the train has seen the strike toward which he is traveling as coming before the one behind him. Question: which of the two observers is correct? If you say both you are left in a sort of logical predicament that would have gotten you tossed out of Aristotle's famed Lyceum. How can both be right if they are not in agreement with one another? Doesn't this violate the law of contradiction and the law of the excluded middle? Nonetheless, both are indeed right because what one sees in a case of this type depends upon the point of reference from which one is doing the viewing.

And Einstein was just getting started.

When he went to the polytechnical school in Switzerland, and after he was out of school and working in the patent office in Berne, one of the most pressing problems for physicists was to reconcile Newton's mechanical world view with new information about light and electromagnetics that was beginning to mount up. At about the middle of the nineteenth century James Clerk Maxwell, taking his cue from the earlier work of Michael Faraday, showed that electricity and magnetic forces were essentially the same as light waves, and that they move at the speed of light, that is 186,000 (in rounded numbers) miles per second. But there is a problem implied by the word "wave." Newton had assumed that light was particles. Faraday and friends

---

[4] Ibid., p. 27.

thought it was waves. Either way, a question arose of how light was propagated.

To understand this, imagine the following. I am standing on one end of a long hallway holding a rope by one end. You are standing at the other end of the hallway holding the other end of the rope. We stretch the rope tightly, then you raise it, and you snap it downward, sending a wave along the rope all the way to the other end. The wave had to have been propagated along something. In this case, it was the rope. Or imagine yourself standing on the seashore watching the waves roll in. In this case it is the water through which the waves are propogated. Take away the medium, and what do you have? Nothing; for the waves cannot exist without the medium through which they are propogated.

Now, assuming light is a wave, what is the medium through which it is propogated? Do not say air, for light can travel just as easily through a vacuum as not. Clearly it cannot be water. What then? The theory (and it goes back to Aristotle) was that there is a substance in space all around us called "aether." It is colorless, odorless, weightless it would seem, and all of creation is bathed in it. This is the medium which propagates light waves throughout the cosmos, or so the theory held. The problem was that in 1887 two American scientists, Albert Michelson and Edward Morley, while trying to show the existence of **aether** inadvertently showed just the opposite. The debunking of the notion of aether, along with other information about the nature of light, led Einstein down the path that would culminate in his monumental theory of special relativity. Quite simply, he wondered how light moved from place to place if there was no aether.

Proved there was no such thing as aether

Aether — or "ether," if you don't like the way the Greeks spelled it — was once thought to bathe the entire cosmos. Nowadays we know that there is no such thing.

But his wondering didn't stop here. Einstein had a particular genius for putting things in their simplest terms by the use of illustrations. The railway passenger is an excellent example. What would happen, he wondered, if he were able to ride a light wave at the speed of light and he were carrying a mirror. Both he and the mirror would be moving at the speed of light, so theoretically the light waves from his face could never catch up with the mirror and his image would never appear in it. Or take a clock. If he were traveling at the speed of light, theoretically it would appear to him that the clock's hands were completely still because the light waves emanating off the clock's face could not catch up to him so that he could see the hands had changed position. Not surprisingly, this one almost caused him to have a nervous breakdown.

Einstein solved this problem, and at the same time opened up the way to special relativity, by referring to an earlier theory of relativity, that of

Galileo. Motion, according to this, cannot be detected without reference to some fixed outside point. If I am traveling on a train, for instance, and the ride is perfectly smooth, I cannot tell that we are moving without looking outside at the countryside whizzing by. If the train is going 75 miles per hour, then how fast am I going. The answer is 75 miles per hour; but my speed is measured with reference to the fix land through which I am traveling.

Suppose now that at some point during my train ride I get up and walked forward the length of the car at the speed of 3 miles per hour relative to the car. How fast am I now traveling relative to a fix point outside the car? The answer is 78 miles per hour, for the 3 miles per hour are added to the 75. To use another illustration, suppose I am driving down the highway at 75 miles per hour and a car is coming toward me at the same rate of speed. How rapidly are we approaching each other? The answer is 150 miles per hour, our two speeds combined.[5] The problem of course — and Galileo realized it — is that there is no such thing as a fixed reference point. We are moving through space at tremendous speed. Nothing is still.

Now comes another of the troubling facts that nearly put Einstein, and other physicists, in straight jackets. In the latter nineteenth century experiments showed conclusively that light traveling through space does not show the sort of cumulative effect that other moving bodies do. To explain, imagine I am riding on a train and you are walking down the embankment beside the tracks. As I pass you, I drop a small rock out the window and it strikes you in the head. There is a good chance that it will kill you, for relative to you the rock was traveling at the speed of the train, and if you were coming toward me when I dropped the rock, you may add your speed to the speed of the rock.

If light travels at 186,000 per second, and it does, and if Galileo was correct, and he certainly appears to have been, then light ought to also show this cumulative effect as it is propogated through space. Thus, if I am on a train traveling toward you at 75 miles per hour, and I direct a beam of light at you, the light ought to travel toward you at 186,000 per second, plus the 75 miles per hour that the train is moving.

But it does not. It travels at 186,000 miles per second.

---

[5] I am indebted for this illustration, and much of what follows, to Gary Zukav whose book *The Dancing Wu Li Masters* is quite probably the finest exposition of modern physics for the neophyte.

If you stand at point "A" and I stand at point "B," and on a given signal we direct two beams of light at a point equidistant between us, the light beams ought to travel toward that point at the combined speed of 372,000 miles per second.

But they do not. The speed is 186,000 per second.

Very well, said Einstein (if you will be gracious enough to allow me to place my thoughts in his head), how are we to make sense of this? He had used Galileo's physics to solve the problem of whether or not he would be able to see his own image in the mirror he was carrying at 186,000 per second. He could see his own image, he said, because he and the mirror were traveling together, thus, relative to one another, they were not moving at all. Therefore, the light would have no difficulty spanning the space between his face and the mirror.

Now, however, things were spinning out of control, and Galileo was falling apart before his very eyes. The same Galileo whose relativity predicted that Einstein should indeed be able to see his face in the mirror, was the Galileo whose laws of motion predicted the cumulative effect of the speed of light. But that didn't work. If the speed of light did not change, what did? Clearly something had to change if any of this was to make sense. There were only so many possibilities. If the speed of light did not change, that left, as the only candidates, time and space.

We might well imagine the young Einstein as he stood face to face with the awesome new realization that time and space might be changed relative to motion. Dare he actually write a paper on the subject and publish it? He is supposed to have said:

> If relativity is proved right the Germans will call me a German, the Swiss will call me a Swiss citizen, and the French will call me a great scientist. If relativity is proved wrong the French will call me a Swiss, the Swiss will call me a German, and the Germans will call me a Jew.[6]

Like it or not, there seemed to be no other way to solve the problem, for as Schwartz and McGuinness have noted, speed is distance divided by time, and if speed were the same in the light experiments, then somehow time and space had to change. If not, then Galileo and Newton were wrong,

---

[6] **Quoted in Schwartz, Joseph and Michael Mcguinness, *Einstein for Beginners,* New York: Pantheon Books, 1979.**

and there were laws in this universe that held sometimes and sometimes did not. Einstein had what appears in retrospect to have been an almost naive faith in the proposition that a law of physics had to hold at all times, in all places, under all conditions. This led to his disagreement with Niels Bohr over quantum mechanics, as we shall see. But that came some twenty years later.

In 1905, before Bohr and Heisenburg,[7] Einstein wrote:

> [T]he unsuccessful attempts to discover any motion of the earth relatively to the light medium suggest that the phenomena of electrodynamics as well as of mechanics possess no properties corresponding to the idea of absolute rest. We will raise this conjecture (the purport of which will be hereafter called the "Principle of Relativity") to the status of a postulate, and also introduce another postulate, which is only apparently irreconcilable with the former, namely, that light is always propagated in empty space with a definite velocity c which is independent of the state of motion of the emitting body. These two postulates suffice for the attainment of a simple and consistent theory of the electrodynamics of moving bodies based on Maxwell's theory for stationary bodies. The introduction of a "luminiferous aether" will prove to be superfluous inasmuch as the view here to be developed will not require an "absolutely stationary space" provided with special properties.[8]

In so many words, my motion relative to the speed of light does nothing to change the speed of light. It is always moving at 186,000 miles per second. But two things do change — time and space. As we speed up, time slows down and space begins to shrink. This is true whether we are in a rocketship going 50,000 miles per hour, or we are simply walking across a room. The reason we don't notice this when walking is that our speed is so slow, relative to the speed of light, that the changes aren't apparent to anything but an extremely sensitive instrument — say an atomic clock. But

---

7 **Bohr and the others did not disprove Einstein. Far from it. They simply showed that when one moves out of interstellar space and down to the subatomic level the rules changes substantially. This is what Einstein could not accept.**

8 **Einstein, Albert, *Annalen der Physik*, 1905, quoted in Schwartz & McGuinness, op.cit.**

if we were able to approach the speed of light we would see the difference in some remarkable ways.

According to Einstein, nothing in the universe can actually travel at the speed of light — except light. So much for intergalactic travel and a good portion of science fiction. At the speed of light, mass becomes infinite, a truth which springs from his famous equation, $e = mc^2$. This is so astounding that it is unbelievable, but repeated experiments under a variety of conditions have confirmed it. People who listened to Democritus expounding his atomic theory must have wondered how anyone could ever explain what was filling up all the empty space that must exist between atoms. Here at long last was a plausible explanation.

Students are no doubt familiar with some of the "what would happen if" stories told about Einstein's theory of special relativity. Assume you are in a space ship and accelerating toward the speed of light. As you approach that impassable barrier everything seems normal to you within the ship, for within the ship and relative to it, all is motionless. Not so for those outside. If they could communicate with you inside the ship, you would find that presidential elections would be occurring five times a week. If they could transmit the sound of their beating hearts, you would hear them only as a high-pitched hum. Going the other way, your heart beats, if transmitted to them, would be spaced twenty minutes apart. Within a few weeks you would receive word that all of your friends on earth were dead.[9]

Einstein welcomes you to a new dimension, that of spacetime. As the poet (myself, of course) has said:

Kindly ignore that apple, Newt.
I'm not so sure it's falling.
There's nothing left that absolute,
And that's downright appalling.

Gravity and Einstein

General relativity is Einstein's theory about gravity.

This brings us to Einstein's general theory of relativity, not so well known or talked about as his special theory, but just as revolutionary. It deals with a subject so basic, and yet so mysterious, that all know about it but no one seems to know what it is. The subject is gravity.

All bodies are affected by gravity, and all fall the same way in a

---

[9] Calder, Nigel, *Einstein's Universe*, New York: The Viking Press, 1979, p. 85.

gravitational field. This is what physicists call the equivalence principle, and it is what Galileo demonstrated in his experiments with falling bodies.[10]

Falling, in a sense, is what gravity is all about. Every body in the universe is falling toward something. So why do some bodies gravitate toward one another? More to the point, why does the earth orbit the sun? Why does the moon orbit the earth? Why doesn't everything just fall apart. Newton had an answer that seemed perfectly logical for years, but that today seems quaint and curious. That is because today we are looking back at Newton with the eyes of Albert Einstein. Newton assumed that all bodies are just naturally attracted toward one another. Einstein thought that the gravitational pull was a property of the space around the bodies.

In 1915 he published his paper on general relativity in which he postulated that space, in effect, is warped by large bodies such as stars or planets as it passes around them. It is this, Einstein said, that attracts a smaller body toward a larger one, and not some sort of force in the two bodies. To get the idea, imagine a stretched elastic sheet with a heavy weight placed at the center. Let the elastic sheet represent space and the weight represent the sun or any other large heavenly body. Now, suppose that we drop a marble onto the sheet. Because the weight is stretching the sheet downward at the center, the marble will roll toward the center and into the heavier weight. To an outside observer it might appear that the two objects were drawn together, but this is not the case. Rather, the smaller object is following the only path possible, given the fact that the sheet is warped downward.

Suppose, however, that we roll the marble very rapidly across the sheet. Though it might be deflected toward the center, if its speed were great enough it would probably continue on passed the larger object and off the sheet on the other side. Or, if the speed of the object were not great enough to allow it to escape, it could go into orbit around the heavy weight in the center; and so long as it maintained the proper speed it would remain in orbit, much as a piece of driftwood will swirl around the outside edge of a whirlpool so long as its speed is great enough. If, for any reason, the smaller body begins to lose speed, then its orbit begins to decay and it is captured by the larger body.

---

10 Some say from the Tower of Pisa, others say he rolled balls down incline planks. It doesn't matter. Either way he demonstrated that objects fall at a uniform rate of speed regardless of their weight, and poor Aristotle took another major hit.

You might wonder what keeps the orbiting body in motion. Why, for example, does the moon continue moving about the earth at the same rate of speed? For this we do not need to consult Einstein. Newton gives us the answer in his first law of motion: A body remains in a state of rest or of uniform motion in a straight line unless compelled by an external force to change that state. This is the law of inertia. If you have always thought of the earth as moving in a circle around the sun, or the moon as moving in a circle around the earth, Einstein invites you to change this way of looking at things. All things are falling through the vacuum of space. The earth has fallen into the space occupied by a larger body, the sun, and is actually traveling in a straight line at a uniform speed; but because it is trapped by the space warped around the sun it is moving straight ahead in the only path possible. It will continue to do so unless, for some reason, it slows down. That shouldn't happen for a few years at least.

Ironically, Einstein was not after showing what was relative. In fact, he wanted to call his theory "invariance theory." According to Nigel Calder,

> [Einstein] discovered what was "absolute" and reliable *despite* the apparent confusions, illusions and contradictions produced by relative motions of the action of gravity. The chief merit of the name "relativity" is in reminding us that a scientist is unavoidably a participant in the system he is studying. Einstein gave "the observer" his proper status in modern science.[11]

Before we leave Einstein and move on to other incredible yet true discoveries by modern physicists, let me divert you with another piece of verse, this by someone other than myself. Earlier I quoted Alexander Pope:

> Nature and nature's laws lay hid in night.
> God said, "Let Newton be," and all was light.

Try this one, written two-hundred years later by J.C. Squire:

> It did not last: the Devil howling, "Ho,
> Let Einstein be," restored the status quo.

Squire obviously thinks that Einstein has plunged us back into the night from which Newton took us. I don't believe it. But it is clear that the simple,

---

[11] Calder, Nigel, *Einstein's Universe*, op.cit., p. 2.

mechanical universe of Newton, Galileo, and Descartes is gone forever.

Max Planck's Quantum Leap

Physicists today say that there are only three constants in the universe. Two of these, the speed of light and gravity, were dealt with by Einstein. The third, Planck's Constant, was discovered by the man for whom it is named. It was this discovery that set in motion the quantum mechanics revolution in modern physics. Planck had broken with long standing notions that light was emitted in a steady stream, and had hypothesized that it actually comes in bursts of energy (quanta) from its source.

Quanta (sing. quantum) is Max Planck's name for energy packets, fired in discontinuous bursts from atoms previously excited by a bombardment of energy.

I am certain that many people, and indeed many students, cannot understand why anyone would spend his or her time fooling around with such things. Light is light, after all, and all we need to know is whether or not it comes on when one throws the switch. But as we have been seeing all along, some people are simply blessed (or cursed) with a more nagging curiosity than others, and it is these, the curious, who change history and win Nobel prizes. Einstein was such a man, as was Max Planck.

In December of 1900, five years before Einstein's epoch-making paper, Max Planck presented a paper to the physics community that troubled him deeply. He had discovered that nature is discontinuous.[12] Big deal, you say. Yes, but this discovery changed everything, and the implications of it are unfolding all around us as cosmologists attempt to fit it into the framework of waking reality. This is metaphysics and physics met together in one confusing swirl of matter and energy.

But to explain. Suppose you pick up the paper one morning, and you read on the front page that a recent survey shows that 15.75 percent of all Americans were born abroad. Now you realize that the 15.75 is merely a statistical device, that there can be no actual 15.75 in people because there is no such thing as a .75 person. People exist only in whole numbers.

Are you still struggling with this one? Try this. Between one person and the second person standing beside him or her there is no continuous line of being. That is, you don't mark out a place halfway between the two and say, "At this point we have one and a half people." No. You have one person, then you jump — you don't slide along a continuum — to two people. You jump from a whole number to a whole number. And that, said

---

12 Once again I find myself indebted to Gary Zukav. I urge all interested parties to pick up his book, *The Dancing Wu Li Masters*.

Planck, is how nature is.

You are still befuddled? Don't worry about it. Come along, and let us be befuddled together.

Planck made his discovery while studying the process by which heated objects take on energy and glow. In his day an atom was thought of as a nucleus to which electrons were attached by tiny spring-like structures. When the atom was heated, the electrons became agitated and began to jiggle up and down, and this was why they glowed and emitted light. The problem with this theory was that it didn't work in practice, which means that it resulted in predictions that did not come to pass, and it resulted in things coming to pass that no one would have predicted. Planck was trying to work out these problems when he made his discovery and opened up to the twentieth century the awesome world of quantum mechanics.

We have all had the experience of watching a piece of metal heated until it begins to glow deep red, then redder, then orange, then yellow. Remove the heat and the color begins to dim, bit by bit, until we are back at the same old dull gray. This process seems continuous, sliding along, and the assumption of physicists up to Max Planck had been that this is precisely what it was. But remember, you cannot have .75 humans, and Planck discovered that heated atoms are exactly the same. The process is a discontinuous one. Atoms absorb energy in packets, and this is how they emit it — in short bursts. To quote Gary Zukav, nature is explosive, not continuous and smooth.

These energy packets that are absorbed and then emitted in short bursts were called "quanta" by Planck. Have you ever heard the term quantum leap? We will get to it in a minute. As the students in my day used to say, "It'll blow your mind." First, let me introduce you in a more intimate fashion to the third remaining constant in our universe, Planck's constant.

Planck discovered that the energy transfer that takes place in discontinuous bursts could actually be calculated. Roughly it is a decimal point, followed by twenty-six zeros, and ending in 6624. The significance of this number is explained in language anyone can understand by the famous Stephen Hawking.

> Heisenberg showed that the *uncertainty* in the position of the particle times the *uncertainty* in its velocity times the mass of the particle can never be smaller than a certain quantity, which is known as Planck's constant. . .
>
> The *uncertainty* principle signaled an end to Laplace's dream of a theory of science, a model of the

> universe that would be completely deterministic: one certainly cannot predict future events exactly if one cannot even measure the present state of the universe precisely![13]

Did I say that anyone can understand this? Forgive me. What I meant to say was that anyone can understand if he or she is willing to apply a little mental effort to the task. You will notice that I italicized the word uncertainty in the passage quoted above. It is this uncertainty, springing from the work of Max Planck and the application of his principles, which gives us Planck's constant and at the same time destroys the naive notion of a deterministic universe. I am sorry, Thomas Hobbes; sorry, Pierre Laplace; sorry, Doctor Skinner — your belief in a determined universe appears to have been shattered forever. It was a neat, and to some, comfortable metaphysical system; but it has fallen to the gun, along with spontaneous generation and the geocentric universe.

The Atom According to Bohr

In 1913, Niels Bohr, Danish physicist, proposed a new theoretical model of the atom, one that was able to account for the findings of Planck. Remember that prior to Planck physicists believed the atom consisted of a nucleus with electrons attached by spring-like things, and that as these were heated they vibrated and emitted light. Planck destroyed this idea by showing that light (energy might be a better way of saying it) is actually absorbed by atoms in whole packets and emitted in discontinuous bursts. Now comes Bohr and says that the atom is actually like a tiny universe. Analogically, the nucleus corresponds to our sun, and the electrons revolving around the nucleus correspond to our planets. This is the atomic model with which most of us are familiar. The electrons orbit the nucleus in particular and fixed orbits, but these orbits can be changed if the atom is bombarded with energy. As energy bombards the atom, and as the electrons absorb this energy, they jumped outward into a new orbit farther from their nuclear center. Then when the energy bombardment ceases they jump back to their original orbits, emitting energy as they do so.

Got it? Jump out as energy is absorbed. Jump back in as energy is emitted. This is the so-called quantum leap. What makes it so unusual, in

---

[13] Hawking, Stephen, *A Brief History of Time: From the Big Bang to Black Holes*, New York: Bantam Books, 1988, p. 55.

fact all but impossible, is that in making the leap the electrons do not traverse time and space. Imagine yourself getting up from the chair in which you are sitting and starting toward the door of the room in which you presently find yourself. You must traverse time and space on the way, which is to say that you must move in a continuous path from point "A" to point "B," and that it will take you a certain amount of time to do so. At any given time on your journey from chair to door you will be one fourth of the distance to your goal; two-thirds of the distance; three-fourths of the distance, and so on. But what if you started from point "A" to point "B," and you were suddenly just there, without moving through time and space at all. This is the famous "quantum leap," first described by Bohr. It can't happen to you,[14] but it happens to electrons all the time.

Remember, as the electron jumps back to its original orbit it emits energy, or light, in a discontinuous burst, a quantum, and this quantum of light is called a photon. But how can this possibly be? Earlier theoreticians such as Faraday and Maxwell, described light as moving in waves; and indeed many experiments have been performed that show that light is just that, and that it possesses all the properties of a wave, including amplitude and frequency. Now we have Niels Bohr talking about light as if it were a particle, and conducting many experiments to show that this is precisely what it is. Light, however, cannot be both a wave and a particle. The two are what logicians call mutually exclusive. But having entered the strange, fairytale land of twentieth century physics why should we find anything strange? As Walt Whitman said on an occasion, "Do I contradict myself? Very well, I contradict myself."

How about a little more self-contradiction? Why should anyone mind if we go from the weird to the positively insane?

Heisenberg and Uncertainty

When we were discussing Planck's constant, I quoted from a book by Stephen Hawking, and I italicized his use of the word uncertainty and promised that we would come back to it. So here we go, off into uncertainty.

In the late 1920's Werner Heisenberg was caught between the theories of Niels Bohr and one Erwin Schrödinger (If you have never heard of Schrödinger's cat, stay with me and I'll introduce you). We have seen what Bohr thought. Schrödinger disagreed because Bohr's theory could not

---

[14] **At least, I don't think it can. If we could move at the speed of light. . .Who knows?**

account for the ways in which light behaves like a wave instead of a particle. As Heisenberg studied the two positions and amassed data on the behavior of electrons he made an interesting discovery: observing electrons changes their behavior.

> You can't observe the position of an electron except by bouncing something — light, for example — off it. In other words, you have to introduce a form of radiation, which has energy of its own, and this energy will disturb the path of the electron to a greater or lesser degree.
>
> In fact, the more precisely you wish to locate the electron, the more you have to disturb its velocity (and thus its momentum), because you have to add more energy. Conversely, if you wish to precisely measure the electron's momentum (expressed in its velocity), you must minimize the interference of the radiation. But by doing so, you make it impossible to precisely locate the electron's position.[15]

What this comes down to is rather simple, but rather troubling. I can calculate the position of an electron, or I can calculate its speed, but I cannot calculate both at the same time because observing the one somehow disturbs the other. Stephen Hawking has said:

> The uncertainty principle had profound implications for the way in which we view the world. Even after more than fifty years they have not been fully appreciated by many philosophers, and are still the subject of much controversy. The uncertainty principle signaled an end to Laplace's dream of a theory of science, a model of the universe that would be completely deterministic: one certainly cannot predict future events exactly if one cannot even measure the present state of the universe precisely. We could still imagine that there is a set of laws that determines events completely for some supernatural being, who could observe the present state of the universe without disturbing it. However, such models of the universe are not of much interest to us ordinary mortals. It seems better to employ the principle of economy known as Occam's razor and cut out all the features of

---

15 Macrone, Michael, *Eureka! What Archimedes Really Meant*, New York: Harper Perennial, 1994, p.103.

> the theory that cannot be observed. This approach led Heisenberg, Erwin Schrödinger, and Paul Dirac in the 1920s to reformulate mechanics into a new theory called quantum mechanics, based on the uncertainty principle. In this theory particles no longer had separate, well-defined positions and velocities that could not be observed. Instead, they had a quantum state, which was a combination of position and velocity.[16]

I would be very surprised (pleasantly so) if the student at this point understood the implications of what we are talking about. As Hawking said in the portion just quoted, after fifty years many philosophers do not fully appreciate them. Nevertheless, anyone who is willing to think about it can see that these physicists have turned our world upside down. At the foundation level, we do not know for certain how to accurately measure reality, and the very idea of a deterministic universe has become passe, a relic left over from a more naive nineteenth century. If we do not live in a materialistic, determined universe, then just how sure can we be that science is a viable method of inquiry, except on a gross level?

Schrödinger and his Weird Cat

The most famous cat in all of science has to be the imaginary one belonging to Erwin Schrödinger. He (the cat) comes up in an interesting thought experiment that illustrates some of the troubling aspects of the world according to quantum mechanics. To understand the experiment we will have to revisit some of our old friends — Einstein, Planck, Maxwell, and one we haven't yet talked about, Thomas Young.

Question: Is light a particle or is it a wave? And remember, logically it cannot be both.

To venture an answer we must first ask, how does a wave behave. Zukav, in *The Dancing Wu Li Masters*, asks us to imagine ourselves looking down from a helicopter at a breakwater protecting a harbor. The entrance to the breakwater is large enough to allow large ocean-going vessels to pass through. If we watch a pattern of waves as they come up to the breakwater we will notice that those waves that go through the opening into the harbor itself have the same pattern as the waves rushing up to the breakwater on the seaward side. The reason is that the harbor entrance is wide enough to allow

---

[16] Hawking, Stephen, *A Brief History of Time, op.cit.*, p. 55.

the waves to go through without being broken up. But suppose the harbor entrance is so small that a rowboat can barely pass through. The waves that rush against the breakwater will be stopped; but those few that go through will form a completely different pattern on the other side. The wave pattern on the harbor side of the breakwater shows a diffracted pattern.

In 1803 Thomas Young reasoned that if light is a wave, then it ought to behave like the wave in the illustration of the breakwater and the harbor. So he tried it and got the results he expected; light passing through a large hole made a pattern on the wall behind it like the hole through which it passed, whereas light passing through a slit made by a razor blade showed a diffracted pattern.

Now we get to Young's famous (assuming you are into reading the sorts of literature in which such things are talked about) double slit experiment. Young set up a light source so that it could direct light against a wall through which one small hole had been drilled. Behind this wall was a second wall with two narrow slits parallel to one another, either of which could be covered over with a piece of cardboard. And behind this was the target area, a blank wall. When Young direct the light at the first wall, and covered over one of the slits in the second wall, the pattern in the target area was the diffracted one we would expect. When he left both slits uncovered, however, so that the light coming through the hole in the first wall passed through both slits in the second wall, the pattern he witnessed in the target area was strange indeed, a series of vertical parallel bars, ranging in brightness from the middle (where the brightest was) out to the darker bars at the edges. This, take it on blind faith, is due to wave interference, and it tended to prove what Young had thought. Light is indeed a wave.

Einstein, however, had shown that light is a particle, a photon. Suppose someone were to re-run the Young experiment. Could it be shown that light is not a wave? Instead of directing a large amount of light at the first wall, so that some gets through the hole but most is stopped by the wall, let us fire light at the hole in discrete bursts, one photon at a time. The hole in the first wall is open, but one of the slits in the second wall is covered. Ready! Fire! The results are eerie. First, the light in this case behaves like a particle, not a wave. Second, the photon hits the target in an area that would be dark if the second slit were open. We do the experiment again, but this time we open both slits in the second wall. Now the photon hits the target in an area where no hits were recorded in the first experiment. The question, according to Zukav, is, *How did the photon in the first experiment know that the second slit was not open*? The question would make no sense if we were flooding the first wall with light; but remember, we fired *only one photon* at the hole in the first wall.

> When we fired our photon and it went through the first slit, how did it "know" that it could go to an area that must be dark if the other slit were open? In other words, how did the photon know that the other slit was closed? . .
>
> There is no definitive answer to this question. Some physicists, like E.H. Walker, speculate that photons may be conscious![17]

Or, as another devotee of our by now notorious cat has said:

> The electrons not only know whether or not both holes are open, they know whether or not we are watching them, and they adjust their behavior accordingly. . .
>
> The physics is impossible, but the math is clean and simple, familiar equations to any physicist. As long as you avoid asking what it means there are no problems. Ask why the world should be like this, however, and the reply is: we have no idea.[18]

Of course, we haven't got to the cat yet; but we shall. All of this is, in a sense, a preliminary. But in this game the preliminaries are just as important, even more so perhaps, than the main event.

Whether light is a wave or a particle appears to depend solely upon how we, the observers, wish to look at it. As with Einstein, the observer becomes a participant in the creation of physical reality. But remember Heisenberg and uncertainty. When we fire a photon at the screen we cannot know exactly where it will land. The most that we can do is state probabilities, and it is this bizarre fact that moves us along toward the cat that exists only in the fertile brain of Erwin Schrödinger.

It is quite possible that the student is not quite clear at this point what is so strange about the double-slit experiment and wave-particle duality. When physicists talk about the photon "knowing" that the second slit is closed or open, the person coming to this for the first time may be genuinely

---

[17] Zukav, Gary, *The Dancing Wu Li Masters*, op.cit., p. 63.

[18] Gribbin, *In Search of Schrödinger's Cat: Quantum Physics and Reality*, New York:

puzzled. The important thing to remember is this — these photons of light are hitting the target area behind the wall with the double slit in patterns that suggest they know how they are supposed to behave if one slit is open, or if both are open.

Now, comes the next important question. Can we calculate where the light will strike the target area? Not actually, for Heisenberg's uncertainty principle intervenes, making statistical probability the best we can do. That is, we can say that there is a sixty-percent probability that the strike will be in a given area, but a forty-percent probability that it will not.

Follow closely, student.

We fire a photon at the first wall, and off it goes at the speed of (what else?) light. While it is in flight either of our two probabilities represent reality, but once it strikes the target one of the possibilities no longer exists. Instantaneously, the one probability wave has collapsed into the other, so that now only one of the two probabilities has become reality. But what controls which area the strike will be made? The answer, nothing but pure chance, was so unsettling to Einstein that he was never able to accept quantum mechanics as viable theory. You may in fact recall his often quoted letter to Max Born on the subject in which he stated he was convinced that God does not play dice.[19] It doesn't matter what Einstein was willing to accept. There are few physicists today who agree with him on this point.

In classical physics, the physics of Newton and Galileo, the double-slit experiment would be seen like this: an actual photon left the light source traveling at the speed of 186,000 per second, went through the hole in the first wall, then through one of the two slits, and struck the target area. Given what Newton — and ultimately Einstein — believed, we should be able to calculate the path of the photon as well as its landing area.

Given what today's physicists know, and given the so-called Copenhagen interpretation of quantum mechanics, the classical physicists are wrong. No actual photon comes from the light source. In this murky never-never land no such thing is possible. A potential photon is there, and will probably hit a certain area, but it is guided by pure chance. And the observer is as much involved in what finally happens as are the photon, its

---

19 This caused Stephen Hawking to quip, "God not only plays dice, he sometimes throws the dice where they cannot be seen." And physicist Joseph Ford: "God plays dice with the universe, but they're loaded dice. And the main objective of physics now is to find out by what rules there were loaded and how we can use them for our own ends." See Gleich, James, *Chaos; Making a New Science,* New York: Viking, 1987.

direction, and its speed. This truth, specifically, is what Schrödinger brought to light, and this gets us to his cat.

In the experiment a cat is placed inside a box, and with it is a device that, if triggered, will release a gas, killing the cat instantly. The triggering mechanism is a random event, such as the light photon hitting the target area; but instead of a photon Schrödinger suggests something that will work just as well — the radioactive decay of an atom. We cannot predict whether or not the decay will take place, so we don't know without looking into the box whether the cat is dead or alive. Which is it? Gary Zukav sums it up as follows:

> According to classical physics, the cat is either dead or it is not dead. All that we have to do is to open the box and see which is the case. According to quantum mechanics, the situation is not so simple.
>
> The Copenhagen Interpretation of Quantum Mechanics says that the cat is in a kind of limbo represented by a wave function which contains the possibility that the cat is dead and also the possibility that the cat is alive. . .
>
> According to classical physics, we get to know something by observing it. According to quantum mechanics, it isn't there until we do observe it! Therefore, the fate of the cat is not determined until we look inside the box.[20]

The moment we look inside the box, says the Copenhagen Interpretation,[21] one of the possibilities collapses and the other becomes reality. It is the act of observation that creates the reality, and up until that time the cat is neither living, nor is it dead.

There is, however, another interpretation, that of Schrödinger himself. Physicists call it the Many Worlds Interpretation. In this view, what has happened inside the unopened box is that the world has actually split into two parts, one in which the cat is dead and one in which it is alive. The moment we open the box and look in, our world also splits into two. In one of these worlds we find a living cat, in the other we find a dead one. Neither world, however, is aware of the existence of the other. We are talking about

---

[20] Zukav, Gary, *The Dancing Wu Li Masters, op.cit.*, pp. 85-86.

[21] This is the school associated with Niels Bohr.

parallel universes, if you are able to handle it.

I feel that by this time the student must have become thoroughly bewildered; not, I trust, because he or she cannot follow what I have been saying, but because it is difficult to believe that intelligent people can actually believe such nonsense. I cannot emphasize strongly enough that this is not nonsense; it is, as I quoted John Gribbin as saying earlier, familiar to any physicist. These are our some of our most brilliant and clear thinking individuals, plying their trade within the most strict of the sciences, the scientist's science. It is just that — to repeat the old cliche — the truth is stranger than fiction. Reality is not what we thought it was.

The Unified Field Theory

A viable unified field theory is the thing all physicists would love to create. It would pull together, in one theory, the worlds of Einstein and the quantum physicists.

Einstein, who refused to believe that God played dice with the universe, went to his grave looking for what has come to be known as the Unified Field Theory. He was, as I have said, a naive man in many ways, and a classical physicist to boot. Newton had formulated his theory of gravity on the belief that the same force that caused the apple to fall from a tree is what guides the planets and stars in their orbits, and that the laws here are equally applicable on the far side of the most remote galaxy. Not only did Newton believe this, but so did Einstein. He refused to believe that there were rules for out there that would not work in here — "in here" being the subatomic world. But so far no one has been able to put things together. What works "out there" does not work "in here," and that is that.

Or maybe it is not.

Einstein was convinced that there could be a Unified Field Theory, one grand, yet simple model that could explain everything and reunify what the quantum physicists had torn apart. Physicists agree with him, and many are looking for it even I as pen these words. As a matter of fact a number of possibilities have been floated, the latest perhaps being the so-called "string theory." But to date there is nothing that has the simplicity, the elegance, the aesthetic beauty that scientists like to see in their theories. Consequently, the search is still on. This might be a good project for one of my students to take up. Find the Unified Field Theory and win the Nobel prize, and someday if I am still alive, I will put you into the fourteenth edition of this book.

Pauli and the Neutrino

The neutrino: an elementary particle with no mass, no weight, and that travels at or near the speed of light — and maybe faster.

The search for the illusive neutrino is another of the odd physical/metaphysical tales of the twentieth century. Its seeker, and finder, always reminds me a bit of Parmenides, who postulated eternal, unchanging being because logic, not common sense, told him this must be the way things are. It takes a great deal of intellectual courage to make this kind of leap; and it took a great deal of courage to do what Wolfgang Pauli did. The leap carried Pauli to international fame among physicists and wrote his name in the stars. But that is really a confusing metaphor, for it wasn't among the stars that Pauli's name was written, but on some of the most minute of the particles making up matter. This is how it happened.

Following Niels Bohr's atomic theory, which he published in 1912, physicists began detailed analyses of the actual structure of atoms. This cannot have been easy, for they could not see the subject of their studies, nor had anyone ever seen them. They were moving forward on theory, using carefully planned and elegant experiments. Things were going along fairly well as long as they were working with some of the simpler atoms, hydrogen for example, which has only a nucleus and one electron. But as they moved on to more complex and heavier elements the theories with which they were working started coming apart at the seams. One area in particular had them all puzzled, that of *beta decay.*

Radioactive decay is just that. An atom explodes, falls apart. Scientists study the process because if they can track and measure all the various parts of the decayed atom they can learn a great deal about how the atom is put together. In the case of beta decay,[22] however, what they were learning was unsettling. When they measured all the parts of the exploded particle, they did not total up to the predecay whole. In short, the predecay particle was greater than the sum of its parts.

There is a principle in science, going back virtually to Democritus, and reemphasized in the eighteenth century by the founder of modern chemistry, Antoine Lavoisier. Let us call it the conservation principle. It says, in so many words, that energy (which is merely mass in a different guise) may change forms but cannot go out of existence. Burn a stick of wood, for example. The stick is changed to something else, but the basic matter is still around. The problem with beta decay was that when the electron under scrutiny decayed, something was missing. Once again, the parts did not add up to the whole.

To get some idea of how puzzled the physicists were by this development, imagine an orange. You peel it, carefully count the sections,

---

[22] **In beta decay an electron shoots out of the nucleus of the atom. If you wish to know more about it than this, take a course in nuclear physics.**

and find that there are eight. Then you separate each section from the whole, tossing them one by one into a dish. Now you count the sections and find that there are only seven. What happened to the eighth section? You try it again with another orange, with exactly the same result. This is ridiculous. It cannot be happening. Yet every time you peel and divide an orange you wind up with less than what you had when the orange was whole. By this time you have a group of scientists working with you, throwing explanations at you faster than you can deal with them. But at the end of the day it all comes down to one simple truth — no one can explain what is happening.

Then a new man shows up, younger than the others, less apt to be intimidated, perhaps, by tradition. He says there can be only one explanation. The part of the orange that is being lost in division is actually invisible. It somehow looks like an eighth section when it is with its mates, but it is really invisible, and it disappears as the orange is taken apart. It may well be there in the dish with the other sections, but you do not know it because it is invisible.

Would you be apt to take such an explanation seriously? What if you were about to throw the youngster out in disgust and he said to you as you were grabbing him by the collar, "Do you have a better explanation?"

The discovery of the neutrino came about in just such a fashion. In 1930 an international group of physicists met to discuss the problems with beta decay and how they might be solved. Wolfgang Pauli, who was only twenty years old, did not attend because he stayed in Zurich to go to a dance, but he sent a letter to his friend Dr. Geiger (of Geiger counter fame) in which he put forth his idea of how the problem could be solved. Geiger read the letter, and was barraged with hostility, insults and skepticism. And it was no wonder. Pauli's solution was outlandish.

> The energy numbers did not balance because one of the exploded parts had been going unobserved. If this particle could be observed, and its energy numbers measured, then they could be added into the equation and balance would result.[23]

Now what is so outlandish about this? It sounds perfectly reasonable until you remember the example of the orange and understand that Pauli is asking us to believe in something that is totally invisible, undetectable,

---

[23] Gale, George, *Theory of Science*, New York, McGraw-Hill, 1979, p. 173.

without weight, mass, or electrical charge. As George Gale has put it:

> [I]n order to balance the electric change equation, the new particle must have no electric charge. Second, in order to balance the mass equation, its mass must be nearly zero, or equal to zero. Third, in order to balance the energy equation, the particle must be extremely small, and travel at or near the speed of light. Thus, this new particle must be neutral in charge, must be vanishingly light in mass and vanishingly small in size, and must travel as fast as can be. In short, the new particle must be, for all practical (indeed, for almost all theoretical) purposes, unobservable.[24]

Over sixty years have gone by, and today Pauli's strange idea no longer seems strange. The Neutrino is accepted as fact, and actually has been observed in a strange way. Since it has no mass, and no physical properties, it cannot be stopped by any sort of matter. Our bodies are being pierced by neutrinos constantly, and we never are aware of them. But if one neutrino collides with another neutrino we can see the results of the collision. V.A. Firsoff has left us with an interesting picture of the world, as it might be seen by a neutrino.

> The universe as seen by a neutrino eye would wear a very unfamiliar look. Our earth and other planets simply would not be there, or might at best appear as thin patches of mist. The sun and other stars may be dimly visible, in as much as they emit some neutrinos. . . A neutrino brain might suspect our existence from certain secondary effects, but would find it very difficult to prove, as we would elude the neutrino instruments at his disposal.
>
> Our universe is no truer than that of the neutrinos — they exist, but they exist in a different kind of space, governed by different laws. . .The neutrino. . is subject neither to gravitational nor to electromagnetic field . . .*It might be able to travel faster than light, which would make it relativistically recede in our time scale.*[25]

---

[24] Ibid., pp. 173-174.

[25] Virsoff, V.A., *Life, Mind and Galaxies*, New York: W.A. Benjamin, 1967. Quoted in Velasquez, Manuel, *Philosophy*, 6th Ed., Belmont, CA: Wadsworth Publishing Co., 1997.

I italicized the final sentence of the Virsoff quote to call your attention to it. It might be able to travel faster than light. Doesn't this violate Einstein's special theory of relativity? Yes, but one of the main reasons nothing in the universe (as we thought we knew it) could travel faster than light is because at the speed of light mass becomes infinite. The neutrino has no mass. If these particles do in fact travel faster than light, then in theory they are receding into our past, which for them is (I suppose) the present.

Obviously the existence of the neutrino creates interesting metaphysical problems for anyone who is seriously questioning the meaning of reality. It seems that, lean on the physical world though we might, when we push down to the foundational level of things we find ourselves in a strange place that bears little resemblance to the reality we thought we knew. As Arthur Koestler has said, "To the unprejudiced mind, neutrinos have indeed a certain affinity with ghosts — which does not prevent them from existing."[26]

So Where Are We Now?

We are living in a strange, exciting universe. Someone once said, "Astronomically speaking, man is nothing;" and one who was standing beside him replied, "Astronomically speaking, man is the astronomer." This is good to remember, for there are times when we look up to the stars, and we consider how small we are in the scheme of things, and we are apt to think of ourselves as nothings. But we are small creatures gifted with marvelous minds, and with these we have been able to go out to the planets, and to dive down to the neutrinos and the elementary particles that make up everything we see around us.

Philosophically speaking, the human is the philosopher, the only one we have on this earth, or are ever likely to have. There is certainly no indication that any other species has the mental capacity to rise to the occasion, so whatever is to be found out about reality and the universe we inhabit will have to be found out by us. Who could have known, a scant hundred years ago, that by this time we would be talking about reality in terms that not even Plato and the early Greeks could have imagined? I began this chapter by saying that the farther along we go, the more blurred become the lines between various metaphysical systems.

---

26 Koestler, Arthur, *The Roots of Coincidence*, New York: Random House, 1972, p. 63.

After reading this brief account of twentieth century physics, I ask you what you think. Are we living in a purely material universe that is determined and obeys the laws of cause and effect? On one level, we are. Are we living in a universe that is idea, or energy, with no clear indication of where cause and effect fit in. On one level, we are. Can we reconcile these two? Not yet, but we are trying. Does God fit into this anywhere? It seems obvious to me that He does, but I will allow others to think about this for themselves. Are we free, or are we determined. Given what twentieth century physicists have discovered, I would say that the model of the human as a free moral agent with a functioning mind, is closer to reality than is the programmed machine of B.F. Skinner. But, once again, I will allow others to think about this for themselves. I often feel like a small child wading in a vast, boundless pool, the depths of which I cannot imagine. So far I have wet myself only up to the knees. The greater discoveries are yet to come.

A Quick Review of Section II

1. Metaphysics has taken on the meaning, for the average person, of something spiritual or other-worldly. But going back to Aristotle, from whose work the term is taken, it means the study of *being qua being.* Metaphysics is the study of reality, what is really there.

2. There are basically only three metaphysical positions — materialism, idealism, and dualism. Materialism holds that everything in the universe is ultimately reducible to some sort of matter. Idealism says that reality is spirit or idea. Dualism says that reality is a blending of the material and the ideal.

3. The materialists, for the most part, hold that we live in a universe in which everything must obey the laws of cause and effect and the Newtonian laws of motion. They are also reductionistic, believing that one reality may be completely explained in the terms of another reality. The materialistic position is basically that of science.

4. The most famous of the recent idealists was George Berkeley, eighteenth-century Irish bishop. All reality, he held, is ultimately a product of mind. He is famous for having asked question, "If a tree falls in the forest, and no one is there to hear it, does it make a sound?" He answered that it does not.

5. Both materialists and idealists are found among the pre-Socratic Greeks. The most famous dualist was Plato. He did not deny the reality of the material world, but he believed that the ideal world of the forms had greater reality, and that to know true truth one had to get behind mere appearance to the ideal.

6. Aristotle was a metaphysical naturalist. Naturalism is materialism. The naturalist holds that there is one level of reality, the physical world that we experience with our physical bodies. To posit a world behind the world, as Plato did, is not necessary according to Aristotle. Later generations of materialists, in agreement with Aristotle, will hold that Plato's ideal world is a violation of Ockham's razor.

7. Dualism became the dominant metaphysical position of the West, primarily because of Christianity's close affinity with the Neoplatonics. This lasted until the nineteenth century, when science and the scientific method began to dominate in intellectual circles.

8. Of all the metaphysical questions that have been asked over the years, none is more pressing and important than the question of whether or not God exists. Philosophers have traditionally attempted to frame rational arguments for the existence of God. These arguments have taken two forms, deductive and inductive.

9. Deductive arguments for the existence of God are variations of what philosophers call the Ontological argument. This is an argument that seeks to prove God's existence from the definition of the word "God." The most famous of the ontological arguments have been those of Anselm, Spinoza, and Descartes.

10. The inductive arguments for God's existence move from the things we see toward the things we do not. Aquinas had five of these. They are still being discussed, over seven-hundred years after he proposed them. The arguments owe a great deal to Aristotle, as do many of Aquinas's arguments. His argument from design, the so-called teleological argument, is particularly powerful, and has appeared in many variations across the years.

11. Those who argue for the existence of God have been troubled across the years by the problem of evil. How can we have evil in a world created by an all-powerful, all-knowing, all-loving God? The answer most frequently given is that evil is the result of humans exercising freedom of choice.

12. We examined other major metaphysical problems, among them, am I free or determined, do I have a mind or only a brain, do I have an essence, or do I not. We saw that how we answer these questions has a great deal to do with what we think of ourselves, and that to have some degree of freedom is necessary if we wish to hold one another responsible for our actions.

13. The twentieth century has not been kind to materialism. Physicists have shown that we live in a universe unlike anything that Newton and Descartes would have postulated in their wildest dreams. Down on the subatomic level things do not obey Newton laws, a fact which troubled Einstein. The quantum leap, the principle of uncertainty, the existence of the neutrino, are just some of the things that have left scientists and philosophers puzzled.

Section III
Epistemology

When the womb parted
we gained immediate wisdom
and spent the next fifty years
conforming to the ignorance
our elders,
and their elders, had
placed before us as a pattern.

We knew things from birth
that our teachers intended to keep from us
until we were old enough to bear them;

and because of our terrible knowledge
we trembled in our dark enclosures
when the light of the moon fell weeping
upon the pale bedclothes.

(Outside the wind crawled along hedgerows.)

In the adjoining room we heard low laughter —
careless rustling.
We believed that we would laugh
when we
became teachers
and moved to the adjoining room.

Chapter 9
Rationalism vs. Empiricism

As I was walking into town
I met a man whose hair was brown.
While coming back the other way
I met him, and his hair was gray.
I saw him in a dream last night.
I vow, his hair had turned snow white.
Answer my riddle if you can.
Who was this strange and phantom man?

What do we actually know? When we say that we know something, what is implied by that affirmation? If there are things that are unknowable, what are they, and how does one differentiate between the knowable and that which is not? Knowledge implies learning — or does it? Perhaps some sorts of knowledge are inborn and needn't be actually learned. On the other hand, maybe all knowledge comes as a result of learning, taking in that which was not there before.

Truth is an important word in the philosopher's lexicon. He or she spends a great deal of time looking for the elusive "truth,"in the hope that once found it will be the key that opens all other doors. But what do we mean by the word? If one says, "That is true,"what is he or she attempting to convey? Can there be different kinds of truth? Is truth for one person falsehood for another, or is truth always the same for all people at all times.

Logic, if properly applied, should certainly get one to truth and knowledge. But what is logic? By what rules am I to frame arguments. Can I tell a sound argument from an unsound argument? If I go along the road marked out by "logical" signposts, will I at long last come to wisdom, the thing all philosophers by definition claim to love? If I behave illogically, am I apt to wander over a cliff?

What is the source of true knowledge? Can I know things about the future by means of dreams, card-reading, gazing into a crystal ball? Socrates said, "Know thyself." How is this to come about? Can seers and astrologists give me any help in this, or am I better off being purely materialistic in my approach?

I am a teacher. That's how I make my living. But the very title "teacher" implies that I am teaching someone something, and that they are learning something from me via my teaching methods. Is this true? What is the best way to get information to people? Or is that the wrong question to ask? Perhaps Socrates was right, and the goal of all true educators is to draw out of the student the knowledge that is already there.

We are about to take up the subject of **epistemology**, that branch of philosophy which investigates knowledge. It takes very little thought to realize that this is at the very foundation of philosophy, and all other academic disciplines; for if knowledge is not possible, or if we do not know how to teach, then we may as well shut the schools and consign ourselves to ignorance. But saying that knowledge is foundational and thus necessary to the philosophical enterprise is not the same as saying that knowledge is possible. Needing something is one thing. Being assured that one can gain what one needs is another. The moment one claims to know something, all sorts of questions arise. Allow me to illustrate with a few stories.

Case 1

In 1944, when the Americans were fighting the Germans on the Western Front, my uncle was seriously wounded when the jeep in which he was riding was strafed by a plane. At this very time (as near as we can tell), half way around the world in Texas, my grandfather woke up in a cold sweat and woke my grandmother. He insisted that something was wrong with their oldest son, that he had been wounded in combat. My grandmother tried to calm him by telling him that he had simply had a bad dream. No, my grandfather said. He *knew* what had happened.

Case 2

About a year ago I got a call from a man I hadn't heard from in years. He was in California, living on welfare, and was suffering from some sort of mental disability. He called me because he was trying to get his disability payments increased by showing that he was paranoid-schizophrenic. He wanted me to provide a written account of his behavior during the period we had been in the Navy together. In the course of our conversations he told me that most of his mental problems went back to his days in a parochial school in Detroit when he had been one of the charges of a particularly cruel nun. The woman, he said, had killed several of his classmates, and had tried to kill him too. When I expressed disbelief, he assured me that it was the truth. When I asked why he had never gone to the police about this, he answered that he had not remembered it until recently when he had recovered it all with the help of a therapist. He *knew* the nun had killed these children.

Case 3

Only a few days ago a group of students and I were discussing suicide as a part of an ethics course I am teaching. The question we were attempting to answer was the obvious one to ask in such a discussion — is suicide ethically and morally right? We had talked about Aquinas's attitude toward suicide, why he said suicide is wrong. Many of the students were unconvinced by Aquinas's argument. I then brought up an interesting argument against suicide by the American novelist Joyce Carol Oates. She said that no one can rationally choose suicide because rational choice implies that one knows and has examined all sides of an issue; and in the case of suicide one cannot know and examine all sides because no one knows what death is. One of my students floored me with the announcement that he knows what death is. When I asked him how he knew, he offered an explanation that had more to do with supposition and belief than with knowledge. But he would not be dissuaded from his avowed knowledge of the experience of death.

In each of these cases we have individuals claiming knowledge of things that it would seem impossible for them to actually know. In the case of the wounded soldier, whereas the event had in fact taken place, the party claiming the knowledge was miles away and had no demonstrable connection to the occurrence. If he knew it, the source of his knowledge is very difficult to determine. In the second case the man is claiming to have known something, to have suppressed the knowledge because it was terribly traumatic, and to have recovered the memory through therapy. In the third case it is not easy to figure out exactly what the student is claiming, except that he says he knows what death is. When I asked him how he knew, he answered that he just knew, that was all.

These three cases are interesting because they all suppose a source of knowledge outside the ordinary. The most obvious way in which we learn anything is through direct experience. In fact I have asked the question of students many times: how do we learn. The vast majority will answer that we learn through experience, and most seem to be highly skeptical of learning by some other means. Have I however made a subtle error somewhere in the course of this paragraph? Have I assumed, without actually saying so, that learning equals knowledge? That is precisely what I have done, therefore we ought to ask whether or not that is true. In at least two of the cases cited above (and perhaps the third) the individuals have claimed knowledge without the benefit of prior learning. They simply "know" without knowing how they know.

It might be helpful if we define knowledge.

According to philosophers, **knowledge** is justified (or warranted) true belief. An examination of the three components of knowledge is, I think, enlightening.

The standard defintion of knowledge, among philosophers, is that knowledge is justified, true belief.

No one can have knowledge of something unless there is warranted evidence for it. This is what Mr. Spock means when he says to Captain Kirk, "It is not logical, Captain." To put it in simple terms: the belief you hold about a given thing is not justified by the existent evidence. In the first section of this book we discussed Aristotle's rules of inference. These rules are critical to the field of epistemology and to the search for the truth, because it is impossible for anyone to seriously hold that he or she knows something if the claimed knowledge violates one of the rules of inference. Example: I know that my car is solid black, and it is also solid green. This assertion violates the law of contradiction. It cannot be both colors at the same time. The statement is not warranted by the evidence, therefore I can have no such knowledge.

But knowledge must also be true. Suppose I state that I know that my car is solid black, but when we look at it we find that it is solid green. I can hardly go on asserting that I know my car is solid black, and I would be thought very strange were I to do so, for knowledge of a thing presuppose that the thing known is actually true.

Finally, it would make little sense to say that I know something if I were to say in almost the same breath that I did not believe it. This sort of language may work in everyday conversation, but no philosopher is apt to take it very seriously. Imagine, if you will, my saying, "I know that my car is parked on the drive in front of my home, but I don't believe it." Anyone who heard this would think it odd, and would immediately ask for some sort of explanation.

Justified, true belief. I have evidence for X. X is true. I believe X. Let us, for the time being, leave aside the question of truth and belief, and let us concentrate on justification. What sort of evidence must we have if we are to accept as justified a particular proposition? Must the evidence be empirical, that is must it be something that we apprehend for ourselves via our senses? If seeing is believing, as we are often told, then what sort of knowledge can we have about things we do not see? Let us go back to the example of my car. I say to you, "My car is both solid black and solid red," and you say, "I know that this is not true." Have you actually seen the car? Must you actually have seen the car in order to reject my proposition? In other words, you have no empirical evidence either for or against my proposition, nor do you need any. You understand, without looking, that my proposition violates the law of contradiction, and that it may be rejected outright as false.

Shall we look at another example? Complete the following equation: 2 + 2 = . . . You immediately said, "Four," and you were, of course, absolutely correct. But think about what you have done. Have you ever actually seen "two?" When I ask this of students, their typical reaction is to hold up two fingers, or to jump up and draw a "2" on the chalkboard. I then tell them that what they have shown me are fingers and a symbol that stands for "2", whereas I asked them if they have ever seen "two." No one would think of responding to my question, "Have you ever seen dog?" by writing "dog" on the chalkboard, because they understand that the letters d, o, g are merely symbols for the four-legged creature that barks, and chases cars. So, back to my original question: have you ever seen "two?" In point of fact, none of us has ever seen two, because two is an abstraction, a concept. And yet, we say with great confidence that two and two equals four, never having seen any of these things.

I have spent a good deal of time on the introductory portion of this chapter because I am actually not just introducing this chapter, but the entire section. What do we know, and how do we know it? We will see that there are actually two general theories about knowledge and how we gain it. One of these asserts that knowledge is inborn or perhaps intuited, and the other asserts that all knowledge comes as a result of experience. The first of these is called **rationalism**; the second, **empiricism**. Both theories have had strong proponents through the years. Neither is thoroughly credible, but both have strong points in their support. We have already touched to some degree on these two positions, because as we have seen it is impossible to discuss metaphysics without referring to epistemology; and it is impossible to talk about the history of western philosophy without talking about epistemology.

Rationalism: the most important knowledge is imborn.
Empiricism: all knowledge comes as a result of sensory experience.

So to the extent that I repeat myself, I beg the indulgence of my students.

Rationalism: Born Knowing

Is it really possible to be born knowing certain things? Some of the greatest thinkers in the history of the West have thought so, including Socrates, Plato, Descartes, Spinoza, Leibniz, and, to a degree, Immanuel Kant. Some have gone so far as to argue that the Socratic dilemma, as stated in the *Meno*, has never been resolved, and that unless some sort of knowledge is present with us it is impossible to account for any scientific discoveries. Bertrand Russell and Alfred North Whitehead, among others, have said that without an appeal to the Platonic forms, in some manner, it is very difficult to account for certain kinds of knowledge, especially mathematical knowledge.[1]

In my experience, however, American students are very lukewarm about the proposition that knowledge is inborn. When I ask about it in class, I will typically get a few who say that such knowledge is possible; but when I ask for examples of inborn knowledge, I usually am treated to a long silence. Finally someone will say something about babies knowing how to nurse at birth. Not a good example, I point out. This is merely a reflex action. What about the way the geese fly north in summer and south in winter? Actually, these are animals. I am asking about humans, and whether or not humans have inborn knowledge. Further, instinctive behavior is not a good example for rationalists to use in bolstering their case, because it is not clear that humans exhibit instinctive behavior in the same way that animals do. Instinct is a sort of *universal* behavior that appears in a species at a certain time, which is clearly not learned and appears to be genetically determined. *Universal* is the key word in the previous sentence. What about intuition?

Ah, perhaps now we are getting somewhere!

Intuition, as in "women's intuition" may be a good candidate for a sort of inborn knowledge. Many students claim to have flashes of intuition that give them real knowledge about the world around them, knowledge

---

[1] Think about it. I asked earlier if anyone has ever seen "two". The obvious answer is no. And yet you have knowledge of this to the extent that you are willing to say you know that two plus two equals four. Whether or not you understand the implications of this, many philosophers would say it argues strongly for some sort of inborn knowledge, and some sort of non-spatial form.

which they have not acquired in the traditional way. Women in particular are supposed to be good at intuiting certain truths. Some of my students however say that this is sexist nonsense, that if intuition is really a sort of inborn knowledge there is no reason to suppose women have it to any greater degree than men. The problem with intuition as an example of inborn learning is that there is no way to isolate and examine it. Perhaps it is nothing more than a synthesizing of a number of things we have learned empirically, and because it is done in a flash it takes on a mysterious quality and appears inborn. If so, this argues more for the position of Immanuel Kant than it does for the earlier rationalists.

Nevertheless, and difficult as it may be to come up with concrete examples, one of the most persistent ideas of western philosophy has been the certain truths are inborn and known to all. The Apostle Paul, for example, writing to the Romans in the early years of the first century, affirmed his belief that the Law of God is written on the heart.

> For when the Gentiles, which have not the law, do by nature the things contained in the law, these, having not the law, are a law unto themselves: Which shew the work of the law written in the hearts, their conscience also bearing witness, and their thoughts the mean while accusing or else excusing one another. (Rom. 2:14-15).

This is an amazing assertion. Paul is affirming that all people know right from wrong, not because they have been taught it by someone, or read it in a written code, or have taken it in in some empirical manner, but because it is written on their hearts. Can this be true? Does everyone know without being taught that it is wrong to steal, lie, and kill? If so, this is an example of rationalism that we can all see in action; and it is interesting to note that Paul was far from the first one to write such a thing. The Greeks were over three-hundred years ahead of him.

Socratic Rationalism

We have already seen that Socrates's epistemological position, and that of his student Plato, sprang from a perceived necessity to demonstrate the unchangeable, eternal quality of truth. The necessity becomes obvious when one stops to think of what it means to say that we know something. Remember how philosophers define knowledge: justified, true belief. If the world and all in it are in constant flux, if there is nothing stable and eternal, then the only truth becomes that there is no truth, and one is unable to believe anything concrete about anything. This, at least, is how Socrates and

Plato saw it, and I must confess that I think they make a good point. Knowledge must be about something with some degree of permanence.

But having admitted to that — if indeed we have — we may be no closer to knowledge; for to say that necessity demands a certain thing is not the same as to say that the demanded thing exists. Because there can be no true knowledge, unless there is such a thing as truth that is eternal and unchanging, may mean nothing more than there can be no true knowledge, and we have to make the best with what we have available. If we go this route, however, we seem to get entangled in sophistry, the very thing that Socrates found appalling. Thus we get the Socratic epistemological proposal, probably the most all-encompassing form of rationalism we have yet seen in the West. The really odd thing about it is that, when looked at without any preconceptions, what Socrates (or Plato) proposed may actually be an odd sort of empiricism, for he states that we are born with true knowledge because in our disembodied state between incarnations we have actually seen and known the forms. Socrates and Plato are the only two philosophers I know of who held to such a position. If this is rationalistic empiricism, we have a philosophical oxymoron if ever we had one. Let me show you why.

Rationalism, to repeat, is the view that knowledge can be gained purely by reason, without relying on the senses. Empiricism is the view that true knowledge can be attained only through experience. Socrates and Plato believed that we are born with all knowledge, and that getting to the knowledge is a process of remembering what we knew before, but forgot during the birth process. Now it truly sounds as if they were rationalists, and indeed they were, if we look only at the process by which they sought to attain knowledge. It is, recall, a drawing out process, facilitated by the Socratic method of teaching, in which teacher and pupil enter into a dialectic and talk their way (or reason their way, if you like that better) toward the truth.

But let us ask the obvious question. How did we gain the knowledge in the first place? If it is inside us waiting to be drawn out, how did it get in there? Here, in a passage from the *Meno*, Socrates gives the answer.

> I have heard wise men and women talk about divine matters. . .The speakers were among the priests and priestesses whose care it is to be able to give an account of their practices. Pindar too says it, and many others of the divine among our poets. What they say is this; see whether you think they speak the truth: They say that the human soul is immortal; at times it comes to an end, which they call dying, at times it is reborn, but it is never destroyed, and one must therefore live one's life as

> piously as possible. . .As the soul is immortal, has been born often and has seen all things here and in the underworld, there is nothing which it has not learned; so it is in no way surprising that it can recollect the things it knew before, both about virtue and other things. As the whole of nature is akin, and the soul has learned everything, nothing prevents a man, after recalling one thing only — a process men call learning — discovering everything else for himself. [2]

Thus Socrates has sought to resolve the problem created by his own theory of learning. If learning is truly recollection then we obviously have to have something to remember; and what can we remember but experiences we have had; and the experiences we are remembering must be actual experiences through which we have lived. Try, for example, to recall the last time you visited the northern polar cap of Mars. Are you having some difficulty with that one? The reason is plain: you have never visited the northern polar cap of Mars. Every recollection you have is of an experience through which you actually have lived.

The word empiricism comes from the Greek *empeiria,* which means experience. Now, if we know the forms and all other truth because we have experienced them on the ideal plane between incarnations, then we did not learn them by recalling them, but we learned them by experiencing them directly; and our recollection of them now that we are again in the body is not true rationalism at all, but (as I have suggested) an odd sort of rationalistic empiricism.

Most philosophical textbooks classify Socrates and Plato as rationalists without ever attempting to resolve this contradiction at the heart of Socratic epistemology.[3] I, however, raise it as a problem because I want the student to think, and to think seriously, about it. Were Socrates and Plato rationalists? They talk as if they were, because they say that we get to truth by using reason rather than by appealing to the senses. But once the issue of recollection is raised, and once we ask what is being recalled, we get

---

[2] Plato, *Five Dialogues,* op.cit., pp. 69-70.

[3] I wish to emphasize, to avoid any misunderstanding, that I am raising this issue in this textbook precisely because it is a learning instrument, and I am attempting to get students to think. I do not know of many philosophers who hold that Socrates and Plato were rationalistic empiricists.

an answer that is purely empirical. We are recalling what we learned through experience.

Clearly, the rationalism of Socrates, and of his gifted student, was of a type unseen in western philosophy before or since. Everyone who has ever looked closely at Socrates's epistemology understands that it is tightly wrapped up in his metaphysics, so much so that it is impossible to untangle the two. This is to say that if his metaphysical position was wrong, then his epistemological position fails along with it. I profoundly hope that the student understands why, but I am prepared to face the possibility that many do not. In fact, it is at points like this that some students get lost and begin wondering why anyone finds philosophy so fascinating. The whole thing can seem downright silly. If I must postulate the ridiculous (in this case the disembodiment of the human soul and the actual existence of the forms in a timeless, non-material, non-spatial never-never land) in order to support my theory of learning and knowledge, perhaps I would be wise to get a new theory, one that doesn't have such shaky underpinnings.

This is precisely what many philosophers have done. I don't know of a single epistemologist who believes that we must buy the Socratic metaphysic in order to seriously espouse a rationalistic position; but there are still many who think that the most important things we know come, not through experience, but as a result of pure reasoning.

Let's take Ockham's razor to Socrates; let's slice away the unnecessary postulations and see what we are left with.

We begin by rejecting the Socratic explanation of how knowledge got into us to begin with. Gone is the idea of reincarnation and the immortality of the soul. Must we reject rationalism along with this metaphysical theory? Not necessarily. But the burden is upon the rationalist to demonstrate the ability to come to knowledge by pure reason and apart from experience?

In the *Meno* Socrates attempted such a demonstration. Rather than quote the passage at length, I will paraphrase. I encourage the student to go to the library, get a copy of the *Meno,* and read the full exchange.[4]

Socrates calls for one of Meno's slaves, a young Greek-speaking boy, and asks him if he knows what a square is. When the boys replies that he does, Socrates asks him to imagine a square which is two feet on either side. If we take two feet twice, Socrates asks him, how many do we have? The

---

[4] I am using Plato, *Five Dialogues,* translated by G.M.A. Grube, which I have cited previously.

slave boy responds that we now have four. Now, suppose we double the sides, so that now the square is twice as big. How long, Socrates asks, is one side now. Four feet, says the lad. And both sides together? Eight, is the answer. And so it goes, for several pages.

It is an engaging discussion, but when it is all over the reader feels (at least this reader does) that what he has actually been witnessing is Socrates's skill as a teacher, not the slave boy recollecting. I can do the same thing and do it much easier. You may demonstrate for yourselves and your own benefit exactly what Socrates was attempting to demonstrate to Meno. Begin by assuming that there are three glasses in a cabinet where you can't see them. You are told that the first glass is ten inches high and has a circumference of five inches. You are told that the second glass is eleven inches high, and that it has a circumference of six inches. Finally, you are told that the third glass, when full, will hold more than the second glass. Now comes the question: which glass will hold the most, the first or the third? This is, as the saying goes, a no-brainer. The third glass will hold more. Stated as a proposition, glass three has a larger capacity than glass one.

Is it fair to say that we know this? If so, we ought to be able to take the philosophical definition of knowledge and apply it. First, do we have justification for the proposition, that is, is it warranted by the evidence? Second, is the proposition true? Third, do we believe the proposition? The answer, in each case, seems to be yes. Thus, we appear to have satisfied the philosophical conditions, and we can say without hesitation we know that glass three is bigger than glass one.

Now, how did we come by such knowledge? The rationalist would reply that we used our reason and only our reason. There was no sensory input, no physical experience of any kind. You did not actually see three glasses. They were hidden from your sight. Are you willing, based purely upon your ability to reason, to have the glasses taken out of the cabinet, to fill each of them with water, and to measure their contents separately to see which glass holds the greatest amount? Of course you are. Assuming fair conditions, there is no question about which glass is larger.

You have just demonstrated rationalism to yourself. Or have you? The empiricists are not so sure, as we shall see. But you have not, at any rate, demonstrated Socrates's metaphysics. You may have demonstrated nothing more than the human mind's ability to synthesize and to abstract. That, of course, is an achievement beyond anything of which any other species is capable.

The Empirical Challenge

Any good empiricist has an answer to the contention that the exercise with the glasses proves rationalism. What are you doing, they would ask, other than using your mental power to work with things that you have learned empirically. You know, after all, what glasses are, what the concepts of larger and smaller are, because you have learned these through experience. Therefore it is relatively easy to perform all the steps necessary to arrive at the correct conclusion in the case of the glasses, and to do so without appealing to some inner knowledge. In short, all learning and all knowledge come through experience.

The Rationalist Response

It is the insistence upon experience as the sole means by which learning takes place that led us down the path with David Hume into a cul-de-sac from which there is no escaping. In short, empiricism is a sure-fire recipe for skepticism. Besides, even if we reject the metaphysics of Socrates, we have to admit that the Socratic dilemma[5] is a formidable obstacle to be overcome if one wishes to be an empiricist. If epistemology is to have any meaning at all, if there is such a thing as knowledge, and if we aspire to knowing the truth, we cannot hope to find answers in empiricism.

The Rationalism of Descartes and Friends

René Descartes is called the father of modern rationalism, as we have seen in the earlier section on the history of western philosophy. You may have heard him called that before. Most of my students who know about René Descartes at all know two things. The first is that he is the father of modern rationalism. The second is that he said, "I think, therefore I am." You are now in a position to know a great deal more about him, for you now know what rationalism is. You also remember Descartes from the first section of this book, and you will recall that his rationalism sprang from a desire to put epistemology on the same footing as geometry. Geometry was, to Descartes, the most exact of all the mathematics, for it deals with material things, but it deals with them according to self-evident axioms. These self-evident axioms were, according to Descartes, *a priori.*

---

[5] **As expressed in the *Meno*, the dilemma is simply either we know the truth already, in which case there is nothing to look for, or else we don't know it, in which case we have no idea what to look for, and probably have no sense of anything lacking.**

Born w/ knowledge
Rational

A *priori* knowledge: knowledge that exists "prior" to experience.
***A posteriori* knowledge: knowledge that comes as a result of experience.**

empirical

A priori is a term with which you should by now be familiar; but I will go over some of the things that I said earlier, when I discussed Descartes within the context of history. If, in looking at the term, you think of the word "prior," you are on the right track. It does mean prior; but prior to what? The answer is, prior to experience. The kind of knowledge comprehended by the term *a priori* is the kind that exists prior to any experience, thus for all practical purposes it is knowledge with which one is born. Its opposite is *a posteriori*, posterior, knowledge that comes after or as a result of experience. We will have more to say about *a posteriori* knowledge when we deal with empiricism, for the empiricists say that all knowledge is *a posteriori.*

A priori knowledge has certain characteristics that make it very attractive to philosophers, especially to those who like Descartes are products of societies cycling through periods of great chaos. *A priori* knowledge, for example, is supposed to be universal. It cannot be one thing in Chicago and another thing in Hong Kong. It is supposed to be certain. Once you have it, you can be assured that it is true and unchanging. It is very much to Descartes's credit that he does not allow himself to get drawn aside into the strange metaphysical system of Socrates by asking how we have come by such knowledge. It is enough for him to demonstrate that we have it, and he is willing to rest on the belief that it is God-given.

With Descartes we are into — please do not forget it — modern rationalism. Not only is he unlike Socrates in his metaphysics, but he is unlike Socrates in assuming that all knowledge is recollection. Descartes believes nothing of the sort, nor do most other modern rationalists. In fact, all of the moderns agree that we learn a great deal from experience. But what we learn from experience is neither universal nor is it certain. It is (and this is definitely Socratic) information about particulars, but not about general principles.

Were I able to interview René Descartes, the first thing I would ask him is the thing I ask all my students when we are discussing rationalism —give me some examples of *a priori* knowledge. And Descartes would surely have answers. Because he hoped to put philosophy on the same footing as geometry, the first examples he would give would probably be geometric. What is the shortest distance between two points? The obvious answer, assuming we are on a place surface, is a straight line. Is this an example of knowledge *a priori*? Descartes thought that it was, as have many other rationalists. A point, for example, is a non-existent entity that no one can claim ever to actually have experienced. Further, when answering the question there is no need to appeal to experience or to anything empirical. Just think about it. Presumably, if you were locked up in a pitch dark dungeon and had nothing but your mental powers to depend upon, you could answer the question correctly just by thinking about it.

Descartes might also refer to Aristotle's rules of inference, the basic laws underlying all logic and correct thinking. How do I know that an object is equal to itself (the law of identification)? How do I know that a thing cannot be itself and not itself at the same time? In every case, he would say, this is a matter of pure logic, pure reason, and no empirical evidence is required. All one has to do is think about these things to discern the truth.

Anselm, Descartes, and Spinoza all constructed *a priori*, ontological arguments for the existence of God, and Descartes went even further, arguing for the self as a thinking, non-material entity which by its very nature can be known only *a priori.*

In fine, for Descartes and other rationalists, the most important truths, those basic to science, philosophy, theology, mathematics, are all *a priori.*

The Trouble With Rationalism

Most of the writers and teachers that I know attempt to be as objective as possible when they present their material. But total objectivity is impossible. No matter how hard one tries, his or her own prejudices and pet theories have a troubling way of inserting themselves into the discussion. So here come some of mine.

I would dearly love to believe that the rationalists are right, for if they are it is easy to demonstrate that the human mind exists as a non-material, free, functioning thing. But try as I might, I can never get over the uncomfortable feeling that rationalism is a complicated, if attractive, violation of that nagging law of parsimony, Ockham's Razor. If one begins by asserting that some kinds of knowledge are *a priori*, prior to sense experience, then one can hardly avoid explaining how such knowledge is possible. It must somehow be inborn, or at least the ability to achieve such knowledge must be inborn. Now notice the interesting either/or aspect of the previous sentence, and get ready to do some thinking.

Either the knowledge is inborn, or the ability to achieve the knowledge is inborn. I can think of no other possibilities. Let's give some thought to the first of them. If knowledge is inborn, then one is left to explain whether this means all knowledge or just some special sorts of knowledge. If one takes the Socratic position that all knowledge is inborn and learning is merely recollection, then one is dragged off in strange directions indeed. When Meno challenges Socrates to explain how this can be, Socrates, as we have seen, answers that we are immortal, have been reincarnated many times, and that we took in knowledge during periods of disembodiment when we were in the place where the forms exist. But this, as I have argued, may not be pure rationalism. It smacks of epistemological hybridism, and the recollection process that has gained Socrates and Plato the rationalistic label may be nothing but a remembrance of what we have experienced.

Of course, Descartes and the modern rationalists do not take the position of Socrates. They only say that some knowledge, the most important sorts of knowledge, is *a priori* and is gained by pure reason. Which brings us to our second possibility: the ability to achieve knowledge is inborn. But in order to believe this, mustn't one believe that certain sorts of knowledge are inborn? How, for example, would I know that the shortest distance between two points is a straight line unless I have a concept of point, line, straight, and distance? Mustn't all thinking, particularly abstract thinking, involve the use of language in some way? If it does not, then we must simply have unlabeled pictures floating around in our minds, a peculiar notion at best. But if language is necessary to thinking, mustn't we have learned the language in some way, and doesn't this imply an empirical process?

This, it seems to me, is the major weakness of rationalism: no matter how you try to explain it or think about it, whether your position is Socratic or Cartesian, you always seem to wind up explaining yourself in empirical terms. If this is the case, then rationalism springs from empiricism, the empiricists are correct in thinking that knowledge is acquired through experience, not inborn, and rationalism as an epistemological system cannot be salvaged in its pure form. It can only be salvaged by proposing some sort of rationalist-empirical amalgam, such as that created by Immanuel Kant. In fact, it seems that the rationalists left us, in the final analysis, with a sort of mixed bag.

Not so the empiricists! But they got us into trouble nonetheless.

More of the Empirical Challenge

Looking at history, one is struck by the fact that some of the brightest lights in the philosophical firmament have been rationalists. Socrates and Plato, Augustine, Descartes, Spinoza, Leibniz, Hegel. Immanuel Kant must also be added to the list, though he, like Socrates and Plato, mixes the two positions. But one is also struck by the fact that all of these are continental Europeans, and all — with the exception of Hegel — were doing their philosophizing in the eighteenth century and before. This might lead one to conclude that as the Age of Enlightenment gave way to the more pragmatic period of the nineteenth century, and as the English began to dominate the world, rationalism was shoved aside by empiricism. And possibly, just possibly, one might conclude that empiricism has come to dominate the western world simply because it is more plausible, easier to explain and to deal with, and not cluttered with the sorts entities that so irked William of Ockham and the scientists that came after him.

The list of empirical philosophers is no less sterling: Aristotle (by implication), Thomas Aquinas, Ockham, Francis Bacon, Hobbes, Locke, Berkeley, Hume, and many of the Anglo-American epistemologists of this century. As the Roman Lucretius said, "What can give us more sure knowledge than our senses? How else can we distinguish between the true and the false?"

Aristotle and Empiricism

Empiricism is the implied epistemological position of Aristotle. He did not work out his epistemology in the same detailed way as did Socrates, but he makes it clear that the forms are not extra-material things with ontological reality.

> What constitutes the substantiality of individual things? Aristotle's answer is that it is the essence — the formal or defining principle of each thing. . .Moreover the universal has no separate existence apart from its particulars (this is a point upon which Aristotle repeatedly insists in his revolt against the Ideal theory). . .Matter and form are always correlative, and. . .never exist apart.[6]

Thus, although we need forms, which he calls universals, if we are to communicate meaningfully, we needn't postulate that they exist apart from particulars. Maleness is the universal which I possess, but it is I who possess it, it is not lurking behind the curtain somewhere giving substance to the particular which is myself. It is because Aristotle believes this that he must opt for a system of learning and knowledge that is at bottom empirical. Cut

---

[6] Aristotle, *Metaphysics,* trans. Hugh Treddenick, *op. cit.*, pp. xxvi, xxvii.

off from a Socratic explanation of knowledge, holding that the human soul does not survive death, he must allow that such learning as is possible takes place during the physical life time of the learner, and that it takes place by observation and experience. And how do we, physical creatures that we are, experience anything if not by means of the senses. *Ergo*: the key to learning is *empeiria*, experience.

In the *Metaphysics* Aristotle refutes Plato's doctrine of forms. The passage is long and complicated, but I will cite a part of it.

> [O]f the ways in which we prove that the Forms exist, none is convincing; for from some no inference necessarily follows, and from some arise Forms even of things of which we think there are no Forms. . .Further, of the more accurate arguments, some lead to Ideas of relations, of which we say there is no independent class, and others introduce the "third man. . ." Above all one might discuss the question what on earth the Forms contribute to sensible things, either to those that are eternal or to those that come into being and cease to be. For they cause neither movement nor any change in them. But again they help in no wise either towards the knowledge of the other things (for they are not even the substance of these, else they would have been in them), or towards their being, if they are not in the particulars which share in them; though if they were, they might be thought to be causes. . .[7]

The "third man"referred to in the passage above is Aristotle's well-known, and generally unsuccessful refutation of Plato's theory of forms. Several arguments against the Platonic forms bore this name. It begins with the assumption that an actual man on earth has a non-spatial, non-material form behind him which gives him substance, then it goes on to show that we cannot stop there. If the physical man, myself for instance, depends on a form, a "second man," to give him reality and substance, then we must postulate a third man standing behind the second to unite the humanity of the two. It's an interesting discussion, but not terribly difficult to deal with. We ought perhaps to call it the "Straw man" theory, for it assumes things which Plato did not, and it knocks down an argument which was not his. In Plato, the second man, the form, is postulated to be the ultimate reality, and

---

[7] Aristotle, *The Pocket Aristotle*, ed. Justin D. Kaplan, *op. cit.*, pp. 130, 131.

therefore he needs nothing standing behind him.

But on with Aristotle. I have said earlier that he was an empiricist by implication. Where are we to look for the implications? The answer is throughout his work, but more immediately in the *Organon.* It is here that he lays down the rules for correct thinking, and the groundwork for what will become science. According to Theodore James, "At the very beginning of chapter one Aristotle takes a stand on the role and function of language which indicates clearly his epistemological realism."[8] Further, in the *Posterior Analytics* of the *Organon,* Aristotle holds that the only propositions that are scientifically known are those which are obtained by a syllogistic process from evident propositions which are necessary, that is always true and never false.

It is this work, perhaps more than any other, that influenced the thinking of the Medieval scholastics, including that most Aristotelian of philosophers, William of Ockham. If you wish to learn something, such men would say in concert with Aristotle, look at the thing about which you wish to learn, study it, then use proper thinking to think about it. Dispense with the unnecessary and hold tightly to the essential. If you wish to learn about general principles, those principles about which Plato speculated and about which he wrote his famous Parable of the Cave, begin by observing particulars, then reason from them toward the general, the universal.

The Scholastics
Pre-empirical Empiricism

The period in which the Scholastics were operating must have been an exciting one in which to be alive. It didn't last long — perhaps two hundred years — but it was fruitful beyond all temporal consideration, for it was during this period that the foundation for the Renaissance was laid, and it was the soil in which modern Western politics was germinated. The European Enlightenment, and consequently the American republic, have their philosophical roots deeply embedded in the High Middle Ages, and in the thoughts of churchmen who could not possibly have foreseen where the thoughts would lead.

---

[8] James, Theodore E., in *Aristotle Dictionary,* ed. Thomas P. Kiernan, New York: Philosophical Library, 1962, p. 17.

Their names were Duns Scotus, Abelard, Bonaventure, Aquinas, Bacon, Ockham. They came from England, Scotland, France, Italy. They had two things in common: their devotion to the Church and their fascination with the newly discovered philosophy of Aristotle. They were in more trouble, potentially, than any of them could have possibly realized, for they were fighting the battle of Plato versus Aristotle, a battle that has continued down to the present day. It is the battle of rationalism versus empiricism. It erupted, as we saw in an earlier chapter, in the Battle of the Universals, a disruption which the Church would dearly have loved to avoid. Not one of the battling philosophers would have admitted to it, though some of them were accused of it, but they were moving the world away from superstition and fear of the unknown toward a confidence in the ability to solve problems by means of correct intellectual application. Nothing like this had been seen in Europe since the burial of the Greeks centuries before.

Because he is so very representative of the early empiricists, and because his principle of parsimony has had such a profound influence on science, I propose to look first and foremost at William of Ockham. In his introduction to the *Philosophical Writings of Ockham*, Philotheus Boehner says of Ockham's epistemology:

> Our cognition starts with the apprehension not of necessary but of contingent facts. **No knowledge of any kind is possible without a direct or indirect contact with some object that is experienced.** . .It is to be noted that the existential judgment is an operation of the intellect alone, and that the intuitive cognition which is at the basis of it, even if it concerns an object of sense, is an intellectual intuitive cognition or a primary intellectual awareness of an object. The intellect could not have an intuitive cognition of a sensible object without the help of sensory cognition, at least in the nature order.[9]

It is interesting to see what Ockham is doing here. He is attempting to retain, it would seem, his posture in both camps, which is not unusual given the intellectual atmosphere of the period in which he lived. But before it is over he will come down solidly on the side of empiricism and science. He cannot help it. He opens his *Prologue to the Exposito super viii libros Physicorum* with a tribute to Aristotle in which he calls him "the great

---

[9] **Ockham, *Philosophical Writings, op. cit.*, pp. xxiv, xxv.**

philosopher," yet admits that while he came to many important truths he also mingled truth with error.[10] He goes on, in this same work, to a lengthy definition of knowledge,[11] which I will avoid quoting because it is quite difficult to follow. But I think the significant part, in the light of subsequent history, is his insistence that knowledge has only two causes, an efficient and a final.

> [K]nowledge has only two essential causes, namely, an efficient and a final cause. Hence, if the statement that all knowledge has a material and formal cause be true, it is so only in an improper and metaphorical sense.[12]

He explains why he rejects the formal and the material as causes of knowledge, but I won't, because of my kindly nature, subject the struggling student to this. I will, however, ask the student, no matter how he or she is struggling or feels put upon, to attend to the brief quote above. This is pure Aristotle. In the *Metaphysics*, Aristotle identifies four causes, the formal, the material, the efficient, and the final. In rejecting the material as a cause of knowledge, it would seem that Ockham is rejecting the objects of cognition and thus empiricism along with them. But this is not the case, as we shall see. The rejection of the formal cause is equally interesting, for with this he seems to be rejecting the knower, even as to reject the formal cause of a piece of art work would be to reject the artist. But this also is not the case. To see precisely what he is rejecting, and what he is retaining, let us return to the example I used in the first section when we were looking at these four Aristotelian causes.

We have before us a statue of Apollo. The statue is marble, the material cause. It was created by an artisan, the efficient cause. The artisan created the statue based upon an idea he had in his mind, the formal cause. And lastly, there is the purpose for which the statue was created, the final cause. If we reject the formal cause, we reject the idea the artisan had in mind, and if we reject the material cause, we reject the marble. That leaves us with the artist himself and the final end of his creation.

---

[10] Ibid., p. 3.

[11] It is significant, and I think the student will find it of some interest, that this particular treatise was written in Latin, and that the Latin word which is translated "knowledge" is "*scientia.*"[12]

Ibid., p. 9.

> [I]n this case "matter"means that with which knowledge is concerned. Yet this is an improper mode of speaking; for in this way I could also say that colour is the matter of vision and that the colour is the material cause of perception and sensation. Likewise, it is only in an improper sense that the distinction between the parts of knowledge is called form; for in this sense I could also say that the three lines are the formal cause of a triangle, and that the hands and feet and the other limbs of man are the formal cause of man, which is not a proper way of speaking. Properly speaking, therefore, knowledge has only two causes, since it lacks a formal and a material cause. . .[N]either the object nor the subject is a material cause of knowledge. Consequently knowledge has no formal cause either.[13]

I am certain that the student found this bewildering passage a delightful thing to read. Perhaps, however, we can untangle it together. Ockham is clearly not rejecting the human mind. This is the efficient cause of knowledge, nor is he rejecting the purpose of knowledge, and that is comforting, for it seems to suggest that getting knowledge for the very sake of getting knowledge is justifiable. What he is rejecting is a more mystical aspect of knowledge. Berkeley and the idealists would not like the passage above; but I feel certain that Hobbes and Locke would love it.

Empiricism and Aquinas

Thomas Aquinas, like Ockham, had to walk a very fine line between truth and heresy. Both were Aristotelian, thus both were empirically inclined. But both were churchmen, thus both were committed to a position that included Plato, the forms as ideas in the mind of God, and a world of authoritarian ecclesiastical pronouncements that sometimes flew in the face of waking reality. It is not strange, therefore, to see both of them saying things that sound, sometimes empirical, sometimes rationalistic. Aquinas, for example, says in the *Summa Theologica* that "although the operation of the intellect has its origin in the senses, yet, in the thing apprehended through the senses, the intellect knows many things which the senses cannot perceive."[14] He is arguing for both an experiential source of knowledge, and

---

[13] Ibid., p. 9

[14] Aquinas, op. cit., p. 335.

an inward one. Nevertheless, his commitment to Aristotle is unshakable, and his grounding in the *Posterior Analytics* of the *Organon* is as solid as was Ockham's, and he consistently asserts his empirical presuppositions. As an example, many know that John Locke, the seventeenth-century English empiricists, said that when humans are born they are intellectually blank slates (*tabula rasa*) upon which experience writes. What many do not know is that the notion originated, not with Locke, but ultimately with Aristotle. Aquinas set it down for posterity in the *Summa Theologica,* and in so doing he cites *De Anima*, III, 4 (430a I).

> [T]he human intellect, which is the lowest in the order of intellects and most remote from the perfection of the divine intellect, is in potentiality with regard to things intelligible, and **is at first like a clean tablet on which nothing is written,** as the Philosopher says. This is made clear from the fact that at first we are only in potentiality towards understanding, and afterwards we are made to understand actually. And so it is evident that with us to understand is in a way to be passive, taking passion in the third sense. And consequently the intellect is a passive power.[15]

It is fairly common knowledge, at least in philosophical circles, that later in life Aquinas experienced some sort of beatific vision that led to his repudiation of his earlier efforts. Or perhaps repudiation is too strong a word. He felt that there was more important knowledge to be had, apparently through some species of intuitive mysticism, and that those who achieve this will forever look back on philosophy as child's play. This is my description of Aquinas's experience and not his own, but my description is fairly accurate.

After his experience, whatever it may have been, he gave up philosophy, and he spent the rest of his life in the sort of mystical contemplation one expects from monks in monasteries. But what was done could never be undone. He and his brother scholastics had changed the intellectual landscape so that it would never again be the same.

---

[15] **Ibid., p. 339.**

Bacon and the Scientific Method

> Francis Bacon of the Elizabethan age is the great forerunner of the spirit of modern life [who as] a prophet of new tendencies. . .hardly receives his due as the real founder of modern thought.[16]

Thus said John Dewey. This is interesting, for there are many philosophers whose works are touted as the real watershed between the ancient and modern worlds. Descartes is supposed to have created the modern attitude of self-consciousness. Newton, a man who in his day would have been labeled a natural philosopher, is thought to have created the general picture of the universe as a machine. Thomas Hobbes is credited with giving us the first thrust toward modern government, with its underlying ideas of freedom and rights. What, then, would be Bacon's claim to occupy a place with these thinkers? Quite simply, it was Bacon who gave us science as we know it today.

In the concluding part of *Novum Organum*, his famous work that was to influence generations of those who came after him, he set out the method of inquiry which would come to be known as the Baconian method of induction. The Baconian method begins with a clear description of the facts. One must then search for positive instances of the phenomenon in question, negative instances of its absence, and instances of its presence in varying degrees. Finally, one must eliminate whatever is not directly connected with the phenomenon under investigation.

The inductive method of inquiry begins with particulars and moves toward generalities. To quote Bacon:

> There are and can be only two ways of searching into and discovering truth. The one flies from the senses and particulars to the most general axioms, and from these principles, the truth of which it takes for settled and immovable, proceeds to judgment and to the discovery of middle axioms. And this way is now in fashion. The other derives axioms from the senses and particulars, rising by a gradual and unbroken ascent, so that it arrives at the most general axioms last of all. This is the correct way, but as yet untried.[17]

---

[16] Quoted in *The Mayfield Anthology of Western Philosophy*, ed. Daniel Kolak, Mountain View, CA: The Mayfield Publishing Co., p. 335.

[17] Ibid., p. 337.

It is the second of these methods that is of particular interest, but both are interesting. Both begin with the senses, and with particulars; thus neither is deductive, properly speaking, and neither is dependent upon *a priori* knowledge. In fact, since Bacon states that there can be only two ways of searching into and discovering truth, and since both of the ways he mentions are grounded in the empirical *a posteriori*, it seems obvious that he has dismissed rationalism as a way of discovering truth.

The second method, however, is, as I have said, of particular interest; for it is this that leads to the Baconian method of induction. Now deduction, as it was understood in those days, was reasoning from the general to the particular. It was also called reasoning *a priori*. It is easy to understand why. If one is to reason from a general rule, one must have somehow established a general rule, a universal and necessary principle, from which to reason. And how would one do this if not by some sort of rational, intuitive process? "I think," is a good example of a general rule used as a premise from which to reason deductively toward the conclusion, "Therefore I am." It is a good example, but Bacon would not agree that it is truly an *a priori* truth, nor would subsequent generations of empiricists.

Inductive reasoning is just the opposite — reasoning from the particular to the general — also called *a posteriori* reasoning, reasoning from the things that we learn from experience. Thus, as deduction fits with rationalism, induction seems to fit with empiricism. But empiricists push things even farther. They say that what is being called deduction also fits with empiricism. To see why, take the ancient and honored syllogism of Aristotle, which is supposed to be a classic example of deduction. The major premise, the universal from which the particular is deduced, is,"All humans are mortal." Empiricists say that this indeed sounds like a universal, and that the process that follows (Socrates is human, therefore Socrates is mortal) sounds like reasoning *a priori*. But the whole pretense is unmasked when one asks how the major premise was established? How, that is to say, do we know that all humans are mortal? The major premise is established through a process of induction, by observing many individual humans and noting that all eventually die.

Bacon believed, as we have seen from the quote from the *Novum Organum*, that axioms were to be established inductively, by beginning with particulars and working upward toward general principles. And once the axioms were firmly, and experimentally, established, they could be used to function as axioms, universals, major premises, to solve particular problems deductively. But one must not get confused about the process. Learning, and the scientific method, were empirical.

Empiricism for the New World

In Book II of his *Essay Concerning Human Understanding* John Locke dismisses the idea of inborn knowledge and states that all knowledge is *a posteriori*, learned from experience via the senses. We have already looked at a portion of Locke's monumental work, but it will do us no substantial harm to see some of it again. Because this is a major contribution to the field of epistemology I will quote from it at some length.

> I know it is a received doctrine, that men have native ideas, and original characters, stamped upon their minds in their very first being. This opinion I have at large examined already; and, I suppose what I have said in the foregoing Book will be much more easily admitted, when I have shown whence the understanding may get all the ideas it has; and by what ways and degrees they may come into the mind; — for which I shall appeal to every one's own observation and experience.
>
> Let us suppose the mind to be, as we say, white paper, void of all characters, without any ideas: — How comes it to be furnished? Whence comes it by that vast store which the busy and boundless fancy of man has painted on it with an almost endless variety? Whence has it all the materials of reason and knowledge? To this I answer, in one word, from experience. In that all our knowledge is founded; and from that it ultimately derives itself. Our observation employed either, about external sensible objects, or about the internal operations of our minds perceived and reflected on by ourselves, is that which supplies our understandings with all the materials of thinking. These two are the fountains of knowledge, from whence all the ideas we have, or can naturally have, do spring.[18]

Here we have the *tabula rasa*, or blank slate, with which Locke is so often associated, but which actually has its origins in much earlier times, as we have seen. It has its origins with Aristotle, was refined and passed on by Aquinas, and appears anew in the writing of John Locke. One might say that the blank-slate theory is an article of faith with all empiricists. They quite simply do not believe in inborn knowledge. In voicing this position they are

---

[18] Locke, John, *Essay Concerning Human Understanding*, op. cit., pp. 25 & 26.

much more strident than are the rationalists. I do not mean that they are strident in a negative sense. I mean that they do not yield ground to the other side at all. The rationalists will admit that there is a great deal of learning that comes about as a result of experience. As a general rule, empiricists do not admit to any sort of inborn knowledge.

Empiricism, as it grew up in England and was later transplanted to America, was truly foundational for the sort of scientific, materialistic society that grew up in the new land across the sea. It fits well with the metaphysical position of naturalism, for it goes along with the idea that there is a real world external to us and not dependent on our perceptions of it for its substantiality. It also works well with science, for it encourages the Baconian position of inductive reasoning based upon observation and moving toward universal principles. Most every science major, during my time as an undergraduate, was thoroughly grounded in the principles of scientific inquiry, beginning with the observation of particulars, the use of experimental and control groups, and the underlying faith that we live in an orderly universe which obeys established physical laws, and which can be studied and understood.

This is the position that took hold in America, and this is the reason that the Continental rationalists sound so strange to many of the American students with which I have to deal. Apply the principle of Ockham's razor to the epistemological question and the resultant empiricism seems almost inevitable. How do we learn? In what is our knowledge grounded? The obvious reply is the one that Locke gave: we learn through experience. To say that knowledge has a source other than this seems to entangle one in problems that cannot be resolved.

And yet things may not be so simple. In fact, Locke may have simplified things to the point of falsifying them. Ockham did not, after all, establish his principle as some sort of ironclad law. Sometimes the most obvious answer may not be the correct one.

Remember George Berkeley, the good Irish bishop who followed, more or less, in John Locke's footsteps? Berkeley thought that physical reality was not in fact reality. He believed, as we have seen, that all reality is mental.

> They who assert that figure, motion, and the rest of the primary or original qualities do exist without mind in unthinking substances do at the same time acknowledge that colors, sounds, heat, cold and such like secondary qualities, do not; which they tell us are sensations, existing in the mind alone, that depend on and are

> occasioned by the different size, texture, and motion of the minute particles of matter. . .Now if it be certain that those original qualities are inseparably united with other sensible qualities, and not, even in thought, capable of being abstracted from them, it plainly follows they exist only in the mind. But I desire anyone to reflect, and try whether he can, by any abstraction of thought conceive the extension and motion of a body without all other sensible qualities. For my own part, I see evidently that it is not in my power to frame an idea of a body extended and moving but I must . . .give it some color or sensible quality, which is acknowledged to exist only in the mind. In short, extension, figure and motion, abstracted from all other qualities, are inconceivable. Where therefore the other sensible qualities are, there must these be also, to wit, in the mind and nowhere else.[19]

This is sometimes difficult for students to grasp. The idealistic position seems to go along much more naturally with a Platonic metaphysics, and when Berkeley is presented as an empiricist and grouped in the company of Locke and Hume, and the very practical Anglo-Americans, he doesn't quite seem to fit. Just remember, he is an empiricist because of how he thinks learning takes place; but he is an idealist because of the way he answers the question of what is really there. Berkeley makes it clear that he is in agreement with Locke — learning comes as a result of experience, and experience has to do with the senses and with the data we are taking in by means of the senses. Reality, however, is another matter. With Berkeley, as with other idealists, reality is idea. We have talked about this in other sections of the book, and it needn't be repeated here. The important thing to note is that epistemologically Berkeley was an empiricist.

Notice that in the above quote Berkeley begins by making reference to primary or original qualities, and how they exist apart from the mind, in the objects of perception themselves. He then says that secondary qualities, such as colors and sounds, do not. He is jabbing at John Locke, without naming him. For this was indeed the position that Locke took. Berkeley did not believe in primary qualities. Instead, he said that all qualities in a perceptible object are products of the perceiving mind, that without a

Primary qualities, for John Locke, were qualities that are in the objects we experience, such as height, depth and weight. Secondary qualities, he thought, were qualities such as color and smell which are in our minds, and which our minds supply to the perception.

---

[19] Berkeley, George, *A Treatise Concerning the Principles of Human Knowledge*, in *The works of George Berkeley*, vol. 1, ed. George Sampson, London: George Bell & Sons, 1897, p. 183.

perceiver nothing would be.

Berkeley's metaphysical position comes close to **solipsism**, the belief that only I exist, and that the rest of the universe is just a creation of my mind. Berkeley escaped from this position by arguing that God is always present, always awake, and always aware. He gets to this in a short work, *Three Dialogues Between Hylas and Philonous,* and it is clear that he is using this as an argument for the existence of God.

> For philosophers, though they acknowledge all corporeal beings to be perceived by God, yet they attribute to them an absolute subsistence distinct from their being perceived by any mind whatever; which I do not. Besides, is there no difference between saying, *There is a God, therefore He perceives all things*; and saying, *Sensible things do really exist; and, if they really exist, they are necessarily perceived by an infinite Mind: therefore there is an infinite Mind or God*?[20]

When we were looking into metaphysics, I detailed some of the better-known arguments for the existence of God. I did not include this one by George Berkeley because I knew we would look at it in epistemology. I do not know of any philosophers today who give serious consideration to this argument. It certainly does not rank with the ontological argument or the teleological argument. But I do find it interesting. It runs something like this.

> 1: Reality exists only in a perceiving mind. And therefore,
>
> 2: If a perceiving mind ceases to perceive something, then the unperceived thing must go out of existence. And therefore,
>
> 3: When anything ceases to be perceived, as for example the tree in the quad in the limerick quoted earlier, it goes out of existence. And therefore,
>
> 4: The solipsistic position must be correct.
>
> 5: But this is a manifest absurdity, thus:

---

[20] **Berkeley, George, *Three Dialogues Between Hylas and Philonous*, Buffalo, NY: Prometheus Books, 1988, p. 55.**

> 6: There must be a least one Mind that is always awake, and aware, and perceiving. But
>
> 7: Only God can be always awake and always perceiving all things at all times. Therefore,
>
> 8: The existence of God is demonstrated by the substantial nature of the universe.

As I have said, I know of no philosophers who today think this is a sound argument; but I believe all would acknowledge that it is a unique one, and it is a fun argument. Students usually enjoy Berkeley, once they get over being shocked by him. You can try him out on your friends. Ask them if they agree that all of reality is basically created by the mind, and if you can get them to this point (most will reject it), try Berkeley's argument for God's existence and see how it works.

Perhaps Knowledge is Impossible

Now we get to the real problem of empiricism: when pushed to its logical conclusions, it leads to skepticism. This was demonstrated by David Hume, who did nothing more than take the arguments of Locke and Berkeley, accept them at face value, then apply rigid logic and follow where the trail led. This is a dreadful situation, perhaps the ultimate *reductio ad absurdum.* We have finally come to an epistemology which says that it is impossible to know whether or not we can actually know.

One would think that David Hume would be utterly rejected by philosophers the world over as a raving nut. Nothing of the kind! Philosophers are not rejected because of the oddness of their conclusions, but only if their conclusions are based upon lines of reasoning that are manifestly flawed. David Hume exhibits no such problem. Thus, he stands as a major thinker in the western philosophical tradition, and a major watershed. Were it not for Hume, there would, in all probability, have been no Kant. Now, let's see just how Hume managed to entangle the thinkers of his day in such an intellectual morass.

He began by accepting the empirical thesis: all knowledge comes from experience, and by experience he meant nothing more or less than sense perception. You learn quite simply by seeing, tasting, hearing, smelling or feeling. There is nothing inborn, nothing to justify the position of the rationalists. He therefore rejects the Cartesian ego as a thinking entity.

Descartes thought of the self as some sort of non-material yet unitary being, a self-evident thing that existed more surely than any of the physical world spreading out around it. Hume, however, acknowledged only the perceptible as the real — or at least the knowable. Thus, he asks, "What do we actually perceive?" He does not perceive an "I" as a non-material homunculus residing somewhere inside him. All he perceives, when he looks within, is a bundle of perceptions, fleeting and ungraspable.

Thus, one cannot be sure of one's existence except as a bundle of impressions and ideas.[21]

But what about impressions and ideas? In a passage we have already considered Hume shows just how flimsy these are.

> Here, therefore, we may divide all the perceptions of the mind into two classes or species, which are distinguished by their different degrees of force and vivacity. The less forcible and lively are commonly denominated *Thoughts* or *Ideas*. The other species want a name in our language, and in most others; I suppose, because it was not requisite for any, but philosophical purposes, to rank them under a general term or appellation. Let us therefore use a little freedom, and call them *Impressions*; employing that word in a sense somewhat different from the usual. By the term *impression*, then, I mean all our more lively perceptions, when we hear, or see, or feel, or love, or hate, or desire, or will. And impressions are distinguished from ideas, which are the less lively perceptions of which we are conscious, when we reflect on any of those sensations or movements above mentioned.[22]

Very well, impressions are our more lively perceptions, and ideas or thoughts are what are left behind. Think of a piece of wet clay into which you have pounded your fist as an impression, and think of the print left in the clay as it erodes over time as the thought or idea. I see an apple before me: an impression. I close my eyes and visualize the apple: an idea. And this is where we get into trouble.

---

[21] It is important to understand that Hume is not denying the existence of the self. He is not denying the existence of God, or of physical reality. He is a skeptic, saying that we cannot know for certain.

[22] Hume, David, *An Enquiry Concerning Human Understanding, op.cit.*, p. 18.

Hume gives every appearance of agreeing with Berkeley. The only reality we know, or can know, is mental reality. The emphasis in this statement, freighted with epistemological significance, is *know*. That there is some sort of external reality, Hume does not appear to seriously doubt. The doubt comes when one asks whether or not the reality is stable and ongoing. In this, we simply cannot know. I look at the world outside my window; but when I close my eyes and turn away how can I know that it continues? Hume's answer: I cannot. In all probability it does. But probability is not the same as knowing. Hume has no God to help him out of his problem. He does not deny the existence of God. He simply says, once again applying his strict empirical standard, that we cannot know.

Woe is me! I find myself adrift, a phantom in a phantom universe. But Hume is not finished. He manages to blow the scientific enterprise out of the water before he lays his pen aside and expires.

Think of Bacon, and the Baconian method of induction. We come to sure and certain knowledge of the world around us by studying particulars and from seeing the way they behave in relation to one another; and we are able, after we have looked at enough particulars, to induce certain general principles that becomes axioms for further study. But one needn't think a great deal about this method to realize that it is dependent for its efficacy upon the supposed law of cause and effect. There must be a causal connection between some things and other things, and this connection must be sure and certain.

Sorry, says Hume, nothing doing. The fact that one thing occurs in company with another, even that it follows the other, is no reason for us to suppose that it will always do so. This is a fallacy, long ago identified by the scholastics and labeled *post hoc ergo propter hoc*. It is habit, and nothing more, that makes us think in these terms. All we can say, once again, is that it is probable that there is some connection. Further no matter how many times a thing happens in a certain way, there is no guarantee that it must continue to do so. Can we really say, for example, that the sun rises (to use the common vernacular) in the east and sets in the west? No. We can only say that so far it always has. Tomorrow it may rise in the west for all we know. We cannot generalize from particulars because we have not observed all the particulars. We can only state probabilities.

So here we are, back on first base again. David Hume left epistemology in tatters, and philosophy in a state of confusion it hadn't seen since the Renaissance had swept scholasticism away.

Coming Out of the Cave

Aside from the parables told by Jesus, Plato's story about the cave is the most well known and most important parabolic creation in the history of the west. He makes Socrates the creator, and he sets the story down in Book VII of the *Republic.*

Socrates asks that you imagine a group of people who have spent their entire lives chained in an underground cave and positioned in such a way that they can see only one wall. Behind them (though they cannot see it) is a large fire, built so as to cast its light on the wall before them; and in front of the fire, but behind the prisoners, are individuals carrying figures of people, animals, and so on. The images of these figures are cast on the wall in the forms of shadows, so that the chained prisoners are merely looking at a shadow play. This is the only reality they have ever known. To them, this *is* reality.

Now, one of the prisoners manages to break free, and turns back to see what is actually happening. At first he is blinded by the light, but as his eyes grow accustomed to it he sees that what he has taken for reality is nothing more than the manipulation of shadows and images. He finally works his way out of the cave and into the sunlight to experience the world as it really is. He is so overwhelmed by the truth of what he has learned that he goes back into the cave to tell his fellow-prisoners and lead them into the light of full reality. They, however, are not interested, desiring the shadow to the reality. They turn on their would-be liberator and kill him. The problem with these prisoners is that they are caught up in the world of particulars and know nothing of ultimate truth — *ergo* the forms behind the particulars. The prisoners in the cave are us. The individual who gains enlightment is that rare person who is able to look behind mere appearance to greater reality.

Plato's point is that gaining knowledge is like struggling up out of a dark cave. It is difficult, sometimes painful, and it can be dangerous. It will cost something to gain wisdom, but for the lover of wisdom no price is too steep to be paid.

We all need to be reminded of this from time to time, because the struggle may sometimes be more difficult than we had ever imagined. If you don't believe it, get ready for Immanuel Kant as he attempts to save epistemology from David Hume.

Chapter 10
Epistemology Revived

Come rescue me from the dark, confining room
Prepared for me by my nemesis, David Hume.
Come show me rainbow light through the dazzling prism
Of Immanuel Kant's transcendental idealism.
I didn't save up my money and go to college
To be told there are no such things as truth and knowledge.

This little verse needn't be taken as actual truth. When did poets ever bother themselves with such things? And even though I am not a poet, but a versifier at best, I claim the right to stretch things a bit in the interest of meter, rhyme and entertainment. Hume didn't actually shut any of us up in a dark room, nor did he deny the existence of truth and knowledge, even when he was saying he wasn't sure we could achieve them. But in a wild and wacky way the verse gets to the heart of the matter, particularly from the point of view of the continental rationalists. Were Kant alive today, and were he writing in English, he might have written the verse himself.

We have already seen that Immanuel Kant characterized himself as one who was wakened from his dogmatic slumber by David Hume. What, precisely, was the dogmatism in which he was slumbering? It was the belief that rationalism was correct, that logic was unassailable, that the truth could be known by pursuing questions logically, and that philosophy was able to gain answers to the deeper problems of humankind. David Hume destroyed all that by showing that inductive reasoning led to only probable conclusions, and that there was not a demonstrable connection between cause and effect. Kant, for one, understood that if anything was to be salvaged for metaphysics, if there were to be any answers to questions about God, morality, beauty, truth, and any solid answers to questions about the world around us, someone had to rise to the challenge and answer David Hume. Someone had to show that knowledge was possible.

Kant, with a degree of humility one might imagine, leaped into the breach.

But how was he to proceed? His first task was to show that there was indeed a connection between cause and effect, and that it was a connection that could not be broken. Secondly, he needed to show that it was possible to make statements that give real information about the world, but that are established completely in the mind, and not as a result of experience. He sets out to do this in his most famous work, *The Critique of Pure Reason.*

> [T]hough all our knowledge begins with experience, it does not follow that it all arises out of experience. For it may well be that even our empirical knowledge is made up of what we receive through impressions and of what our own faculty of knowledge (sensible impressions serving merely as the occasion) supplies from itself. If our faculty of knowledge makes any such addition, it may be that we are not in a position to distinguish it from the raw material, until with long practice of attention we have become skilled in separating it.[1]

Good old Kant! He always leaves you wondering why you're too stupid to understand the first thing about philosophy. But, then, good old Immanuel Kant is only deceptively difficult; once you get your bearings and understand some of the terms that he uses the light begins to shine through, and you find yourself thinking it was worthwhile to work at him a bit. Take the passage we have just read. All knowledge begins with experience, but it doesn't follow that it all arises out of experience, because there is something that we bring to the task of knowing, something in our own minds that is not in the raw, incoming sense data of pure experience.

Were you able to follow what I just wrote any better than the passage from Kant? Look at it like this. The external world, that world outside of you, bombards you constantly with sense data, things you see, hear, smell, and so on. They are tumbling in upon you in a jumbled mass. Now suppose David Hume and the empiricists are correct and that all knowledge is derived purely from sense experience. If so, your own mind is a passive participant, taking in the data and recording it, but nothing more. Let us go back to an earlier example I gave, that of a baseball game. The pitcher winds up, throws the ball to homeplate, where it pops into the catcher's mitt. Ten-thousand of us are watching, and we all see the same thing. If we did not,

---

[1] **Kant, Immanuel, *The Critique of Pure Knowledge*, tran. Norman Kemp Smith, New York: Random House, 1958, p. 25.**

then the game would make no sense, the announcer wouldn't be able to announce, the catcher wouldn't be able to catch the ball, the umpire wouldn't be able to call the pitch a ball or a strike. But what did we see? We saw a ball, moving through time and space, from point A to point B. Further, we saw a ball that was caused to move in this direction because it was thrown by a pitcher. We experienced time and space; and we experienced cause and effect.

But how did time and space, cause and effect get in to the game? Did anyone ever see time? Did anyone ever see space? Did anyone ever have a sensory experience of cause and effect? Are any of these available to any of the senses? And yet, are they not absolutely necessary to the events we have just seen, that of the ball speeding from the pitcher to the catcher?

When Kant says that knowledge doesn't necessarily arise out of experience he is saying that a portion of knowledge is something that we bring with us; it is not just incoming sense data. We need the sense data, and Kant acknowledges as much when he says that all knowledge begins with experience. But we need something more than just incoming sense data. In arguing that concepts such as time and space (Kant calls them categories) are inborn, Kant brings rationalism and empiricism together in a sort of synthesis and, to many philosophers, saves philosophy from Humean skepticism. He demonstrates that true *a priori* knowledge is possible, and he shows that the human mind exists as a functioning thing, and as a necessary thing.

Early in *The Critique* he makes another distinction that is important. There are, he says, *a priori* and *a posteriori* judgments, and there are corresponding analytic and synthetic judgments. He illustrates this by first asking a question.

> This, then, is a question. . .whether there is any knowledge that is thus independent of experience and even of all impressions of the senses. Such knowledge is entitled *a priori*, and distinguished from the empirical, which has its sources *a posteriori*, that is in experience. . .[2]

All right, we knew this from our earlier readings. In this Kant is merely using the definitions of the epistemologists who have gone before him. But he also goes on to make the case that *a priori* judgments are universal and necessary, to wit:

---

[2] Ibid., p. 25.

> [I]f we have a proposition which in being thought is thought as *necessary*, it is an *a priori* judgment; and if, besides, it is not derived from any proposition except one which also has the validity of a necessary judgment, it is an absolutely *a priori* judgment. Secondly, experience never confers on its judgments true or strict, but only assumed and comparative *universality*, through induction. We can properly only say, therefore, that, so far as we have hitherto observed, there is no exception to this or that rule. When, on the other hand, strict universality is essential to a judgment, this indicates a special source of knowledge, namely a faculty of *a priori* knowledge. Necessity and strict universality are thus sure criteria of *a priori* knowledge, and are inseparable from one another.[3]

Very well. . .*a priori* judgments are both universal and necessary, and are, as we have seen, judgements that arise prior to sense experience. It then follows that *a posteriori* judgements are judgments that arise through sense experience, that are neither universal nor necessary. But, once again, Descartes said the same thing, and all epistemologists understand the definitions he is using.

Can there actually be *a priori* judgments? The empiricists did not think so, but Kant says that there can be, that there must be, that without them there can be no knowledge, but only jumbled data. But Kant says something more, something about which the earlier epistemologists had been silent. He says that judgments can be, not only *a priori* or *a posteriori*, but can also be analytic or synthetic.

Analytic statement: one in which the subject contains the predicate. In a synthetic statement the subject does not contain the predicate, and the statement must be empirically verified.

Difficult as this may be, I must insist that the student apply his or her considerable intelligence to understanding what Kant is about. Believe me when I tell you that it is important.

Let's take up **analytic** and **synthetic** judgments. I will not quote from Kant directly, but will merely paraphrase. An analytic judgment or proposition is one in which the subject contains the predicate. Example: my brother is a male. Notice that the statement, my brother is a male, is also *a priori*, that is to say, it is universal, it is necessary, and it needn't be confirmed empirically. But also notice that it conveys no real information about the world. It is what philosophers call a tautology, an empty truism.

---

[3] Ibid., pp. 28-29.

A synthetic proposition is one in which the subject does not contain the predicate. Thus, the proposition must be verified empirically. Example: the shirt is blue. Notice that "the shirt is blue" is *a posteriori*, that is to say, it is not universal (many shirts are not blue), nor is it necessary (shirts can be many different colors), and it must be confirmed empirically. But it does give one real information about the world. However, if the only meaningful statement one can make is a synthetic *a posteriori*, then the empiricists were correct, and Hume's criticism of them was correct, and we are left bogged down in skepticism.

But notice what Kant brilliantly proceeds to do. It is easy to see the *a priori* analytic, and the *a posteriori* synthetic. It is also easy to see that there can be no *a posteriori* analytic, because there are no *a posteriori* propositions that are universal and necessary. But can there be propositions that are *a priori* synthetic? That is, are there some propositions, verifiable by experience, that are also universal and necessary? It is in seeking to answer this question that Kant becomes one of the greatest of the western epistemologists. He says that there can be, and he offers a number of examples, including those we considered earlier. Cause and effect, according to Kant, is an example of the synthetic *a priori*. It begins with experience, because it must have sense data to work with, but it doesn't arise from experience, because there is no sensory experience of cause and effect. This is one of the categories supplied by the mind. The human mind, in effect, creates reality from incoming data that would otherwise be a mass of confusion.

Kant called his philosophy transcendental idealism, and he likened it to the Copernican Revolution. Remember that Copernicus opened up modern astronomy by suggesting that we simply look at things a bit differently — instead of placing the earth at the center of the universe, we should place the sun there. Kant did much the same thing for epistemology and the human mind. Instead of making the mind a passive recipient of incoming sense data, he gave it a creative function, made it an active participant in the creation of reality as we know it.

Kant and God

Immanuel Kant was himself a religious man, and a strict pietist; but his work had the ironic effect of making the philosophical proof of God's existence a dubious enterprise. Since his time, few philosophers outside of theological seminaries have attempted to prove the existence of God. If God exists, his existence is in the noumenal world[4], which cannot be known by us. You simply can't get there from here, because all knowledge must begin with experience, and there is no experience of God.

If a proof of God's existence is possible, it must be purely mental, an ontological argument such as that of Anselm or Descartes; and Kant undertakes, in *The Critique of Pure Reason*, to refute the ontological argument by showing, basically, that existence is not an actual predicate of anything, but that it is merely a relational word. To say God exists is to say no more than God is; but the question becomes, God is what? And the moment one begins to fill in the blank by answering the question one runs into the problem of having no experience to fall back on. The true statement implied by the ontological argument is, "If there is a God, then God is that being greater than which none other can be conceived." But this is a conditional, predicates nothing, and is not a synthetic judgment.

We will leave Kant at this time, but we will come back to him again when we get to the section on ethics. Like all great philosophers, he provided much to think about and to respond to, and his philosophy gave rise to others.

The Logical Positivists and the Analytic Philosophers

The philosophical efforts of Immanuel Kant were influential in the development, in the late nineteenth century, of analytical philosophy, and a little later of logical positivism.

To understand logical positivism, go back to Kant and think about his two types of judgments: a judgment may be analytic or it may be synthetic. An analytic judgment is one in which the subject contains the predicate. A synthetic judgement is one in which the subject does not contain the predicate, but the subject-predicate connection must be verified empirically. This is not to say that we will always have the means to verify the connection. It is to say, however, that we must always be able to state the means whereby such a connection could be verified. Or — even more importantly to some philosophers — we can always state the means whereby a proposition can be falsified. The logical positivists constructed a school of epistemology based upon these premises.

---

[4] **Go back and review Section I to see what Kant said about the noumenal world and the phenomenal world.**

The logical positivists came to prominence during the first half of the twentieth century. I think it is fair to say that their influence has waned during the latter half, but they have remained very influential in the areas of logic and epistemology. The problem with logical positivism, as with some of Aquinas's arguments for God, is that the basis for the philosophy is refuted by its own major premise. We shall look at this later.

Analytic philosophy and logical positivism sprang from the work of certain mathematicians and logicians. Gottlob Frege comes immediately to mind, and Wittgenstein, and Rudolph Carnap. ***Fin de siecle*** Vienna was the place where many of these intellectuals of the late nineteenth century came together, and the so-called Vienna Circle was to become the famous breeding ground for logical positivists. When the young Wittgenstein approached the aging Frege and asked to be allowed to study and work with him, Frege responded that he was too old and too tired, and he suggested Wittgenstein contact a younger man, a Cambridge philosopher-mathematician named Bertrand Russell, who along with Alfred North Whitehead had written an important work on logic, *Principia Mathematica.* The result was a flowing together of thoughts of Continental analytical philosophers and British mathematicians. The wedding proved fruitful.

***Fin de siecle* is French, and means literally, "End of the cycle." Normally, when you see the term, it will refer to the period near the end of the 19th century in Europe. But in a broader sense, it can mean the end of any defined period.**

The analytical philosophers were very interested in what they considered the correct use of language — or the incorrect use of language — depending upon the emphasis one wished to give to the inquiry. Why, they wondered, do we have so much confusion in philosophy? The answer they gave is instructive. Much of the confusion has to do with the incorrect use of language, and once this problem is cleared up much of the confusion is cleared up along with it. To quote Bertrand Russell:

> The most important [thing]. . .consists in criticizing and clarifying notions which are apt to be regarded as fundamental and accepted uncritically. As instances I might mention: mind, matter, consciousness, knowledge, experience, causality, will, time. I believe all these notions to be inexact and approximate, essentially infected with vagueness, incapable of forming part of any exact science.[5]

The logical positivists had, they thought, the answer to the problem.

---

[5] Russell, Bertrand, "Logical Atomism," quoted in Velasquez, Manuel, *Philosophy*, op.cit., p. 279.

All propositions that could be reduced to the analytic or the synthetic form were philosophically meaningful, and all those that could not were philosophically meaningless and ought to be rejected as such.

> I divide all genuine propositions into two classes: those which, in this terminology, concern "relations of ideas," and those which concern "matters of fact." The former class comprises the *a priori* propositions of logic and pure mathematics, and these I allow to be necessary and certain only because they are analytic. That is, I maintain that the reason why these propositions cannot be confuted in experience is that they do not make any assertion about the empirical world, but simply record our determination to use symbols in a certain fashion. Propositions concerning empirical matters of fact, on the other hands, I hold to be hypotheses, which can be probable but never certain. . .I require an of empirical hypothesis. . .that some possible sense-experience should be relevant to the determination of its truth or falsehood. If a putative proposition fails to satisfy this principle, and is not a tautology, then I hold that it. . .is neither true nor false, but literally senseless.[6]

From this statement by the well-known logical positivist A.J. Ayer it is clear that the logical positivists are, for all practical purposes, empiricists. Some would disagree with this, and in so doing they would point to the connection of these twentieth century logicians to mathematicians such as Frege and mathematical philosophers such as Russell and the young Wittgenstein. What could be more rationalistic, they would protest, more typical of the sort of knowledge for which Descartes and Leibniz stood, than mathematics. It should be clear, my opponents would doubtless say, that the logical positivists were rationalists who also believed, as did Descartes and company, that a good deal of learning and knowledge comes via experience. In further proof of their position, they would doubtless point to the very word "logic" (as in logical positivists) and remind me that it would be difficult to find a more obviously rationalistic enterprise than the field of logic, with its pure, self-evident axioms.

Sorry. The logical positivists were and are empiricists. It is true that they find analytic propositions meaningful; but it is also true that they find them basically empty of informational content. The statement, "My brother

---

[6] Ayer, Alfred J., *Language, Truth and Logic*, 2nd ed., New York: Dover, 1952, p. 31.

is a male," gives me no genuine information about the world. It is a tautology, a truism, that needn't be verified empirically because it only tells one what has been universally agreed to as the symbols that stand for certain things. Only synthetic propositions give one meaningful information about the world and experience, and these statement must, by their very nature as *a posteriori* judgments, be empirically verifiable.

> The criterion which we use to test the genuineness of apparent statements of fact is the criterion of verifiability. We say that a sentence is factually significant to any given person if, and only if, he knows how to verify the proposition which it purports to express — that is, if he knows what observations would lead him, under certain conditions, to accept the proposition as being true, or reject it as being false. If, on the other hand, the putative proposition is of such a character that the assumption of its truth, or falsehood, is consistent with any assumption whatsoever concerning the nature of his future experience, then, as far as he is concerned, it is, if not a tautology, a mere pseudoproposition. The sentence expressing it may be emotionally significant to him; but it is not literally significant. . .[7]

We must not, however, allow ourselves to suppose that every meaningful proposition is immediately verifiable. This misses the point, which is that one need only be able to tell in a reasonable manner how such a proposition could be verified. Again, we hear from A.J. Ayer on the subject.

> [I]t is necessary to draw a distinction between practical verifiability and verifiability in principle. Plainly we all understand, in many cases, believe, propositions which we have not in fact taken steps to verify. Many of these are propositions which we could verify if we took enough trouble. But there remain a number of significant propositions concerning matters of fact which we could not verify even if we chose, simply because we lack the practical means of placing ourselves in the situation where the relevant observations could be made. A simple and familiar example of such a proposition is the proposition that there are mountains on the further side of the moon. No rocket has yet been invented which would enable me to go and look at the further side of the

---

[7] **Ibid., p. 35.**

> moon, so that I am unable to decide the matter by actual observation. But I do know what observations would decide it for me, if, as is theoretically conceivable, I were once in a position to make them. And therefore I say that the proposition is verifiable in principle, if not in practice, and is accordingly significant.[8]

I think this is clear enough. A meaningful synthetic proposition is one that is verifiable in principle if not in fact. One might even go so far as to say that if a proposition is not verifiable, at least in principle, it cannot be called a true synthetic proposition, for it gives one no true information. As to the statement above, written in 1936, we have now gone to the far side of the moon and have confirmed its truth. But we needn't stop there. How about this for a proposition: there is, on the northern polar cap of Jupiter, a cage that houses a living pink gorilla with green spots. Is this a valid synthetical proposition? Yes it is, for anyone can look at it and can tell the method by which it may be confirmed, even if the method is not available to us just now. If we had the necessary equipment (and we might for all I know), and the desire, we could put a satellite with a powerful camera in orbit around the northern Jupiter pole and take close up pictures of it. I use this example to show that the unverifiability of the proposition is what makes it unmeaningful, not its ridiculousness .

But what would be an example of a meaningless proposition, one that could not be properly called synthetic? Ayer has the answer for that question too.

> [S]uch a metaphysical pseudoproposition as "the Absolute enters into, but is itself incapable of, evolution and progress," is not even in principle verifiable. For one cannot conceive of an observation which would enable one to determine whether the Absolute did, or did not, enter into evolution and progress. Of course it is possible that the author of such a remark is using English words in a way in which they are not commonly used by English-speaking people, and that he does, in fact, intend to assert something which could be empirically verified. But until he makes us understand how the proposition that he wishes to express would be verified, he fails to communicate anything to us.[9]

---

[8] **Ibid., p. 36.**

[9] **Ibid., p. 36.**

Very well, in what Ayer calls a pseudoproposition, we have a failure to communicate anything meaningful. So what would be some other examples of meaningless statements? According to the logical positivists, and most of the analytical philosophers, all metaphysical statements are meaningless.

> The non-theoretical character of metaphysics would not be in itself a defect; all arts have this non-theoretical character without thereby losing their high value for personal as well as for social life. The danger lies in the deceptive character of metaphysics; it gives the illusion of knowledge without actually giving any knowledge. This is the reason why we reject it.[10]

It is probably true that the analytic philosophers and the logical positivists do not have in mind, when they use the term "metaphysics," the broader definition of metaphysics which we examined in the last section. If we are discussing reality, and if in the course of that discussion we bring up quantum physics, they would doubtless say that since the scientists engaged in that enterprise are actually using mathematics and the experimental method to do their investigations they are not to be lumped into the same category as the metaphysicians of old, those speculating about the immortality of the soul. But it is not clear to me what they mean by this. How, in fact, are we to interpret the Copenhagen School of quantum physics? And how the multiple worlds theory of Schrődinger? Are these not bordering on the meaninglessness which Ayer and Carnap (quoted above) decry? In insisting on the purely analytic and the purely synthetic, are these philosophers not narrowing their epistemology so that it cuts out much meaningful inquiry and research?

But there is a more telling argument against Ayer and company, and it has to do, as I have stated, with the fact that the premise upon which their entire system is constructed is self-contradictory. Think about it for a moment. What is the major premise of the logical positivistic edifice? In order for a statement to be philosophical meaningful it must be either analytic or synthetic. Very well, let us take them at their word. Their major premise, by definition, is philosophically meaningless. Is it an analytic statement? That is, does the subject contain the predicate? No, it does not.

---

[10] Carnap, Rudolph, "The Rejection of Metaphysics," in *Twentieth-Century Philosophy: The Analytic Tradition*, ed. Morris Weitz, New York: The Free Press, 1966, pp. 215-216.

Is it a synthetic statement? That is, can someone please tell me what it would take to verify the statement empirically? It is not empirically verifiable. It must be taken on faith, at best. At worst, any attempt to explain or justify the statement winds up begging the question. And once we have admitted that this statement does not fit the logical positivists's definition of meaningful, but that it is nevertheless useful to accept it on pragmatic (or whatever) grounds, we have opened the door for the acceptance of other non-verifiable statements on the same grounds. Wittgenstein saw the problem and in later years distanced himself from the logical positivists, even though he always had serious questions about the metaphysical statements.

> But how many kinds of sentences are there? Say assertion, question, and command? — There are countless different kinds of use of what we call "symbols," "words," "sentences." And this multiplicity is not something fixed, given once for all; but new types of language, new language-games, as we may say, come into existence, and others become obsolete and get forgotten. . .Here the term "language game" is meant to bring into prominence the fact that the *speaking* of language is part of any activity, or of a form of life.[11]

Thus, whether or not metaphysical propositions are meaningful, or carry real information, or may be said to convey knowledge, may have something to do with the sort of "language game" that is being played at the time. The logical positivists would not find this line convincing, but they have problems of their own that are not likely to be resolved unless they can restate their thesis in a non-contradictory manner. I, for one, don't see how that can be done, but I will leave it to them to try.

Before we leave the subject of the logical positivists and the analytic philosophers and go on to other epistemological considerations, I wish to look at an interesting variation on verifiability, because it bears upon our next area of epistemological inquiry — science. In fact, it also bears upon an area of epistemology we will be taking up in Chapter 12 — logic. To understand this variation, consider the following piece of hypothetical logic:

---

[11] **Wittgenstein, Ludwig, *Philosophical Investigations*, trans. G.E.M. Anscombe, 3rd ed., New York: Macmillan, 1953, 11e.**

> If it is raining, then the pavement is wet.
> But the pavement is wet.
> Therefore it is raining.

The error in this logic is fairly obvious, but to give it a name, it is called affirming the consequent. In a hypothetical of this type one may either affirm the antecedent (*modus ponens*) or deny the consequent (*modus tollens*), but one may not turn this order around without making an elementary error in logic. When one affirms the consequent, as in the above example, the error becomes immediately clear — there are many things other than rain that can wet pavement. The problem is that many propositions, particularly of a scientific type, are stated in the hypothetical form; and when one reaches conclusions about unseen things based upon that which is seen and observed, more often than not an affirming of the consequent takes place.

> If oxygen is present in this mixture, then it
> ought to ignite when I place a match in it.
> But it does ignite when I place a match in it.
> Therefore, there is oxygen in the mixture.

In order to avoid this sort of problem some scientists, including Karl Popper, suggest that the proper thing to do, assuming that one wishes to use this experimental format, is to opt for falsifiability rather than verifiability. In this sort of arrangement one is not asked, as with Ayer, what would it take to verify a proposition, but rather, what would it take to falsify it. This doesn't get logical positivism around its basic problem of self-contradiction, but it does, it seems to me, get it around an equally serious logical problem.

Many metaphysical and theological problems are exposed by this approach, not as meaningless (since what is or is not meaningful is often a subjective judgment), but as irresolvable. If, for instance, I say that God always answers my prayers, and you ask me what it would take to falsify that proposition, I might be stuck for an answer. If I pray for a big, red Cadillac and don't get it, then I can say that God answered the prayer, No. This may well be true, but it is not likely that many philosophers will be persuaded.

Science as an Epistemology

Now that I have broached the subject, we may as well talk about science. In fact we have already discussed science when we were looking at the development of empiricism in the last chapter. We saw that science as a method of inquiry owes a great deal to Aristotle, and later to such thinkers as Ockham and Bacon. We also saw that the Baconian method was inductive, reasoning from particulars to general principles. But we also saw that induction, and the very law of cause and effect upon which so much of Bacon's thought and system were based, was seriously undermined by the brilliant, if skeptical, thought of David Hume. So why, if Hume was right, has science been so successful? And why do so many people think of science as the highest type of knowledge we can have? Perhaps we have been thinking all along that science is something that it is not.

Back in my undergraduate days I had several teachers (one of them was the Skinnerian with whom I disagreed over the Kent State affair) who were scientists, and who were deeply committed to science — so much so that for them reality was science, and science was reality. To say that they were philosophically naive is true, if perhaps intellectually snobbish. Every one of them, with the exception of one rather brilliant and well-known experimental psychologist, believed that Bacon was essentially the final word on knowledge and truth. But Bacon was an inductionist, and not all scientific theorists agree that inductive reason is efficacious in getting to the truth. Many very fine scientists are actually rationalists. To demonstrate why, ask yourself a simple question: what is a theory, and how is it used in science?

To put it bluntly, a theory is nothing more than an educated guess about the way things work. The theory may then be used to generate hypotheses for testing. Or sometimes the theory begins as an hypothesis, which expands to theory, and ultimately into paradigm. And finally, once certain things have been confirmed through repeated testing and observation, we may actually get to general laws that purport to state with some degree of certainty how things actually work. Take as an example Aristotle's theory of falling bodies. He began with the postulation that there are four elements, and only four — earth, air, fire, and water. He postulated that earth and water are the heavier elements, and that air and fire are the lighter elements. He went on to guess that the heavier elements will always fall through the lighter elements, and that the lighter elements will rise above the heavier elements. Now all of this is theory, and from it we can extract certain hypotheses. If I drop a stone it will fall to the earth because it is composed of earth and water, and we would expect the heavier elements to fall through the lighter element of air. We drop the stone, and we get exactly the result we expected, proof positive that the theory is correct.

Or is it?

Let's go back and check this again. Hypothesis: heavier elements fall through lighter ones. If a stone is composed of heavier elements, then it will fall if I drop it because the air through which it is falling is lighter. I drop the stone, and observe that it does in fact fall, thus I have shown that it is, as hypothesized, composed of heavier elements. Now I hope you were paying close attention when I was dealing with falsifiability a few pages back. This entire business with the falling stone is marred by an obvious logical fallacy. It is called affirming the consequent. But that is only the beginning of our woes if we buy into the Aristotelian law of falling bodies.

If Aristotle is correct then heavier bodies ought to fall faster than lighter ones. That is to say, if I simultaneously drop a stone weighing ten pounds and one weighing five pounds, the one weighing ten pounds ought to fall twice as fast as the five pound stone. You are probably familiar with the experiments of Galileo, and you probably wondered when you read of these why no one prior to Galileo had thought to perform the simple yet epoch-making experiment. I suppose the answer has something to do with reverence for authority. At any rate, Galileo tried the experiment, discovered that the stones fall at the same rate of speed, and in so doing laid the groundwork for our present law of falling bodies. Galileo did something else right too. He structured his experiment so that he denied the consequent, or, to use language of which Karl Popper would approve, he falsified rather than verified.

You may be thinking that Galileo demonstrated the correct usage of the scientific method of inquiry, and you may be wondering what point I am attempting to make. The point is that theory, if it is any good at all, will yield testable hypotheses. Did Aristotle have a theory of falling bodies? Yes he did. Did the theory yield testable hypotheses? Yes it did. Did the hypotheses, once tested, confirm the theory. No, they did not. In fact, the entire theory was scrapped in favor of another, and that is how science ought to work.

Earlier I stated that many theorists do not think inductive reasoning is a useful way to get to the truth. I also said that many fine scientists are, or have been, rationalists. Now we are in a position to see why. Where did Aristotle's theory come from? It came from the fertile mind of Aristotle, and the minds of his Greek predecessors. And how did they get it? If Bacon is correct, and if science really works in a Baconian fashion, it should have begun with a series of observations, from which certain general principles were derived, principles that were used to construct the theory. But in fact it had no such genesis, and this ought to give all strict empiricists something to think about. Of all the great scientific theories I know about, not one was derived in the Baconian fashion — that is, by testing particulars and reasoning from the results towards generalization — but rather by what appear to have been flashes of insight, leaps of faith.

Take Gottfried Liebniz for example. Back in the seventeenth century he and a number of other philosophers were working on theories of light and reflection. What path will light take if it originates at point "A," is reflected from a mirror, and terminates at point "B." Leibniz stated that, from a number of available possibilities, it would take the shortest path, because God was an able and efficient architect, and thus nature would always act in the optimum fashion. Subsequent testing showed that Leibniz was absolutely correct. Now his initial hypothesis was not established empirically, but rationally, and only afterwards was it empirically confirmed. As George Gale has noted:

> The rationalist epistemology has as its central claim the belief that human reason, independently of and prior to experiment, can reach scientific knowledge about the natural world. Experimental results are to function only as corroborative evidence of the truth and validity of the deductive statements reached by reason. . .Leibniz has deduced a prediction about the way the world behaves, and he apparently has reached this prediction prior to doing any experiment.[12]

If you do not like the example of Leibniz, perhaps you will feel more comfortable with Charles Darwin, although my experience is that many students have come to college with strong prejudices against the man. Regardless of how many people feel about him, there is no question that he has given us one of the most useful and fruitful theories of recent years, the theory of evolution through natural selection. But how did he come up with the theory? Certainly not through observation and induction. He never saw evolution occurring, and by definition he could not have seen it. What he did was to study a number of living species, and then ask himself how they had become what they are. His answer was not arrived at inductively, but more by a sort of insight that then functioned deductively as an explanation for what he saw. This is very troubling to those who do not really understand theory, or logic, or science. In fact it is one of the criticisms usually aimed at Darwin: he calls himself a scientist, but he violates the first law of science, the law of empirical observation. This is simply not true.

---

[12] Gale, George, *Theory of Science*, op.cit., p. 17.

Empirical observation is an important feature of science, but it is not its first law. In fact, as I hope I am demonstrating, rationalism and deduction can be just as important to science as empiricism and induction.

Finally there is Einstein. We have already seen the impact his thinking and his theories have had on twentieth century physics. No one would question his credentials as a scientist, so we ought to at least pay close attention to how he formulated his theories. A story told by George Gale (probably apocryphal, but delightful nevertheless), illustrates the way in which the great physicist operated.

> The director of one of the world's largest and most complete experimental laboratories extended to Mrs. Einstein an invitation to tour their site. She came one day, and was escorted through acre after acre of huge, complicated, and obviously expensive high-energy equipment. After the tour, the director approached her, and said, "This equipment, then, is what we are using to unlock the secrets of nature." To this Mrs. Einstein replied, in a rather puzzled fashion, "But that is what my husband does too, unlocks the secrets of nature. But he does it with a pencil on the back of an envelope!"[13]

It is almost as if Einstein and the others knew what they were looking for to begin with, or at least had strong suspicions, and this has amazing epistemological implications. We seem to be back at square one, asking how we know, how we learn, what knowledge is, what counts for truth. Indeed, we have returned to the Socratic dilemma as expressed in the *Meno*: we either know the truth already, or we cannot possibly even recognize that we do not know it.

> It seems that discovery — that is, reaching new knowledge and information — is not possible. This conclusion is derived from the argument that discovery results from an inquiry either about something we already know, or about something we do not already know. But it is easily seen that discoveries cannot result from inquiries about what we already know, since if we already know something, it cannot be considered to be a discovery. On the other hand, discoveries cannot be results of inquiries about that which we do not know,

---

[13] **Ibid., pp. 18-19.**

> since if we do not know something, we cannot even inquire what it is we are inquiring about. You can see that this argument depends upon the fact that we can know something only if we can recognize it as being what it is. But we can recognize it only if we already know what it is.[14]

This is entangling, and I can imagine many students wondering who could possibly care about this sort of thing. If we learn, we learn, it's just that simple. Why make more of it? I'll tell you exactly why more must be made of it. Assuming we actually wish to get to truth, we cannot begin by laying a weak foundation. To do this is to run the risk of building up what looks like a solid structure, only to have it crumble and fall in the first high wind. No better example is needed than that of Aristotle. For many years he was received as absolute authority on most anything that he bothered to deal with. But a relatively soft nudge by Galileo, and down he went. The days of citing Aristotle as an authority in matters of physics and science are long past, for he appears to have violated some of his own cardinal principles, those that have to do with accurate observation and recording.

The truth is, neither rationalism nor empiricism standing alone appears to be able to account for how we learn and how we know. Both are important, but in the final analysis knowing and learning are apparently more complex operations than can be accounted for by any one theory. Maybe we can clarify matters by getting away from theories altogether, and by asking simply, "What works?"

The Pragmatic Approach

Pragmatism. The word comes from the Greek, *pragma*, meaning act or consequence.

An individual who is pragmatic is one who is thought to be practical. In fact, the word pragmatism, coined by Charles Sanders Peirce, comes from the Greek, *Pragma,* meaning act or consequence. It is rather difficult to imagine how we have worked it around to its present definition, but perhaps a look at the way in which the philosophers developed it can clear matters up.

Pragmatism is the one, the only, philosophy that is purely American; and I suppose that shouldn't surprise any of us, for the Americans are nothing if not pragmatic. The one thing any American is sure to want to know about any item under the sun is, "Does it work?" If it works, then we

---

[14] Ibid., p. 101.

use it. If it doesn't work, then we don't wish to be bothered with it. In the next chapter, when we are looking at the various theories of truth, we will have more to say about the Pragmatists. Just now, the subject is epistemology, theories of learning and knowledge, and the Pragmatists have something of value to add to this debate.

Think back to the ongoing argument, beginning with the Greeks and continuing to the present, about how knowledge is gained. We saw that even in science, the one field where knowledge seems to be solid and certain, difficult questions are still waiting for answers. At one point I suggested that some students would find the ongoing disagreements tiresome; that they would say that we ought to use what works and not be worried about why it works. I said this because the students I am addressing are Americans, and I think I know American students, or Americans of any type for that matter. I made it clear that there are sound reasons for being concerned about why something works; but now I am about to introduce a group of men, Americans every one, who aren't so certain. The names of the more famous Pragmatists are Peirce, William James, and John Dewey. They lived and worked in the latter nineteenth and early twentieth centuries. They had a strong influence over American thought during that period, though the influence in other countries has been much less. Today most of the pragmatists are older men and women who are ready to retire, if they haven't retired already. I am personally acquainted with no young philosophers who designate themselves as Pragmatists. But we might be able to learn something from Peirce and his followers. Even if they seem to have passed into history, they left some sizeable ripples on the pond on their way down. Perhaps the best way to understand Pragmatism, at least from an epistemological standpoint, is by looking at the pragmatists's theory of meaning. In some ways, they sound very like the analytic philosophers, for like them the pragmatists are interested in language and in how we assign meaning to words. But unlike the analytic philosophers and the logical positivists, the pragmatists do not say that statements must be either analytic or synthetic to be meaningful. They say that whether or not a word is meaningful all depends upon how it tests out in experience. According to Charles Peirce, "Our idea of anything is our idea of its sensible effects."

Idea is important to epistemology. Think about it for a moment. When you hear the word, of what do you think? Probably of a comic strip character with a light bulb going on his head, a signal that he or she just intuited something of great importance in one monumental flash of insight. But philosophers don't typically use the word in that way. For the British empiricists, ideas were mental impressions left by sense experience, and when we look at what Peirce has to say, he seems to be thinking along the same lines.

> Now this sort of consideration, namely, that certain lines of conduct will entail certain kinds of inevitable experiences is what is called a "practical consideration." Hence is justified the maxim, belief in which constitutes [pragmaticism]; namely, *In order to ascertain the meaning of an intellectual conception one should consider what practical consequences might conceivably result by necessity from the truth of that conception; and the sum of these consequences will constitute the entire meaning of the conception.*[15]

Notice the use of the word "pragmaticism" in the passage quoted above. Peirce used this to signal his philosophical disagreement with William James, and his intention to disassociate himself from James and the others who were coming along and trading on what Peirce considered his ideas. One would think that philosophers would be above such pettiness, but one would be wrong. But back to our story.

Peirce felt that all meaning, and thus all knowledge, is context dependent, and that to cut oneself off from context was to commit a fatal mistake. The mistake of René Descartes and other dualists, according to Peirce, was that this was the very thing they did, created systems that floated in a sort of mental never-never land without being tied down to the earth and to actual experience. What pragmatic epistemology finally comes down to is this: if words, ideas, concepts, make no practical difference in the world in which we live, they are meaningless and ought to be consigned to the rubbish heap. In the words of William James, "Pragmatism is the attitude of looking away from first things, principles, categories, supposed necessities; and of looking towards last things, fruits, consequences, facts."

> The pragmatic method is primarily a method of settling metaphysical disputes that otherwise might be interminable. Is the world one or many? — fated or free? — material or spiritual? — here are notions either of which may or may not hold good of the world; and

---

[15] Peirce, Charles Sanders, *Collected Papers of Charles Sanders Peirce, vol. 5*, ed. Charles Hartshorne and Paul Weiss, Cambridge, Mass.: Harvard University Press, 1931-35, p. 6.

> disputes over such notions are unending. The pragmatic method in such cases is to try to interpret each notion by tracing its respective practical consequences. What difference would it practically make to anyone if this notion rather than that notion were true? If no practical difference whatever can be traced, then the alternatives mean practically the same thing, and all dispute is idle. Whenever a dispute is serious, we ought to be able to show some practical difference that must follow from one side or the other's being right.
>
> A pragmatist turns his back resolutely and once and for all upon a lot of inveterate habits dear to professional philosophers. He turns away from abstraction and insufficiency, from verbal solutions, from bad *a priori* reasons, from fixed principles, closed systems, and pretended absolutes and origins. He turns toward concreteness and adequacy, toward facts, toward action and toward power.[16]

The whole thing can be summed up in less than a dozen words: if something works use it, if it doesn't abandon it. If, as James says above, nothing practical would result from my assuming something is true as opposed to not being true, then why would I waste my time trying to prove anything about it? Philosophy, John Dewey says repeatedly in so many words, is about solving problems, not creating them.

Pragmatism has a certain down-to-earth, commonsensical appeal that can be refreshing after one has been wandering in the labyrinth of European epistemology. And that, when all the cards are called in, is precisely its weakness: it is so down to earth that it finally answers nothing, though I am sure it would have appealed to my farming, East Texas forbearers. Imagine, if you will, two sixteenth-century men discussing the heliocentric as opposed to the geocentric theories of the universe. Now, imagine a passerby stopping, listening for a moment, and saying, "Gentlemen, I think we ought to take a pragmatic approach to whole thing by asking what practical difference it makes if one of you is right or if the other is." Not many people in the sixteenth century would have thought anything being argued by Galileo and Kepler made any practical difference; but those of us who have the advantage of four-hundred years of hindsight can see that the dispute

---

[16] James, William, *The Will to Believe and Other Essays in Popular Philosophy,* 1897. Reprinted in *Human Immortality: Two Supposed Objections to the Doctrine,* New York: Dover, 1956, pp. 146-47.

was important, that who was right made an enormous difference.

To further illustrate the strange position to which one is brought by the pragmatic method, imagine yourself sitting in a lecture hall in Harvard listening to William James. He takes the podium and says:

> Pragmatism. . .asks its usual question, "Grant an idea or belief to be true," its says, "what concrete difference will its being true make in any one's actual life? How will the truth be realized? What experiences will be different from those which would obtain if the belief were false? What in short, is the truth's cash-value in experiential terms?"
>
> The moment pragmatism asks this question, it sees the answer: True ideas are those that we can assimilate, validate, corroborate and verify. False ideas are those that we cannot. That is the practical difference it makes to us to have true ideas; that, therefore, is the meaning of truth, for it is all that truth is known as. . .
>
> Our account of truth is an account of truths in the plural, of processes. . .Truth for us is simply a collective name for verification-processes.[17]

After the lecture you approach him and ask for some clarification. You have been reading his work, and that of his colleagues Peirce and Dewey, and you have become somewhat confused. If truth is a context related concept, and if the test of any theory's truth depends upon our ability to assimilate and verify it, mustn't truth then be a thing relative to the individual holding it, and doesn't this drive us toward solipsism? Should he respond by saying that you have misapplied his intentions, you would probably ask him for some clarification. Truth, he would say, is a man-made language, but that the making is something of a corporate one, something that groups — not individuals — must agree on.

> Any idea upon which we can ride, so to speak; any idea that will carry us prosperously from any one part of our experience to any other part, linking things satisfactorily, working securely, simplifying, saving labor, is true for just so much, true in so far forth, true instrumentally.[18]

---

[17] James, William, *Pragmatism*, in *William James: Writings 1902-1910*, New York: Library of America, 1987, pp. 573.

[18] James, William, *Pragmatism*, New York: Longmans, Green, 1907, p. 58.

But you would probably fail to see how this clarifies things. What he has actually said is that there is no such thing as truth, or that truth is a creation of expedience at best; and if this is the case, then why is his conception a truthful one, and what would cause us to accept his definition above another. Because it works, he would respond. Well, you might say, it works only as long as you choose to live within a framework that accommodates it (the particular truth one is discussing). Certainly all men once believed the earth was flat, and that seemed to work at the time. Are we to agree that there was a time when the earth was flat, but that it became round only when someone said, "Flat earth no longer works?"

At this point in your discussion, Dr. James would probably excuse himself, politely, and suggest that you do some more reading before you come back to see him again. But I, for one, would applaud you; for it would seem to me that you had raised some interesting, and even obvious, objections to his philosophy.

One must remember that any particular philosophy is a product of the time and place in which it is produced. René Descartes, as we have seen, produced his rationalistic dualism in a time and place rife with revolution and confusion, and he clearly was looking for something stable onto which to hang his thoughts. The pragmatists were Americans, philosophizing during a time of great material growth and optimism. They truly felt that they were on their way to solving the problems that had plagued humankind for centuries, and they were willing to toss aside as useless anything that did not fit their immediate program. To say that things have changed since that time would be as weak an understatement as I could conjure up on short notice. Some of you may have said, as you read what has gone before, that the pragmatists were nothing but empiricists; and you may have wondered why I gave a separate place to them. The reason is that they were not just simple empiricists. They sound like empiricists, insisting that things be empirically verified, but their definitions of truth and idea are not those of standard empirical philosophy. The test of true knowledge, as they say over and over, is whether or not it will work. John Locke and David Hume would never hold to such a notion.

If, however, we go back to a simple definition of empiricism, and if we ask how one learns, how one comes by knowledge, the pragmatists do indeed sound very empirical. Remember our definition of knowledge, however, the one we talked about at the first of our inquiry into epistemology. Knowledge is warranted (or justified), true belief. What would justify a concept for the pragmatist? What would make it true? Once again, we come back to expedience, utility, things that all Americans understand as commonsensical, but that few would agree to over the long run. So while it never hurts to study pragmatism, particularly if the students are Americans and wish to know how their own country has developed intellectually, pragmatism seems in retrospect a brief stop on the journey, one that lasted barely long enough for a coffee break. Nevertheless, we will see the pragmatists again in the next chapter, and we may gain a new respect for them as we see them dealing with some of the problems that have baffled philosophers for centuries, free will among them.

What do Existentialists Know?

While at first glance no one seems farther apart than the pragmatists and the existentialists, some of the things William James said sound almost Kirkegaardian. Take the following statement, from *The Will to Believe.*

> All the magnificent achievements of mathematical and physical science — our doctrines of evolution, of uniformity to law, and the rest — proceed from our indomitable desire to cast the world into a more rational shape in our minds than the shape into which it is thrown there by the crude order of our experience. . .I, for one, feel as free to try conceptions of moral as of mechanical or logical rationality. If a certain formula for expressing the nature of the world violates my moral demand, I shall feel as free to throw it overboard, or at least doubt it, as if it disappointed my demand for uniformity of sequence, for example; the one demand being, so far as I can see, quite as subjective and emotional as the other is. The principle of causality, for example — what is it but a postulate, an empty name covering simply a demand that the sequence of events shall one day manifest a deeper kind of belonging of one thing with another than the mere arbitrary juxtaposition which now phenomenally appears? It is as much an altar to an unknown god as the one Saint Paul found at Athens. All our scientific and philosophic ideals are altars to unknown gods. Uniformity is as much so as is free will.[19]

There is a certain existential ring to this, a certain appeal to the subjective side of truth and knowledge that Kierkegaard would appreciate.

---

[19] James, William, *The Will to Believe,* op.cit., p. 31.

But it also rings of David Hume, and perhaps even of Immanuel Kant. Perhaps it is philosophical eclecticism at its finest. But while James certainly had read Hume and Kant, it is doubtful that he had even heard of Søren Kierkegaard, so the quote above cannot be attributed to any possible influence by the Dane. Perhaps "subjectivity" as truth was simply an idea whose time had come. Here is Kierkegaard on the subject.

> As soon as subjectivity is taken away, and passion from subjectivity, and infinite interest from passion, there is no decision whatever, whether on this issue or any other. All decision, all essential decision, is rooted in subjectivity. At no point does an observer (and that is what the objective subject is) have an infinite need for a decision, and at no point does he see it. This is the *falsum* of objectivity and the meaning of mediation as a passing through in the continuous process in which nothing abides and in which nothing is infinitely decided either, because the movement turns back on itself and turns back again, and the movement itself is a chimera, and speculative thought is always wise afterward. Objectively understood, there are more than enough results everywhere, but no decisive result anywhere. This is quite in order, precisely because decision is rooted in subjectivity, essentially in passion, and *maxime* in the infinitely interested, personal passion for one's eternal happiness.[20]

Students generally bog down on polysyllables in about the first two lines of Kierkegaard and get no further. Well, no one ever said it would be easy. In order to understand this passionate Dane, you have to begin by understanding that his main emphasis is upon action. Not what one understands, but what one does is the important thing. And in the above passage we see him talking about that which moves one to make decisions, of a religious nature to be sure, but the same thing will work for any decisions one is called upon to make.

The problem with the mid-nineteenth century European world of Søren Kierkegaard, as he saw it, was that there was a lack of passion, and lack of commitment. People were disengaged from life to the point that they

---

20 Kierkegaard, Søren, *Concluding Unscientific Postscript to Philosophical Fragments, Vol. 1*, trans. Howard V. Hong and Edna H. Hong, Princeton, N.J.: Princeton University Press, 1992, pp. 33, 34.

were simply going through the motions, when the most momentous of issues were pressing upon them, begging to be decided. It is subjective, not objective, truth that will move people to action, and there will be no meaningful action apart from this.

Kierkegaard is generally misunderstood when he talks about truth being subjective. He is not denying, nor did he ever deny, that there is objective reality, and that what one person experiences is more or less what the other experiences. He is not an idealist of the Berkeley mold, nor a skeptic like Hume. When he talks about subjective truth he has in mind taking the truth in so that it becomes a part of me in an experiential — or, better, in an existential — manner. Kierkegaard was tremendously impressed by the biblical story of Abraham and Isaac. It moved him that this man, on a word from God, would take his son Isaac to Mount Moriah and offer him up as a slain sacrifice. The standard teaching about Abraham, that this action showed his great faith, was not lost on Kierkegaard; but neither was a greater truth lost on him: the faith that Abraham had was an interior one. He knew certain things that others did not, and because of what he knew, he was willing to sacrifice his son.

Now this gets us to the heart of the matter. What did Abraham know, and how did he know it? It is easy to say that he knew something about God, but this hardly explains the sacrifice he was willing to make. It is as if Abraham had taken the empiricists and turned them around backward. Whereas they all would have said that seeing is believing, Abraham was beginning with belief, acting as if believing was seeing. Abraham's action is an example of the famous "leap," of which Kierkegaard speaks again and again.

> Therefore, anyone who wants to demonstrate the existence of God (in any other sense than elucidating the God-concept and without the [ultimate reservation] that we have pointed out — that the existence itself emerges from the demonstration by a leap) proves something else instead, at times something that perhaps did not even need demonstrating, and in any case never anything better.[21]

The leap, an idea he picked up from the German philosopher Lessing, seems to have fascinated Kirkegaard, for he wrote of it in a number

---

[21] Kierkegaard, Søren, *Philosophical Fragments*, trans. Howard V. Hong and Edna H. Hong, Princeton, N.J.: Princeton University Press, 1985, p. 43.

of works all through his productive years. Notice that demonstrating God's existence is impossible, other than through the leap. But demonstrating God's existence to whom? Clearly, the demonstration is to oneself; and this is true not only in demonstrating God, but as one moves through the stages of life. One can live the aesthetic life, a life given to hedonism and the accumulation of things, or one can, by an act of the will, make the leap to a higher life, the ethical life. One can go on in the ethical life, or one can leap still higher, to the life of faith. In each case a decision is called for. In each case, the leap is undertaken, not on the basis of any objective evidence, but for purely subjective reasons.

In *Fear and Trembling*, Kierkegaard characterizes his Knight of Faith as an individual who outwardly appears to be just like other people; but inwardly he is wrestling with infinite matters.

> [I]f one didn't know him it would be impossible to set him apart from the rest of the crowd; for at most his hearty, lusty psalm-singing proves that he has a good set of lungs. In the afternoon he takes a walk in the woods. He delights in everything he sees, in the thronging humanity, the new omnibuses, the Sound — to run across him on Strandveien you would think he was a shopkeeper having his fling, such is his way of taking pleasure. . .Towards evening he goes home, his step tireless as a postman's. . .He smokes his pipe in the evening: to see him you would swear it was the cheesemonger opposite vegetating in the dusk. . .and yet this man has made and is at every moment making the movement of infinity.[22]

The epistemological implications of Kierkegaard's philosophy are not immediately so apparent as are those of some of the other philosophers at whom we have looked. Usually an epistemologist calls himself or herself by that name, whereas Kierkegaard never did. It is only when he is seen as the forerunner of the twentieth-century existentialists that it becomes clear how crucial epistemological issues were to him. Some have wondered why he, a Christian, had such strong influence over many of the existential atheists. The reason is clear — it was Kierkegaard who identified and attempted to deal with the problems that these twentieth-century thinkers have identified as crucial, not the least of which is how we know and what it means when

---

22 Kirkegaard, Søren, *Fear and Trembling*, trans. Alastair Hannay, London: Penguin Books, 1985, p. 69.

we use the term truth.

The Phenomenologists

The next link in the existential chain are the phenomenologists, and there is no question about their interest in epistemology. To see how they follow from Kierkegaard, let us begin by assuming that Kierkegaard was onto something important, that truth is not truth until it is taken in, made subjective, and can move one to action. From the very outset the phenomenologists were interested in many of the same things that interested Søren Kierkegaard and (to a lesser extent) Friedrich Nietzsche. Underlying all their epistemological concerns is the conviction that if one wishes to know reality one must begin by focusing on the human condition. Just as Kierkegaard turned his attention to the experience of what it is to be human, the phenomenologists concentrated on what it meant for a human to perceive anything. As Manuel Velasquez has said:

> The phenomenologist and the existentialist try to approach reality from the inside, by focusing on reality as it is subjectively revealed by our human condition and human consciousness. And they attempt to approach reality not by relying on theoretical presuppositions but by trying to examine and describe reality as it presents itself to our unprejudiced view. Truth about our human existence cannot be grasped and repeated by means of neat objective statements. We experience truth, like everything else, through living; the truth is within, not without.[23]

The truth is within, not without. Kierkegaard couldn't have said it better.

Phenomenology was founded by Edmund Husserl (1859-1938). One cannot read his writing, particularly his diary entries, without thinking that he shared much of the passion for certainty that we have seen in René Descartes. In his *Kant to Wittgenstein and Sartre*, W.T. Jones quotes from Husserl's diary and comments as follows:

> The animating force in Husserl's life and thought was a deep need for certainty. In 1906 he wrote in his diary, "I have been through enough torments from lack of clarity

[23] Velasquez, Manuel, *Philosophy*, op.cit., p. 265.

> and from doubt that wavers back and forth. . .Only one need absorbs me: I must win clarity, else I cannot live; I cannot bear life unless I can believe that I shall achieve it." It was this passion that led Husserl from mathematics to logic and from logic to philosophy, always in search of absolutely secure foundations.[24]

Jones points out that there are considerable differences between Husserl's approach and that of the existentialists who preceded him, specifically Kierkegaard and Nietzsche. Both of them were willing to tolerate uncertainty as the best that a human could hope for. This accounts for Kierkegaard's insistence on the leap of faith. As for Nietzsche, he not only tolerated it, he revelled in it, considering an insistence on certainty a sign of neurosis. For Husserl, this would not do, nor would the relativism of the pragmatists. To say, in effect, that something is true if it works was not the sort of certainty he was looking for. He attacked the pragmatists at the very point they were the most vulnerable, which they, ironically, thought was their strongest point. Relativism is not certainty. The pragmatism led to the sort of natural science with which Dewey and James felt comfortable, but Husserl was not interested in natural science. In fact, writing in 1935, he stated that the crisis in Europe, as evidenced by the rise of fascism, was a result of a blind allegiance to the methods of natural science. He urged a return to pure, theoretical science.

Like many philosophers, Husserl is a bit difficult to understand when read in the original. So I shall give a general summary of his position. First, notice that when someone begins talking about certainty he or she is talking about epistemology, the study and theory of knowledge, what we can know and how we can know it. Second, notice, as I have already pointed out, that Husserl sounds something like Descartes, that while he expresses some of the same concerns as the early existentialists, he departs from their epistemological position. Third, he rejects the epistemology of pragmatism as being relativistic and given to the promotion of a thing he despises, natural science.

This third point is worth talking more about. What, precisely, is Husserl calling natural science? He mainly has sociology and psychology in mind. And what is wrong with these? Neither, according to Husserl, is

---

[24] **Jones, W.T., *Kant to Wittgenstein and Sartre, 2nd ed.*, New York: Harcourt, Brace & World, 1952, pp. 390-91.**

purely scientific, and in the case of psychology a more basic error has been committed — having distinguished between minds and bodies, psychologists treated minds as if they were bodies.[25]

Now we come to phenomenology, as Husserl argued for it. He wishes to disconnect from what he calls the "fact-world" of natural science, the world that is out there. It is not that he is denying the existence of the fact-world, but that he wishes to somehow get around it to the thing that is really there. Does this sound like Immanuel Kant? It does indeed, but you may notice that the new philosophy is called "*pheno*menology" not "*nou*menology." Still, in understanding Husserl, it might be helpful to go back and review Kant a bit. Remember that Kant did not believe we can ever know the world as it actually is, the noumenal world; we can only know the world as it appears to us, the phenomenal world. This, Kant held, is because the human mind has a formative effect on reality, taking the incoming, noumenal raw matter, and putting it into meaningful form in accordance with the inborn categories, which he saw as synthetic *a priori.*

Now, consider Husserl. He wishes to get behind the fact-world and get to the underlying world of pure being as it reveals itself to our consciousness, which is also pure being and not the physical things imagined by the psychologists. To do this, Husserl uses a device he calls "bracketing." Imagine you are holding a red apple in your hand. You may see the apple, its shiny surface, touch its smoothness, smell its distinctive odor. But, now, suppose we bracket each of these sense events, by which Husserl means we place brackets around them and set them aside. We take them out of play as it were, assuming for the time being that they are making no claims on our cognitive process. If we do this, what we are left with is consciousness, or ultimate reality. This, I will freely admit, has always seemed impossible to me. Perhaps it can be done. But I have tried and tried, and I have yet to achieve anything like the experience Husserl seems to have thought awaited me. It has an almost mystic ring. But while I haven't achieved any sort of enlightenment, Jean Paul Sartre's hero Roquentin, the protagonist of *Nausea,* claims to have had it. In the latter portion of his well-known novel, Sartre has Roquentin sitting in a garden, looking at the roots of an old chestnut tree, when ultimate reality swims into his view. It is indeed nauseating.

> Never until these last few days have I understood the meaning of existence. . .And then all of a sudden, there it

[25] See Velasquez, *Philosophy,* op.cit., p. 266.

> was, clear as day: existence had suddenly unveiled itself. It had lost the harmless look of an abstract category; it was the very paste of things, this root was kneaded into existence. Or rather the root, the park gates, the bench, the sparse grass, all that had vanished: the diversity of things, their individuality, were only an appearance, a veneer. This veneer had melted, leaving soft monstrous masses, all in disorder — naked, in a frightful, obscene

The veneer which had melted away before Roquentin's eyes, leaving monstrous, naked reality, was presumably what we can voluntary bracket and set aside in our study of reality.

One might well ask, at this point, why Husserl is important enough to deserve mention in an overview of epistemology. The answer is, not because of what he was in himself, but because of what he led to. It is those who were influenced by Husserl who were to become critical to the development of twentieth century philosophy, namely Heidegger and Sartre, the later existentialists.

Twentieth-Century Existentialism

When one thinks of the twentieth-century existentialists, one normally thinks of bearded, depressed individuals sitting in cafes on the left bank of the Seine, staring into glasses of beer and muttering that existence is absurd, that one must strive to retain one's authenticity, that the universe is a frightful, meaningless place in which one is forever an alien, forever seeking to affirm oneself. Actually, existentialism in this century grew first out of epistemological concerns, and only afterward addressed the issues that we normally associate with Kierkegaard and Nietzsche.

These issues need not concern us in this chapter. The only questions we need to ask are, how have this century's existentialists dealt with the problem of knowing? How do they define truth? True to form, they have typically been very subjective in their definitions, but this is not to say that they have tended toward relativism or solipsism. As we saw earlier with Kierkegaard, the existentialists do not deny the reality of the world around us, nor did the phenomenologists. They come at epistemology more from a pragmatic angle. Now this can be easily misunderstood, for the pragmatists

[26] Sartre, Jean-Paul, *Nausea,* trans. L. Alexander, New York: New Directions, 1959, p. 173.

really do wind up stating that, for all practical purposes (and practical purposes are the only ones that ultimately matter for them), something is true if it works. While this may have a certain commonsensical aura that some in the working world might find attractive, it has troubling implications, as do most of the more subjective theories of truth and knowledge. We shall examine this more carefully in the next chapter. For now, let us ask whether or not the existentialists, who admittedly take a very subjective approach to just about everything, have a more plausible epistemological stance.

We might begin by asking, what, finally, is their epistemological stance. At the risk of oversimplifying what is fairly complicated, I will repeat that epistemologically they are a great deal like the phenomenologists from whom they draw so much of their initial inspiration. Maurice Merleau-Ponty, phenomenologist turned existentialist, says in his Phenomenology of Perception, "The aim of phenomenology is described as the study of experiences with a view to bringing out their 'essences,' their underlying reason."[27] Now the student is within reason at this point to ask what, precisely, this means; and in seeking an explanation he or she will certainly find the words "study of experiences" standing in a very central position.

Sartre, the most prolific and well-known spokesman for existentialism has addressed the issue of essentialism versus existentialism by saying that man first exists, he is, and that his essence follows after, a product of the existent being making choices. Thus, the experiences in Merleau-Ponty's statement, and the existence in the writings of Sartre, are different sides of the same coin, for experiences must spring from existence. And it is within the existential milieu that epistemological concerns arise. Whose experience am I supposed to be studying, assuming I set out to follow Merleau-Ponty's lead? It can be none other than my own, for my own is all that I know. Sartre makes this clear in *Being and Nothingness.*

> [S]elf-consciousness we ought to consider not as a new consciousness, but as *the only mode of existence which is possible for a consciousness of something.*[28]

---

[27] Pivcevic, Edo, ***Husserl and Phenomenlogy***, **London: Hutchinson University Library, 1970, p. 11.**

[28] **Sartre, Jean-Paul, *Being and Nothingness*, op.cit., p. 14.**

This brings us back, once again, to the subjective nature of existential epistemology, and to the consideration that I can know my own experience and none other. But this is not to say that my experience of being will somehow differ from yours, for reality, that massive, inert other which Sartre calls being-in-itself, is there for you as well as for me. The difference, finally is in how each of us chooses to know reality, and in how we choose to react to what we come to know. This — how we react, the choices we make — is what will ultimately determine what we are, our essence. Thus, for Sartre as for Kierkegaard, knowledge issues forth in action, choice. If it does not, it is difficult to say that it is true knowledge. One is either propelled to the leap, or one hovers suspended in inauthenticity. This is the final irony, and existentialists do not shrink from irony, they revel in it. What one knows is evident only in what one is willing to do; but doing always has a subjective, irrational aspect to it. It is a plunge off a cliff into nothingness, with the expectation that someone will catch me. Is it God. If God does, in fact, catch me, then I can say with Abraham, "I know God, for I have experienced Him."

Chapter 11
Pilate's Question

Place your right hand on the Bible.
Repeat, with solemnity, after me:
I, Pilate, as best I am able,
As a student of theology,
Will tell the unmitigated truth. . .
Hold on! Desist! What does that mean?
Define "truth" or I take the Fifth.
Is it Coherence? Correspondence?
Something between?

ilate's question is contained in the Gospel of John, in the New Testament. When Jesus said, "Everyone who is of the truth heareth my voice," Pilate responded with a question, "What is truth?" This question lies at the very heart of philosophy, particularly that part of philosophy that has to do with knowledge and learning. Epistemology has, from the beginning, been concerned with answering the question, what is truth? But as I cleverly attempted to suggest in the verse above, the answer is not always easy to get at. When someone says, "Truth," what does he or she mean? Some students will think this is just more philosophical hair-splitting. Anyone knows what truth is.

Do they?

Very well, you tell me. What do you mean when you say of some proposition, "That is the truth?" Have you ever said this? Of course you have. We all have. But I have spent many years teaching students philosophy, have asked this question of them many times, and have yet to have one single student, when the question is initially introduced, leap confidently up and say, "I know exactly what that means." In every case it takes a good deal of discussion to elicit an answer, and even then confusion remains. Some seem to think that the answer is self-evident. It is not. If it were, then there would have been no reason for philosophers over the years to have asked the question and to have attempted to answer it; and there would certainly be no explaining the disagreement that has arisen over the proper definition.

Look back at Pilate's question. Why would he ask such a thing? Was it to avoid, by means of philosophical wrangling, facing a truth he did not wish to deal with? Was it the cynical expression of a world-weary man who had traveled widely, been exposed to many cultures, and heard many conflicting versions of truth? Or was he, perhaps, a genuine seeker of the truth eagerly awaiting a reply? If so, Jesus's failure to respond to the question, and Pilate's failure to press him on the subject, are both puzzling.

Regardless of what Pilate was after, I will assume that all my students are genuine truth seekers, and I will proceed accordingly. Let's return to our definition of knowledge as justified, true belief. If this is a definition worthy of acceptance, then we must acknowledge that truth lies at the very heart of things. For if truth is not possible, and if we cannot even agree on what truth is, then by definition we can have no knowledge.

It may surprise some students to learn that there are actually theories of truth, and that these theories tend to go along with, and be supportive of, the theories of learning that we have already examined. The theory that has grown up alongside rationalism is called the **coherence theory** of truth. That which supports empiricism is called the **correspondence theory**. A third theory of truth, arising out of pragmatism and existentialism, has come to be called the **pragmatic theory** of truth. There are others as well. Follow along and we shall see where the road takes us.

But Does it Hang Together?

Suppose we are looking at a picture puzzle that has been assembled, all except for one piece. You are given the task of determining which piece fills in the blank, and you are given ten pieces from which to choose. Do you think you would have difficulty picking out the correct piece? You probably would not — assuming, that is, that one of the pieces does fit. You would simply look for the piece that has the right shape, the right pattern, the right colors. In other words, you would look for the piece that goes along with the other pieces. This is precisely what the **coherence theory** of truth proclaims: a proposition is true if it coheres, fits with, hangs together with, other known truths. This theory of truth is particularly suited for use if one wishes to argue for a form of rationalism and what we have been calling *a priori* knowledge and analytic propositions.

Coherence theory of truth: a proposition is true if it "hangs together" with other propositions known to be true.

Think about how one would go about gaining knowledge if

rationalism is a correct epistemological position, and if there is innate knowledge to be ferreted out, and you can see why rationalists have generally held to some form of the coherence theory of truth. If you have difficulty understanding the why of this, don't worry. It will become clear once we set it alongside and compare it with a rival theory of truth, the correspondence theory. Before we do that, however, it might help matters if we look at another prime example of the coherence theory at work.

Courts of law are important forums for determining truth; and though we are apt to think of lawyers as sophists willing to argue anything for a price, this is not really how things are supposed to work. You have heard, I'm sure, of circumstantial evidence. Some people express surprise when they are told that an individual may be convicted on circumstantial evidence. Actually, many times circumstantial evidence is strong enough to convince most anyone who weighs it impartially and intelligently, and circumstantial evidence is an excellent example of the coherence theory of truth at work.

Suppose you are walking down a hall in school one day, when suddenly you hear what sounds like a gunshot in one of the rooms. You rush into the room in which you think you heard the shot, and there you find, much to your distress, one of your close friends lying dead on the floor with a bullet hole in his head, and another of your close friends standing over him with a smoking gun, a .45 automatic. Your friend with the gun begins by saying, "I know this looks bad. . ." And you acknowledge that it certainly does. Eventually you are called to testify at your friend's trial, and you hear his lawyer state before the jury that the case against his client, your friend, is purely circumstantial. The district attorney says that it certainly is circumstantial, but he goes on and says to the jury, "Let's examine the circumstances." He elicits testimony from you that you heard the sound of the gun go off, that you rushed into the room by the only door. It was a second floor room, and there was no way in or out except by the door, for the windows were small and high on the wall. Further, you were in the room in a matter of seconds after you heard the gun. You found your one friend dead and your other friend standing over him with a smoking gun.

More evidence is presented. A paraffin test done on the accused showed that he had fired a gun. Ballistics tests prove the bullet removed from the victim's head was fired from the .45 automatic the accused had been holding. Fingerprint experts testify under oath that his fingerprints were on the murder weapon.

But it gets worse. Two people come forward to testify that they heard an argument between the victim and the accused the day before, during which the accused had angrily said he would kill the victim if he got a chance. And then, to make matters still worse, the accused failed a lie detector test.

Put it all together and what conclusion would an intelligent man or woman reach. To the proposition, The accused shot and killed the victim on May 13, in room 214 of the Liberal Arts building, your verdict must surely be that the proposition is true.

But notice that only the accused knows exactly what went on in room 214, and he isn't talking except to plead not guilty. The proposition must be adjudged true or false on some basis other than the testimony of an eye witness. If it is true that John Smith shot Bill Williams on the morning of May 13 in room 214 of the Liberal Arts building, that truth has been established using the coherence theory of truth: the proposition is true because it coheres, hangs together, with other propositions that we know are true.

But hold on! Stop the presses! How do we know the other propositions are true? And if we do not, then what does the unknown proposition have to cohere with? This brings in another theory of truth, the most commonsensical theory, the one which (according to its adherents) is foundational to the coherence theory. It is called, as we have seen, the correspondence theory.

As Any Fool Can See. . .

"As any fool can see, and I can plainly see. . ." So runs the quote from a once popular comic strip called *L'il Abner.* This is the gist of the **correspondence theory** of truth, and this is what most people mean when they talk of truth -- at least in my experience. I mentioned at the beginning of this chapter that I frequently ask students what truth is, and how they have trouble answering the question. When they finally think and argue their way toward an answer, this is invariably the answer they give, in so many words: a proposition is true if it corresponds with the facts. For example, the proposition, "There is a yellow tom cat sitting in the middle of my desk," is true if, and only if, a yellow tomcat is sitting there. And how would we know? We look. We verify the proposition empirically. Thus, as any fool can see, the correspondence theory of truth is most nearly compatible with the empirical epistemological position, with the theory that all knowledge is *a posteriori* and with synthetic propositions. For this reason, it is the most popular theory of truth; it is the theory that most

Correspondence theory of truth: a proposition is true if it corresponds with observable facts.

people hold with, when they are pushed enough to actually give a definition of truth. Seeing (or hearing, tasting, etc.) is believing, we like to say, and this is correspondence.

Proponents of this theory like to point out, as I have suggested, that all truth is ultimately arrived at by means of verifying a proposition's correspondence with empirical fact, for without an appeal to such fact, in some form, there would be no demonstrable truths to cohere with one another. Let us go back to the example of the picture puzzle. In this case, one is able to determine which piece, of the ten left over, goes into the blank spot only because one is able to see the blank spot, to see the available pieces, and to make a judgment based upon empirical evidence. And this, correspondence theorists say, is not actually coherence at all. It is correspondence.

Let us set that one aside and come back to it. What about the case of the killing and the conviction based on circumstantial evidence. Is this not a good example of the coherence theory at work? No more so, the correspondence theorists reply, than is that of the picture puzzle. The same criticism applies. In the killing we have what amounts to a picture puzzle, with a series of pieces fitted into place, verified empirically, with one central piece missing. Now we are hypothetically presented with a group of possible pieces to fill in the blank: who killed Bill Williams? Was it Professor Plum, Butler Higgins, or John Smith. There is only one piece that fits properly, and that is the one marked John Smith. But does this show the strength of the coherence theory? Perhaps it is a better example of coherence than is that of the picture puzzle; but it supports even better the idea that correspondence, not coherence, is the correct theory of truth. The entire picture of the killing that was built for us, piece by piece, by the prosecution was empirically substantiated. Each proposition, save the final one, was determined to be true by showing that it "corresponded" with the available facts. The final verdict, that Smith killed Williams, may not actually be true at all, since there was no eye witness. It is only the best available proposition we have.

So is the coherence theory down for the count? No, for there are coherence theorists who argue that what we are calling correspondence can only be understood as the perception is seen within the larger whole. Note the following, by the well-known coherence theorist Brand Blanshard.

> Suppose we say, "the table in the next room is round"; how should we test this judgment? In the case in question, what verifies the statement of fact is the perceptual judgment that I make when I open the door and look. But then what verifies the perceptual judgment

> itself? . .To which the reply is, as before, that a judgment of fact can be verified only by the sort of apprehension that can present us with a fact, and that this must be a further judgment. And an agreement between judgments is best described not as correspondence, but as coherence.[1]

But the equally famous Bertrand Russell, a committed correspondence theorist, has different notions.

> Thus a belief is true when it corresponds with a certain associated complex, and false when it does not. Assuming, for the sake of definiteness, that the objects of the belief are two terms and a relation, the terms being put in a certain order by the "sense" of the believing, then if the two terms in that order are united by the relation into a complex, the belief is true; if not, it is false. This constitutes the definition of truth and falsehood that we were in search of. Judging or believing is a certain complex unity of which a mind is a constituent; if the remaining constituents, taken in the order which they have in the belief, form a complex unity, then the belief is true; if not, it is false.[2]

As with the debate between rationalists and empiricists, there are some propositions that can be best handled by an appeal to coherence, and there are some that can best be handled by an appeal to correspondence. Perhaps our most illuminating approach to an understanding of which is more useful, and under which cases, would be to set the two alongside one another and see how they compare.

Pattern and Formula

We are all familiar with the sorts of problems one is asked to solve in I.Q. tests. A series of words or numbers are presented, followed by a blank, and the respondent is asked what goes into the blank. For example: 1,2,2,3,3,3,4 ___. The blank space should obviously contain the number "4". Try this one: red apple green apple yellow apple blue ______. If you

---

1 Blanshard, Brand, "The Nature of Thought," *In Philosophical Interrogation*, ed. Sidney and Beatrice Rome, New York: Holt, Rinehart & Winston, 1964, p. 210.

2 Russell, Bertrand, *The Problems of Philosophy*, London: The Oxford University Press, 1912, p. 285.

filled in the blank with anything other than "apple" you lose. These simple cases illustrate the coherence theory doing what it does best, account for truth when the question is one of pattern or wholeness.

But is this really a case for coherence, or is it a case for correspondence? Look back to the quote by Russell and ask yourself what he would say about the patterns above. Suppose we reduce the first example to propositional form by saying, "Given the string of numbers presented, the blank ought to be filled with the number four." Blanshard would certainly hold that coherence accounts for the truthfulness of the proposition, but Russell would not; he would say, as he has said, "[I]f the remaining constituents, taken in the order which they have in the belief, form a complex unity, then the belief is true, if not, it is false."

Perhaps we need to look elsewhere for a clear example of coherence theory at work, for correspondence seems able to handle the two cases above, plus a great deal more. This is why, as George Gale has put it, "Correspondence theory is relatively intuitive, and most likely is the theory we all believe up until the time philosophers start to mess around with our minds."[3] So kindly allow me to mess with your minds. Intuitive or not, commonsensical or not, backed by popular opinion or not, the correspondence theory of truth simply cannot handle mathematical truth, and I for one have always been somewhat surprised that a mathematician of Russell's brilliance could not see this. This becomes particularly puzzling when one considers that Russell understood the need to appeal to the Platonic forms in explaining mathematical truth. Now that I have committed two serious sins in one paragraph (one, messing with your minds; and two, challenging Bertrand Russell), I need to give some serious thought to how I plan to atone. Perhaps I can do it by showing you why we need the coherence theory of truth if we wish to say so much as 2 + 2 = 4.

To see why this common mathematical proposition demands the existence of the coherence theory, think a moment of what the correspondence theory says: a proposition is true if, and only if, it corresponds to the observed facts. The problem with trying to use the correspondence theory to explain the truth of mathematics is precisely that there are no observable facts. George Gales puts it like this.

> Consider, to paraphrase Plato, the numerical statement "2 + 2 = 4." Certainly we must all admit that it is intuitively true. But how can we explain its truth in terms

---

[3] Gale, George, *Theory of Science*, op.cit., p. 221.

> of the correspondence theory? If it is true, then "2" must refer to some object, and so also must "4," "+," "=," and so on. If there are no such objects, then the statement cannot correspond to them -- in fact it cannot correspond to anything at all -- and hence it cannot be true. This follows from the fact that a statement is true only if it corresponds to what it refers to, and "2 + 2 = 4" does not refer to anything, since there is nothing there to be referred to. Thus, how can we possibly claim that "2 + 2 = 4" is true?[4]

I hope that the student is able to see exactly what Gale is getting at here, for, to use an outworn phrase, he has just laid bare the Achilles Heel of the correspondence theory. One may attempt to argue one's way around the difficulty by saying that the truth of this equation can only be understood by an appeal to correspondence, for the concepts of "2" and "4," of "+" and "=," are abstracted from actual things which have been learned empirically. This is, of course, the sort of argument used by Locke and other empiricists; it purports to show that the entire structure of Continental rationalism was predicated upon the false premise that abstract concepts are somehow intuited rather than created by humans using ideas obtained from sense data. To me, this argument has a vague air of question begging about it. Of course, if we know in advance that abstract concepts are constructed using incoming sense data as raw material, then the argument is sound; but that is the very thing the argument is attempting to prove, and it cannot be used as a premise in the argument.

The correspondence theory simply cannot handle mathematics well, and some theorists, Gale among them, have thought that it was a vain attempt to salvage the correspondence theory, in some form, that led Plato to postulate his invisible world of forms. There is a much better way to handle it, Gales suggests, one that is much more in keeping with reality, one that does not fall before the relentless slashing of Ockham's razor — abandon correspondence in favor of coherence.

> If this be done, then one need no longer believe in the existence of a nonmaterial, ideal world, a world peopled by "2," "4," "+." and later, of course, Lucifer and all the other angels and heavenly beings. Many philosophers and mathematicians have felt more comfortable doing without this other, ephemeral world. But a further

---

[4] **Ibid., p. 221.**

> difficulty remains: What theory can we put in the place of the now-discarded correspondence theory? Coherence theory seems to be most likely candidate: "2 + 2 = 4" is true simply because it coheres, this is, it is logically consistent, with the entirety of the conceptual system of arithmetic. "2 + 2 = 5" is not true, is false, because it is not logically consistent with the rest of the arithmetical system. On this point, then, coherence theory is very useful for the philosophy of mathematics.[5]

If, however, one wishes to argue that, nonetheless, the coherence theory is simply incorrect, that when we are talking truth we are talking some form of correspondence, then the entire mathematical system, as we know it, can be shown to be truthful only if we assume the existence of Plato's forms. This is why Bertrand Russell got boxed in to a defense of something that he must have felt rather uncomfortable with from time to time.

If mathematics is a good example of coherence theory, Euclidean geometry is an even better one. In fact to Brand Blanshard this is one of the most perfect examples of coherence that has ever been constructed. Each part contributes to the whole, is sustained by the whole, and also contributes to the whole, to the extent that to change even one of the propositions would be to alter the entire system.

So far it seems that correspondence, the most obvious approach to truth, is not doing well. It seems to be a poor stepchild, dragged out to do service for its more glamorous sibling, then pushed back into the pantry. This is, of course, not so. As we have seen Russell saying, most philosophers, particularly since the days of Locke and Hume, have thought that the correspondence theory is the correct one, and that coherence, the glamorous sibling, is all surface beauty with no inner core. Or, perhaps more to the point, push through the facade of coherence and one will invariably find correspondence lurking at its core. To see whether or not this is the case, return with me to Russell's *The Problems of Philosophy.*

Russell's Three Requisites

In This well-known work, Russell posits three requisites which he says are necessary for any theory of truth, and which he says are frequently

---

[5] Ibid., pp. 221-222.

overlooked by epistemological theorists. First, any theory of truth must be able to admit of its opposite, falsehood. Second, an adequate theory must exist within a world of beliefs. Third, the truth or falsehood of any belief must always depend upon something which lies outside the belief itself. It is the third of these requisites, according to Russell, which must lead us to adopt some form of the correspondence theory of truth.[6] These three requisites must be taken as a whole, each leading to the next, if we are to accept the final conclusion. We might put them together in this fashion:

> Premise 1: A theory of truth must admit of the possibility of falsehood; therefore
>
> Premise 2: The theory must exist within a milieu of belief; and therefore
>
> Premise 3: The truth or falsehood of a belief must depend upon something that lies outside of the belief itself; and therefore
>
> Conclusion: Only the correspondence theory meets the full conditions necessary for a working theory of truth.

There is an important sub-premise attached to premise 2, and that is that in a world of mere matter, one in which there are no beliefs but only facts, truth would not be possible. There is no doubt that students, coming to this business for the first time, have difficulty seeing just how it all fits together, and how it leads to the conclusion that Russell has reached. There is also no doubt that all students are students because they wish to learn new things, or someone else wishes they would. This cannot happen unless there is some exposure to new things and some mental application; so I propose that we take Russell's argument and apply ourselves to understanding exactly what he is getting at. It could lead us to some profitable discoveries about the universe in which we live.

First, think about what he says with regard to truth and falsehood. One of my graduate-school professors used to ask, "Would it make any sense to talk of truth if you had no concept of falsehood?" The answer, it seems to me, is obvious. If there were no such thing as falsehood, if the possibility of falsehood did not exist, if you possessed no concept of

---

[6] See Russell, Bertrand, *The Problems of Philosophy*, op.cit., pp. 283-284.

falsehood, then the whole idea of truth would become meaningless.[7] Now, moving right along, if knowledge is justified, true belief, then truth and belief are inseparably bound up together, and both truth and belief must exist together in a world that makes room for falsehood, or at least for its possibility. So, what sort of world would this be? This leads into the second premise, and more particularly to its sub-premise.

A world which must have beliefs that admit of falsehoods must be a world of something more than mere matter. A world of matter, Russell says, would contain many facts, but no possibility of belief, or (he adds) of statements. This is a bit more difficult to understand than the first premise, but perhaps a grammatical example will help. You have all been taught that a sentence, in order to be correct, must at the bare minimum have a subject and a predicate, that the subject is a noun, and that the predicate must consist of a verb and either another noun or an adjective. Put in other terms, a statement (philosophers sometimes call it a "proposition") must be predicating something of something. To understand what Russell means when he talks about a world of mere matter, one in which there are facts but no truths, imagine a world in which all predicates were removed.

Is this helpful?

In our world of no predicates there are a good deal of things. I might, for instance, take the ring from my left index finger, lay it on the desk before you, and simply stand there looking at you. Is there anything in this situation that calls for a judgment of truth or falsehood? Obviously not. Obviously some sort of language is called for.

Very well, I take the ring from my finger, lay it on the desk and say, "Ring." Is there now anything in the situation that calls for a judgment of truth or falsehood? Think carefully and you will see that there is not. All I have done is present you with a piece of matter. Suppose I add the definite article to the noun. Now we have, "the ring," which doesn't help at all. What I must obviously do, in order to create the sort of world that admits of the possibility of truth or falsehood, is to say something about the ring.

Here we go again: "The ring is gold." Now the possibility of truth has become real, and along with it the possibility of falsehood. Now a universe of something more than mere matter has been created. We now

---

[7] This, interestingly enough, is the same argument (with a few different applications) used by theologians such as Hick, and even Augustine, to show the necessity of evil in a universe created by a good God. No evil -- no good.

have established a universe in which belief is possible. But this is not enough. According to Russell, there is a third thing that we need. The truth or falsehood of a belief must always depend upon something that lies outside the belief itself. Once again, this is not easy, but understanding it can be extremely useful.

To illustrate this proposition, Russell gives the example of the execution of Charles I. If I believe he died on the scaffold, I believe correctly; whereas, if I believe he died in bed, I believe falsely. In either case, the truthfulness or the falsehood of my belief has nothing to do with something intrinsic in the belief itself, but rather in events or conditions that lie outside the belief — in this case, in an historical event. From here, it is relatively easy to take the next step, and to say that the belief is true or false depending upon whether or not it corresponds with facts extrinsic to the particular belief, statement, or proposition.

It seems to me that Russell's approach to a theory of truth is, as common jargon has it, so far so good. He has done what a competent philosopher would do, laying out his reasoning in premises that move from one to another, each building on the one that went before, and ending with a conclusion that appears to follow from the premises. I wonder, however, if there is a student out there who is bold enough at this point to challenge Lord Russell and to say that the conclusion isn't quite as solid as it may initially seem.

Sparring with Russell

The correspondence theory of truth works well when one is dealing with propositions that are immediately and empirically verifiable. At least it seems to. If I say, as I did earlier, that there is a yellow tomcat sitting in the middle of my desk, I have all the conditions that Russell has laid down as requisites for a theory of truth: (1) it is possible that the proposition is true, possible that it is false; (2) a belief has been expressed in the form of a statement; (3) the truth or falsehood of the statement does not depend upon something intrinsic within the statement itself. I look, there sits the tomcat, the statement corresponds with observable facts, I judge the statement to be true. This is correspondence, pure and simple.

Well. . .maybe.

Go back to the assertion of Brand Blanshard that we looked at earlier, and you will notice that he takes no less obvious an example than that of the tomcat (the table in the next room is round), and uses it to argue for coherence. How could this possibly be the case? Are either, or both, of these rather intelligent gentlemen in need of some sort of mental healing? Not actually. What we see demonstrated is that both theories have their strengths, both have their weaknesses, and we probably need both to account for something as basic to philosophy as "truth."

Blanshard's point is that correspondence can account for the simple observation of the table (or tomcat), and for the judgment that it is what the proposition claims that it is, and that it is located where the proposition places it. But when one pushes matters farther by asking, "But how do you understand that this table is round, or that the animal in the middle of the desk is a tomcat?" — one has nothing to which to refer but to past experience, to the concept of roundness, to the concept of maleness; and this sort of judgment calls for an agreement between judgments, which is best described, to use Blanshard's words, not as correspondence but as coherence. In other words, we know what we see (correspondence), but we judge it to be round because it fits in with what we already know about such shapes (coherence).

Now where does this leave us? We have correspondence theorists pointing to coherence theory as weak because it basically depends upon correspondence; and we have coherence theorists point to correspondence theory as weak because it basically depends upon coherence; and we are left standing between the two wondering which direction to go. As a rule of thumb, coherence theory works well with mathematics, geometry, abstract concepts, whereas correspondence theory works well with anything that calls for empirical observation, and finally each seems to need the other.

When we were looking at rationalism and empiricism we saw much the same thing. Neither theory of knowledge and learning can fully account for what we seem to know, but we do seem to learn and to know, so how do we account for the existence of these basic components of philosophy, truth and knowledge? Perhaps we had better bring in Søren Kirkegaard and ask him to clear the matter up, for we seem to have gone soaring off into the ethereal world of thought, and we may need to be brought back to earth.

Get Real, Fellows!

We all know Kierkegaard by now, assuming we have been paying attention to the fascinating story of western philosophy. But for those who may have been sleeping. . . Kierkegaard is the Dane who broke up with his sweetheart, Regine Olsen, went to the University of Berlin, sat through a few lectures, and came back with a permanent chip on his shoulder for anything that resembled Hegel. He is the man whom Jean-Paul Sartre said ought always to be placed in opposition to Hegel, for he is the man who stands for the individual against the Hegelian collective.

There is also a very real sense in which Kierkegaard stands for the common man and woman, although you wouldn't know it from reading his books. He is the one who said, as it were, "I read Hegel, and I see the work of a brilliant man, a genius, who somehow misses what it is to be a living individual in the world of waking reality." Now this is not what Kierkegaard said, but these are the words I have put into his mouth because they represent his attitude toward philosophical systems. Kierkegaard was interested in how individuals actually experience living in a world that seems, in so many cases, to be dark and hostile and indifferent to their presence. I believe that if we had Kierkegaard here with us, and if we put to him the theoretical question of how one accounts for truth, he would refer us back to our own experience. He would probably say that truth is what one experiences as one goes through life, that he or she learns personally what truth is by the act of living, and that truth is, when all is said and done, what works for one. This might be a less than satisfactory solution, for it seems to suggest that truth is a totally subjective thing, which is not what Kierkegaard believed. He understood that the external world is really there; but he consistently argued that what mattered were the sorts of choices we make, our freedom to make them, and our responsibility for our choices. To this end, what one perceives as the truth makes a great deal more difference than what the truth actually is by a test of, say, correspondence. If, for instance, I believe that the world is flat, and that if I travel too far in any direction I will fall off into the abyss, will this have a restricting effect on my physical movements? The obvious answer is that it will. My choices become a function of my understanding of truth, and thus for all practical purposes truth is a creation of my own understanding.

If this is what Kierkegaard were to argue (and I feel certain that he would), he would sound very much like the American Pragmatists who would be on the scene a half-century after his death, operating in a country far away to the west. The major difference in Kierkegaard and the pragmatists is seen in their motivation. He was an inward type, interested in the individual's mode of existence and development in a world that, for him, had become indifferent to, even destructive of, individuality. The pragmatists, on the other hand, were progressives who thought that philosophy ought to be used to solve social and economic problems, and who optimistically assumed that this could be done if proper application were made.

The pragmatic theory of truth: a proposition is true if it works, proves out in practice.

Proper application was obviously not being made, from their point of view — or from Kierkegaard's. There could have been no better example of failure to apply knowledge properly than this endless wrangling over theories of truth. As we saw in the last chapter, the pragmatists had a simple definition of truth: truth is what works. If it works, then treat it as truth and use it. This seems so ordinary after all that we have been considering that we are apt to reject it outright as unworthy of our intellectual attention. But let's not be hasty. We have been comparing coherence and correspondence. To make things interesting, let's add the **pragmatic theory** of truth and see how it stands up. First, let us hear from a pragmatist as he talks about truth and how we actually recognize truth when we see it. This is a quote from the famous William James.

> Truth, as any dictionary will tell you, is a property of certain of our ideas. It means their "agreement," as falsity means their disagreement, with "reality." Pragmatists and intellectualists both accept this definition as a matter of course. They begin to quarrel only after the question is raised as to what may precisely be meant by the term "agreement," and what by the term "reality," when reality is taken as something for our ideas to agree with.[8]

This is nice and non-troublesome. Well, almost. It seems at first that James is going to admit that he is a simple correspondence theorist, but by the end of the statement he admits to having some trouble when the terms agreement and reality are raised. Must we indeed quarrel over this? James thinks that we must. Rather than quote him at length (if the student wishes to read James, we have a library on campus), I will cut to the chase.

> Grant an idea or belief to be true. . .what concrete difference will its being true make in any one's actual life? How will the truth be realized? What experiences will be different from those which would obtain if the belief were false? What, in short, is the truth's cash-value in experiential terms? . . .The moment pragmatism asks this question, it sees the answer: True ideas are those that we can assimilate, validate, corroborate and verify. False ideas are those that we can not. This is the practical

---

[8] **James, William, *Pragmatism: A New Name for some Old Ways of Thinking*, New York: Longmans, Green, 1907, p. 198.**

> difference it makes to us to have true ideas; that, therefore, is the meaning of truth, for it is all the truth is known as.[9]

All right, but I am still having trouble seeing how what he says differs substantially from what a correspondence theorist might say. At the next paragraph he lays out his "thesis."

> . . .The truth of an idea is not a stagnant property inherent in it. Truth happens to an idea. It becomes true, is made true by events. Its verity is in fact an event, a process: the process namely of its verifying itself, its veri-*fication.* Its validity is the process of its valid-*ation.*[10]

What it finally comes down to is this, truth is not something that relates to some sort of external reality, but rather what works, or as James puts it "what makes a practical difference in our lives." If no practical difference flows from my acceptance, or rejection, of an idea, then the idea is false. This is an odd way of looking at truth, assuming one is a Platonic and believes that truth is something set in concrete and that never changes. Perhaps, however, it can be useful in the workaday world. As I said earlier, let's throw it into the arena with correspondence and coherence and see how it fares.

Balancing the Book

We begin with a mathematical proposition: 2 + 2 = 4. Is this true, and if so why? It is true, say the correspondence theorists because it corresponds with the facts. It is true, say the coherence theorists, but not for the reasons the correspondence theorists have put forth. There are actually no external facts in a mathematical formula for the proposition to correspond with. The formula is true because it coheres with other tried and proven systems of truth. Now come the pragmatists. It is true, they say, simply because it works and for no other reason. What it coheres or corresponds with doesn't matter and completely misses the point. It is true because it makes a practical difference to us all. It has been tried and shown to be useful.

---

[9] **Ibid., p. 198.**

[10] **Ibid., p. 199.**

To me, American though I am, this rather strange American theory has always suffered from one of the major flaws in theories of knowledge we saw in the last chapter — there is really no way to falsify it so far as I am able to tell. Remember Karl Popper and the falsifiers? They made the case, and a rather sound one I think, that if one takes a position that cannot be falsified then the position is in reality a non-position. It is philosophically meaningless. A pragmatist might argue that the correspondence and the coherence theories suffer from exactly the same defect. They would be wrong. There are clearly cases which correspondence doesn't handle well, and there are cases which coherence doesn't handle well, but I can't think of a single case which can't be accounted for by an appeal to the pragmatic theory. It will always work, but this is not a strength of the theory. Rather, it is a major weakness. To demonstrate why this is so we will bring the three theories to bear on one of the major questions of the Renaissance.

Where is the Center?

How is the universe in which we live actually structured? Answer: the earth is fixed and flat, positioned at the center, and the heavenly bodies are all moving around us. The truth of that answer has been affirmed by each of our theories at some time in the past, and yet today no reasonable person believes it. It is quite simply false. But who could have convinced Aristotle of its falsity? Think about it, not from the point of view of a denizen of the late twentieth century, but as a simple observer of things around us. The earth, as you observe it, appears to be flat. The sun appears to rise in the east, move across the heavens and set in the west. The moon and the stars seem to be whirling in the heaven above us, and there clearly appears to be an up and a down to things. As a matter of fact, by all appearance the entire universe seems to be revolving around me (the so-called ego-centric predicament). Now the correspondence theorists may argue as long as they like that the geocentric position does not correspond with facts, but what they really mean is that it does not correspond with facts as we now know them. Given our present state of knowledge it is easy to affirm, by the correspondence theory, that the geocentric position is wrong, has always been wrong, will always be wrong. Ah, for the wisdom brought on by hindsight! There was probably not a correspondence theorist walking the earth in the eleventh century (and by implication there were many of them), who would not have adhered to the geocentric position. Why? Because it corresponded with what appeared to be facts.

Now how about the coherence theory? It didn't fare much better, and yet it seems that the coherence theory is the one that eventually led to the heliocentric position. For a period of fifteen hundred years or so the Ptolemaic system was considered the true one, precisely because it was the one that seemed to pull things together into a coherent whole. But by the time of Copernicus, with new methods of observation including improved telescopes, it was increasing clear that there was something wrong with the theory. It could not account for the motion of the stars and planets through the heavens, and in order to salvage it astronomers of the day were having to construct evermore cumbersome additions and corrections. The whole thing was becoming unwieldy. In short, the Ptolemaic theory was being falsified by new observations. Now the correspondence theorists may say that the Ptolemaic theory was abandoned because it was shown not to fit the facts; but it seems to me that coherence is a more apt way of explaining things. A theory of this type ought to be able to pull together a great many particular observations, coordinate and explain them, make predictions. It should, in other words, do all the things that a theory does, as we saw in an earlier chapter. If it doesn't, then there is something wrong with the theory and it has to be changed or scrapped. But is this correspondence? I don't think so. This is more accurately described as coherence.

Now, how would the pragmatic theory of truth deal with the question of the heliocentric versus the geocentric universe? The pragmatic theorist would have to say that as long as the geocentric theory worked, that is as long as practical consequences flowed from it, it was true. It ceased being true when it would no longer work, and it ceased working as we got more and better information about what was actually out there. This is correct, as a description of what happened, but it probably seems to be a weak theory of truth to most of us. If it works, call it truth and use it. When it no longer works, call it a falsehood and stop using it. To repeat myself, how could one ever falsify this theory? And if there is no way to falsify it, can it really be a meaningful theory?

We have seen that in some cases correspondence and coherence lap into one another so that each is dependent upon the other for support. I challenge the student to ask himself or herself whether the pragmatic theory of truth stands as an independent theory, or if it is not, in fact, a variation of the coherence theory? That which coheres with other known truths so that it fits as a part of the whole could be said to "work." It seems that little is gained from the pragmatic positions, and that a great deal might be lost; and in this regard it is worth noting that there are few philosophers nowadays who are arguing the pragmatic position as it was argued by William James.

In fact, some pragmatists are now saying that truth is not the sort of thing we ought to be attempting to define. A contemporary pragmatist, Richard Rorty, sees the ongoing debate as rather pointless.

> We pragmatists. . .are making the purely *negative* point that we would be better off without the traditional distinctions between knowledge and opinion, construed as the distinction between truth as correspondence to reality and truth as a commendatory term for well-justified belief. Our opponents call this negative claim "relativistic" because they cannot imagine that anybody would seriously deny that truth has an intrinsic nature. So when we say that there is nothing to be said about truth save that each of us will commend as true those beliefs which he or she finds good to believe, the realist is inclined to interpret this as one more positive theory about the nature of truth: a theory according to which truth is simply the contemporary opinion of a chosen individual or group. Such a theory would, of course, be self-refuting. But we pragmatists do not have a theory of truth, much less a relativistic one. . .[We hold] the ethnocentric view that there is nothing to be said about either truth or rationality apart from descriptions of the familiar procedures of justification which a given society, ours, uses in one or another areas of inquiries.[11]

It is interesting that in the passage quoted above Rorty admits that "we do not have a theory of truth." I doubt that William James would have said such a thing, but perhaps he would have. To believe in truth, to use the term truth in one's conversations, or even in one's philosophical dialogues, is not the same as having a theory of truth, because theories are more complex things than are mere propositions. Rorty and company are obviously satisfied that they know what they mean when they say truth, and that they are able to define the term — at least to their own satisfaction.

But what, when all the cards are called in, have they finally said? That truth is what works. That truth is that from which practical consequences flow. Ultimately, that truth is really an ethnocentric thing, and that communities and groups establish what is truth for them on the basis of what has been shown to meet their needs. Thus, it is meaningless to talk of the

---

[11] Rorty, Richard, "Science as Solidarity," in *Dismantling Truth*, ed. Hilary Lawson and Lisa Appignanesi, New York: St. Martin's Press, 1989, p. 11.

heliocentric cosmological position as the true position if one is in a society structured around the belief in a geocentric cosmos, for what has proved out in practical experience for the latter group would be totally at odds with the former. But by the same token, would it not be meaningless to talk of quantum physics, of the Copenhagen and the "many worlds" positions, to most people?

I generally try to be as objective as possible in teaching any introductory philosophy course. I want the students to think, not to simply imbibe my opinions and ideas. So perhaps I had better stop this discussion at this point, leaving the student to meditate on the three theories of truth we have been looking at. Which of them best handles the idea of truth as we use the term? When we say that a proposition is true, what are we saying? There are at least three possibilities? First, we can be saying that the proposition corresponds with the observable facts. Second, we can be saying that the proposition coheres with a system of known truths. Third, we can be saying that the proposition has been proved out in experience, that it works, that practical consequences flow from it. That all three theories have useful features, none would deny. That all three can account for truth is also clear. That all three give an equally good account of truth under any and all cases is, as we have seen, not at all clear; but the pragmatic account seems to have no limitations. Under it, most anything that one wishes to hold as truth can in fact be dignified as truth, so long as one has proved it out in some arena or another, and found that it has some practical consequences. A definition this broad is a weak definition, for it admits of no possibility of falsehood, and as Bertrand Russell has said (correctly it seems to me), any theory of truth must admit of its opposite, falsehood.

Perhaps It's All Relative

It is possible that the search for the truth must finally end in failure, if by truth we mean something close to what Plato had in mind. Just as learning is a process carried on for and by humans, so truth is a particularly human enterprise. I can hear all the animal lovers shouting at me from the wings, wondering why I am so willing to assume that animals cannot learn, that animals cannot benefit from or recognize, in some limited fashion, the truth. I am very sorry to have to tell you this, but learning and truth are both words, the processes they describe are largely linguistic in nature, and if you remove the exclusive human ability to use language from the mix it is very difficult for me — obtuse as I may be — to see how you can talk meaningfully of either learning or truth. Grant my point, however, and put the human in the very center of the epistemological enterprise, and you may have introduced the very element that makes Platonic truth an impossibility.

This may be the ultimate irony of the whole matter. The very creature necessary to establish the concept of truth is the one who makes it impossible to ever know for certain what truth is. Perhaps the pragmatic definition, weak as it may be, is the best we can do in establishing our truth theory; for we must face the possibility that truth is relative, not just to the society, but to the individual. Truth, like beauty, may be in the eye of the beholder, and it may be molded so that even the beholder is not able to believe his eyes.

In a study done in 1951, psychologist S.E. Asch asked students to judge the length of lines. There was only one actual experimental subject in each group, and the rest of the students were confederates of the experimenters. They had been told to say something which was directly at odds with the truth, as the correspondence theory would have it. For example, two lines would be put on the board, one longer than the other, and the students would be asked which line was longest. The group, working with the psychologist, would report just the opposite to what actually appeared. The purpose of the experiment was to see whether or not the experimental subject would deny his or her own perception in order to conform with the group. In most cases this is exactly what happened. Several years later the experiment was repeated, and the subjects were allowed to express their opinions anonymously rather than openly. Even under these anonymous conditions most of them reported what they group had said.[12]

If this is truly the way humans look at the world, the wonder is that we can come to any true judgments at all. And perhaps we cannot. This is precisely the point of a famous short story, "Rashomon," written by the Japanese author Ryunosuke Akutagawa.[13] The story concerns a mountain bandit who murders a traveler and rapes the traveler's wife. Seven individuals who were eyewitnesses to the event, including the murdered man via a

---

[12] Reported in Morgan, Clifford T., & Richard A. King, *Introduction to Psychology*, New York: McGraw-Hill, 1966, pp. 580-581.

[13] The story, translated by Takashi Kojima, was published in a collection of Akutagawa's stories. It was turned into a movie, a play, and was also produced as a western under the title *The Outrage*, starring Paul Newman, Lawrence Harvey, and Edward G. Robinson. If you wish to read it, the title of the book is *Rashomon and Other Stories*, New York: Liveright, 1952.

medium, come forward to give sworn testimony to what occurred. Surely with all of these individuals claiming to see what happened the High Police Commissioner can get to the simple facts. But as we see each witness come forward, and as we listen to them, we find that they agree on very little. Each is a compelling witness. Each appears to be telling the truth. None however can agree on what actually occurred, and we come to realize that in each case the truth of what happened becomes a function of what the witness wanted to happen. Or, perhaps, they experienced what they expected to experience, what they were prepared to experience. It is not that any of them is lying, but rather that they are unwittingly twisting the truth to fit their own prejudices.

The first of the witnesses, a **woodcutter**, gives very exact testimony, but it is the sort of eyewitness testimony which reports only the barest of facts. He saw what he saw, and he reads very little into it, other than the notion that the deceased must have put up a good fight because the grass and bamboo was trampled down all around him.

Second comes a traveling **Buddhist priest**. Rather than looking at the physical evidence, he appears to have been more interested in the people. At least he has a degree of interest in them. He saw the husband and wife traveling together. The priest had wonderful recall of the colors of clothes, but very little of the woman herself. He is a priest, after all, and cannot be expected to take note of such things.

The third witness is **a local policeman**. Most of his testimony is about the alleged murderer, one Tajomaru, and the policeman talks at great length about him. There is no doubt that the policeman believes him to be an evil and violent man, but his conclusions about what actually happened to the man and his wife are obscured by the fact that he didn't actually see any of it. His testimony is confident and he is obviously telling the truth as he sees it, but beyond that his testimony has little evidentiary value.

Fourth comes the **mother** of the raped woman, the mother-in-law of the murdered man. She is old and honorable, but her testimony is all about the character of her children. They are fine and upstanding citizens who couldn't possibly have done anything to have caused Tajomaru to attack them as he did. The truth, for her, is that her children were righteous and Tajomaru was not.

Finally **Tajomaru** takes the stand in his own defense. Now we are going to get the truth — or are we? The story he tells is at odds with that told by the others, but not exactly in the way that we would expect. His testimony runs on for some thirteen paragraphs, much longer than any of the others. He freely admits to killing the man. He is a bandit, after all. What should he be expected to do? He presents himself as a bold and fearless highwayman who joined himself to the traveling couple because he was bewitched by the woman's beauty. Through a series of events he disarms the man, ties him up, then rapes the woman — but only because that was what she wanted him to do. She then begged him, Tajomaru, to either kill her husband or himself, for she could not bear to have her shame known to two men. Being the honorable soul that he was, Tajomaru turned the husband loose, they fought a duel, the husband lost.

This is not, needless to say, the way **the woman** saw it. She showed up sometime after the killing at the Shimizu Temple, dishevelled and distressed. Her story is in agreement with that of Tajomaru up to a point. She agrees that the bandit tied up her husband and raped her. Then she drops the bomb. It wasn't the bandit who killed her husband but she herself. After the rape the husband, still tied up, looked at her with disgust and loathing and said, "Kill me," for he cannot live with the shame that he has suffered. So, to make get to the heart of the matter, that is exactly what she did, although her memory of the incident is very vague.

The final witness is **the murdered man**. He speaks through a spiritual medium. This obviously requires a suspension of disbelief, and it would not occur in American courts, although sometimes one wonders if a medium wouldn't be preferable to some of those who claim to be alive, well, and eyewitnesses. Anyway, the medium speaks for the murdered man. According to him, his wife was absolutely shameless. She egged the bandit on to tie him up, had sex with him willingly, then begged the bandit to take her with him. After they two of the had run off together, the poor deceived husband managed to free himself from his bonds, and he killed himself.

The end.

This story has had a tremendous popularity, and one feels the need to ask why. The answer appears to be that there is in the situation that which says something important about the human condition, and about the very critical human concept of truth. Which of our theories of truth can best account for the strange stories told by the various witnesses in this case, and how do we judge who has spoken truthfully and who has not?

By the correspondence theory of truth there is little to be said about the first four witnesses. They are obviously telling the truth as best they know it, although it is clear that their perceptions of the truth, or what actually happened, are limited and slanted, both by their own expectations and by their social identities. They saw only a small part of what happened, and they gave only superficial analysis to that.

The last three witnesses leave the correspondence theory all in tatters. All that we can say, if a true proposition is one that is in agreement with the facts, is that at least two of our witnesses, and maybe all of them, are lying. It cannot be true that the victim was murdered by the bandit, by his wife, and by himself. This does violence to all we think we know of logic, for the laws of contradiction and of the excluded middle are violated if we accept all three statements as true.

The coherence theory of truth doesn't deal with the killing much better, but it is a bit more useful than the correspondence theory. By the coherence theory we would also agree that only one person of the three can be telling the truth, and that perhaps none of them is, but we can at least gather what facts are available and attempt to see, within the pattern of facts, which version of the killing is most likely to be the true one.

Shall we give it a try? Who killed the poor traveller? Our quest for the answer to the question is complicated by the fact that each of the three final witnesses points to himself, or herself, as the actual killer, and we are left to wonder what motivated each of them to confess to murder, when it is clear that in two of the three cases the witnesses are confessing to something which, by the correspondence and the coherence theories, they did not do. I have studied the story "Rashomon" for years, and I quite confess that there is not sufficient circumstantial evidence for me, applying the coherence theory of truth, to come to a conclusion. The pattern is too confused. In fact, there seems to be no pattern, other than the pattern created by each individual in and for himself or herself.

So we come back to the statement that stands at the head of this section — Perhaps it's all relative. To push things farther, perhaps only the pragmatic theory of truth can handle this case. If so, then allow me to point out that the truth might be found in all versions of the killing presented by the final three witnesses. It is obvious that for reasons too complex to be easily understood each of them has assumed the burden of guilt for what went on. The bandit, Tajomaru, must certainly consider himself guilty, for had he not accosted the couple in the first place the man would still be alive and be with his wife. The wife considers herself guilty because at some point during the episode she seems to have yielded to the bandit and realized that she did not love her husband. It is possible that she considers herself an adulteress, and thinks her infidelity is what caused the death of her husband. Thus, whether or not she struck the blow that killed him, she is the guilty party. And whether or not he actually took his own life, the husband was shamed to the point that he no longer wanted to live. Even if his wife was raped, she apparently did not struggle enough to suit him. And even if he put up a good fight, it was not good enough to protect him and his wife. He cannot live with the dishonor, but cannot admit that his life is being taken by another, so in his eyes his death has to have been self-inflicted.

Each of those who was directly involved in the rape and killing has told a story that "works" from his or her point of view. But which one is true. If we are only looking at the individuals, and if we accept the pragmatic definition of truth, all of them must be. But if we broaden the field to take in the society in which the killing occurred, then most pragmatists would say the truth is the bandit did the killing. Why? Because if there is to be social stability, then there must be structure and laws. Experience shows only too well that society cannot tolerate anarchy, banditry, violation of the family structure. To set the bandit free to kill again would be to create a situation threatening to the social structure. What works in this case, once we have asked what is good from the greater point of view of the society in which the murder took place, is a verdict of guilty for the bandit, with whatever punishment the society deems appropriate.

It is strange, but true, that in the world of "Rashomon" only the pragmatic theory of truth appears to bring any kind of satisfactory closure to the incident. Most philosophers however would not accept the proposition, "The bandit killed the traveler and raped his wife," as a true statement. What they would say is that there is not sufficient evidence to come to a conclusion, that in reaching a conclusion prematurely we have sacrificed truth on the altar of expediency, and that we are no closer to the actual truth now than we were when we began.

The instrumentalist view of truth: in science, the view that a theory is true if it allows us to predict what will happen.

Scientific Truth

Before we close out this chapter I wish to touch briefly on truth as it is seen by scientists. The student might think that scientists are committed to the correspondence theory of truth, pure and simply, but this is not the case. There are three major scientific positions with regard to truth, and each of them is a variation of the three theories of truth which we have been considering.

The realist view of truth: in science, the view that the entities postulated by any theory must exist in actuality.

The so-called **instrumentalist** view of truth, closely related to the pragmatic theory, holds that any scientific theory is true only to the extent that it allows us to predict what will happen. The **realist** view is like the instrumentalist view insofar as it too posits that a theory must lead to accurate prediction. But whereas the instrumentalist view does not posit the actual existence of any invisible entities the theory may predict, the realist view says that if the theory is true such entities must exist in actuality. The realist view has a good deal in common with the correspondence theory of truth. Finally, the **conceptual relativist** view, science's version of the coherence theory, says that a theory is true if it coheres with the conceptual framework of scientific truth established by the community of scientists. The important thing for the student to notice is that science, that field of endeavor which so many look to as the very bastion of truth, has an ongoing philosophical disagreement about what constitutes truth, and about which theory of truth is most viable. Ultimately, science is as dependent upon philosophy as is any other field of inquiry, and what scientists accept as true finally comes down to the philosophical stance they take.

The conceptual relativist view: in science, the view that a theory is true if it coheres within the framework of scientific truth established by the scientific community.

In Fine

The theory of truth with which an individual feels most comfortable will undoubtedly depend upon what truth he or she is attempting to reach. If one is a scientist, involved in experiments that call for observation of particulars and reasoning toward general principles, then he or she will probably feel strongly that the correspondence theory of truth is the proper one to employ. If one is a mathematician, or perhaps a policeman attempting to put evidence together to reach conclusions, the coherence theory of truth would be most useful. Poets and artists might find the pragmatic theory of truth more to their liking, for they might feel that they are dealing with truth on a level that one cannot reach with the other theories.

Our conclusion must probably be that the various theories of truth complement each other and that we need all of them in one way or another if we are ever to make any sense of the universe in which we live.

Chapter 12
A Quick Look at Logic

A moment of your time, sir, if you please.
Madam, the merest moment, if you please.
You perceive, do you not, the alabaster bottle
I hold. My friends, it may be little
And ordinary to the sight, but it's filled
With an amazing elixir, a potion distilled
From an ancient Greek recipe.
It is the essence of esoteric wisdom.
I call it the Aristotelian syllogism.
And here's a second vial which contains
Another product of Hellenic brains,
Straight to you from the west's pedagogic
Whiz-kids, I give you inductive logic.

All logicians will be offended that I am treating logic as if it were nothing more than a subfield of epistemology. The truth is that it began its career within the confines of epistemology, but that it long ago broke away and became a separate philosophical discipline in its own right. Some forms of logic have even separated from mother to the extent that they are arguably closer to mathematics than they are to philosophy. But there will always be a familial resemblance between logic and epistemology. After all, if the pursuit of knowledge and truth is not what logic is all about, then what is it? So I have included it here, if only in one brief chapter, so that the student may gain some idea of what philosophers mean when they use the term logic. As with other disciplines that grew up in philosophy and were eventually taken over by the outside world, we will find that what outsiders call logic, and what philosophers mean when they use it, are often two different things. This chapter will deal with a great deal more than logic however. I propose to look at a whole series of false arguments and logical fallacies, as well as some simple categorical and truth function logic; and I trust that by the time we have gone through this chapter the student will have some basis for accepting good arguments and rejecting bad ones.

Arguments and Non-arguments

We are bombarded everyday of our lives with claims of various sorts. Television and radio, magazines and newspapers, politicians and pundits, all are, in their own ways, trying to sell us something. We like to think of ourselves as discerning and intelligent, discriminating and sophisticated; but the truth is that most of us are easily manipulated by those who make it their business to know how such things are done. Metaphorically speaking, we tend to think with our hearts and our guts as often as we do with our brains, and this is why we go down the primrose path after whatever pied piper comes along with a song that sounds good. But help is available. One of the reasons for going to school is to gain, not just knowledge, but wisdom, and to learn how to separate the intellectual wheat from the chaff. So follow along.

Question: what does it take to convince you of something? If you say, "A good reason, or a good argument," what do you mean by that? In philosophical terms, an **argument** must have at least two parts, a **premise** and a **conclusion**. A conclusion is the thing that one is trying to prove, and the premise is the reason one gives for believing the conclusion. If the conclusion does not flow from the premise (or the premises, for frequently an argument will contain more than one) we have what philosophers call a *non sequitur*. In any analysis of an argument we begin by identifying the conclusion, a task that is not always as easy as it seems. Next we identify the premises, and we ask ourselves whether or not the one logically flows from the others. If not, we have a faulty argument.

An argument, in philosophical terms, must have at least a premise, and a conclusion.

Over the years philosophers have been very interested in good arguments and bad arguments, and how one separates between the two. Faulty arguments have been categorized and labelled. There are only so many after all, and they keep coming up over and over again. Because many of these were originally identified by philosophers in medieval universities, and because Latin was the accepted language for all instruction in these schools, the faulty arguments usually have Latin names. Without attempting to exhaust the subject, I have picked out some of the most often heard, and utilized, bad arguments. In my experience, students have lots of fun with these because if there is any part of philosophy that one can put to work almost immediately this is it.

Rotting Fish Always Stink

Red herring: a false logical fallacy in which a false issue is raised in an attempt to divert one's opponent from the actual subject under discussion.

I am sure that you have heard the term "**red herring**" applied to bad reasoning, but chances are you don't know what the term means or why it is used. It actually goes back to the early days of this country, and to the experience of the very wise people who lived in the woods and survived by tracking and hunting. They knew that a herring fish cured in salt turns a red color, and develops a rather distinctive smell. They also knew that if one drags a red herring across the trail of an animal being tracked by dogs, the dogs will give up chasing the animal and follow the trail of the salt cured fish. Thus, in logic and critical thinking the term "red herring" came to mean the practice of deliberately introducing a false issue into a discussion to obscure the real issue. You drag a red herring across the trail in the hope that those following the quarry will go off in a wrong direction. We see this sort of thing all the time. I am always surprised to see how well it works, how easily people are deceived and turned aside, following a false trail for miles, until they finally forget what they were after to begin with.

Most of the false arguments we will be looking at may be considered red herrings, for they obscure issues and lead down blind alleys and dead end streets. Thinkers, beware!

Why You Ugly Devil. . .

Ad hominem: literally, "to the man." In this logical fallacy the individual is attacked personally, and the argument is ignored.

Have you ever heard two people engaged in an argument, and suddenly the one who is getting the worst of it begins to call the other names or impugn his intelligence? This is the fallacy known as *ad hominem*, Latin for "to the man." It should go without saying that what I am personally has nothing to do with the cogency of the argument I have constructed. I may be an absolute scoundrel, dishonest and vicious, even unsanitary, but when I argue for a certain position it is my argument, and only my argument, that ought to be answered. In order to understand why, and in order to understand why the *ad hominem* is so effective when it ought to be utterly ignored, it is necessary that we go back and look again and what an argument is and how it differs from other exchanges that take place among humans.

An argument, to repeat, consists of two parts, premises and conclusion. It purports to give us a reason why a certain thing is true or ought to be believed. In this, it is different than a mere explanation. Suppose, for instance, someone asks why the light in the dining room does not come on when the switch is flipped to the "on" position, and I state that it doesn't because the light bulb is burned out. This is not an argument, it is only an explanation. To push matters further, it is a physical explanation. But suppose I say that I have unscrewed the bulb to keep it from coming on because too much light in an area where one is eating causes one to digest one's meals poorly. I have gone far beyond a simple explanation, although an explanation is contained in what I have just said. I have offered an argument, with a conclusion. The conclusion, however, that one ought not to eat where there is too much artificial light, is only implicit in what I have said. Why? Because (and here we get the premise) too much light in an area where one is eating causes one to digest one's meals poorly.

This is a rather interesting, if simple, example of deductive logic. You may have noticed that the premise is itself the conclusion of an unstated argument, and were you and I involved in this exchange you would probably ask why I think too much light in a dining area causes one to have poor digestion. In other words, you would be questioning the premise of my original argument, knowing full well that if my premise is false so is my conclusion. Perhaps I have at hand a well-documented study performed by scientists in a major university that serves as a premise to my first conclusion. Or perhaps I say that my grandmother told me so, and I always believed my grandmother. Now you may do one of two things. You may accept my argument and agree with me that the lights in the dining room ought to remain off, or you may challenge my premises by offering counter evidence. But what you cannot do, if you wish to argue honestly and effectively, is say, "I have always thought you are stupid, and you have just proved it." This response of yours is a false argument, an *ad hominem*, that attacks the person making the argument and not the argument itself.

Ad hominem arguments are so common that almost all one has to do to hear one is turn the television to a panel discussion in which political opponents are arguing some question. The worst part about these is that politicians are generally lawyers, and anyone who has been to law school knows better than to argue *ad hominem*. But they also know that most people haven't been to law school, and if they can convince the listeners by attacking the man rather than his argument they will do it and laugh all the way to the polls.

Well You Did it Too. . .

***Tu quoque.* In this false argument the respondent answers a charge by saying, in effect, "Well, you did the same thing."**

Closely related to the *ad hominem* argument is another false argument that philosophers call ***tu quoque***, Latin for "you too." In this pseudo-argument the attack comes not against the other person but the other person's behavior. An individual tells a lie, for example, and when asked why responds by saying, "Well, you did the same thing," or "That guy over there lied about it, and you did nothing to him." If lying is wrong, and to this aging teacher of philosophy it certainly is, one is not relieved of the responsibility for having told a lie by pointing out that someone else did the same thing.

Yet this is one of the most common defenses offered, and it is one of the most common of false arguments. This can only be because it is rather effective, and will continue to be until the public learns that it simply will not work. It springs, no doubt, from an underlying desire for fairness, a desire to see to it that no one is discriminated against; but it leads to undesired conclusions.

Closely related to the *tu quoque* is an type of argument that philosophers call a **pseudorefutation.** A master of this type of false refutation is a talk show host with a large national following, Rush Limbaugh. In fact, Mr. Limbaugh is a master of many of the false arguments we will look at. A current textbook on critical thinking cites an interesting example of Limbaugh's use of the pseudorefutation[1] to attack a popular movie star who made a speech in support of environmentalism. The movie star, Tom Cruise, spoke in New York's Central Park on Earth Day, calling for recycling and an end to environmental pollution. Limbaugh's response was that Cruise had made a movie in which he had destroyed thirty-five cars, burned thousands of gallons of gasoline, and wasted dozens of tires. Limbaugh says that if he could talk to Cruise he would point this out to him, and say, "Now you're telling other people not to pollute the planet? Shut up, sir."

Well, Mr. Limbaugh, your refutation of Cruise is a pseudorefutation, so shut up, sir.

If Limbaugh really wishes to refute Tom Cruise, and if he wants me to give any attention to what he has to say, he will have to deal with Cruise's argument and not with Cruise's behavior. All he has done with his pseudorefutation is call attention to the possibility that Cruise doesn't feel as strongly about the environmental problem as he pretends to; but even that does not get to the real issue of whether or not the original argument is sound.

---

[1] **The book is Moore, Brooke Noel and Richard Parker, *Critical Thinking, 5th ed.*, Mountain View, CA.: Mayfield Publishing Co., 1998. The example is given on page 167,**

The Genetic Fallacy

The **genetic fallacy** is a sort of *ad hominem* attack, except it goes not to the individual, nor to the behavior of the individual, but to the group with which the individual may be associated. Some of these groups are questionable in their political or philosophical stance, and some are not, but in any case the individual who is attempting to argue down a point commits the genetic fallacy when he ignores the argument being made to concentrate on the source (genesis) of the argument. Recently, to raise an obvious example, a book was published which purported to show, among other things, that intelligence is inborn and that certain racial groups score higher as groups on intelligence tests than others.[2] Predictably the book was widely criticized and attacked, and just as predictably many of the attacks were weakened by the poor quality of the counterarguments. The authors were labelled as "conservatives" and known members of the political right. The *ad hominem* nature of this counterargument is clear enough, but it is equally clear that it is an *ad hominem* of a special variety. The attack is not aimed directly at the individual, but at the group of which the individual is a member.

The genetic fallacy is a sort of *ad hominem*, but it is aimed at the group with which the arguer is associated rather than the arguer.

The American scene abounds with groups and associations which many of us no doubt find disgusting for a variety of reasons. Please do not misunderstand me, I am not indicating that I find the political right or left disgusting, or that I am beating the drum for liberals as opposed to conservatives. I am saying that in our society we make room for all sorts of beliefs, opinions, political groups, and outright kooks. A sound thinker is never, and I emphasize *never*, turned aside from examining an argument by the consideration of the source of that argument. An argument stands on its own, and no matter how we may react to the individual framing the argument, he or she deserves to be heard. Even odd people espousing strange causes can come up with cogent arguments from time to time.

According to the Bishop. . .

Now, suppose we go in the opposite direction. We have seen an obvious, and often-used, method of attempting to win arguments by attacking and denigrating the arguer or his source, but it is just as easy to attempt to put one's own ideas across by appealing to someone or to some

---

2 Herrnstein, Richard J. & Charles Murray, *The Bell Curve: Intelligence and Class Structure in American Life*, New York: The Free Press, 1994.

Ad vericundiam: an appeal to authority. Ad populum: an appeal to the people. Both of these are false arguments.

group that is admired or credited with the possession of impressive credentials. The two most common false arguments of this type are called *ad verecundiam* (to authority) and *ad populum* (to the people). I am always amazed how easily deceived people are by these two red herrings; drag them across the trail, and a good portion of the pack will go bounding off after them. But perhaps my amazement is displaced. Perhaps the normal thing to do is to follow after authority and the group, and perhaps the amazing thing is that there are always some who are not turned aside.

A professor of mine once told me that veneration for print is such that one can prove most anything by pointing it out in a book. I might add that the veneration for authority is such that there is scarcely anything more common than to support one's arguments by showing that Dr. So-and-So says. . .and then follows the thing one is seeking to prove. I suppose that one ought to pay due deference to authority, assuming that the authority is being exercised in the appropriate field; but this does not mean that authority is everything or that the correctness of an argument finally turns upon the number of authorities one can cite.

The first thing one ought to do when confronted with authority is to ask the rather obvious question, "In what field is this supposed authority authoritative?" The fact is that authority has a way of generalizing itself, and we find Albert Einstein making theological pronouncements. Einstein may well be an authority in physics, but even in that field his disagreement with Niels Bohr over quantum mechanics has generally been resolved in Bohr's favor. Now, to extend Einstein's authority to theology and philosophy, and to listen to him in those areas as though he were anything other than an enlightened layman, could be dangerous.

But we go even further. On most any given day in our enlightened republic we can turn on the television and find movie starlets airing their views on the state of the economy, foreign affairs, family relations. The troubling part of all this is that because they are famous they tend to be listened to. Not long ago two famous movie stars were called in to testify before a House Committee investigating agricultural problems. Their credentials: both had played farmers wives in movies. It is laughable but true. This is the *ad verecundiam* fallacy at work in the highest echelons of government.

Ad populum is much the same. The difference is that with *ad populum* one appeals to the crowd rather than to an authority. This fallacy can take a number of forms, such as the **appeal to belief**, in which one is exhorted to believe a certain thing because everyone else does, or the **appeal**

to common practice, in which one is told in so many words that everyone else is doing it. Sometimes the *ad populum* takes the form of a **peer pressure** argument, and sometimes it is the familiar **bandwagon** argument (get on this one; it's a sure winner). It seems scarcely believable that anyone could fall victim to arguments so obviously fallacious, but the truth is it happens all too often.

One of the most common forms the *ad populum* argument has taken in recent history is that of the poll. Both advertisers and politicians love this one, in fact it seems that whether or not something is right or wrong can simply be determined by taking a poll. Eight-five percent of those surveyed believe that. . . the implication being that if you disagree there must be something wrong with you. History, however, tells us only too clearly that the people are frequently wrong, and are easily manipulated. It was, I believe, Arnold Toynbee who said, "It is doubtful that the majority has ever been right."

Whenever you hear such phrases as, "Everyone knows that. . .", or "Two out of three surveyed said that . . .", you know you are on the business end of an *ad populum* argument, and the warning lights in your brain ought to instantly go on.

The Case of Chauntecleer

Sooner or later everyone who goes to college gets a chance to read Geoffrey Chaucer's marvelous Middle-English poem, *The Canterbury Tales.* Among the tales told is one by the Nun's Priest of a rooster, Chauntecleer, who has the extraordinary notion that he makes the sun come up by his crowing. His logic is, of course, impeccable, and if you don't believe it just listen to him and observe the real world. He appeals to empirical fact in a way that would make a correspondence theorist proud. Every morning before daybreak he sits on the fence rail and crows with all his might, and shortly thereafter the sun rises. It is perfectly obvious to Chauntecleer, and to any reasonable person, that he is the cause of the sun's rising. This laughable story introduces us to the logical fallacy known by philosophers as ***post hoc ergo propter hoc*** or the **cause and effect fallacy.**

It (whatever "it" is) preceded that (whatever "that" is), therefore this caused that. This fallacy is at the roots of many superstitions.

Just because something follows something else, or just because two things occur in close proximity to one another (either in space or in time), does it follow that the one caused the other? Those who employ the fallacy would like for you to think so, and perhaps they even think so themselves. This is how many superstitions get started. Example, I was walking down the street the other day when suddenly a black cat ran across my path, and shortly thereafter I slipped on a banana peel and fell. This proves once again the old notion that one will have bad luck if a black cat crosses one's path. Certainly it does. . .and I'm Marie of Romania.

We know from what we were able to learn from David Hume that under the best of conditions it is difficult to establish the cause and effect connection. Those who commit the *post hoc ergo propter hoc* fallacy establish it at the drop of a hat — and usually when it isn't warranted. The next time you hear someone arguing that one thing caused another simply because it preceded it, stop and ask yourself whether or not there is a demonstrable connection between the two. Often you will find that there is not. Poverty, for example, is often put forward as a cause of crime, when the simple truth is that there is no evidence to show that poverty causes anything, other than poor people.

Post hoc ergo propter hoc is associated with another fallacy that is so similar as to be virtually identical. It is called the guilt-by-association fallacy. Keep your eyes and ears open and you will surely find these two lurking in many an unsuspecting argument.

Life is Like this Glass of Beer

You may have heard the story of the two men who were sitting at a bar, each silently absorbed in his own thoughts, when one of them suddenly said, "Life is like this glass of beer." The other asked why, and the first replied, "How should I know, I'm not a philosopher." Even though he couldn't finish the line he had opened, the man was utilizing a tool which philosophers have found useful for centuries, and will doubtless find useful for centuries yet to come. The tool is called analogy, and the type of reasoning involved is analogical reasoning. It is the technique of getting to a truth that is obscure by setting up an analog, a comparison, which is much clearer. The idea is that what is true of the analog must also be true of the thing we are examining. But this technique is only as good as the analogy that is used.

I don't imagine that anyone knows exactly what I'm talking about, so I'll give an example. In a well known essay Judith Jarvis Thomson is arguing that even if the fetus is a human being, the woman carrying it has a right to an abortion if she chooses. How could one possibly prove something this difficult? She attempts a proof by constructing an analogy. Suppose that you wake up one morning to find that overnight you have been physically hooked up to a violin player who is suffering from renal failure. The doctors explain that the violin player will need to use your body only for nine months, then his own kidneys will be functional and he can be on his own. But if he is not allowed the use of your body during the interim he will die. The question is, are you morally obligated to allow the violin player to use your body? If you say that you are not — and Thomson is convinced you will — then she will say that your position *vis a vis* the violin player is analogically like that of a woman who is pregnant. She has no moral obligation to allow a fetus to use her body, even if it is a human being.[3]

The problem with this analogical argument is that it may not be a very good analogy. No analogy compares perfectly with the case under consideration, but some are so far out that they are really misleading and have to be put down as faulty reasoning. This is the error of the **false analogy.**

Some students may remember the year 1990 when both houses of Congress were debating the issue of whether or not to give the president the authority to go into Kuwait to throw out the Iraqi invaders. Surely this was a momentous issue and an important vote, and all the representatives wanted to do the right thing. But what was the right thing to do? Those who were against the invasion said that it was just like Vietnam, and that once we got in we were apt to find ourselves bogged down in a long, drawn-out, bloody land war. But was the analogy correct. It seems to have been weak at best. Vietnam was a completely different country, topographically and ethnically, than Kuwait, and the sorts of problems that got the Americans mired in Vietnam can hardly have been said to exist in Kuwait.

But the other side of the debate had some problems as well. They said that Saddam Hussein was just like Hitler, and that the situation was analogous to Hitler's remilitarizing the Rheinland in 1936. Had the nations of the west moved then, before Hitler had grown strong, they could have put and end to him. But they vacillated, and when they finally were forced to move, after the invasion of Poland three years later, it was too late to get out with a quick victory. It took over five years to stop Nazi Germany.

This analogy suffers from weaknesses, just as the first did. There is a good deal of difference in Saddam Hussein and Adolf Hitler, and attempting to compare the two borders on the ludicrous.

I could multiply examples, but I trust that these will suffice. An analogical argument is easy to spot, because the arguer will be making a

---

[3] **Thomson, Judith Jarvis, "A Defense of Abortion: A Compromise View, *Philosophy and Public Affairs,* vol. 1, no. 1, 1975 Princeton University Press.**

comparison between the thing he is trying to prove and something else which either needs no proof or seems self-evident. When you hear an analogical argument make sure that the analogy fits the case or you may well wind up a victim of false reasoning.

Petitio Principii

To "beg the question" is to assume, as a premise of one's argument, the very thing one is trying to prove.

Don't let the Latin fool you; it's just a fancy way of saying something much more down to earth and, I might add, about as common in arguments as earth. I remember distinctly the first time I ever heard the term "**begging the question.**" I was in an introductory philosophy class, and two students were arguing the question of whether or not God exists. At some point the professor, who had up to this time been content to simply sit and listen, intervened and said to one of the students, "So-and-So, you're begging the question." I didn't know exactly what he meant by that, and it took me a number of years to learn. I have since heard many people use this term, and most of them are misusing it, or at least are not using it in the way that philosophers do. I have often watched reporters interviewing someone on television, and the one being interviewed will make a statement of some sort, to which the interviewer will respond, "But, sir, that begs the question. . ." and then he or she will put another question to the one being interviewed. All the reporter means is that the statement made raises another question. This is not the meaning of the term in philosophy. Begging the question is a logical fallacy in which the arguer attempts to use as a premise in his argument the very thing that he is trying to prove. One individual will say, for example, that the Bible is the word of God, and when asked to prove it he will quote a passage of scripture as proof: "It says right here that all scripture is given by inspiration of God. . ." Now this begs the question. The very issue being argued is whether or not the Bible is the word of God, and if it is not then it will hardly do to use it to prove its own validity.

In a sense, begging the question is arguing in a circle. In fact, in Medieval times a form of this fallacy was known as *Circulus in Probando.* He: I know he is telling the truth. She: how do you know it. He: because he is an honest person and he always tells the truth.

How about this one, another interesting version of question begging. Why can't an ostrich fly? Because his body is not aerodynamically designed to get off the ground. Oh, really? He can't fly because he can't get off the ground. How very enlightening!

I hereby serve notice, in the most solemn of tones, that this logical fallacy may be found in many of the arguments that are passed off as valid everyday of our lives. It isn't always easy to recognize, but with a little practice and a little attention to what is being said anyone who wishes can learn to spot it. It is called, once again, begging the question.

Either it is or it Ain't

Some arguments are based upon the faulty logical premise that something either is something or it is something else, when in fact there are a multitude of other things that it might be. When I was in high school, for instance, my father insisted that I go to college. When I asked him why, he said something like, "Well, do you want to be digging ditches the rest of your life?" This interesting argument has to be analyzed to be appreciated. Suppose we reduced it to the form of a disjunctive: P or Q, but not P, therefore Q. Now there is nothing wrong with this type of reasoning so long as we make sure that there are genuine alternatives which cannot exist together at the same time and under the same conditions. Disjunctive reasoning is at the heart of that foundational law of logic called the law of the excluded middle. Either he passed the test, or he failed the test; but he did not pass the test, therefore he failed the test.

The error comes when the arguer (deliberately perhaps) poses two possibilities and only two, when in fact there are a good many more. My father, in the personal example above, was not deliberately misleading me. He was a product of the Great Depression, and he genuinely believed that education was the key to staying out of the misery he had lived through. It followed for him as the night does the day that the uneducated individual — and this meant not possessing a college degree — would wind up doing menial labor, whether or not it was ditch digging. Nevertheless, he was committing the **either-or fallacy**, the fallacy of assuming only two possibilities when in fact there are many others. To illustrate the fallacy to yourself, consider all the people who did not go to college but who are nevertheless rich and successful.

The either-or fallacy comes when one structures an argument so as to give only two choices, when in fact there may be others.

This is also sometimes called the **black-white fallacy**, and it is closely related to another piece of pseudoreasoning called the **false dilemma**. When someone tells you that something is either one way or another, and that there are no shades of gray between, take a closer look or you may fall victim to this old trick.

Leaping to Conclusions

This is one of which you have all heard, but you may not know that like so many of the things we take for granted in our intellectual world, it

To commit the *secundum quid* fallacy is to move to general conclusions with too few particulars to justify such a move.

had its source in philosophy. They don't call it leaping to conclusions, however, they call it ***secundum quid.*** Now there are a number of different versions of the *secundum quid* fallacy, but I will deal with only the simplest type, that of leaping to general conclusions based on particular observations, but with too few particulars to justify the leap.

This error has its genesis in the perfectly legitimate area of logic that philosophers call induction, that method of thinking employed by Bacon and others to establish the rules that scientists have used for centuries. As we have seen, David Hume thought that all inductive logic was flawed by the fact that one can never observe enough particulars to justify the conclusion as certain. All we can state, at best, are probabilities. Still, we can state some fairly solid probabilities. Based on my observations, for example, I feel safe in saying that I shall physically die someday.

The problem, and the *secundum quid* fallacy, arises from leaping to generalities with too few particular observations to justify the leap. This is the error behind much racial prejudice and has caused a great deal of grief that could have easily been avoided if there had been someone around to counsel a slower approach, further observation and consideration.

The Slippery Slope

A **slippery-slope** argument (sometimes called an **entering-wedge** argument) is not always fallacious. In fact, none of these arguments always yield false conclusions. In every case one might, by using them, stumble onto the truth; but usually it will be purely accidental. Of all the arguments I am dealing with as false arguments or pseudoreasoning, the slippery slope argument is the most difficult to dismiss as one to be avoided. Truth is, there are times when it can be used very persuasively.

Suppose, to illustrate, we are considering passing a law which says that all mentally-defective people ought to be sterilized so that they cannot produce offspring that are similarly defective. As the debate heats up someone takes the floor to say that in Nazi Germany there were laws of this type preceding any of the racial laws that later were used with such deadly results. You begin by devaluing human life in the case of mentally-defective people, then it is easier to take the next step, then the next. . .and you wind up in Dachau. In other words, once you get on the slippery slope you can't get off it, and you ride down hill with gathering momentum.

The slippery-slope argument shows up in many arguments, from anti-abortion to anti-euthanasia. What makes it so compelling is that in some cases it can be used to explain why something that started off in an innocent attempt to actually do something helpful winds up in heartache and bloodshed. And it can serve as a reminder that we ought to proceed with great caution into certain areas.

But as often as not the slippery-slope argument is misused, and when it is it can yield results that are almost ridiculous. Try this one. Let the gun-control people get their way, and the next thing you know you'll be disarmed and your home will be invaded by goon squads from the government. Somehow I rather doubt it.

The lesson is, beware of slippery slopes, both those that are real, and those that are merely the creations of faulty reasoning.

A Brief Interlude

We have just looked at twelve of the most common types of false arguments. This treatment is far from exhaustive, but it should give you a good idea of what to watch for when you are involved in a debate, or when you listen to others debating an issue. We need to move on now and look at some simple logic. Perhaps some of you are surprised, and may even be saying to yourselves that you thought we had already been looking at logic. It is true that these false arguments are sometimes called logical fallacies, by myself and others; but strictly speaking, while they are certainly illogical arguments that ought to be avoided if one wishes to reach sound conclusions, they are not "logic" in a formal sense. Of course, it may be a simple matter of definition. If one wishes to define a good argument as logical and a false argument as illogical, then in that sense we have been talking about logic. I do not choose this definition, however, and neither do most of the philosophers I know.

Logic is a much more structured affair than anything we have yet seen. It deals with claims and statements, with the way in which sentences are structured and the manner in which they are juxtaposed; it deals with premises and conclusions, antecedents and consequents; and its claims and statements are typically reduced to symbolic form in accordance with rules that have developed over many hundreds of years and are by now a universal language.

In a course of this type we are not going to cover the subject in detail, but I do feel it is important that any introduction to philosophy offer at least a brief treatment of formal logic. So here it is. We will be looking only at three types, categorical logic, truth-functional logic, and inductive logic. Obviously no student will achieve expertise as a logician by the end of this section of the chapter, but all should have at least some appreciation of what formal logic is all about.

Categorical Logic

Categorical logic: A type of deductive logic based upon inclusion in, or exclusion from, classes or categories.

Categorical logic is a special type of deductive logic based upon inclusion in, or exclusion from, classes (or categories). We use this type of logic everyday of our lives whether or not we realize it, for the very structure of our language demands it; but unless we are careful and listen to exactly what is being said it is easy to become confused. Suppose for example I say, "Only black birds are ravens." Someone hears this and repeats it as, "The only black birds are ravens." The only difference in the two claims is that the first omits the definite article "the" whereas the second begins with it. But the omission or addition of that simple word completely changes the meaning of the claim. It is precisely failure to attend to slight differences of this type, or perhaps the lack of understanding that there is a critical difference, that makes for so much confusion. The first claim, awkward as it may sound, is true, for it says that a raven is a blackbird. The second claim is false, for it holds that ravens are "the only" blackbirds. Take the first claim, change the opening "the" to an "all" and you have a false claim again. Let us examine some of the inner workings of the fascinating world of categorical logic, something that is never far from any of us but is frequently misused by all of us.

The Four Claims

All categorical logic is structured on four basic claims, the A Claim, the E Claim, the I Claim, and the O Claim. These are easy enough to remember because they are labelled with the first four vowels you learned when you were in grade school: A, E, I, O. But these letters are actually taken from two Latin words, *affirmo* (affirmative) and *nego* (negative). Two of the claims, the A and the I, are affirmative claims, and two, the E and the O, are negative claims. Take note.

A. All ____________ are ____________.
(Example: *All freshmen are undergraduates.*)

E. No ____________ are ____________.
(Example: *No seniors are freshmen.*)

I. Some ____________ are ____________.
(Example: *Some freshmen are females.*)

O. Some ____________ are not ________.
(Example: *Some freshmen are not females.*)

Notice that the A and the I claims are affirmative, and that the E and the O claims are negative. Also notice that every claim is a complete sentence, that it contains a subject and a predicate. These are called the terms of the claim. In the "A" claim example above, for instance, the subject term is freshmen and the predicate term is undergraduates. Now it is important to understand that only nouns or noun phrases can properly serve as terms for a claim. The reason, while not immediately apparent, becomes clear once you begin working with the converse forms of claims. To do this you must be able to switch the subject and predicate terms and still have the claim make sense, and this cannot be the case if the predicate, for instance, is an adjective. Try it. "All ravens are black" becomes "All black are ravens." The problem is easily corrected by changing "black" to the noun phrase "black birds."

These four categorical claims are amazingly versatile, and with them one can construct arguments that are logically valid and logically sound (valid and sound do not mean the same thing in logic); but this depends, of course, upon one's knowing what one is doing. To this very end, most undergraduate logic courses spend several weeks analyzing categorical claims. Students learn how to use Venn diagrams as well as a tool called the Square of Opposition, then move into conversion, obversion, contraposition, and finally get to the various forms of the categorical syllogism. We are going to skip most of this and spend our time with the categorical syllogism, since that is something with which you are somewhat familiar, and since it is such an ever-present part of philosophy as it has developed in the west.

First, a quick review of the three laws of inference to which I have made reference throughout this book. Like so much of classical logic, these are the work of Aristotle, and they are absolutely critical to logic in any form. The most elementary of the three is the law of identification, a thing is equal to itself, or in symbolic terms A = A. The second, called the law of the excluded middle, states that a thing either is or it is not. In symbolic terms, A v ~ A (read A wedge non-A). Either I am in this room, or I am not in this room. Finally, we have the law of contradiction, sometimes called the law of non-contradiction: a thing cannot be and not be at the same time and under the same conditions. Either I am in the room, or I am not in the room, but I am not in the room and not in the room at the same time.

These three laws seem so obvious that any student who is encountering them for the first time is apt to feel that I am needlessly stating the obvious. If so, then let me state the obvious, because, as I have said, categorical logic is based upon a thing's inclusion within or exclusion from certain classes (categories), and if the laws of inference do not hold then the entire edifice comes tumbling down like the walls of Jericho.

Sorting out the Claim

The first thing that we must do if we wish to use categorical logic effectively is to sort out the claim, by which I mean that we must identify the subject and the predicate, and make sure we have an actual sentence that is making a claim. In simple sentences the subject will precede the predicate, but in actual language, as it flows from lips and pens, this is often not the case. Just remember that the subject will always be a noun (a person, place, or thing), and the predicate will be a noun or noun phrase connected in some way to a verb (action, being, or state of being). The following statement, for example, is easy to put into the form of an "A" claim.

Every college graduate has a degree.

This becomes, "All college graduates have degrees," an "A" claim that is predicating something positive about all graduates. Now try this one:

Some college graduates have B.A. degrees.

Once again, this presents no problem. It is a positive claim, predicating something about some of those who go to college, but not all. It is, therefore, an "I" claim. Likewise, we would have no difficulty identifying this statement as an "E" claim. Notice that it is a negative claim.

No illiterate people are college graduates.

And finally, here is a negative statement that is easily recognized as an "O" claim:

Some college graduates are not males.

If only all statements were this simple, then recognizing the type of claim that is being made would be equally simple. Unfortunately, however, they are not, and one of the main problems that confronts logicians is deciding exactly what is being said. To illustrate, what kind of claim is this?

Ed Smith is a politician.

This is, believe it or not, an "A" claim, but it has to be rewritten and put into the proper form. Translation:

All people identical to Ed Smith are politicians.

Of course, there is only one person in the subject class, but that doesn't matter. The subject is, as logicians say, distributed, because everyone in the class is covered.

Making sense from statements can be difficult sometimes, but there are some useful rules. For one, a claim about a single individual, such as the one above, can generally be treated as an "A" or an "E" claim, depending upon whether the claim is positive or negative. Second, the word "only" in a sentence introduces the predicate term of an "A" claim, whereas the words "the only" introduce the subject term of an "A" claim. Knowing the difference can be critical to understanding what is actually being said. Take the following statement: Only American citizens are eligible voters. How are we to understand this statement, if we write it as a categorical claim? There are two possibilities:

All American citizens are eligible to vote

and

All eligible voters are American citizens.

If you think these claims say the same thing you are mistaken. The first says that anyone who is an American citizen may vote, while the second says that in order to vote one must be an American citizen. Going back to our rule of thumb, we note that the word "only," standing by itself, introduces the predicate terms of an "A" claim. The second statement, therefore, is the correct one.

The Categorical Syllogism

The categorical syllogism is nothing in the world but a series of three claims put together in such a way as to lead to an incontrovertible conclusion. Now notice that I said it is three claims. This is not to say that all arguments are composed of three claims. You may pick up almost any philosophical journal and find lengthy arguments in which one premise leads to the next, and then another, and so on for ten and twelve premises before a conclusion is ever reached. Then the conclusion of an argument can become a premise for the next argument. But these long arguments, while they may be constructed of categorical claims, do not constitute a syllogism. In a categorical syllogism there can only be three claims; two of them are premises, and the final claim is the conclusion, and they are put together in such a way that if the premises are true the conclusion cannot be false.

Before we look at some examples of categorical syllogisms to see what makes them valid or invalid, I need to reintroduce the topic of deductive logic. All through this book I have been mentioning deductive as opposed to inductive logic, and I have said that deductive reasoning is reasoning from the general to the particular, while inductive reasoning is reasoning from the particular to the general. But I have also said that this is an old-fashioned sort of definition to which logicians no longer hold. Now it is time for me to tell you why. As a rule of thumb, deduction, when it is placed in the syllogistic form, does move from the general to the particular; but there are cases when it does not. Take this argument, as an example.

> John is a half foot taller than Max, and Max is a half foot taller than Bill, therefore John is a foot taller than Bill.

This is clearly a deductive argument, and it is valid, but there are no general or universal statements in it. It is all about particulars. So the definition of deduction, that it is reasoning from the general to the particular, is not actually correct, although it is useful in a loose sort of way.

Now look at this argument:

> I have gone to the baseball game five times, and my team lost every single time. Tomorrow they are playing a team that has already beat them twice. It is probable that they will lose again.

This is an inductive argument, but once again there are no universals introduced into the argument; it is all about particulars. This leads us to the definition of inductive and deductive reasoning that is generally agreed upon by logicians nowadays. A deductive argument is either valid, or is intended to be. An inductive argument, while persuasive, is neither valid, nor is it intended to be.

Now, having said all that, it is still good to keep in mind that categorical syllogisms are deductive, and most of the time they are structured to reason from the general to the particular. The standard example of a categorical syllogism, one that has come down to us from Aristotle and has appeared in textbooks on logic for centuries, is the one to which I have already made reference, to wit:

Humans are mortal.
Socrates is human.
Therefore, Socrates is mortal.

Now if you have been paying attention you have already seen that this syllogism is composed of three separate "A" claims, two of which are flawed. The first claim is flawed because the predicate is not a noun nor a noun phrase; and the third is flawed for exactly the same reason. But we can fix both statements easily by adding the word "being" after mortal, or by simply adding the letter "S" to mortal, thus turning it into a plural noun. Suppose we rewrite it and put it into proper form.

All humans are mortal beings.
All those identical to Socrates are humans.
Therefore, all those identical to Socrates
are mortal beings.

The elegance and the beauty of the syllogism are a joy to behold. This is deductive reasoning at its best and most sophisticated, but also at its simplest and clearest. The first two statements, both of which are "A" claims, are called the premises. The final statement, also an "A" claim, is the conclusion. Now notice that if the premises are correct the conclusion must be correct. Accept the premises, and you are stuck with the conclusion. This is what philosophers call a valid piece of reasoning.

There is a major difference in a "valid" argument and a "sound" argument. When philosophers say an argument is valid," they mean only that it is properly formulated. When they say it is sound, they mean that it is true.

In order to be a **valid argument**, a syllogism must be structured in a certain way, and to determine that it has the proper structure we must learn certain terms and see the elements to which those terms are applied.

The **major term** of the syllogism is that term which occurs as the predicate term in the syllogism's conclusion; the **minor term** is the term which occurs as the conclusion's subject; the **middle term** is that term which occurs in both the premises but is absent from the conclusion.[4]

There is another definition which you will find useful in determining whether or not a syllogism is valid, and that is the term "distributed." If a

[4] Frequently the first claim in a syllogism is called the major premise, the second is called the minor premise, and the third is called, of course, the conclusion.

term is distributed it covers every possible member of the category, and is frequently designated in the claim by the word "all." This is not always the case, however, and sometimes a careful analysis is necessary to determine whether or not a term is distributed.

Here are four easy-to-remember rules that will help you to determine whether or not a syllogism is valid.

1. The middle term must be distributed in at least one of the premises.

2. If either term in the conclusion is distributed, it must be distributed in the premises.

3. Both premises must not be negative.

4. If one of the premises is negative, then the conclusion must be negative.

Suppose we apply these rules to our syllogism about Socrates to see whether or not it is valid. First, the middle term, that term which is present in both premises but is absent from the conclusion, is the word "human." Is it distributed in at least one of the premises? Yes, it is distributed in the major premise, to wit: *All* humans are mortal beings. Second, is there a distributed term in the conclusion? Yes, there is, though we had to look closely to find it. The term is "Socrates," which is read as, "All those identical to Socrates. . ." Is the term also distributed in the premises? Yes it is. Finally, rules three and four do not apply as there are no negatives in the syllogism, either in the premises or in the conclusion. Therefore the syllogism is valid.

Suppose we changed the minor premise to: Socrates is not human (or, no one identical to Socrates is human). Then the conclusion must be changed to a negative to make the syllogism valid (rule four).

Try this one:

1. Some humans are oriental.
2. Some humans are caucasians.
3. Therefore, some orientals are caucasians.

The problem is immediately apparent. The middle term is not distributed in either premise.

Now let us take one of the arguments for the existence of God that we looked at when we were studying metaphysics, reduce to a syllogistic form, and see whether or not it is valid.[5]

> God is that being greater than which none can be conceived, therefore God exists.

How can we reduce this to a syllogism? Simply by writing down the minor premise, which is clearly implied in the argument. Thus we have.

> God is that being greater than which none can be conceived.
>
> A being greater than which none can be conceived must exist.
>
> Therefore: God exists.

The argument is valid (whether or not it is "sound" is another matter), as can be easily determined by application of our four rules. Is the middle term distributed? Yes it is. Is the minor term, "God," distributed in both the conclusion and in the major premise? Yes it is. The argument is valid.

But is the **argument sound**? Quite possibly it is not. The soundness of an argument and the validity of an argument are two different things. A valid argument is one which is properly constructed, so that *if* the premises are true, *then* the conclusion must be true. If either of the premises is false then one would have good reason to reject the argument as unsound, particularly in the case of a categorical syllogism. This is why, when listening to an argument, it is imperative that one identify the premises of the argument. If not, then there is always the chance of wandering over the cliff's edge, or being led down the primrose path, or being taken for a ride, or. . . You fill in the metaphor which you think fits best.

Truth-Functional Logic

Truth-functional logic is logic based upon the structure of sentences, specifically, conjunctions, disjunctions, and conditionals.

Not all logic is based upon categorical propositions; in fact, since the time of the Stoics we in the west have been working with a type of logic that has come to be called **truth-functional** logic, or sometimes **propositional** or **sentential** logic. Though the Stoics were the first to recognize that the

---

5 I am indebted to Manuel Velasquez, op.cit., for this example.

classical logic of Aristotle did not begin to do all that logic should, and though they were the ones who introduced us to this logic based upon the structure of sentences, it wasn't until the nineteenth century that truth-functional logic began to truly come into its own. Like categorical logic, truth-functional logic can sometimes seem, when one is first introduced to it, an exercise in the obvious. Don't be fooled by appearances. What we will be covering will merely scrape the surface of the subject. Truth-functional logic is the basis for set theory, electrical circuitry, and digital computers. It is also useful, as the Stoics intended it to be, for analyzing many arguments.

First, a simple observation: not all linguistic statements are of the categorical type. In fact, most of the things we say are probably not categorical statements. We make many compound statements, statements that involve the bringing together of simpler ones, and whether or not those statements are true has something to do with the way they are structured. That's the logic of it. For example, take the following statement: Bill is in the room. This is a simple statement saying something about the location of the individual identified as Bill. Here is another one: Sam is in the room. We can put these together and we have a compound statement. But if we wish to make a single sentence of the two, and if we wish to have it make sense, we will have to add some language. Suppose we use the little word "and." This is a conjunction, and thus the compound statement that it forms when we used it to join two simple sentences is called a **conjunctive statement.** "Bill is in the room, and so is Sam," we might say. Or, in a more strained form, "Bill is in the room, and Sam is in the room." Now if we let the letter B represent the first statement, Bill is in the room, and if we let the letter S represent the second statement, Sam is in the room, we can symbolize the entire thing thusly: B & S.[6]

We are now into what philosophers call symbolic logic. We saw some of this when we were looking at categorical logic; but truth-functional logic carries symbolic logic to a level of sophistication that is truly amazing.

But why is this type of logic called truth-functional? To answer that, ask yourself what truth value the statement Bill is in the room might have. Clearly there are only two possibilities — it may be either true or it may be false. The same may be said of the statement about Sam. We can therefore construct a truth table, once again using only symbols.

---

[6] Frequently instead of the ampersand (&), logicians will represent the word "and" with a "." which they call simply "dot." Read aloud the statement would be, "B dot S."

	B	S
1.	T	T
2.	T	F
3.	F	T
4.	F	F

Believe me, when these two statements are put together as a compound statement, the table above represents the totality of possible truth values they can have. First, both statements can be true (line 1), B can be true and S false (line 2), B can be false and S true (line 3), or both can be false (line 4). Now, let me share a wonderful truth with you. *For a conjunctive statement to be true, both of its conjuncts must be true.* That is, for the statement B & S to be true, both B and S individually must be true; and there is only one condition in the table above that meets that requirement, that shown on line 1. Think about it. If someone says Bill is in the room, and Sam is in the room, if either of those conjuncts is false, the statement is false.

A conjunctive statement is a compound statement in which two simple statements are brought together with the simple word "and." The disjunctive is a compound statement composed of two simple statements brought together by the word "or".

Now let's look at another compound statement, very similar to the **conjunctive statement** but with very different truth value. It is the statement of the "either/or" variety, and we call it the **disjunctive** compound. Sometimes one wishes to say something like this: Either it will rain today or the sun will shine. Once again, it is easy to see that this compound statement is made up of two simpler statements called disjuncts, It will rain today, and the sun will shine today. If we let R represent the first disjunct and S represent the second, we may symbolize the whole thing like this: R v S.[7]

Suppose now that we construct another truth table. It will be like the one above, with one major difference. To show the difference, I will include the truth values for the compound along with the truth values for the two simple statements.

	R	S	R v S
1.	T	T	T
2.	T	F	T
3.	F	T	T
4.	F	F	F

Notice that the first three of these conditions have a compound truth value of "true," and only the fourth one is "false." This is because, *with a*

---

[7] Logicians call the small "v" wedge, so that the statement, if read aloud, would be, "R wedge S."

disjunctive statement, the statement is false if, and only if, both disjuncts are false. If you doubt this, test it by putting it back into language. I say either it will rain today or the sun will shine. Suppose that it rains, and the sun shines as well. Then my disjunctive compound is true. Suppose that it rains but the sun doesn't shine. The disjunctive statement is still true. What if it doesn't rain, but the sun shines? The disjunctive statement is still true. There is only one condition under which the disjunctive can be false. It must not rain, and the sun must not shine.

A conditional is also called a hypothetical statement. It is a claim of the "if-then" variety. If this happened, then this resulted.

Now there is one more compound statement that we need to look at, and it is called a **conditional statement**, or sometimes a hypothetical statement. It is a compound that is formed by two simpler statements and the words "if" and "then." If it rains, then the pavement will be wet. Supposing we allow "R" to represent the hypothetical, "If it rains," and "W" to represent, "Then the pavement is wet." We may write this conditional statement in symbols as follows R —> W. The first term, "R" is called the antecedent, and the second, "W" is called the consequent; and we have a rule for establishing the truth value of a conditional proposition. A conditional is false if, and only if, the antecedent is true and the consequent is false. If I say, "If it rains, the pavement is wet," and if it rains but the pavement remains dry, then the statement was a false statement.

With these three types of statements — the conjunctive, the disjunctive, and the conditional — and with the rules for establishing their truth values, we have the basis for truth-functional logic, a type of deductive logic that is, as I have said, at the heart of mathematics, set theory, and computers. If you ever take a class in advanced symbolic logic you will learn a great deal more than I have been able to cover in this short space, and you will see formulae that run on and on, sometimes for pages, but it will all be based on the simple rules we have just covered.

Modus Ponens/Modus Tollens

Before we leave this subject I wish to share some important information with you, information about how to use — and to misuse — the conditional "if/then" we have just been considering. You will have noticed that with both the conditional and the disjunctive something more is called for than the simple statement itself. This is not true with a conjunctive statement, for the proposition, "Ann is in the room, and Mary is in the room," is true if observation confirms both women are in the room. But if we are to come to any conclusion about the truth of the other two types of statements we need more statements. Suppose I say, for example, "Either

Mary is in the room, or Mary is not in the room." I may then say, "But Mary is in the room." It then must be that the statement, "Mary is not in the room," is a false statement. But what about the conditional. Take note.

1. If it is raining, then the pavement is wet.
2. But it is raining.
3. Therefore, the pavement is wet.

This is called a *modus ponens*, and it is valid assuming that premises 1 and 2 are true.

We can turn this into a *modus tollens* in the following fashion:

1. If it is raining, then the pavement is wet.
2. But the pavement is not wet.
3. Therefore it is not raining.

The *modus ponens* is an affirmative claim, whereas the *modus tollens* is a negative. I frequently tell students to remember them by remembering *ponens* begins with the letter "P" for positive, and the *tollens* begins with the letter "T" for taking away, or negative. If a negative appears in either of the premises, then your conclusion must be negative, and you will have a *modus tollens*; but if the premises are all positive, then your conclusion will be an affirmative and you will have a *modus ponens*. However, you must be very careful how the argument is constructed or you will produce a flawed argument.

In constructing a hypothetical syllogism — for this is what *modus ponens* and *modus tollens* are called — you must either affirm the antecedent or deny the consequent. A *modus ponens* affirms the antecedent and produces a valid affirmative conclusion, whereas a *modus tollens* denies the consequent and produces a valid negative conclusion. If you get these turned around you wind up with a flawed argument. For example, consider this.

1. If it is raining, then the pavement is wet.
2. But it is not raining.
3. Therefore the pavement is not wet.

The fallacy in this argument is called denying the antecedent, and the conclusion it reaches is manifestly false. Denying the antecedent will always yield a false conclusion. Look at this one, which we hear in one form or another all the time.

1. If capital punishment deters crime, then we ought to use it.
2. But capital punishment does not deter crime.
3. Therefore we ought not to use it.

Perhaps we shouldn't use capital punishment, but the case can't be made from arguments of this type.

Now let's see what happens when we affirm the consequent. Back to our old friends the rain and the pavement.

1. If it is raining, then the pavement is wet.
2. But the pavement is wet.
3. Therefore, it is raining.

Once again we have a flawed argument and a resultant conclusion that one needs only to look at to reject as fallacious. Not all hypotheticals will yield results that are immediately recognizable as false, but no matter how they look, logicians learned long ago that denying the antecedent or affirming the consequent in hypotheticals results in a failed argument.

I hope that I have at least managed to whet your appetites for the subject of logic, even in the brief time we have been able to spend in this fascinating field. If you should ever take advanced courses in logic, then you will doubtless look back to this chapter and realize just how elementary it truly is. But you will also realize that getting the elements, the basics, down well is the first step in going on to things more difficult. Clear, logical thinking is never easy, but it pays rich dividends, and it is something we need now as we never needed it before.

A Quick Review to Section III

1. Epistemology is that part of philosophy which seeks to deal with the questions about knowledge. What do we know, and how do we know it? How do we learn? What do we mean when we say something is true? Logic, which deals with correct thinking and the proper forms of arguments, falls beneath the penumbra of epistemology.

2. Philosophers define "knowledge" as justified (or warranted) true belief. In other words, if we say we know something we must believe it, it must be true, and we must have some justification for what we are saying. If any, or all, of these conditions are missing from a proposition, then philosophers will generally say that the proposition falls short of being actually known.

3. Rationalism is the name of the epistemological position which holds that some knowledge is — for want of a better term — inborn. This can include some of our most important forms of knowledge, such as mathematics, logical principles, and even, according to some, our knowledge of God and morality.

4. Some of our most important philosophers have been rationalists. These include Plato (and, by extension, Socrates), Augustine, and more recently Descartes and Leibniz. Knowledge of the type postulated by the rationalists is called *a priori* knowledge, meaning that it is "prior" to sense experience.

5. René Descartes is called the father of modern rationalism. His most famous single statement is, "I think, therefore I am," or, in Latin, "*Cogito ergo sum.*" His epistemology is an attempt to place philosophy on the same footing as geometry by discovering axioms from which we can reason, deductively, to universal truths.

6. The word "empiricism" comes from a Greek root which means to experience. Empiricists believe that all learning, and therefore all knowledge, is a result of experience. This means that which is taken in, in the form of sense data, via our senses. If we know it, then we must have seen it, felt it, smelled it, heard it, or tasted it. Empirical knowledge is called *a posteriori*, meaning that it comes after (post), or as a result of, experience.

7. Some famous empiricists are Aristotle, Thomas Aquinas, William of

Ockham, Francis Bacon, and in more recent times the so-called British empiricists John Locke, George Berkeley, David Hume. Empiricism is the foundational position of much of science and experimentation. Of the two theories, it appears to be much the more obvious and commonsensical.

8. Empiricism, if pushed to its logical conclusions, can lead to trouble. This was demonstrated by David Hume, who with relentless logic showed that skepticism, a position of epistemological uncertainty, is the best we can hope for. Hume left philosophy in a tattered state, and it took the German, Immanuel Kant, to salvage it.

9. Kant attempted to show that both the empiricists and the rationalists were, to some degree, correct. He did this by arguing that the human is more than a passive recipient of incoming sense data, that it plays an active role in the forming of reality as we experience it.

10. The concept of truth is a part of epistemology, as is easily seen from the philosophical definition of knowledge: justified, true belief. There are three theories of truth: the correspondence theory, the coherence theory, and the pragmatic theory.

11. The correspondence theory is related to empiricism, whereas the coherence theory is related to rationalism. The pragmatic theory of truth is closely related to existentialism. Each of these theories of truth has its weaknesses and its strengths. The correspondence theory of truth, which says that a proposition is true if it corresponds with observable facts, is the theory most people seem to hold to.

12. Logic, while it is typically treated as a field of its own, clearly arose out of, and is closely associated with, epistemology. It has to do with the way we think and argue, and with what are proper arguments and what are not.

13. A number of fallacious arguments were identified long ago, but keep cropping up in arguments to this day. Among these are *ad hominem* arguments, which attack the person rather than the argument the person is making, *secundum quid,* the fallacy of over generalizing, begging the question, the fallacy of assuming as a part of the argument the very thing one is trying to prove, and the *post hoc ergo propter hoc* argument, the fallacy of assuming that because one thing follows another it was caused by the thing it follows.

14. Two types of formal logic are categorical logic and truth-functional logic. The first, which includes the deductive argument called a syllogism, has to do with the inclusion or exclusion of a thing in certain categories. The second, also called sentential logic, has to do with the way sentences are structured.

15. Deductive arguments are valid, or are intended by the arguer to be so, whereas inductive arguments are neither valid nor are they intended to be.

Section IV
Ethics

There was a young fellow named Bruce
Whose morals were known to be loose.
When asked to explain,
He said, "I'm insane."
I think that's a sorry excuse.

There was a young man from Shanghai
Who gouged out another man's eye.
When asked if he did it,
He said, "I'll admit it,
"But I am an unfortunate victim
"Of a dysfunctional home,
"And a misspent youth,
"Ergo, I am not responsible
"For my actions,
"And the true culprit, Society,
"Must therefore undertake to
"Clothe, feed, rehabilitate,
"And in general look out for me,
"Till the day I fall over and die."

Chapter 13
Do The Right Thing -- Whatever it Is

There was a young man from Bulgaria
Who claimed he came down with malaria.
His wife said,"It ain't
"Pray, cease your complaint.
"You're a victim of moral hysteria."

he question about what is or is not proper behavior is, for all I know, as old as the race. Certainly it is as old as philosophy and philosophers. But it is also as new and as relevant as today's newspapers. Like so many of the things that philosophers talk about, ethics is also something that most non-philosophers talk about — if not constantly, then often enough. But unlike some of the other things that philosophers talk about, ethics is actually one of the fields in which people seem to have very definite opinions. Mention metaphysics, epistemology, logic, and most, while they might offer a few guarded thoughts, would certainly not think of themselves as being experts. Ethics is different. When it comes to proper behavior, experts abound on every corner. If you don't believe it, just keep your ears open.

Think of the ethical questions that are swirling around us at this very moment. Is abortion right or wrong? Should we execute those convicted of capital crimes? Is euthanasia right for those who are suffering from terminal and painful illness? What are we to say to those who may be contemplating suicide if they say to us that their lives are their own, and if they wish to end them then it would be wrong for anyone else to interfere? Is war right? Is it always wrong to tell a lie? What are we to say about adultery, homosexuality, premarital sex?

Clearly ethics is critical to any discussion of philosophy, for if philosophy tells me anything it ought to tell me how to behave toward my fellow humans, and even toward animals and the environment. Ethics is the one area of philosophy that involves all of us, for the moment ethical questions are raised the question of the "other" is raised along with them. One cannot be ethical in a room by oneself. In order to be ethical one must engage, be in some sort of relationship to at least one other person or being, even if that being is the Ponderosa Pine in one's backyard.

Morals: rules governing behavior within groups, or from one country to another.

Ethics: an academic discipline, a study not of what people do, but of what they ought to do.

Before we go any farther we need to get a definition of ethics, and we need to differentiate it from a word often used as its synonym, morals. These do not necessarily denote the same things. Ethicists generally define **morals** as rules governing behavior within certain groups and in certain countries. Morals are descriptive in nature. Ethics, on the other hand, is an academic discipline, a study not of what people do, but of what they ought to do. Morals is practical; ethics is theoretical. The moralist says, "That ain't the way we do it down in Texas," whereas the ethicists says, "The way you do it down in Texas might work in a society given over to some hedonistic form of consequentialism, but it can't be justified by any deontological position of which I am aware."

Don't worry about it. We'll figure it all out as we go along.

One other thing we need to get clear on before we plunge into the fascinating world of ethics. Ethics is one of those rare words which ends in an "s" but is a singular. So whether or not ethics "are" or ethics "is" must be determined by the context in which the word is found. I say this to mute the anticipatory shouts of those who might think I wasn't paying attention in freshman English.

All right, let's get to it. A famous itinerant carpenter said on an occasion, "Judge not that ye be not judged." The same man, on another occasion, said, "Let he who is without sin among you be the first to cast a stone." How am I to understand these two commands, and what application am I to make with them? This becomes rather perplexing when one considers that the same man, Jesus of Nazareth, considered by many to be the absolute and final word on any moral (note that I avoided the use of the word "ethical") questions, also said that he did not come to destroy the Law but to fulfill it; that whoever breaks the least of the commandments (by implication, the Mosaic Law) and teaches others to do so will be called the least in the Kingdom. But the law does not ask me to turn the other way and refuse to judge bad behavior. In fact, under the Mosaic Law, which Jesus said he did not come to destroy, the adulterous woman of the eighth chapter of John's gospel was guilty of a capital crime and ought to have been executed.

Woe is me! What I am to do?

Well, there is certainly nothing that would prevent my thinking, and bringing the problem of what is or is not proper behavior, into the philosophical process. There is no reason why you and I cannot engage one another in an ethical dialectic and attempt to resolve the problems of right and wrong that confront us everyday. We might even find that we can come up with some answers, and we might come to understand that ethics is foundational to the establishment of any sort of social order. I can think of nothing more important, for if we cannot agree on what is right and what is wrong, then it takes little reflection to realize that the human race cannot survive for long.

Let's give it a go! First, a bit of the language of philosophical ethics that we will find useful.

What is Axiology?

I love things that can be answered simply and quickly! **Axiology** is the study of values.

Axiology: the most simple and direct definition is that it is a study of values. Since ethics has to do with values, axiology is basic to ethics.

I hate things for which simple and quick answers are inadequate! There is no quick and simple answer to the question, what are values.

Obviously a value is something we value or assess to be of worth,[1] but that answer is tautological and tells us precisely nothing. According to Ayn Rand, a value is anything we will work to get and to keep.[2] Thus, for Rand, a value is not something that one desires or wants, but what one acts to achieve. There is a difference. Rand's definition is useful, if not conclusive, although it doesn't necessarily do what Rand wanted it to do. Clearly, within this definition there is a good deal of room for motion, and good deal of room for some sort of relativistic valuation. That is to say, what I will work to get and to keep, and what someone else will work to get and to keep, are two different things.

Is relativism, then, the final word in values?

Rand didn't think so, and she spent a good deal of time attempting to show that proper values are grounded in what one is, and in the

---

1 This is the definition given in more than one textbook used in introductory philosophy courses.

2 Rand, Ayn, *For the New Intellectual*, p. 13. Quoted in Merrill, Ronald E., *The Ideas of Ayn Rand*, Chicago: Open Court, 1993, p. 100. Merrill notes that Rand's ideas about the source of values are similar to those of Ralph Barton Perry. And, of course, as with any of Rand's ideas, there is a strong Aristotelian influence.

teleological consideration of what one is becoming. What one ought to value depends upon what one is, and what one is is largely biologically determined. Humans are not apes, for example, and therefore will not value the same things.

Extrinsic value: something we value because it leads to something else; as opposed to intrinsic value: something we value for its own sake.

But where does this leave me? Do I really have a choice in what I ought to value? And if so, where ought I to concentrate my efforts? Philosophers distinguish between things with **extrinsic value** and those with **intrinsic value**, and it is in judging between these two that one may obtain an answers to the question, what am I to value.

An extrinsic value is one that I value as a means to an end. I don't desire it, but rather I desire what it can get me. An intrinsic value is something that I value for its own sake; it is an end, not a means to an end. Money, for example, has only extrinsic value. Unless I am a bit kinky, I don't value money for its own sake. Do I, for example, pile coins on the floor and roll around on them because I get some sort of kick out of it? Not likely. I value money only because of what it can get me, and what it can get me, presumably, is something with intrinsic value. Now, what would that be.

Possibly the most basic intrinsic value is happiness. Aristotle thought so, as we shall see when we look at his classic, *The Nicomachean Ethics*. If he was right, and I must admit that I lean toward thinking that he was, then we value happiness as an end in itself, not because it leads to something else. For Aristotle, happiness is the ultimate good. It takes little reflection to realize that getting or doing good, as opposed to getting or doing bad, brings us into the arena of ethics. It also takes little thought to realize that good and bad are difficult, if not impossible, to define, and that saying something is ethically good and saying something is good to eat or drink are not the same. Still, values are the basic things of which ethics is made, and we cannot talk of ethics without talking, at least briefly, of values.

Normative ethics: ethics that propose to say what is right and wrong, what one ought to do, by establishing some sort of norms for behavior; as opposed to nonnormative ethics, ethics that do not propose "oughts," but rather are descriptive or scientific.

Normative versus Nonnormative

When you think of the word "norm" you probably also think of the word "normal," and this is not just by accident. The two words are very closely related. A norm is a sort of measuring staff by which one may judge something; and that which is normal is by definition that which measures up or conforms to the norm. Thus, we can think of a **normative ethics** as one which tells us, or at least tries to tell us, what we *ought* to do.

The word "ought" is critical to the business of ethics, for not all ethical theories tell us what we ought to do. Many, those that we call **nonnormative ethics**, make no such attempt, and may even teach that this is not the business of ethics, that it is not even possible to construct a normative ethical theory. There are many examples. Cultural relativism is non-normative, and is what some call a descriptive ethics. Metaethics come in a number of different packages. G.E. Moore, whose well-read and much-commented-upon *Principia Ethica* appeared in the early part of this century, is an example of a metaethicist. The emotivism of R.M. Hare and others holds that ethical language is normative only to the extent that those who use it are attempting to control behavior by raising emotional responses in its hearers. Calling behavior "bad," for example, does not imbue it with any particular quality, but rather it is intended to cause those who hear the word to withdraw from contact with that sort of behavior and those who engage in it.[3]

Normative ethics, on the other hand, are exactly what the word implies, ethical theories (there are several) which purport to tell one what one ought to do if one wishes to do the right thing. Some normative ethicists are **absolutists,** that is they hold to the position that there are clearly things that are right and things that are wrong, and that the right and wrong are in the action itself. That which is right, for them is always right, and that which is wrong is always wrong. There are ethicists, however, who believe that the act itself cannot be called either right or wrong, but that it is the result of the act that we should concentrate on. If the act results in that which is good, then it is a good act; but if it results in that which is bad, then the act is bad. These ethicists are called **consequentialists,** and they might be either utilitarians or egoists, depending upon whom they feel the act ought to be good or bad for.

Ethical absolutism: the theory that what is ethical is determined by something that is, in effect, written in stone. Right is right, and wrong is wrong.

Consequentialism: a theory that right or wrong of an action is determined by the action's results.

Virtue ethics is an interesting normative ethics that revives the ancient Greeks. If it is not a form of absolutism, it is close enough that I could never tell the difference, and I shall treat it as such.

Finally, ethical relativism, while clearly a normative ethics is not an absolutist ethics. In fact, it is at the opposite end of the ethical spectrum, being closely related to cultural relativism, separated from it only by that interesting little word "ought."

---

3 This brief and all too inadequate description of emotivism is clearly not exhaustive. In fact, many emotivists would probably take immediate issue and wish to point out all that I have *not* said. My response — please do. I cannot go into a more detailed treatment in a book of this type.

The naturalistic fallacy is the fallacy of attempting to extract a value from a fact without going through a process of logic or reasoning.

Making the leap from non-normative to normative Trying to get an "ought" out of an "is" w/o using logic.

The Is/Ought Problem

If you have never yet encountered the is/ought problem, you are about to. There is a fallacy in philosophy, long ago identified by our old buddy David Hume, that has come to be called the **naturalistic fallacy**. It is the fallacy of attempting to extract a value from a fact, or an "ought" from a mere "is." Suppose we allow the Scottish skeptic to speak for himself.

> I cannot forbear adding to these reasonings an observation which may, perhaps, be found of some importance. In every system of morality which I have hitherto met with, I have always remarked that the author proceeds for some time in the ordinary way of reasoning, and establishes the being of a god or makes observations concerning human affairs; when of a sudden I am surprised to find that instead of the usual copulation of propositions *is* and *is not*, I meet with no proposition that is not connected with an *ought* or an *ought not*. This change is imperceptible, but is, however, of the last consequence. For as this *ought* or *ought not* expresses some new relation or affirmation, it is necessary that it should be observed and explained; and at the same time that a reason should be given for what seems altogether inconceivable, how this new relation can be a deduction from others which are entirely different from it.[4]

If you do not get the point and therefore do not see the problem, let me aid you by reducing the matter to more palatable language. What it comes to is this — Hume has noticed that individuals with whom he is arguing ethics will be talking indicatively about how things are, and that they slip, without so much as a by-your-leave into the imperative by asserting how things ought to be. It is as if I asked you why you place your fork to the left side of the plate in a table setting, and that you responded that it is done because it is right, and that anyone who wishes to be right does it that way. I might reply that, maybe it should be done that way, but that I would need something more than your saying, "That is the way we do it," before I would be convinced that that is the way it ought to be done.

The naturalistic fallacy is an ever-present danger to those who enter the realm of ethics, because there is always a great temptation to see the way

---

[4] Hume, David, *A Treatise on Human Nature*. Quoted in Peter Singer in *The Expanding Circle*.

we do things as the way they ought to be done.

Now that we have looked at values, normative and nonnormative ethics, and one of the major ethical problems, the naturalistic fallacy, we can begin to look at some of the major ethical theories. We will leave metaethics for another course, and will devote the bulk of this section to the normative ethics, with one exception. Cultural relativism, though it is nonnormative, a descriptive ethics, is of considerable interest and has made strong enough inroads into the ethical dialectic that we will spend some time with it. In fact, relativism, whether cultural or ethical, is of considerable importance to the ongoing question of what is right and what is wrong. We will look at it first.

Relativism

When I was in school I attended a seminar in Washington, D.C. in which ethics was being widely discussed. I announced that I was an ethical absolutist (yes, I'll admit to it, I was and still am; but this doesn't mean that any of my students have to be), only to be set upon by what seemed bands of howling fellow students who demanded to know what sort of bigot had come among them. All of them seemed committed to the idea that ethical relativism was a theory chiselled in stone by the finger of God and brought down from Mount Sinai. Fortunately all of them were either literature or psychology students, and I didn't take them very seriously. But they took me seriously — as a plague that ought to be eradicated. As I pushed them on the subject I learned what I had suspected — not one of them was a relativist as philosophers define the term. They were more properly ethical skeptics, or perhaps, if one insists on using the term relativists to describe them, they were individual relativists. What they meant when they used the word was that each individual has a duty to determine for himself or herself what is right and wrong, and that none dare judge them against any sort of standard outside of themselves.

This is not ethics; it is bedlam. Not only do I know of no philosophers who are holding to this nearly indefensible position, but I know of no one who is actually living by it, though there are some who profess to. Think about it. If I come to your home while you are not there and take all of your belongings, are you apt to find persuasive my protests that for me, given my personal code of behavior, it was the right thing to do? Or how about an individual who plants a bomb in a school, kills and maims forty or fifty children, then says he was striking a blow for freedom. Do you find his action defensible on the grounds that he truly believes it was right?

One of the questions I like to ask my students early in the semester before they have been corrupted by my teaching has to do with ethical relativism. "How many of you agree with this statement," I begin. "It is wrong for one to impose one's moral values on others." In most cases nearly every hand in the room will go up, for they all wish to appear liberal and open minded. I then point out to the them that the statement with which they have just agreed is self-contradictory. *It is wrong for one to impose one's moral values on others* by itself constitutes the imposition of a moral value, namely something that it is wrong to do. So if it is wrong to do it, why would you, or anyone else do it to me? But more importantly, we impose moral values on others all the time. When we find someone guilty of theft and lock him or her up, we are in fact imposing a moral value on them. Thou shalt not kill is a moral pronouncement that springs from a moral value, namely that it is wrong to kill. As a society we seem to have no problem imposing this value.

But the individual relativist is not yet defeated. When cornered in this fashion, he or she will typically say something like this: it is wrong to hurt other people, but so long as you are doing nothing to hurt someone else you may do anything you like. Notice, however, that the statement *it is wrong to hurt other people* is actually a moral absolute, very out of place in the arsenal of one who considers himself or herself an ethical relativist. And even then, I have noticed that the so-called relativist tends to be an ethical relativist when it comes to his or her own behavior, an ethical absolutist when it comes to the behavior of others.

I have nothing more to say on the subject of individual relativism, or ethical bedlam as I call it. But there is more to be said on the subject of relativism. In fact, there is good reason to believe that relativism is a viable ethical theory, even when it is pursued only in a scientific and descriptive fashion.

When In Rome. . .

Cultural relativism: the theory that morals are relative to the culture in which one lives. It is strictly a nonnormative ethics.

We all know the old saying, "When in Rome, do as the Romans." This is a good way of introducing what we call cultural relativism. **Cultural relativism** is a nonnormative ethics which holds, in so many words, that right behavior and wrong behavior are culturally determined, and that one cannot properly judge the behavior of those within a given cultural group against another group. One of the best known proponents of cultural relativism is the anthropologist Ruth Benedict. Like many of those who have spent their lives studying diverse cultural groups, Benedict feels that morals are purely a function of how and where one was raised, and that it is a mistake to think in terms of right and wrong if one wishes to judge from a position outside the group.

> The vast proportion of all individuals who are born into any society always and whatever the idiosyncrasies of its institutions, assume, as we have seen, the behaviour dictated by the society. This fact is always interpreted by the carriers of the culture as being due to the fact that their particular institutions reflect an ultimate and universal sanity. The actual reason is quite different. Most people are shaped to the form of their culture because of the enormous malleability of their original endowment. They are plastic to the moulding force of the society into which they are born. It does not matter whether, with the Northwest Coast, it required delusions of self-reference, or with our own civilization the massing of possessions. In any case the great mass of individuals take quite readily the form that is presented to them.[5]

There are many other examples of cultural relativism which we might look at, but this passage serves as well as any to illustrate what the cultural relativists are all about. Certainly there is something to be said for the position they take. One need only look at one's own society and compare it with others to see that what we do here is not exactly what is done there. I come from a small town in East Texas. I can guarantee that what is acceptable behavior there and what is acceptable behavior in New York City are two different things. Of course, those in New York City look down on us as unlettered, ill-manner hicks, and we look at them in no less favorable a light. But people who can think a bit, whether they are in East Texas or New York City, are apt to realize that it is difficult to tag the behavior of either them or us with terms such as good and bad. We do what we do, in many cases, for the same reasons that we speak with a local accent — it is how we were formed when we were at our most plastic, and when we were in the hands of those who had the greatest influence over us.

This is cultural relativism. Morals (I did not say ethics, though cultural relativism is an ethical theory) are determined by the culture in which one is born and raised. Please note that the cultural relativist is not

---

[5] **Benedict, Ruth, *Patterns of Culture*, Boston: Houghton Mifflin Co., 1934.**

beating the drum for the sort of ethical grab-bag that the individual relativist thinks ought to be dangled before us all. In fact, a society generally will have hard and fast rules that hold, and very strict definitions of what is right and what is wrong. Many societies, if not most, have moral absolutes which one cannot violate with impunity. But those are for them, not for others. At least, they should not be for others.

Another example of cultural relativism might be useful, although the student can think of many examples for himself or herself, particularly if he or she has done any traveling to other countries. The Greek historian Herodotus told of the Persian king Darius, who heard of strange things from people who lived within the borders of his vast kingdom. The Greeks cremated their dead, while an Indian tribe, the Callatians, disposed of their dead by eating them. Both groups, when informed of the other, were horrified by what they considered strange behavior. Herodotus's conclusion: custom is king.

Ethical relativism, as opposed to cultural relativism, is a normative ethics. It leaves the area of cultural relativism and becomes ethical relativism when one asserts that this is how things "ought" to be.

Now watch carefully as we moved from **cultural relativism** into **ethical relativism** by inserting one little word — ought. And true to the warning of David Hume, this word usually slips into the dialectic without so much as being noticed. It is one thing to be a cultural relativist, a descriptive ethicist who merely tells how one social group behaves and how it differs from another group. It is quite another to say that this is how things ought to be. This is, however, precisely what Ruth Benedict does. In a 1934 article, "Anthropology and the Abnormal," she tells a story of some American Indians on the Northwest Coast in which the sister of a chief was drowned in an accident on a trip to Victoria. The chief raised a war party, set out, found seven men and two children asleep, and killed them. He then said he felt much better. He did this, according to Benedict, because within this culture any death, even a natural death, was seen as a sort of affront that ought to be retaliated against. Not only did the chief, in this instance, see his actions as morally good, but most of the tribe felt the same way.[6] "The concept of the normal," Benedict says, referring to this incident, "is properly a variant of the concept of the good. It is that which society has approved." The subtle shift from cultural to ethical relativism is not lost on Rosenstand (among others), who says:

---

[6] Reported by Nina Rosenstand in *The Moral of the Story*, Mountain View, CA: Mayfield Publishing Co., 1997, p. 81.

> Benedict is taking a giant leap from expressing cultural relativism to expressing ethical relativism. She moves from a description of what the people do to the statement that it is normal and thus good for them to do it — in their own cultural context. . .Those individuals who somehow can't conform (and they will always be the minority, because most people are very pliable) become the abnormals in that culture.[7]

Now I want to make sure before we go farther that the student understands the difference between individual relativism, cultural relativism, and ethical relativism. The individual relativist — and I emphasize once more for effect that I know of no philosophers who hold to this position — thinks that the individual makes up his or her own rules, and that what is right for him or her is effectively what is right. The cultural relativist understands that the individual is bound by moral rules outside himself or herself, but thinks that the rules are determined by the culture in which the individual lives. This is purely a descriptive, thus a nonnormative, ethics. The ethical relativist takes cultural relativism one step further by introducing an "ought" into things. Not only is morality culturally determined, but this is the way it ought to be, *ergo* this is good.

Evaluating Relativism

Individual relativism needs little comment, for it takes little effort to refute it. Indeed it is refuted everyday by those who claim to believe it. It is one thing to be big-hearted, liberal-minded, and tolerant; it is another to be foolish. We do not live our lives as if everyone ought to decide what is right and what is wrong on an individual basis because we *cannot* live that way. If some sort of social arrangement is necessary for the survival of the species, and if the coherence of the social arrangement depends upon our getting along with one another, then we must hold to certain rules of behavior. This means imposing upon individuals who make up the order certain standards of behavior that have been shown by thousands of years of trial and error to be necessary. Societies which cannot do this, those in which rule and order break down, disintegrate and die, and the individuals within them either die or move into other more stable societies.

Case closed on individual relativism.

---

[7] Ibid., p. 81.

The case on cultural relativism, however, is still open. There is little that one can say against it, so long as we are talking of ethics in anthropological terms. The anthropologist or social scientist observes, records, describes, and we all are able to learn from her efforts or his how the society under examination behaves, how the behavior may have evolved, and how it differs from the moral behavior of other societies, including our own. There is clearly a great deal to be gained from studies of these types, and we can probably agree that tolerance for one another's customs and beliefs can go a long way toward healing long-standing disagreements.

Moreover, there is good reason to believe that beneath the idiosyncratic and cultural dressing that changes from one society to another, there are certain core values that are universal and unchanging. In another context I have called these core values the big four, and have suggested that they are found in every culture, albeit they are sometimes interpreted differently from culture to culture.

1. A prohibition against lying.
2. A prohibition against theft.
3. A prohibition against murder.
4. A prohibition against sexual immorality, chiefly incest.

The well-known ethicist James Rachels has reduced them to three, as follows:

1. A policy of caring for enough infants to insure the continuation of the group.
2. A rule against lying.
3. A rule against murder.

But now we slip over into the murkier and more troublesome world of ethical relativism, a world which may be entered only with difficulty and careful thought. For with ethical relativism we begin to argue that whatever morals exist within a given society are those which ought to exist, and that they are good and right for that society. There is even an implicit, if not explicit, notion that those in one society (ours, let us say) have no business saying that the morals of another society are wrong. One must be careful at this point of that great ogre that threatens to swallow up the would-be ethicist, the naturalistic fallacy. Remember, according to those who believe the fallacy is truly fallacious, one cannot get a value out of a fact with nothing more than the fact to go on. Just because something "is," does this mean that it "ought" to be? Not necessarily. And the ethical relativist has some work to do if he or she wishes to convince this student of ethics that just because a certain Northwestern tribe thinks natural death ought to be avenged, then proceeds to slaughter seven or eight innocent members of a neighbor tribe, that this is by definition good and ought to be accepted as right. Surely such a theory cannot be taken seriously, for if we push it to its logical conclusion by the process we call *reductio ad absurdum* we find ourselves in all sorts of trouble.

Suppose, for example, we find ourselves in Nuremberg, Germany in 1946 interviewing several officers in the Germany army who are now prisoners of war. We ask them about the Nuremburg Laws which effectively made Jews non-citizens within the Reich. We ask them about the seizing of the property of Jews and political dissidents. We ask about a number of the more notorious prison camps, including Buchenwald, Dachau, and Treblinka. We find, much to our amazement, that they are not the least bit troubled by any of this, and when we talk to them about the wrongness of it, they respond that it is wrong only when judged by an outside standard, an American standard, or some other standard foreign to Nazi Germany. To them everything that they did was not only legal but correct and morally right. They then claim to hold to an ethical theory that supports everything they are saying: they are ethical relativists.

Does it occur to you that if ethical relativism is the correct theory, then we have nothing more to say to these men? We might mumble that we certainly don't do it that way, but we have no come back when they say, "Well, we don't do it your way either."

A recent case into which this country was dragged, probably against its wishes, illustrates the problem of ethical relativism even more powerfully. You may remember reading of it in the newspapers. A woman from one of the East African nations was living in this country with her two small daughters. Her husband, the children's father, was back in Africa. Now this was a country which practiced what we call female circumcision. When a girl in this culture reaches puberty, a portion of her clitoris is cut away in an operation that can only be traumatic and painful. But there is more. The labia are sewn together, the obvious motive being to preserve her virginity intact until marriage.

In this case, the father insisted that the girls, his daughters, be brought home so that they could be put through this ordeal, which in his society is thought to be good and proper. There, in fact, it would be shameful for a woman not to have this done. The mother refused to go back, stating that she was not going to have done to her daughters what was done to her, and she applied for a permanent residency permit so that she and her daughters could stay in this country. The whole thing became something of a *cause célèbre*, with scarcely anyone, least of all the ethical relativists, lining up on the father's side. In short, the mother and daughters stayed in this country.

How are we to deal with this situation? It is easy to say that ethically it may be proper to circumcise women in certain parts of East Africa, but now the girls are here, and it is not proper here. I don't believe this consideration saves the day for ethical relativism, because there is little question that judgment has been pronounced, and that the practice of female circumcision has been found monstrous. Neither the Nazis nor the East African circumcisers can be given a moral pass because that's how things are done in their countries.

We see things all the time in other countries that are not morally acceptable, and we have little hesitancy in calling them wrong. Child labor in China. Violations of human rights in Africa. We could hardly question any of these practices if we were truly ethical relativists. And what about ethical problems in our own country? Not only will ethical relativism not allow us to deal with moral violations around the globe, but it makes it impossible to condemn those which occur right here.

Witness the civil rights movement of the 1960's. Martin Luther King and others were particularly effective because they were able to hold a moral mirror up to the society in which they lived, and to ask people in that society to judge themselves. But if ethical relativism is an ethical theory to be championed, why would anyone seriously question the Jim Crow laws of the South? True, there were many who found the racial policies of the South abhorrent, but those policies were nothing but the outgrowth of long established custom and belief, and just because things weren't done that way in Oregon can't be used, under ethical relativism, to condemn the behavior of the Texans and Georgians.

And the Verdict Is. . .

The verdict is that ethical relativism is a theory with serious problems. Certainly customs differ from one place to another, and certainly there is much to be said for allowing people in one place to have their ways of doing things, and to show some tolerance toward others. But ethical relativism commits the naturalistic fallacy right up front, then goes on to call "right" and "good" behaviors that most of us would wish to see condemned and outlawed — genocide, for instance, and genital mutilation.

Ethical relativists begin their system with a supposition that isn't necessarily true — that there is no universal moral code that is binding for all peoples, in all places, at all times. If asked how they know this, they simply point to the obvious fact that people do things differently from one culture to another. This may prove something, or it may prove nothing. Clearly what it does not prove, but what ethical relativists wish to imply, is that any moral code is just as good as any other moral code. I wish to go on record as saying that a moral code that allows for genocide and genital mutilation is *not* as good as a moral code that condemns such things.

Another major problem with ethical relativism is that any moral system that grows up within a group is going to be basically a product of the majority of the group members. Minorities are not apt to be heard, or even to be taken seriously. This can be a little bit frightening, for someone has said,[8] "It is doubtful that the majority has ever been right." Societies and systems that make no provision for hearing the ideas and concerns of the minorities within their borders frequently wind up doing things harmful to those minorities.

Finally, as we have seen, ethical relativism does not provide us with any basis for condemning immoral behavior within our own society. No doubt what is socially acceptable in the South and what is socially acceptable in the North may not be the same. But long and bitter experience shows us that allowing the South to have slaves, or to treat blacks as if they are subhuman, is immoral no matter where it is done. Ethical relativism needs to be polished up, or it needs to be gotten rid of.

But where does this leave us?

Moses Comes off the Mountain

This leaves us with an obvious need to look for some other solution to our ethical questions, something that will give more substantial answers to the questions, "What ought we to do?" and "What ought our values to be?" One of the most obvious sources of ethics is religion, and one of the oldest and most universal of ethical theories, is called religious absolutism. Do not be fooled by the word "universal" in the preceding sentence. The theory is universal only in its barest outline. It does not yield results that are universally agreed upon, as we shall see shortly.

---

[8] Elsewhere, I have attributed this quote to Arnold Toynbee. My head tells me, however, that it is not sure of this, and I cannot seem to find the source.

A religious absolutist believes that right behavior is always right, wherever and whenever it appears, and that wrong behavior is always wrong. The reason for this is simple: ethics has its genesis in divine commandments, and divinities are not in the habit of issuing suggestions. Moses brought the law down from Mount Sinai, for example, and in that law one reads, "Thou shalt not steal." It does not say, "Thou shalt not steal *much.*" Nor does it say, "Maybe thou shalt not steal, but sit down and we'll talk about it." It is characteristic of religious absolutism that it cuts one no slack whatever. This is its strength, and this is one of its weaknesses.

The Judeo-Christian ethics is the one with which most westerners are familiar, and the one to which many claim to hold. The rules of conduct are from God. Depending to a great degree upon what one believes God intended, this code of conduct is sweeping, broad, and covers things that some of us at least can hardly believe one would expect to find in a code of this type. Am I wrong, for instance, if I eat a ham and cheese sandwich, or if I do not use a separate plate for dairy products? One answer is that God intended these dietary rules for the nation of Israel and not for all peoples. Very well, then what part of the Mosaic Law is intended for me?

This question has been a subject of discussion among Christians for the past two-thousand years, virtually since the Jerusalem conference (Acts 15) declared that the provisions of the law having to do with Sabbath keeping and circumcision were not binding on gentile Christians. But if certain portions of the law were intended only for Jews, what about those parts that seem to have more universal application, those that proscribe murder, theft, lying, adultery? For that matter (and here we reach the heart of the problem of any system of religious moral absolutes), what do Jews and Christians have to say to Moslems, Hindus and Buddhists about morality? Any system of religious absolutism depends for its force upon the adherence of individuals to its basic principles, including the belief in the existence of its source. In other words, the God of Abraham, Isaac, and Jacob may make moral demands upon one only so long as one believes that this God exists and that the written record is what it purports to be, commands that come directly from him. Those who do not fall beneath the penumbra of this system of belief are apt to have their own religious absolutes that differ markedly from those of Jews and Christians.

Imagine, if you will, a religion which worships a god totally different from the God of Jews and Christians. There are many such deities out there, or at least there have been. Suppose this god is conceived to be four feet tall, green with purple hair, and an inhabitant of a certain oak tree in Montana.

In order to be right, with this god, one is obliged to steal everything one can, to lie at every opportunity, to kill at least one innocent human a day, and to engage in sex with wild animals. I do not believe there is such a god, but I can assure any who wishes to undertake the necessary research that history is littered with conceived gods no less strange. The point is that the individual who believed in this god would also be a religious absolutist, but he or she would have a different set of absolutes than the ones to which most of us adhere; and they would be no less certain of their absolutes as any of us might be of ours.

Cultural relativism can handle a situation of this type. Indeed, cultural relativism was fashioned just to handle such situations. Religious absolutism, however, runs into a serious problem — it is called the law of contradiction, and we have it from our old friend Aristotle. The two positions are in radical disagreement with one another, and both cannot be right (though both may be wrong). If one of them is right, then the other, to the extent that it is disagreement with the right position, is simply wrong.

There is little more that needs to be said about religious absolutism. The ethical absolutes a religion offers are only as solid as the religion itself. And to push matters further, the absolutes of a religion are only as strong as the faith of the believers. God may well have sent Moses down from the mountain in possession of a divine moral code, and that code may indeed be the absolute truth, binding upon all living humans; but most of the world's people, then and now, don't believe this, and for this reason the absolutes of the faith have no obvious effect upon them, for good or for bad.

Understand, now, that if Moses was right, and if his message was from God, then all those who are in violation of the code are simply wrong, whether they believe it or not. That is the nature of a moral absolute. But philosophers, engaged in a rational dialectic and intent upon answering questions about right and wrong conduct, are apt to balk at such a suggestion because it is all but impossible to prove this case with sound logic and reason.

Ethics: the Human Enterprise

One might be tempted at this point to throw up one's hands and declare the whole thing a waste of time. As we look around the world there appear to be dozens of religions and religious gurus, each claiming to be right and calling for a type of behavior utterly different from the others, assuring whoever will listen that he or she is right and the others are wrong. Or perhaps he assures us that we are all right, each in our own way, when it is manifestly apparent to any reasonable observer that all cannot be right, particularly when they contradict one another.

We see that both ethical relativism and religious absolutism have problems that leave us bewildered, wandering in circles. Like so many things philosophical, ethics seems to be an exercise in confusion.

The problem is that we must pursue this quest because ethics is as critical to human survival as anything we can imagine. All you have to do to convince yourself of this is to think of a society without ethics of any kind. There is something else too. As I have already said, ethics is a human enterprise. Take out the human and you take out the ethics along with him or her. Remove the human, and you remove the ethical dimension from the universe. God is not ethical nor is he required to be: God simply is, and whatever he does is right by definition because he does it.[9] Animals are not ethical, nor are they required to be. Imagine, for instance, someone saying to an eagle who is eating a field mouse, "You evil devil — that might be someone's mother." Humans, on the other hand, are at the heart of the entire ethical dialectic, the creators of the very concept of ethics, the teachers of morality, the ones who have structured language to include the stated concepts of right, wrong, and what one ought to do.

There will never be an abandonment of ethics, though there are times when it may look as if this is precisely what we have done. If relativism and absolutism cannot work, then perhaps we can go in another direction. But go we must, for we seem driven to seek out the answers to our questions about proper conduct. Suppose, then, we try another approach.

The problem with ethical relativism and with religious absolutism seems to be that there is wide diversity among peoples, and that diversity breeds different beliefs and different behaviors. Perhaps we ought to be asking if there are things that all people have in common; and if we can find and isolate such things, perhaps we can use these in some foundational way to build an ethical structure that will be applicable to all. Do we now see light at the end of the tunnel? Ethics, the human enterprise, may begin with a question of what things we all have in common, rather than in looking at

---

[9] An interesting question: Does God do something because it is right, or is it right because God does it. Wittgenstein, when asked the question, answered immediately, "It is right because God does it." This is true, if God is truly God. God cannot be subservient to anything, even to a moral code. Rather, God defines the moral by what he is and does. All of this assumes, of course, that one accepts the theistic definition of God.

our differences. Certainly one of the things we have in common is our ability to use reason. Assuming that the human brain functions in the same manner for everyone, no matter where he or she may have been born, and assuming that there are certain *a priori* rules of thinking that do not vary from one society to another (two plus two must equal four, for example, at the North Pole as well as in sub-Saharan Africa), we ought to be able to construct some sort of rational ethics that all humans who can think rationally will agree on. What could be more human?

It is not surprising that three major ethical theories were born within metaphorical spitting distance of one another — England, Germany and France — and that they all sprang from that time period we call the Enlightenment. The Enlightenment, after all, is a philosophical movement centered in northwestern Europe, a movement flowing out of the earlier time we call the Renaissance, a humanistic period in which there was great confidence in the ability of people, by using their thought processes, to solve all problems. Science was pushing back the physical darkness on every side. Why shouldn't philosophy push back other types of darkness. Surely those willing to use their minds could solve the old problem of the question of right and wrong.

It is also significant, I think, that each of these theories is a normative theory of ethics.[10] The optimism of the Enlightenment thinkers seems, from our historical vantage point, both touching and naive, for there has been a great deal of destruction and disillusionment since then. But we must applaud the conviction of these philosophers that through the application of reason the Kingdom could be brought to reality upon earth. It is not without significance the United States of America is a child of the Enlightenment. And it is also not without significance that another product of the Enlightenment, bloody and terrible, was the French Revolution. Executing hundreds of people on the guillotine is not very nice, and not, let me add, very ethical either. But that is another story.

Natural Law Ethics

One of the most famous sons of the Enlightenment was the third president of the United States, Thomas Jefferson. Of all the documents ever

---

[10] Nonnormative ethics will come into its own in the late nineteenth and early twentieth centuries, as a result of expanded anthropological interests and new-found tolerance of the customs of others.

Natural law, as a theory, is found first in the work of Thomas Aquinas. But it is implied in the Stoics. The idea is that that which is natural is that which is good, and that humans are doing good when they follow human nature.

written few are so universally known and widely quoted as the preambular portions of the document declaring the American colonies independent of Great Britain. I have already quoted part of this in an earlier portion of the book, but let's look at it again, for it makes reference to one of the theories of ethics that had great currency during this time, and that is still useful, the theory of **natural law**.

> When, in the course of human events, it becomes necessary for one people to dissolve the political bands which have connected them to another, and to assume, among the powers of the earth, the separate and equal station to which the *laws of nature and nature's God*[11] entitle them, a decent respect to the opinions of mankind requires that they should declare the causes which impel them to the separation. We hold these truths to be self-evident, that all men are created equal, that they are endowed by their Creator with certain unalienable Rights, that among these are Life, Liberty, and the pursuit of Happiness. . .

Kindly direct your attention to the words I have emphasized in the fifth line of the quote: "laws of nature and nature's God," and ask yourself what point Jefferson is wishing to make in appealing to such laws. Human law was useless in this case because Jefferson and his colleagues were in clear violation of human law. They were rebelling against their sovereign, a monstrous act in most civilized circles of the day. Jefferson could only appeal to a higher law, one to which human law must bend the knee, and that was the natural law.

We might wonder why he did not appeal to the law of God. The wording of Jefferson's statement is very subtle and very deliberate. It is the law of nature, and of nature's God, that he cites, not divine law, and the difference is interesting. Had Jefferson's appeal been to divine law, and were his ethics a derivative of such law, then he would be a normative ethicist and a religious absolutist basing his case upon divine commands. This might not have worked so well, because this was precisely the basis upon which the kings of the earth were arguing the divine right of kings to rule.[12] Jefferson veers every so slightly, away from faith and toward reason, and in so doing he becomes a natural-law ethicist. This is also a normative ethics, and must

---

[11] The italics are mine.

[12] See Romans 13 for example.

be seen as a form of religious absolutism; but it is an absolutism which is an expected product of an enlightenment philosopher. Jean-Jacques Rousseau held to a theory of natural law. So did John Locke. So, obviously, did Jefferson. So, in more recent times, have Henry David Thoreau, Mohandus Gandhi, and Martin Luther King. These and others have dusted off an ancient theory, brought it up to date, and clothed it in modern garb. The natural-law ethicist does not say, "God said it and that settles it." Rather, he or she says in so many words, "Look around you and then think about it."

In its embryonic form, natural-law ethics is at least as old as the stoic Epictetus, who wrote on an occasion:

> The chief concern of a wise and good man is his own reason. . .The business of a wise and good man is to use the phenomena of existence conformably to nature. Now, every soul, just as it is naturally formed to assent to truth, dissent from falsehood, and to suspend judgment with regard to things uncertain, so it is moved by a desire of good, an aversion from evil, and an indifference to what is neither good nor evil. . .Apparent good at first sight attracts, and evil repels. Nor will the soul any more reject an evident appearance of good, than Caesar's coin.[13]

Epictetus, an obvious essentialist, is saying that there is a nature within every human being that is attracted to that which is good and repelled by that which is evil, and the morally-good person is the one who is led by these natural tendencies. Now if such a nature is actually present, it follows that it was put there by God — assuming that one believes in God — and that in obeying one's nature one is obeying God. I needn't point out that this can have some frightening implications. But remember, if you were to challenge Epictetus on this by citing a case of one who obeyed his nature and wound up killing and dismembering twenty-five people, Epictetus would say that this killer was going against his nature, not with it. Okay, so he's begging the question. Don't we all sooner or later?

Natural-law ethics was, in a sense, very natural to the Christian philosophers, and it is not surprising to see Saint Augustine arguing the position in his famous *City of God.* But it took the Medieval saint, Thomas

---

[13] Epictetus, *Discourses,* Book III, Chapter 3, trans. Thomas Wentworth Higginson, Roslyn, N.Y.: Walter J. Black, 1944, p. 180.

Divine law is God's law, and it governs the entire universe. Natural law is that portion of divine law which applies directly to humans and which we can see in operations around us.

Aquinas, to fully develop the theory. According to Aquinas there is such a thing as **divine law**, law as established by God and which governs the entire universe, the great, overriding rule to which everything but God is subservient. Underneath that comes **natural law**, which gives rise to natural law ethics, and which is that portion of the divine law which is directly applicable to humans. Because this law is applicable to humans, we may say that we see this law at work all around us, and that we witness it within ourselves. Finally comes **human law**, law made by people. Now notice that of these three, only one, human law, may turn out to be an unjust law; the other two, coming from God, must be just and good. Human law, however, is just and good if, and only if, it conforms to natural and divine law. Aquinas wrote at length on virtue and law in the *Summa Theologica.* What follows is excerpted from Question 91, On the Various Kinds of Law (in six articles).

> [L]aw is nothing else but a dictate of practical reason emanating from the ruler who governs a perfect community. Now it is evident, granted that the world is ruled by divine providence, as was stated in the First Part, that the whole community of the universe is governed by the divine reason. Therefore the very notion of the government of things in God, the ruler of the universe, has the nature of a law. And since the divine reason's conception of things is not subject to time, but is eternal, according to *Prov.* viii. 23, therefore it is that this kind of law must be called eternal.[14]

In the very next article he gets to the existence of the natural law, which gives rise to natural law ethics.

> [S]ince all things subject to divine providence are ruled and measured by the eternal law, as was stated above, it is evident that all things partake in some way in the eternal law, in so far as, namely, from its being imprinted on them, they derive their respective inclinations to their proper acts and ends. . .[The rational creature] has a natural inclination to its proper act and end; and this participation of the eternal law in the rational creature is called the natural law.[15]

---

[14] Aquinas, Thomas, *Summa Theologica*, ed. Anton C. Pegis, op. cit, pp. 610-11.

[15] Ibid., p. 618.

I know of no reason to assume that Aquinas was influenced by Epictetus, but he is amazingly in agreement with him. The rational creature has a natural inclination toward proper behavior, and toward proper ends. This shows the Aristotelian influence, and is teleological in intent. Humans, for Aquinas, have moral motions within them because that is how they have been made, and because they have been made this way they are always tending in the direction of morality. To be immoral is to go against the grain, to swim upstream against the current of human nature. Living in accordance with nature is the moral thing to do. This language is mine, but it gets to the heart of what Aquinas believes, and natural law ethicists are in agreement with him.

Let us suppose that someone is about to commit suicide, and that he comes to a natural law ethicist and asks if suicide is right or wrong. The answer is that suicide is wrong because it is in violation of natural law, which is to protect life and to stay alive. How would one reach such a conclusion? Well, if Aquinas is right, and if natural law is that portion of the divine law which is applicable to and evident in the behavior of humans, then one would reach the conclusion that suicide is wrong by appealing to experience. Do living things normally kill themselves? The answer is that they do not. Of course there are exceptions ("What about the lemmings," someone at the back of the room shouts every time I raise the issue), but the rule is that given a choice between life and death living things will almost always opt for life, will struggle and fight to stay alive. This is because, Aquinas and others would say, the natural law, written in the very being of the living thing, bids it stay alive.[16]

What else might one derive from the theory as to the rightness and wrongness of behavior? A great deal, according to proponents of natural law ethics. It is right for a man and woman to marry, to produce children, to stay together and raise those children, protecting them and nurturing them. It is right to produce an orderly society, one which will aid in the protection of both families and individuals. It is right that individuals be treated with respect, that they not be deprived of life, liberty or property without good cause, and that they be able to pursue happiness, each in his or her own way.

It seems almost predictable that as individuals began questioning the notion that kings have a right to rule other people, as they did in the seventeenth and eighteenth centuries, they would return to some form of

---

16 This is precisely what Aquinas does say, in *Summa Theologica.*

natural law ethics. This is precisely what happened. Both Thomas Hobbes and John Locke raised the issue of natural law as binding upon all people, and Jean-Jacques Rousseau did it too, both in *The Social Contract* and In *Emile.* Of the many examples one might cite, the following is perhaps representative.

> All the duties of the natural law, which were almost erased from my heart by the injustice of men, are recalled to it in the name of the eternal justice which imposes them on me and sees me fulfill them. I no longer sense that I am anything but the work and the instrument of the great Being who wants what is good, who does it, and who will do what is good for me through the conjunction of my will and His and through the good use of my liberty. I acquiesce in the order that this Being establishes, sure that one day I myself will enjoy this order and find my felicity in it; for what felicity is sweeter than sensing that one is ordered in a system in which everything is good?[17]

Now it isn't surprising to find Hobbes and Locke (more the latter than the former) using the theory of natural law to argue for freedom and equality among humans; and it is certainly not surprising to see the American revolutionaries tending in this direction. What is somewhat surprising is to see how often, throughout American history, an appeal has been made to natural law when some theory has been needed to support revolution, rebellion, or even new legislation, and how few of those making the appeal actually know the philosophical reasons behind it. Human rights is an idea rooted and grounded in natural law ethics, but few seem to realize it. I have often asked students where human rights come from, only to be told that they are granted by the Constitution. Not so, I reply, for if the written law grants rights, then written law can take them away. Jefferson, and others, felt a need to appeal to rights that were much more basic, *ergo* inborn and unalienable. These are the rights granted to humans under the unwritten, but perhaps genetically encoded, laws of nature.

In more recent times natural-law ethics has provided the basis for the thinking of Gandhi and King. These individuals were involved in acts of civil disobedience, breaking written laws while appealing to a higher law.

---

[17] Rousseau, Jean-Jacques, *Emile or On Education*, tran. Allan Bloom, Basic Books, Inc., p. 292.

The higher law was that of God, and the reasoning was as old as Augustine and Aquinas. In fact, in his famous "Letter from a Birmingham Jail," King makes reference to both of these Medieval philosophers in justifying his defiance of laws which he says are "unjust."

> There are just and unjust laws. I would agree with Saint Augustine that "An unjust law is no law at all." Now what is the difference between the two? How does one determine when a law is just or unjust? A just law is a man-made code that squares with the moral law or the law of God. An unjust law is a code that is out of harmony with the moral law. To put it in the terms of Saint Thomas Aquinas, an unjust law is a human law that is not rooted in eternal and natural law.[18]

Thomas Jefferson couldn't have said it better. The appeal of natural-law theory to those who are about to violate human law (thus to all revolutionaries) is obvious. Problematically, however, as with any ethical theory, one cannot have one's cake and eat it too. Natural-law theory is rooted and grounded in Divine Command theory, is thus normative and absolutist, and makes no room for ethical relativism. We will see why this is so presently.

Though it may draw sustenance from Divine-Command theory, there are substantial differences between a religious absolutist and a natural law theorist, and the differences often make natural law attractive to those who reject the idea of God issuing commands that must be obeyed. As Manuel Velasquez has said:

> Clearly, natural law theory does not raise all of the problems that scriptural divine command theories raise. For example, natural law theory does not have to deal with the problem that many different scriptures exist, each claiming to tell us what God commands. In fact, one of the most important advantages of natural law theory is that one does not even have to believe in God in order to accept the theory. For the theory claims that morality is based on living in accordance with our human nature, and this claim does not require belief in God. All people,

---

[18] King, Martin Luther, Jr., "Letter from Birmingham Jail," in *Civil Disobedience: Theory and Practice*, ed. Hugo Adam Bedau, New York: Pegasus, 1969, pp. 77-78.

> whether they believe in God or not, can discover what morality requires by reflecting on their own human nature.[19]

What, then, are the problems with natural-law theory, and why should we not all accept it with alacrity?

Is Unnatural Abnormal?

Mark Twain is supposed to have said on an occasion, "If the Lord had wanted us to run around naked, he would have made us without clothes." Perhaps this gets to the real problem with natural-law ethics: is the natural thing always the right, or even the desirable, thing? Natural-law ethicists sometime seem to have a strange myopia when it comes to things natural, even as Rousseau did about the "noble savage," and returning to nature. He genuinely thought that civilization had corrupted us all, and that the thing to do was to return to an earlier, edenic time, when, he supposed, people lived in harmony with one another and life, for all its basic simplicity, was joyous and carefree. A closer look at humans in their natural state (if by "natural" one means untouched by civilization) may serve to dispel these notions. Savages do in fact kill one another, steal from one another, violate one another's basic rights. In fact, one might argue that the natural thing to do is to take over my neighbor's garden and home, if I can do it and get away with it; and that it takes something unnatural, human law, to restrain me.

Applied to such a basic thing as sex, natural law ethics can easily be used to show that any sex act which does not result in the potential production of children is unethical, since this is clearly the natural function of sex. Homosexuality, oral sex, masturbation would all be condemned by natural law ethics — so far as I am able to tell — and abortion for any reason, as well as active euthanasia. Now there are many people who have no problem with this, who indeed feel that such acts are wrong and ought to be condemned as unnatural and thus unethical. But think about it. Are you really willing to condemn as unethical a sex act undertaken purely for pleasure or merely to express love for one's partner? If not, natural law ethics need some serious adjustments.

And there is more to be said. If we all know right and wrong because

---

[19] Velasquez, *op.cit.*, p. 480.

these are encoded in us at birth, or because we can see what is the natural thing and thus the right thing, why have so many people, in so many different cultures, over so many years, done things that seem wrong by the most charitable of evaluations? And having done these things, why do they seem not the least bit troubled by their actions? When we look at history, we see what appears to be one long, unbroken chain of atrocity, brutality, viciousness, with little concern for the rights of those who are the victims of this behavior. Can you imagine Atilla the Hun's reaction if you stood between him and someone he was getting ready to decapitate and pled for the intended victim's life on the grounds that his natural rights were being violated?

Slavery has been practiced in most every country, in most every culture, in most every period of history that we know anything about. It clearly overrides a right to liberty and self-determination that most all natural-law ethicists agree is fundamental to morality. But is slavery itself unnatural?

Here, then, is another problem that all natural-law ethicists have difficulty solving. How does one resolve disagreements when one portion of the natural law comes into conflict with another? This is why there is an ongoing debate about abortion. The mother's rights to liberty and the pursuit of happiness seem to be in conflict with the fetus's right to life, if indeed the fetus has such rights, and we have what one theorist has called a clashing of absolutes. It is one thing to say that your fist ends at the beginning of my nose, or that one may pursue one's own happiness until the pursuit encroaches upon the happiness of another, but it is quite another thing to say that this principle is a product of natural law.

Perhaps there is no more obvious expression of natural law than what we call the golden rule: do unto others as you would have them do unto you. On the other hand, this may be neither obvious nor natural, and we may need another route if we wish to get to this place. Immanuel Kant thought so, as we shall see.

Summing Up

So far we have taken a look at normative and nonnormative ethics. We have seen that there is such a thing as cultural relativism, which is purely a descriptive ethics and nonnormative, and we have seen how it has been extended into a normative ethics called ethical relativism. We have also seen that ethical relativism has problems, particularly when it comes to making judgments about right and wrong in societies other than one's own. We have looked at religious absolutism, and another type of absolutism called natural- law ethics. Both of these have promising features, but both also have serious shortcomings. Ought we to throw up our hands at this point and retreat into some sort of individual relativism? Take heart. There is more ground yet to cover.

Chapter 14
The Consequentialists

Said the Guru to the Seeker,
"Listen closely to me, lad.
"If the deed results in goodness,
"It can't possibly be bad."
Said the Seeker to the guru,
"I believe I've understood.
"If the deed results in badness
"It can't possibly be good."

Said the Guru to the Seeker,
"You play loosely with my word,
"When your lips reflect my message
"It seems just a bit absurd."
Said the seeker, "Holy father,
"I accept thy reprimand.
"Teach to me this holy wisdom;
"And thy wish is my command."

With utilitarianism we have another of the major ethical systems which came from the period of the Enlightenment. We also have one of the most common ways I know of judging right from wrong. The poem above gets to the heart of the matter: if an action has good results, then we judge it to have been good; if it has bad results, then we judge it to have been bad. This is ethical consequentialism at its simplest, and I don't believe I am far from the mark when I say that this is the way most people tend to determine whether or not something ought to be done, or ought not to be done.

Now I began the first paragraph with a word you may never have heard within this context — utilitarianism. I couldn't have said that consequentialism began during the Enlightenment, for this wouldn't have been true. Ethical consequentialism has been around for centuries in one form or another, but utilitarianism is relatively new, created by politician *cum* philosopher, Jeremy Bentham, and brought to its highest form by his brilliant protege, John Stuart Mill. The first philosopher who actually used the term utilitarian to apply to the sort of normative ethics that judges actions by their consequences was, you guessed it, David Hume. He was a utilitarian, although there was no formal utilitarian ethics until Jeremy Bentham created it. Utilitarianism is a type of consequentialism, but only one type. All utilitarianism is consequentialism, but not all consequentialism is utilitarianism. Now, to explain.

Define the word "consequences" for yourself. You are probably saying that consequences are things that result from certain actions, and you are right. If I jump from a ten-story building without a parachute, and with nothing under me but the pavement, the consequences will not be good. Now if we are talking about normative ethics, asking what one ought or ought not to do, it seems almost too obvious that someone, sooner rather than later, will point out that the act itself cannot be the important thing; that we ought not focus on the act at all, but rather on the results of the act; and that there is no way of judging the rightness or wrongness of an act but by its results. This is ethical consequentialism. You may hear this type of ethics called teleological ethics, and for the very same reasons given above. You will remember from what we saw about Aristotle that *teleos* is a Greek word suggestive of ends or consequences. Thus, teleological ethics bids us look at the ends rather than the means, the results of actions rather than the actions themselves.

This raises some questions, however, and it is the answering of the questions that gives us a variety of approaches to ethical consequentialism. When we talk of consequences, for instance, we might immediately ask, "Consequences for whom?" Or we might ask, "When you talk of 'good,' how do you define the word?" The definition of good, and the question of whose good ought to concern us, are among the problems consequentialists have faced over the years. You may not agree with their solutions, but I trust you will find the discussion intellectually invigorating.

Why Do You Call Me Good?

Some of you will recognize the question above as the one Jesus put to the rich young ruler who came running up to him and addressed him as, "Good Master." You might also remember that he went on to say that no one is good, except for God. I suppose we could end the discussion right here, but for the fact that we use the word all the time to describe all sorts of things in this world, including our own behavior. So let's slide down from the cosmic level to the mundane and ask the question like this: why do we call anything good? What is it that we are trying to convey when we use the term? Like so many common terms, this one is not easy to define — or at least philosophers have not found it to be. G.E. Moore thought good and bad were undefinable primaries. R.M. Hare, the prescriptivist, suggests (as stated previously) that words such as good and bad carry heavy emotional weight, and are used more often than not to control behavior. But he also thinks that the words can have descriptive uses as well as prescriptive ones, and that the meanings we derive from them have a good deal to do with the context and manner in which they are used.

I trust that you all understand how important it is for a consequentialist to carefully define the basic words good and bad. If one grounds one's ethics on the primary thesis that an act is good if it results in that which is good (or bad, etc.), and if, when asked, he or she cannot tell what good means, then the entire structure falls apart. How can I say the result of some act was good unless I know what good is? Now my experience with students is that often, at this point, they will become a bit disgusted, throw up their hands, and say something to the effect that this is just like a bunch of philosophers, arguing over how many angels can dance on a pin's head. Everyone knows what good means. "Great!" I usually say. "Then you define it for me," only to experience a heavy silence as the students look from one to another waiting for the resident genius to speak.

One of the most plausible and useful definitions of good was offered centuries ago by the ancient Greeks. In fact, the definition was so useful that Jeremy Bentham and the utilitarians picked it up and used it when they formulated their system. They defined good as pleasure, or, by a sort of logical extension, the absence of pain, or the reduction of pain. Isn't this pure hedonism. Maybe, but what's wrong with that?

Hedonism: if it feels good, do it!

Hedonism is the pleasure principle, the philosophy which says that one ought to pursue pleasure, either physical or mental, or both.

Surely no one would ground a philosophy on such a lowly and superficial principle. Ah, but they would. And, besides, who says the principle is either lowly or superficial? Certainly not those who espouse some form of hedonism. Of course, hedonism didn't begin with philosophers. There is no reason to suppose that the earliest ancestors of the race were not hedonists, seeking pleasure and fleeing from pain. But it took philosophers to come along and say that this is what we ought to do, and then get busy proving their point.

The word **hedonism** comes from the Greek, *hedone*, meaning pleasure, and the philosophy, also traceable back to the Greeks, equates pleasure with good and pain with bad. Only a short while ago I was asking how we might define good. These early Greeks thought they had the answer. Nothing that brought one pleasure could, for them, be bad.

Ethical hedonism: one ought to seek pleasure. Psychological hedonism: at any rate one will seek pleasure because he or she is psychogically "wired" to do so.

Philosophers have typically distinguished between two basic types of hedonism, ethical and psychological. **Ethical hedonism** says that one ought to seek pleasure and seek to avoid pain. **Psychological hedonism** says that, at any rate, this is what you will do because you can't help it. This is how you are wired up. Notice that these two types of hedonism are like the two types of ethics; one of them (psychological) is a nonnormative, descriptive hedonism, while the other (ethical) is normative, assigning a value, an ought, to the seeking of pleasure and avoidance of pain. If it is true that we are psychologically programmed to seek pleasure and avoid pain, then we might be wise to construct an ethical theory around this drive, for we are going to obey it whether we wish to or not. This, as we shall see later, is precisely what Jeremy Bentham did.

Cyrenaic hedonism: named for Aristippus of Cyrene. It holds that nothing that brings physical pleasure can be bad.

This is, to put it in other terms, the pleasure principle, and it has had many philosophical adherents over the years. One of the earliest of whom we have record is one Aristippus, who lived in the North African city of Cyrene four centuries before Christ. For reasons that I don't know, the system of belief he left us took its name from his hometown instead of him. We call it **Cyrenaic hedonism**, and for all of you party animals Aristippus must be your philosophical godfather. When he said pleasure, he meant physical pleasure, and when he was asked to distinguish between pleasures he had a simple answer: whatever pleases me the most at the time is the highest good. This leads to what is known as hedonistic utility, the principle that bids us maximize pleasure and minimize pain.

Notice that this is a self-centered philosophy. I am under no obligation to define pleasure (i.e. good) for you, and you are under no such obligation to me. It was inevitable, however, that someone would come along and attempt to do so. The idea that it is good by definition if one finds pleasure in getting drunk and rolling in the gutter is not palatable for much of the civilized world, and so we get the attempts to define some pleasures as higher, or more worthy of consideration, than others. One of the first major philosophers to do this was Epicurus of Samos, who gave his name to Epicureanism, the philosophy typically associated with the pleasure principle.

Ataraxia: peace of mind.

Ironically, Epicurus was anything but pleasure mad. He taught moderation, and a state of mental balance called **ataraxia**.

> Because of the very fact that pleasure is our primary and congenital good we do not select every pleasure; there are times when we forgo certain pleasures, particularly when they are followed by too much unpleasantness. Furthermore, we regard certain states of pain as preferable to pleasures, particularly when greater satisfaction results from our having submitted to discomforts for a long period of time. Thus every pleasure is a good by reason of its having a nature akin to our own, but not every pleasure is desirable. In like manner every state of pain is an evil, but not all pains are uniformly to be rejected. At any rate, it is our duty to judge all such cases by measuring pleasures against pains, with a view to their respective assets and liabilities, inasmuch as we do experience the good as being bad at times and, contrariwise, the bad as being good.[1]

So much for rolling in the gutter. If you wake up with a bad hangover, your money and shoes missing, sitting in a jail cell with a possibility of doing ninety days on the chain gain, then your brief pleasure can hardly have been worth the price you paid. Epicurus clearly draws a distinction between types of pleasures, reserving the higher type as the ones that ought to be the objects of our pursuits.

> Thus when I say that pleasure is the goal of living I do not mean the pleasures of libertines or the pleasures inherent in positive enjoyment, as is supposed by certain persons who are ignorant of our doctrine or who are not in agreement with it or who interpret it perversely. I mean, on the contrary, the pleasure that consists in freedom from bodily pain and mental agitation. The pleasant life is not the product of one drinking party after another or of sexual intercourse with women and boys or of the seafood and other delicacies afforded by a luxurious table. On the contrary, it is the result of sober thinking — namely, investigation of the reasons for every act of choice and aversion and elimination of those false ideas about the gods and death which are the chief source of mental disturbances.[2]

Suppose, however, that we press the matter a bit by asking whether

---

1 **Epicurus, *Letter to Menoceceus*, pp. 7ff.**

2 **Ibid., p. 8.**

or not I have some obligation to seek the good, or pleasure, of others. Given the fact that most of us have grown up in a Judeo-Christian setting that bids us love our neighbors as ourselves, we tend to shrink from the position that one has an ethical obligation to seek pleasure for oneself. Looking out for number one is usually not the sort of behavior one expects from a moral philosopher. But there are those who think this is what we ought to be doing. They are called egoists.

Ethical Egoism — First Me, Then You

Ethical egoism is a consequential ethics which holds that that action is good which results in good for the individual performing it.

Remember, ethical consequentialism may take one of two forms, depending upon whose good one is seeking. There are those who say one's first obligation is ever and always to oneself, in fact it is immoral not to think first of oneself. These are consequentialists who judge every action by one question, will it result in good for me. The term **egoist** is attached to them for obvious reasons. I never think of ethical egoists without thinking of Ambrose Bierce's amusing definition of an egoist, from his *Devil's Dictionary*. Egoist: a person of low moral calibèr, more interested in himself than me. The fact is that most of us have been taught most of our lives that it is not nice to think of oneself first; that one ought always to be altruistic and think of others; that egoists are persons of (as Ambrose Bierce suggests, tongue in cheek) low moral caliber. It is somewhat surprising, therefore, to find philosophers who think that there is nothing wrong with thinking of oneself first, and that it is evil not to do so.

As with hedonism, so with egoism — it may be divided into ethical and psychological. The ethical egoist says that we ought to look out for ourselves. The psychological egoist says that what we ought or ought not to do aside, we are so constituted that we will always do that which is in our own self-interest. One of the earliest proponents of psychological egoism was Glaucon, one of Socrates's adversaries. In Book Two of *The Republic* he tells of the story of the ring of Gyges, a shepherd who finds a ring that he learns can make him invisible. The point of the story, as it unfolds, is that we do what we think is good only for fear of getting caught, and that if we had no such fear then we would unabashedly do the thing which we wish to do, which is ever and always that which is best for us. In fact, Glaucon goes so far as to say that if we give one of these rings to a known scoundrel and one to a so-called just person, both will behave equally badly. It is all a question of what we know we can get away with.

This, in an embryonic form, is what psychological egoism is all about: we do the thing that benefits us because that is human nature. Ethical egoism goes further: you ought to do the thing that results in what is good for you.

The most famous ethical egoist is probably the novelist Ayn Rand, whose books *The Fountainhead* and *Atlas Shrugged* have raised her to a cult-figure status. You have an ethical obligation, according to Rand, to look out for yourself, and it is downright evil to do anything less.

> The great treason of the philosophers was that they never stepped out of the Middle Ages: they never challenged the Witch Doctor's code of morality. They were willing to doubt the existence of physical objects, they were willing to doubt the validity of their own senses, they were willing to defy the authority of absolute monarchies, they were willing (occasionally) to proclaim themselves to be skeptics or agnostics or atheists — but they were not willing to doubt the doctrine that man is a sacrificial animal, that he has no right to exist for his own sake, that service to others is the only justification of his existence and that self-sacrifice is his highest moral duty, virtue and value.[3]

Ethics that demand one live one's life for others, altruistic ethics, is consistently seen by Rand as an ethics of non-moralists. In *The Fountainhead* she has her hero Howard Roark saying:

> Altruism is the doctrine which demands that man live for others and place others above self. . .
>
> The man who attempts to live for others is a dependent. He is a parasite in motive and makes parasites of those he serves. The relationship produces nothing but mutual corruption. It is impossible in concept. The nearest approach to it in reality — the man who lives to serve others — is the slave. If physical slavery is repulsive, how much more repulsive is the concept of servility of the spirit? The conquered slave has a vestige of honor. He has the merit of having resisted and of considering his condition evil. But the man who enslaves himself voluntarily in the name of love is the basest of creatures. He degrades the dignity of man and he degrades the conception of love. But this is the essence of altruism.[4]

---

[3] Rand, Ayn, *For the New Intellectual*, New York: Signet Books, 1961, p. 35.

[4] Ibid., pp. 79-80.

Finally, let's hear from John Galt in *Atlas Shrugged.*

> Man's life is the standard of morality, but your own life is its purpose. If existence on earth is your goal, you must choose your actions and values by the standard of that which is proper to man — for the purpose of preserving, fulfilling and enjoying the irreplaceable value which is your life.
>
> Since life requires a specific course of action, any other course will destroy it. A being who does not hold his own life as the motive and goal of his actions, is acting on the motive and standard of death. Such a being is a metaphysical monstrosity, struggling to oppose, negate and contradict the fact of his own existence, running blindly amok on a trail of destruction, capable of nothing but pain.[5]

By means of fictional characters and situations Rand makes her point repeatedly, and brilliantly, though she has an army of detractors who profess to be horrified at what she holds as morality. Joseph Fletcher, for example, has called hers a "jungle morality." Of course, his own situational ethics would be what she would call "parasite ethics."

Rand is probably the purest Aristotelian since William of Ockham, but her ethics are not Aristotle's. Notice that she does not believe in psychological egoism at all. She feels that people have been hoodwinked over the years into thinking that the right thing is a total absence of self-interest, and that all moral people will exhibit this sort of selflessness. On the contrary, she says, if there is anything a human ought to be doing it is surviving, and this can be done only if the human has his or her own interest at heart. To abandon this is to become a metaphysical monstrosity, a creature confused about the one basic truth of what the human must do.

Ayn Rand does not teach (despite what her detractors have charged her with over the years) that one ought to hurt or harm others, be discourteous to or ignore the needs of others. What she teaches is a normative, consequentialism that says the right thing to do in every case is that which is in your own self-interest. It is easy to see that in many cases my own self-interest lies in helping others, being charitable, and in always dealing honestly with others. Fine, Rand would say, if this is in your interest, then do it. But what one never does, if one wishes to be truly moral, is turn

---

[5] Ibid. pp. 122-23.

oneself into a sacrificial animal by forsaking his or her own interest as the primary motive for any behavior.

Call it enlightened self-interest.

Egoism Criticized

I must admit that I think there is something to be said for what Ayn Rand says in general, and for ethical egoism in particular. I well remember the summer of 1960 when the woman who was to become my wife wrote to me that I simply had to read *Atlas Shrugged.* And I well remember reading it, passing it on to my friends, and how we spent that entire summer discussing it. Since that time I have re-read the book numerous times, and have read *The Fountainhead* and others of her books as well. She is a stimulating, thought-provoking philosopher who chose to write in a fictional format, and who has had tremendous influence in this country and around the world. Many members of the Libertarian Party trace their beginnings back to her.

But is the ethics of egoism viable, or must I, more often than not, sacrifice my own self-interest if I am to do the right thing? It is precisely at this point that one of the main problems of ethical egoism emerges — it is a theory which it is difficult to actually falsify. And if this is true of ethical egoism it is even more true of its nonnormative relative psychological egoism.

Suppose, for example, that I am, like Glaucon in *The Republic*, a psychological egoist. That is, I believe that everyone will always behave in a way that is in his or her own interest. How could such an idea possibly be shown to be false? Whatever I do may be seen as in my own interests, and if I do something which is manifestly not in my interest, there will be a host of amateur psychologists waiting to explain that it is purely a matter of perception. Why did Mother Theresa leave everything and go to India to live among the poor? Obviously because she wanted to, it gave her pleasure, *ergo* it was in her own interest. There is no behavior that cannot be explained in this way as egoistic, and ultimately a theory that accounts for everything accounts for nothing.

But suppose there is some way to get around this problem of non-falsifiability. We have a more basic problem. Ethical egoism appears to be self-contradictory. An ethical theory ought to be able to provide answers about what I am to do. It ought to resolve moral issues when they arise; and when there are moral conflicts between individuals — and there invariably are — it ought to be able to suggest a way to settle the conflict. Ethical egoism not only does not do this, it can actually make matters worse. Consider a case in which two individuals, male and female, have foolishly gotten together and conceived a child out of wedlock and are now faced with a question of what to do. The man comes to you for counselling, and you, being an ethical egoist, advise him to do the thing that is in his own best interests. His entire life at this moment is aimed toward completing a degree in electrical engineering, going to graduate school, and taking a job with his rich uncle's firm in Hong Kong. The problem is that to do this he must be single with no dependents. If the baby comes his whole career goes down the tubes. His decision, therefore, based upon your counselling, is to have the child aborted.

A day later the lady comes to see you. You, being an ethical egoist, advise her to do the thing which is in her self-interests. She is a strong Catholic, and thinks that abortion is murder and a mortal sin. She wants the baby, but she cannot afford to raise the baby by herself. It is in her interest for the husband of her child to marry her; but if he will not she intends to file a paternity suit, take him to court, and make him support the child.

Both are following your advice, the advice takes them in opposite directions, and you have two people pursuing opposite courses, based upon one theory coming from one theorist. To salvage something for the theory one might say that actually there is a resolution of sorts, because one of the two will ultimately win out, and that even the loser has done the right thing in pursuing his or her own interests. This is weak. The truth of the matter is that the theory has resulted, in practical terms, in two people going in completely opposite directions in the name of that which is good. This seems to violate our old friend, the law of contradiction, which Aristotle formulated. Remember, Ayn Rand was Aristotelian. Were she alive I would like to ask her to respond to this.

But wait! What about egoism's reciprocal, altruism? In this theory everyone gives up his or her own interests to work for the interest of others. Apply that to the case above and you get exactly the same problem produced by egoism, each working at cross purposes attempting to do the right thing for the other. Aside from producing a warm feeling in the heart of the altruist who is sacrificing himself for the other, it is difficult to see that this theory gains us anything; and frankly, if all I get for my efforts is a warm feeling, I much prefer egoism and my own interests taken care of.

Now that I have confessed in print to being the very sort of lowlife Bierce lampooned in his wacky definition, let me redeem myself somewhat by saying that we are not forced into an either/or. We don't have to opt for egoism or altruism. There are other ethical theories we may consider. In fact, there is another consequentialist theory we may look at. It is called utilitarianism.

Working for the Majority

Abraham Lincoln is supposed to have said, "I am for what does the most good for the greatest number of people." That, in a loose form, is what utilitarianism is all about, and that is what morality is all about for many people. Consequentialism as an ethical theory is very alluring because it sounds so right, and because it is so simple to explain and to understand. Unlike the more burdensome thought of Immanuel Kant (we'll get to him in the next chapter), the theory of Jeremy Bentham bids us simply ask ourselves, before we do something, will what I am about to do result in good or bad.

Question: what is good and what is bad?

Ah, the early Greeks have answered this one for us, as we saw a few pages ago. Good is that which results in pleasure, or the reduction of pain. Bad is that which results in pain, or the reduction of pleasure.

Second question: What is the target? Or, to put it more bluntly, good or bad for whom?

Well, it is obvious that it cannot be myself, for that would bring us right back to egoism, a theory many of us might like to steer clear of. The answer is, good or bad for the majority of the population. If the action results in the increase in pleasure, or the reduction of pain, for at least fifty-one percept of the people, then according to Bentham you have done a good thing. This is pure hedonism, but what of it. Bentham was convinced that this is the mainspring of human motivation.

> I. Nature has placed mankind under the governance of two sovereign masters, *pain* and *pleasure*. It is for them alone to point out what we ought to do, as well as to determine what we shall do. On the one hand the standard of right and wrong, on the other the chain of causes and effects, are fastened to their throne. They govern us in all we do, in all we say, in all we think: every effort we can make to throw off our subjection, will serve but to demonstrate and confirm it. In words a man may pretend to abjure their empire: but in reality he will remain subject to it all the while. The *principle of utility* recognizes this subjection, and assumes it for the foundation of that system, the object of which is to rear the fabric of felicity by the hands of reason and of law.

> Systems which attempt to question it, deal in sounds instead of sense, in caprice instead of reason, in darkness instead of light.[6]

Notice that Bentham, in the opening chapter of *Introduction to the Principles of Morals and Legislation*, appeals to psychological hedonism as the foundation for his ethical hedonism. Pleasure and Pain are the two sovereigns under which we have been placed, and regardless of what we think we ought to do, we will be driven psychologically to gain pleasure and avoid pain. He calls it, "the principle of utility."

Now the principle of utility could apply to an individual, and it could apply to a group, and it is in applying it to the group that one moves away from egoism and toward utilitarianism. He makes this clear a little later in the same opening chapter.

> II. The principle of utility is the foundation of the present work: it will be proper therefore at the onset to give an explicit and determinate account of what is meant by it. By the principle of utility is meant that principle which approves or disapproves of every action whatsoever, according to the tendency which it appears to have to augment or diminish the happiness of the party whose interest is in question: or, what is the same thing in other words, to promote or to oppose that happiness; I say of every action whatsoever; and therefore not only of every action of a private individual, but of every measure of government.
>
> III. By utility is meant the property in any object, whereby it tends to produce the benefit, advantage, pleasure, good, or happiness (all this in the present comes to the same thing) to prevent the happening of mischief, pain, evil, or unhappiness to the party whose interest is considered; if that party be the community in general, then the happiness of the community: if a particular individual, then the happiness of that individual. . .
>
> VI. An action then may be said to be conformable to the principle of utility or, for shortness sake, to utility (meaning with respect to the community at large), when the tendency it has to augment the happiness of the

---

[6] **Bentham, Jeremy, *Introduction to the Principles of Morals and Legislation*, Oxford: Oxford University Press, 1823 ed., p. 1.**

> community is greater than any it has to diminish it.
>
> VII. A measure of government (which is but a particular kind of action, performed by a particular person or persons), may be said to be conformable to or dictated by the principle of utility, when in like manner the tendency which it has to augment the happiness of the community is greater than any which it has to diminish it.[7]

A Bit of History

Philosophy does not spring from a vacuum, but from the times during which it arises. Utilitarianism was an idea whose time had come. Bentham was a politician, not a philosopher, whose time had come. The time was the end of the period of the Enlightenment, when the Industrial Revolution was sweeping England, bringing in its wake not only undreamed of prosperity, but also undreamed of problems and changes. Whole populations had been displaced from the farms where they had worked as tenants, and had crowded into the large urban areas, such as London and Manchester, to labor in the factories. Slums grew, and crime, and the population went up and up with no end in sight.

At about the time of Bentham another thinker, Thomas Malthus, floated a theory concerning food supply and population growth, which stated in its simplest terms that populations would inevitably outgrow food supplies because food supply was growing arithmetically (1, 2, 3, etc.) while population was growing geometrically (1, 2, 4, 8, etc.). The result would be wide spread starvation, with all of the problems attendant thereunto.[8] Malthus and other free-marketers thought the best thing that could be done was to leave things alone and let natural forces — disease, famine, and so on — decrease the surplus population. Social programs that fed the poor at government expense were, for Malthus, very ill advised. They did not cure the problem; they only prolonged it.

Into this mix came Jeremy Bentham, a politician and a reformer, who genuinely thought that progressive legislation could cure social problems.

---

[7] Ibid., pp. 2-5

[8] In case you are wondering why Malthus's predictions did not come to pass, supporters of his theory say that the surplus population was displaced to America, Canada and Australia. Now that there is nowhere for the growing populations of the Third World to go, we may get a chance in our lifetimes to see if Malthus was correct.

And what sort of laws ought to be passed? That is precisely what his theory of utility is all about, and it is what the ethical theory of utilitarianism was created to deal with. Obviously no one could hope to cure every single problem of every single individual in a given society. So what one must do is ask, what is best for the majority? What is that action (enactment, law) which will increase the pleasure and decrease the pain for the majority of the society. By definition, this is good.

Take note. I said this before, but it bears repeating. The good is not the act itself. The act, in and of itself, is morally neutral. It is only the end, the consequence of the act, that defines it.

Let's Calculate It

But how are we to tell whether or not one act produces more good than another? That is, suppose we have a choice between two acts, both of which will yield some good and some misery, and we wish to know which of the two we ought to put into practice. We have, for example, a slum in which people are living. We are asked to improve the slum, upgrade the living conditions, so that the people will have a better place in which to live. Or, we are asked to tear down the slum to make room for a major highway that will greatly enhance the income of the manufacturing firms in the area. What should we do? Jeremy Bentham had this problem figured out too.

He constructed what he called a hedonic (or hedonistic) calculus, which assigned numerical values to actions, and by which one could actually come up with a score for the level of pleasure of any given act. Seven elements made up the calculus. Four of them affect pleasure or pain themselves, two affect action related to pleasure or pain, and one is based on the number of people affected. They are:

1. *Intensity.* How strong is the pleasure?
2. *Duration.* How long will the pleasure last?
3. *Propinquity.* How soon will the pleasure occur? (Nearness)
4. *Certainty.* How likely or unlikely is it that the pleasure will occur?
5. *Fecundity.* How likely is it that the proposed action will produce more pleasure? (Fruitfulness)
6. *Purity.* Will there be any pain accompanying the action?
7. *Extent.* How many other people will be affected?

Hedons were Bentham's units of pleasure, used in his hedonic calculus to determine the amount of pleasure an act would produce.

The idea is to take the particular act, attach the requisite **hedons** (Bentham's pleasure units) to it, based upon the elements above, and compare the resulting totals. If the calculation results in more units of pleasure than pain, then we ought to do it; if more units of pain than pleasure, then we ought not to do it.

> Take an account of the *number* of persons whose interests appear to be concerned; and repeat the above process with respect to each. *Sum up* the numbers expressive of the degrees of *good* tendency which the act has, with respect to each individual. . .do this again with respect to each individual, in regard to whom the tendency of it is *bad* upon the whole. Take the balance; which, if on the side of pleasure, will give the general *good tendency* of the act, with respect to the total number or community of individuals concerned; if on the side of pain, the general *evil tendency*, with respect to the same community.[9]

Is this guy kidding me? Just how many mathematicians does he think we have out there? And just how many does he think will stop before undertaking an action, whip out a notebook, and calculate the hedons attaching to the proposed action? This might have some relevance to someone sitting in an office on Capitol Hill pondering some legislation, but it will hardly do for the man or woman in the market place who has to think and think fast about the choices that confront them.

And then there is the problem with the hedons themselves, and with their values. It has probably already occurred to you that someone has got to assign the numerical values to these units of so-called pleasure, and that the assignment has got to be somewhat arbitrary. Who is to act as our presumed expert in this area, and how is one to say that the pleasure of drinking a glass of fine wine is greater than an evening at the opera? Questions about the hedonic calculus of Bentham lead to a raft of questions that make a reformation of utilitarianism necessary if it is to be of a formal use. Fortunately, there are always reformers waiting in the wings.

John Stuart Mill, Polished Utilitarian

John Stuart Mill (1806-1873) was the right man, in the right place, at the right time, and with the right equipment to undertake the reformation of utilitarianism. His father, James Mill was a close friend and co-laborer of Jeremy Bentham, and when John Mill was little more than a babe in arms the two men made him what I can only describe as a guinea pig in an

---

[9] Bentham, Jeremy, op. cit., ch. 4, sec. 5.

educational experiment. Where Mrs. Mill was during this period might make an interesting book in its own right. Apparently she and her husband were estranged, while continuing to occupy the same home, each in an opposite wing; and if she ever protested her husband's right to make use of her son in this way, I am not aware of it.

James Mill and Bentham had a theory of learning, empirical to be sure, which held that all human minds were equal, and that the only difference in a genius and a dunce was the intellectual matter to which each was exposed — and the sooner, the better. Accordingly, John learned arithmetic and Greek when he was three years old, Latin, geometry, and algebra at eleven, and logic and philosophy at twelve.

All agree that John Stuart Mill was a genius; all agree that he paid a terrific price for his genius. According to Mill himself, he never really had a boyhood, was never around other children, had no actual moral conscience, and lived in a state of fear of his surrogate conscience, his father.[10] "Mine was not an education of love but of fear," said Mill in an early version of his *Autobiography*. "My father's children neither loved him, nor, with any warmth of affection, anyone else."[11] This is sad. Mill had help waiting in the wings, but it, or more properly she came after he had lived through an experience that nearly destroyed him.

When he was about twenty years old Mill suffered what he described as a dry, heavy dejection. We would call it a nervous breakdown. Because it is important, I beg the students's indulgence while I quote him at some length.

> I was in a dull state of nerves, such as everybody is occasionally liable to, one of those moods when what is pleasure at other times becomes insipid or indifferent; the state, I should think, in which converts to Methodism usually are when smitten by their first "conviction of sin." I seemed to have nothing left to live for. At first I hoped that the cloud would pass away of itself; but it did not. A night's sleep, the sovereign remedy for the smaller vexations of life, had no effect upon it. In vain I sought relief from my favourite books, those memorials of past nobleness and greatness from which I had always hitherto drawn strength and animation. I read them now without feeling, or with the accustomed feeling minus all

---

[10] **The student is directed to Mill, John Stuart, *Autobiography*, New York: Columbia University Press, 1971.**

[11] **Quoted in Soccio, p. 416, op.cit.**

> its charm; and I became persuaded that my love of mankind, and of excellence for its own sake, had worn itself out. . .
>
> I was. . .left stranded at the commencement of my voyage, with a well equipped ship and rudder, but no sail; without any real desire for the ends which I had been so carefully fitted out to work for; no delight in virtue or the general good, but also just as little inanything else. . .[12]

In his *Autobiography*, the same work from which the above quote is taken, he describes an emotional experience in which he breaks down and cries after reading the memoirs of a French writer, and his own father's death. Being able to cry was, for Mill, a cathartic thing, and after that he began the long climb out of the pit in which he had been living. He also met a woman.

Harriet Taylor

Harriet Taylor was older than Mill, and was married to a wealthy merchant older than herself. Her relationship with Mill began as a platonic one centered around books and intellectual ideas. Harriet wanted to become a writer, and she was interested in the young Mill, who was brilliant to say the least. At first they spent hours talking together in the Taylor home. Then, as Mill began spending more and more of his time there, it became obvious to all, including Mr. Taylor, that what had begun as an intellectual union had become a romantic one.

It was to last for life. Two years after Mr. Taylor died John Stuart Mill married Harriet Taylor, and for seven years, until her death, they lived happily together. There can be little doubt that Harriet was a major influence on John Stuart, if not intellectually, certainly psychologically and emotionally. He became a major reformer, an early and passionate advocate of women's rights, and a libertarian ahead of his times. And he reformed the utilitarianism of Bentham, giving an altruistic cast to the pleasure principle that was missing in the older man's work.

---

12 **Mill, John Stuart, *Autobiography*, ed. J.D. Stillinger, London: Oxford University Press, 1971, pp. 83-84, 97-98.**

When Is Pleasure Not Pleasant?

There is pleasure, and there is pleasure, but is pleasure always pleasant, and is that which brings pleasure always worth pursuing? If we listen to Bentham, and to the Greek hedonists, we are apt to come away believing that one man's meat is another's poison, and if a majority of the people wish to poison themselves then we must not only let them do it, but define that as good. Of course, Bentham's hedonic calculus, if applied correctly, might be used to steer one away from that poison which is cloaked in the outer integuments of meat; but, as we have seen, the hedonic calculus can be confusing and can yield ambiguous results.

To bring the problem into focus, imagine that we have two courses of actions open before us. In the first, we all go out, get roaring drunk, and roll in the gutter together like swine. In the second, we all stay at home, read a good book, get a good night's sleep, and wake up in the morning refreshed. Getting drunk and rolling in the gutter may leave us hung over and miserable the following morning, but if the pleasure of the action is intense enough we might opt for it and call it good. We might, but Mill would call us fools. All pleasures, he holds are not equal, regardless of what his mentor Jeremy Bentham thought. Some pleasures are higher than others. In his classic, *Utilitarianism*, published in 1863, he undertakes to make this case. He goes back to the much-misunderstood Epicureans, generally maligned, in his view, as pure hedonists, and shows that they were nothing of the sort, that they recognized and taught that not all pleasures are equal.

> There is no known Epicurean theory of life which does not assign the pleasures of the intellect, of the feelings and imagination, and of the moral sentiments, a much higher value as pleasure than those of mere sensation.[13]

Clearly, there are those who enjoy behaving like swine, but to say that this is the good to which the human ought to aim is a "doctrine worthy of swine." As humans, people have aspirations that go far beyond those of pigs, or even of human fools. Mill's famous statement, from the Utilitarians, is, "It is better to be a human being dissatisfied than a pig, satisfied, better to be Socrates dissatisfied than a fool satisfied. And if the fool, or the pig, are of a

---

[13] **Mill, John Stuart, *Utilitarianism*, in *The Utilitarians*, Garden City, N.Y.: Dolphin Books, 1961, p. 407.**

different opinion, it is because they only know their own side of the question. The other party to the comparison knows both sides."[14]

This business of knowing both sides of the question is important for Mill. If we wish to know which of two pleasures is the higher, qualitatively, then we must ask someone who has experienced them both, and be guided by what they tell us. And even this will not be decisive. Some individuals, because of poor learning, poor habits, badly-formed character, cannot be relied upon to know what is actually best. Mill was a great believer in education, for he saw in it a formative factor in guiding people to those sorts of pleasures that are best and highest.

Politically, Mill was what we would today call a libertarian, and that in the word's truest sense. All of his life he was committed to the belief that utilitarianism, if properly applied, could be used to do the right thing, to improve lives, to better society. He was convinced that this was the ethical theory that really worked.

But is it?

The Problems With Utilitarianism

If you are an old movies buff, you may recall a movie called *The Young Lions*, made from Irwin Shaw's novel by that name; and you may remember Marlon Brando, as a young Nazi officer in occupied Paris, saying to a young French girl who questioned him about how many people he had killed, "I have killed no one; but if I have to sacrifice a few lives in order to bring peace, including my own, I will do it — *ja!*" This is a utilitarian sentiment if I ever heard one, and it certainly has a noble ring to it — to everyone but those whose lives are to be sacrificed. I am not sure all of them would feel about it the way Brando did. There is an old saying: The end doesn't justify the means. Of course, no utilitarian could say that, because utilitarians believe that the end does, in fact, justify the means. More than that, the end actually defines the means. If the end is good — that is, increases pleasure or decreases pain for the majority — then we call the means to that end good. This, to me, has always been the Achilles heel of utilitarianism. Within certain limits I can agree that the utilitarians have made a good case for consequential ethics. I can even agree that most of us, at one time or another, use consequentialism. Who hasn't stopped to consider the supposed results of his or her actions, then gone ahead only

[14] Mill, John Stuart, *Utilitarianism*, quoted in Nina Rosenstand, *The Moral of the Story*, *op.cit.*, p. 173.

upon being convinced that good will result. But there are times when, no matter how good the results, the means become too monstrous to be entertained. In his classic *The Brothers Karamozov*, Dostoyevsky has Ivan Karamazov saying to his brother Alyosha:

> "Imagine that you are creating a fabric of human destiny with the object of making men happy in the end, giving them peace and rest at last. Imagine that you are doing this but that it is essential and inevitable to torture to death only one tiny creature — that child beating its breast with its fist, for instance — in order to found that edifice on its unavenged tears. Would you consent to be the architect on those conditions? Tell me. Tell the truth."
>
> "No, I wouldn't consent," said Alyosha softly.
>
> "And can you accept the idea that the men for whom you are building would agree to receive their happiness from the unatoned blood of a little victim? And accepting it would remain happy forever?"
>
> "No, I can't admit it," said Alyosha suddenly, with flashing eyes.

And yet, let us admit it, the utilitarianism of Bentham, and even Mill, demands nothing less under these circumstances than the sacrifice of the infant. Most of us would say, with Alyosha, "I can't admit it." There must be something very wrong with a theory that would call for such a sacrifice and call it good.

A second problem with utilitarianism is precisely that it does not respect, indeed cannot respect, the rights of minorities. The principle of utilitarianism is that one should always act in such a way as to maximize pleasure and minimize pain for the majority of the people. What then of the minorities? They are just out of luck. Now of course, anyone might, at any given time, wind up in the minority; and isn't democracy predicated upon the principle of majorities ruling through the vote. The answer is, yes. But this was one of the major reasons that Plato rejected democracy as a system of government. He had stood by and watched his friend, Socrates, condemned to death by a majority vote of the Athenian Counsel, and it soured him on democracy for the rest of his life. Mob rule, he called it.

> Of course I saw in a short time that [the Thirty] made the former government look in comparison like an age of gold. Among other things they set an elderly man, Socrates, a friend of mine, who I should hardly be ashamed to say was the justest man of his time. . .against

> one of the citizens. . .Their purpose was to connect Socrates to their government whether he wished or not. . .When I observed all this — and some other similar matters of importance — I withdrew in disgust from the abuses of those days.[15]

We can all think of instances in which the majority have simply been wrong, and the minority have been right, and in working for the happiness of the majority wrong things were done. No better examples exist than those of Nazi Germany during the period from 1933 to 1945, or of our own society in its treatment of the American Indians. The fact is that it was very utilitarian to move the Indians off their lands so that those who were greater in number and wanted the land could have it. This worked for the pleasure of the majority, and the minority needed to understand that it was all good — by a utilitarian definition. But was it actually good? I remain unpersuaded.

Finally, none of us is a prophet, but that is what is required if we are to do things based upon what the results will be. If we enact a law and say it will be a good law, on what basis are making that assessment? On the basis that there is something inherently good in the law itself? Hardly. We are doing it because we say the law will result in good things. But this is frequently not what happens. History is littered with laws that someone was convinced would be good, but that turned out to be very bad. What's the problem. The problem is that we can't look into the future, and we can't always tell what the results of our actions will be. And if we cannot, then it is really impossible to ever say of an action — applying the utilitarian principle — this action is good. We just don't know.

Ethicists have made attempts to correct the first two problems — those of manifest evils done to produce good results, and the need to respect the rights of minorities — but there is no correcting this third problem, unless and until someone shows up who is able to look into the future. All we can say is that we do the best we can to judge the results of our actions.

Act and Rule Utilitarianism

The perceived necessity to get around problems like the one described by Ivan Karamazov caused some utilitarians to break ranks with their classical brethren and to propose a new kind of utilitarianism. The

15 Plato, *Letter: VII*, 324E, trans. L.A. Post, in *Plato: The Collected Dialogues*, p. 1575.

Act utilitarianism: that act is good which results in the greatest good for the greatest number.

Rule utilitarianism: that type act (or rule) is good which results in the greatest good for the greatest number.

classical utilitarians, those who remain true to Bentham and Mill, are known as Act Utilitarians. The breakaway group are called Rule Utilitarians. In order to understand the difference in the two, we will give again the classical definition of utilitarianism. An act is good if it results in the greatest pleasure or reduction of pain for the greatest number of people. By this definition, and as understood by classical utilitarians, an act that results in good cannot possibly be bad. And this, incidentally, is **act utilitarianism**. Notice that it is the individual act that we are judging, and the individual consequences that flow from the individual act. The same act, given different circumstances and consequences might be judged bad. The act itself is always morally neutral for the act utilitarian.

But as we have already seen this can lead us down some strange intellectual alleys, such as the one presented by Ivan Karamazov. It is difficult, if not morally repugnant, to many people to call the torturing to death of a child good, and this has led many people to abandon utilitarianism as untenable. But the rule utilitarians think they can still salvage something, and they propose the following change to the definition of utilitarianism: a type of act that results in the greatest pleasure or reduction of pain for the greatest number is a good type of act. I realize that my phrasing of this principle is a bit awkward, but I want the student to see that the insertion of a single word can make a great difference in the meaning of a claim or proposition. The word "type" takes us from act to **rule utilitarianism.**

It is the type of act, or the rule, that we ought to be looking at, say the **rule utilitarians,** and not just the individual act alone. The rule is that we do not torture innocent victims in order to benefit the rest of us, because we have learned over time that this does not lead to good things for us all. It leads ultimately to disaster. The final two statements are necessary if we wish to preserve consequentialism in anything like its pristine form. I'll have more to say about this in a moment.

Let's have a little fun by setting up an imaginary situation into which we plunge two ethicists, an act utilitarian and a rule utilitarian. Same situation, same set of facts, different moral conclusions. Two students of philosophy are drafted into the army in 1943, and ultimately wind up as lieutenants in the same airborne outfit that makes the jump over Saint Lo on D-Day. One of them happens to be an act utilitarian and the other is a rule utilitarian. They manage to survive the jump, and along with the survivors of their unit they fight their way inland through the hedgerow country. Within a week they have captured several square miles of territory, and with it they have taken fifteen German prisoners. But all is not well. They have also been cut off from their main unit. They don't know exactly where they are, nor do they know exactly where they are going, but they know there are Germans all around them. To make matters worse, they are running short on both food and ammunition.

Question: What are they to do with the German prisoners?

They can't keep them because they can't feed them. If they turn them loose, there is every reason to believe that the Germans will rejoin their units and lead them against the isolated Americans, with the result that the Americans will probably be killed, or, if not, taken prisoner. That evening the two officers meet with their sergeants to discuss what they ought to do.

The act utilitarian is convinced that there is only one right thing to do. They must kill the prisoners. The rule utilitarian is shocked at the very suggestion. They can't kill unarmed prisoners; not only is it against the Geneva Convention's rules of lawful conduct for warring parties, but it is immoral. The act utilitarian argues however that their first duty is to themselves and to their unit, and they cannot in good conscience let the prisoners go knowing that the probable results will be the death of many of their own men.

This is an example of what philosophers call dilemma ethics, a situation one hopes never to be in. These men are clearly on the horns of a dilemma, and it seems that there is no right answer, and no wrong one. In the one case, act utilitarianism bids them kill the prisoners. In the other, rule utilitarianism bids them not kill the prisoners. What shall they do? What would you do?

The same sort of problems come up in so-called lifeboat ethics. You probably all know the scenario. A ship is sunk, and a handful of survivors manage to save themselves in one lifeboat. In the lifeboat they have enough food and water to sustain ten people until they can manage to get to the nearest land; but there are fifteen people in the boat. Some of these are very sick, and probably can't make it to land at any rate; but it is clear that if an attempt is made to save all, most, if not all, will perish. A situation very much like this one actually occurred, and provided the raw material for a 1957 movie, *Abandon Ship*, starring Tyrone Power. For the act utilitarian, there is no question about what must be done in this case. The sick individuals must be thrown overboard in order that those who are able to row the boat be given a chance to live. We sacrifice some to save many. The act is good by definition.

But how are we to distinguish the dissenting party as rule utilitarians?

Wouldn't a divine command theorist say it is wrong to throw the weaker and sick overboard? This is why I earlier pointed out that how one establishes the "rule" to be followed is what makes one a rule utilitarian rather than some species of absolutist. If I say it is wrong to kill the weak and sickly in this case, and the reason it is wrong is because God has said it is wrong, then I am not a rule utilitarian. In fact, classical utilitarians would be quick to point out that some rule utilitarians have basically abandoned utilitarianism in establishing their rules, or their types of acts that one ought to follow. The true rule utilitarian, however, has an answer for them.

Rules, or types of acts, are established in consequential fashion. The rule utilitarian holds that his rules are not those handed by God to Moses, but rather they are rules that have been shown over many years of experience to result in the greatest good for the greatest number. Whereas violating the rules thus established has proven in the long run to be detrimental to the greatest number.

The Idealists

There may be however more to be said about the basic values underlying utilitarianism. Pleasure and pain are useful as the primary values presumably because that is what good and bad are ultimately reducible to, and because there is some indication that these are universal and intrinsic values. Everyone is after pleasure, and everyone is trying to avoid pain. But is it possible to identify other things that might have intrinsic worth, that humans might seek as ends in themselves? Some modern utilitarians have suggested that there are.

Departing from Bentham and Mill, ethicists such as G.E. Moore and Hastings Rashdall, have suggested that power, knowledge, beauty, or moral qualities have intrinsic value, and that any of these might well serve as ends to be sought. In other words, an act would be good if it led to knowledge or beauty. This position is sometimes called **ideal utilitarianism.**

Ideal utilitarianism has the advantage that it extends the base of utilitarianism so as to weaken the charges that utilitarians are pure hedonists and nothing more. Yet finally it is not clear that it does anything of the sort. Aristotle, one of the first philosophers to formally tie happiness and good together, and to say that happiness[16] is the thing we all are after, was clear to distinguish between things we value for themselves and things we value because they lead to something else. To push matters — do we desire

---

[16] The hedonists, who came after Aristotle, were the ones who replaced happiness with pleasure. But it is not clear whether this is a replacement or merely a redefining. Perhaps happiness and pleasure do not equate, if by pleasure one means purely physical enjoyment. Still, the two are similar enough that they might pass for fraternal, if not identical, twins.

knowledge for its own sake, or because it leads to something else, namely a species of pleasure? Do we desire power or beauty for their own sake? In fact, isn't pure pleasure what all beauty seekers are finally after? Would they really be after beauty if they derived pain from it?

Pleasure and pain are bedrock for classical utilitarians. It is these, they say, that motivate us all, and it is these that give value to the ethical theory to which the utilitarians hold.

Utilitarianism: a Postscript

One of the things I keep trying to do with students, especially in the area of values and ethics, is to get them to see that ethics is not simply a matter of opinion and personal taste. We can think logically, rationally about ethics, just as we do with any other area of philosophy. Some ethical systems are better than others, and they are better because they have a greater degree of internal consistency, because they lead to better solutions to ethical problems, and because over the years they have been proven viable in the market place of human experience.

In science, one of the things that is asked of any theory is whether or not it has generated research. A theory that generates a great deal of research is considered important, whether or not it is ultimately thrown out. By this standard alone utilitarianism is an enormously important theory. And utilitarianism is not about to be thrown out. Most any current philosophical journal devoted to ethical issues will contain essays either by utilitarians or espousing some sort of consequentialism, and most every legislative body meeting in the world is enacting laws on the supposition that they will result in the greatest good for the greatest number. All of us, at one time or another, will find ourselves making use of the principle of utility in reaching ethical decisions. But what are we to do when we cannot use it — as in the story told by Ivan Karamazov? Perhaps Immanuel Kant has the answer.

Chapter 15
Deontological Ethics

I am feeling both philosophical and rhetorical.
I am about to define that imperative which is categorical.
The categorical imperative is an absolute moral law
Which bids me neither steal from my neighbor, nor break his jaw,
Lest I set up thereby a universal moral reaction
That leaves me beside him, bankrupt and in traction.

ne day two men, Smith and Jones, became involved in an argument so heated that Smith vowed to kill Jones. Smith went home, got a loaded pistol, and went to the home of Jones, hiding in the bushes beside the front porch and waiting for him. By the time Jones came home it was night, there was no moon, and it was very dark. But Smith was certain he recognized Jones as he bounded up the steps and onto the front porch. He opened fire, and killed. . . And this is where the story becomes interesting, and loaded with heavy ethical baggage.

Within minutes sirens wailed and police cars drove up. Then, surprised, Jones came out of his home. The man lying face down in a pool of his own blood was not Jones at all, but someone of nearly the same size and dressed in the sorts of clothes Jones typically wore. The police identified the dead man as Green, a dangerous homicidal maniac recently escaped from the locked criminal ward of a nearby mental hospital. He was suspected in the deaths of five people since his escape, and there is little doubt (for it turned out he was armed with a handgun) that he intended to kill Jones and his entire family.

Smith was hailed as a hero, feted and lionized. He had, with courage and by putting himself at risk, done the sort of thing of which movies and books are made. He was quoted in the local newspapers as saying modestly, "Shucks, it was nothin'."

The statement, "It was nothin'," hardly begins to tell the whole story. It was something all right, but it was not ethical and it was not heroic. It was cold-blooded murder.

Wasn't it?

Well, that depends upon who is doing the talking. A utilitarian would have to say that it was a good act because it led to that which was good for an entire family, and at the same time it rid society of a dangerous madman. Even a rule utilitarian, looking solely at the action, would probably have to say that the deed was a good one, assuming that there is a rule (unwritten but understood) that one has a duty to defend innocent people when they are threatened with death.

But what do you say? Has Smith done an ethical thing? You would probably say that he has not because at some point the matter of intention must be given consideration, and the intention of Smith was not to save Jones, but to kill him. Smith did the right thing purely by accident, and there are few of us who would assign the designation good to Smith's action. "It was nothin'," he said, and from an ethical standpoint he is right. He is an ethical zero. Or perhaps he has slid down into the minus column, and ethically he is minus twenty. One thing is certain, by going about playing the role of the modest hero he is only compounding things by adding lying to his already sorry behavior. These sorts of situations lead to the formulation of a principle that may be of some value in determining whether an action is right or wrong. The principle is that intention has something to do with ethics. If one intends to do a bad thing, as Smith did, it seems strange to credit him with behaving ethically just because it came out right by accident. Conversely, if someone sets out to do a good thing, things go wrong, and the whole thing winds up rather badly, don't we nevertheless give him or her some credit for good intentions? If any of this makes sense to you, then you are looking at the world of ethics from Immanuel Kant's point of view.

Kant, you will remember, was a philosopher committed to the idea that rational thought was the way to arrive at truth. He was the one who felt the need to answer David Hume's skepticism. It is not surprising to find him bringing logic and rational thought to bear on the problem of ethics. He certainly did not agree with the utilitarians, for he could see all sorts of problems with an end-defines-the-means sort of theory. But his main problem was that utilitarians left out the critical element of intention. If one did not intend to do the right thing, or if he or she did the right thing only because of how they thought their actions would turn out, Kant saw nothing ethical in the action at all.

He applauded the utilitarian effort to put ethics on a logical basis; for he was well aware that religious absolutism was vulnerable to attack from those who, for what ever reason, refused to accept the religious source of the absolutes. And yet he was firmly convinced that there was such a thing as right and wrong, and that these definitions did not change with circumstances or cultures. Was it possible to establish a **rational absolute**, one that any reasonable person, anywhere, anytime would be able to apply? He intended to make the attempt. The result is the famous categorical imperative, one of the most widely discussed and written-about moral principles in the history of western philosophy. It is a system based upon the idea of one doing one's duty,[1] regardless of consequences.

A Good Will is Truly Good

It is interesting — at least I have always thought it so — that Immanuel Kant produced his deontological ethical theory in the Enlightenment, the same period of history during which Jeremy Bentham was formulating utilitarianism; and I have wondered what it was about this period that spawned so many important philosophical ideas. Possibly it was because this was the period during which absolutism in government was falling to the gun, self-government was on the rise, and there was a need for rational answers to questions which had up till now been answered by authorities. If King Louis is not around to tell me what is right and wrong, then I may have to think for myself.

Immanuel Kant, as we have seen, left us a rational ethical absolute of such importance that, in the humble opinion of this teacher of philosophy, who wrote his dissertation in ethics, one must have some knowledge of it to be considered educated. So stay with me and I will tell you all about it, and then you can swagger around showing off your wisdom to your more poorly instructed friends. "Your behavior is in obvious violation of the categorical imperative. . ." They'll learn to love you for it.

Kant formulated his principle in one of his most famous works, *The Groundwork of the Metaphysical of Morals*, sometimes called simply the *Metaphysic of Morals*, and sometimes simply the *Groundwork*.[2] Like all of Kant's work, it is difficult to follow; but, also like all of Kant's work, making the effort to follow it will pay rich dividends. Early in the book he defines

---

[1] Greek = *deon* = duty. Thus, Kant's is called deontological ethics.

[2] Depending upon which translation you may get, the book is called *The Groundwork of the Metaphysic of Morals*, or *The Foundations of the Metaphysic of Morals*.

good, and his definition is nothing like that of Bentham and Mill. Pleasure — forget it.

> Nothing in the world — indeed nothing even beyond the world — can possibly be conceived which could be called good without qualification except a *good will.* Intelligence, wit, judgment, and the other talents of the mind, however they may be named, or courage, resoluteness, and perseverance as qualities of temperament, are doubtless in many respects good and desirable. But they can become extremely bad and harmful if the will, which is to make use of these gifts of nature and which in its special constitution is called character, is not good. It is the same with the gifts of fortune. Power, riches, honor, even health, general well-being, and the contentment with one's condition, which is called happiness, make for pride and even arrogance if there is not a good will to correct their influence on the mind and on its principles of action so as to make it universally conformable to its end. It need hardly be mentioned that the sight of a being adorned with no feature of a pure and good will, yet enjoying uninterrupted prosperity, can never give pleasure to a rational impartial observer. Thus the good will seems to constitute the indispensable condition even of worthiness to be happy.[3]

Bentham had begun his formulations with the supposition that good equals pleasure. Mill later refined this somewhat by talking about happiness. Aristotle would have been in agreement with Mill, the hedonists would have been in agreement with Bentham. Kant is in agreement with neither, and the question of intent lies at the heart of the reason for his disagreement. In saying that a "good will" is the only thing that is good without qualification, he has brought internal motive into the discussion. In order to be an ethical person, one must set out to do the right thing, must have a will set on doing that which is good. Without good will, the intent to do that which is good, no matter what one does or how it turns out, he or she cannot be called ethical.

You probably also noticed, in the passage from Kant quoted above, that he specifically talks about happiness. This cannot have been by accident.

---

[3] **Kant, Immanuel, *Foundations of the Metaphysic of Morals,* trans. Lewis White Beck, Indianapolis: Bobbs-Merrill, 1959, p. 9.**

Kant was well aware of Aristotle's *Nicomachean Ethics*, and must also have known of the work of British philosophers, who leaned heavily on pleasure and happiness as objects of actions in their morals systems. Kant says that without a good will one can't even be happy. What doth it profit a man if he gain the whole world and lose his soul?

I must say that even at this early stage I have a problem with what Kant has said, and I might as well get it off my chest. He hasn't defined good, as did Aristotle and Bentham, but appears to assume that we all know what he is talking about when he says a good will. Maybe we do, and maybe we don't, but this failure leads to some pointed criticism from one of the most famous utilitarians, John Stuart Mill. We will see this later on. In the meantime let's get back to Kant's fascinating argument. Intent is the important thing, as he makes clear, without regard to results.

> The good will is not good because of what it effects or accomplishes or because of its adequacy to achieve some proposed end; it is good only because of its willing, i.e., it is good of itself. And, regarded for itself, it is to be esteemed incomparably higher than anything which could be brought about by it in favor of any inclination or even of the sum total of all inclinations. Even if it should happen that, by a particularly unfortunate fate or by the niggardly provision of a stepmotherly nature, this will should be wholly lacking in power to accomplish its purpose, and if even the greatest effort should not avail it to achieve anything of its end, and if there remained only the good will (not as a mere wish but as the summoning of all the means in our power), it would sparkle like a jewel in its own right, as something that had its full worth in itself. Usefulness or fruitlessness can neither diminish nor augment this worth.[4]

This is really extraordinary. The good will becomes the crown jewel in Kant's system, or, to mix metaphors, the foundation stone upon which everything is based. Without a good will there can be no ethics, for there will be no motivation for one to be ethical (i.e., do the right thing); but with a good will, even if one is prevented from doing the right thing, he or she is counted ethical by Kant, and the good will shines like a jewel in a rubbish

---

[4] Ibid., p. 10.

pile.

But there must be more to it than this, otherwise I could sit around from now on basking in the goodness of my intentions and never get anything done. "Remember, boy," said one of my elders on an occasion, "that the road to hell is paved with good intentions." Kant knows this, and that is why he says parenthetically, "Not as a mere wish but as a summoning of all the means in our power." It is not enough simply to intend good, one must actively, and with all the means in one's power, get out and try to do good. In fact, it is one's duty to do good, and this leads us to the next stone in the foundation.

England Expects Every Man, Etc.

". . . to do his duty." So runs the full quote. I assume of course that all of my students know about Lord Nelson and his victory over the French fleet at Trafalgar. Suppose we amend Nelson's famous signal as follows: Kant expects each human to do his or her duty. As a matter of fact, if one's will is good, then the doing of one's duty can be taken for granted.

> We have, then, to develop the concept of a will which is to be esteemed as good of itself without regard to anything else. It dwells already in the natural sound understanding and does not need so much to be taught as only to be brought to light. In the estimation of the total worth of our actions it always takes first place and is the condition of everything else. In order to show this, we shall take the concept of duty. It contains that of a good will, though with certain subjective restrictions and hindrances; but these are far from concealing it and making it unrecognizable, for they rather bring it out by contrast and make it shine forth all the brighter.[5]

A good will is impossible, in any ethically meaningful sense, unless it has an objective. Without that it becomes like some sort of fragmented sentence with a subject but no predicate; and the object of a good will is duty. What is one to do with one's good will? One is to do one's duty. It is this that gives the label deontological to Kant's ethical theory.

I never come to this point in teaching Kant's ethics without thinking of Spike Lee's movie *Do the Right Thing.* This is a film I think worth seeing,

---

[5] **Ibid., p. 13.**

because it raises so many ethical questions without being preachy, and because the concepts right and wrong, while important to the meaning of the film, seem to be lost on the individuals caught up in the strange events that transpire on a hot summer day in Brooklyn. Early in the movie the main character, Mookie, meets "Da Mayor," a confused but well-meaning old man, who tells him that he must always do the right thing. By the time the movie is over Mookie, and others, have trashed Sal's pizzeria, threatened to do the same thing to a store owned by a Korean, and the police have killed Radio Raheem.

At the end of the movie I found myself thinking, "Do the right thing. . .but what is the right thing to do?"

This is precisely the question Kant wishes to answer. I am to do my duty. Now, will someone tell me what my duty is. Kant proceeds to do that very thing, but a certain warning is implicit in his formulation. If he tells me my duty, then he expects me to do it. If I say I cannot, he has an answer for me: Ought implies can. This famous statement is another of those gems that lie near the heart of Kantian ethics. That which I *ought* to do (in this case, my duty) I *can* do, and to say that I cannot is to reveal that I am lacking in the most important quality of all — a good will.

Universal Morality

How different is my duty from yours when we are in the same circumstances and an ethical decision is called for? Kant's answer is, none at all. We both have the same duty, for we are bound by a moral principle that is universal, and that is discoverable by rational thought and by the asking of a simple question. The question is, what would I do if I knew that my action would become a universal moral law for everyone in this same circumstance? To illustrate how this might work, let me tell you two true stories.

When I was thirteen years old my friend, also thirteen, won a trip to Colorado Springs by selling subscriptions to a local newspaper. He and the other winners made the trip on a bus, staying at motels along the way. My friend did what many people do, at each motel he loaded up his suitcase with whatever he could put his hands on, and by the time he reached Colorado Springs he had a satchel full of washcloths, towels, ashtrays. Then one evening when he was out someone broke into his motel room and stole his suitcase of stolen goods. Outraged, he sshouted, "Some dirty, no good thief. . ."

Or, if that one wasn't amusing enough for you, try this. I was recently standing in the lobby at the local YMCA talking to the receptionist. She told me an irate mother had called the day before to complain that someone had stolen her son's towel. She couldn't believe that at the YMCA, of all places, someone would steal a towel. "Now just a minute," said the receptionist. "Maybe it's not stolen. Maybe it's only misplaced. What did it look like and I'll see if I can find it." With no apparent embarrassment the woman said, "It was large, white, and had 'Hilton' printed across it."

The problem with these two individuals is that they are attempting to bind others to a moral code from which they have exempted themselves. When we see something like this, the behavior of the individuals involved is so ridiculous that we laugh, because the inconsistency is so obvious that it is funny. I could tell this story virtually anywhere in the world, and assuming my audience is a rational one I would get the same laugh I do from students in this country. Why is this? Because, Kant would say, there is a universal, inborn idea of morality, and it starts with the unassailable truth that the behavior one expects from others ought to be no different from what one is willing to perform. If I steal from other people, it seems very strange that I would attempt to raise some sort of moral outrage in others when I am stolen from. The same is true of lying, murdering, or anything else of the sort. What I give is what I ought to be willing to get.

Now this treatment of the categorical imperative is admittedly a shallow one, but it will do to get the student into the proper frame of mind. Now, let's hear from Kant again.

> [T]he pre-eminent good can consist only in the conception of the law in itself (which can be present only in a rational being) so far as this conception and not the hoped-for effect is the determining ground of the will. This pre-eminent good, which we call moral, is already present in the person who acts according to this conception, and we do not have to look for it first in the result.
>
> But what kind of law can that be, the conception of which must determine the will without reference to the expected result? Under this condition alone the will can be called absolutely good without qualification. Since I have robbed the will of all impulses which could come to it from obedience to any law, nothing remains to serve as a principle of the will except universal conformity of its action to law as such. That is, *I should never act in such a way that I could not also will that my maxim should be a universal law.* Mere conformity to law as such (without assuming any particular law applicable to certain actions) serves as the principle of the

> will, and it must serve as such a principle if duty is not to be a vain delusion and chimerical concept. The common reason of mankind in its practical judgments is in perfect agreement with this and has this principle constantly in view.[6]

The categorical imperative is Kant's universal moral absolute: act always so that you can will that your action become a universal moral law.

Look back to the second paragraph of this quote to the portion that I have italicized. This is the **categorical imperative.** Never act in such a way that you cannot also will that the maxim of your behavior should become a moral law; or, as he puts it later, and in a positive form: *act always so that you can will the maxim of your behavior to become a universal law.* In a footnote, Kant defines "maxim" as the principle of subjective volition. This is precisely what my friend, and the woman with the towel, were not doing. They had stolen, but they did not want anyone to steal from them, which means that they could not will the maxim of their behavior to become universal law. Consequently, they had violated the categorical imperative and had behaved immorally. Their duty might easily have been pointed out to them had anyone been there to give them a bit of guidance. Are you willing to have people steal from you? Are you willing to establish a society in which theft is a way of life? Remember that whatever rule you establish will, in theory, become the rule by which the rest of the universe will operate — in this case, if you see something you want, take it, and do not bother to ask whose it is. If you do not feel that you can live in a society that operates on this principle, then you are not allowed to establish the principle. Only when you can rationally say, "Yes," to a principle, thereby raising it to a universal, are you allowed to act upon it. In fact, it is stronger than this. When you say, "Yes," to a principle it is your duty to act upon it.

Kant is convinced that any rational human, anywhere in the world, in any time period, will, if he or she is honest, come up with the same answer.

Notice the broad sweep of the categorical imperative. It can handle, not only the question of whether or not I ought to steal, but of whether or not I ought to tell the truth, whether or not I am allowed to cheat, murder the innocent, rape, and so on. Further, I never let a group of students get away from me without making sure they understand that this is *the* categorical imperative, not *a* categorical imperative. The use of the definite article, rather than the indefinite, is of critical importance; for there is only one, not many. This single rational absolute is meant by Kant to govern the

---

[6] *Ibid.*, pp. 17, 18.

entire ethical life of all humans, now and forever. Does it? We shall see.

Another thing that one needs to see and understand is that this is a matter of being rational, of thinking correctly. If one violates the categorical imperative, as did my friend and the towel lady, and if he or she goes on to defend the behavior as correct, then they are guilty of self-contradiction, thus of being irrational. This is a bit more difficult to grasp that anything that has gone before because it is not exactly what one expects. But think of a self-contradictory statement. Remember, for example, the claim, "It is wrong for one to impose one's moral values on others." The statement contradicts itself; it is itself an imposition of a moral value. Here is another: "There are no such things as absolutes." The statement is contradictory, being itself an absolute. Now take the thief, and his implied maxim: stealing is right. If so, then why are you reacting in anger when someone steals from you? You are demonstrating that you do not think stealing is right, and you are contradicting yourself.

In the *Foundations* Kant uses another example that shows just how useful the categorical imperative can be as a moral principle, that of making a promise one does not intend to keep. Because the passage contains several important points, and also one large problem, I will quote from it at length, with apologies to the student who wishes to finish quickly and watch television.

> May I, when in distress, make a promise with the intention not to keep it? I easily distinguish the two meanings which the question can have, viz., whether it is prudent to make a false promise, or whether it conforms to my duty. Undoubtedly the former can often be the case, though I do see clearly that it is not sufficient merely to escape from the present difficulty by this expedient, but that I must consider whether inconveniences much greater than the present one may not later spring from this lie. Even with all my supposed cunning, the consequences cannot be so easily foreseen. Loss of credit might be far more disadvantageous than the misfortune I now seek to avoid, and it is hard to tell whether it might not be more prudent to act according to a universal maxim and to make it a habit not to promise anything without intending to fulfill it. But it is soon clear to me that such a maxim is based only on an apprehensive concern with consequences.
>
> To be truthful from duty, however, is an entirely different thing from being truthful out of fear of disadvantageous consequences, for in the former case the concept of the action itself contains a law for me, while

> in the latter I must first look about to see what results for me may be connected with it. For to deviate from the principle of duty is certainly bad, but to be unfaithful to my maxim of prudence can sometimes be very advantageous to me, though it is certainly safer to abide by it. The shortest but most infallible way to find the answer to the question as to whether a deceitful promise is consistent with duty is to ask myself: Would I be content that my maxim (of extricating myself from difficulty by a false promise) should hold as a universal law for myself as well as for others? And could I say to myself that everyone may make a false promise when he is in a difficulty from which he otherwise cannot escape? I immediately see that I could will the lie but not a universal law to lie. For with such a law there would be no promises at all, inasmuch as it would be futile to make a pretense of my intention in regard to future actions to those who believe this pretense or — if they overhastily did so — who would pay me back in my own coin. Thus my maxim would necessarily destroy itself as soon as it was made a universal law.[7]

In this passage we see Kant distinguishing between his deontological ethics and any form of ethical consequentialism. That which is done with an eye on the results, and not from a sense of duty, is not truly ethical. That imperative which commands from a position of duty is categorical. That imperative which commands from a position of consequences is, according to Kant, a "hypothetical imperative." To command hypothetically (i.e., "If you want this, then do this") is to play to the purely selfish side of the human. Even the most immoral of humans can do good if they expect to get good back for their efforts. But to command categorically is to play to the most rational and noble feature in human character; the individual thus motivated is asked to do his or her duty because it is the right thing, without regard to consequences. Here we see just how important intention is to Immanuel Kant.

There is, however, a snake lurking in the garden. You may have notice that in the quoted passage, after talking at length about doing one's duty without looking at the consequences, Kant finally ends up talking about the consequences, thus suggesting that one cannot get away from

---

[7] ***Ibid.*, pp. 18, 19.**

consequential considerations. This, too, will make him vulnerable to Mill, who will argue that Kant's deontological ethics is really a form of utilitarianism.

How This Works in Practice

Kant obviously can't cover all the possibilities of human conduct in a work this short, but it is an indication of the genius of the man and the brilliance of his theory that he doesn't have to. If he has indeed discovered a universal moral principle, as he claims to have done, one ought to be able to state it simply but apply it broadly. Having stated that one ought always to act so he might will the maxim of his behavior to become a universal moral law, he goes on to give some examples, breaking them down into four categories, perfect duties to oneself, perfect duty to others, imperfect duties to oneself, and imperfect duty to others. First, let us look at perfect duties to oneself, applying the categorical imperative.

> **Perfect duties to oneself.** A man who is reduced to despair by a series of evils feels a weariness with life but is still in possession of his reason sufficiently to ask whether it would not be contrary to his duty to himself to take his own life. Now he asks whether the maxim of his action could become a universal law of nature. His maxim, however, is: For love of myself, I make it my principle to shorten my life when by a longer duration it threatens more evil than satisfaction. But it is questionable whether this principle of self-love could become a universal law of nature. One immediately sees a contradiction in a system of nature whose law would be to destroy life by the feeling whose special office is to impel the improvement of life. In this case it would not exist as nature; hence that maxim cannot obtain as a law of nature, and thus it wholly contradicts the supreme principle of all duty.[8]

Now, just as there are perfect duties to oneself, there are perfect duties to others, to wit:

> **Perfect duty to others.** Another man finds himself forced by need to borrow money. He well knows that he will not be able to repay it, but he also sees that nothing will

---

[8] Ibid., pp. 39, 40.

> be loaned him if he does not firmly promise to repay it at a certain time. He desires to make such a promise, but he has enough conscience to ask himself whether it is not improper and opposed to duty to relieve his distress in such a way. Now, assuming he does decide to do so, the maxim of his action would be as follows: when I believe myself to be in need of money, I will borrow money and promise to repay it, although I know I shall never do so. Now this principle of self-love or of his own benefit may very well be compatible with his whole future welfare, but the question is whether it is right. He changes the pretension of self-love into a universal law and then puts the question: How would it be if my maxim became a universal law? He immediately sees that it could never hold as a universal law of nature and be consistent with itself; rather it must necessarily contradict itself. For the universality of a law which says that anyone who believes himself to be in need could promise what he pleased with the intention of not fulfilling it would make the promise itself and the end to be accomplished by it impossible; no one would believe what was promised to him but would only laugh at any such assertion as vain pretense.[9]

These perfect duties are predicated upon the believe that, as Kant says, one **could not will** that these actions (suicide and lying) become universal moral laws without at the same time contradicting oneself. The imperfect duties, which we shall now consider, are those that could, without self-contradiction, become universal moral laws, but that a good person would not will to be universal moral laws. The student may find it a bit difficult to draw a distinction between the two, but it is at least worth a try. Here we go.

> **Imperfect duty to oneself.** A third finds in himself a talent which could, by means of some cultivation, make him in many respects a useful man. But he finds himself in comfortable circumstances and prefers indulgence in pleasure to troubling himself with broadening and improving his fortunate natural gifts. Now, however, let him ask whether his maxim of neglecting his gifts besides agreeing with his propensity to idle amusement, agrees also with what is called duty. He sees that a system of

---

[9] Ibid., p. 40.

> nature could indeed exist in accordance with such a law, even though man (like the inhabitants of the South Sea Islands) should let his talents rust and resolve to devote his life merely to idleness, indulgence, and propagation — in a word, to pleasure. But he cannot possibly will that this should become a universal law of nature or that it should be implanted in us by a natural instinct. For, as a rational being, he necessarily wills that all his faculties should be developed, inasmuch as they are given to him for all sorts of possible purposes.[10]

Finally, we get:

> **Imperfect duty to others.** A fourth man, for whom things are going well, sees that others (whom he could help) have to struggle with great hardships, and he asks, "What concern of mine is it? Let each one be as happy as heaven wills, or as he can make himself; I will not take anything from him or even envy him; but to his welfare or to his assistance in time of need I have no desire to contribute." If such a way of thinking were a universal law of nature, certainly the human race could exist, and without doubt even better than in a state where everyone talks of sympathy and good will, or even exerts himself occasionally to practice them while, on the other hand, he cheats when he can and betrays or otherwise violates the rights of man. Now although it is possible that a universal law of nature according to that maxim could exist, it is nevertheless impossible to will that such a principle should hold everywhere as a law of nature. For a will which resolved this would conflict with itself, since instances can often arise in which he would need the love and sympathy of others, and in which he would have robbed himself, by such a law of nature springing from his own will, of all hope of the aid he desires.[11]

Each of these only serves as an example. Kant believed that any ethical questions that arose could be put to this test, and that in every case one could identify one's duty, either the perfect or the imperfect duty, and

---

[10] Ibid., pp. 40, 41.

[11] Ibid., p. 41.

that one could then, assuming he or she had a good will, proceed to do one's duty. But the categorical imperative has another aspect that may be even more important.

Further Developments

Kant goes on to identify what he calls necessary and contingent duties, both to oneself and to others. Because these duties flow from one of the most important moral principles ever enunciated, I ask the student's indulgence while I once again quote at length.

> Now, I say, man and, in general, every rational being exists as an end in himself and not merely as a means to be arbitrarily used by this or that will. In all his actions, whether they are directed to himself or to other rational beings, he must always be regarded at the same time as an end. All objects of inclinations have only a conditional worth, for if the inclinations and the needs founded on them did not exist, their object would be without worth. The inclinations themselves as the sources of needs, however, are so lacking in absolute worth that the universal wish of every rational being must be indeed to free himself completely from them. Therefore, the worth of any objects to be obtained by our actions is at all times conditional. Beings whose existence does not depend on our will but on nature, if they are not rational beings, have only a relative worth as means and are therefore called "things"; on the other hand, rational beings are designated "persons" because their nature indicates that they are ends in themselves, i.e., things which may not be used merely as means. Such a being is thus an object of respect and, so far, restricts all [arbitrary] choice. Such beings are not merely subjective ends whose existence as a result of our action has a worth for us, but are objective ends, i.e., being whose existence in itself is an end. Such an end is one for which no other end can be substituted, to which these being should serve merely as means. For, without them, nothing of absolute worth could be found, and if all worth is conditional and thus contingent, no supreme practical principle for reason could be found anywhere.[12]

Kant was onto something here that would have been a monumental achievement if he had done nothing else. He was affirming the absolute

---

[12] Ibid., pp. 46-47.

value of the individual, the rational creature, and he was affirming, as a part of his categorical imperative, the principle that humans are ends in themselves and ought never to be used merely as means to ends. Having grown up under a system of government that at least pays lip-service to this principle, we are apt to think that it is, as Thomas Jefferson, claimed for his inalienable rights, self-evident. In fact, it is truly revolutionary. No king alive in Kant's day — and there were many — would have dreamed of holding to such an outlandish rule. Imagine all the servants, slaves, day-laborers claiming to have value in and of themselves, demanding to be treated as if they were something other than things to be used. Kant affirmed that this was so, and it was a critical component of the categorical imperative.

> Thus if there is to be a supreme practical principle and a categorical imperative for the human will, it must be one that forms an objective principle of the will from the conception of that which is necessarily an end for everyone because it is an end in itself. Hence this objective principle can serve as a universal practical law. The ground of this principle is: rational nature exists as an end in itself. Man necessarily thinks of his own existence in this way; thus far it is a subjective principle of human actions. Also every other rational being thinks of his existence by means of the same rational ground which holds also for myself; thus it is at the same time an objective principle from which, as a supreme practical ground, it must be possible to derive all laws of the will. The practical imperative, therefore, is the following: *Act so that you treat humanity, whether in your own person or in that of another, always as an end and never as a means only.* [Italics mine][13]

In order to understand the importance of this principle, stop and ask yourself if you, in all of your life, were ever used by someone else. If you were (and I think it is a rare person who would answer, "No," to this one), then try to remember how you felt about it. You may have been angry, hurt, you may have felt cheapened by the affair, and you probably wanted to confront the individual who did the using to demand of them just who they thought they were, just why they would have treated you as if you were nothing more than a thing.

---

[13] Ibid., p. 47.

Martin Buber once wrote a book, now considered a classic, called *I and Thou* (*Ich und Du* in German), in which he deals with some of the problems that arise from the using of humans as if they are nothing more than things. I relate to things in the world as I-it. But I relate to another human — or I ought to at least — as I-thou. Everything in the world has either a value or a dignity. Rational creatures, according to Kant (and Buber picks up on this and develops it further), have dignity. There is no price that can be put on them. They are ends in themselves.

From this consideration, we get a new set of duties, similar in some ways to the perfect and imperfect duties that flow from the initial version of the categorical imperative, but particularly fashioned around the obligation to treat rational beings as ends in themselves and not merely as means to ends.

Now a necessary duty is one which rises to the level of a universal law, one which cannot be violated without creating some basic — if only symbolic — breach in nature. A contingent duty does not rise to this level, but is clearly one that the moral human understands ought to be performed. To illustrate, Kant uses the same four situations we have already seen: the man who is contemplating suicide; the individual who is seeking a loan that he knows he can't repay; the individual who is too lazy or self-indulgent to develop his natural talents; and the individual who is wondering whether or not to help those who are less fortunate than himself.

> [A]ccording to the concept of necessary duty to one's self, he who contemplates suicide will ask himself whether his action can be consistent with the idea of humanity as an end in itself. If, in order to escape from burdensome circumstances, he destroys himself, he uses a person merely as a means to maintain a tolerable condition up to the end of life. Man, however, is not a thing, and thus not something to be used merely as a means; he must always be regarded in all his actions as an end in himself. Therefore, I cannot dispose of man in my own person so as to mutilate, corrupt or kill him.[14]

I find this intriguing. Kant makes the case that just as I cannot use another human as a means to an end, neither can I use myself in this way. I have the same obligation to myself as I do to every other human, the same

---

[14] Ibid., p. 47.

obligation to every human that I have to myself.

Now, just as there are necessary duties to myself, as illustrated above, there are necessary duties to others.

> Second, as concerns necessary or obligatory duties to others, he who intends a deceitful promise to others sees immediately that he intends to use another merely as a means, without the latter containing the end in himself at the same time. For he whom I want to use for my own purposes by means of such a promise cannot possibly assent to my mode of acting against him and cannot contain the end of this action in himself. This conflict against the principle of other men is even clearer if we cite examples of attacks on their freedom and property. For then it is clear that he who transgresses the rights of men intends to make use of the persons of others merely as a means, without considering that, as rational beings they must always be esteemed at the same time as ends, i.e., only as beings who must be able to contain in themselves the ends of the very same action.[15]

Contingent duties to oneself also flow from the prohibition of not using oneself merely as a means to an end.

> Third, with regard to contingent (meritorious) duty to one's self, it is not sufficient that the action not conflict with humanity in our person as an end in itself; it must also harmonize with it. Now in humanity there are capacities for greater perfection which belong to the end of nature with respect to humanity in our own person; to neglect these might perhaps be consistent with the preservation of humanity as an end in itself but not with the furtherance of that end.[16]

And finally, we get the contingent duties to others.

> Fourth, with regard to meritorious duty to others, the natural end which all men have is their own happiness. Humanity might indeed exist if no one contributed to the happiness of others, provided he did not intentionally detract from it; but this harmony with humanity as an

---

[15] **Ibid., p. 48.**

[16] **Ibid., p. 48.**

> end in itself is only negative rather than positive if everyone does not also endeavor, so far as he can, to further the ends of others. For the ends of any person, who is an end in himself, must as far as possible also be my end, if that conception of an end in itself is to have its full effect on me.[17]

It boils down to this. We must be able to will that the maxim of our action become a universal law. There is one class of duties consisting of actions that, according to Kant, could not even be conceived as universal laws, nor could we possibly will them as such. These are the necessary or perfect duties, depending upon which version of Kant's imperative one applies. There are another class that could be conceived as universal laws, but we could not will them to be. These are the contingent or imperfect duties.

I could have paraphrased all of this, and this might have made it easier for you to understand, but I decided against it. I wanted you to get the flavor of what Kant actually wrote, and to get a real chance to struggle with his language and his thoughts. But now we can wrap the matter up by repeating the categorical imperative in its two-fold manifestation; and the student can fully appreciate what Kant has done, for the categorical imperaative is easy to remember and can be taken wherever one goes. Act always so that you can will the maxim of your behavior to become a universal moral law. Act always so as to treat rational beings, whether yourself or someone else, as ends in themselves and never merely as means to ends.

Is This The Golden Rule?

It has been noted that the categorical imperative bears a striking resemblance to the golden rule, and there can be no doubt that in the golden rule we have an ethical law so basic that it is all but universally recognized. It is precisely the universal character of the principle that interests Kant, for it demonstrates that there really is, operative on the purely rational level, a moral law that seems to be inborn in humans. You probably have heard that the golden rule, or its cousin the silver rule,[18] can be found in every culture

---

[17] **Ibid., pp. 48 49.**

[18] **Gold: do unto others as you would have them do unto you. Silver: what you don't want done to yourself, do not do to others. There is a difference in the two statements which I will allow the student to mull over. But they are close enough to one another to illustrate the point Kant wishes to make.**

and religion of the world. Whether or not this is true, the two rules certainly are widespread.

So What's the Problem?

There's always a problem, isn't there? Even in Eden the snake slithers in. The categorical imperative has been around for many years, and during that time philosophers have had ample opportunity to look at it from just about every angle. All agree that Kant made a major contribution to ethical theory; but all agree that the categorical imperative has its limitations. In some cases the categorical imperative just doesn't seem to work, and this has to mean that the universal moral principle Kant thought he had discovered isn't really universal.

You be the judge.

Consequentialism Rehashed?

Kant had no time for consequentialism if one intended thereby to define what was ethical and what was unethical. An imperative can command either categorically, or it can command hypothetically. The former commands because the right or wrong of an action resides in the action itself, and one is duty-bound to do the right thing. The latter commands because of what one expects to gain from performing the act — implicitly good consequences. The world's most loathsome degenerate will act to gain what he or she perceives as good, but it takes a truly noble person to act out of duty without regarding the results of the action. If I tell the truth, for example, because I profit thereby, I have done nothing worthy of note. If I tell the truth even when it costs me dearly, when it is against my interests, then I am an individual to be lauded.

But when carefully analyzed, isn't his theory consequentialism cloaked in absolutist language? John Stuart Mill thought so, and so have others. Consider, for example, the individual who borrows money, promising to repay it, when he knows that he can't do so. One cannot will that this sort of action become a universal law for behavior, says Kant, because what would happen, after all, if everyone started making promises with no intention of keeping them. What is Kant doing, Mill wishes to know, if not considering consequences? "What would happen if. . ." are the words that give the whole thing away. Mill thought that while ostensibly rejecting consequential ethics Kant had actually created an ethical theory that was propped up by the ultimate consideration of consequences.

Kant was never able to respond to Mill's criticism, because Kant was dead long before Mill had risen to challenge him. Thus, one can only speculate about what Kant might have said in reply. No doubt it would have been something like this: I am not dealing with consequences of actions, but with internal inconsistencies in principles. The consequences are not important; logical consistency is. Maybe Kant could have talked his way around Mill in this way, but there are more problems ahead.

The Dreaded Dilemma

Most ethics teachers like to use dilemma ethics occasionally, purely as a device for getting students to think about how they make ethical decisions. A dilemma is not, as many students seem to think, a problem and nothing more. By definition it is being stuck between a rock and a hard place, or the devil and the deep blue sea. Two roads diverge in a wood, and one is forced to travel one or the other, not both, and neither looks that appealing. How do you solve a ethical problem that forces you to choose between the lesser of two evils? And remember, someone has said, "The lesser of two evils is still evil."[19]

Kant dealt with this problem only to the extent of assuming that ethical conflict is always between duty and inclination. If that were indeed the case, then the categorical imperative could provide a solution to the problem by pointing us to duty and urging us, when inclinations conflict, to do our duty. But many times things are just not that simple. What happens when we are stuck between two duties, both of which we know we ought to do, but one of which must be left undone if we are to do the other? As an example, let us return to an earlier story, that of the lifeboat.

We have a lifeboat adrift some fifty miles off the coast of, let us say, West Africa. In the boat there is sufficient water and food to sustain fifteen people, assuming that all are rowing toward the coast, and assuming it will take about sixty hours to reach the coast, rowing steadily. The problem is that there are not fifteen people in the boat — there are twenty-five, and ten of these are injured to the extent that they cannot row. All they can do, in fact, is consume food and water that must go to the healthy individuals who are able to row the boat ashore. Any rational person can compute the situation and realize that not all of those in the boat can be kept alive, and any attempt to keep them alive will result in the deaths of everyone.

---

[19] **I have heard the remark attributed to Ayn Rand, but I have also heard it attributed to others. Frankly, I don't know where it originated. But I do find it useful.**

What are we to do?

Utilitarianism can answer the problem: the ten injured people will have to go overboard in order that the greater number may be saved. The categorical imperative leaves one on the horns of the dilemma. One cannot sacrifice the injured people, because to do so would be to deal with them as means to an end rather than as ends in themselves. On the other hand, since the injured people cannot be sacrificed, the healthy people that might otherwise be saved will be sacrificed, and all ultimately will die. It seems that the whole bunch are being used as means to an end, the end being that of proving the efficacy of the categorical imperative.

Hey, man, cut me some slack

There are times when all of us need a little room in which to move, but the categorical imperative gives not an inch. Duty is duty, case closed, and to not do one's duty is to show a lack of good will, or cowardice, or both. But surely there are times when reason demands we do something that in most cases would be considered unethical — lying for instance. Take the following case.

I am sitting in my office one fine afternoon when one of my students, Bill, comes rushing in and out of breath and asks me to hide him. Mary, it seems, is after him with a meat axe. I tell him to get in the closet and keep quiet, which he does. Shortly thereafter Mary rushes in, wild-eyed and angry, brandishing a meat axe, and demanding to know if I have seen Bill. I tell her, as calmly as I can, that I have not seen him, and I suggest that he has probably left the campus and gone to Texas for the weekend. Mary goes her way. Within a few days Mary has calmed down, Bill is still alive, and I am able to tell Mary that Bill had been in my office, hiding in the closet, but that I was afraid to tell her for fear that she would hurt Bill and perhaps kill him.

"Why, Dr. Miller," says Mary, "I am shocked and surprised that you lied to me. What would Immanuel Kant say?"

Good question. What *would* Immanuel Kant say?

He would probably get out of the difficulty by saying that the maxim is not what we think it is. We have apparently constructed the maxim thusly: can one lie in order to extricate one's self from a difficult position. The correct maxim, Kant would probably say, is may one sacrifice innocent victims in order to save oneself. When seen in that light, I have made Bill an innocent sacrifice in order to save myself from the raging Mary, and this is not permissible. One could not conceive of this as a universal law, nor could one will it to be such. But it is not clear that this gets us out of trouble.

Instead, it only raises another problem which opponents of Kant long ago recognized as a flaw in the categorical imperative.

The Loophole

One day an individual named Sam goes into a liquor store with a pistol, threatens to blow off the proprietor's head unless he immediately hands over all his money, and, having been given the money, leaves by the front door. The whole thing is video-taped, an all-points bulletin goes out, Sam's picture is shown over television to the local broadcasting area, and he is picked up by the police within twenty-four hours of the robbery.

Sam admits to the robbery, but says that he is doing it because he knows both the prosecuting attorney and the judge before whom the case will be tried. They are old school friends of his, and they all spent many hours together discussing philosophy. They were particularly interested in Immanuel Kant's categorical imperative. Sam is sure that, even having admitted to the holdup, he can reason his way out of a conviction by appealing to the judge's philosophical convictions.

Now imagine Sam defending himself before his old friend by saying that while he did in fact hold up the liquor store he can prove by means of the categorical imperative that it was the right thing to do under the circumstances. The prosecuting attorney, assuming he is willing to rise to the challenge, might point out that it would be impossible to justify a liquor store robbery by means of Immanuel Kant's theory.

Don't be too sure.

One would say, *prima facie*, that the attorney is right. The maxim, according to the attorney, is that if one has no money one may take it from others. One could not possibly will that this become a universal law for behavior, therefore the act is wrong. But must that actually be the maxim? The accused says that the attorney has the maxim wrong, but that he can hardly be blamed, for he doesn't know the full story.

The accused, as he tells the story, is not just financially broke, he also broken emotionally and spiritually. He was fired from his job after having been falsely accused by an envious fellow worker who bribed witnesses to confirm the false accusation. After his dismissal, his wife left him for another man, he was evicted from his home and had his car repossessed, and to make matters worse he has custody of his only child, a girl, who is suffering from a disease from which she would die if she could not get medicine. He, of course, could not afford to buy the medicine. The robbery of the liquor store was a last-ditch effort to obtain medicine for his suffering daughter.

Having told his story, Sam proposes a maxim quite different from the one proposed by the prosecuting attorney: if one finds oneself. . .And Sam reels off his personal story. Is it permissible to steal under these circumstances? The story is reminiscent of Jean Valjean's in *Les Miserables.* Sam has effectively constructed a maxim tailored to his situation, one that fits him and only him; and then he has invited the rational person to judge whether or not he has done the right thing. I can't imagine that his old school friend, now the judge, will actually let him off; but I can imagine that he will draw a much lighter sentence than he otherwise would have, and I can imagine both the judge and the prosecuting attorney getting together after the trial to discuss what went wrong with the categorical imperative.

What went wrong is that Immanuel Kant envisioned universal moral laws based upon rather general maxims. But there is nothing in his theory to prevent one's fine-tuning maxims, as Sam has done, until we have our ethical universe cluttered with laws and rules to fit situations so exact that they are apt to occur only once in a lifetime. Kant would have little time to spare for such intellectual shenanigans, and would no doubt accuse the persons so inclined of lacking good will and being more interested in justifying themselves than doing their duty. This may be true in some cases, but I am reluctant to say that it is true in all of them. Jean Valjean's story has universal appeal precisely because most people agree that stealing a loaf of bread to feed one's starving children may not always be the wrong thing to do, and certainly is not the sort of action that ought to land one in the galleys on the end of an oar. In cases such as this, or that of Sam the liquor store robber, some sort of consequentialism — in other words the hypothetical imperative — seems better able to handle the question of right or wrong. Or one might argue that duty (since we are discussing deontological ethics) must go first to the welfare of one's children and only later to the question of universal and abstract moral laws. This is precisely what Carol Gilligan thinks and has argued in *In a Different Voice.*

This is the sort of discussion that makes many students tired. Why, they want to know, must philosophers nitpick one another to death? We have in Kant's theory one which seemed so solid, so useful, when we first read it; now the critics come in, like the sharks on the big fish in *The Old Man and the Sea,* and when they are finished there is little left but the skeleton. Like it or not, this is what philosophy is all about, and it is in the ongoing dialectic that theories are refined, sharpened, made more useful, or, in the case of some, finally discarded as useless. The better ones stand up and the weaker ones are done in. Kant's categorical imperative is one of the better ones. It has stood up well, in spite of its weaknesses, and this is why we are still discussing it, two hundred years after its formulation.

But What About Those "Things"

All of the criticism we have seen so far is aimed squarely at that part of the categorical imperative which says you ought always to act so that you can will the maxim of your action to become a universal moral law. As we have seen, however, there is more to the categorical imperative, a second feature having to do with one's behavior toward his or her fellow humans: act always so as to treat humans, whether yourself or others, as ends in themselves and never merely as means to ends. In other words, never treat humans as mere things. Actually, Kant broadened this rule to read, instead of humans, rational beings. Or perhaps he didn't broaden it. Perhaps he shrank it. This is where the discussion becomes interesting.

Rational beings might include things other than humans, assuming there are other creatures possessed of rationality. If this is what Kant intended, then he broadened his law. But when I look around I am hard-pressed to find anything in our immediate universe, other than humans, who can be said to possess rationality. Do the great apes come in for a slice of the pie? How about computers?[20]

But is this what Kant intended? His writing makes it possible, but it appears that his actual intent is to narrow the law so that it takes in only rational adult humans. What about children and brain-damaged adults? Are they to be excluded? And if they are, does this make them mere things? Kant leaves us no clear answer, and we are left to speculate.

It is instructive that in this particular imperative he used the word "merely," otherwise the imperative itself would be unworkable. For example, if I pull into a service station and ask the attendant to fill up the tank of my ancient Volkswagen, are he and I not in truth using one another? Don't we use one another everyday? I recently saw Gloria Steinem and Hugh Hefner, seated together with a moderator in between, discussing their turbulent intellectual warfare, she as a passionate advocate for women's rights, he as the editor of a magazine, *Playboy*, that, if one believes the femi-

---

[20] **The question of artificial intelligence is one which philosophers have found fascinating for many years. A great deal has been written on the subject. Unfortunately we have neither the time nor the space to go into it here. The interested student will have no difficulty however finding reams of material. See, for example, *Computers, Minds, and Robots*, by William S. Robinson.**

nists, has exploited women for the most gross of purposes. It was a meeting ready-made for Immanuel Kant. At some point she raised the issue of women as sex objects, and he responded that there is nothing wrong with being an object, we are all objects (he said) for someone. "I don't wish to be an object for anyone," Ms. Steinem responded.

Kant would have pronounced both right, and both wrong. Hefner is correct in saying that we are all objects for others, but should have added, "To some extent." Steinem is right that no one should be an object for others, but should have added, "Merely." Insert those few words into the dialectic and the disagreement disappears, though I can't imagine Hefner and Steinem making peace on that basis.

None of this however answers the more basic question of what one must do to be considered rational, and whether or not rationality implies a certain standard of intelligence. If it is rational creatures who have dignity and not mere value, who must be treated as ends in themselves and not merely as means to ends, then how do we define rational. Kant, and even Bentham and Mill, share, along with the classic Greeks, an assumption that people are people, that all have the ability to reason, that there is a rough sort of intellectual parity between any member of the race and any other member, that they are all therefore capable of functioning at the necessary philosophical level to be included within the rational community. This is typical of the Enlightenment thinkers, typical of the founders of the American republic, typical of all those who believe in the principle of one man one vote. Is it justified? Perhaps not, but it may be the best we can do if we wish to set up a system that deals fairly with all.

I have always thought that one of the most important things anyone can learn from Immanuel Kant is the very principle we have been discussing. Always act so as to treat humanity, whether yourself or others, never as a mere means to an end, but always as ends in themselves. This is a major contribution to ethics.

Wrapping it Up

The *Groundwork of the Metaphysic of Morals* is without a doubt a work of great importance to anyone interested in the area of ethics — and that should be all of us. Immanuel Kant was disturbed to see ethics sliding away into a sort of utilitarianism which he felt pandered to one's self-interest. True ethical behavior demands a great deal more of one, he thought, and he insisted that to be ethical one must always do the right thing. But if one is to do the right thing, then one must know what to do.

Kant tried his best to established a rational (to avoid the complications of religion) universal moral principle, one that would work in all places, at all times, for anyone who was willing to think. It is possible that he went farther in this direction than anyone before or since.

We have seen, however, that the categorical imperative has its limitations, just as other ethical systems do. It is this that causes many people to throw up their hands in disgust and opt out of the dialectic with the conclusion that there are no such things as ethical standards, and that some type of relativism is all that is possible. This cannot be true, for it leaves us with ethical anarchy, and no society can long survive which goes this direction. The greater wisdom is to choose some form of ethical pluralism, which means being familiar with a variety of ethical theories and knowing when and how to apply them. There are times when one needs to take a consequential approach by considering what will result from certain actions. There are times when one must stand on principle and do the right thing regardless of the results. And there are times when one can profit from going back to the Greeks, as we shall see in the next chapter.

Chapter 16
Back to the Greeks

Round in a circle we go, we go,
Back where we started from.
Following footnotes to old Plato,
A long, long road we've come.
Now back we go to the golden Greeks,
The living and the dead.
He who discovers is he who seeks.
Fly fast to the fountain head.

Prior to this century there were few women in any of the academic fields. But during the latter part of the twentieth century women have made tremendous contributions to learning, particularly in philosophy, and particularly in the area of ethics. Virtue ethics, a rediscovery of the ethics of the Greeks, is primarily the work of women. Men like to draw up rules of conduct. Women seem much more interested in character. Now that I've made what may appear to some a sexist statement, let me tell you that I am taking my cue from some very brilliant women, particularly from Carol Gilligan.

But what, exactly, is virtue ethics?

In a recent political campaign, one of the candidates was accused of sexual misbehavior. There was nothing new in this, but there was something different in the way in which this candidate's supporters responded. "We don't wish to talk about character," they said. "We wish to talk about the issues." But on the other side the attackers were saying, "Character is the issue." Should character indeed be an issue in politics, or is what one does in one's on time no one else's business? Virtue ethicist Janet Smith answers like this:

> Most may agree that some true generalizations could be made about adulterers that would lead us to think that in general adultery is not compatible with the moral virtues that we admire. The reaction of the American public to

> the the extra-marital affairs of Jim Bakker and Gary Hart reveal well the widespread view that lying predictably accompanies the act of adultery and that adulterers are not to be trusted. Certainly, if someone told us that he or she wanted to be an honest, trustworthy, stable and kind individual with good family relationships, and wanted to know if an adulterous affair would conflict with this goal, we would have little

What is this business of character, and what does it have to do with ethics? To begin to answer this question, let's look back to the Janet Smith quote. Adulterers are not to be trusted, she says, because lying accompanies the act of adultery. Crucial to the understanding of what we in this century call virtue ethics is the conviction that unethical behavior flows from a flawed character, and that if the character is flawed all sorts of improper behavior can be expected, not just the particular behavior that has come to our attention.

I often introduce the subject of virtue ethics to my students with a question: is a man a liar because he lies, or does he lie because he is a liar. Push it farther. Is a woman a thief because she steals, or does she steal because she is a thief. Sometimes I have to wait for the answer while the students think about the difference in the two possibilities. If you say that someone is a liar because he or she has committed the act of lying it is probably because you have been raised within the Judeo-Christian tradition. To understand virtue ethics you must return to the world of the pre-Christian Greeks, and you have to get into their philosophical frame of reference. For them, one lies because he or she is a liar. It is a question of character. The liar will also steal from you and cheat you, because there is something deficient in his character, or in hers. Something wrong was done to this person during the period of growth and nurturing, and we now have a flawed product on our hands.

Friedrich Nietzsche, the German who declared the death of God, believed that since we have slain God we may no longer depend upon him as the source of morals and *a priori* goodness. In his famous work on ethics, *Beyond Good and Evil*, Nietzsche anticipates the question of what sort of ethics we can possibly hold to if, as he assumes, there is no God to issue and

---

[1] **Smith, Janet, "Moral Character and Abortion," in *Doing and Being*, Janet Graf Haber, New York: Macmillian, 1993, pp. 442-456.**

sustain rules and laws of conduct. Nietzsche urges a return to the Greeks, in whose society

> It is obvious that everywhere the designations of moral value were at first applied to men, and were only derivatively and at a later period applied to actions.[2]

Nietzsche was not a virtue ethicist, but some of his pronouncements are the sorts to which they might put an amen, as, for example, the one above. Among the classical Greeks, a good man was good because of what he was, not because of what he did; but because he was good he was expected to behave in a good way. This may be difficult for young Americans to follow, but perhaps as we look in greater depth at this old Greek idea of ethics, resurrected and brought back to serve our needs, there will be something in it that will find lodging in a few hearts as, I humbly confess, it has in mine.

Aristotle and Arete

Arete (Greek) and virtu (Latin): words which are difficult to translate. The best rendering is probably excellence. We are talking about character.

The Greek word, ***arete***, has no English equivalent, nor does its Latin cousin, ***virtu***. One can see, however, that it is the source of the English, "virtue," and this is how it has been translated by most scholars working with Greek texts. This is unfortunate, because "virtue" has picked up some negative baggage over the years, so that today we are apt to think of a virtuous person as something of a prig, a goody-two-shoes, one a bit too good for other people, in a conceited, superior way. This is not how the Greeks saw things.

Impossible to translate with just a word, *arete* meant excellence, virtue, goodness, rightness, completeness, competence. Or, better yet, for the Greek male, *arete* meant the incomparable hero Odysseus, the man who embodied everything a free Greek citizen ought to be. Greek religion had no revelator, no holy book, no central figure. The closest to any of these were the two epics of Homer, *The Odyssey* and *The Iliad*, which defined, for the Greeks, what they were as a people, and what anyone was if he (Odysseus) or she (Penelope) was to be respected as proper and correct. There were certain qualities one was expected to have, and these qualities, either inborn or built in by training, were ethical bedrock. One was not good because one

---

2 Nietzsche, Friedrich, *Beyond Good and Evil*, in *The Philosophy of Nietzsche*, New York: Random House, 1927, p. 579.

Virtue ethics: ethics that go back to the Greeks, and that are based upon certain cardinal virtues that go to make up that elusive thing called character.

did the right thing. Rather, one did the right thing because one was good. And one was good because he or she possessed *arete*. Call it virtue if you must.

Virtue ethics is a normative ethics, and it is a good example of ethical absolutism, though it is not religious absolutism, nor is it rational absolutism. But getting students to understand the difference may take some time.

Greeks, Jews and Christians

A few sentences back I said that if you think someone is liar because he or she lies it is probably because you have been raised within a Judeo-Christian ethical milieu, or words to that effect. Let me show you why I think this is so. Several years ago I was teaching a course in ethics, and when we came to the section on virtue ethics I found myself, as usual, struggling to get the students to see where the virtue ethicists were coming from. One of the students who always sat near the front stated, at one point, that he was Jewish, and that in the Jewish faith one was counted right or wrong because of one's actions. He had hardly finished speaking when another student, this one a Christian, said that he agreed, that this is what he had been taught all his life.

It was like a light bulb went on in my head! I have frequently said that, whether or not I have taught them anything, I have learned a great deal from my students.

Jews, Christians and Moslems all fell out of the same ethics tree, and this is why they have trouble understanding Greek ethics. In Judeo-Christian ethics, which swept the Mediterranean area during the first century A.D., certain precepts are placed before someone and he or she is told to follow them.[3] They are good if they do, bad if they don't. This way of thinking, picked up by the Romans and subsequently encoded in the western legal tradition, has been so deeply ingrained in the western psyche that it is difficult for westerners to see ethics in any other way. But maybe we have got it backwards. Maybe goodness is not what you do, but what you are, and the doing comes afterward. Maybe good people do good things because they are good people.

But a question arises, and it is the same one that plagued Bentham,

---

[3] I do, in fact, understand the concept of grace. The present treatment has to do with the way we relate to one another in the world.

Mill and Kant. How do we define good? What qualities are we to look for in the good person, and why do we call those qualities good rather than others? The Greeks of course had an answer, and it is the answer that defined for them that elusive thing called *arete*, without which no Greek could be called good.[4]

Neither modern day philosophers nor the Medieval philosophers who were strongly influenced by Aristotle have been in complete agreement with him on what constitutes a virtue. Aristotle had a much broader definition, one much more capable of fitting a number of situations, than perhaps we would feel comfortable with. As Philippa Foot has put it:

> For us there are four cardinal moral virtues: courage, temperance, wisdom and justice. But Aristotle and Aquinas call only three of these virtues moral virtues; practical wisdom (Aristotle's *phronesis* and Aquinas's *prudentia*) they class with the intellectual virtues, though they point out the close connexions between practical wisdom and what they call moral virtues; and sometimes they even use *arete* and *virtus* very much as we use "virtue."[5]

Actually, Aristotle has, as I have said, an even broader definition of virtue, one that bears close scrutiny. Virtue is hitting the mark, and the mark is a mean point between excess and deficiency.

The Nicomachean Ethics

The Nicomachean Ethics, so called because they were put together from lecture notes after Aristotle's death by his son Nicomachus, are another major contribution to western ethics. Like Socrates before him, Aristotle thought that good behavior was first of all a matter of good teaching. One had to be taught to aim at the proper mark before one could be held accountable for not hitting it. Aristotle begins the Nicomachean Ethics by dealing with the question, what mark should we be aiming at?

> Every art of applied science and every systematic investigation, and similarly every action and choice, seem to aim at some good; the good, therefore has been well

---

4 *Eudaimonia* is the Greek word for what I keep calling good. It literally means "good spirit." This flowed from a balanced personality, as we shall see.

5 Foot, Philippa, "Virtue Ethics," from *Virtues and Vices*.

> defined as that at which all things aim. But it is clear that there is a difference in the ends at which they aim: in some cases the activity is the end, in others the end is some product beyond the activity. In cases where the end lies beyond the action the product is naturally superior to the activity. . .
>
> Now, if there exists an end in the realm of action which we desire for its own sake, an end which determines all our other desires; if, in other words, we do not make all our choices for the sake of something else — for in this way the process will go on infinitely so that our desire would be futile and pointless — then obviously this end will be the good, that is, the highest good. Will not the knowledge of this good, consequently, be very important to our lives? Would it not better equip us, like archers who have a target to aim at, to hit the proper mark? If so, we must try to comprehend in outline at least what this good is and to which branch of knowledge or to which capacity it belongs.[6]

Axiologists (those who study values) talk, as we have seen, of things having intrinsic value and extrinsic value. We pursue things with extrinsic value because they help us to gain other things that we value, but we pursue things with intrinsic value because we value them alone. They are ends in themselves. Without saying so directly, Aristotle, in the passage above, is urging us toward the things with intrinsic value, for he recognizes what many less wise than he do not, that if we spend our time in a frantic search for things with extrinsic value, we will never know true happiness. If you doubt this, ask the man who spent his life chasing money and wound up at the end rich, bitter, and alone.

Aristotle proceeds then to answer the next, and the most obvious question: what is the intrinsic value that one ought to pursue?

> To resume the discussion: since all knowledge and every choice is directed toward some good, let us discuss what is in our view the. . .highest good attainable by action. As far as its name is concerned, most people would probably agree: for both the common run of people and cultivated men call it happiness, and understand by "being happy" the same as "living well" and "doing well." But when it

---

[6] **Aristotle, *The Nicomachean Ethics*, tran. Martin Oswald, Indianapolis: Bobbs-Merrill, Co., 1962, pp. 3, 4.**

> comes to defining what happiness is, they disagree, and the account given by the common run differs from that of the philosophers. The former say it is some clear and obvious good, such as pleasure, wealth, or honor; some say it is one thing and others another, and often the very same person identifies it with different things at different times. . .[7]

Aristotle's assertions invite discussion. Let us review what he has told us so far to see whether or not we can agree with him. The good is that at which things aim. The highest good is that which we value for its own sake, not as a means to something else. And the thing that we value for its own sake and to which, he seems to suggest, all other "goods" are subservient, is happiness. Suppose you say to Aristotle that the highest good is love, and that it is love to which all aspire. Aristotle will respond that you desire love only because it makes you happy; if love made you miserable you would wish to avoid it, as the poets have repeatedly advised us to do. In fact, most of the things we consider as having intrinsic value (power, honor, wisdom, etc.) are, according to Aristotle, merely means to a greater end, that of happiness. Happiness is that thing at which we are all aiming.

Now I would be very surprised if no one was wondering at this point what any of this has to do with ethics. Let me show you.

The subject is virtue ethics, and for Aristotle virtue is defined as hitting the mark. This means that if one wishes to be virtuous, one must be able to hit the mark, and if one is to hit the mark, one must know what one is aiming at. As the saying goes, aim at nothing and that is what you will hit. Or as another saying has it, if you don't know where you're going, any road will take you there.

A virtuous person hits the mark. The mark is happiness. Thus — if Aristotle is correct — if one wishes to be happy one must be virtuous, for the two go together like Babe Ruth and Lou Gehrig. Lacking the *arete* of Aristotle, dooms one to misery.

Having said all this, however, Aristotle seems to have talked all around the subject without getting right down to, as the old-timers used say, brass tacks. Aim at happiness. All right, I will; but happiness is elusive, and at some point I have to determine what will actually make me happy. Happiness is one of those abstract things which philosophers hold so dear

---

[7] **Ibid., p. 6.**

and which all other people abominate. What will actually make me happy, if not money, power, love, beauty, etc. . ?

Pleasure might seem an obvious candidate, and many philosophers across the years have opted for this and called it the highest good. Jeremy Bentham did, as we have already seen. The hedonists, beginning with Aristippus the Cyrenaic, made an entire philosophy out of the pleasure principle, by which they meant nothing more complicated than pure physical pleasure, whatever its source.

Aristotle is not convinced. For him, a thing, anything, achieves happiness when it fulfills the purpose for which it was intended. This is, of course, his theory of *entelechy*, which we have already considered. His ethics, like his metaphysics, are teleological, and the four causes that he outlines in the *Metaphysics* are also applicable to his ethics.

The four causes are the material, the efficient, the formal, and the final. Take a loaf of bread as an example. The material cause of its existence is flour, water, and so on. The efficient cause is the baker. The formal cause is the recipe the baker used. The final cause is the purpose for which the bread is baked, namely as food for people. The fourth, or final cause, is the one of particular interest to the subject of ethics, for this is the target at which one is aiming. One might say that the final cause of any ethical behavior, so far as Aristotle is concerned, is happiness, and virtue equals happiness. But then, as any fourth grade student of mathematics can tell you, given the correctness of this formula, the obverse is also true: happiness equals virtue.

Let's forget earthworms, trees, spotted owls, snail darters, and bighorn sheep. Each of them has its own *entelechy*, and each of them is completed and perfected as it achieves the end for which it was intended. But let's talk about people. What is the end of the human; for it is in answering this question that we answer the question of what makes for happiness. What is the human *entelechy*, and what goal must the human attain if he or she is to be fulfilled and therefore happy? It occurred to me as I was writing the previous sentence that there is probably no more important question that a human could ask than this one; this is the question philosophers and sages have been trying to answer across the ages. And though I repeat myself *ad nauseam*, allow me to remind you that for Aristotle this brings us to the heart of ethics. One cannot know what virtuous behavior is until one first knows something about the creature whose behavior is being monitored.

If I placed an acorn before you and asked what its *entelechy* — its basic purpose — is, you would no doubt say to become an oak, which is a tree that grows, has leaves, produces shade, other acorns, and other oaks. I place an egg before you and ask what its purpose is. You might say, "Ham and eggs." No, I say this is the egg of a bald eagle. Ah, then its purpose is to hatch into an eaglet, and then to grow into an eagle, a creature with keen vision that can fly above the clouds. Now, what about humans?

> Man cannot survive except through his mind. He comes on earth unarmed. His brain is his only weapon. Animals obtain food by force. Man has no claws, no fangs, no horns, no great strength of muscle. He must plant his food or hunt it. To plant, he needs a process of thought. To hunt, he needs weapons, and to make weapons — a process of thought. From this simplest necessity to the highest religious abstraction, from the wheel to the sky-scraper, everything we are and everything we have comes from a single attribute of man — the function of his reasoning mind.[8]

Thus said Ayn Rand, one of the more famous of contemporary Aristotelians, whom we looked at when we were discussing egoism.

I call your attention to something you may have forgotten by now, because it was in one of the earlier chapters. Aristotle was an essentialist, which is to say that he believed that things, humans included, are possessed of certain core qualities which make them what they are and which drive them toward their final and ultimate goals. In other words, the *entelechy* of a thing depends upon its essence. Now, in the case of a human, what is this essence, this quality that sets the human apart from other creatures and without which the human would not be human? For Aristotle, and very certainly for Ayn Rand, the answer is obvious — it is the marvelous human mind. The human is the rational animal, and for this reason the human is never happier than when developing and using the intellectual powers at his or her disposal. The human mind is the thing that the human possesses which sets him or her apart from every other creature, and it is in the use of the mind that the human will reach happiness.

> To call happiness the highest good is perhaps a little trite, and a clearer account of what it is, is still required. Perhaps this is best done by first ascertaining

[8] **Rand, Ayn, *The Fountainhead*, in *For the New Intellectual*, op.cit., p. 78.**

> the proper function of man. . .Should we not assume that just as the eye, the hand, the foot, and in general each part of the body clearly has it own proper function, so man too has some function over and above the functions of his parts? What can this function possibly be? Simply living? He shares that even with plants, but we are now looking for something peculiar to man. Accordingly, the life of nutrition and growth must be excluded. Next in line there is a life of sense perception. but this, too man has in common with the horse, the ox, and every animal. There remains then an active life of the rational element. The rational element has two parts: one is rational in that it obeys the rule of reason, the other in that it possesses and conceives rational rules. . .
>
> The proper function of man , then consists in an activity of the soul in conformity with a rational principle or, at least, not without it. . .[I]f we take the proper function of man to be a certain kind of life, and if this kind of life is an activity of the soul and consists in actions performed in conjunction with the rational element, and if a man of high standards is he who performs these actions well and properly, and if a function is well performed when it is performed in accordance with the excellence appropriate to it; we reach the conclusion that the good man is an activity of the soul in conformity with excellence or virtue, and if there are several virtues, in conformity with the best and most complete.[9]

You cannot have missed the reference to excellence and virtue in the passage just quoted. This is the *arete* of which we have been speaking. What makes this so important is that, for reasons not unlike those of Immanuel Kant, Aristotle begins with an assumption that humans are rational, and that rationality lies at the foundation of all virtue. If you wish to express your virtue in behaving well, then you must be prepared to think about what you are doing. And this should not be troubling to any human. On the contrary, it is the most natural thing in the world, the thing which the human does best, the activity which is the most satisfying, fulfilling, and which is most likely to bring the sort of happiness that Aristotle equates with good.

Once again, there is something very Socratic in this man, who disagreed with Socrates on so many things. But Aristotle and Socrates are in

---

[9] Aristotle, *Ethics*, pp. 16, 17.

agreement at least on this: one cannot be virtuous unless one is willing to think, and to make rational thought a goal, a lifetime project. Bad behavior, so far as Socrates is concerned, comes as a result of ignorance. While he doesn't say the same thing in just those words, Aristotle appears to agree with his intellectual grandfather. It is an unwillingness to think which gets people into moral trouble — and other trouble too.

The Greeks and Balance

We will return to Aristotle shortly and give some time to his theory of the "golden mean." But first we need to take a backward step and review Plato's position on what it is to be well-balanced, for without balance one can never think properly, can never aim at the right mark, and can never be virtuous.

In the *Phaedrus*, as we have already seen, Plato has Socrates dividing the human soul into three parts, and using to illustrate their separate functions the figure of a charioteer driving a chariot pulled by two spirited horses, one noble and one ignoble. The charioteer corresponds to reason, the noble horse to spirit (or sometimes Plato calls it willpower), and the ignoble horse corresponds to appetites. It is interesting that each of these also corresponds to one of the virtues. The charioteer, reason, represents the virtue of wisdom; the noble horse, spirit, represents courage; and the ignoble horse, appetite, represents temperance.

Now if you were paying attention earlier you will recall that Philipa Foot said the Greeks believed there were four cardinal virtues, and you are probably wondering where justice comes in. Justice quite simply results when one has control of his two horses by means of reason, for then we have a truly well-balanced individual, and a virtuous one to boot. The place of reason in this is clear, and it is critical. Now, let's get back to Aristotle and to the *Nicomachean Ethics*.

The Golden Mean

Aristotle also believed that the human soul was divided into three parts, the vegetative, the appetitive, and the rational. For the purposes of understanding his ethics, these parts may be said to correspond very closely to the three different parts of the Platonic soul.

If virtue is hitting the mark, as Aristotle believed, then by logical extension, vice is missing the mark. Aristotle thought one could miss the mark in two ways: he could overshoot it, in which case we have excess; he could undershoot it, in which case we have deficiency. Here, then, we have

Aristotle's definition of vice, but we are still not sure what this means, nor are we sure how the critically important factor of reason comes into play. He clarifies matters in Book II of the *Ethics*, from which I now intend to quote at some length. This is not an apology; it is a warning.

> Of every continuous entity that is divisible into parts it is possible to take the larger, the smaller, or an equal part, and these parts may be larger, smaller, or equal either in relation to the entity itself, or in relation to us. The "equal" part is something median between excess and deficiency. By the median of an entity I understand a point equidistant from both extremes, and this point is one and the same for everybody. . .
>
> If this, then, is the way in which every science perfects its work, by looking to the median and by bringing its work up to that point — and this is the reason why it is usually said of a successful piece of work that it is impossible to detract from it or to add to it, the implication being that excess and deficiency destroy success while the mean safeguards it. . .[A]nd if virtue, like nature, is more precise and better than any art, we must conclude that virtue aims at the median. I am referring to moral virtue: for it is moral virtue that is concerned with emotions and actions, and it is in emotions and actions that excess, deficiency, and the median are found. . .
>
> We may thus conclude that virtue or excellence is a characteristic involving choice, and that it consists in observing the mean relative to us, a mean which is defined by a rational principle, such as a man of practical wisdom would use to determine it. It is the mean by reference to two vices: the one of excess and the other of deficiency. It is, moreover, a mean because some vices exceed and others fall short of what is required in emotion and in action, whereas virtue finds and chooses the median. Hence, in respect of its essence and the definition of its essential nature virtue is a mean, but in regard to goodness and excellence it is an extreme.[10]

Aristotle goes to some length to illustrate exactly how this works in practical terms, and we can do no better than to use his own illustrations. Suppose we take one of the cardinal virtues, courage. We find, says

---

[10] **Aristotle, *Ethics*, op.cit., pp. 42-44.**

Aristotle, that it is actually a mean value between the extreme of foolhardiness and the deficiency of cowardice. The coward runs away, the foolhardy person behaves rashly and gets himself and others killed. Neither of these is a virtue. The courageous person stands her ground, even when faced with danger and fear, and behaves as she knows she ought to behave, but she does not take foolish chances. This is an example of being well-balanced, and this is virtue.

How about wisdom? The excess in its case is (get ready for a surprise) cleverness.[11] Think in this regard of the sorts of sophistry against which Socrates taught, the sorts of things that one sometimes sees in American courts of law, and you can gain some insight into why cleverness might be wisdom, or practical wisdom, as Aristotle calls it, pushed to the extreme of a vice.

Aristotle wrote at some length to demonstrate how virtue was indeed the mean between two vices. Loyalty is the mean between the excess of uncriticalness and the deficiency of disloyalty. Patience is the mean between the excess of passivity and the deficiency of impatience. Honesty is the mean between the excess of being rude and the deficiency of lying. Generosity is the mean between the excess of prodigality and the deficiency of stinginess. To wrap matters up, temperance is called for in all things. Temperance is the virtue that makes one seek the mean between the vices of excess and deficiency, and wisdom is that virtue that one needs if one is to recognize the mean between the two extremes. And, finally, it is courage that one must possess if one is to behave virtuously in all things, for being virtuous often costs one a great deal. Thus, the cardinal virtues are those upon which all the others depend.

A virtuous character is built slowly, bit by bit, action by action. We become virtuous, not as a result of a single action (One swallow does not make a summer, said Aristotle), but as a result of doing the right thing, in a variety of situations, until it becomes a habit. The honest man is not honest because he tells the truth from time to time, but because he has been trained up to be honest and has that particular virtue built in as a result.

> Intellectual virtue or excellence owes its origin and development chiefly to teaching, and for that reason requires experience and time. Moral virtue, on the other hand, is formed by habit, *ethos*, and its name, *ethike*, is therefore derived, by a slight variation, from *ethos*. This

---

[11] **Ibid., p. 169.**

> shows, too, that none of the moral virtues is implanted in us by nature, for nothing which exists by nature can be changed by habit. For example, it is impossible for a stone, which has a natural downward movement, to become habituated to moving upward, even if one should try ten thousand times to inculcate the habit by throwing it in the air; nor can fire be made to move downward, nor can the direction of any nature-given tendency be changed by habituation. Thus, the virtues are implanted in us neither by nature nor contrary to nature: we are by nature equipped with the ability to receive them, and habit brings this ability to completion and fulfillment.[12]

It is obvious, is it not, that virtue ethics involves something much deeper than superficial rules and regulations. It goes down into the heart and the soul of the individual, and it springs from the well-balanced person, the one who is well-taught, who has ***eudaimonia*** and ***sophrosyne***, who has, more importantly, *arete.* It is pointless to tell the flawed person to do the right thing; he or she, when the chips are down, will not do the right thing. Doing the right thing is the action of a person who is virtuous, who knows the mark and how to hit it.

***Sophrosyne* is the Greek word for moderation, a concept which figures prominently in the philosophy of Aristotle.**

Aquinas and Virtue

With Thomas Aquinas we get, in the very midst of the Christian world, a renewal in the interest of things Greek, and thus a renewed interest in virtue ethics, although neither Aquinas nor his contemporaries would have given their ethics that label. In fact, from our vantage point, he appears to have been a sort of eclectic who shows traces of utilitarianism and natural-law ethics. Nevertheless, as with many philosophers of the high Middle Ages, Aquinas was enthusiastically Aristotelian, and it is hardly surprising to find him commenting upon, and championing, the ethics of the one he called The Philosopher.

Aquinas agrees that there are four cardinal virtues, which he divides into intellectual (prudence, or wisdom), and moral (justice, temperance, and fortitude).

> First, as existing in the consideration itself of reason, and thus we have one principal virtue called *prudence.*— Secondly, according as the reason puts its order into something else, and this either into operations, and then

---

12 Ibid., p. 33.

> we have *justice*, or into passions, and then we need two virtues. For the need of putting the order of reason into the passions is due to their thwarting reason; and this occurs in two ways. First, when the passions incite to something against reason, and then they need a curb, which we thus call *temperance*; secondly, when the passions withdraw us from following the dictate of reason, *e.g.*, through fear of danger or toil, and then man needs to be strengthened for that which reason dictates, lest he turn back, and to this end there is *fortitude*.[13]

But we should also not be surprised to find him expanding Aristotle's cardinal virtues from four to seven.[14] To this end, he adds three theological virtues — faith, hope, and charity.

> [T]he theological virtues direct man to supernatural happiness in the same way as by the natural inclination man is directed to his connatural end. Now the latter direction happens in two respects. First, according to the reason or intellect, in so far as it contains the first universal principles which are known to us through the natural light of the intellect, and which are reason's starting point, both in speculative and in practical matters. Secondly, through the rectitude of the will tending naturally to the good as defined by reason. . .
>
> First, as regards the intellect, man receives certain supernatural principles, which are held by means of a divine light; and these are the things which are to be believed, about which is *faith*. — Second, the will is directed to this end, both as to the movement of intention, which tends to that end as something attainable, — this pertains to *hope* — and as to a certain spiritual union, whereby the will is, in a way, transformed into that end — and this belongs to *charity*.[15]

Human virtue is, for Aquinas as for Aristotle, a matter of habit.

---

[13] Aquinas, op.cit., pp. 588-89.

[14] The number seven has powerful symbolic significance for Jews and Christians. It is the number of completeness or perfection. There are also seven deadly sins — pride, lust, envy, anger, covetousness, gluttony, and sloth.

[15] Ibid., p. 594.

> Virtue denotes a certain perfection of a power. Now a thing's perfection is considered chiefly in relation to its end. But the end of power is act. Therefore power is said to be perfect according as it is determined to its act. Now there are some powers which of themselves are determined to their acts, for instance, the active natural powers. And therefore these natural powers are in themselves called virtues. But the rational powers, which are proper to man, are not determined to one particular action, but are inclined indifferently to many; but they are determined to acts by means of habits, as is clear from what we have said above. Therefore human virtues are habits.[16]

Aquinas became the official philosopher of the Catholic Church, and ostensibly retains that title, but his influence as an ethicist lags far behind his influence in the areas of theology and metaphysics. The reasons for this are two-fold. One is that Christians have, in the writings of the Apostles and the Church fathers, and in the Old Testament, a well-established ethical tradition that runs somewhat against the grain of the Greeks. The second is that Aquinas's strength is also his weakness. He was the great synthesizer, the one who wedded Aristotelian philosophy with Christian faith; and the results are, as I have already suggested, eclectic to the point that one is able to find in him some suggestions of just about every ethical theory we have. He is teleological, appeals to natural law, cites the cardinal virtues, is clearly an absolutist, and was confident enough in the ability of reason to get humans to divine truth that he would probably fit in well with Immanuel Kant. Consequently, Aquinas was not the one to truly revive Greek ethics. That would take a generation of twentieth-century philosophers, many of them women. They would look back to Aristotle and find in him and his teaching something that they found lacking in the work of modern ethicists — the appeal to character.

Virtue Ethics Revived

It is interesting that the revival of virtue ethics has taken place in this century, against a backdrop of moral laxity and what is generally presented as ethical relativism. It sometimes seems that the worst thing anyone can say about anyone else is that he or she is "judgmental," as if to question the

---

[16] Ibid., p. 561.

rightness or wrongness of someone's actions is itself morally wrong and subject to condemnation. The virtue ethicists come onto the scene asking us to pass judgment, not just on actions, but more importantly on the conditions of the soul that produced the actions. But perhaps conditions of the soul is not quite what I, in this modern era, ought to be saying. Perhaps I ought to be talking about bad habits, learned at an early age and never unlearned, that are now being acted out publicly by individuals who demonstrate a lack of virtue.

The virtue ethicists are, regardless of how they see themselves, ethical absolutists in a very important sense — there are values one ought to hold to and virtues that one must express, and these are non-negotiable. This may, as we shall see, constitute a major weakness of their theory; but, on the other hand, it may be one of its strengths. For there do seem to be certain virtues — call them cardinal virtues if it pleases you — that are all but universal. Aren't courage, generosity, honesty, love prized in most any society in the world? Christina Hoff Summers says:

> In ethics classes one thing should be made central and prominent: right and wrong do exist. This should be laid down as uncontroversial, lest one leave an altogether false impression that *everything* is up for grabs. . .British philosopher G.J. Warnock speaks of "moral facts" that are as plain as the fact that "snow is white." Have we not learned a thing or two over the past several thousand years of civilization? We know that gratuitous cruelty and political repression are wrong. We know that kindness and political freedom are right and good. Why should we be the first society in history afraid of passing along its moral tradition to the next generation?[17]

Notice in this passage the appeal to "moral tradition," the suggestion that as beings under a process of civilization for thousands of years we ought to have learned something by now about right and wrong conduct, and we ought to be willing to pass what we have learned on to our children. What we should have learned, Sommers contends, is that honesty, kindness, political freedom, are right things. Who would deny it?

Constrained as I am by both time and space, I cannot go into a more

---

[17] Sommers, Christina Hoff, "What Ever Happened to Right and Wrong?", in *Imprimis*, November, 1991.

lengthy apologetic for virtue ethics. The interested student will find ample material from which to choose should he or she wish to learn more of this rather fascinating ethical theory. Plato and Aristotle are of course rich sources of information. Among contemporary ethicists, Alasdair MacIntyre has also urged a return to the traditional values of society. I have already mentioned Philippa Foot, the British ethicist, and I have quoted from her best known work, *Virtues and Vices.* She places a strong emphasis upon intention, much as Immanuel Kant did. But she differs from Kant in at least one important respect. Suppose one is tempted to do good and resists the temptation. Suppose that we set beside him another person who, facing the same situation, is not even tempted. Which person is the most moral. Kant would say the first, for he or she has to actually struggle to do the right thing, therefore the act of doing the right thing has greater value. Foot says, in agreement with Aristotle, that the second person is the most virtuous, because he or she has the relevant virtue ingrained to the point that the temptation to do wrong is simply rejected without difficulty.

A recent book by virtue-ethicist William Bennett became a surprise best-seller. In *The Book of Virtues* Bennett goes back to one of the most time-honored methods of teaching virtue, that of the fairy tale and the fable, and in ten chapters champions such virtues as compassion, courage, honesty, loyalty, faith.

The Problem with the Virtues

It would be wonderful if someone would come along and create an ethical theory — or a philosophical theory of any kind — which is perfect and which leaves no room for criticism. It would be wonderful for everyone but the philosophers, for if such a theory emerges there will be nothing left for them to do, but to learn and comment upon the theory. Fortunately, or unfortunately, no such theory is in place or is ever likely to be, and virtue ethics is no exception. Generally, the criticism of virtue ethics takes two forms, an intrinsic criticism having to do with the theory itself, and an extrinsic one having to do with those beings who are asked to put the theory to work — namely ourselves.

The problem with virtue ethics, according to those who see its intrinsic flaws, is that it assumes certain things are virtues, and insists upon seeing these built into the human psyche, when in fact there is no reason *a priori* to make any such assumptions. Aristotle's virtues were obviously the virtues of the upperclass Greek society from which he came, but they wouldn't necessarily be considered virtues in our own culture. In fact, some of the things Aristotle put forward as virtues would be rejected by contemporary westerns as downright evil. Aristotle's theory of justice, for instance, was a great deal like that of his mentor Plato. Justice meant everybody getting what he or she had coming, and this depended strictly upon who or what the individual was. A slave had one thing coming. A woman had something else coming. A free Greek male had something coming. A foreign male had something else coming. A manual laborer could not expect the same treatment as a scholar walking the shaded paths of the Lyceum. Now, if one cannot agree on what the virtues are, how can one possibly teach them to someone else.

The obvious response is that we need not be controlled by the Greeks. Brilliant as they may have been, we are able to see where they were wrong and to make the necessary corrections. Just because they thought that slavery was proper, and that slaves had no rights, it does not follow that we have to think this and act accordingly. The obvious thing to do is to look at Greek ethics from a more universal point of view, taking from them the overall system and the general virtues which we can all agree are necessary — i.e., honesty, loyalty, courage, temperance.

But this doesn't solve the problem, it merely prolongs it. What the Greeks considered courageous might differ considerably from our definition, and at this point we slide away into a sort of cultural relativism, with all the problems and weaknesses attendant thereunto.

To put it in simple language: what are the cardinal virtues, and who makes the decision?

The other problems that critics of virtue ethics have raised are extrinsic. That is, they have less to do with the theory than they do with the subjects of the theory, those creatures who have to put it to work.

To begin with, aren't we much better off to simply draw up rules, tell people to obey them, and agree that those who obey are good and those who don't are not? Ask why this might be a better approach and the response is immediate and difficult to argue against: it's better because there are a whole host of people out there who, for whatever reason, are simply deficient in the area of character. In making proper conduct depend upon the person, we put tremendous pressure on the weakest point — the flawed creature. If, on the other hand, we draw up a list of rules and tell people to keep them, we haven't totally removed the pressure from the individual (they are still told to keep the rules), but we have at least removed the pressure of requiring them to make decisions about what is right and wrong, drawing all the while upon a reservoir of character that, for many, is rather shallow.

Remember Immanuel Kant? He assumed that every human was rational and was able by applying his or her God-given sense to reach precisely the same answer to the question, is this right. But this is an assumption one can reasonably make only in some cases. There are many whose behavior, indeed whose mental capacity, leaves one to wonder whether or not they possess the requisite rationality to fit Kant's criterion for a free moral agent. For these, as for the individuals of low or deficient character, it would seem that rules and regulations may be the best way to assure ethical behavior.

Another extrinsic problem with virtue ethics is suggested by Thomas Aquinas. Many ethicists treat Brother Thomas as a sort of reborn virtue ethicist simply because he is so very Aristotelian in so many ways. I would challenge those who do this to go back and re-read the *Summa Theologica.* Aquinas is, as I said earlier, rather eclectic in his ethics. Sometimes he sounds very much the virtue ethicist, sometimes not; sometimes the consequentialist, sometimes not. But always he sounds like the Christian intellectual building upon the foundation of scripture and the Church fathers.

> Therefore, just as the primary goodness of a natural thing is derived from its form, which gives it its species, so the primary goodness of a moral action is derived from its suitable object; and so some call such an action good in its genus. . .
>
> A fourfold goodness may be considered in a human action. First, that goodness which, as an action, it derives from its genus; since as much as it has of action and being, so much has it of goodness, as was stated above. Secondly, it has goodness according to its species, which is derived from its befitting object. Thirdly, it has goodness from its circumstances, — its accidents, as it were. Fourthly, it has goodness from its end, to which it is compared as to the cause of its goodness.[18]

Now, throw Christian ethics in and you see immediately the problem Aquinas would have with the theory of virtue ethics, as the Greeks proposed it and as it exists today. Remember that he not only spelled out the seven virtues, but the seven deadly sins as well; and one of those sins was the sin of pride. For Aquinas, as for Christians before and since, the development

---

[18] **Aquinas, op.cit., pp. 527-28.**

of human character was as much a matter of God's grace than it was of human striving. In fact, to suppose that one could, by human effort, improve oneself was to be guilty of a grievous sin. This is why the virtue ethics of the Greeks was not only replaced by Christian ethics, but has been fighting something of an uphill battle ever since Christianity came in.

But for all its weaknesses and perhaps unresolvable problems, there is something very attractive about virtue ethics, and I for one am thankful to those who renewed and revised it as a theory. Character is important, and character weakness can result in wide variety of behavior problems ranging from lying, through theft, to abusive behavior, to murder. Jesus seems to have had this in mind when he said, "That which cometh out of the man, that defileth the man. For from within, out of the heart of men, proceed evil thoughts, adulteries, fornications, murders, thefts, covetousness, wickedness, deceit, lasciviousness, an evil eye, blasphemy, pride, foolishness: All these evil things come from within, and defile the man."

That pretty well covers the ten commandments.

Feminist Ethics

Are men more ethical than women? If you did not like that question, perhaps we could please you by turning it around. Are women more ethical than men? If you do not like either question, seeing both as sexist, then perhaps this would please you better — do men and women look at ethics differently? If you are a classical feminist, such as Simone de Beauvoir or Mary Wollstonecraft, you will find the third question just as offensive as the first two, because it implies that there is something in the ethical makeup of people that is sexually determined, or, if not sexually determined, then culturally determined by a society that insists on raising women and men differently.

Feminism has come a long way, and has undergone some changes in the process. Many feminists today say that the classical feminists are mistaken, that there are differences in the way woman and men approach many questions, including ethical ones, and that not all of these differences can be dismissed by saying that it's just a matter of learning.

The December, 1981 issue of *Ms.* carried an interview by Martha Saxton with psychologist Carol Gilligan under the title, "Are Women More Moral Than Men?" In the course of the interview, the question is never answered; in fact, it is never actually asked. What Gilligan makes clear is that, in her opinion, women approach ethics from a different position than men. Men are rule-makers, impersonal, objective. Women's ethics is more likely to be an ethics of caring, of establishing and maintaining relationships.

This was something of a departure from the standard approach of both women and men, and since it isn't likely that the editors of *Ms.* woke up one day and said, "Why not get an interview with Carol Gilligan; maybe she'll say something interesting," we may well ask what *did* impel them to the interview — and why the provocative title? Gilligan had just published a book called *In a Different Voice*, in which she responded at length to the work of psychologist Lawrence Kohlberg. Kohlberg had conducted, over a period of several years, a study in ethical development, and had basically concluded that women are inferior ethically to men.[19] According to Kohlberg, humans pass through six separate stages of ethical development, beginning with the most basic stage, goodness is power, and going up to the highest stage, goodness is based on universal principles of justice and equality.[20] The lowest level on the scale is where children are found. Few people ever develop, even as adults, to the sixth level, the highest level of ethical maturity; and women, according to Kohlberg, rarely get beyond the first three levels. If Kohlberg is correct — and his theory is based upon a great deal of research — then the question posed by the Gilligan interview may be answered with a sound, "No." In fact, men are more ethical than women. It is in dealing with the question of which gender is more ethical that Gilligan departs from the position of the classical feminists, and at the same time opens up a whole new dimension to the ongoing ethical dialectic. Gilligan says that neither group is more ethical than the other, but that there are two ways of looking at ethics, and that one of these ways is a masculine way and one is a feminine way. The first of these she calls an ethics of justice; the second an ethics of care.

---

[19] In all fairness to Kohlberg, he does not actually say that women are inferior, and were he questioned would probably say that he never intended such a thing. Nevertheless, it is difficult to read his findings and not come up with the notion that men are morally-superior beings.

[20] Kohlberg's developmental stages are, to be more accurate, three with two sub-stages in each. Goodness is power, and goodness satisfies my needs are what Kohlberg calls the preconventional stage. Goodness comes from pleasing and helping others, and goodness is doing our duty to ensure law and order make up the conventional stage. Goodness is a matter of fairness according to a social contract like the Constitution, and goodness is based on universal principles of justice and equality — the ethic of justice is the postconventional stage.

> Over the past ten years I have been listening to people talking about morality and about themselves. Halfway through that time, I began to hear a distinction in these voices, two ways of speaking about moral problems, two modes of describing the relationship between other and self. . .
>
> The different voice I describe is characterized not by gender but by theme. Its association with women is an empirical observation, and it is primarily through women's voices that I trace its development. But this association is not absolute, and the contrasts between male and female voices. . .highlight a distinction between two modes of thought and. . .focus [on] a problem of interpretation rather than represent a generalization about either sex.[21]

It is worth noting that she does not say that Kohlberg was totally wrong; she simply says that his study is biased by the waters in which he fished (the metaphor is mine, not Gilligan's) — his studies were done using mainly men as his subjects, and from a bias that, as we shall see, appears to be slanted toward men. An example is what Kohlberg called in his study the *Heinz dilemma.*

Heinz's dilemma is that his wife is desperately ill, and he cannot afford the medicine she needs if she is to be made well. Should he steal it? Kohlberg put the question to two eleven-year-olds, Jake and Amy. For Jake, there was no doubt about it; the life of Heinz's wife was far more important than any ethical rule about stealing. Heinz should steal the medicine. Amy said that he should not. What if he got caught? He would go to jail, then who would care for his wife? Amy suggested that the thing for Heinz to do is go to the pharmacist, explain the situation to him, and see if they could work out some way for Heinz to get the medicine now and pay later.

Kohlberg's analysis of the way these two children solved the Heinz dilemma is interesting. He said that Jake sees clearly what is involved, rights and justice, whereas Amy's grasp of the situation is fuzzy at best. Carol Gilligan gives a very different analysis, and it is the difference that is instructive, and that leads to what Gilligan calls an ethics of care. Gilligan says that the two children didn't even respond to the same question, although the question was posed to both in exactly the same language. Jake

---

21 Gilligan, Carol, *In a Different Voice: Psychological Theory and Women's Development*, Cambridge, Mass.: Harvard University Press, 1982, pp. 1-2.

answered the question, *Should Heinz steal the drug or not?* Amy answered the question, *Should Heinz steal the drug, or should he do something else?* Jake concentrated on justice: the wife's right to receive the medicine overrode the law against stealing. Amy concentrated on relationships, Heinz and his wife, Heinz and the pharmacist, Heinz and his wife and society.

The real problem, says Gilligan, is not that Jake is right and Amy wrong, or that Amy is right and Jake is wrong. The problem is that women tend to look at things differently, and that for thousands of years men have dominated the discussion and have assumed, as Kohlberg seems to, that the feminine point of view is one that needn't be bothered with. The fact is that philosophers, going all the way back to Aristotle, have associated correct thinking with a sort of Apollonian rationality that purports to rise above emotion. Emotion, in fact, is seen as weakness when one wishes to get to the truth, and emotion is associated with women. Philosophers have distrusted feeling, and have traditionally described women as being given to feeling and emotion, unable to set these aside and to think dispassionately about problems.

> Classical Christian spirituality viewed man as a "rational spirit." The male alone was said to fully possess this "human nature" in its essence. The male alone was made in the "image of God," modeled in his inward being after the intellectual Logos. . .Woman was thereby modeled after the rejected part of the psyche.[22]

Gilligan's approach to ethics constitutes are major breakthrough in the ongoing debate about what is right and what is wrong. She has not been universally hailed by those involved in the women's movement, however, because what she is saying goes against the grain of the classical feminists. Women and men are not the same, the difference goes much deeper than the mere possession of certain genitalia, and in order to have a full ethics, one that treats of every aspect of right and wrong, both the feminine and the masculine points of view must be considered.

Psychologist Alison Jaggar has weighed in on the side of Gilligan, arguing that emotions are vital to anyone's picture of reality, and that in seeing emotion as inferior to reason, something to be shunned and kept down, philosophers have managed to falsify human experience and cut themselves off from one of the most important aspects of human experience.

---

[22] **Rosemary Radford Ruether. Quoted in Soccio, op.cit.**

Over the years I have found that women and men do seem to have different approaches to ethics, and that women, much more often than men, are concerned about forming and preserving relationships. The man lays down the rule; the woman tends to be willing to break the rule to preserve the relationship. I can remember a situation during the late 60's when the war in Vietnam was roaring. A student burned his draft card and his father disowned him. "Your mother is a woman," he said. "She'll love you no matter what you do. But I no longer have a son." I have thought of this many times when considering the feminine ethics of caring and opposed to the masculine ethics of justice.

Women and Virtue Ethics

The ethics of justice, about which Carol Gilligan has so much to say, has grown out of the Judeo-Christian tradition and western jurisprudence. The ancient Greeks would never have created this sort of ethics because their theory of justice would not have sustained it. To prove this to yourself, define justice, then sit down and read *The Republic*, and ask yourself, when you have finished the last chapter and laid the book aside, whether or not Plato's republic is the sort of place in which you would like to live and work.

How do you define justice? I have asked this of many students over the years, and I always get the same answer, in so many words. It is an answer that John Rawls would appreciate. Rawls is a Harvard social philosopher, justly famous for his theory that justice is fairness. There you have it. Whatever else justice is, justice is fairness, and an unfair society is an unjust society. But, assuming you would have defined justice in this way, what do you mean when you say fairness? Do you mean that everything is equally distributed, that everyone gets what he or she has coming, and that whatever one has coming is just as good as what the next fellow gets? If this is fairness, then there has never been, and will never be, a just society, and everyone, no matter who or where they are, has a complaint to lodge before whatever judge listens to complaints of this type. John Rawls spends a good deal of time defining exactly what he means by fairness, simply because it is ostensibly impossible to make things equal, and those societies that have tried it (post-revolutionary France and Soviet Russia, to name two) have wound up in chaos. This is why Gilligan, and other feminists, have seen the necessity to establish ethics on some other basis than rules and justice. Justice can be hard and harsh. Sometimes one wants mercy. This is why we need an ethics of caring.

> The potential error in justice reasoning lies in its latent ego-centrism, the tendency to confuse one's perspective with an objective standpoint or truth, the temptation to define others in one's own terms by putting oneself in their place. The potential error in care reasoning lies in the tendency to forget that one has terms, creating a tendency to enter into another's perspective and see oneself as "selfless" by defining oneself in others' terms. The two types of error underlie two common equations that signify distortions or deformations of justice and care; the equation of human with male, unjust in its omission of women; and the equation of care with self-sacrifice, uncaring in its failure to represent the activity and agency of care.[23]

But, if Gilligan is right, the ethics of caring has its shortcomings as well, and what is finally needed is something that combines the best features of both justice and caring, while eliminating the problems of both. Perhaps it is this need for an ethics that can somehow represent both justice and caring that has led many women, and not a few men, back to the Greeks and to virtue ethics.

Because Aristotle, and other Greek philosophers, had such a low opinion of women (Aristotle thought they were deformed men), and because women were excluded from much of the civic life in the Greek city states, it is tempting to view the Greek women as little more than doormats. This would be a mistake. Women too had their *arete*, as illustrated by Penelope, wife of Odysseus, and a number of other Greek women who made contributions to moral philosophy, particularly to what we would call applied ethics. Perictione, the supposed mother of Plato, has left us the following fragment on the harmonious woman.

> One must deem the harmonious woman to be full of wisdom and self-control; a soul must be exceedingly conscious of goodness to be just and courageous and wise, embellished with self-sufficiency and hating empty opinion. Worthwhile things come to a woman from these — for herself, her husband, her children, her household, perhaps even for a city. . .
>
> I think a woman is harmonious in the following

---

[23] Kittay, Eva Feder and Diane T. Mayers, ed. *Women and Moral Theory*, Totowa, N.J.: Rowman and Littlefield, 1987, pp. 19-33.

> way: if she becomes full of wisdom and self-control. For this benefits not only her husband, but also the children, relatives, slaves; the whole house, including possessions and friends, both fellow-citizens and foreign guest friends. Artlessly, she will keep their house, speaking and hearing fair things, and obeying her husband in the unanimity of their common life, attending upon the relatives and friends who he extols, and thinking the same things sweet and bitter as he — lest she be out of tune in relation to the whole.[24]

The recurring theme of Perectione's writing is that of the virtues, the same virtues that Aristotle talked about as cardinal, justice and courage, wisdom and self-control. Writing in about 420 B.C., another woman philosopher, Phintys of Sparta, argued, not only for these same virtues, but that it was foolish to believe that women were not as capable as men of cultivating these virtues, and demonstrating them in their conduct. Thus, female moral philosophers seem to have been interested in what we would call virtue ethics long before Aristotle was on the scene.

At the risk of being accused of oversimplifying matters, I would like to opine that virtue ethics has appealed so broadly to today's women philosophers precisely because it is neither justice ethics, nor is it caring ethics, but it is sort of an mingling together of the best of both those ethical theories. It is normative, has clearly defined absolutes, and therefore avoids the weakness of an ethics of pure caring. And yet it appeals much more to the heart and soul of the individual than do pure justice ethics, which are comparatively superficial, and thus does not lead to the sort of harshness that we see, for example, in the individuals who insisted that the woman taken in adultery be stoned because the Mosaic Law said she should be.

Further, the emphasis upon the development of character through teaching and proper development, is something that is really not so alien to most of us. Virtue ethics may turn out to be the most important contribution to the ethical dialectic since those of Bentham and Kant; and we owe much gratitude to those women and men who urged us to go back to the Greeks and take it up anew.

---

[24] Perictione, *On the Harmony of women,* Fragment 1, trans. Vicki Lynn Harper in *A History of Women Philosophers,* vol. I, 600 B.C.-500 A.D., ed. Mary Ellen Waithe, Dordrecht: Martinus Nijhoff Publishers, 1987, pp. 32-34.

The Future of Ethics

The future of ethics is bound up with the future of philosophy. The questions that humans have been asking throughout recorded history are the same questions that they will continue to ask, because they are the questions that go to the heart of what it is to be human. Ethical questions will always be among these, for the ethicist is a human, and ethics, as philosophy, is a human enterprise.

No doubt what is considered proper and improper behavior will change somewhat as one generation dies and another comes on the scene; but it is difficult to imagine that the core virtues we have been discussing will ever go out of style. For future generations, as for us and the ancient Greeks, honesty, courage and loyalty will probably always be defined as the sorts of things one ought to demonstrate if one is to be considered virtuous. If not — if these become "old-fashioned" — it is not likely that the human race can survive.

A Quick Review of Section IV

1. At the root of ethics is values. The study of values is called axiology. The most basic definition of a value is that it is anything in which we place worth. According to Ayn Rand, it is anything that we will work to gain and keep.

2. There are two general types of ethics — normative and nonnormative. Normative ethics tell one what one ought to do. Nonnormative ethics do not deal in "ought," but usually take a scientific or descriptive approach.

3. One of the major fallacies connected with ethics was first identified by David Hume. It is the naturalistic fallacy, the fallacy of attempting to extract a value from a fact.

4. Relativism takes several forms. Cultural relativism says that ethics are relative to the culture in which one lives. Ethical relativism is a normative ethics that says, in so many words, that cultural relativism is good. Individual relativism, or ethical skepticism, is not a theory that most philosophers are willing to argue for.

5. Ethical absolutism takes several forms. The most common is religious absolutism: a thing is right because God commands it. Immanuel Kant's categorical imperative is an example of rational absolutism. Virtue ethics is also a type of absolutism. An ethical absolutist believes that right is right, and wrong is wrong, and that the rightness and wrongness are in the act.

6. Ethical consequentialism holds that an act is right or wrong depending upon what results it produces. Utilitarianism and ethical egoism are types of consequentialism.

7. Hedonism, the pleasure principle, goes back to the ancient Greeks. It is also the foundation for the utilitarianism of Jeremy Bentham, who held that an action is good if it results in the greatest pleasure (or reduction of pain) for the greatest number.

8. Natural-law ethics has its roots in the writings of Thomas Aquinas, and also of John Locke. There are, according to Aquinas, three kinds of law, divine law (God's law over the cosmos), natural law (that portion of the divine law which pertains directly to humans), and human law (law made by humans). In natural-law ethics, that act is good which conforms with human nature.

9. Act always so that you could will the maxim of your behavior to be a universal moral law. This is Kant's categorical imperative. Also, he said that one should never use a human, whether oneself or someone else, merely as a means to an end.

10. Virtue ethics is a return to the ethics of the Greeks, particularly to Aristotle. The virtue ethicist insists that there are cardinal virtues which ought to be built into a person as he or she is educated, and that proper behavior flows from a person of high moral character.

Selected Bibliography

Aquinas, St. Thomas, *Introduction to Saint Thomas Aquinas*, ed. Anton C. Pegis, New York: Random House, 1948.

Aristotle, *The Metaphysics*, trans. Hugh Tredennick, Cambridge, Mass.: Harvard University Press, 1980.

The Nicomachean Ethics, Indianapolis: Bobbs-Merrill Co., 1962.

On Man in the Universe, trans. William Ogle, ed. Louise Ropes Loomis, New York: Walter J. Black, 1943.

The Pocket Aristotle, ed. Justin D. Kaplan.

Ayer, Alfred J., *Language, Truth and Logic*, 2nd ed., New York: Dover, 1952.

Bainton, Roland, *Here I Stand: A Life of Martin Luther*, New York: Mentor Books, 1963.

Benedict, Ruth, *Patterns of Culture*, Boston: Houghton Mifflin Co., 1934.

Bentham, Jeremy, *Introduction to the Principles of Morals and Legislation*, Oxford: Oxford University Press, 1823.

Berkeley, George, *Three Dialogues Between Hylas and Philonous*, Buffalo, NY: Prometheus Books, 1988.

A Treatise Concerning the Princples of Human Knowledge, in *The Works of George Berkeley*, vol. I, ed. George Sampson, London: George Bell & Sons, 1897.

Blanshard, Brand, "The Nature of Thought," *In Philosophical Interrogation*, ed. Sidney and Beatrice Rome, New York: Holt, Rinehart& Winston, 1964.

Calder, Nigel, *Einstein's Universe*, New York: The Viking Press, 1979.

Campbell, C.A., *On Selfhood and Godhood,* New York: Macmillan.

Copleston, Frederick, *A History of Philosophy* , Garden City, New York: Image Books, 1962.

Descartes, René *Discourse on Method,* trans. Laurence J. Lafluer, Indianapolis: Bobbs-Merrill Co., 1960.

Einstein, Albert, *Relativity, the Special and General Theory,* trans. Robert W. Lawson, New York: Crown Publishers, 1961.

Epictetus, *The Enchiridion,* in *Discourses of Epictetus,* trans. Thomas Wentworth Higginson, Roslyn, New York: Walter J. Black, Inc., 1944.

Epicurus, Fragment 221, in Giovanni Reale, *A History of Ancient Philosophy, vol. 3, The Systems of the Hellenistic Age,* ed. and trans. John R. Catan, Albany: State University of New York Press, 1985.

Gale, George, *Theory of Science,* New York, McGraw-Hill, 1979.

Gaunilon, *In Behalf of the Fool,* in *Medieval Philosophy,* ed. Herman Shapiro, New York: The Modern Library, 1964.

Gilligan, Carol, *In a Different Voice: Psychological Theory and Women's Development,* Cambridge, Mass.: Harvard University Press, 1982.

Greene, Norman N., *The Existentialist Ethic,* Ann Arbor: University of Michigan Press, 1966.

Hawking, Stephen, *A Brief History of Time: From the Big Bang to Black Holes,* New York: Bantam Books, 1988.

Hegel, G.W. *Encyclopedia of Philosophy,* trans. Gustav Emil Mueller, New York: Philosophical Library, 1959.

Hobbes, Thomas, *Leviathan,* ed. Francis B. Randall, New York: Washington Square Press.

Holbach, P., Baron d', *The System of Nature*, London, 1795.

Hume, David, *Dialogues Concerning Natural Religion*, ed. Henry D. Aiken, New York: Hafner Press, 1977.

An Enquiry Concerning Human Understanding, LaSalle, Illinois: Open Court Publishing Co., 1956.

A Treatise of Human Nature, ed. D.G.C. Macnabb, New York: World Publishing Co..

James, William, *Pragmatism*, in *William James: Writings 1902-1910*, New York: Library of America, 1987.

Pragmatism: A New Name for some Old Ways of Thinking, New York: Longmans, Green, 1907.

The Will to Believe and Other Essays in Popular Philosophy, 1897. Reprinted in *Human Immortality: Two Supposed Objections to the Doctrine*, New York: Dover, 1956.

Jones,W.T., *Kant to Wittgenstein and Sartre*, New York: Harcourt, Brace & World, 1952.

Kant, Immanuel, *Critique of Practical Reason*, New York: Liberal Arts Press, 1956.

Critique of Pure Reason, trans. Norman Kemp Smith, New York: The Modern Library, 1958.

Foundations of the Metaphysic of Morals, trans. Lewis White Beck, Indianapolis: Bobbs-Merrill, 1959.

Prolegomena to Any Future Metaphysics, trans. Lewis White Beck, Indianapolis: Bobbs-Merrill Co., 1976.

Kierkegaard, Søren, *Concluding Unscientific Postscript to Philosophical Fragments, Vol. 1*, trans. Howard V. Hong and Edna H. Hong, Princeton, N.J.: Princeton University Press, 1992.

Fear and Trembling, trans. Alastair Hannay, London: Penguin Books, 1985.

Søren Kirkegaard's Journal and Papers, trans, & ed. Howard V. Hong and Edna H. Hong, Bloomington, Indiana:Indiana University Press, 1967.

Philosophical Fragments, trans. Howard V. Hong and Edna H. Hong, Princeton, N.J.: Princeton University Press, 1985.

King, Martin Luther, Jr., "Letter From a Birmingham Jail," in *Civil Disobedience: Theory and Practice*, ed. Hugo Adam Bedau, New York: Pegasus, 1969.

Kittay, Eva Feder and Diane T. Mayers, ed. *Women and Moral Theory*, Totowa, N.J.: Rowman and Littlefield, 1987.

Koestler, Arthur, *The Roots of Coincidence*, New York: Random House, 1972.

Lamm, Robert C. & Neal M. Cross, *A Search for Human Values*, Vol. I, 9th Ed., Dubuque, Iowa: Brown & Benchmark, 1993.

Leibniz, G.W., *Theodicy*, Ontario: J.W. Dent & Sons, 1966.

Locke, John, *Essay Concerning Human Understanding*, ed. Mary Whiton Calkins, La Salle, Illinois: Open Court, 1905.

Two Treatises of Government, ed. Peter Laslett, New York: New American Library, 1965.

Macrone, Michael, *Eureka! What Archimedes Really Meant*, New York: Harper Perennial, 1994.

Marcus Aurelius, *Meditations*, trans. George Long, Roslyn, New York: Walter J. Black, Inc., 1945.

Mill, John Stuart, *Autobiography*, ed. J.D. Stillinger, London: Oxford University Press, 1971.

Human Worth, eds. Richard Paul Janaro and Darwin E. Gearhart, New York: Holt, Rinehart & Winston, 1972.

Utilitarianism, New York: Bobbs-Merrill, 1957.

Nietzsche, Friedrich, *Also Sprach Zarathustra*, Munich: Wilhelm Goldmann Verlag.

Beyond Good and Evil, in *The Philosophy of Nietzsche*, New York: Random House, 1927.

The Birth of Tragedy in *The Philosophy of Nietzsche*, New York: Modern Library, 1927.

Paley, William, *Natural Theology*, in *The Works of William Paley*, Philadelphia: Crissy & Markley, 1857.

Pascal, Blaise, *Pensees*, trans. William F. Trotter, ed. H.S. Thayer and Elizabeth Thayer, New York: Washington Square Press, 1965.

Peirce, Charles Sanders, *Collected Papers of Charles Sanders Peirce, vol. 5*, ed. Charles Hartshorne and Paul Weiss, Cambridge, Mass.: Harvard University Press, 1931-35.

Penrose, Roger, *The Emperor's New Mind*, Oxford: Penguin Press, 1989.

Pivcevic, Edo, *Husserl and Phenomenlogy*, London: Hutchinson University Library, 1970.

Plato, *The Apology*, in *Five Dialogues*, trans. G.M.A. Grube, Indianapolis, Indiana: Hackett Publishing Co.

The Meno, in *Plato: Five Dialogues*, trans. G.M.A. Grube, Indianapolis, IN: Hackett Publishing Co., 1981.

Phaedo, In *Plato: Five Dialogues*, trans. G.M.A. Grube, Indianapolis, IN: Hackett Publishing Co., 1981.

The Republic, Book VI, trans. B. Jowett, New York: Doubleday, 1989.

Rand, Ayn, *For the New Intellectual*, New York: Signet Books, 1964.

Royce, Josiah, *The Spirit of Modern Philosophy*, Boston: Houghton Mifflin, 1892.

Russell, Bertrand, *The Problems of Philosophy*, London: The Oxford University Press, 1912.

Sartre, Jean Paul, *Being and Nothingness*, trans. Hazel E. Barnes, New York: Washington Square Press, 1992.

The Humanism of Existentialism, trans. Bernard Frechtman, *The Fabric of Existentialism: Philosophical and Literary Sources*, ed. Richard Gill and Ernest Sherman, Englewood Cliffs: N.J.: Prentice-Hall, 1973.

Nausea, trans. L. Alexander, New York: New Directions, 1959.

Skinner, B.F., *Beyond Freedom and Dignity*, New York: Alfred A. Knopf, 1971.

Soccio, Douglas, *Archetypes in Wisdom.*, New York: Wadsworth Publishing Co., 1995.

Spinoza, Baruch, *Ethics*, New York: Hafner Press, 1974.

Tipler, Frank J., *The Physics of Immortality*, New York: Doubleday, 1994.

Trefil, *The Dark Side of the Universe: A Scientist Explores the Cosmos*, New York: Macmillan Publishing Co., 1988.

Velasquez, Manuel, *Philosophy*, 6th ed., Belmont, Ca.: Wadsworth Publishing Co., 1997.

Warnock, G.J., *Berkley*, London: Penguin Books, 1953.

White, Andrew Dickson, *A History of the Warfare of Science and Theology*, Gloucester, Mass.: Peter Smith, 1978.

William Ockham, *Philosophical Writings*, trans. Philotheus Boehner, Indianapolis: Bobbs-Merrill Co., 1976.

Wittgenstein, Ludwig, *Philosophical Investigations*, trans. G.E.M. Anscombe, 3rd ed., New York: Macmillan, 1953.

Wollstonecraft, Mary, *A Vindication of the Rights of Women*, in *A Wollstonecraft Anthology*, ed. Janet M. Todd, Bloomington, IN: Indiana University Press, 1977.

Zukav, Gary, *The Dancing Wu Li Masters*, New York: Bantam Books, 1980.

Index

A

B

C

D

E

F

G

H

P

Q

R

S